KU-477-290

CLASSIC TRAVEL STORIES

CLASSIC
TRAVEL STORIES

INTRODUCTION BY
FIONA PITT-KETHLEY

Classic Travel Stories

This edition published in 1996 by Leopard, a division of Random House UK Ltd, Random House, 20 Vauxhall Bridge Road, London SW1V 2SA.

All rights reserved.

This publication may not be reproduced, stored in a retrieval system or transmitted, in any form or by any means, electronic, mechanical, photocopying or otherwise, without the prior written permission of the publishers.

ISBN 1 85891 328 4

Printed and bound in Guernsey by The Guernsey Press Co. Ltd

CONTENTS

CONTENTS

INTRODUCTION

From the earliest times Man has travelled and come back with wonderful stories of his adventures. In prehistoric days, these narratives passed by word of mouth and thus many interesting tales were lost. With the invention of alphabets travel-writing came into being. Every person brought up as a Christian will be familiar with *Exodus* in The Bible, although that text is not represented here. The Egyptians that the Jews got away from had their own travel writing too. It is certainly one of the earliest forms of literature.

For those of us who can buy food from a supermarket rather than going out hunting in search of it, travel may be considered a luxury. But in early times it was sometimes a necessity for tribes to move on or emigrate to more fertile areas where a better quality of life was possible, one unharassed by other nations. Wars between neighbouring tribes often involved marches or rides across their territories, or voyages to unknown lands.

Travelling alone or in a small group is an unusual phenomenon. It takes a rare temperament to venture out into the unknown. Few of us realize what travelling in unmapped and often hostile areas can involve. The courage and ingenuity of the explorers of the past is an example to us all.

In the last decade or two everyone has become an armchair traveller with the aid of television, and package holidays have become part of most people's lives. These days it is absolutely necessary, therefore, that a travel writer speaks the truth. The audience can catch him or her out. We've seen it all on television, or out there, for ourselves. What the narratives of other travellers can provide though, is detail. The tastes and smells of other countries are as much part of the whole picture as the visual details which can be recorded in a photograph.

Classic Travel Stories contains more than sixty-five travel stories and covers all the continents and every kind of terrain from the flattest of deserts to the summit of Everest. A great many of the narratives are first-hand accounts. They are grouped in sections according to the nationalities of the authors. The writing spans over three thousand years – from Ancient Egypt up to the beginning of the present century – and covers the wanderings of women travellers as well as men. While many of us will have visited the more obvious places contained in the book, none of us can return to the past without the help of a vivid raconteur to guide our imagination. It is the sense of what a place was like at a precise moment in history that can only be gleaned from travel writing.

Most of the journeys described in this book were embarked upon with a clear sense of purpose. The authors were very rarely tourists or holiday makers. Some of the earliest narratives – that from an Egyptian papyrus and Xenophon, for instance – describe the travel of warriors. Other pieces recount the adventures of pilgrims. Ibn Batuta's account of his bad luck on the way to Mecca is fascinating. Christian pilgrim tours like those of Antoninus of Placentia or St Silvia of Aquitaine, on the other hand, have a great many of the qualities of package holidays. While there was no travel agent's representative standing around, there is a distinct feel that Christians of the Dark Ages could move amongst a crowd of nuns, monks and hermits while seeing all the Biblical sites in perfect safety. In such narratives as these, it's the detail not the danger that's interesting. For instance, the fact that the salt-formation known as 'Lot's Wife' might have been used as a cattle-lick and reduced in size by passing beasts is an intriguing and amusing idea.

In later times, travel became more a matter of education than a devotional act. Those who were not there to do business toured a circuit of mainly European sites, both Christian and pagan, then returned, poorer but wiser to their own countries. Occasionally, travellers stayed and grew to love other lands. Like Lady Hesther Stanhope in the Lebanon, an outsider may feel more at home as a permanent exile.

One of the most curious accounts in the book is that of Belzoni. He and his wife were circus performers. He had also invented a hydraulic scheme but failed to sell the idea of its usefulness for controlling the Nile to Mohammed Ali. Thus, he found himself in Egypt with an extraordinary commission from the English consul to bring back the colossal granite bust of Rameses II to England. He went in with just a few poles and a lot of locally hired manpower, shifting the statue at first by road, then by boat on its long journey to the British Museum. It's proof positive for all those physics students who doubted the power of leverage.

The least safe voyages recorded in this volume are those of the explorers who pioneered beyond the limits of human knowledge. Sometimes trade went hand in hand with exploration, as in Nicolas de Menonville's account of bringing cochineal from Mexico. Curiously, the story-telling is often at its most dead-pan when these traveller-explorers are taking their greatest risks. Scott's account of his Antarctic exploration is one of the most touching of these pieces. Less likeable are those of missionaries. The reader is left eternally conscious of a host of poorly-rewarded natives carrying bundles, and droves of animals being shot and eaten to satisfy hearty Victorian appetites. Yet, these pieces are worth reading as a record of an archaic way of thinking.

Even if the traveller is not likeable we can empathize with his predicament. Travel is an apt metaphor for life. There is a mystical side to any difficult journey to a destination we have not visited before. While travelling we are most strongly impressed with the fact that life cannot be wholly planned and controlled, however much we prepare in advance for our own futures.

Fiona Pitt-Kethley

ANCIENT EGYPT

THE JOURNEYING OF THE MASTER OF THE CAPTAINS OF EGYPT[1]

(*Fourteenth century* B.C.)

THOU hast put horses to the chariots; thy horses are as swift as jackals: their eyes flash: they are like a hurricane bursting; thou takest the reins, seizest the bow: we contemplate the deeds of thy hand. I send thee back the Mohar's portrait: and make thee know his actions. Didst thou not then go to the country of the Kheta? Hast thou not seen the land of Aup? Knowest thou not Khatuma, Ikatai, likewise? How is it? The Tsor of Sesortris, the city of Khaleb in its vicinity? How goes it with its ford? Hast thou not made an expedition to Qodesh and Tubakkhi? Hast thou not gone to the Shasous with the auxiliary body? Hast thou not trampled the road of Pamakar: the sky was dark on the day when there flourished the cypresses, the oaks and cedars, which reached up to heaven: there are many lions, wolves, and hyænas which the Shasous track on all sides.

Didst thou not ascend the mountain of Shaoua? Hast thou not travelled, thy arms placed on the back of thy car separated from its harness by the horses drawing it? Oh! come to . . . barta. Thou hastenest to get there: thou crossest its ford. Thou seest a Mohar's trials. Thy car is placed in thy hand: thy strength fails. Thou arrivest at the night: all thy limbs are knocked up: thy bones are broken: thou fallest asleep from excess of somnolence: thou wakest up—'Tis the hour when sad night begins: thou art absolutely alone. Comes there not a thief to rob the things left aside: he enters the stable: the horses are agitated: the thief goes back in the night, carrying away thy clothes. Thy servant awakes in the night; he perceives the thief's actions; he takes away the rest: he goes among the bad ones, and joins the tribes of the Shasous, and transforms himself to an Asiatic. The enemy comes to plunder: he finds only the wreck. Thou wakest, dost thou not find them in their flight? They take thy baggage. Thou becomest an active and quick-eared Mohar.

I also describe to thee the holy city, whose name is Kapaon [Gabal]. How is it? Of their goddess [we will speak] another time. Therein hast thou not penetrated? Come then to Berytus, to Sidon, to Sarepta. The ford of Nazana, where is it? Aoutou, how is it? They are neighbours of another city on the sea. Tyre the port is its name: water is carried to it in barks: it is richer in fish than in sands.

[1] From *Records of the Past*, translated from a papyrus in the British Museum.

I will speak to thee of the towns other than the preceding ones. Wentest thou not to the land of Takhis, to Cofer-Marlon, to Tamena, to Qodesh, to Dapour, to Adjai, and to Harnemata? Hast thou not seen Keriath-Anab, near to Beith-Tuphar? Knowest thou not Odulam and Tsidphoth? Knowest thou not the name of Khaouretsa, which is in the land of Aup? 'Tis a bull on his frontier, the place where one sees the battle [*mêlée*] of the brave ones.

Come then to the image of Sina: let me know Rohob: represent to me Beith-Sheal as well as Keriathaal. The fords of the Jordan, how does one cross them? Let me know the passage to enter Mageddo, whereof it remains to speak.

Thou art a Mohar expert in courageous deeds. Is there found a Mohar like thee to march at the head of the soldiers, a Marina superior to thee to shoot an arrow! Take care of the gulf in the ravine two thousand cubits deep, full of rocks and rolling stones. Thou makest a *détour*: seizest thy bow, preparest the iron in thy left hand, showest thyself to the good chiefs. Their eye looks down at thy hand: Slave, give camel for the Mohar to eat. Thou makest thy name of Mohar known, Master of the Captains of Egypt: thy name becomes like that of Kadjarti, the Chief of Assur, after his encounter with the hyænas in the wood, on the defile infected by the wood-hidden Shasous. Some of these were four cubits from the nose to the heel: fierce without mildness, not listening to caresses.

Thou art alone, no guide with thee, nor troop behind thee. Didst thou not meet the Marmar? He makes thee pass: thou must decide on departing, and knowest not the road. Anxiety seizes thee, thy hair bristles up, thy soul places itself in thy hand: thy way is full of rocks and rolling stones, no practicable passage: the road is obstructed by hollies, nopals, aloes, and bushes called *dog-wolf's shoes*. On one side is the precipice, on the other rises the vertical wall of the mountain. Thou must advance going down. Thy car strikes the wall and thy horses are startled by the rebound: they stop at the bottom of the harness; thy reins are precipitated and left behind; all fall down; thou passest on. Thy horses break the pole and move it out of the path: you cannot think of refastening them, cannot repair them. The seats are precipitated from their places; the horses refuse to be loaded with them. Thy heart fails thee. Thou beginnest to reel: the sky is clear: thirst torments thee: the enemy is behind thee: thou beginnest to quake: a thorny bush hinders thee: thou placest it aside: the horses wound themselves. At this moment thou art stretched flat.

Entering Joppa, thou seest a verdant inclosure in a ripe state. Thou makest an opening for eating the fruit. Thou findest a pretty young girl who takes care of the gardens: she yields herself to thee as a companion; and yields to thee her secret charms. Thou art perceived: thou art subjected to an interrogatory: thou art recognized as a Mohar. Thy tie of sweet servitude is settled by a compromise.

Each night thou liest down, a rug of hair is on thee: thou imprudently fallest asleep, a robber takes away thy bow, thy dagger, and thy quiver: thy reins are cut in the night, and thy horses run away. Thy valet takes a sliding path: the road mounts before him: he breaks thy car in pieces. . . . Thy armour-pieces fall on the ground. They sink in the sand. Thou must have recourse to prayers, and thou gettest puzzled in thy address. Give me victuals and water, and I shall reach my safety. They pretend to be deaf; they do not listen: they do not consent. Thou orderest:

"Pass to the forge! Pass through the workshops!"

Workmen in wood and metals, and workmen in leather come before thee: they do all thou wishest. They repair thy car, leaving aside all unserviceable pieces: they nail on again a new pole: they replace the fittings: they replace the leathers of the harness, and at the back they consolidate thy yoke: they replace the metallic ornaments: they incrust the marquetry: they put on the handle of thy whip and arrange the thongs. Thou leavest very hastily to fight at the perilous post, to perform valiant deeds.

Mapou, O chosen scribe! Mohar, who knows his hand, Conductor of the Arunas, Chief of Tsebaou, Explorer of the most distant limits of the land of Pa, thou dost not answer me any how: thou givest me no account; come let me tell all that happened to thee at the end of thy road.

I begin for thee at the dwelling of Sestsou [Rameses]: hast thou not forced thy way therein? Hast thou not eaten fishes of [. . .]? Hast thou not bathed therein? O come, let us describe Atsion to thee: where is its fortress? Come to the house of Ouati; to Sestsouem-paif-nakhtou-Ousormara;[1] to Sats . . . aal, also to Aksakaba. I have pictured to you Aïnini. Knowest thou not its customs? Nekhai and Rehobroth, hast thou not seen them since thy birth, O eminent Mohar? Raphia, how about its entrenchment? It covers the space of an *aour* going towards Gaza.

Answer quickly, and speak to me of what I have said of a Mohar concerning thee. I have thunderstruck the strangers at thy name of Marina: I have told them of thy fierce humour, according to which word thou saidst, "I am fit for all works; I have been taught by my father, who had verified his judgment millions of times. I can hold the reins, and also and skilful in action. Courage never forsakes my limbs: I am of the race Mentou."

I have mutilated the end of thy book, and I send it to thee back, as thou

[1] A fortress built by Rameses II. The name means "Rameses II in his Victories."

didst request: thy orders accumulate on my tongue, they rest on my lips: but they are difficult to understand; an unskilful man could not distinguish them; they are like the words of a man of Athou with a man of Abou. Yet thou art a scribe of Pharaoh; whose goodness reveals the essence of the universe.

Be gracious when seeing this work, and say not, "Thou hast made my name repugnant to the rabble, to all men." See I have made for thee the portrait of the Mohar: I have travelled for thee through foreign provinces. I have collected for thee nations and cities after their customs. Be gracious to us: behold them calmly: find words to speak of them when thou wilt be with the Prince Ouah.

OF SOME STRANGE ANIMALS AND OF AN ISLAND THAT LIES BEYOND THE PEPPER COUNTRY [1]

COSMAS OF ALEXANDRIA [2]

(*fl.c.* A.D. 548)

CAMELEOPARDS are found only in Ethiopia. They also are wild creatures and undomesticated. In the palace one or two that, by command of the King, have been caught when young, are tamed, to make a show for the King's amusement. When milk or water is set before these creatures in a pan, as is done in the King's presence, they cannot, by reason of the great length of their legs and the height of their breast and neck, stoop down to the earth and drink, unless by straddling with their forelegs. They must therefore, it is plain, in order to drink, stand with their forelegs wide apart. This animal also I have delineated from my personal knowledge of it.[3]

The Agriobous, or Wild Ox, is a large Indian animal, and from it is got what is called the *toupha*, with which commanders of armies decorate their horses and banners when taking the field. If his tail, it is said, catches in a tree, he does not seek to move off but stands stockstill, having a strong aversion to lose even a single hair of his tail. So the people of the place come and cut off his tail, and then the beast, having lost it all, makes his escape. Such is the nature of this animal.

The Monoceros, or Unicorn, I cannot say that I have seen. But I have seen four brazen figures of him set up in the four-towered palace of the King of Ethiopia. They speak of him as a terrible beast and quite invincible, and say

[1] From *The Christian Topography*, translated from the Greek and edited by J.W. McCrindle (Hakluyt Society, No. 98 (1897)).

[2] An Egyptian monk, surnamed Indicopleustes, or "the Indian Navigator."

[3] In the original manuscript is a drawing by Cosmas of the cameleopard (or giraffe).

that all his strength lies in his horn. When he finds himself pursued by many hunters and on the point of being caught he springs up to the top of some precipice whence he throws himself down, and in the descent turns a somersault so that the horn sustains all the shock of the fall, and he escapes unhurt. And scripture in like manner speaks concerning him, saying, *Save me from the mouth of lions, and my humility from the horns of unicorns.* And again: *And he that is beloved as the son of unicorns;* and again in the blessings of Balaam wherewith he blessed Israel, he says for the second time: *God so led him out of Egypt even as the glory of the unicorn;* thus bearing complete testimony to the strength, audacity, and glory of the animal.

The hog-deer I have both seen and eaten. The hippopotamus, however, I have not seen, but I had teeth of it so large as to weigh thirteen pounds, and these I sold here. And I saw many such teeth both in Ethiopia and in Egypt.

Concerning the Island of Taprobanê

This is a large oceanic island lying in the Indian sea. By the Indians it is called Sielediba, but by the Greeks Taprobanê, and therein is found the hyacinth stone. It lies on the other side of the pepper country. Around it are numerous small islands, all having fresh water and cocoanut trees. They nearly all have deep water close up to their shores. The great island, as the natives report, has a length of three hundred *gaudia*—that is, of nine hundred miles—and it is of the like extent in breadth. There are two kings in the island, and they are at feud the one with the other. The one has the hyacinth country, and the other the rest of the country where the harbour is and the centre of trade. It is a great mart for the people in those parts. The island has also a church of Persian Christians who have settled there, and a presbyter who is appointed from Persia, and a deacon and a complete ecclesiastical ritual. But the natives and their kings are heathens. In this island they have many temples, and on one, which stands on an eminence, there is a hyacinth as large as a great pine-cone, fiery-red, and when seen flashing from a distance, especially if the sun's rays are playing round it, a matchless sight. The island being, as it is, in a central position, is much frequented by ships from all parts of India and from Persia and Ethiopia, and it likewise sends out many of its own. And from the remotest countries, I mean Tzinista and other trading-places, it receives silk, aloes, cloves, sandalwood, and other products, and these again are passed on to marts on this side, such as Male, where pepper grows, and to Calliana, which exports copper and sesame logs and cloth for making dresses, for it also is a great place of business. And to Sindu also, where musk and castor is procured and androstachys, and to

Persia and the Homerite country, and to Adulê. . . .

Now I must here relate what happened to one of our countrymen, a merchant called Sopatrus, who used to go thither on business, but who to our knowledge has now been dead these five-and-thirty years past. Once on a time he came to this island of Taprobanê on business, and, as it chanced, a vessel from Persia put into port at the same time with himself. So the men from Adulê with whom Sopatrus was went ashore, as did likewise the people of Persia, with whom came a person of venerable age and appearance. Then, as the way there was, the chief men of the place and the custom-house officers received them and brought them to the king. The king having admitted them to an audience and received their salutations, requested them to be seated. Then he asked them: "In what state are your countries, and how go things with them?". To this they replied, they go well. Afterwards, as the conversation proceeded, the king inquired: " Which of your kings is the greater and the more powerful?" The elderly Persian, snatching the word, answered: "Our king is both the more powerful and the greater and richer, and indeed is King of Kings, and whatsoever he desires that he is able to do." Sopatrus on the other hand sat mute. So the king asked: "Have you, Roman,[1] nothing to say?" "What have I to say," he rejoined, "when he there has said such things? But if you wish to learn the truth you have the two kings here present. Examine each and you will see which of them is the grander and the more powerful." The king on hearing this was amazed at his words and asked, "How say you that I have both the kings here?" "You have," replied Sopatrus, "the money of both—the nomisma of the one and the drachma—that is, the miliarision—of the other. Examine the image of each, and you will see the truth." The king thought well of the suggestion, and, nodding his consent, ordered both the coins to be produced. Now, the Roman coin had a right good ring, was of bright metal, and finely shaped, for pieces of this kind are picked for export to the island. But the miliarision, to say it in one word, was of silver, and not to be compared with the gold coin. So the king after he had turned them this way and that, and had attentively examined, both, highly commended the nomisma, saying that the Romans were certainly a splendid, powerful, and sagacious people. So he ordered great honour to be paid to Sopatrus, causing him to be mounted on an elephant and conducted round the city with drums beating and high state. These circumstances were told us by Sopatrus himself and his companions, who had accompanied him to that island from Adulê; and as they told the story the Persian was deeply chagrined at what had occurred.

[1] *Roomi*, the name given in India to whatever power held Constantinople—Roman, Christian, or Mohammedan.

But in the direction of the notable seats of commerce already mentioned there are numerous others of less importance both on the coast and inland, and a country of great extent. Higher up in India, that is, farther to the north, are the White Huns. The one called Gollas when going to war takes with him, it is said, no fewer than two thousand elephants and a great force of cavalry. He is the lord of India, and oppressing the people forces them to pay tribute. A story goes that this king once upon a time would lay siege to an inland city of the Indians which was on every side protected by water. A long while he sat down before it, until what with his elephants, his horses, and his soldiers all the water had been drunk up. He then crossed over to the city dryshod and took it. These people set great store by the emerald stone and wear it set in a crown. The Ethiopians, who procure this stone from the Blemmyes in Ethiopia, take it into India, and with the price it fetches they invest in wares of great value. All these matters I have described and explained partly from personal observation and partly from accurate inquiries which I made when in the neighbourhood of the different places.

ANCIENT GREECE

EXPLORERS OF THE LIBYA DESERT[1]

HERODOTUS

(c. 485–425 B.C.)

Now for a voyage and land journey of four months, the Nile is known, in addition to the part of the stream that is in Egypt. For upon computa tion, so many months are known to be spent by a person who travels from Elephantine to the Automoli. This river flows from the west and the setting of the sun; but beyond this no one is able to speak with certainty, for the rest of the country is desert by reason of the excessive heat. But I have heard the following account from certain Cyrenæans, who say that they went to the oracle of Ammon, and had a conversation with Etearchus, king of the Ammonians; and that, among other subjects, they happened to discourse about the Nile—that nobody knew its sources: whereupon Etearchus said, that certain Nasamonians once came to him; this nation is Libyan and inhabits the Syrtis, and the country for no great distance eastward of the Syrtis; and that when these Nasamonians arrived, and were asked if they could give any further information touching the deserts of Libya, they answered, that there were some daring youths amongst them, sons of powerful men; and that they, having reached man's estate, formed many other extravagant plans, and moreover chose five of their number by lot to explore the deserts of Libya, to see if they could make any further discovery than those who had penetrated the farthest. (For as respects the parts of Libya along the Northern Sea, beginning from Egypt to the promontory of Solois, where is the extremity of Libya, Libyans and various nations of Libyans reach all along it, except those parts which are occupied by Grecians and Phœnicians: but as respects the parts above the sea, and those nations which reach down to the sea, in the upper parts Libya is infested by wild beasts; and all beyond that is sand, dreadfully short of water and utterly desolate.) They further related "that when the young men deputed by their companions set out, well furnished with water and provisions, they passed first through the inhabited country; and having traversed this, they came to the region infested by wild beasts; and after this they crossed the desert, making their way towards the west; and when they had traversed much sandy ground, during a journey of many days, they at length saw some trees growing in a plain; and that they approached and began to gather the fruit that grew on the trees; and while they were

[1] From *The History*, translated by Henry Cary (1847).

gathering, some diminutive men, less than men of middle stature, came up, and having seized them carried them away; and that the Nasamonians did not at all understand their language, nor those who carried them off the language of the Nasamonians. However, they conducted them through vast morasses, and when they had passed these, they came to a city, in which all the inhabitants were of the same size as their conductors, and black in colour: and by the city flowed a great river, running from the west to the east, and that crocodiles were seen in it."

Thus far I have set forth the account of Etearchus the Ammonian; to which may be added, as the Cyrenæans assured me, "that he said the Nasamonians all returned safe to their own country, and that the men whom they came to were all necromancers."

CONCERNING THE BEASTS OF EGYPT [1]

Herodotus

(*c.* 485–425 B.C.)

Egypt, though bordering on Libya, does not abound in wild beasts; but all that they have are accounted sacred, as well those that are domesticated as those that are not. But if I should give the reasons why they are consecrated, I must descend in my history to religious matters, which I avoid relating as much as I can. They have a custom relating to animals of the following kind. Superintendents, consisting both of men and women, are appointed to feed every kind separately; and the son succeeds the father in this office. All the inhabitants of the cities perform their vows to the superintendents in the following manner: having made a vow to the god to whom the animal belongs, they shave either the whole heads of their children, or a half, or a third part of the head, and then weigh the hair in a scale against silver, and whatever the weight may be, they give to the superintendent of the animals; and she in return cuts up some fish, and gives it as food to the animals: such is the usual mode of feeding them. Should anyone kill one of these beasts, if wilfully, death is the punishment; if by accident, he pays such fine as the priests choose to impose. But whoever kills an ibis or a hawk, whether wilfully or by accident, must necessarily be put to death.

Although the domestic animals are many, they would be much more numerous were it not for the following accidents which befal the cats. When the females have littered, they no longer seek the company of the males, and

[1] From *The History*, translated by Henry Cary (1847).

they, being desirous of having intercourse with them, are not able to do so; wherefore they have recourse to the following artifice: having taken the young from the females, and carried them away secretly, they kill them; though when they have killed them, they do not eat them. The females being deprived of their young, and desirous of others, again seek the company of the males; for this animal is very fond of its young. When a conflagration takes place, a supernatural impulse seizes on the cats. For the Egyptians, standing at a distance, take care of the cats, and neglect to put out the fire; but the cats, making their escape, and leaping over the men, throw themselves into the fire; and when this happens great lamentations are made among the Egyptians. In whatever house a cat dies of a natural death, all the family shave their eyebrows only; but if a dog die, they shave the whole body and the head. All cats that die are carried to certain sacred houses, where being first embalmed, they are buried in the city of Bubastis. All persons bury their dogs in sacred vaults within their own city; and ichneumons are buried in the same manner as the dogs: but field-mice and hawks they carry to the city of Buto; the ibis to Hermopolis; the bears, which are few in number, and the wolves, which are not much larger than foxes, they bury wherever they are found lying.

The following is the nature of the crocodile. During the four coldest months it eats nothing, and though it has four feet, it is amphibious. It lays its eggs on land, and there hatches them. It spends the greater part of the day on dry ground, but the whole night in the river; for the water is then warmer than the air and dew. Of all living things with which we are acquainted, this, from the least beginning, grows to be the largest. For it lays eggs little larger than those of a goose, and the young is at first in proportion to the egg; but when grown up it reaches to the length of seventeen cubits, and even more. It has the eyes of a pig, larger teeth, and projecting tusks, in proportion to the body: it is the only animal that has no tongue: it does not move the lower jaw, but is the only animal that brings down its upper jaw to the under one. It has strong claws, and a skin covered with scales, that cannot be broken on the back. It is blind in the water, but very quick-sighted on land; and because it lives for the most part in the water, its mouth is filled with leeches. All other birds and beasts avoid him, but he is at peace with the trochilus, because he receives benefit from that bird. For when the crocodile gets out of the water on land, and then opens its jaws, which it does most commonly towards the west, the trochilus enters its mouth and swallows the leeches: the crocodile is so well pleased with this service that it never hurts the trochilus.

With some of the Egyptians crocodiles are sacred; with others not, but they treat them as enemies. Those who dwell about Thebes, and Lake Mœris, consider them to be very sacred; and they each of them train up a crocodile, which is taught to be quite tame; and they put crystal and gold earrings into their ears, and bracelets on their fore-paws; and they give them appointed and sacred food, and treat them as well as possible while alive, and when dead they embalm them, and bury them in sacred vaults. But the people who dwell about the city of Elephantine eat them, not considering them sacred. They are not called crocodiles by the Egyptians, but "champsæ"; the Ionians give them the name of crocodiles, because they thought they resembled lizards, which are also so called, and which are found in the hedges of their country.

The modes of taking the crocodiles are many and various, but I shall only describe that which seems to me most worthy of relation. When the fisherman has baited a hook with the chine of a pig, he lets it down into the middle of the river, and holding a young live pig on the brink of the river, beats it; the crocodile, hearing the noise, goes in its direction, and meeting with the chine, swallows it; but the men draw it to land: when it is drawn out on shore, the sportsman first of all plasters its eyes with mud; and having done this, afterwards manages it very easily; but until he has done this he has a great deal of trouble. The hippopotamus is esteemed sacred in the district of Papremis, but not so by the rest of the Egyptians. This is the nature of its shape. It is a quadruped, cloven-footed, with the hoofs of an ox, snub-nosed, has the mane of a horse, projecting tusks, and the tail and neigh of a horse. In size he is equal to a very large ox: his hide is so thick that spear-handles are made of it when dry. Otters are also met with in the river, which are deemed sacred: and amongst fish, they consider that which is called the lepidotus and the eel sacred; these they say are sacred to the Nile; and among birds, the vulpanser.

There is also another sacred bird called the phœnix, which I have never seen except in a picture; for it seldom makes its appearance amongst them, only once in five hundred years, as the Heliopolitans affirm: they say that it comes on the death of its sire. If he is like the picture, he is of the following size and description: the plumage of his wings is partly golden-coloured, and partly red; in outline and size he is very like an eagle. They say that he has the following contrivance, which in my opinion is not credible. They say that he comes from Arabia, and brings the body of his father to the temple of the sun, having enclosed him in myrrh, and there buries him in the temple. He brings him in this manner: first he moulds an egg of myrrh as large as he is able to carry; then he tries to carry it, and when he has made the experiment, he hollows out the egg, and puts his parent into it, and stops up with some more myrrh the hole through which he had introduced the body, so when his father is put inside, the weight is the same as before: then, having covered it over, he carries him to the temple of the sun in Egypt. This they say is done by this bird.

In the neighbourhood of Thebes there are sacred serpents not at all hurtful to men: they are diminutive in size, and carry two horns that grow on the top of the head. When these serpents die they bury them in the temple of Jupiter, for they say they are sacred to that god. There is a place in Arabia, situated very near the city of Buto, to which I went, on hearing of some winged serpents; and when I arrived there I saw bones and spines of serpents in such quantities as it would be impossible to describe: there were heaps of these spinal bones, some large, some smaller, and others still less; and there were great numbers of them. The place in which these spinal bones lie scattered is of the following description: it is a narrow pass between two mountains into a spacious plain; this plain is contiguous to the plain of Egypt: it is reported, that at the beginning of spring, winged serpents fly from Arabia towards Egypt; but that ibises, a sort of bird, meet them at the pass, and do not allow the serpents to go by, but kill them: for this service the Arabians say that the ibis is highly reverenced by the Egyptians; and the Egyptians acknowledge that they reverence these birds for this reason. The ibis is of the following description: it is all over a deep black, it has the legs of a crane, its beak is much curved, and it is about the size of the crex. Such is the form of the black ones, that fight with the serpents. But those that are commonly conversant among men (for there are two species) are bare on the head and the whole neck; have white plumage, except on the head, the throat, and the tips of the wings and extremity of the tail; in all these parts that I have mentioned they are of a deep black; in their legs and beak they are like the other kind. The form of the serpent is like that of the water-snake; but he has wings without feathers, and as like as possible to the wings of a bat. This must suffice for the description of sacred animals.

THE MARCH OF THE TEN THOUSAND [1]

(401 B.C.)

XENOPHON

(c.430 B.C.-?)

[*In 401* B.C., *intent upon wresting the throne of Persia from his elder brother, Artaxerxes II, Cyrus the Younger set out from Sardis with a vast*

[1] From *The Anabasis, or Expedition of Cyrus.*

army in which went over thirteen thousand Greeks under the leadership of Clearchus. Within a few days' march of Babylon the Persian host came suddenly into view, and in the battle of Cunaxa Cyrus was killed. His own troops at once dispersed, and the Greeks thus found themselves stranded in the midst of an unknown country, more than a thousand miles from home, and hundreds of miles from the sea. Halted by the river Zabatus, Clearchus and the other officers in command were negotiating for a safe conduct when they were treacherously murdered by the Persian satrap Tissaphernes.]

THEN were the Greeks in great perplexity, reflecting that they were distant from Greece not less than ten thousand stadia; that there was no one to guide them; that impassable rivers would intercept them in the midest of their course; that the Barbarians who had gone up with Cyrus had deserted them; and that they were left utterly alone: reflecting, I say, on these circumstances, and being disheartened at them, few of them tasted food for that evening, few kindled fires and many did not come to the place of arms during the night, but lay down to rest where they severally happened to be, unable to sleep for sorrow and longing for their country, their parents, their wives and children, whom they never expected to see again.

There was in the army a certain Xenophon, an Athenian, who accompanied it neither in the character of general, nor captain, nor common soldier, but it had happened that Proxenus, an old guest-friend of his, had sent for him from home, giving him a promise that, if he came, he would recommend him to the friendship of Cyrus.

When this perplexity occurred, Xenophon was distressed as well as the other Greeks, and unable to rest, but having at length got a little sleep, he had a dream, in which, in the midst of a thunderstorm, a bolt seemed to him to fall upon his father's house, and the house became all in a blaze. Being greatly frightened, he immediately awoke, and considered his dream as in one respect favourable (inasmuch as, being in troubles and dangers, he seemed to behold a great light from Jupiter), but in another respect he was alarmed (because the dream appeared to him to be from Jupiter who was a king, and the fire to blaze all around him), lest he should be unable to escape from the king's territories.

As soon as he awoke the thought than first occurred to him was, "Why do I lie here? The night is passing away. With daylight it is probable that the enemy will come upon us. Yet no one concerts measures for our defence. From what city then do I expect a leader? What age am I waiting for to come to myself? Assuredly I shall never be older if I give myself up to the enemy to-day."

After these reflections he arose, and called together the captains.

[*New leaders are chosen, Xenophon himself being one of them, and it is at once resolved that they shall try to force their way northward to the Euxine Sea. Still harassed by the enemy, they reach the Tigris, "a river of such depth that when they sounded it their spears did not rise above the water," while passage along its banks was barred by the Carduchian Mountains*]

The next day (therefore) they retreated back towards Babylon, to some unburnt villages, having first set fire to those which they abandoned; so that the enemy did not come up to them, but watched them, and seemed to be wondering which way the Greeks would turn themselves, and what they had in their mind. The rest of the soldiers then turned their thoughts to getting supplies; but the generals and captains held another council, and, bringing together the prisoners, questioned them as to be whole country around, what each part was. They said that the parts towards the south were on the road toward Babylon and Media, through which the Greeks had come; that the road towards the east led to Susa and Ecbatana; that the one across the river, towards the west, led to Lydia and Ionia; and that the other over the mountains, towards the north, led to the Carduchi. The generals, having heard these statements, kept apart by themselves those who said that they knew the road in each direction, not letting it be known which way they intended to go. It appeared necessary to the generals, however, to make their way over the mountains into the country of the Carduchi; for the prisoners said that after passing through this they would come to Armenia, a large and rich country, of which Orontes was governor, whence it would be easy for them to go whichever way they pleased.

Their entrance upon the territory of the Carduchi they made in the following manner. When it was about the last watch, and enough of the night was left to allow them to cross the plain under cover of darkness, they arose at a given signal, and, marching onwards, reached the hills by break of day. Here Cheirisophus took the lead of the army, having with him both his own men and all the light-armed; while Xenophon brought up the rear with the heavy-armed troops, having not a single light-armed soldier. Cheirisophus mounted the summit before any of the enemy perceived him; he then led slowly forward; and each portion of the army, as it passed the summit in succession, followed him to the villages which lay in the windings and recesses of the mountains. The Carduchi, in consequence, quitting their dwellings, fled to the hills. There was plenty of provisions left for the Greeks to take; and the houses were furnished with great numbers of brazen utensils, none of which the Greeks took away.

But when the rear of the Greeks was descending from the hills into the villages, being now overtaken by darkness (for as the way was narrow their ascent of the heights and descent to the villages had lasted the entire day), some of the Carduchi, collecting together, attacked the hindmost, and killed and wounded some of them with stones and arrows: They were but few; for the Greek troops had come one them unawares; but had they assembled in greater numbers, a great part of the army would have been in danger of being destroyed. For this night, accordingly, they took up their abode in the villages; and the Carduchi lighted a number of fires around them on the hills.

As soon as it was day the generals and captains of the Greeks, meeting together, resolved to reserve only such of the baggage-cattle as were most necessary and most able, abandoning the rest, and to dismiss all the slaves that had been recently captured; for the cattle and the slaves, being numerous, rendered their progress slow. When they had breakfasted, and were on the march, the generals, taking their stand in a narrow part of the way, took from the soldiers whatever of the things mentioned they found had not been left behind; and the men submitted to this, unless any of them, smitten with desire of a handsome boy or woman, conveyed them past secretly. Thus they proceeded during this day, sometimes having to fight a little, and sometimes resting themselves. On the next day a great storm arose; but they were obliged to pursue their march, for they had not a sufficient supply of provisions. Cheirisophus continued to lead, and Xenophon had charge of the rear. The enemy pressed steadily upon them, and where the passes were narrow, came close up, and used their bows and their slings; so that the Greeks, somethings pursuing and sometimes retreating, were compelled to march but slowly; and Xenophon, when the enemy attacked them violently, had frequently to pass the word for a halt. Cheirisophus on one occasion did not halt, but hurried on rapidly, and passed the word to follow, so that it was manifest that there was something extraordinary; but there was no time to go forward and ascertain the cause, and the march of the rear-guard became like a flight.

When they arrived at the place of encampment Xenophon immediately proceeded, just as he was, to Cheirisophus, and blamed him for not having halted. Cheirisophus answered, "Cast your eyes upon those mountains, and observe how impassable they are. The only road which you see is steep; and close upon it you may perceive a great multitude of men, who, having occupied the pass, keep guard at it. For these reasons I hastened on, and therefore did not wait for you, to try if I could get the start of the enemy before the pass was seized; and the guides whom we have say that there is no other road."

Xenophon rejoined, "I have two prisoners, for when the enemy molested us we placed an ambush, which enabled us to recover breath and to take some alive that we might use them for guides."

Immediately after, bringing forward the two men, they inquired of them separately whether they knew of any other road then that which was open to their view. The one denied that he knew of any other, though many threats were held out to him; and as he would give no useful information he was put to death in sight of the other. The survivor said that he himself would lead them by a road that might be passed even by beasts of burden. Being then asked if there was any spot in it difficult to be passed, he replied that there was one height, and that unless a party secured it beforehand it would be impossible for them to pass. Upon this it was thought proper to call together the captains and to acquaint them with the prospect of affairs, and ask whether any of them was willing to prove himself a man of valour and engage to go on this service as a volunteer. Aristonymus of Methydrium and Agasias of Stymphalus, both Arcadians, offered themselves; and Callimachus of Parrhasia, also an Arcadian, disputed the honour with them, and Aristeas of Chios presented himself, a man who had often proved himself of great value to the army for similar services.

It was now afternoon, and the generals desired the party to take some refreshment and set forward. Having bound the guide, they put him into their hands, and arranged with them, that if they should gain the summit, they should keep guard at that post during the night, and give a signal by trumpet at break of day, and that those on the height should then charge the enemy in possession of the apparent egress, and those below should issue forth and come in a body to their assistance as soon as they were able.

When they had made this arrangement, the party set out, being in number about two thousand; and there was heavy rain at the time. Xenophon, taking the rear-guard, led them towards the apparent egress, in order that the enemy might turn their attention in that direction, and that those who were going round might as much as possible escape notice. But when the rear-guard came to a ravine, which they had to pass to gain the ascent, the Barbarians then rolled down masses of rock, each big enough to load a waggon, with other stones greater and smaller, which striking in their descent against the rocks, were hurled abroad in all directions; and it was utterly impossible even to approach the pass. Some of the captains, when they could not succeed in this part, made attempts in another, and continued their efforts till darkness came on. When they thought that they might retire unobserved, they went to get their supper; for the rear-guard had been dinnerless that day. The enemy, however, being evidently in fear, continued to roll down stones through the whole of the night.

Those, meanwhile, who had the guide, taking a circuitous route, surprised a guard of the enemy sitting round a fire, and, having killed some of them and put the rest to flight, remained on the spot, with the notion that they were in possession of the summit. But in possession of it they were not; for there was a small hill above them, round which lay the narrow pass at which the guard had been posted. However, there was a way from thence to that party of the enemy who were stationed at the open egress. Here they remained during the night.

As soon as day began to dawn they advanced in regular order, and with silence, against the enemy; and as there was a mist, they came close upon them before they were perceived. But when they caught sight of one another, the trumpet sounded on the side of the Greeks, who, raising the shout of battle, rushed upon the enemy. The Barbarians did not stand their charge, but quitted the pass and fled; only a few of them were killed, for they were active in moving off. At the same time the party of Cheirisophus, hearing the sound of the trumpet, marched immediately up the plain track; while others of the officers proceeded by untrodden paths, where each happened to be, and, climbing up as well as they could, drew up one another with their spears.

[*Having fought their way through the Carduchi, they came at last to the river Centrites.*]

[And] the Greeks abode in the villages above the plain near the river Centrites, the breadth of which is about who hundred feet, and which forms the boundary between Armenia and the territory of the Carduchi. Here they took some rest, being glad to see a piece of level country. The river is distant from the mountains of the Carduchi about six or seven stadia. It was with great satisfaction that they stayed here, for during seven days that they had been marching among the Carduchi they had been constantly fighting.

At daybreak, however, they perceived on the other side of the river a body of cavalry, in complete armour, ready to prevent them from crossing, and on the high banks above the cavalry, another of foot prepared to hinder them from entering Armenia. These were Armenians, Mardians, and Chaldæans, mercenary troops of Orontes and Artuchas. The high banks on which these forces were drawn up, were three or four hundred feet from the river; and the only road that was visible was one that led upward, apparently a work of art. Here the Greeks endeavoured to cross, but as the water rose above their breasts, and the bed of the river was rough with large and slippery stones, and as it was impossible for them to carry their arms in the water, or, if they attempted to do so, the river swept them away (while if any of them took their arms on their heads they became exposed to the arrows and other missiles of the enemy), they in consequence retreated, and encamped at the side of the river.

They now perceived the Carduchi assembled in great numbers under arms on the spot where they themselves had been on the previous night. Hence great despondency was felt by the Greeks. This day, therefore, and the following night they remained where they were in great perplexity. Xenophon, however, had a dream; he thought that he was bound in fetters, but that they fell off him of their own accord, so that he was set at liberty, and walked securely whithersoever he pleased.

While-Xenophon was at breakfast two young men came running up to him, for every one knew that it was allowable to approach him whether breakfasting or supping, and to wake him and speak to him even when asleep, if they had anything to tell of affairs relating to the war. The youths informed him that they had been gathering sticks for their fire, and had chanced to see on the opposite side of the river, among the rocks that reached down to the stream itself, an old man, a woman, and some girls, depositing in a cavernous rock what appeared to be bags of clothes; that when they saw this, they thought it would be safe to cross, as the ground at that point was inaccessible to the enemy's horse; that having taken off their clothes, and taken their daggers in their hands, they went over undressed, in expectation of having to swim, but that as they went on, they reached the other side before they were wet to the middle, and, having thus forded the stream, and taken the clothes, they came back again. Xenophon immediately therefore made a libation, and ordered the young men to join in it, and to pray to the gods who had sent the dream and pointed out the ford, to complete what was wanting to their success. After the libation, he at once conducted the youths to Cheirisophus, and to him they gave the same account. Cheirisophus on hearing it, made a libation also.

When the libation was over they gave orders to the soldiers to get their baggage ready; while they themselves, calling the rest of the generals together, consulted with them how they might cross the river to the best advantage, and how they might defeat the enemy in front, and suffer no damage from those in the rear. It was then resolved that Cheirisophus should take the lead, and cross over with half of the army, that the other half should stay behind with Xenophon, and that the baggage-cattle and camp followers should go over between the two. When these matters were fairly arranged, they began to move, the young men acting as guides, and keeping the river on the left, the distance to the ford being about four stadia. As they proceeded, the lines of the enemy's cavalry advanced abreast of them on the opposite bank; and when they came to the ford, and the margin of the river, they halted, laying down their arms; and then Cheirisophus himself, placing a chaplet upon his head, and laying aside his outer garments, took up his arms and commanded the rest to follow his example, directing the captains to lead their troops in files, some on his left hand, and some on his right. The augurs at the same time sacrificed victims over the river; while the enemy plied their bows and slings, but did not reach the Greeks. As the sacrifices appeared favourable, all the soldiers sang the pæan and raised a shout, and all the women (for there were a number of the men's mistresses in the army) joined in the cry.

Cheirisophus and his men then entered the stream, and Xenophon, taking the most active of the rear-guard, marched at full speed back to the ford opposite the outlet into the mountains of Armenia, making a feint that the meant to cross the river there, and thus cut off the cavalry that were on the bank; when the enemy, seeing Cheirisophus and his men crossing over with ease, and Xenophon and his party hurrying back, were afraid of being intercepted, and fled with precipitation to gain the outlet that led up from the river, and as soon as they came to that passage, they directed their course up into the mountains. Lycius, who had command of the troop of horse, set off in pursuit of them, but Cheirisophus made his way up the high banks that reached down to the river, to attack that portion of the enemy that were on the more elevated ground.

Xenophon, when he saw that all was going well on the other side, returned with all possible speed to join that part of the army which was crossing over; for the Carduchi were evidently descending into the plain, with the view of falling upon the rear. Turning towards the Carduchi, [Xenophon] halted and ordered the captains to form each his own company into divisions of five-and-twenty men, bringing round each division in line towards the left; and he directed both the captains, and the officers of the divisions of five-and-twenty, to advance facing the Carduchi, and the rearmost to halt facing the river.

Cheirisophus, when he saw that all was safe on his own side, sent the peltasts and the slingers and archers to Xenophon. Xenophon, seeing them beginning to cross, sent a messenger to desire that they should remain where they were, and that, when his own party should begin to cross, they should come forward into the water on each side opposite to him, the javelin-men holding their weapons by the thong, and the archers with their arrows on the string. His own men he ordered to raise the pæan and rush towards the enemy; and he directed that when the enemy should take to flight, and the trumpeter should sound, the rear should wheel to the right, run forward as fast as possible and cross over at the part where each happened to be stationed, telling them that he would be the best man who should first reach the opposite side. The Carduchi, seeing that those who were left were but few, began to press forward boldly, and to use their slings and bows. The Greeks then sang the pæan, and rushed upon them at full speed; and the Barbarians did not stand the charge. At this juncture the trumpeter sounded, when the enemy fled still faster, and the Greeks, turning in the opposite direction, made their way over the river with all possible speed.

When they had crossed, and had ranged themselves in order about noon, they proceeded through the country of Armenia, consisting wholly of plains and gently sloping hills, a distance of not less than five parasangs. The village at which they at length arrived was of considerable size, and provisions were in great plenty.

Hence they proceeded, who days' journey, a distance of ten parasangs, until they passed round the sources of the river Tigris. From hence they advanced, three days' journey, fifteen parasangs, to the river Teleboas, a stream not large, indeed, but of much beauty; and there were many villages on its banks. This part of the country was called Western Armenia. Hence they proceeded, three days' march, a distance of fifteen parasangs, through a plain. They then came to a palace, with several villages around it stored with abundance of provisions. While they were encamped there fell a great quantity of snow in the night, so that it covered both the arms and the men as they lay on the ground. The snow cramped the baggagecattle, and they were very reluctant to rise; for, as they lay, the snow that had fallen upon them served to keep them warm. But when Xenophon was hardy enough to rise without his outer garment, and to cleave wood, some one else then rose, and, taking the wood from him, cleft it himself. Soon after the rest got up, and lighted fires and anointed themselves, for abundance of ointment was found there.

Hence they dispatched in the night Democrates of Temenos, giving him a detachment of men, to the hills, where stragglers said they had seen fires. Having gone, he said he saw no fires, but he brought with him a captive having a Persian bow and quiver, and a short battleaxe, such as the Amazons have. Being asked of what country he was, he said that he was a Persian, and that he was going from the army of Tiribazus to get provisions. They then asked him how large the army was and for what purpose it was assembled. He said that Tiribazus had his own troops and some mercenaries from the Chalybes and Taochians, and that he was prepared to attack the Greeks in their passage over the mountains, at a narrow defile through which lay their only road.

The generals, on hearing this, proceeded to march without delay, taking the man that had been captured for their guide. After they had passed the mountains, the peltasts, who were the first to discover the enemy's camp, ran forward with a shout to attack it. The Barbarians, hearing the noise, fled; some of them, however, were killed, and about twenty horses taken, as was also the tent of Tiribazus, and in it some couches with silver feet, and drinking-cups, and some prisoners who said that they were bakers and cupbearers.

The next day it was thought necessary to march away as fast as possible, before the enemy's force should be reassembled, and get possession of the pass. Collecting their baggage at once, therefore, they set forward through a deep snow, and, having the same day passed the height on which Tiribazus had intended to attack them, they encamped. Hence they proceeded three days' journey through a desert tract of country, a distance of fifteen parasangs, to the river Euphrates, and passed it without being wet higher than the middle. From hence they advanced three day's march, through much snow and a level plain, a distance of fifteen parasangs; the third day's march was extremely troublesome as the north wind blew full in their faces, completely parching up everything and benumbing the men. The depth of the snow was a fathom, so that many of the baggage-cattle and slaves perished, with about thirty of the soldiers. They continued to burn fires through the whole night, for there was plenty of wood at the place of encampment.

From hence they marched through snow the whole of the following day, and many of the men contracted the *bulimia*. Xenophon, who commanded the rear, finding in his way such of the men as had fallen down with it, knew not what disease it was. But as one of those acquainted with it told him that they would get up if they had something to eat, he went round among the baggage, and wherever he saw anything eatable he gave it out, and sent such as were able to run to distribute it among those diseased, who, as soon as they had eaten, rose up and continued their march. As they proceeded Cheirisophus came just as it grew dark to a village, and here, as many of the troops as could come up, encamped; but of the rest, such as were unable to get to the end of the journey, spent the night on the way without food or fire; and some of the soldiers lost their lives on that occasion. Some of the enemy too, who had collected themselves into a body, pursued our rear, and seized any of the baggage-cattle that were unable to proceed, fighting with one another for the possession of them. Such of the soldiers, also, as had lost their sight from the effects of the snow, or had their toes mortified by the cold, were left behind. It was found to be a relief to the eyes against the snow, if the soldiers kept something black before them on the march, and to the feet, if they kept constantly in motion, and allowed themselves no rest, and if they took off their shoes in the night; but as to such as slept with their shoes on, the straps worked into their feet, and the soles were frozen about them; for when their old shoes had failed them, shoes of raw hides had been made by the men themselves from the newly-skinned oxen. From such unavoidable sufferings, some of the soldiers were left behind, who, seeing a piece of ground of a black appearance, from the snow having disappeared there, conjectured that it must have melted; and it had in fact melted in the spot from the effect of a fountain, which was sending up vapour in a woody hollow close at hand. Turning aside thither, they sat down and refused to proceed farther. Xenophon, who was with the rear-guard, as soon as he heard this, tried to prevail on them by every art and means not to be left behind, telling them, at the same time, that the enemy were collected, and pursuing them in great numbers. At last he grew angry; and they told him to kill them, as they were quite unable to go forward. He then thought it the best course to strike a terror, if possible, into the enemy that were behind, lest they should fall upon the exhausted soldiers. It was now dark, and the enemy were advancing with a great noise, quarrelling about the booty that they had taken; when such of the rear-guard as were not disabled, started up, and rushed towards them, while the tired men, shouting as loud as they could, clashed their spears against their shields. The enemy, struck with alarm, threw themselves among the snow into the hollow, and no one of them afterwards made themselves heard from any quarter.

Xenophon, and those with him, telling the sick men that a party should come to their relief next day, proceeded on their march, but before they had gone four stadia, they found other soldiers resting by the way in the snow, and covered up with it, no guard being stationed over them. They roused them up, but they said that the head of the army was not moving forward. Xenophon, going past them, and sending on some of the ablest of the peltasts, ordered them to ascertain what it was that hindered their progress. They brought word that the whole army was in that manner taking rest. Xenophon and his men, therefore, stationing such a guard as they could, took up their quarters there without fire or supper.

When it was near day, he sent the youngest of his men to the sick,telling them to rouse them and oblige them to proceed. At this juncture Cheirisophus sent some of his people from the villages to see how the rear was faring. The young men were rejoiced to see them, and gave them the sick to conduct to the camp, while they themselves went forward, and, before they had gone twenty stadia, found themselves at the village in which Cheirisophus was quartered. When they came together, it was thought safe enough to lodge the troops up and down in the villages. Cheirisophus accordingly remained where he was, and the other officers, appropriating by lot the several villages that they had in sight, went to their respective quarters with their men.

Xenophon made the chief man of his village sup with him, and told him to be of good courage, assuring him that he should not be deprived of his children, and that they would not go away without filling his house with provisions in return for what they took, if he would but prove himself the author of some service to the army till they should reach another tribe. This he promised, and to show his goodwill, pointed out where some wine was buried. This night, therefore, the soldiers rested in their several quarters in the midst of great abundance, setting a guard over the chief. The following day Xenophon went with him to Cheirisophus, and wherever he passed by a village, he turned aside to visit those who were quartered in it, and found them in all parts feasting and enjoying themselves; nor would they anywhere let them go till they had set refreshments before them; lamb, kid, pork, veal, and fowl, with plenty of bread, both of wheat and barley. Whenever any person, to pay a compliment, wished to drink to another he took him to the large bowl, where he had to stoop down and drink, sucking like an ox.

When they came to Cheirisophus they found his men also feasting in their quarters, crowned with wreaths made of hay, and Armenian boys, in their Barbarian dresses, waiting upon them. When Cheirisophus and Xenophon had saluted one another, they both asked the chief man, through the interpreter who spoke the Persian language, what country it was. He replied that it was Armenia, and added that the neighbouring country was that of the Chalybes, and told them in what direction the road lay.

When the eighth day was come Xenophon committed the guide to Cheirisophus, [and he] conducted them through the snow, walking at liberty. When he came to the end of the third day's march, Cheirisophus was angry at him for not guiding them to some villages. He said that there were none in that part of the country. Cheirisophus then struck him, but did not confine him; and in consequence he ran off in the night.

After this occurrence they proceeded seven days' journey, five parasangs each day, till they came to the river Phasis, the breadth of which is a plethrum. Hence they advanced two days' journey, ten parasangs; when, on the pass that led over the mountains into the plain, the Chalybes, Taochi, and Phasians were drawn up to oppose their progress. Cheirisophus accordingly ordered the other officers to bring up their companies, that the whole force might be formed in line.

When the rear-guard was come up, he called together the generals and captains, and spoke to them as follows:

"The enemy, as you see, are in possession of the pass over the mountains. It is my opinion, therefore, that we should direct the troops to get their dinner, and that we ourselves should hold a council whether it is advisable to cross the mountain to-day or to-morrow."

"It seems best to me," exclaimed Cleanor, "to march at once, as soon as we have dined and resumed our arms."

After him Xenophon said: "I am of opinion that we ought to make our arrangements so as to fight with the greatest advantage. The range of hills, as far as we see, extends more than sixty stadia in length, but the people nowhere seem to be watching us except along the line of road; and it is therefore better, I think, to try to seize unobserved some part of the unguarded range. Nor do I think it at all impracticable for us to steal a way for ourselves, as we can march by night, so as not to be seen. We seem likely, too, if we make a pretended attack on this point, to find the rest of the range still less guarded, for the enemy will so much the more probably stay where they are. But why should I speak doubtfully about stealing? For I hear that you Lacedæmonians, O Cheirisophus, practise stealing from your boyhood, and it is not a disgrace, but an honour, to steal whatever the law does not forbid; while in order that you may steal with the utmost dexterity, and strive to escape discovery, it is appointed by law that, if you are caught stealing, you are scourged. It is now high time for you, therefore, to give proof of your education, and to take care that we may not receive many stripes."

"But I hear that you Athenians also," rejoined Cheirisophus, "are very clever at stealing the public money, though great danger threatens him that steals it, so that it is time for you likewise to give proof of your education."

"I am then ready," exclaimed Xenophon, "to march with the rearguard, as soon as we have supped, to take possession of the hills."

Cheirisophus then said, "But why should you go, and leave the charge of the rear? Rather send others, unless some volunteers present themselves."

Upon this Aristonymus of Methydria came forward with his heavy-armed men, and Aristeas of Chios and Nicomachus of Œta with their light-armed; and they made an arrangement that as soon as they should reach the top, they should light a number of fires.

When they had taken their supper, and night came on, those appointed for the service went forward and got possession of the hills; the other troops rested where they were. The enemy, when they saw the heights occupied, kept watch and burned a number of fires all night. As soon as it was day, Cheirisophus, after having offered sacrifice, marched forward along the road, while those who had gained the heights advanced by the ridge. Most of the enemy, meanwhile, stayed at the pass, but a part went to meet the troops coming along the heights. But before the main bodies came together, those on the ridge closed with one another, and the Greeks had the advantage, and put the enemy to flight. At the same time the Greek peltasts ran up from the plain to attack the enemy drawn up to receive them, and Cheirisophus followed at a quick pace with the heavy-armed men. The enemy at the pass, however, when they saw those above defeated, took to flight. The Greeks, as soon as they had gained the ascent, and had sacrificed and erected a trophy, went down into the plain before them, and arrived at a number of villages stored with abundance of excellent provisions.

From hence they marched five days' journey, thirty parasangs, to the country of the Taochi, where provisions began to fail them; for the Taochi inhabited strong fastnesses, in which they had laid up all their supplies. Having at length, however, arrived at one place which had no city or houses attached to it, but in which men and women and a great number of cattle were assembled, Cheirisophus, as soon as he came before it, made it the object of an attack, and when the first division that assailed it began to be tired, another succeeded, and then another; for it was not possible for them to surround it in a body as there was a river about it. When Xenophon came up with his rear-guard, peltasts, and heavy-armed men Cheirisophus exclaimed, "You come seasonably, for we must take this place, as there are no provisions for the army, unless we take it."

Xenophon asking what hindered them from taking the place, Cheirisophus replied, "The only approach to it is the one which you see, but when any of our men attempt to pass along it, the enemy roll down stones over yonder impending rock."

"But if they expend all their stones," rejoined Xenophon, "is there anything else to prevent us from advancing? The space through which we have to pass is, as you see, only about a hundred and fifty feet in length, and of this about a hundred feet are covered with large pine-trees in groups, against which, if the men place themselves, what would they suffer either from the flying stones or the rolling ones? The remaining part of the space is not above fifty feet, over which, when the stones cease, we must pass at a running pace."

"But," said Cheirisophus, "the instant we offer to go to the part covered with trees the stones fly in great numbers."

"That," cried Xenophon, "would be the very thing we want, for thus they will exhaust their stones the sooner. Let us then advance, if we can, to the point whence we shall have but a short way to run, and from which we may, if we please, easily retreat."

Cheirisophus and Xenophon, with Callimachus of Parrhasia, one of the captains, who had that day the lead of all the other captains of the rear-guard, then went forward, all the rest of the captains remaining out of danger. Next about seventy of the men advanced under the trees, one by one, each sheltering himself as he could. Agasias of Stymphalus, and Aristonymus of Methydria, who were also captains of the rear-guard, with some others, were at the same time standing behind, without the trees, for it was not safe for more than one company to stand under them. Callimachus then adopted the following stratagem: he ran forward two or three paces from the tree under which he was sheltered, and when the stones began to be hurled, hastily drew back; and at each of his sallies more than ten cartloads of stones were spent. Agasias, observing what Callimachus was doing, and that the eyes of the whole army were upon him, and fearing that he himself might not be the first to enter the place, began to advance alone, and passed by all the rest. Callimachus, seeing him rushing by, caught hold of the rim of his shield, and at that moment Aristonymus of Methydria ran past them both, and after him Eurylochus of Lusia, for all these sought distinction for valour, and were rivals to one another; and thus in mutual emulation they got possession of the place, for when they had once rushed in not a stone was hurled from above. But a dreadful spectacle was then to be seen; for the women, flinging their children over the precipice, threw themselves after them; and the men followed their example. Thus very few prisoners were taken, but a great number of oxen, asses, and sheep.

Hence they advanced, seven days' journey, a distance of fifty parasangs, through the country of the Chalybes. These were the most warlike people of all that they had passed through, and came to close combat with them. They stayed in their villages till the Greeks had passed by, when they pursued and perpetually harassed them. They had their dwellings in strong places, in which they had also laid up their provisions, so that the Greeks could get nothing from that country, but lived upon the cattle which they had taken from the Taochi.

The Greeks next arrived at the river Harpasus, the breadth of which was four plethra. Hence they proceeded through the territory of the Scythini, four days' journey, making twenty parasangs, over a level tract, until they came to some villages, in which they halted three days, and collected provisions. From this place they advanced four days' journey, twenty parasangs, to a large, rich, and populous city, called Gymnias, from which the governor of the country sent the Greeks a guide, to conduct them through a region at war with his own people. The guide, when he came, said that he would take them in five days to a place whence they should see the sea; if not, he would consent to be put to death.

On the fifth day they came to the mountain, and the name of it was Theches. When the men who were in the front had mounted the height, and looked down upon the sea, a great shout proceeded from them; and Xenophon and the rear-guard, on hearing it, thought that some new enemies were assailing the front. But as the noise still increased and drew nearer, and as those who came up from time to time kept running at full speed to join those who were continually shouting, the cries became louder as the men became more numerous, it appeared to Xenophon that it must be something of very great moment. Mounting his horse, therefore, and taking with him Lycius and the cavalry, he hastened forward to give aid, when presently they heard the soldiers shouting, "The sea, the sea!" and cheering on one another. They then all began to run, the rear-guard as well as the rest, and the baggage-cattle and horses were put to their speed; and when they had all arrived at the top, the men embraced one another, and their generals and captains, with tears in their eyes.

[*Thus, in a few more days, they reached Trebizond, having been five months upon the march.*]

ANCIENT ROME

THE JOURNEY TO BRUNDUSIUM[1]

QUINTUS HORATIUS FLACCUS

(65-8 B.C.)

HAVING left mighty Rome, Aricia received me in but a middling inn: Heliodorus the rhetorician, most learned in the Greek language, was my fellow-traveller : thence we proceeded to Forum-Appî, stuffed with sailors and surly landlords. This stage, but one for better travellers than we, being laggard we divided into two ; the Appian Way is less tiresome to bad travellers. Here I, on account of the water, which was most vile, proclaim war against my belly, waiting not without impatience for my companions whilst at supper. Now the night was preparing to spread her shadows upon the earth, and to display the constellations in the heavens. Then our slaves began to be liberal of their abuse to the watermen, and the watermen to our slaves. "Here bring to." "You are stowing in hundreds ; hold, now sure there is enough." Thus while the fare is paid and the mule fastened, a whole hour is passed away. The cursed gnats, and frogs of the fens, drive off repose, while the waterman and a passenger, well soaked with plenty of thick wine, vie with one another in singing the praises of their absent mistresses. At length the passenger being fatigued, begins to sleep, and the lazy waterman ties the halter of the mule turned out a-grazing to a stone, and snores, lying flat on his back.

And now the day approached, when we saw the boat made no way, until a choleric fellow, one of the passengers, leaps out of the boat, and drubs the head and sides of both mule and waterman with a willow cudgel. At last we were scarcely set ashore at the fourth hour. We wash our faces and hands in thy water, O Feronia. Then, having dined, we crawled on three miles ; and arrive under Anxur, which is built upon rocks that look white to a great distance. Mæcenas was to come here, as was the excellent Cocceius, both sent ambassadors on matters of great importance, having been accustomed to reconcile friends at variance. Here, having got sore eyes, I was obliged to use the black ointment. In the mean time came Mæcenas and Cocceius, and Fonteius Capito along with them, a man of perfect polish, and intimate with Mark Antony, no man more so.

Without regret we passed Fundi, where Aufidius Luscus was prætor, laughing at the honours of that crazy scribe, his prætexta, laticlave, and pan

[1] From *Satires*, I, v, translated by C. Smart.

of incense. At our next stage, being weary, we tarry in the city of the Mamurræ, Murena complimenting us with his house, and Capito with his kitchen.

The next day arises, by much the most agreeable to all, for Plotius and Varius and Virgil met us at Sinuessa ; souls more candid ones than which the world never produced, nor is there a person in the world more bound to them than myself. Oh what embraces and what transports were there! While I am in my senses, nothing can I prefer to a pleasant friend. The village, which is next adjoining to the bridge of Campania, accommodated us with lodging at night, and the public officers with such a quantity of fuel and salt as they are obliged to by law.

From this place the mules deposited their pack-saddles at Capua betimes in the morning. Mæcenas goes to play at tennis, but I and Virgil to our repose, for to play at tennis is hurtful to weak eyes and feeble constitutions.

From this place the villa of Cocceius, situated above the Caudian inns, which abounds with plenty, receives us. Now, my muse, I beg of you briefly to relate the engagement between the buffoon Sarmentus and Messius Cicirrus, and from what ancestry descended each began the contest. The illustrious race of Messius—Oscan ; Sarmentus's mistress is still alive.[1] Sprung from such families as these, they came to the combat.

First, Sarmentus : "I pronounce thee to have the look of a mad horse."

We laugh, and Messius himself says :

"I accept your challenge," and wags his head.

"Oh !" cries Sarmentus, "if the horn were not cut off your forehead, what would you not do, since, maimed as you are, you bully at such a rate ?"

For a foul scar has disgraced the left part of Messius's bristly forehead. Cutting many jokes upon his Campanian disease and upon his face, Sarmentus desired him to exhibit Polyphemus's dance, that he had no occasion for a mask or the tragic buskins.

Cicirrus retorted largely to these : he asked whether he had consecrated his chain[2] to the household gods according to his vow, though he was a scribe, he told him, his mistress's property in him was not the less. Lastly he asked him how he ever came to run away, such a lank meagre fellow, for whom a pound of corn a-day would be ample.[3] We were so diverted that we continued that supper to an unusual length.

[1] Sarmentus had been a slave.

[2] A freed slave consecrated his chains to Saturn. For Saturn Messius substitutes the *Dii Lares*, or *Viales*, the gods of the highway, thereby implying Sarmentus was a fugitive.

[3] A slave was allowed a pound of corn a day.

Hence we proceed straight on for Beneventum, where the bustling landlord almost burned himself in roasting some lean thrushes, for the fire falling through the old kitchen floor, the spreading flame made a great progress towards the highest part of the roof. Then you might have seen the hungry guests and frightened slaves snatching their supper out of the flames, and every body endeavouring to extinguish the fire.

After this Apulia began to discover to me her well-known mountains, which the Atabulus scorches with his blasts, and through which we should never have crept unless the neighbouring village of Trivicus had received us, not without a smoke that brought tears into our eyes—occasioned by a hearth's burning some green boughs with the leaves upon them. Here, like a great fool as I was, I wait till midnight for a deceitful mistress ; sleep, however, overcomes me whilst meditating love, and disagreeable dreams make me ashamed of myself and every thing about me.

Hence we were bowled away in chaises twenty-four miles, intending to stop at a little town, which one cannot name in a verse,[1] but it is easily enough known by description ; for water is sold here, though it is the worst in the world ; but their bread is exceedingly fine, insomuch that the wary traveller is used to carry it willingly on his shoulders, for the bread of Canusium is gritty, which place was formerly built by the valiant Diomedes. Here Varius departs dejected from his weeping friends.

Hence we came to Rubi, fatigued, because we made a long journey, and it was rendered still more troublesome by the rains. Next day the weather was better, the road worse, even to the very walls of Barium that abounds in fish. In the next place, Egnatia, which seems to have been built on troubled waters, gave us occasion for jests and laughter, for they wanted to persuade us that at this sacred portal the incense melted without fire. The Jew, Apella, may believe this, not I ! For I have learned from Epicurus that the gods dwell in a state of tranquillity ; nor, if nature effect any wonder, that the anxious gods sent it from the high canopy of the heavens.

Brundusium ends both my journey and my paper.

[1] Equotuticum.

OF THE ILE OF BRYTAINE AND OF THOSE THAT ENVIRON IT[1]

Gaius Julius Solinus

(*fl. third century* A.D.)

THE Sea coast of *Gallia* had beene the ende of the worlde, but that the Ile of Brytaine for the largenesse thereof every way deserveth the name almoste of an other Worlde, for it is in length eyght hundred myles and more, so we measure it to the angle of Calydon, in which nooke an Alter engraven with Greek Letters for a vowe, beareth witnes that *Ulisses* arrived at Calydon. It is environed with many Iles and those not unrenowned, whereof Ireland draweth neerest to it in bygnesse, uncivill for the savage manners of the inhabiters, but otherwise so full of fat pasture, that if theyr Cattell in Sommer season be not now and then kept from feeding, they should run in danger of bursting. There are no Snakes, and fewe byrdes : the people are harbourless, and warlike. When they have overcome theyr enemies, they first besmeere their faces in the blood of them that be slayne, and then drinke of it. Be it right or be it wrong, all is one to them. If a woman be delivered of a manchilde shee layes his firste meate uppon her Husbands sworde, and putting it softlie to his pretie mouth, giveth him the first hansell of his foode uppon the very point of the weapon, praying (according to the manner of their Countrey) that he may not otherwise come to his death, then in battel and among weapons.

The Sea that is betweene Ireland and Brytaine being full of shallowes and rough all the yeere long, cannot be sayled but a fewe dayes in the Sommertime. They sayle in Keeles of wicker doone over with Neats leather. How long soever their passage continueth, the passengers abstaine from meate.

The Ile Thanatos is beaten upon with ye French Sea, and is divided from Brytaine with a very narrowe cutte, luckie for corne fieldes and fatte soyle, and not onely healthful to it selfe, but also to other places. For inasmuch as there is no snake creeping there, the earth therof to what place soever it bee carried from thence, killeth snakes. There bee many other Iles about Brytaine, of which Thule is ye furthest of, wherin, at such time as the Sun is at the hyghest in Sommer, and passeth through the signe of Cancer, there is almost no night at all. Againe in the deade of wynter when the Sunne is at the lowest, the day is so shorte, that the rysing and going downe of the Sunne is both together. Beyond Thule wee learne is a deade and frozen Sea. . . .

[1] From *Collectanea ; or, The excellent and pleasant worke of Julius Solinus, Polyhistor,* translated by Arthur Golding, Gent. (1587).

THE CREDULOUS TOURIST[1]

ANTONINUS OF PLACENTIA

(*fl. c.* A.D. 570)

THE blessed Antoninus the Martyr going on his way together with his companion, after he left Placentia, I will take care to explain in what parts I travelled, desiring to follow the footsteps of Christ, and see [the sites of] the miracles of the prophets.

So starting from Placentia,[2] we came to Constantinople, from which we came to the island of Cyprus, to the city of Constantia,[3] where St Epiphanius rests. It is a beautiful and agreeable city, and is adorned with date-palms. Thence we came into the parts of Syria, to the island of Antaradus;[4] and thence we came to Tripolis,[5] in Syria, where St Leontius rests, which city, together with some others, was destroyed by an earthquake in the time of the Emperor Justinian. Thence we came to Byblus,[6] which city also was destroyed with its inhabitants ; and likewise to the city of Trieris,[5] which also was similarly destroyed. Next we came to the most magnificent city of Berytus,[8] in which there was recently a school of literature, and which also was destroyed. We were told by the bishop of the city, who knew the sufferers personally„that without counting strangers, thirty thousand persons, in round numbers, here miserably perished. The city itself lies at the foot of Lebanon.

From Berytus we came to Sidon,[9] which itself was partly ruined, and which is near to the slope of Lebanon. The people in it are very wicked. There flows the river Asclepius,[10] and there is the source from which it rises. From Sidon we came to Sarepta,[11] which is a small and very Christian city. In it is the chamber which was built for Helias, and the bed upon which he lay, and a marble trough in which the widow [in Scripture] made her bread. In this place many offerings are made, and many miracles wrought. Leaving Sarepta, we came to the city of Tyre[12] seven miles from Sarepta. The city of Tyre contains influential men : the life there is very wicked, the luxury is such as cannot be described ; there are public brothels; and silk and other kinds of clothing are woven. Thence we came to Ptolemais,[13] a respectable city, where we found good monasteries.

[1] From *Of the Holy Places visited by Antoninus Martyr,* translated by Aubrey Stewart, for the Palestine Pilgrims' Text Society, 1885.

[2] Piacenza. [3] The ancient Salamis, on the east coast of Cyprus.

[4] The island of Ruad, off the coast of Syria. [5] Tarabulus. [6] Jebeil.

[7] Now probably Enfeh. [8] Beirût. [9] Now Saida.

[10] Probably the Bostrenus, Nahr el Auly.

[11] On the coast, about a mile from Surafend. [12] Now Sûr. [13] Acre.

Opposite Ptolemais, six miles off, is a city which is named Sycaminus,[1] under Mount Carmel, where, a mile from Sycaminus, are the hamlets [*castra*] of the Samaritans; and above the hamlets, a mile and a half away, is the monastery of Helisæus[2] the prophet, at the place where the woman met him, whose child he raised from the dead. On Mount Carmel is found a stone of small size and round, which when struck, rings because it is solid. This is the virtue of the stone : if it be hung on to a woman or to any animal, they will never miscarry. About six or seven miles off is the city of Porphyrion.[3]

From Ptolemais, by the seaside, we came to the borders of Galilee, to the city of Diocæsarea,[4] in which we adored with reverence the pail and basket of Blessed Mary. In that place, also, was the chair in which she was sitting when the angel came to her. Three miles farther we reached Chana, where our Lord was at the wedding ; and we reclined upon His very couch, upon which I, unworthy that I am, wrote the names of my parents. There are two water-jars there : one of them I filled with water, and brought forth from it wine ; and I raised it when full upon my shoulder, and carried it to the altar; and we bathed in the fountain for a blessing.

Thence we came to the city of Nazareth, in which there are many excellent things. In the synagogue there is still the book from which our Lord was set to learn ABC. In the synagogue, too, is the bench upon which our Lord used to sit with the other children. This bench can be moved and lifted up by Christians ; but Jews cannot by any means stir it ; nor does it permit itself to be carried out of doors. The house of the Blessed Mary is a basilica, and many cures are wrought in it by her garments. In the city the beauty of the Hebrew women is so great, that no more beautiful women are found among the Hebrews ; and this they say was granted them by the Blessed Mary, who they say was their mother. And though the Hebrews have no love for Christians, yet these women are all full of charity for them. This province is like a park, in corn and produce it is like Egypt ; but it excels in wine and oil, fruits and honey. Millet too is there unnaturally tall, higher than the stature of a tall man.

From Nazareth we came to Mount Tabor, which mountain rises from the centre of the plain : it is formed of productive earth, and is six miles in circuit, three in ascent, and has a plain of one mile on the top. . . .

From Tabor we came to the Sea of Tiberias . . . to a city which in former times was called Samaria, but which is now called Neapolis, in which there is the well from which our Lord asked the woman of Samaria for water. There

[1] Haifa el 'Atîkah, or Tell es Semak.

[2] Elijah.

[3] Porphyrion has been identified with Khan Neby Yûnas.

[4] Sepphoris, the modern Seffûrieh.

a church has been built in honour of St John the Baptist, and the well itself is placed before the rails of the altar, and in the same place is the water-pot from which the Lord is said to have drunk. Many sick persons come there and are healed.

Thence we came to the city of Tiberias, in which are hot baths of salt water; for the water of the sea itself is sweet—which sea is eight miles in circumference. Thence we came to the city of Capharnaum, to the house of blessed Peter, which is now a church. Thence passing hamlets or villages, or cities, we came to two fountains, that is to say, Jor and Dan, which flow into one stream and are called Jordan. The river is small where it enters the sea ; it flows through the whole sea, and runs out on the opposite shore. Returning, we came to the place where the Jordan leaves the sea, and at that place we crossed the Jordan, and came to a city named Gadara, which is also called Gabaon. . . . There died John of Placentia, the husband of Thecla.

And then we descended through Galilee along the banks of the Jordan, passing through many cities which are mentioned in Scripture, and reached the chief city of Galilee, which is named Scythopolis,[1] and stands upon a mountain, in which St John performed many miracles. Thence we descended through various places in Samaria and Judæa to the city of Sebaste,[2] in which Helisæus the prophet rests. Through the open country, cities, and villages of the Samaritans, and in the streets along which we passed, the Jews followed us with straw, burning our footsteps. These people have such a hatred for Christ, that they will scarcely give an answer to Christians ; and their custom is, that you must not touch anything that you wish to buy of them before you have given them its price ; but if you touch it and do not buy it, they will be offended immediately. And outside their city they have a building in which is a person who answers visitors. Also they will not take coins from your hand, but you must cast them into water ; and they announce this to you when you enter their city. Do not spit, for if you spit they will be offended. In the evening they cleanse themselves with water, and so enter their village or city.

Thence we came to the place where our Lord, with five loaves and two fishes, fed five thousand men, not counting women and children, which lies in a wide plain on which are olive and palm groves. Thence we came to the place where the Lord was baptized. In that very place the children of Israel crossed over Jordan, and the sons of the prophets lost their axe; and from that very place Helias was carried up into heaven. . . . In the valley itself Helias was found, when the raven used to bring him bread and meat. On the sides

[1] Beisan, the Biblical Bethshean, which did not, however, stand upon a mountain.

[2] Sebustîyeh.

of the valley live a multitude of hermits. . . .

We celebrated the Epiphany by the side of the Jordan, and wonders take place on that night in the place where the Lord was baptized. There is there a mound surrounded with railings; and at the place where the water returned to its bed, a wooden cross is fixed standing in the water; and upon the banks on each side marble steps descend into the water. Upon the eve of the Epiphany great vigils are held there, a vast crowd of people is collected, and after the cock has crowed for the fourth or fifth time, matins begin. After matins, as day begins to dawn, the deacons begin the holy mysteries and celebrate them in the open air; the priest descends into the river, and at the hour when he begins to bless the water, at once the Jordan, with a mighty noise, rolls back upon itself, and the water stands still until the baptism is completed. And all the men of Alexandria who have ships, with their crews, holding baskets full of spices and balsams, at the hour when the priest blesses the water, before they begin to baptize, throw those baskets into the river, and take thence holy water, with which they sprinkle their ships before they leave port for a voyage. After the rite of baptism is completed, all descend into the water for a blessing, clothed in linen cloths and various other kinds of clothing, which they preserve to be used for their burial. When all is finished, the water returns to its own bed; and from the place where the Jordan rises from the Sea of Tiberias, to the Salt Sea where it ends, is one hundred and thirty miles. . . .

From the Jordan to Jericho is six miles. Jericho appears to the eyes of all like a park [*paradisus*]. The walls have been destroyed by an earthquake. The house of Raab still stands, which is an inn; and the very chamber in which she hid the spies, which is a chapel of the Blessed Mary. The stones which the children of Israel took from the Jordan are placed in a church not far from the city, behind the altar; and before the church is the holy field of the Lord, in which the Lord sowed with His own hand, casting in seed to the amount of three measures [*modii*], which is still reaped twice in the year, but in the month of February, in order that it may be afterwards eaten as sacramental bread at Easter. When it has been reaped, it is ploughed, and a second time reaped together with the harvest from the other fields. Then it is ploughed again. . . .

Leaving Jericho, we travelled towards Jerusalem. Not far from the city of Jericho is the tree into which Zacchæus climbed that he might see the Lord; and it is inclosed in an oratory, and when looked at from above through the roof appears withered. So leaving Jericho, proceeding from the east towards the west, we had on our left hand the ashes of Sodom and Gomorrha, over which country there always hangs a dark cloud with a sulphurous odour. But as for what they say about Lot's wife, that she is diminished in size by being licked by animals, it is not true; but she stands just in the same condition as she originally was. . . .

Bowed to the earth and kissing the ground, we entered the holy city, through which we proceeded with prayer to the tomb of our Lord. The tomb itself, in which the Body of the Lord Jesus Christ was laid, is cut out of the natural rock. A brazen lamp, which was then placed at His head, burns there day and night; from which lamp we received a blessing and replaced it. Into the tomb earth is carried from without, and those who enter it bear away a blessing with them from it when they depart. The stone by which the tomb was closed lies in front of the tomb. The natural colour of the rock, which was hewn out of the rock of Golgotha, cannot now be discerned, because the stone itself is adorned with gold and precious stones. The stone of the tomb is as large as a millstone; its ornaments are innumerable. From iron rods hang armlets, bracelets, chains, necklaces, coronets, waistbands, sword-belts, and crowns of the emperors made of gold and precious stones, and a great number of ornaments given by empresses. The whole tomb, which has the appearance of the winning-post on a race course, is covered with silver; an altar is placed in front of the tomb, under some golden suns. . . .

Journeying through the desert, on the eighth day, we came to the place where Moses brought forth water from the rock, and after that we came to the mountain of God, Horeb, from which place we removed, that we might ascend Mount Sinai. Here, behold a multitude of monks and hermits! Bearing crosses and singing psalms, they came to meet us, and, falling upon the ground, they did reverence to us. We also did likewise, shedding tears. Then they led us into the valley between Horeb and Sinai, at the foot of which mountain is the fountain at which Moses was watering his sheep when he saw the burning bush, which fountain is now within the monastery. The monastery is surrounded by walls, and in it are three abbots learned in tongues—that is to say, Latin, Greek, Syriac, Egyptian, and Persian—and many interpreters of each language. In it are dwellings of monks. We ascended the mountain unceasingly for three miles, and came to the place of the cave in which Helias was hidden when he fled before Jezebel. Before the cave rises a fountain, which flows down the mountain. Thence we ascend unceasingly for three miles farther, to the topmost peak of the mountain, upon which is a small chapel, having six feet, more or less, in length and in breadth. In this no one is permitted to pass the night; but after the sun has risen, the monks ascend thither and perform the Divine Office. In this place many, out of devotion, cut off their hair and beard, and throw them away; and there I also trimmed and cut my beard.

Mount Sinai is stony, with earth only in a few places. Round about it are the cells of many servants of God, and likewise in Horeb. They say that Horeb means 'clean earth.' . . .

Between Sinai and Horeb is a valley, in which at certain times dew descends from heaven, which they call manna. It thickens and becomes like grains of mastic, and is collected. Jars full of it are kept upon the mountain, and they give away small bottles of it for a blessing; and they gave us five sextarii [pint and a half] of it. They also drink it as a relish; and they gave some of it to us, and we drank it. Upon those mountains feed lions and leopards, wild goats and mules, and wild asses together, and none of them are hurt by the lions because of the vastness of the desert. . . .

From the Mount Sinai to the city of Arabia, which is called Abila,[1] is eight stages. To Abila come ships from India, bringing various spices. We, however, determined to return through Egypt. So we came to the city of Phara,[2] in which Moses fought with Amalech, where is a chapel, the altar of which is placed upon the stones which they placed under Moses when he prayed. In that place is a city fortified with walls made of brick, and the place is very bare of everything except water. There, women with children met us, bearing in their hands palms and flasks of oil of roses; and kneeling down at our feet, they anointed the soles of our feet and our heads, singing in the Egyptian tongue the hymn, "Blessed are ye of the Lord, and blessed is your coming: Hosanna in the highest." This is the land of the Midianites, and they are the dwellers in the city; it is said that they descend from the family of Jethro, the father-in-law of Moses.

Thence we came to Magdolum[3] and Sochot, and to a place where there are seventy palm-trees and twelve fountains; and we rested there for two days, being fatigued with such great toils and with the greatness of the desert. In this place is a small castle, which is named Surandela,[4] and it contains nothing but a church with its priest and two hospices for the use of travellers. In this place I saw a pepper-tree, and gathered pepper from the tree itself. Thence we came to the place where the children of Israel marked out their camp after passing the Red Sea, and here likewise is a small castle with a hospice. And thence we came to the place on the shore of the sea, where the children of Israel crossed over and came out of the sea. There is the oratory of Moses; and there is a small city, named Clysma,[5] whither also ships come from India. At

[1] Elath, or Ailath, now 'Akabah.
[2] Phara stood where now is Feirân,
[3] Wâdy Mughârah.
[4] Wâdy Gharandel.
[5] Suez.

that part of the sea where they crossed over, a gulf reaches out from the main sea, and runs in for many miles, for the tide rises and falls. When the tidefalls, all the marks of the army of Pharaoh, and even the tracks of his chariot-wheels, appear; but all the arms seem to have been turned into stone. . . .

Thence we came through the desert to the cave of blessed Paul, which is named Syracumba, near a fountain, which up to the present time waters the whole place. Thence journeying again through the desert, we came to the cataracts of the Nile, where the water rises to a mark, a register made by the hand of man, which has twelve steps. Near the cataract upon either bank of the Nile are two cities, which the daughters of Lot are said to have built; one of them is named Babylonia. Then we came through the plains of Tanis,[1] to the city of Memphis,[2] and to Antinoe,[3] where Pharaoh lived, from which cities the children of Israel went out. At these places are the granaries of Joseph, twelve in number, full of wheat. . . .

Descending through Egypt, we came to the city of Athlibis,[4] and. . . thence . . . to Alexandria in boats over the marsh. In the marsh itself we saw a great number of crocodiles. . . .

We came again to Jerusalem where I remained sick for a long time, evidently for the increase of my faith. Then I saw in a vision blessed Antonius and blessed Euphemia; when the vision appeared it healed me. Leaving Jerusalem, I went down to Joppa[5] . . . thence I came to Cæsarea Philippi. Thence we went up through Galilee, and came to Damascus. There is there a monastery at the second milestone, where St Paul was converted in the street which is called Straight, where many miracles are wrought. Thence we came to Heliopolis,[6] and thence to Emesa,[7] where there is the head of John the Baptist in a glass jar, and we with our own eyes saw it within the jar and adored it. Thence passing through the cities of Larissa,[8] Arethusa,[9] and Epiphania,[10] we came to the most magnificent city of Apamia,[11] in which dwell all the nobles of Syria.

Leaving that place we came to the greater Antioch, where rests St Babylas and three children, St Justina and St Julian; thence we came down into Mesopotamia to the city of Chalcis.[12] Thence we came to Carrha,[13] where Abraham was born; and descending came to the city of Barbarissus,[14] thence

[1] Sân. [2] Near Bedrasheyn.
[3] Sheikh Abideh. Antoninus has misplaced his towns. [4] Probably Athribis.
[5] Jaffa. [6] Baalbek. [7] Homs.
[8] Kala'at Seijar. [9] Restan. [10] Hamah.
[11] Kala'at el Medyk. Antoninus again disarranges his towns.
[12] Kinnisrin. [13] Harran. [14] Barbalissus, now Kala'at Balis.

to Sura,[1] through the midst of which runs the river Euphrates, which is there crossed by a bridge.

Having seen so many places full of wonders throughout so many cities, castles, villages, houses, and roads, wearied with so long a journey, we began to return. Crossing the sea, we came to Italy, our own country, by the help of our Lord Jesus Christ. With joy we came to Placentia, our own city.

[1] Surieh.

ARABIA

OF A PROPHECY AND ITS FULFILMENT [1]

(A.D. 1325)

IBN BATUTA

(1304-78)

[*Abu Abdullah Mohammed, surnamed Ibn Batuta, set out upon his travels at the age of twenty-two. For twenty-eight years he wandered through Arabia, East Africa, India, China, South Russia, Palestine, Egypt, Andalusia (or Spain), etc., making, in addition, the pilgrimage to Mecca four times. In 1355 he dictated the story of his travels to Mohammed Ibn Juzayy, who thus concludes the narration: "It is plain to any man of intelligence that this shaykh is the traveller of the age: and if one were to say 'the traveller par excellence of this our Muslim community' he would be guilty of no exaggeration."*

The episodes here given tell of a prophecy made to him on his setting out in 1325 and of its fulfilment seventeen years later when the Sultan Muhammad sent him as envoy to China.]

I

I LEFT Tangier, my birthplace, on Thursday, 2nd Rajab, 725 (14th June, 1325), being at that time twenty-two years of age, with the intention of making the Pilgrimage to the Holy House (at Mecca) and the Tomb of the Prophet (at Madína). I set out alone, finding no companion to cheer the way with friendly intercourse, and no party of travellers with whom to associate myself. Swayed by an over-mastering impulse within me, and a long-cherished desire to visit those glorious sanctuaries, I resolved to quit all my friends and tear myself away from my home. As my parents were still alive, it weighed grievously upon me to part from them, and both they and I were afflicted with sorrow.

On reaching the city of Tilimsán (Tlemsen), whose sultan at that time was Abú Táshifín, I found there two ambassadors of the Sultan of Tunis, who left the city on the same day that I arrived. One of the brethren having advised me to accompany them, I consulted the will of God in this matter, and after a stay of three days in the city to procure all that I needed, I rode after them with all speed. I overtook them at the town of Miliána, where we stayed ten days, as both ambassadors fell sick on account of the summer heats. When we set out again, one of them grew worse, and died after we had stopped for three nights

[1] From *Travels of Ibn Batuta*, translated by H. A. R. Gibb, in the "Broadway Travellers" series, 1929.

by a stream four miles from Miliána. I left their party there and pursued my journey, with a company of merchants from Tunis. On reaching al-Jazá'ir (Algiers) we halted outside the town for a few days, until the former party rejoined us, when we went on together through the Mitíja to the mountain of Oaks (Jurjúra) and so reached Bijáya (Bougie). . . . At Bijáya I fell ill of a fever, and one of my friends advised me to stay there till I recovered. But I refused, saying,

"If God decrees my death, it shall be on the road, with my face set toward Mecca."

"If that is your resolve," he replied, "sell your ass and your heavy baggage, and I shall lend you what you require. In this way you will travel light, for we must make haste on our journey, for fear of meeting roving Arabs on the way."

I followed his advice and he did as he had promised—may God reward him!

On reaching Qusantínah (Constantine) we camped outside the town, but a heavy rain forced us to leave our tents during the night and take refuge in some houses there. Next day the governor of the city came to meet us. Seeing my clothes all soiled by the rain, he gave orders that they should be washed at his house, and in place of my old worn headcloth sent me a headcloth of fine Syrian cloth, in one of the ends of which he had tied two gold dinars. This was the first alms I received on my journey. From Qusantínah we reached Bona where, after staying in the town for several days, we left the merchants of our party on account of the dangers of the road, while we pursued our journey with the utmost speed. I was again attacked by fever, so I tied myself in the saddle with a turbancloth in case I should fall by reason of my weakness. So great was my fear that I could not dismount until we arrived at Tunis. The population of the city came out to meet the members of our party, and on all sides greetings and questions were exchanged, but not a soul greeted me as no one there was known to me. I was so affected by my loneliness that I could not restrain my tears and wept bitterly, until one of the pilgrims realized the cause of my distress and coming up to me greeted me kindly and continued to entertain me with friendly talk until I entered the city.

The Sultan of Tunis at that time was Abú Yahyá, the son of Abú Zakaríya II, and there were a number of notable scholars in the town. During my stay the festival of the Breaking of the Fast fell due, and I joined the company at the Praying-ground. The inhabitants assembled in large numbers to celebrate the festival, making a brave show and wearing their richest apparel. The Sultan Abú Yahyá arrived on horseback, accompanied by all his relatives, courtiers, and officers of state walking on foot in a stately procession. After the recital of the prayer and the conclusion of the Allocution the people returned to their homes.

Some time later the pilgrim caravan for the Hijáz was formed, and they nominated me as their qádí (judge). We left Tunis early in November, following the coast road through Súsa, Sfax, and Qábis, where we stayed for ten days on account of incessant rains. Thence we set out for Tripoli, accompanied for several stages by a hundred or more horsemen as well as a detachment of archers, out of respect for whom the Arabs kept their distance. I had made a contract of marriage at Sfax with the daughter of one of the syndics at Tunis, and at Tripoli she was conducted to me, but after leaving Tripoli I became involved in a dispute with her father, which necessitated my separation from her. I then married the daughter of a student from Fez, and when she was conducted to me I detained the caravan for a day by entertaining them all at a wedding party.

At length on April 5th (1326) we reached Alexandria. It is a beautiful city, well built and fortified with four gates and a magnificent port. Among all the ports in the world I have seen none to equal it except Kawlam (Quilon) and Cálicút, in India, the port of the infidels (Genoese) at Súdáq in the land of the Turks, and the port of Zaytún in China. . . . I went to see the lighthouse on this occasion and found one of its faces in ruins. It is a very high square building, and its door is above the level of the earth. Opposite the door, and of the same height, is a building from which there is a plank bridge to the door; if this is removed there is no means of entrance. Inside the door is a place for the lighthouse-keeper, and within the lighthouse there are many chambers. The breadth of the passage inside is nine spans and that of the wall ten spans; each of the four sides of the lighthouse is 140 spans in breadth. It is situated on a high mound, and lies three miles from the city on a long tongue of land which juts out into the sea from close by the city wall, so that the lighthouse cannot be reached by land except from the city. On my return to the West in the year 750 (1349) I visited the lighthouse again, and found that it had fallen into so ruinous a condition that it was not possible to enter it or climb up to the door. Al-Malik an-Násir had started to build a similar lighthouse alongside it, but was prevented by death from completing the work. Another of the marvellous things in this city is the awe-inspiring marble column in its outskirts which they call the "Pillar of Columns." It is a single block, skilfully carved, erected on a plinth of square stones like enormous platforms, and no one knows how it was erected there nor for certain who erected it.

One of the learned men of Alexandria was the qádí, a master of eloquence, who used to wear a turban of extraordinary size. Never either in the eastern or the western lands have I seen a more voluminous head-gear. Another of them was the pious ascetic Burhán ad-Din, whom I met during my stay and whose hospitality I enjoyed for three days. One day as I entered his room he said to me:

"I see that you are fond of travelling through foreign lands."

I replied, "Yes, I am" (though I had as yet no thought of going to such distant lands as India or China).

Then he said, "You must certainly visit my brother Faríd ad-Din in India, and my brother Rukn ad-Dín in Sind, and my brother Burhán ad-Din in China, and when you find them give them greeting from me."

I was amazed at his prediction, and the idea of going to these countries having been cast into my mind, my journeys never ceased until I had met these three that he named and conveyed his greeting to them.

During my stay at Alexandria I had heard of the pious Shaykh al-Murshidí, who bestowed gifts miraculously created at his desire. He lived in solitary retreat in a cell in the country where he was visited by princes and ministers. Parties of men in all ranks of life used to come to him every day and he would supply them all with food. Each one of them would desire to eat some flesh or fruit or sweetmeat at his cell, and to each he would give what he had suggested, though it was frequently out of season. His fame was carried from mouth to mouth far and wide, and the Sultan too had visited him several times in his retreat. I set out from Alexandria to seek this shaykh and passing through Damanhúr came to Fawwá (Fua), a beautiful township, close by which, separated from it by a canal, lies the shaykh's cell. I reached this cell about mid-afternoon, and on saluting the shaykh I found that he had with him one of the sultan's aides-de-camp, who had encamped with his troops just outside. The shaykh rose and embraced me, and calling for food invited me to eat. When the hour of the afternoon prayer arrived he set me in front as prayer-leader, and did the same on every occasion when we were together at the times of prayer during my stay. When I wished to sleep he said to me:

"Go up to the roof of the cell and sleep there" (this was during the summer heats).

I said to the officer: "In the name of God," but he replied (quoting from the Koran):

"There is none of us but has an appointed place."

So I mounted to the roof and found there a straw mattress and a leather mat, a water vessel for ritual ablutions, a jar of water, and a drinking-cup, and I lay down there to sleep.

That night while I was sleeping on the roof of the cell I dreamed that I was on the wing of a great bird which was flying with me towards Mecca, then to Yemen, then eastwards, and thereafter going towards the south, then flying far eastwards, and finally landing in a dark and green country, where it left me. I was astonished at this dream and said to myself, "If the shaykh can interpret my dream for me, he is all that they say he is."

Next morning, after all the other visitors had gone, he called me and when I had related my dream interpreted it to me saying:

"You will make the pilgrimage [to Mecca] and visit [the Tomb of] the Prophet, and you will travel through Yemen, 'Iráq, the country of the Turks, and India. You will stay there for a long time and meet there my brother Dilshád the Indian, who will rescue you from a danger into which you will fall."

Then he gave me a travelling-provision of small cakes and money, and I bade him farewell and departed. Never since parting from him have I met on my journeys aught but good fortune, and his blessings have stood me in good stead.

II

The King of China had sent valuable gifts to the Sultan, including a hundred slaves of both sexes, five hundred pieces of velvet and silk cloth, musk, jewelled garments and weapons, with a request that the Sultan would permit him to rebuild the idol-temple which is near the mountains called Qarájil (Himalaya). It is in a place known as Samhal, to which the Chinese go on pilgrimage; the Muslim army in India had captured it, laid it in ruins and sacked it. The Sultan, on receiving this gift, wrote to the King saying that the request could not be granted by Islamic law, as permission to build a temple in the territories of the Muslims was granted only to those who paid a poll-tax; to which he added, "If thou wilt pay the *jizya* we shall empower thee to build it. And peace be on those who follow the True Guidance." He requited his present with an even richer one—a hundred thoroughbred horses, a hundred white slaves, a hundred Hindu dancing- and singing-girls, twelve hundred pieces of various kinds of cloth, gold and silver candelabra and basins, brocade robes, caps, quivers, swords, gloves embroidered with pearls, and fifteen eunuchs. As my fellow-ambassadors the Sultan appointed the amír Zahítr ad-Din of Zanján, one of the most eminent men of learning, and the eunuch Káfúr, the cup-bearer, into whose keeping the present was entrusted. He sent the amír Muhammad of Herát with a thousand horsemen to escort us to the port of embarkation, and we were accompanied by the

Chinese ambassadors, fifteen in number, along with their servants, about a hundred men in all.

We set out therefore in imposing force and formed a large camp. The Sultan gave instructions that we were to be supplied with provisions while we were travelling through his dominions. Our journey began on the 17th of Safar 743 (22nd July, 1342). That was the day selected because they choose either the 2nd, 7th, 12th, 17th, 22nd, or 27th of the month as the day for setting out. On the first day's journey we halted at the post-station of Tilbat, seven miles from Delhi, and travelled thence through Bayána, a large and well-built town with a magnificent mosque, to Kúl (Koel, Aligarh), where we encamped in a wide plain outside the town.

On reaching Koel we heard that certain Hindu infidels had invested and surrounded the town of al-Jalálí. Now this town lies at a distance of seven miles from Koel, so we made in that direction. Meanwhile the infidels were engaged in battle with its inhabitants and the latter were on the verge of destruction. The infidels knew nothing of our approach until we charged down upon them, though they numbered about a thousand cavalry and three thousand foot, and we killed them to the last man and took possession of their horses and their weapons. Of our party twenty-three horsemen and fifty-five foot-soldiers suffered martyrdom, amongst them the eunuch Káfúr, the cup-bearer, into whose hands the present had been entrusted. We informed the Sultan by letter of his death and halted to await his reply. During that time the infidels used to swoop down from an inaccessible hill which is in those parts and raid the environs of al-Jalálí, and our party used to ride out every day with the commander of that district to assist him in driving them off.

On one of these occasions I rode out with several of my friends and we went into a garden to take our siesta, for this was in the hot season. Then we heard some shouting, so we mounted our horses and overtook some infidels who had attacked one of the villages of al-Jalálí. When we pursued them they broke up into small parties; our troop in following them did the same, and I was isolated with five others. At this point we were attacked by a body of cavalry and foot-soldiers from a thicket thereabouts, and we fled from them because of their numbers. About ten of them pursued me, but afterwards all but three of them gave up the chase. There was no road at all before me and the ground there was very stony. My horse's forefeet got caught between the stones, so I dismounted, freed its foot and mounted again. It is customary for a man in India to carry two swords, one, called the stirrup-sword, attached to the saddle, and the other in his quiver. My stirrup-sword fell out of its scabbard, and as its ornaments were of gold I dismounted, picked it up, slung it on me and mounted, my pursuers chasing me all the while. After this I came to a deep nullah, so I dismounted and climbed down to the bottom of it, and that was the last I saw of them.

I came out of this into a valley amidst a patch of tangled wood, traversed by a road, so I walked along it, not knowing where it led to. At this juncture about forty of the infidels, carrying bows in their hands, came out upon me and surrounded me. I was afraid that they would all shoot at me at once it I fled from them, and I was wearing no armour, so I threw myself to the ground and surrendered, as they do not kill those who do that. They seized me and stripped me of everything that I was carrying except a tunic, shirt and trousers, then they took me into that patch of jungle, and finally brought me to the part of it where they stayed, near a tank of water situated amongst those trees. They gave me bread made of peas, and I ate some of it and drank some water. In their company there were two Muslims who spoke to me in Persian, and asked me all about myself. I told them part of my story, but concealed the fact that I had come from the Sultan. Then they said to me: "You are sure to be put to death either by these men or by others, but this man here (pointing to one of them) is their leader." So I spoke to him, using the two Muslims as interpreters, and tried to conciliate him. He gave me in charge of three of the band, one of them an old man, with whom was his son, and the third an evil black fellow. These three spoke to me and I understood from them that they had received orders to kill me. In the evening of the same day they carried me off to a cave, but God sent an ague upon the black, so he put his feet upon me, and the old man and his son went to sleep. In the morning they talked among themselves and made signs to me to accompany them down to the tank. I realized that they were going to kill me, so I spoke to the old man and tried to gain his favour, and he took pity on me. I cut off the sleeves of my shirt and gave them to him so that the other members of the band should not blame him on my account if I escaped.

About noon we heard voices near the tank and they thought that it was their comrades, so they made signs to me to go down with them, but when we went down we found some other people. The new-comers advised my guards to accompany them but they refused, and the three of them sat down in front of me; keeping me facing them, and laid on the ground a hempen rope which they had with them. I was watching them all the time and saying to myself: "It is with this rope that they will bind me when they kill me." I remained thus for a time, then three of their party, the party that had captured me, came up and spoke to them and I understood that they said to them: "Why have you not killed him?" The old man pointed to the black, as though he were excusing himself on the ground of his illness. One of these three was a pleasant-looking youth, and he said to me: "Do you wish me to set you at liberty?" I said "Yes," and he answered " Go." So I took the tunic which I was wearing and gave it to him and he gave me a worn double-woven cloak which he had, and showed me the way. I went off but I was afraid lest they should change their minds and overtake me, so I went into a reed thicket and hid there till sunset.

Then I made my way out and followed the road which the youth had shewn me. This led to a stream from which I drank. I went on till near midnight and came to a hill under which I slept. In the morning I continued along the road, and sometime before noon reached a high rocky hill on which there were sweet lote-trees and zizyphus bushes. I started to pull and eat the lotus berries so eagerly that the thorns left scars on my arms that remain there to this day. Coming down from that hill I entered a plain sown with cotton and containing castor-oil trees. Here there was a *bá'in*, which in their language means a very broad well with a stone casing and steps by which you go down to reach the water. Some of them have stone pavilions, arcades, and seats in the centre and on the sides, and the kings and nobles of the country vie with one another in constructing them along the highroads where there is no water. When I reached the *bá'in* I drank some water from it and I found on it some mustard shoots which had been dropped by their owner when he washed them. Some of these I ate and saved up the rest, then I lay down under a castor-oil tree. While I was there about forty mailed horsemen came to the *bá'in* to get water and some of them entered the sown fields, then they went away, and God sealed their eyes that they did not see me. After them came about fifty others carrying arms and they too went down into the *bá'in.* One of them came up to a tree opposite the one I was under, yet he did not discover me. At this point I made my way into the field of cotton and stayed there the rest of the day, while they stayed at the *bá'in* washing their clothes and whiling away the time. At night time their voices died away, so I knew that they had either passed on or fallen asleep. Thereupon I emerged and followed the track of the horses, for it was a moonlit night, continuing till I came to another *bá'in* with a dome over it. I went down to it, drank some water, ate some of the mustard shoots which I had, and went into the dome. I found it full of grasses collected by birds, so I went to sleep in it. Now and again I felt the movement of an animal amongst the grass; I suppose it was a snake, but I was too worn out to pay any attention to it.

The next morning I went along a broad road, which led to a ruined village. Then I took another road, but with the same result as before. Several days passed in this manner. One day I came to some tangled trees with a tank of water between them. The space under these trees was like a room, and at the sides of the tank were plants like dittany and others. I intended to stop there until God should send someone to bring me to inhabited country, but I recovered a little strength, so I arose and walked along a road on which I found the tracks of cattle. I found a bull carrying a pack-saddle and a sickle, but after all this road led to the villages of the infidels. Then I followed up another road, and this brought me to a ruined village. There I saw two naked blacks, and in fear of them I remained under some trees there. At nightfall I entered the village and found a house in one of whose rooms there was something like a large jar of the sort they make to store grain in. At the bottom of it there was a hole large enough to admit a man, so I crept into it and found inside it a layer of chopped straw, and amongst this a stone on which I laid my head and went to sleep. On the top of this jar there was a bird which kept fluttering its wings most of the night—I suppose it was frightened, so we made a pair of frightened creatures. This went on for seven days from the day on which I was taken prisoner, which was a Saturday. On the seventh day I came to a village of the unbelievers which was inhabited and possessed a tank of water and plots of vegetables. I asked them for some food, but they refused to give me any. However, in the neighbourhood of a well I found some radish leaves and ate them. I went into the village, and found a troop of infidels with sentries posted. The sentries challenged me but I did not answer them and sat down on the ground. One of them came over with a drawn sword and raised it to strike me, but I paid no attention to him, so utterly weary did I feel. Then he searched me but found nothing on me, so he took the shirt whose sleeves I had given to the old man who had had charge of me.

On the eighth day I was consumed with thirst and I had no water at all. I came to a ruined village but found no tank in it. They have a custom in those villages of making tanks in which the rainwater collects, and this supplies them with drinking-water all the year round. Then I went along a road and this brought me to an uncased well over which was a rope of vegetable fibre, but there was no vessel on it to draw water with. I took a piece of cloth which I had on my head and tied it to the rope and sucked the water that soaked into it, but that did not slake my thirst. I tied on my shoe next and drew up water in it, but that did not satisfy me either, so I drew water with it a second time, but the rope broke and the shoe fell back into the well. I then tied on the other shoe and drank until my thirst was assuaged. After that I cut the shoe and tied its uppers on my foot with the rope off the well and bits of cloth which I found there. While I was tying this on and wondering what to do a person appeared before me. I looked at him, and lo! it was a black-skinned man, carrying a jug and a staff in his hand, and a wallet on his shoulder. He gave me the Muslim greeting "Peace be upon you," and I replied, "Upon you be peace and the mercy and blessings of God." Then he asked me in Persian who I was, and I answered, "A man astray," and he said, "So am I." Thereupon he tied his jug to a rope which he had with him and drew up some water. I wished to drink, but he saying "Have patience." opened his wallet and brought out a handful of black chick-peas fried with a little rice. After I had eaten some of this and drunk he made his ablutions and prayed two prostrations, and I did the same. Thereupon he asked me my name. I answered, "Mohammad," and asked him his, to which he replied, "Joyous Heart." I took this as a good omen and rejoiced at it. After this he said to me, "In the name of God accompany me." I said, "Yes," and walked on with him for a little, then I found my limbs giving way, and as I was unable to stand up I sat down. He said, "What is the matter with you?" I answered, "I was able to walk before meeting you, but now that I have met you I cannot." Whereupon he said, "Glory be to God! Mount on my shoulders." I said to him, "You are weak and have not strength for that," but he replied, "God will give me strength. You must do so." So I got up on his shoulders and he said to me, "Say *God is sufficient for us and an excellent guardian.*" I repeated this over and over again, but I could not keep my eyes open, and regained consciousness only on feeling myself falling to the ground. Then I woke up, but found no trace of the man, and lo! I was in an inhabited village. I entered it and found it was a village of Hindu peasants with a Muslim governor. They informed him about me and he came to meet me. I asked him the name of this village and he replied, "Táj Búra." The distance from there to Koel, where our party was, is two farsakhs. The governor provided a horse to take me to his house and gave me hot food, and I washed. Then he said to me: "I have here a garment and a turban which were left in my charge by a certain Arab from Egypt, one of the soldiers belonging to the corps at Koel." I said to him, "Bring them; I shall wear them until I reach camp." When he brought them I found that they were two of my own garments which I had given to that very Arab when we came to Koel. I was extremely astonished at this; then I thought of the man who had carried me on his shoulders and I remembered what the saint Abú 'Abdalláh al-Murshidí had told me, as I have related in the first journey, when he said to me: "You will enter the land of India and meet there my brother Dilshád, who will deliver you from a misfortune which will befall you there." I remembered too how he had said, when I asked him his name, "Joyous Heart," which, translated into Persian, is *Dilshád*. So I knew that it was he whom the saint had foretold that I should meet, and that he too was one of the saints, but I enjoyed no more of his company than the short space which I have related.

The same night I wrote to my friends at Koel to inform them of my safety, and they came, bringing me a horse and clothes and rejoiced at my escape.

THE SNOWS OF BARBARIE[1]

Leo Africanus

(*c.* 1494-1552)

[*Al Hassan Ibn Mohammed Al Wezaz Al Fasi, later to be known as Johannes Leo or Leo Africanus, was a Moor of noble family, born probably at Granada. He had spent seven years in travel when, in 1520, he was captured by pirates and presented as a slave to Pope Leo X (Giovanni de' Medici). The Pope, having persuaded him to become a Christian, stood sponsor at his baptism, giving him his own names—Giovanni and Leo.*]

All the Region of Barbarie, and the Mountaines contained therein, are subject more to cold then to heat. For seldome commeth any gale of wind which bringeth not some Snow therwith. In all the said Mountaines there grow abundance of Fruits, but not so great plentie of Corne. The Inhabitants of these Mountaines live for the greatest part of the yeere upon Barley Bread. The Springs and Rivers issuing forth of the said Mountaines, representing the qualitie and taste of their native soyle, are somewhat muddie and impure, especially upon the confines of Mauritania. These Mountaines likewise are replenished with Woods and loftie Trees, and are greatly stored with Beasts of all kinds. But the little Hills and Valleys lying betweene the foresaid Mountaines and Mount Atlas are farre more commodious and abounding with Corne. For they are moistened with Rivers springing out of Atlas, and from thence holding on their course to the Mediterran Sea. And albeit Woods are somewhat more scarce upon these Plaines, yet are they much more fruitfull, then be the plaine Countreys situate betweene Atlas and the Ocean Sea, as namely, the Regions of Maroco, of Duccala, of Tedles, of Temesna, of Azgara, and the Countrey lying towards the Straights of Gibraltar.

The Mountaines of Atlas are exceeding cold and barren, and bring forth but small store of Corne, being woody on all sides, and engendring almost all the Rivers of Africa. The Fountaines of Atlas are even in the midst of Summer extremely cold; so that if a man dippeth his hand therein for any long

[1] From *Description of Africa*, translated by Master John Pory in A.D. 1600.

space, he is in great danger of losing the same. Howbeit the said Mountaines are not so cold in all places: for some parts thereof are of such milde temperature, that they may be right commodiously inhabited: yea, and sundry places thereof are well stored with inhabitants.... Those places which are destitute of Inhabitants be either extremely cold, as namely, the same which lie over against Mauritania: or very rough and unpleasant, to wit, those which are directly opposite to the Region of Temesna. Where notwithstanding in Summer time they may feed their great and small Cattell, but not in Winter by any meanes. For then the North wind so furiously rageth, bringing with it such abundance of Snow, that all the Cattell which till then remaine upon the said Mountaines and a great part of the People also are forced to lose their lives in regard thereof: wherefore whosoever hath any occasion to travaile that way in Winter time, chuseth rather to take his Journey betweene Mauritania and Numidia. Those Merchants which bring Dates out of Numidia for the use and service of other Nations, set forth usually upon their Journey about the end of October: and yet they are oftentimes so oppressed and overtaken with a sodaine fall of Snow, that scarcely one man among them all escapeth the danger of the tempest. For when it beginneth to snow over night, before the next morning not only Carts and Men, but even the very Trees are so drowned and overwhelmed therein, that it is not possible to finde any mention of them. Howbeit the dead Carkasses are then found, when the Sunne hath melted the Snow.

I my selfe also, by the goodnesse of Almightie God, twice escaped the most dreadful danger of the foresaid Snow; whereof, if it may not be tedious to the Reader, I will here in few words make relation. Upon a certaine day of the foresaid moneth of October, travelling with a great companie of Merchants towards Atlas, wee were there about Sunne going downe weatherbeaten with a most cold and snowy kind of Hayle. Here we found eleven or twelve Horse-men (Arabians to our thinking) who perswading us to leave our Carts and to goe with them, promised us a good and secure place to lodge in. For mine owne part, that I might not seeme altogether uncivill, I thought it not meet to refuse their good offer; albeit I stood in doubt lest they went about to practise some mischiefe. Wherefore I bethought my selfe to hide up a certaine summe of gold which I had as then about me. But all being readie to ride, I had no leisure to hide away my Coyne from them; whereupon I fained that I would goe ease my selfe. And so departing a while their companie, and getting me under a certaine Tree, whereof I tooke diligent notice, I buried my money betweene certaine stones and the roote of the said Tree. And then we rode on quietly till about mid-night. What time one of them thinking that he had stayed long enough for his Prey, began to utter that in words which secretly he had conceived in his mind. For he asked whether I had any money about me or no? To whom I answered, that I had left my money behind with one of them which attended the carts, and that I had then none at all about me. Howbeit they being no whit satisfied with this answer, commanded me, for all the cold weather, to strip my selfe out of mine apparell. At length when they could find no money at all, they said in jesting and scoffing wise, that they did this for no other purpose, but onely to see how strong and hardy I was, and how I could endure the cold and tempestuous season.

Well, on we rode, seeking our way as well as wee could that darke and dismall night; and anon we heard the bleating of Sheepe, conjecturing thereby that wee were not farre distant from some habitation of people. Wherefore out of hand we directed our course thitherwards: being constrained to leade our Horses thorow thicke Woods, and over steepe and craggie Rockets, to the great hazard and perill of our lives. And at length after many labours, wee found Shepheards in a certaine Cave: who, having with much paines brought their Cattell in there, had kindled a lustie fire for themselves, which they were constrained, by reason of the extreme cold, daily to sit by. Who understanding our companie to be Arabians, feared at the first that we would doe them some mischiefe: but afterward being perswaded that we were driven thither by extremitie of cold, and being more secure of us, they gave us most friendly entertainment. For they set bread, flesh, and cheese before us, wherewith having ended our Suppers, we laid us along each man to sleep before the fire. All of us were as yet exceeding cold, but especially my selfe, who before with great horrour and trembling was stripped starke naked. And so we continued with the said shepheards for the space of two days: all which time we could not set forth, by reason of continual Snow. But the third day, so soone as they saw it leave snowing, with great labour they began to remoove that Snow which laybefore the doore of their Cave. Which done, they brought us to our Horses, which wee found well provided of Hay in another Cave. Being all mounted, the shepheards accompanied us some part of our way, shewing us where the Snow was of least depth, and yet even there it touched our Horse bellies. This day was so cleere, that the Sunne tooke away all the cold of the two dayes going before.

At length entring into a certaine Village neere unto Fez, wee understood, that our Carts which passed by, were overwhelmed with the Snow. Then the Arabians seeing no hope of recompence for all the paines they had taken (for they had defended our Carts from Theeves) carryed a certaine Jew of our

Companie with them as their Captive, (who had lost a great quantitie of Dates, by reason of the Snow aforesaid) to the end that he might remayne as their Prisoner, till he had satisfied for all the residue. From my selfe they took my Horse, and committed me unto the wide World and to Fortune. From whence, riding upon a Mule, within three daies I arrived at Fez, where I heard dolefull newes of our Merchants and Wares, that they were cast away in the Snow. Yea, they thought that I had beene destroyed with the rest; but it seemed that God would have it otherwise.

PERSIA

HOW ABD-ER-RAZZAK SAMARQANDI JOURNEYED INTO INDIA [1]

(A.D. 1442)

ABD-ER-RAZZAK SAMARQANDI

(A.D. 1413-82)

IN this year 845 (A.D. 1442), the author of this narrative, Abd-er-Razzak, the son of Ishak, in obedience to the orders of the sovereign of the world, set out on his journey towards the province of Ormuz and the shores of ocean. . . .

In pursuance of the orders of Providence, and of the decrees of that Divine prescience, the comprehension of which escapes all the calculations and reflections of man, I received orders to take my departure for India; and how shall I be able to set forth the events of my journey with clearness, seeing that I have wandered at haphazard into that country devoted to darkness. His majesty, the happy Khakan, condescended to allot to me my provisions and post horses. His humble slave, after having made the necessary preparations, started on his journey on the first day of the month of Ramazan (January 13th), by the route of Kohistan. In the middle of the desert of Kerman, he arrived at the ruins of a city, the wall of which and four bazaars could still be distinguished; but no inhabitant was to be found in all the country round. . . .

On the eighteenth day of Ramazan (January 30th) I reached the city of Kerman; it is a pleasant place, as well as one of great importance. The *darogah* (governor), the Emir Hadji-Mohammed-Kaiaschirin, being then absent, I was compelled to sojourn in this city until the day of the feast. The illustrious Emir Borhan-Eddin-Seid-Khalil-Allah, son of the Emir Naim-Eddin-Seid-Nimet-Allah, who was the most distinguished personage of the city of Kerman, and even of the whole world, returned at this time from the countries of Hindoostan. He loaded me with attentions and proofs of his kindness. On the fifth day of Schewal (February 16th) I quitted the city of Kerman. . . . Continuing my journey, I arrived towards the middle of the month at the shore of the Sea of Oman, and at Bender-Ormuz. The prince of Ormuz, Melik-Fakhr-Eddin-Touranschah, having placed a vessel at my

[1] From *The Voyage of Abd-er-Razzak, Ambassador from Shah Rukh, A.H. 845, A.D. 1442,* translated from the Persian into French by M. Quatremère, rendered into English by R. H. Major, and published (1857) in *India in the Fifteenth Century* (Hakluyt Society, No. 22).

disposal, I went on board of it, and made my entry into the city of Ormuz. I had had assigned to me a house, with everything that I could require, and I was admitted to an audience of the prince.

Ormuz, which is also called Djerrun, is a port situated in the middle of the sea, and which has not its equal on the surface of the globe. The merchants of seven climates, from Egypt, Syria, the country of Roum, Azerbijan, Irak-Arabi, and Irak-Adjemi, the province of Fars, Khorassan, Ma-wara-annahar, Turkistan, the kingdom of Deschti-Kaptchack, the countries inhabited by the Kalmucks, the whole of the kingdoms of Tchin[1] and Matchin, and the city of Khanbâlik,[2] all make their way to this port, . . . they bring hither those rare and precious articles which the sun, the moon, and the rains have combined to bring to perfection, and which are capable of being transported by sea. . . .

I sojourned in this place for the space of two months; and the governors sought all kinds of pretexts to detain me; so that the favorable time for departing by sea, that is to say the beginning or middle of the monsoon, was allowed to pass, and we came to the end of the monsoon, which is the season when tempests and attacks from pirates are to be dreaded. Then they gave me permission to depart. As the men and horses could not all be contained in the same vessel, they were distributed among several ships. The sails were hoisted, and we commenced our voyage.

As soon as I caught the smell of the vessel, and all the terrors of the sea presented themselves before me, I fell into so deep a swoon, that for three days respiration alone indicated that life remained within me. When I came a little to myself the merchants . . . cried with one voice that the time for navigation was passed, and that every one who put to sea at this season was alone responsible for his death, since he voluntarily placed himself in peril. All, with one accord, having sacrificed the sum which they had paid for freight in the ships, abandoned their project, and after some difficulties disembarked at the port of Muscat. For myself, I quitted this city, escorted by the principal companions of my voyage, and went to a place called Kariat, where I established myself and fixed my tents, with the intention of there remaining . . . . In consequence of the severity of pitiless weather and the adverse manifestations of a treacherous fate, my heart was crushed like glass and my soul became weary of life, and my season of relaxation became excessively trying to me.

At the moment when, through the effect of so many vicissitudes, the mirror of my understanding had become covered with rust, and the hurricane

[1] China. [2] Pekin.

of so many painful circumstances had extinguished the lamp of my mind, so that I might say in one word I had fallen into a condition of apathetic stupidity, on a sudden I one evening met a merchant who was on his return from the shores of Hindoostan. I asked him whither he was going? he replied: "My only object is to reach the city of Herat." When I heard him utter the name of that august city I went very nearly distracted. The merchant having consented at my request to tarry awhile, I threw off the following verses upon paper:

When in the midst of strangers, at the hour of the evening prayer I set me down to weep,
I recall my adventures, the recital of which is accompanied with unusual sighs.
At the remembrance of my mistress and of my country I weep so bitterly
That I should deprive the whole world of the taste and habit of travelling.
I am a native of the country of the Arabs, and not of a strange region.
O mighty God, whom I invoke! vouchsafe to bring me back to the companionship of my friends. . . .

At the time that I was perforce sojourning in the place called Kariat, and upon the shores of the ocean, the new moon, of the month of Moharrem of the year 846 (May 1442), showed me in this abode of weariness the beauty of her disk. Although it was at that time spring, in the season in which the nights and days are of equal length, the heat of the sun was so intense that it burned the ruby in the mine and the marrow in the bones; the sword in its scabbard melted like wax, and the gems which adorned the handle of the khandjar were reduced to coal.... The extreme heart of the atmosphere gave one the idea of the fire of hell. As the climate of this country is naturally opposed to human health my elder brother, a respectable and learned man, Maulana-Afif-Eddin-Abd-el-Wahhâb, the rest of my companions and myself, fell sick, in consequence of the excessive heat, and we resigned our fate into the hands of Divine goodness.... The constitution of each one of us had undergone so sad a change; trouble, fatigue, sickness, and the burning of the fever went on increasing every day. This cruel condition was prolonged for the space of four months; our strength gave way by degrees, and the malady increased....

In the meanwhile I was informed that in the environs of the city of Kalahat, there was a place called Sour, which offered a salubrious temperature and agreeable waters. In spite of my extreme weakness I went on board the vessel, and departed for Kalahat. No sooner had I arrived than my malady increased; in the daytime I was consumed by the fire of a burning fever, and in the night I was devoured by the anguish of chagrin.... I was torn to pieces by the torments of absence, by the sorrows of exile... and my soul was on the point of quitting the asylum of my body . . . and abandoned its fate to the goodness of the living and merciful God.

My respectable brother, Maulana-Afif-Eddin-Abd-Wahhâb, in obedience to that maxim "Man knows not in what country he must die," and in obedience to that other sentence, "Wherever thou mayst be death shall reach thee," committed his soul into the hands of the Deity, and was buried in the neighbourhood of that place of pilgrimage where some of the illustrious companions of the prophet repose.

The grief of this loss, and the pain of this separation, produced a deep impression upon me, which it is impossible to describe or to represent by words....

Unhappy me! detaching myself from life, and regarding the past as having never occurred, I determined to continue my voyage in a vessel which was leaving for Hindoostan. A few strong men carried me on board the ship.... The air of the sea... gave me the hope of a perfect cure: the morning of health began to dawn upon the longing of my hopes; the wounds caused by the sharp arrows of my malady began to heal, and the water of life, hitherto so troubled, recovered its purity and transparency. Before long a favourable breeze began to blow, and the vessel floated over the surface of the water with the rapidity of the wind.... Finally, after a voyage of eighteen days and as many nights, by the aid of the supreme king and ruler, we cast anchor in the port of Calicut....

As soon as I landed at Calicut I saw beings such as my imagination had never depicted the like of.

> Extraordinary beings, who are neither men nor devils,
> At sight of whom the mind takes alarm;
> If I were to see such in my dreams
> My heart would be in a tremble for many years.
> I have had love passages with a beauty, whose face was like
> the moon; but I could never fall in love with a negress.

The blacks of this country have the body nearly naked; they wear only bandages round the middle.... In one hand they hold an Indian poignard, which has the brilliance of a drop of water, and in the other a buckler of ox-hide, which might be taken for a piece of mist. This costume is common to the king and to the beggar. As to the Mussulmauns, they dress themselves in magnificent apparel after the manner of the Arabs, and manifest luxury in every particular. After I had had an opportunity of seeing a considerable number of Mussulmauns and Infidels I had a comfortable lodging assigned to me, and after the lapse of three days was conducted to an audience with the king. I saw a man with his body naked, like the rest of the Hindus. The sovereign of this city bears the title of

Sameri. When he dies it is his sister's son who succeeds him, and his inheritance does not belong to his son, or his brother, or any other of his relations. No one reaches the throne by means of the strong hand....

When I obtained my audience of this prince, the hall was filled with two or three thousand Hindus, who wore the costume above described; the principal personages amongst the Mussulmauns were also present. After they had made me take a seat, the letter of his majesty, the happy Khakan, was read, and they caused to pass in procession before the throne, the horse, the pelisse, the garment of cloth of gold, and the cap to be worn at the ceremony of Nauruz. The Sameri showed me but little consideration. On leaving the audience I returned to my house. Several individuals, who brought with them a certain number of horses, and all sorts of things beside, had been shipped on board another vessel by order of the King of Ormuz; but being captured on the road by some cruel pirates, they were plundered of all their wealth, and narrowly escaped with their lives. Meeting them at Calicut, we had the honour to see some distinguished friends.

> Thanks be to God we are not dead, and we have seen our very dear friends;
> we have also attained the object of our desires.

From the close of the month of the second Djoumada (beginning of November 1442), to the first days of Zou'lhidjah (middle of April 1443), I remained in this disagreeable place, where everything became a source of trouble and weariness. During this period, on a certain night of profound darkness and unusual length, in which sleep, like an imperious tyrant, had imprisoned my senses and closed the door of my eyelids, after every sort of disquietude, I was at length asleep upon my bed of rest, and in a dream I saw his majesty, the happy Khakan, who came towards me with all the pomp of sovereignty, and when he came up to me said: "Afflict thyself no longer." The following morning, at the hour of prayer, this dream recurred to my mind and filled me with joy. . . .

My reflections led me to the hope, that perhaps the morning beam of happiness was about to dawn upon me from the bosom of Divine goodness, and that the night of chagrin and weariness had nearly reached its close. Having communicated my dream to some skilful men, I asked them its interpretation. On a sudden a man arrived, who brought me the intelligence that the King of Bidjanagar, who holds a powerful empire and a mighty dominion under his sway, had sent to the Sameri a delegate charged with a letter, in which he desired that he would send on to him the ambassador of his majesty, the happy Khakan. . . .

The humble author of this narrative having received his audience of dismissal, departed from Calicut by sea. After having passed the port of Bendinaneh, situated on the coast of Melibar, he reached the port of Mangalor, which forms the frontier of the kingdom of Bidjanagar. After staying there two or three days he continued his route by land. At a distance of three parasangs from Mangalor he saw a temple of idols, which has not its equal in the universe. It is an equilateral square, of about ten ghez[1] in length, ten in breadth, and five in height. It is entirely formed of cast bronze. It has four *estrades*. Upon that in the front stands a human figure, of great size, made of gold; its eyes are formed of two rubies, placed so artistically that the statue seems to look at you. The whole is worked with wonderful delicacy and perfection.

After passing this temple I came each day to some city or populous town. At length I came to a mountain whose summit reached the skies, and the foot of which was covered with so great a quantity of trees and thorny underwood, that the rays of the sun could never penetrate the obscurity, nor could the beneficial rains at any time reach the soil to moisten it. Having left this mountain and this forest behind me, I reached a town called Belour, the houses of which were like palaces, and its women reminded one of the beauty of the Houris. . . .

Having sojourned in this town for the space of two or three days we continued our route, and at the end of the month of Zou'lhidjah (end of April) we arrived at the city of Bidjanagar. The King sent a numerous *cortège* to meet us, and appointed us a very handsome house for our residence.

The preceding details forming a close narrative of events, have shown to readers and writers that the chances of a maritime voyage had led Abd-er-Razzak, the author of this work, to the city of Bidjanagar. He saw a place extremely large and thickly peopled, and a king possessing greatness and sovereignty to the highest degree, whose dominion extends from the frontier of Serendib to the extremities of the country of Kalbergah. From the frontiers of Bengal to the environs of Belinar (Melibar) the distance is more than a thousand parasangs. The country is for the most part well cultivated, very fertile, and contains about three hundred harbours. One sees there more than a thousand elephants, in their size resembling mountains, and in their forms resembling devils. . . . .

The city of Bidjanagar is such that the pupil of the eye has never seen a place like it, and the ear of intelligence has never been informed that there existed anything to equal it in the world. It is built in such a manner that seven

[1] Cubits.

citadels and the same number of walls enclose each other. Around the first citadel are stones of the height of a man, one half of which is sunk in the ground while the other rises above it. These are fixed one beside the other, in such a manner that no horse or foot soldier could boldly or with ease approach the citadel. If any one would wish to find what point of resemblance this fortress and rampart present with that which exists in the city of Herat, let him picture to himself that the first citadel corresponds with that which extends from the mountain of Mokhtar and Direh dou Buraderim (the Valley of the Two Brothers) as far as the banks of the river and the bridge of Mâlan, situated east of the town of Ghinan, and west of the village of Saiban. . . . The space which separates the first fortress from the second, and up to the third fortress, if filled with cultivated fields, and with houses and gardens. In the space from the third to the seventh one meets a numberless crowd of people, many shops, and a bazaar. At the gate of the King's palace are four bazaars, placed opposite each other. On the north is the portico of the palace of the *raï*. Above each bazaar is a lofty arcade with a magnificent gallery, but the audience hall of the King's palace is elevated above all the rest. The bazaars are extremely long and broad. The rose merchants place before their shops high *estrades*, on each side of which they expose their flowers for sale. In this place one sees a constant successionof sweet smelling and fresh looking roses. These people could not live without roses, and they look upon them as quite as necessary as food. . . .

The author of this narrative, having arrived in this city at the end of the month of Zou'lhidjah (the end of April 1443) took up his abode in an extremely lofty house, which had been assigned to him, and which resembled that which one sees in the city of Herat, over the King's gate, which gate serves as a passage for the entire population. He rested himself for several days from the fatigues of his journey. It was on the first day of Moharrem (May 1st, 1443) that I took up my abode in this great city. One day some messengers sent from the palace of the King came to seek me, and at the close of that same day I presented myself at Court, and offered for the monarch's acceptance five beautiful horses, and some *tokouz* of damask and satin. The prince was seated in a hall, surrounded by the most imposing attributes of state. Right and left of him stood a numerous crowd of men ranged in a circle. The King was dressed in a robe of green satin, around his neck he wore a collar, composed of pearls of beautiful water and other splendid gems. He had an olive complexion, his frame was thin, and he was rather tall; on his cheeks might be seen a slight down, but there was no beard on his chin. The expression of his countenance was extremely pleasing. On being led into the presence of this prince I bowed my head three times. The monarch received me with interest, and made me take a seat very near him. When he took the august letter of the emperor, he handed it to the interpreter, and said: "My heart is truly delighted to see that a great king has been pleased to send me an ambassador." As the humble author of this narrative, in consequence of the heat, and the great number of robes in which he was dressed, was drowned in perspiration, the monarch took pity on him, and sent him a fan, similar to the khata which he held in his hand. After this a salver was brought, and they presented to the humble author two packets of betel, a purse containing five hundred *fanoms*, and twenty *mithkals* of camphor. Then, receiving permission to depart, he returned to his house. . . .

When the *fête* of *Mahanadi* was ended, at the hour of evening prayer, the monarch sent to summon me. . . . He questioned me on particular points respecting his Majesty the happy Khakan, his emirs, his troops, the numbers of his horses, and also respecting his great cities, such as Samarcand, Herat, and Shirez. He expressed towards the emperor sentiments of the greatest friendship, and said to me:

"I shall send, together with an able ambassador, some rows of elephants, two *tokouz* [twice nine] of eunuchs, and other presents." . . .

At this period Daiang, the vizier, who manifested towards the author of this work the most lively interest, set out on an expedition into the kingdom of Kalberga. . . . The King had admitted into his council, to supply the place of Daiang, a Christian named Nimeh-pezir. This man thought himself equal to a vizier; he was a creature of small stature, malicious, ill-born, mean, had stern. All the most odious vices were united in him, without one finding in him any counterbalancing estimable quality. This wretch, as soon as he had defiled by his presence the seat of authority, suppressed, without any reason, the daily allowance which had been assigned to us. Soon after, the inhabitants of Ormuz, having found a favourable occasion, manifested without reservation that diabolical malignity which was stamped upon their character, and the conformity of their perverse inclinations having united them intimately with the vizier Nimeh-pezir, they said to that man: "Abd-er-Razzak is not an ambassador sent by his Majesty the happy Khakan; he is but a merchant who has been charged with the conveyance of a letter from that monarch." They also circulated amongst the idolators a variety of falsehoods, which produced a deep impression upon their minds. For a considerable time the author, placed as he was in the midst of a country inhabited by infidels, remained in a painful position, and doubtful as to what course he ought to follow. While all these perplexities, however, were hanging over me the King, on several occasions when he met me on his road, turned towards me with kindness and asked after my welfare. He is in truth a prince who possesses eminent qualities.

> If we say that he is just in everything, such an eulogium is sufficient.

Daiang, after having made an invasion upon the frontiers of the country of Kalberga, and taken several unfortunate prisoners, had retraced his steps. He expressed to Nimeh-pezir some keen reproaches for the neglect he had shown in the author's affairs, to whom, on the very day of his arrival, he caused to be paid a sum of seven thousand *varahahs*, for which he delivered him an order upon the mint. Two persons, Kojah-Masood and Kojah-Mohammed, both natives of Khorassan, who had fixed their abode in the kingdom of Bidjanagar, were appointed to undertake the duties of ambassadors, and variouspresents and stuffs were accordingly sent to them. . . .

On the day of the audience of dismissal the King said to the humble author of this work:

"It has been asserted that thou wast not really sent by his majesty Mirza-Schah-Rokh, otherwise we should have shown thee greater attentions; if thou comest back on a future occasion into my territories, thou shalt meet with a reception worthy of a king such as we are."

But the author said to himself mentally:

> If, when once I have escaped from the desert of thy love, I reach my own country,
> I will never again set out on another voyage, not even in the company of a king. . . .

The Sun of the Divine Majesty displayed itself above the horizon of happiness. The star of fortune arose to the east of my hopes. The bright glimmer of joy and satisfaction showed itself in the midst of the darkness of night. . . .

With a heart full of energy, and with vast hopes, I set out on my journey, or, rather, I committed myself to the goodness and compassion of God. On the twelfth day of the month of Schaban (December 5th, 1443), accompanied by the ambassadors, I left the city of Bidjanagar to commence my journey. After travelling eighteen days, on the first day of the month of Ramazan (December 23rd, 1443), I reached the shores of the Sea of Oman and the port of Maganor. There I had the honour of being admitted to the society of the Sheriff-Emir Seid-Ala-eddin-Meskhedi, who was a hundred and twenty years old. . . .

After having celebrated in the port of Maganor the festival which follows the fast, I made my way to the port of Manor [Honawer] to procure a vessel, and I laid in all the provisions necessary for twenty persons during a voyage of forty days. One day, at the moment that I was on the point of embarking, I opened the *Book of Fates*, the author of which was the Iman Djafar-Sadek, and which is composed from verses of the *Alcoran*. There I found a presage of joy and happiness, for I lighted upon this verse:

Fear nothing, for thou hast been preserved from the hand of unjust men.

Struck with the coincidence of this passage with my situation, I felt all those anxieties disappear from my heart, which had caused me alarm in the prospect of encountering the sea. Abandoning myself entirely to the hope of a happy deliverance, I embarked on the eighth day of the month of Zu'lkadah (February 28th, 1444) and put to sea. . . .

The eye of sad events and of misfortunes was gone to sleep, Fortune appeared to have given herself up to indolence, and we were surrounded with happiness.

The ship, after a million of shocks, reached the open sea.

On a sudden there arose a violent wind on the surface of the sea, and on all sides were heard groaning and cries.

The night, the vessel, the wind, and the gulf presented to our minds all the forebodings of a catastrophe. On a sudden, through the effect of the contrary winds, which resembled men in their drink, the wine which produced this change penetrated even to the vessel. The planks of which it was composed, and which by their conformation seemed to form a continuous line, were on the point of becoming divided like the separate letters of the alphabet. . . .

The sailor who, with respect to his skill in swimming, might be compared to a fish, was anxious to throw himself into the water like an anchor. The captain, although familiarized with the navigation of all the seas, shed bitter tears, and had forgotten all his science. The sails were torn, the mast was entirely bent by the shock of the wind. The different grades of passengers who inhabited this floating house threw out upon the waves riches of great value, and, after the manner of the Sofis, voluntarily stripped themselves of their worldly goods. Who could give a thought to the jeopardy in which their money and their stuffs were placed, when life itself, which is so dear to man, was in danger? For myself, in this situation, which brought before my eyes all the threatening terrors which the ocean had in its power to present, with tears in my eyes I gave myself up for lost. Through the effect of the stupor, and of the profound sadness to which I became a prey, I remained, like the sea, with my lips dry and my eyes moist, and resigned myself entirely to the Divine Will. At one time, through the driving of the waves, which resembled mountains, the vessel was lifted up to the skies; at another, under the impulse of the violent winds, it descended like divers to the bottom of the waters. . . .

Many times I said to myself, and it was in language dictated by my situation that I repeated, this verse:

A dismal night! the fear of the waves, and so frightful an abyss!

What judgment can they who are so peaceful on shore form of our situation?. . . .

Overwhelmed at every point, and seeing the gate of hope shut on every side against me, with an eye full of tears and a heart full of burning chagrin, I addressed myself to God with the expression of this verse:

Oh, our Lord, place not upon us a burden which is too heavy for our strength to bear!. . . .

In the midst of this sad position I reflected and put the question to myself: "What, then, is this catastrophe, which has made fortune in her revolution fall so heavily upon me?". . . .

I was in the midst of these reflections, and everything about me spoke of dejection and trouble, when at length, by virtue of that Divine promise: *"Who is He who hears the prayers of the afflicted, and drives away his misery?"* on a sudden the zephyr of God's infinite mercy began to blow upon me from that point which is indicated by these words: *"Despair not of the mercy of the Most High."* The morning of joy began to dawn from the East of happiness, and the messenger of a propitious fate brought to the ears of my soul these consolatory words: *"Since on your behalf we have divided the sea, we have saved you."* The impetuous hurricane was changed to a favourable wind, the tossing of the waves ceased, and the sea, in conformity with my desires, became completely calm. My fellow-passengers, after having celebrated at sea the feast of victims, gained sight, at the close of the month of Zu'lhidjah (middle of April 1444), of the mountain of Kalahat, and found themselves at length in safety from all the perils of the deep. At this period the new moon of the month of Moharrem, of the year 848 (20th April, 1444), like a beneficent spirit looked on us with a friendly eye. . . .

The vessel still remained at sea for several days. On our arrival at the port of Muscat we cast anchor.

After having repaired the damages which the vessel had suffered through the effect of the storms, we re-embarked, and continued our voyage.

After leaving Muscat, the vessel arrived at the port of Jurufgan, where it put in for a day or two. On this occasion we felt during one night such excessive heat, that at daybreak one would have said that the heavens had set the earth on fire. So intense was the heat which scorched up the atmosphere, that even the bird of rapid flight was burnt up in the heights of heaven, as well as the fish in the depths of the sea. I re-embarked and set sail from the port of Jurufgan, and reached Ormuz on the forenoon of Friday, the eighth day of the month of Safar (28th May, 1441). Our voyage from the port of Honawer to Ormuz had lasted sixty-five days.

HOW DON JUAN OF PERSIA TRAVELLED TO MUSCOVY [1]

(A.D. 1599)

DON JUAN OF PERSIA

(1560-1605)

AT about this same time there arrived at the Court of the Sháh . . . that Englishman . . . called Sir Anthony Sherley, with his suite of thirty-two attendants, and they halted at Qasvín. He gave himself out as a cousin of the Scottish King James, saying that all the kings of Christendom had recognized him as such, and had now empowered him as their ambassador to treat with the King of Persia, who should make a confederacy with them in order to wage war against the Turk, who was indeed the common enemy of all of them. Now this Christian gentleman had by chance arrived in the very nick of time, for the King of Persia was then himself preparing to send an ambassador with many gifts to the King of Spain, by way of the Portuguese Indies. Sir Anthony, however, brought it to the knowledge of the Sháh that there were, besides his Catholic Majesty of Spain, many other Christian kings in Europe and the West, who being most powerful monarchs would willingly join him against the Turk: hence it would now be proper to send also with his ambassador letters and presents to each of these other kings. Sir Anthony succeeded so well in setting forth this matter as urgent, that the Sháh was satisfied to do as he advised, and gave orders forthwith that arrangements for these embassies should be set on foot, proposing that Sir Anthony should accompany his envoy the Persian ambassador. To all this Sir Anthony readily agreed, thanking his Majesty for the honour he was doing him, and he proceeded to name the Christian Powers, to the number of eight, to whom he and the Persian ambassador were to be accredited; and these were: the Roman Pontiff, the Emperor of Germany, the King of Spain, the King of France, the King of Poland, the Signiory of Venice, the Queen of England, and the King of Scotland. . . .

Now, in coming to Persia Sir Anthony had made his voyage through Greece (and the Ottoman Empire) in the dress of a Turk, being a man cognizant of the Turkish language, but it was not possible or advisable for him to seek to return home by that route. On the other hand, the way by India would demand too long a sea journey, and it was in consequence determined that the voyage of the present embassy should be taken through Tartary and Muscovy.

[1] From *Don Juan of Persia*, translated by G. Le Strange, in the "Broadway Travellers" series, 1926.

All needful preparations having thus been made, his Majesty granted his patents and orders for free provisions throughout all his lands and territories where the embassy should pass; further, the needful credits with orders for cash to pay our travelling expenses, and the same was done for the Englishman—all to be thus defrayed at the charge of the King of Persia. The Persian gentlemen who were as secretaries to accompany the ambassador being also now duly appointed, we took leave in audience of Sháh 'Abbás in Isfahán, where the Court was then in residence, and started on our journey, it being Thursday evening, the 9th day of July, in the year of the Incarnation 1599. Now, those who thus went out from the royal palace travelling at the King's command and expense, were all grandees of his Court, of high rank, and they were habited and accoutred suitably for their voyage. The Persian ambassador was called Husayn 'Ali Beg, and with him were four gentlemen the secretaries of embassy [1] and fifteen servants. Next came the two Friars, and then Sir Anthony with five interpreters, and fifteen other Englishmen. There were withal thirty-two camels carrying the presents, besides the needful number of riding-horses for those who went the journey, and the usual sumpter-beasts required for carrying the baggage of the various persons already mentioned. Diverse were the feelings in the hearts of those who were thus departing, and different their expression: for some set forth most joyfully, but others very dolefully. To all the King had graciously given his royal word to bestow on us at our return many favours, but such were the tears of our relatives, the sad faces shown by our friends, the sorrow and despair expressed differently but grievously by wives, fathers, and children, that we had perforce at last hurriedly to conclude and depart, and that evening leaving the capital, we forthwith took the road to the city of Káshán, our first stage.

The journey from Isfahán to Káshán occupied us four days; we rested there two, and then went on to the town of Qum; and the next morning we reached the city of Sávah. From Sávah we travelled during three days, coming to the city of Qazvín, formerly the capital city of Persia. . . . Here we remained eight days, for the Sháh had ordered us to procure from here certain articles for gifts that we were to present to the kings of the Christians, these in addition to those with which from Isfahán we were already in charge; this matter therefore we now attended to. After leaving Qazvín, we came in five days to Gílán, a territory and province where a different language to Persian is spoken, although. . . . it is indeed an integral part of the kingdom of Persia. This province lies along the coast of the Sea of Bákú, also called Qulzum, which

[1] One of whom was Uruch Beg, who upon his conversion to the Catholic Faith took the name of Don Juan of Persia.

is the Caspian Sea of the ancients, and as here we had to embark aboard ship, we were delayed ten days while the necessary arrangements were being completed. Now many of our friends and relations had come out accompanying us hither on the road from Isfahán, and when we had at last embarked in our ship very sorrowfully we bade them good-bye, we standing on board, and finally set sail.

The Caspian Sea was not very well known to the ancients, who till after the times of Cæsar Augustus believed it to be a bay of the Ocean; but the Arabs knew it to be otherwise and called it the "Closed Sea." It is 800 miles in length, and 600 in breadth; it receives into its waters many copious rivers, and although there is no lack of those who have stated that for this cause the water of the same is neither bitter nor salt, I who sailed over it, and once or twice tried to essay its taste, can affirm that it is gross, bitter, and salt, being indeed anything but palatable. The chief rivers that flow into this sea are the Chessel, the Geicon the Teuso, the Coro, and the Volga. This last is in those parts known as the Eder, and on this river, as will later be described, we were destined to take our journey inland to Russia. Now, having, as already said, got on board our ship, we put out to sea, and in a day and a night reached a little island far from the land, where a number of fisher-folk are wont to live, for the fish here are abundant and of many kinds. More especially they catch hereabout great quantities of dog-fish, and the same provide the fish-skins which being first dried are afterwards used as bags for holding olive-oil, and these skins are sold for a great price. Here we stayed a day and the night, waiting for fine weather, and the following day, as the sea appeared calm, we set sail. Very soon, however, it was manifest how little the seamen knew of the weather, for, after sailing three or four miles, a tempest arose, and the violence of the wind split our sails, whereby more than once one might have thought that we should all drown. But in truth we Persians are so entirely unused to sea-faring, that most of us were now unapprehensive of either danger or death; and we laughed heartily at the Portuguese Friars, who had fallen to weeping, being apparently prepared to die. The storm lasted the whole of that night, and in the morning we found ourselves back once again at that port and town, in Gílán, where we had embarked some days before.

It appeared to some who were faint-hearted that we should best now disembark and return to Isfahán, for it seemed to them as though it were not the will of Heaven that we should undertake this long journey. But in sooth we all feared too much the wrath of Sháh 'Abbás, and as fine weather had set in we again put to sea, in two days retraced the way already gone, and in another day, proceeding forward, reached a port where there were indeed no houses, but a settlement of folk of divers tribes. These men were all living, as is the fashion we see among the nomad Moors of Morocco, in the midst of their flocks and camels; they are of the Tartar nation, and the country goes by the name of the Land of the Great Tamerlane of Tartary; though, in fact, it is subject to the King of Persia. The manner of life of these people is quite barbarous, and they talk little that is matter of sense; they go almost naked, wearing only fisher-breeches, or a very short shirt. They are poor and very humble folk in their ways, and welcome anybody who comes to their country. They treated us well, giving us of their flocks a liberal and sufficient entertainment during the fortnight that we were delayed here, for by reason of the dead calm which lay upon the sea, it was impossible for the ship to set sail all this time. In this country, which otherwise is called Manquishlágh (and lies on the east coast of the Caspian), there is a native Persian Idol very greatly venerated by the folk of the land, also by strangers, and to this Idol, we, offering many gifts, forthwith made sacrifice, that the Idol might grant to us a favourable wind. We met here with a Persian, who begged to join us, and having at last a favourable wind we again made sail. None the less, during the next two months we were constantly set back by foul weather; so we coasted the shore, and had we but had a favourable wind, in twelve days we should easily have accomplished this our journey across the Caspian.

At the end of these two months we came into what is an arm of the Caspian, where the water is clearer and less salt than out at sea, and, indeed, Giovanni Botero has already remarked this matter in his book, but this gulf is a separate arm of the Caspian and it is no part of the main sea. And here it is proper to point out that the water is thus less salt here by reason of the rivers which flow into this bay or estuary; but, as proving clearly that the water of the Caspian is truly salt, when a storm wind drives the waters back through this estuary, of which we are speaking, into the river mouths, their waters then become as bitter as gall, and of this fact I satisfied myself by experiment. The people of the country call this river, which is the Volga, by the name of Idel. Thirty leagues up this bay or estuary, sailing north we began to enter the territories which the Muscovites occupy in Asia, and the first inhabited place we came to was a town of the Christians, which is called Astrakhan. One of our Persians and an Englishman, with some of the sailors to row, now got into a small boat and went to wait upon the captain-general of the town, which lay thirty leagues above where the ship had come to anchor, for the water above here is so shallow that she could not have passed the bar without running aground. Now as we lay here, by a change of wind our vessel was in great risks, for though of considerable size, when a squall fell on us, she was all but overset, and we already accounted ourselves as doomed men. Immediately we began to throw overboard first a thousand bushels of wheat and flour, next many provisions with which we had been supplied, many boxes of clothes, lastly some chests of valuable gifts, whereby finally, and by the loss thereof, the tempest came to be appeased, and the ship saved.

This danger being overpassed, those who had gone up to the city returned, and with them the captain-general had sent down to us many gentlemen, aboard four galleys, with provisions and refreshments. We now transshipped and were taken on board their galleys, and our ship weighing anchor, sailed away, leaving us. On arriving at the city we disembarked from the galleys, when they gave us a very great and solemn reception, for there was a mighty assembly of folk present. Here we found another ambassador from the King of Persia, especially accredited to Muscovy, who was on his way thither, and in his suite 300 persons. In Astrakhan we sojourned for sixteen days, for they gave us excellent entertainment, and it being the autumn season, there was in that country an abundance of melons and apples of very good quality. Also not only was the land pleasant, but the people likewise, for the captain-general, whom the Grand Duke of Muscovy had appointed here as governor, had caused it to be proclaimed that no one should presume to demand money for anything that we might need or desire, and this under pain of 200 lashes for disobedience.... Astrakhan stands on the bank of the Volga, or Eder, and is much frequented by merchants coming from Muscovy, Armenia, Persia, and Turkey, and its chief commerce is in salt. Botero states that the township lies one day's sail by boat from the Caspian, but I, who have been there, say that with a very good wind you may only reach it thence with difficulty in two days....

Having sojourned sixteen days in Astrakhan, and the five galleys being now ready which had been prepared for our accommodation, and for that of that other Persian ambassador whom we had joined company with in Astrakhan, we all now came together and embarked—namely, we Persians and the Englishmen and the Friars. Along with us were sent a hundred soldiers of the Duke of Muscovy, who were to serve us as guard and escort, by order of the captain-general at Astrakhan. The galleys were very well built, and each had a crew of a hundred rowers. We got on board down at the strand of that river, which, as already said, is called the Eder, otherwise the Volga, the stream here having a width across of half a Spanish league. The land is well inhabited on either bank by the Tartar folk, who are divided up into hordes or tribes, and who for the most part live out in the countryside among their flocks, which supply them with their chief sustenance and livelihood....

They live as do the nomad Moors fo Morocco, changing their habitations with the four seasons, even as those men are wont to do. They go by the name of the Nogay, and when the pasturage fails on the one side, and is to be found only on the other bank of the river, since there are no bridges by which to carry over their flocks, it is their custom to make the passage over the river breadth during the month of August, when the water is at its lowest. To accomplish this fording of the river, they have contrived a method as follows. The horses and camels are tied together by their tails one to another, thirty by thirty, or fifty by fifty, and then being driven into the water their number enables them to struggle against the force of the current, and thus they get over. For the sheep to cross they lay over the surface of the water great pieces of coarse frieze which have been tarred, as is done to the sides of ships, and these being strongly linked together, they push these across one after the other with poles, like the pans in a turning-table, and thus the rams and ewes, having been set on them, may be got over. But as the distance across the stream is very great, it is not uncommon for half the flock to get drowned, for, indeed, in the narrowest places the river here is a league from bank to bank....

During the two months following we now travelled in our galleys up the Volga, but every ten days we disembarked and went ashore to some village, for all along the river bank there are small settlements with houses that are built of wood. At each stopping place we changed some of our rowers, taking on fresh men to row the galleys. All this was done under command from the soldiers who accompanied us by an order sent from the Duke of Muscovy. The hills which the Volga has on either side its banks are very high, and are populated with settlements. We saw on these hills numerous bears, lions, and tigers, also martens of many species. Every hundred leagues or so along the river there stand cities of the Duke of Muscovy, and the first that we came to was called Cherny Yar, the next Tzaritzyn, the third Samara, and so on with the rest we do not name. When there was a contrary wind blowing down the river, the boatmen would land the horses on one or other bank, and these towed the galleys with great ropes. Every night we were wont to land to sleep comfortably ashore in the fields, and our escort of a hundred soldiers then kept watch and ward for us. At the end of two months' journeying by river we came to a very great city of the Duke of Muscovy called Kazan, and its population, numbering over 50,000 householders (or 225,000 souls), are all Christians. This town is extremely full of churches, each having many great bells, and on the vesper of feast days no one can sleep or indeed stay in the city for the noise. On the day when we arrived at this city so great a concourse of people came out to meet us and wonder at the sight, that we scarcely could pass through the squares and streets. We stayed in Kazan eight days, and they provided us with such abundant supplies that the food we could not eat had to be thrown out of the windows and wasted.

In this country none are poor, for the victuals are so cheap, that any that are hungry go out to find it in the highways. What they lack is good wine, and they have only one kind of drink, which is made from wheat or barley, and this is so strong that those who drink it are often drunk. For this reason there is a law and ordinance that no officer may carry any kind of weapon, otherwise they would be killing each other every other moment. The climate here is extremely cold, hence all go clothed in marten skins, which are to be had in abundance. They have no succulent fruits, only crabapples, and no plenty even of these, and they are not sweet, being indeed quite sour. The people of Kazan are a fine race: the men are fair, tall, and stout, and the women, as a rule, good looking. They appear very well dressed in the marten furs of which the robes and hoods that they wear are made. They have great use for stoves, and in each house is a dog, as big as a lion, for they fear robbery by night from him who might be an enemy. In the day-time the dogs are chained up, but at the first hour of the evening the bells ring to warn people that the dogs are about to be let loose in the streets, and thus the passengers abroad must take care. For they now set their dogs free, and no one then dare go out of his house, lest he should be torn to pieces by them.

All the houses of Kazan are made of wood, but there is a great fort, very strongly built with stone walls; it is garrisoned by soldiers, and they keep watch here at night in their quarters, as is done with us in Spain, Italy, and Flanders. This guard was first established because it was the evil custom formerly of the Turks and Tartars to come in by night and, having set fire to the houses, plunder the people.

From Kazan we set forth in seven galleys with which the captain of the city supplied us, together with a guard of a hundred soldiers ordered to conduct us safely to the Court of the Duke of Muscovy. We continued to travel up the same stream, and advancing north-ward, began the more to feel the rigour of the climate of that region; and six days after leaving Kazan we came to a town on the same river bank, which is called Cheboksary. That same night the Volga, or Eder river, was frozen so thick all along where we were about to go, that perforce we had to change our way of travelling. The people here now carried on shore all our luggage and goods that we were taking in the galleys, and next provided us with horse-sleighs and sleds for the transport of baggage, thus enabling us to proceed on to the Court without delay....

The horse-sleighs... were a fashion of portable chairs, like small litters, or little coaches, set on runners made of smoothed wooden beams. These sleds are, in appearance, just like the sleighs which the Flemings make use of in the Low Countries or in Flanders on the Meuse and Scheldt when the waters freeze, and in Italy also by the people who live round the sources of the river Po, except that those which the Muscovites make use of on the Volga are much larger, and run smoothly without cutting into the frozen surface, as those of Germany are wont to do. The form of sled here used is after this wise. There is a square box like a little turret, and inside of it two seats; the roof ends above in a pyramidal form, being covered over by skins with the fur left on. In front there is a stool, or half-seat, where the man can sit who drives the horse which draws the sled, while inside are safely accommodated the two travellers who are making the journey. At the back, as it were on the shoulder of the square box, is a kind of shelf, where some of the luggage may be carried. The horse is driven swiftly, and they go twelve or fifteen leagues in a day; but as each sled can accommodate but two passengers, to transport all our people and goods more than five hundred of these sleighs were required. After this fashion, therefore, we travelled beyond Kazan till we came to a city called Nizhni Novgorod, which holds a population of about 8000 householders (or 36,000 souls). The houses, as elsewhere on the Volga, are of wood, but the city has a stone wall round it, which on one side overhangs the river bank. As soon as we had arrived here, an order came from the Duke of Muscovy—to whom news had been sent of our approach—that we should delay a month, remaining stationary here, and so for that time we postponed further travelling....

At the end of the month... orders came for us to proceed, and we set out for the Court. We travelled in the manner arranged by one of the majordomos of the Duke, who had come to Nizhni for us, in sleighs with covered chairs similar to those we had already used; and were now accompanied by the captain-general of the fortress at Nizhni. This fort is held by a garrison of 6000 soldiers, who night and day keep ward here against the Turks and Tartars....

During six days we now travelled on, keeping always the banks of the river Eder in sight, and then came to a town which is called Murom. This is a large place and very populous, but as we were travelling post-haste, we were unable to enjoy much of the curious amenities of that city....

We passed by the city of Murom, therefore, and in three days reached Vladimir, travelling as formerly up towards the source of the Volga, in other sleighs, but like those already described. This town is of larger size than Murom, being of 12,000 householders (or some 54,000 inhabitants), and it has the appearance of a well-organized community and one that is well governed. The women here are extremely beautiful, but their mode of dress is so ugly and eccentric, and they display so little taste for a suitable combination of colours, that their clothes do not favour them. The men are very tall and stout. The natural character of the place is much the same as that of other towns we passed through since leaving the borders of the Caspian Sea; and as we stayed no longer in Vladimir than one day, we were unable to profit by its amenities. From this place onwards we began to lose sight of the river Eder, leaving it on the right hand. Travelling still after the fashion above described, under the escort of the captain-general and the majordomo of the Duke, who had with them a guard of two hundred soldiers, after three more days we finally arrived at the Court of the Grand Duke, who is the Sovereign of Muscovy....

On a certain Friday, at about ten o'clock in the morning, in the month of November, we entered the capital, and there came out, very courteously, to meet us an infinity of people, for the Muscovites are folk much given to ceremony. Thus on the day when any prince or foreign ambassador comes to the Court of their Duke, or, indeed, should one such enter any city of his that is a seat of government, holiday is proclaimed by public edict, and none shall that day do any work. Further, everybody must then appear, dressed each in his best and finest clothes, in order to go out to the place of reception at the entry of the city....

The number of noblemen who thus came out to meet us, in accordance with the command and ordinance of the Duke—all of them grandees and men of title, lords of many vassals, and gentlemen of position—their number, I say, appeared to me to exceed six thousand. And to bring us in, the Duke had sent two hundred little carriages or litters, each drawn by a well-favoured horse, every carriage being covered in for warmth, the coachmen well dressed, and the horse furnished out in lion and tiger skins; all this, on the one hand for the due pomp of the occasion, and on the other to keep horse and man from the cold, which is very severe in those parts at this season. Half a league before we reached the city gate we found the men of the Duke's bodyguard drawn up to receive us, and next by his order they lined the roadway to right and left along which we passed. The bodyguard are all infantry and matchlockmen, and not counting other soldiers armed with bows and arrows, those who carried matchlocks must have numbered 10,000. Through their line we made our way, and every soldier of the bodyguard stood to attention holding his match lighted.

GREAT BRITAIN

HOW WILLIBALD WENT TO THE HOLY LAND AND TO THEODORIC'S HELL[1]

(A.D. 718)

WRITTEN FROM HIS OWN RECITAL BY A NUN OF HEIDENHEIM

[*Willibald, a son of St Richard, was an Anglo-Saxon, born about the year* A.D. *700. He set out upon his journey when he was eighteen, travelling with his father, his brother Wunibald, and his sister Walpurgis. Arrived at Lucca, the father died. Going on to Rome, the others were seized with fever, on recovering from which they determined upon a pilgrimage to Jerusalem.*]

AFTER the ceremonies of Easter were ended, the active champion of Christ prepared for his voyage with his two companions, and left Rome. They first went eastward to the town of Daterina,[2] where they remained two days; and thence to Cajeta, on the coast, where they went on board a ship and sailed over to Nebule.[3] They here left the ship, and remained a fortnight. These are cities belonging to the Romans; they are in the territory of Beneventum, but subject to Rome. There, after waiting anxiously, in constant prayer that their desires might be agreeable to heaven, they found a ship bound for Egypt, in which they took their passage, and sailed to the land of Calabria, to the town which is called Rhegia,[4] and there remained two days; and then proceeded to the island of Sicily, in which is the town of Catania, where the body of St Agatha, the virgin, reposes. And there is Mount Etna; in case of an eruption of which, the inhabitants of Catania take the veil of St Agatha, and hold it up towards the fire, which immediately ceases. They made a stay of three weeks at this place, and then sailed to the isle of Samos, and thence to the town of Ephesus, in Asia, which is one mile from the sea. They walked thence to the place where the seven sleepers repose; and onward thence to John the Evangelist, in a beautiful locality by Ephesus. They next walked two miles along the seaside to a large village which is called Figila, where they remained one day, and, having begged bread, they went to a fountain in the middle of the town, and, sitting on the edge, they dipped their bread in the water, and so made their meal. They next walked along the sea-shore to the town of Strobole, seated on a lofty hill, and thence to the place called Patera, where they remained till the rigour of winter was past.

After this, going on shipboard, they came to the town which is called

[1] From *Early Travels in Palestine*, edited by T. Wright (1848).

[2] Probably Terracina. [3] Naples (?). [4] Reggio.

Melitena,[1] which had been nearly destroyed by an inundation; and two hermits lived there on a rock, secured by walls, so that the water could not reach them. And there they suffered much from hunger, from which they were only relieved by God's providential mercy. They sailed thence to the isle of Cyprus, which is between the Greeks and the Saracens, to the town of Papho, where they passed the first week in the year. And thence they went to the town of Constantia, where St Epiphanius reposes, and there they remained till after the Nativity of St John the Baptist. They then put to sea again and came into the region of the Saracens to the town of Tharratas,[2] by the sea; and thence they walked a distance of nine to twelve miles to a castle called Archæ, where there was a Greek bishop; and there they had divine service according to the Greek custom. Thence they walked twelve miles to the town which is called Emessa, where there is a large church built by St Helena, in honour of John the Baptist, whose head was long preserved there. This is in Syria.

Willibald's party had now increased to eight in number, and they became an object of suspicion to the Saracens, who, seeing that they were strangers, seized them and threw them into prison, because they knew not of what country they were, and supposed them to be spies. They carried them as prisoners before a certain rich old man, that he might examine them; and he inquired whence they came and the object of their mission; whereupon they related to him the true cause of their journey. The old man replied, "I have often seen men of the parts of the earth whence these come, travelling hither; they seek no harm, but desire to fulfil their law." And upon that they went to the palace, to obtain leave to proceed to Jerusalem.

While they were in prison it happened, by a manifest intervention of Divine Providence, that a merchant residing there was desirous, as an act of charity, and for the salvation of his soul, to purchase their deliverance, that they might pursue their way, but he was not allowed to carry his generous design into effect; nevertheless, he sent them daily their meals, and on Wednesdays and Saturdays sent his son to them in prison, who took them out to the bath, and brought them back again. And on Sunday he took them to church through the market, that they might see the shops, and whatever they seemed to take a liking to he afterwards bought for them at his own expense. The townsmen used then to come there to look at them, because they were young and handsome, and clad in good garments.

Then, while they were still remaining in prison, a man, who was a native of Spain, came and spoke with them, and inquired earnestly who they were

[1] Miletus. [2] Tortosa, now Tartus.

and from whence they came, and they told him the object of their pilgrimage. This Spaniard had a brother in the king's palace, who was chamberlain to the king of the Saracens; and when the governor who had thrown them into prison came to the palace, the captain in whose ship they had sailed from Cyprus, and the Spaniard who had spoken to them in prison, went together before the king of the Saracens, whose title is Emir-al-Mumenin, and, when their cause came on, the Spaniard spoke to his brother, and begged him to intercede with the king for them. After this, when all three came before the king, and told him the case, he asked whence the prisoners came. And they said, "These men come from the west country, where the sun sets; and we know of no land beyond them, but water only." And the king replied, "Why ought we to punish them? They have not sinned against us: give them leave, and let them go." And even the fine of four deniers, which the other prisoners had to pay, was remitted to them. The Cyprians were then situated between the Greeks and the Saracens, and were not in arms: for there was great peace and friendship between the Greeks and Saracens. It was a great and extensive region and had twelve bishops.

As soon as they had obtained leave the travellers went direct to Damascus, a distance of a hundred miles. St Ananias reposes there, and it is in the land of Syria. They remained there one week. And at two miles from the city was a church, on the spot where St Paul was first converted, and the Lord said to him, "Saul, Saul, why persecutest thou me?" etc. And after praying there they went into Galilee, to the place where Gabriel first came to St Mary and said, "Hail, full of grace," etc. A church now stands there, and the village which contains the church is Nazareth. The Christians repeatedly bought that church of the pagans, when the latter were about to destroy it. And having there recommended themselves to the Lord they proceeded to the town of Cana, where our Lord turned water into wine. A large church stands there, and near the altar is still preserved one of the six vessels which our Lord commanded to fill with water to be turned into wine; and the travellers drunk wine out of it. They remained there one day, and then continued their journey to Mount Tabor, the scene of our Lord's transfiguration, where there is now a monastery and a church consecrated to our Lord, and Moses, and Elijah. And those who dwell there call it Hagemon (the Holy Mount). After praying there, they proceeded to the town of Tiberias, which stands on the shore of the sea on which our Lord walked with dry feet, and on which Peter tried to walk but sank. Here are many churches and a synagogue of the Jews. They remained there some days, and observed where the Jordan passes through the midst of the sea. And thence they went round the sea, and by the village of Magdalum to the village of Capernaum, where our Lord raised the prince's daughter. Here was a house and a great wall, which the people of the place told them was the residence of Zebedæus with his sons John and James. And thence they went to Bethsaida, the residence of Peter and Andrew, where there is now a church on the site of their house. They remained there that night, and next morning went to Chorazin, where our Lord healed the demoniacs, and sent the devil into a herd of swine. Here was a church of the Christians.

Having performed their devotions there they went to the place where the two fountains, Jor and Dan, issue from the earth, and flowing down from the mountain are collected into one, and form the Jordan. And there they passed the night between the two fountains, and the shepherds gave them sour ewes' milk to drink. The sheep are of an extraordinary kind, with a long back, short legs, large upright horns, and all of one colour. There are deep marshes in the neighbourhood, and when the heat of the sun in summer is oppressive, the sheep go to the marsh, and immerse themselves in the water all but the head. Thence they proceeded to Cæsarea, where there was a church and a multitude of Christians. They next went to the monastery of St John the Baptist, where there were about twenty monks, and remained one night there, and next day went the distance of a mile to the spot in the river Jordan where our Lord was baptized. Here is now a church raised upon stone columns, and under the church it is now dry land where our Lord was baptized. They still continue to baptize in this place; and a wooden cross stands in the middle of the river, where there is small depth of water, and a rope is extended to it over the Jordan. At the feast of the Epiphany, the infirm and sick come thither, and, holding by the rope, dip in the water. And women who are barren come thither also, and thus obtain God's grace. Willibald here bathed in the Jordan, and they remained at this place one day.

Thence they went to Galgala, a journey of five miles, where is a moderate-sized wooden church, in which are the twelve stones which the children of Israel carried out of the Jordan to Galgala, and placed there as a memorial of their passage. Here also they performed their devotions, and then proceeded to Jericho, above seven miles from the Jordan, and saw there the fountain which was blessed by the prophet Elisha, and hence to the monastery of St Eustochium, which stands in the middle of the plain between Jericho and Jerusalem.

On their arrival at Jerusalem they first visited the spot where the holy cross was found, where there is now a church which is called the Place of Calvary, and which was formerly outside of Jerusalem; but when St Helena found the cross, the place was taken into the circuit of the city. Three wooden crosses stand in this place, on the outside of the wall of the church, in memory of our Lord's cross and of those of the other persons crucified at the same time. They are without the church, but under a roof. And near at hand is the garden in which was the sepulchre of our Saviour, which was cut in the rock. That rock is now above ground, square at the bottom, but tapering above, with a cross on the summit. And over it there is now built a wonderful edifice. And on the east side of the rock of the sepulchre there is a door, by which men enter the sepulchre to pray. And there is a bed within, on which our Lord's body lay; and on the bed stand fifteen golden cups with oil burning day and night. The bed on which our Lord's body rested stands within the rock of the sepulchre on the north side, to the right of a man entering the sepulchre to pray. And before the door of the sepulchre lies a great square stone, in the likeness of the former stone which the angel rolled from the mouth of the monument. Our bishop[1] arrived here on the feast of St Martin, and was suddenly seized with sickness, and lay sick until the week before the Nativity of our Lord. And then, being a little recovered, he rose and went to the church called St Sion, which is in the middle of Jerusalem, and, after performing his devotions, he went to the porch of Solomon, where is the pool where the infirm wait for the motion of the water, when the angel comes to move it; and then he who first enters it is healed. Here our Lord said to the paralytic, "Rise, take up thy bed, and walk." St Mary expired in the middle of Jerusalem, in the place called St Sion; and as the twelve apostles were carrying her body, the angels came and took her from their hands and carried her to paradise.

Bishop Willibald next descended to the valley of Jehoshaphat, which is close to the city of Jerusalem, on the east side. And in that valley is the church of St Mary, which contains her sepulchre, not because her body rests there, but in memory of it. And having prayed there, he ascended Mount Olivet, which is on the east side of the valley, and where there is now a church, where our Lord prayed before his passion, and said to his disciples, "Watch and pray, that ye enter not into temptation." And thence he came to the church on the mountain itself, where our Lord ascended to heaven. In the middle of the church is a square receptacle, beautifully sculptured in brass, on the spot of the Ascension, and there is on it a small lamp in a glass case, closed on every side, that the lamp may burn always, in rain or in fair weather, for the church is open above, without a roof; and two columns stand within the church, against the north wall and the south wall, in memory of the two men who said, "Men of Galilee, why stand ye gazing up into heaven?" And the man who can creep between the wall and the columns will have remission of his sins.

[1] Willibald, who became Bishop of Eichstadt, *c.* A.D. 740.

He next came to the place where the angel appeared to the shepherds, and thence to Bethlehem, where our Lord was born, distant seven miles from Jerusalem. The place where Christ was born was once a cave under the earth, but it is now a square house cut in the rock, and the earth is dug up and thrown from it all round, and a church is now built above it, and an altar is placed over the site of the birth. There is another smaller altar, in order that when they desire to celebrate mass in the cave they may carry in the smaller altar for the occasion. This church is a glorious building in the form of a cross. After prayers here Willibald came to a large town called Thecua, where the children were slain by Herod, and where there is now a church; here rests one of the prophets. And then he came to the valley of Laura, where there is a large monastery; here the abbot resides in the monastery, and he is porter of the church, with many other monks who belong to the monastery, and have their cells round the valley on the slope of the mountain. The mountain is in a circle round the valley, in which the monastery is built. Here rests St Saba. He next arrived at the place where Philip baptized the eunuch, where there is a small church, in an extensive valley between Bethlehem and Gaza, where the travellers prayed. Thence they went to St Matthew, where there is great glory on the Sunday. And while our Bishop Willibald was standing at mass in this church he suddenly lost his sight, and was blind for two months. And thence they went to St Zacharias, the prophet, not the father of John, but another prophet. They next went to the castle of Aframia, where the three patriarchs, Abraham, Isaac, and Jacob repose, with their wives, and thence he returned to Jerusalem, and there, entering the church where the holy cross of our Lord was found, he recovered his sight.

After remaining some time at Jerusalem, Willibald set out on another journey, and came first to St George, at Diospolis, which is ten miles from Jerusalem, and then to a town where there is a church of St Peter the apostle, who here restored to life the widow named Dorcas. He went thence to the coast, far away from Jerusalem, to Tyre and Sidon, which stand on the seashore six miles from each other; after which he passed over Mount Libanus, to Damascus, and so again to Cæsarea, and a third time to Jerusalem, where he passed the following winter. And then he went to the town of Ptolemais, on the extreme bounds of Syria, and was obliged by sickness to remain there all Lent. His companions went forward to the king of the Saracens, named Emir-al-Mumenin, with the hope of obtaining letters of safe conduct; but they could not find the king, because he had fled out of his kingdom. Upon this, they came back, and remained together at Ptolemais until the week before Easter.

Then they went again to Emessa, and asked the governor there to give them letters, and he gave them a letter for each two, because they could not travel in a company, but only two and two, on account of the difficulty of obtaining food. And then they went to Damascus, and returned a fourth time to Jerusalem, where they remained a short period.

They now left Jerusalem by another route, and came to the town of Sebaste, which was formerly called Samaria, and they call the castle Sebastia. Here repose St John the Baptist, and the prophets Abdiah and Elisha; and near the castle is the well at which our Lord asked for water of the Samaritan woman, and over which well there is now a church. And near is the mountain on which the Samaritans worshipped; for the woman said to our Lord, "Our fathers worshipped in this mountain, and ye say that in Jerusalem is the place where men ought to worship." Here the travellers performed their devotions, and then they proceeded to a large town on the farthest borders of Samaria, where they reposed that night. And thence they continued their journey over an extensive plain covered with olive trees, and they were accompanied by a black with two camels and a mule, who was conducting a woman through the wood. And on their way they were met by a lion, which threatened them much with fearful roaring; but the black encouraged them, and told them to go forward; and when they approached it, the lion, as God willed, hurried off in another direction, and they soon heard his roaring in the distance. They supposed he came there to devour people who went into the wood to gather olives. At length they arrived at a town called Thalamartha, on the sea-coast; and they proceeded onwards to the head of Mount Libanus, where it forms a promontory in the sea, and where stands the tower of Libanus. Nobody is allowed to pass this place without letters of safe conduct, for there is a guard in it; those who are without such letters are seized and sent to Tyre. That mountain is between Tyre and Thalamartha. And so the bishop arrived again at Tyre.

Willibald had formerly, when at Jerusalem, bought balsam, and filled a gourd with it, and he took a gourd that was hollow, and had flax, and filled it with rock oil; and poured some in the other gourd, and cut the small stalk, so that it fitted exactly and closed up the mouth of the gourd. So, when they came to Tyre, the citizens stopped them, and examined their burthens to see if they had any thing concealed; for if they had found any thing, they would immediately have put them to death. But they found nothing but Willibald's gourd, which they opened, and, smelling the rock oil in the stalk, they did not discover the balsam that was within. So they let them go. They remained here many days waiting for a ship, and when they had obtained one they were at sea all the winter, from the day of St Andrew the apostle till a week before Easter, when they reached Constantinople. Here repose in one altar the three saints, Andrew, Timothy, and Luke the evangelist; and the sepulchre of John Chrysostom is before the altar where the priest stands when he performs mass. Willibald remained there two years and was lodged in the church, so that he might behold daily where the saints reposed. And then he came to the town of Nice, where the Emperor Constantine held a synod, at which three hundred and eighteen bishops were present. The church here resembles the church on Mount Olivet, where our Lord ascended to heaven, and in it are the pictures of the bishops who were at the synod. Willibald went thither from Constantinople, that he might see how that church was built, and then returned to Constantinople.

At the end of the two years they sailed, in company with the envoys of the pope and the emperor, to the isle of Sicily, to the town of Syracuse, and thence to Catania, and so to the city of Regia, in Calabria; and thence to the isle of Vulcano, where is Theodoric's Hell. And when they arrived there they went on shore to see what sort of a hell it was; and Willibald especially, who was curious to see the interior, was wishful to ascend to the summit of the mountain where the opening was; but he was unable to accomplish his wish, on account of the cinders which were thrown up from the gulf, and settled in heaps round the brim, as snow settles on the ground when it falls from heaven. But though Willibald was defeated in his attempt to reach the summit he had a near view of the column of flame and smoke which was projected upwards from the pit with a noise like thunder. And he saw how the pumice-stone, which writers use, was thrown with the flame from the hell, and fell into the sea, and was thence cast on the shore, where men gathered it and carried it away. After having witnessed this spectacle, they sailed to the church of St Bartholomew the apostle, which stands on the seashore, and came to the mountains which are called Didymi. Thence they went by sea to Naples.

THE FIRST VOYAGE MADE BY MASTER ANTHONIE JENKINSON, FROM THE CITIE OF LONDON, TOWARD THE LAND OF RUSSIA, BEGUNNE THE TWELFTH OF MAY, IN THE YEARE 1557 [1]

ANTHONY JENKINSON

(*Died.* 1584)

FIRST, by the grace of God, the day and yeare above mentioned, I departed from the said Citie, and the same day at Gravesend, embarked my selfe in a good ship, named the *Primrose*, being appointed, although unworthy, chiefe Captaine of the same, and also of the other three good ships—to say, the *John Evangelist*, the *Anne*, and the *Trinitie*—having also the conduct of the Emperour of Russia, his Ambassadour named Osep Nepea Gregoriwich, who passed with his company in the said *Primrose*. And thus our foure tall ships being well appointed, as well for men, as victuals, as other necessary furniture, the said twelfth day of the moneth of May, we weighed our Anchors, and departed from the said Gravesend, in the after-noone, and plying downe the Thames, the wind being Easterly, and faire weather, the thirteenth day we came a ground with the *Primrose*, upon a sand called the blacke tayle, where wee sate fast untill the fourteenth day in the morning, and then God bee praysed, shee came off: and that day we plyed downe as farre as our Ladie of Holland, and there came to an Anchor, the wind being Easterly, and there remayned untill the twentieth day: then wee weyed and went out at Goldmore gate. . . .

[And] the twelfth day of the . . . moneth of July all our foure ships arrived in safety at the Road of Saint Nicholas, in the Land of Russia, where we anchored, and had sayled from London unto the said Road seven hundred and fiftie leagues. The Russian Ambassadour and his companie with great joy got to shoare, and our ships heere forthwith discharged themselves: and being laden againe, and having a faire winde, departed toward England the first of August.

The third of the said moneth I with other of my companie came unto the Citie of Colmogro, being an hundred verstes from the Bay of Saint Nicholas, and in the latitude of 64 degrees, 25 minutes. I tarried at the said Colmogro untill the fifteenth day: and then I departed in a little Boat up the River of Duina, which runneth very swiftly, and the selfe same day passed by the mouth of a River called Pinego, leaving it on our left hand fifteene verstes from Colmogro. On both sides of the mouth of this River Pinego is high Land,

[1] From *Purchas his Pilgrimes*.

great Rockes of Alabaster, great Woods, and Pine-apple trees lying along within the ground, which by report have lyen there since Noes flood. And thus proceeding forward the nineteenth day in the morning, I came into a Towne called Yemps, an hundred verstes from Colmogro. All this way along they make much Tarre, Pitch, and ashes of Aspen trees.

From thence I came to a place called Ustiug, an ancient Citie, the last day of August. At this Citie meet two Rivers: the one called Iug, and the other Sucana, both which fall into the aforesaid River of Duina. The River Iug has his spring in the Land of the Tartars, called Cheremizzi, joyning to the Countrey of Permia: and Sucana hath his head from a Lake not farre from the Citie of Vologda. Thus departing from Ustiug, and passing by the River Sucana, we came to a Towne called Totma. About this place the water is very shallow, and stonie, and troublesome for Barkes and Boats of that Countrey, which they call Nassades and Dosneckes, to passe that way: wherein merchandise are transported from the aforesaid Colmogro to the Citie of Vologda. . . .

The twentieth of September I came unto Vologda, which is a great Citie, and the River passeth through the midst of the same. The houses are builded with wood of Firre trees, joyned one with another, and round without: the houses are foure square without any Iron or stone worke, covered with Birch barkes, and wood over the same: Their Churches are all of wood, two for every Parish, one to be heated for Winter, and the other for Summer. On the tops of their houses they lay much earth, for feare of burning: for they are sore plagued with fire. This Vologda is in 59 degrees, 11 minutes, and is from Colmogro, one thousand verstes.

All the way I never came in house, but lodged in the Wildernesse, by the Rivers side, and carried provision for the way. And he that will travell those wayes, must carrie with him an Hatchet, a Tinder boxe, and a Kettle, to make fire and seethe meat, when he hath it: for there is small succour in those parts, unlesse it be in Townes.

The first day of December I departed from Vologda in poste in a Sled, as the manner is in Winter. And the way to Moscua is as followeth. From Vologda to Commelski, seven and twentie verstes; so to Olmor five and twentie verstes, so to Teloytske twentie verstes, so to Ure thirtie verstes, so to Voshanske thirtie verstes, then to Yeraslave thirtie verstes, which standeth upon the great River Volga, so to Rostove fiftie verstes, then to Rogarin thirtie verstes, so to Peraslave ten verstes, which is a great Towne, standing hard by a faire Lake. From thence to Dowbnay, thirtie verstes, so to Godoroke thirtie verstes, so to Owdsay thirtie verstes, and last to the Mosco five and twentie verstes, where I arrived the sixt day of December. . . .

The tenth day of December I was sent for to the Emperours Castle by the said Emperour, and delivered my Letters unto the Secretarie, who talked with mee of divers matters, by the commandement of the Emperour. And after that my Letters were translated, I was answered that I was welcome, and that the Emperour would give mee that I desired.

The five-and-twentieth day, being the day of the Nativitie, I came into the Emperours presence, and kissed his hand, who sate aloft in a goodly Chaire of estate, having on his head a Crowne most richly decked, and a staffe of Gold in his hand, all apparelled with Gold, and garnished with Precious stones. There sate distant from him about two yards his Brother, and next unto him a Boy of twelve yeeres of age, who was Inheritor to the Emperour of Casan, conquered by this Emperour eight yeeres past. Then sate his Nobilitie round about him, richly apparelled with Gold and stone. And after I had done obeysance to the Emperour he with his owne mouth calling me by my name, bade me to dinner, and so I departed to my lodging till dinner-time, which was at sixe of the clocke, by Candle light.

The Emperour dined in a faire great Hall, in the midst whereof was a Pillar foure square, very artificially made, about which were divers Tables set, and at the uppermost part of the Hall sate the Emperour himselfe, and at his Table sate his Brother, his Uncles sonne, the Metropolitan, the young Emperour of Casan, and divers of his Noblemen, all of one side. There were divers Embassadours, and other strangers, as well Christians as Heathens, diversly apparelled, to the number of sixe hundred men, which dined in the said Hall, besides two thousand Tartars, men of warre, which were newly come to render themselves to the Emperour, and were appointed to serve him in his warres against Lief-landers, but they dined in other Halls.

I was set at a little Table, having no stranger with mee, directly before the Emperous face. Being thus set and placed, the Emperour sent mee divers bowles of Wine and Meade, and many dishes of Meate from his owne hand, which were brought mee by a Duke, and my Table served all in Gold and Silver, and so likewise on other Tables, there were set bowles of Gold, set with Stone, worth by estimation 400 pounds sterling one cup, besides the Plate which served the tables.

There was also a Cupboard of Plate, most sumptuous and rich, which was not used; among the which, was a piece of Gold of two yards long, wrought in the top with Towers, and Dragons heads, also divers barrels of Gold and Silver, with Castles on the bungs, richly and artificially made. The Emperour, and all the Hall throughout was served with Dukes: and when dinner was ended, the Emperour called mee by name, and gave mee drinke with his owne hand, and so I departed to my lodging. Note, that when the Emperour drinketh, all the companie stand up, and at every time he drinketh or tasteth of a dish of meate he blesseth himselfe. Many other things I saw that day, not here noted.

The fourth of Januarie, which was Twelf-tide with them, the Emperour, with his brother and all his Nobles, all most richly apparelled with Gold, Pearles, Precious stones, and costly Furres, with a Crowne upon his head, of the Tartarian fashion, went to the Church in Procession, with the Metropolitan, and divers Bishops and Priests. That day I was before the Emperour againe in Russe apparell, and the Emperour asked if that were not I, and his Chancellour answered, yea. Then he bad me to dinner: then came hee out of the Church, and went with the Procession upon the River, being all frozen, and there standing bare-headed, with all his Nobles, there was a hole made in the Ice, and the Metropolitan hallowed the water with great solemnitie and service, and did cast of the said water upon the Emperours sonne, and the Nobilitie. That done, the people with great thronging filled pots of the said water to carrie home to their houses, and divers children were throwne in, and sicke people, and plucked out quickly againe, and divers Tartars christned: all which the Emperour beheld. Also there were brought the Emperours best Horses, to drinke at the said hallowed water. All this being ended hee returned to his Palace againe, and went to dinner by Candle light, and sate in a woodden house, very fairly gilt. There dined in the place, above three hundred strangers, and I sate alone as I did before, directly before the Emperour, and had my Meat, Bread, and Drinke sent mee from the Emperour.

The citie of Mosco is great, the houses for the most part of wood, and some of stone, with windowes of Iron, which serve for Summer time. There are many faire Churches of stone, but more of wood, which are made hot in the Winter time. The Emperours lodging is in a faire and large Castle, walled foure square of Bricke, high, and thicke, situated upon an Hill, two miles about, and the River on the South-west side of it, and it hath sixteene gates in the walls, and as many Bulwarkes. His Palace is separated from the rest of the Castle, by a long wall going North and South, to the River side. In his Palace are Churches some of stone, and some of wood, with round Towres fairely gilded. In the Church doores, and within the Churches are Images of Gold: the chiefe Markets for all things are within the said Castle, and for sundry things sundry Markets, and every science by it selfe. And in the Winter there is a great Market without the Castle, upon the River being frozen, and there is sold Corne, earthen Pots, Tubs, Sleds, etc. The Castle is in circuit two thousand and nine hundred paces. . . .

The Countrey is full of marish ground, and Playne, in Woods and Rivers abundant, but it bringeth forth good plentie of Corne. This Emperour is of great power: for he hath conquered much, as well of the Lieflanders, Poles, Lettoes, and Swethens, as also of the Tartars, and Gentiles, called Samoeds, having thereby much inlarged his Dominions. Hee keepeth his people in great subjection: all matters pass his judgement, bee they never so small. The Law is sharpe for all offenders.

The Metropolitan dealeth in matters of Religion, as himselfe listeth, whom the Emperour greatly honoureth. They use the Ceremonies and Orders of the Greeke Church. They worship many Images painted on Tables, and specially the Image of Saint Nicholas. . . . They have foure Lents in the yeere, and the weeke before Shrovetide they call the Butter weeke, etc.

They have many sorts of meats and drinks, when they banket and delight in eating of grosse meates, and stinking fish. Before they drinke they use to blow in the Cup: their greatest friendship is in drinking: they are great Talkers and Lyars, without any faith or trust in their words, Flatterers and Dissemblers. . . .

They use saddles made of wood and sinews, with the tree gilded with damaske worke, and the seat covered with cloth, sometimes of gold, and the rest Saphian leather, well stitched. They use little drummes at their saddle bowes, by the sound whereof their horses use to runne more swiftly.

The Russe is apparelled in this manner: his upper garment is of cloth of gold, silke, or cloth, long, downe to the foot, and buttoned with great buttons of silver, or else laces of silke, set on with Brooches, the sleeves thereof very long, which he weareth on his arme, ruffed up. Under that he hath another long garment, buttoned with silke buttons, with a high coller standing up of some colour, and that garment is made straight. Then his shirt is very fine, and wrought with red silke, or some gold, with a coller of pearle. Under his shirt he hath linnen breeches, upon his legs, a pair of hose without feet, and his bootes of red or yellow leather. On his head hee weareth a white Colepeck, with buttons of silver, gold, pearle or stone, and under it a black Foxe cap, turned up very broad. When he rideth on horse-back to the warres, or any journey, he hath a sword of the Turkish fashion, and his Bowe and Arrowes of the same manner. In the Towne he weareth no weapon, but onely two or three paire of knives, having the hafts of the tooth of a Fish, called the Morse.

In the Winter-time the people travell with Sleds, in Towne and Countrey, the way being hard, and smooth with snow: the waters and Rivers are all frozen, and one horse with a Sled, will draw a man upon it foure hundred miles in three dayes: but in the Summer-time, the way is deep with myre, and travelling is very ill.

The Russe, if he be a man of any abilitie, never goeth out of his house in the winter, but upon his Sled, and in summer upon his Horse: and in his Sled he sits upon a Carpet, or a white Beares skin: the Sled is drawne with a Horse well decked, with many Foxes and Woolves tailes at his necke, and is conducted by a little boy upon his backe. . . .

The most part of the women use to ride a-stride in Saddles with stirrops, as men doe, and some of them of Sleds, which in Summer is not commendable. The Husband is bound to find the Wife colours to paint her with all, for they use ordinarily to paint themselves: it is such a common practice among them, that it is counted for no shame; they grease their faces with such colours, that a man may discerne them hanging on their faces almost a flight shoot off: I cannot so well liken them as to a Millers Wife, for they looke as though they were beaten about the face with a bagge of Meale, but their Eye browes they colour as blacke as Jeat. The best propertie that the women have is that they can sewe well, and imbroider with Silke and Gold excellently.

When any man or woman dyeth, they stretch him out, and put a new paire of shooes on his feet, because he hath a great Journey to goe: then doe they wind him in a sheet, as wee doe, but they forget not to put a testimonie in his right hand, which the Priest giveth him, to testifie unto Saint Nicholas that he dyed a Christian man or woman. . . . They that bee hanged or beheaded, or such like, have no testimonie with them: how they are received into Heaven, it is a wonder, without their Pasport.[1] . . .

HOW THE MASTER ORGANIST OF QUEEN ELIZABETH VISITED THE GRAND TURK [2]

(1599)

THOMAS DALLAM [3]

THE shipp whearin I was to make my voyege to Constantinople, Lying at Graves ende, I Departed from London in a pare of ores, with my chiste and suche provition as I had provided for that purpose, the nynthe of Februarie 1598 (1599), being Frydaye.

[1] These last two paragraphs are "taken out of another mans Relation of the same Voyage."

[2] From *Early Voyages and Travels in the Levant*, edited by Theodore Bent (Hakluyt Society, No. 87 (1893)).

[3] Dallam, the Master-organist, had himself made the organ as a present from the Queen to Sultan Mahomed III.

Comminge to Graves ende, I wente aborde our shipp, Called the Heckter, and thare placed my chiste, my beddinge, and a pare of virginals, which the martchantes did alow me to carrie, for my exersize by the waye. Other comoditis I carriede none, savinge one grose of tin spounes, the which coste me nyne shillinges; and thirtie pounde of tin in bares, which coste me 18*s*. The shipe beinge verrie unreddie, and no cabbins appoynted for passingeres, I was constrainede to go into the towne for my Lodginge and Diette till the thirtenthe Daye in the After nowne, at which time anker was wayed and we under sayle, untill we came to Deale Castell.

Cominge to Deale Castell, thare we came to an anker, for the wynde sarved not to pass by Dover. Thar our ship stayed foure dayes for a wynde. In the meane time we wente a shore into the towne of Deale, and also to Sandwiche, to make our selves merrie. When the wynde came fayer, it was in the nyghte, and diverse of us that weare passingers, and also som saylers, weare in the towne of Deale, wheare som of our company had dranke verrie moche, espetialy one of our five Trumpeters, who, beinge in Drinke, had Locked his Chamber dore; and when he that came from the ship to call us went under his chamber wyndoe and caled him, he Came to the wyndoe and insulted him; whear upon we wente all a waye a borde our ship, and lefte that Dronkerde be hinde. Thar the wynde sarvinge well, we sayled merraly by Dover, and so alonge the Sleve.[1]

But beinge aboute thirty leages at sea, sodonly thare cam a contrarie wynde, the which did prove a marvalus greate storme for the space of eyghte and fortie houres. In the nyghte we did not only louse our pinis caled the *Lanerett*, who was to goo with us to the gulfe of Venis, but we also loste our selves, not knowinge whear we weare by Reason the fogge was so greate that we could se no son. When it began anythinge to cleare, we founde our selves to be harde upon the ponie stones[2] betwyxt Ingland and Ierlande, a verrie dangerus place. Than our mariners did Labur to gitte into the mayn otion againe, but the storme not altogether seacinge, but the foge more Increasinge, we wear the next Daye at a non plus againe, not knowinge wheare we weare, but beinge under sayle, and the foge verrie thicke. Upon a sodon we saw the seae breake a gainste the shore, the which was verrie greate Rockes, and we weare so neare the shore that it was not possible to caste aboute in time to save ourselves from shipwracke, but it pleased almyghtie God so to defend us from harme that we weare juste befor the harbur at Dartmouthe, a verrie straite entrie betwyxte greate Rockes that ar on bothe sides of that entrie. Than weare we all verrie joyfull, and entred in thare verrie willingly. Thare

[1] La Manche.

[2] Probably the Pommier Rocks, in the Casquets.

we stayed four dayes. In the meane time the Mr and Martchantes sent postes aboute to all the haven townes upon that coste to inquier of our pinis, the *Lanerett*. In the End word was brought that presently, after the storme, three or four sayle of Dunkerkes had her in chace, and in the storme her top-maste was broken, so that, to save her selfe from beinge taken, she Ron a shore at Falmouthe. Havinge thar goten a new topmaste, she sente word by the mesinger that she would meet us in Plimmouthe sounde. This worde beinge broughte, Anker was wayed, and we under sayell; when we cam Ryghte before Plimmouthe a peece was discharged to call our pinis; but even at that time the wynd came contrarie, so that we moste needes also goo in thare, and cam to an anker in Catt water, wheare we founde our pinis. Thar we stayed sevene dayes for a wynde.

The 16th day of Marche, beinge verrie could wether, the wynde came fayer, and as we weare under sayle in Plimmouthe-sounde, thare came in a little carvell with salte, who no sonner was come to the shore, and hearinge the name of our shipe, but they caused a parlie to be sounded be a trumpett, whearupon sayle was storouk, and tow sailers of that carvell came aborde our shipe, advisinge our Mr not to goo to seae with oute good store of companye; for they wente to seae in a man of ware from Plimmouthe, caled the Plow, and theye weare taken by seven sayell of Dunkerkes, who Did straitly examon them if they could tell weare the *Heckter* was, or whether she weare gone her voyage or no, but they protested that they never hard of such a shipp. Som of these men thei put to death, to feare otheres. Whate they did with the Reste of theire men they knew not. They touke theire ship from them, and gave sixe of them that litle carvell to bringe them home.

When our Mr and captaine had harde these men speake, he toulde them that he would not staye one houre for any more companye than God alreddie had sente him, the which was only our pinis and tow shipes that weare goinge for New found Land, and for there owne saftie mad haste after us. Saylinge forthe before a faire wynde, our ship sayled so well that we could spare the pinis our mayne saile, and yeate the nexte morninge our pinnis was verrie far behind. About 8 of the clocke, one in our maine tope discried three sayle, the which did ly close by our fore porte, a little after he saw four more, which lay the same cource, and these weare the seven sayell which we weare tould of. Then we began to Louke aboute us, our goneres made Reddie there ordinance, our faightes[1] oute, and everie man his bandaleare and muskett. We hade the wynde of them, and needed not to have spoken with them, but our Captaine thoughte it not fitt to show our selves fearfull or cowardly; Leaste

[1] Fights—*i.e.*, waistcloths.

the wynde should sodonly turne, or scante upon us, and our flyinge would incurridge our enemyes to com the more bouldly upon us. Than he caled the botson and bid him beare towardes them, the which he willingly wente aboute; so we bore Towardes them, and when we came so neare them that we myghte well disarne the hulke of there amberall and of their vizamberall, and they cam bouldly upon us, our Mr bide the botswayne stow them a brood side; for our mayne sayle was so brode, that they could not se the stoutnes of our ship; for may hape, cothe he [mayhap, quoth he], they may take our ship to be one of the Quene's and yf we doo hapen to heale them, or theye us, they which make answer maye say our ship is caled the *Seven Stars*, for the Quene as yeate hathe none of that name; but assowne as they sawe the brode side of our ship, thinking us in dede to be one of the Quene's ships, they presently turned them aboute to flye away. Than we gave chace to them, havinge almoste loste sighte of our pinis, and all other shipes savinge those which we gave chace unto. They made all the sayle they coulde, and yeat with in halfe an hour we weare come with in shott of them. Than our captain bid the Mr goner give them a chace peece[1] shout at the amberall, but hitt him not, so the Mr goner gave him a shott cloce by his fore bowe; yeat would they nether strike sayle, not show any flagge, but made away with all the sayle they had, drablings[2] and topgalands. . . .

Marche 1599

The 20th Day, the wynde sarvinge well, we paste the Northe Cape, and entered the bay of Portingale. The 23 we Recovered the Soothe Cape.[3] Than we weare becalmed for a time. The 24 thare came an Infinite company of porposis aboute our ship, the which did leape and Rone [run] marvalusly. The 25 we saw 2 or 3 great monstrus fishis or whales, the which did spoute water up into the eayere, lyke as smoke dothe assend out of a chimnay. Sometime we myghte se a great parte of there bodye above the water. The calme did yeate continue. The 27, havinge a verrie fayer wynde, the which did blow a good gale aboute 12 or one of the clocke, we entered the straytes of Marie-medeteranum in Dispite of our enymyes. . . .

The seventhe of Aprill beinge Easter eve, we saw verrie strainge lyghtninge in the skie, or in the eire. It was verrie wonderfull and strainge, for we myghte se the eayre open and a fier lyke a verrie hote iron taken out of a smythe's forge, somtimes in liknes of a roninge worme, another time lyke a horsshow, and agine lyke a lege and a foute. Also the Thunder clapes weare also

[1] Chase-piece, a gun placed in the bows during a fight. [2] Drabler.
[3] Cape Finisterre.

exseding greate. The seventhe daye we passed by a place caled Morrottome.[1] The 18th, by a hudge mountaine, which is an Ilande in the seae, close by the shore. This ilande is called Simberrie.[2] Upon that shore, over againste it, was somtime the Cittie of Carttag, but some wryteres caled it Carthage. Aboute five leagues further we sawe the cape, or forte, caled Debone.[3] At the weste sid of it thar is a greate and large Tovne, caled Tonis,[4] by some peopell Thunes. Thare dothe lye some parte of the Turkes gallis. The 14th we sayelled by a famous iland Caled Sissillia,[5] cloce by the shore of it. This ilande, they saye, is threscore leages in lengthe; a verrie frutfull and pleasante iland. It dothe yelde greate store of corne and all maner of frute. At the weste End Thare Dothe alwayes ly at the leaste nyne gallies, and at the easte end ten or more.

Neare unto the easte ende of this Cissillie there is a verrie heie mountayne, the which they do cale Montabell, but the ryghte name of it is mounte Ettna. In the Daye time we that sayle by it maye se the topp of it covered with snow, but in the nyghte we did see many flashis of fiere, to our thinkinge about the mydle of the mountaine. . . .

JUNE

The firste of June Thar was letters convayede verrie straingly from Alippo to Sçandaroune, the which is thre score and twelve myles distance. After I hade bene thare a little whyle, I persaved that it was an ordinarie thinge. For, as we weare sittinge in our marchantes house talkinge, and pidgons weare a feedinge in the house before us, thare came a whyte cote pidgon flyinge in, and lyghte on the grounde amongeste his fellowes, the which, when one of the marchantes saw, he sayd: Welcom, Honoste Tom, and, takinge him upe, thare was tied with a thred under his wynge, a letter, the bignes of a twelve penc., and it was Dated but four houres before. After that I saw the lyke done, and alwayes in 4 houres. . . .

In the time of our being at Scandaroune, our longe boote wente everie Frydaye to Tharschus, the cittie or towne wheare the appstele St Pale was borne, for that was ther markett Daye, and she wente to buy vittals. Tharshus is but 16 myles from Scandaroune, and aboute the myd waye, or somwhat nearer to Scanderowne, is the place wheare Jonas was caste out of the whales bellie, as the Turkes and Greekes tould us. . . .

The tenthe of this monthe we departede from Scandaroune towardes Constantinople, the wynde beinge direcktly againste us, bordinge it from shore to shore. . . .

[1] Probably Marabout.
[2] Zembra el Jamoor, over against Carthage.
[3] Cape Bon.
[4] Tunis.
[5] Sicily.

AUGUST

The 15th day, beinge Wednesday, we arived at Constantinople.

The 16th our shipp Came neare to the Seven Towers, which is the firste porte that we com unto of the surralia [seraglio] which doth joyne close to the Cittie. From that poynte or corner of the surralia unto the Cittie it is almoste tow myles; thare our shipp cam to an anker, and the nexte daye she begane to be new payntede.

The 17th we wente aborde our ship for the presente, and carried it to our imbassaders house in the Cittie of Gallata, in the vines of Peara; and because there was no roome heie enoughe to sett it up in his house, he caused a roome to be made with all speed withoute the house in the courte, to sett it up in, that it myghte there be made perfitt before it should be carried to the surralia.

The twentethe daye, beinge Mondaye, we begane to louke into our worke; but when we opened our chistes we founde that all glewinge worke was clene Decayed, by reason that it hade layne above sixe monthes in the hould of our ship, whicte was but newly bulte, so that the extremetie of the heete in the hould of the shipe, with the workinge of the sea and the hootnes of the cuntrie, was the cause that all glewinge fayled; lyke wyse divers of my mettle pipes weare brused and broken.

When our Imbassader, Mr Wyllyam Aldridge, and other jentlmen, se in what case it was in, theye weare all amayzed, and sayde that it was not worthe *2d.* My answeare unto our Imbassader and to Mr Aldridge, at this time I will omitt; but when Mr Alderidge harde what I sayede, he tould me that yf I did make it perfitt he would give me, of his owne purss, 15 *li.*, so aboute my worke I wente. . . .

The 28, the *Heckter*, our ship, made hire salutation to the Great Turke, thare called the Grande Sinyor, on the northe side of the Surralya, the Grande Sinyor beinge in his Cuske [kiosk], upon the wale which is close to the sea.

The salutation was verrie strange and wonderfull in the sighte of the Great Turke and all other Turkes. She was, as I have saide before, new paynted (upon everie topp an anshante[1]—viz., mayne top, fore top, myssen top, sprid saile top, and at everie yardes arme a silke penante). All her braurie[2] I cannot now relate; her faightes was oute, and in everie top as many men, with their musketes, as coulde stande conveniently to descharge them.

Anker was wayed, the Daye verrie calme and fayere. Althinges beinge reddie, our gonores gave fiere, and discharged eighte score great shotte, and betwyxte everie greate shott a vallie of smale shott; it was done with verrie

[1] Ancient—*i.e.*, standard. [2] Bravery.

good decorume and true time, and it myghte well desarve commendations.

But one thinge I noteed, which perswaded my simple consaite that this great triumpte and charge was verrie evile bestowed, beinge done unto an infidell. Thare was one man sicke in the ship, who was the ship carpinder, and wyth the reporte of the firste greate peece that was discharged he died.

SEPTEMBER

The 11th Daye, beinge Tusdaye, we Carried our instrament over the water to the Grand Sinyors Courte, Called the surralya, and thare in his moste statlyeste house I began to sett it up. This watere which we crosed from Galletta to Surralia is a streame that comethe from the Blacke Sea, and is called Hellisponte, which partethe Asia and Thratia, and as it comethe Downe by Galletta, a creke of that rever goethe up into the contrie aboute sixe myles, which partethe the tow Cittis of Constantinople and Galletta; they maye go betwyxte them by lande, but it is twelve myle, and to cross the water it is but one myle. At everie gate of the surralia thare alwayes sitethe a stoute Turke, abute the calinge or degre of a justis of the peace, who is caled a chia; not withstandinge, the gates ar faste shut, for thare pasethe none in or oute at ther owne pleasures.

Beinge entered within the firste gate, thare was placed righte againste the gate five greate peecis of brass, with Christians armes upon them. . . . Than we passed throughe verrie Delitfull walkes and garthins; the walkes ar, as it weare, hedged in with statly siprus tres, planted with an equale Distance one from thother, betwyxte them and behinde them, smaler tres that bearethe excelente frute; I thinke thare is none wanting that is good. The garthenes I will omite to wryte of at this time. The waye from the firste gate to the seconde wale is som thinge risinge up a hill, betwyxte wales aboute a quarter of a myle and better. The gates of the seconde wale was also shutt, but when we came to the gate, my Intarpreter caled to those that kepte it within. Thoughe they had Knowledge of our cominge, yeat would they not open the gates untill we had caled and tould them our busines. These gates ar made all of massie iron; tow men, whom they do cale jemeglans, did open them.

Wythein the firste wales ar no housis but one, and that is the bustanjebasha his house, who is captaine of a thousande jemeglanes, which doo nothinge but kepe the garthens in good order; and I am perswaded that thare is none so well kepte in the worlde. Within the seconde wales thar is no gardens, but statly buildinges; many courtes paved with marble and such lyke stone. Everie ode[1] or by corner hath som excelente frute tre or tres growing in them;

[1] Compartment.

allso thar is greate abundance of sweete grapes, and of diveres sortes; thar a man may gather grapes everie Daye in the yeare. . . .

Cominge into the house whear I was appoynted to sett up the presente or instramente; it seemed to be rether a churche than a dwellinge house; to say the truthe, it was no dwellinge house, but a house of pleasur, and lyke wyse a house of slaughter; for in that house was bulte one litle house, verrie curius bothe within and witheout; for carvinge, gildinge, good Collors, and vernishe, I have not sene the lyke. In this litle house, that emperor that rained when I was thare, had nyntene brotheres put to deathe in it, and it was bulte for no other use but the stranglinge of everie emperors bretherin.

This great house it selfe hathe in it tow rankes of marble pillors; the pettestales [pedestals] of them ar made of brass, and double gilte. The wales on three sides of the house ar waled but halfe waye to the eaves; the other halfe is open; but yf any storme or great wynde should hapen, they can sodonly Let fale suche hanginges made of cotten wolle for that purpose as will kepe out all kinds of wethere, and sudenly they can open them againe. The fourthe side of the house, which is close and joynethe unto another house, the wale is made of purfeare [porphyry], or suche kinde of stone as when a man walketh by it he maye se him selfe tharin. Upon the grounde, not only in this house, but all other that I se in the Surraliae, we treade upon ritch silke garpites, one of them as muche as four or sixe men can carrie. Thare weare in this house nether stouls, tables, or formes, only one coutch of estate. Thare is one side of it a fishe ponde, that is full of fishe that be of divers collores.

The same Daye, our Imbassader sente Mr Paul Pinder, who was then his secritarie, with a presente to the Sultana, she being at hir garthen. The presente was a Coatche of six hundrethe poundes vallue. At that time the Sultana did Take greate lykinge to Mr Pinder, and after wardes she sente for him to have his private companye, but there meetinge was croste.

The 15th, I finished my worke in the Surraliao, and I wente once everie daye to se it, and dinede Thare almoste everie Daye for the space of a monthe; which no Christian ever did in there memorie that wente awaye a Christian.

The 18 daye (stayinge somethinge longe before I wente), the Coppagaw [Capougee] who is the Grand Sinyor's secritarie, sente for me that one of his frendes myghte heare the instramente. Before I wente awaye, the tow jemaglanes, who is keepers of that house, touke me in theire armes and Kised me, and used many perswations to have me staye with the Grand Sinyor, and sarve him. . . .

The 24, at nyghte our ambassodor Caled me into his Chamber and gave me a greate Charge to goo the next morninge betimes to the surralia and make the instrumente as perfitt as possibly I could, for that daye, before noune, the Grand Sinyor would se it, and he was to Deliver his imbassage to the Grand Sinyor; after he hade given me that charge he toulde me that he had but done his dutie in tellinge me of my dutie, and cothe he: Because yow shall not take this unkindly, I will tell you all and what you shall truste unto.

The Imbassadores spetche unto me in Love after he had given me my charge:

Yow ar come hether wythe a presente from our gratious Quene, not to an ordinarie prince or kinge, but to a myghtie monarke of the worlde, but better had it bene for yow yf it had bene sente to any Christian prince, for then should yow have bene sure to have receaved for yor paines a greate rewarde; but yow muste consider what he is unto whom yow have broughte this ritche presente, a monarke but an infidell, and the grande Enymye to all Christians. Whate we or any other Christians can bringe unto him he dothe thinke that we dow it in dutie or in feare of him, . . . and tharfore yow muste louke for nothinge at his handes. Yow would thinke that for yor longe and wearriesom voyege, with dainger of lyfe, that yow weare worthie to have a litle sighte of him; but that yow muste not loake for nether; for yow se wheat greate preparinge we made and have bene aboute ever sense your cominge, for the credite of our contrie, and for a Deliveringe of this presente and my imbassadge, the which, by Godes helpe, to-morrow muste be performede. We cale it kisinge of the Grand Sinyor's hande; bute when I come to his gates I shalbe taken of my horse and seartcht, and lede betwyxte tow men holdinge my handes downe close to my sides, and so lede into the presence of the Grand Sinyor, and I muste kiss his kne or his hanginge sleve. Havinge deliverede my letteres unto the Coppagawe, I shalbe presently ledd awaye, goinge backwardes as longe as I can se him, and in payne of my heade I muste not turne my backe upon him, and therefore yow muste not louke to have a sighte of him. I thoughte good to tell yow this, because yow shall not heareafter blame me, or say that I myghte haue tould yow so muche; lett not your worke be anythinge the more carlesly louked unto, and at your cominge home our martchantes shall give yow thankes, yf it give the Grand Sinyor contente this one day. I care not if it be non after the nexte, yf it doo not please him at the firste sighte, and performe not those thinges which it is Toulde him that it can Dow, he will cause it to be puled downe that he may trample it under his feete. And than shall we have no sute grantede, but all our charge will be loste.

After I had given my Lorde thankes for this frindly spetche, thoughe smale comforte in it, I tould him that thus muche I understoode by our martchantes before my cominge oute of London, and that he needed not to Doubte that thare should be any faulte ether in me or my worke, for he hade sene the triall of my care and skill in makinge that perfickte and good which was thoughte to be uncurable, and in somethinges better than it was when Her Maiestie sawe it in the banketinge house at Whyte Hale.

The nexte morninge, being the 25, I wente to the Surralia, and with me my mate Harvie, who was the ingener, Mr Rowland Buckett the paynter, and Myghell Watson the joyner.

Aboute an houre or tow after my lorde was reddie, and sett forwarde towardes the surralya, he did ride lyke unto a kinge, onlye that he wanted a crowne. Thare roode with him 22 jentlmen and martchantes, all in clothe of goulde; ye jentlemen weare these: Mr Humfrye Cunisbye, Mr Baylie of Salsburie, Mr Paule Pinder, Mr William Alderidg, Mr Jonas Aldridge, and Mr Thomas Glover. The other six weare martchantes; these did ride in vestes of clothe of goulde, made after the cuntrie fation; thare wente on foute 28 more in blew gounes made after the Turkie fation, and everie man a silke grogren cape,[1] after the Ittallian fation. My Livery was a faire clooke of a Franche greene, etc.

Now when I had sett all my worke in good order, the jemyglanes which kepte that house espied the Grand Sinyor cominge upon the water in his goulden Chieke [caïque], or boate, for he cam that morning six myles by water; whear I stoode I saw when he sett foote on the shore.

Than the jemyglanes tould me that I muste avoyd the house, for the Grand Sinyor would be thare presently. It was almoste halfe a myle betwyxte the water and that house; but the Grand Sinyor, havinge a desier to se his presente, came thether wythe marvalus greate speed. I and my company that was with me, beinge put forthe, and the Dore locked after us, I hard another Dore open, and upon a sodon a wonderfull noyes of people; for a litle space it should seme that at the Grand Sinyore's coming into the house the dore which I hard opene did sett at libertie four hundrethe persons which weare locked up all the time of the Grand Sinyore's absence, and juste at his cominge in theye weare sett at libertie, and at the firste sighte of the presente, with greate admyration did make a wonderinge noyes.

The Grand Sinyor, beinge seated in his Chaire of estate, commanded silence. All being quiett, and no noyes at all, the presente began to salute the Grand Sinyor; for when I lefte it I did alow a quarter of an houre for his cominge thether. Firste the clocke strouke 22; than The chime of 16 bels went of, and played a songe of 4 partes. That beinge done, tow personagis which stood upon to corners of the seconde storie, houldinge tow silver trumpetes

[1] Grosgrain.

in there handes, did lifte them to theire heades, and sounded a tantarra. Than the muzicke went of, and the orgon played a song of 5 partes twyse over. In the tope of the orgon, being 16 foute hie, did stand a holly bushe full of blacke birds and thrushis, which at the end of the musick did singe and shake theire wynges. Divers other motions thare was which the Grand Sinyor wondered at. Than the Grand Sinyor asked the Coppagawe yf it would ever doo the lyke againe. He answered that it would doo the lyke againe at the next houre. Cothe he: I will se that. In the mean time, the Coppagaw, being a wyse man, and doubted whether I hade so appoynted it or no, for he knew that it would goo of it selfe but 4 times in 24 houres, so he cam unto me, for I did stand under the house sid, wheare I myghte heare the orgon goo, and he asked me yf it would goo againe at the end of the nexte houre; but I tould him that it would not, for I did thinke the Grand Sinyor would not have stayed so longe by it; but yf it would please him, that when the clocke had strouk he would tuche a litle pin with his finger, which before I had shewed him, it would goo at any time. Than he sayde that he would be as good as his worde to the Grand Sinyor. When the clocke began to strick againe, the Coppagaw went and stood by it; and when the clocke had strouke 23, he tuched that pinn, and it did the lyke as it did before. Than the Grand Sinyor sayed it was good. He satt verrie neare unto it, ryghte before the Keaes [keys], wheare a man should playe on it by hande. He asked why those keaes did move when the orgon wente and nothinge did tuche them. He Tould him that by those thinges it myghte be played on at any time. Than the Grand Sinyor asked him yf he did know any man that could playe on it. He sayd no, but he that came with it coulde, and he is heare without the dore. Fetche him hether, cothe the Grand Sinyor, and lett me se how he dothe it. Than the Coppagaw opened that Dore which I wente out at, for I stoode neare unto it. He came and touke me by the hande, smylinge upon me; but I bid my drugaman aske him what I should dow, or whither I shoulde goo. He answered that it was the Grand Sinyore's pleasur that I should lett him se me playe on the orgon. So I wente with him. When I came within the Dore, That which I did se was verrie wonderful unto me. I cam in direcktly upon the Grand Sinyore's ryghte hande, som 16 of my passis [paces] from him, but he would not turne his head to louke upon me. He satt in greate state, yeat the sighte of him was nothinge in Comparrison of the traine that stood behinde him, the sighte whearof did make me almoste to thinke that I was in another worlde. The Grand Sinyor satt still, behouldinge the presente which was befor him, and I stood daslinge my eyes with loukinge upon his people that stood behinde him, the which was four hundrethe persons in number. Two hundrethe of them weare his princepall padgis, the yongest of them 16 yeares of age, som 20, and som 30. They weare apparled in ritche clothe of goulde made in gowns to the mydlegge; upon theire heades litle caps of clothe of goulde, and som clothe of Tissue; great peecis of silke aboute theire wastes instead of girdls; upon their leges Cordivan buskins, reede. Theire heades wear all shaven, savinge that behinde Their ears did hange a locke of hare like a squirel's taile; theire beardes shaven, all savinge theire uper lips. Those 200 weare all verrie proper men, and Christians borne.

The thirde hundrethe weare Dum men, that could nether heare nor speake, and theye weare likwyse in gouns of riche Clothe of gould and Cordivan buskins; bute theire Caps weare of violett velvett, the croune of them made like a lether bottell, the brims devided into five picked [peaked] corneres. Som of them had haukes in theire fistes.

The fourthe hundrethe weare all dwarffs, big-bodied men, but verrie low of stature. Everie Dwarfe did weare a simmeterrie [scimitar] by his side, and they weare also apareled in gowns of Clothe of gould.

I did moste of all wonder at those dumb men, for they lett me understande by theire perfitt sins [signs] all thinges that they had sene the presente dow by its motions.

When I had stode almost one quarter of an houre behouldinge this wonder full sighte, I harde the Grande Sinyore speake unto the Coppagaw, who stood near unto him. Than the Coppagaw cam unto me, and touke my cloake from aboute me, and laye it Doune upon the Carpites, and bid me go and playe on the organ; but I refused to do so, because the Grand Sinyor satt so neare the place wheare I should playe that I could not com at it, but I muste needes turne my backe Towardes him and touche his Kne with my britchis, which no man, in paine of deathe, myghte dow, savinge only the Coppagaw. So he smyled and lett me stande a litle. Than the Grand Sinyor spoake againe, and the Coppagaw, with a merrie countenance, bid me go with a good curridge, and thrusts me on. When I cam verrie neare the Grand Sinyor, I bowed my heade as low as my kne, not movinge my cape, and turned my backe righte towardes him, and touched his kne with my britchis.

He satt in a verrie ritche Chaire of estate, upon his thumbe a ringe with a diamon in it halfe an inche square, a faire simeterie by his side, a bow, and a quiver of Arros.

He satt so righte behinde me that he could not se what I did; tharfore he stood up, and his Coppagaw removed his Chaire to one side, wher he myghte se my handes; but, in his risinge from his chaire, he gave me a thruste forwardes, which he could not otherwyse dow, he satt so neare me; but I thought he had bene drawinge his sorde to cut of my heade.

I stood thar playinge suche thinge as I coulde untill the cloke stroucke, and then I boued my heade as low as I coulde, and wente from him with my backe towardes him. As I was taking of my cloake, the Coppagaw came unto me and bid me stand still and lett my cloake lye; when I had stood a litle whyle, the Coppagaw bid me goo and cover the Keaes of the organ; then I wente Close to the Grand Sinyor againe, and bowed myselfe, and then I wente backewardes to my Cloake. When the company saw me do so theye semed to be glad, and laughed. Than I saw the Grand Sinyor put his hande behind him full of goulde, which the Coppagaw receved, and broughte unto me fortie and five peecis of gould called chickers,[1] and than was I put out againe wheare I came in, beinge not a little jotfull of my good suckses. . . .

The laste of September I was sente for againe to the surralia to sett som thinges in good order againe, which they had altered, and those tow jemoglans which kepte that house made me verrie kindly welcom, and asked me that I would be contented to stay with them always, and I should not wante anythinge, but have all the contentt that I could desier. I answered them that I had a wyfe and Childrin in Inglande, who did expecte my returne. Than they asked me how long I had been married, and how many children I hade. Thoughe in deede I had nether wyfe nor childrin, yeat to excuse my selfe I made them that Answeare.

Than they toulde me that yf I would staye the Grand Sinyor would give tow wyfes, ether tow of his Concubines or els tow virgins of the beste I Could Chuse my selfe, in Cittie or contrie.

The same nyghte, as my Lorde was at supper, I tould him what talke we had in the surralya, and whate they did offer me to staye thare, and he bid me that by no meanes I should flatly denie them anythinge, but be as merrie with them as I could, and tell them that yf it did please my Lorde that I should stay, I should be the better contented to staye; by that meanes they will not go about to staye you by force, and yow may finde a time the better to goo awaye when you please. . . .

The nexte daye our shipp caled the *Heckter*, beinge reddie to departe, I wente to carrie my beed and my Chiste aborde the shipp. Whylste I was aborde the shipp, thar came a jemoglane or a messenger from the surralia to my lord imbassador, with an express command that the shipp should not departe, but muste stay the Grand Sinyores pleasur. When my lord hard this messidge, with suche a comande, he begane to wonder what the Cause should be. He thoughte that thare hade bene som forfitt made, or that som of the chips company had done horte or given som greate offence unto som greate person;

[1] Sequins.

but, what so ever it was, he knew that the Grand Sinyores comande must be obayed; tharefore, when he had stodied longe what the cause myghte be, and beinge verrie desirus to know the truthe, he wente to the messenger and desiered him to tell him the cause whye the Grand Sinyor had sente this comande, or whearfore it should be.

The messenger tould him that he did not know the cause whye, nether whearfore, but he did hearde the chia say that yf the workman that sett up the presente in the surralia would not be perswaded to stay be hind the shipe, the ship muste staye untill he had removed the presente unto another place.

When my lord had got thus muche out of him, he began to be somwhat merrie . . . and sente one to the ship whear I was, who tould me that I muste com presently to my Lorde; so when I came to my lorde I found with him another messinger, who broughte the sartaintie of the matter that it was for no other cause but for my stainge to remove the organ; but when my lord tould me that I muste be contented to staye and Lette the ship goo, than was I in a wonderfull perplixatie, and in my furie I tould my lorde that that was now com to pass which I ever feared, and that was that he in the end would betray me, and turne me over into the Turkes hands, whear I should Live a slavish Life, and never companie againe with Christians, with many other suche-like words. . . .

November

The 12th of November I wente to Adranople gate, that is the farthest gate of Constantinople, towardes Adranople. Upon a goodly plaine withoute that gate, I se a carravan of the Taleste [tallest] Camels that ever I had sene in all my time. Than we returned into the Cittie to see Diverse monymentes, the which I would not for anything but that I had sene them. I have not time now to wryte them, but of force muste leave them un named untill a time of better Leasur.

This daye, in the morninge, I put on a pare of new shoues, and wore them quite oute before nyghte; but this daye I touke a great could with a surfett, by means whearof I was sore troubled with a burninge fever, and in great dainger of my Life. When I was somthinge recovered, by the helpe of God and a good fisition, it hapemed that thar was good Company reddie to com for Inglande, suche as in tow or three years I could not have had the lik, if I had stayed behinde them, and they weare all desierus to have my company. My Lord was verrie unwillinge that I should goo at that time, because I was verrie wayke, not able to goo on foute one myle in a daye. But I desiered my lord to give me leve, for I had rether die by the way in doinge my good will to goo home than staye to die thare, wheare I was perswaded I could not live if I did staye behinde them.

[*At Zant Dallam picked up his old ship, the "Heckter." On April the 1st he was in the Gulf of Lyons, hearing the "crye of a mearmaide," and at some date unknown reached England*].

Than we wente a shore at Dover, and our trompetes soundinge all the waye before us into the towne, wheare we made ourselves as merrie as Could, beinge verrie glad that we weare once againe upon Inglishe ground.

HAZARDS OF THE WAY [1]

(1716)

LADY MARY WORTLEY MONTAGU

(1689-1762)

I

LEIPSIG

Nov. 21 (O.S.) (1716)

I BELIEVE, dear sister, you will easily forgive my not writing to you from Dresden, as I promised, when I tell you that I never went out of my chaise from Prague to that place.

You may imagine how heartily I was tired with twenty-four hours' post travelling, without sleep or refreshment (for I can never sleep in a coach, however fatigued). We passed by moonshine the frightful precipices that divide Bohemia from Saxony, at the bottom of which runs the river Elbe; but I cannot say that I had reason to fear drowning in it, being perfectly convinced that, in case of a tumble, it was utterly impossible to come alive to the bottom. In many places the road is so narrow that I could not discern an inch of space between the wheels and the precipice. Yet I was so good a wife not to wake Mr W——, who was fast asleep by my side, to make him share in my fears, since the danger was unavoidable, till I perceived, by the bright light of the moon, our postilions nodding on horseback, while the horses were on a full gallop, and I thought it very convenient to call out to desire them to look where they were going. My calling waked Mr W——, and he was much more surprised than myself at the situation we were in, and assured me that he had passed the Alps five times in different places, without ever having gone a road so dangerous. I have been told since it is common to find the bodies of travellers in the Elbe; but, thank God, that was not our destiny; and we came

[1] From *Letters of Lady Mary Wortley Montagu.*

safe to Dresden, so much tired with fear and fatigue, it was not possible for me to compose myself to write.

II

DOVER

Oct. 31 (O.S.) (1718)

I am willing to take your word for it, that I shall really oblige you by letting you know, as soon as possible, my safe passage over the water. I arrived this morning at Dover, after being tossed a whole night in the packet-boat, in so violent a manner that the master, considering the weakness of his vessel, thought it prudent to remove the mail, and gave us notice of the danger. We called a little fisher boat, which could hardly make up to us; while all the people on board us were crying to Heaven; and 'tis hard to imagine one's self in a scene of greater horror than on such an occasion; and yet, shall I own it to you? though I was not at all willing to be drowned, I could not forbear being entertained at the double distress of a fellow-passenger. She was an English lady that I had met at Calais, who desired me to let her go over with me in my cabin. She had bought a fine point head, which she was contriving to conceal from the custom-house officers. When the wind grew high, and our little vessel cracked, she fell very heartily to her prayers, and thought wholly of her soul. When it seemed to abate, she returned to the worldly care of her headdress, and addressed herself to me: "Dear madam, will you take care of this point? if it should be lost!—Ah, Lord, we shall all be lost!—Lord have mercy on my soul!—Pray, madam, take care of this headdress." This easy transition from her soul to her headdress, and the alternate agonies that both gave her, made it hard to determine which she thought of greatest value. But, however, the scene was not so diverting but I was glad to get rid of it, and be thrown into the little boat, though with some hazard of breaking my neck. It brought me safe hither; and I cannot help looking with partial eyes on my native land. That partiality was certainly given us by nature, to prevent rambling, the effect of an ambitious thirst after knowledge, which we are not formed to enjoy. All we get by it is a fruitless desire of mixing the different pleasures and conveniences which are given to different parts of the world, and cannot meet in any one of them. After having read all that is to be found in the languages I am mistress of, and having decayed my sight by midnight studies, I envy the easy peace of mind of a ruddy milkmaid, who, undisturbed by doubt, hears the sermon with humility every Sunday, having not confused the sentiments of natural duty in her head by the vain enquiries of the schools, who may be more learned, yet, after all, must remain as ignorant. And, after having seen part of Asia and Africa, and almost made the tour of Europe, I think the honest English squire more happy, who verily believes the Greek wines less delicious than March beer; that the African fruits have not so fine a flavour as golden-pippens; and the becafiguas of Italy are not so well tasted as a rump of beef; and that, in short, there is no perfect enjoyment of this life out of Old England. I pray God I may think so for the rest of my life; and since I must be contented with our scanty allowance of daylight, that I may forget the enlivening sun of Constantinople.

I am, etc., etc.

RARE ADVENTURES [1]

(1796)

MUNGO PARK

(1771-1806?)

[*In 1793, "having learnt that the noblemen and gentlemen, associated for the purpose of prosecuting discoveries in the interior of Africa, were desirous of engaging a person to explore that continent by way of the Gambia River," Mungo Park offered himself "for that service." Reaching the Gambia on June 21, 1795, he went up the river for a hundred miles, and on December 2 set off into the unknown interior of Africa. A journey fraught with hardship and danger brought him on March 6, 1796, to the Negro village of Samee, and "Fancy had already placed" him "on the banks of the Niger" (the aim of his journey), "and presented to my imagination a thousand delightful scenes in my future progress," when he was seized by Ali, the Moorish chief of Ludamar, whose captive he remained for four months.*]

ON the afternoon of the Ist of July, as I was tending my horse in the fields, Ali's chief slave and four Moors arrived at Queira, and took up their lodging at the Dooty's house. My interpreter, Johnson, who suspected the nature of this visit, sent two boys to overhear their conversation, from which he learnt that they were sent to convey me back to Bubaker. The same evening two of the Moors came privately to look at my horse, and one of them proposed taking it to the Dooty's hut, but the other observed that such a precaution was unnecessary, as I could never escape upon such an animal. They then inquired where I slept, and returned to their companions.

All this was like a stroke of thunder to me, for I dreaded nothing so much as confinement again among the Moors, from whose barbarity I had

[1] From *Travels in the Interior of Africa.*

nothing but death to expect. I therefore determined to set off immediately for Bambarra, a measure which I thought offered almost the only chance of saving my life, and gaining the object of my mission. I communicated the design to Johnson, who, although he applauded my resolution, was so far from showing any inclination to accompany me that he solemnly protested he would rather forfeit his wages than go any farther. He told me that Daman had agreed to give him half the price of a slave for his service, to assist in conducting a coffle of slaves to Gambia, and that he was determined to embrace the opportunity of returning to his wife and family.

Having no hopes therefore of persuading him to accompany me I resolved to proceed by myself. About midnight I got my clothes in readiness, which consisted of two shirts, two pair of trousers, two pocket-handkerchiefs, an upper and under waistcoat, a hat, and a pair of half boots; these, with a cloak, constituted my whole wardrobe. And I had not one single bead, nor any other article of value in my possession, to purchase victuals for myself, or corn for my horse.

About daybreak Johnson, who had been listening to the Moors all night, came and whispered to me that they were asleep. The awful crisis was now arrived when I was again either to taste the blessing of freedom or languish out my days in captivity. A cold sweat moistened my forehead as I thought on the dreadful alternative, and reflected that, one way or the other, my fate must be decided in the course of the ensuing day. But to deliberate was to lose the only chance of escaping. So taking up my bundle, I stepped gently over the Negroes, who were sleeping in the open air, and having mounted my horse, I bade Johnson farewell, desiring him to take particular care of the papers I had intrusted him with, and inform my friends in Gambia that he had left me in good health on my way to Bambarra.

I proceeded with great caution, surveying each bush, and frequently listening and looking behind me for the Moorish horsemen, until I was about a mile from the town, when I was surprised to find myself in the neighbourhood of a korree belonging to the Moors. The shepherds followed me for about a mile, hooting and throwing stones after me; and when I was out of their reach, and had began to indulge the pleasing hopes of escaping, I was again greatly alarmed to hear somebody halloo behind me, and looking back, I saw three Moors on horseback coming after me at full speed, whooping and brandishing their double-barrelled guns. I knew it was in vain to think of escaping, and therefore turned back and met them, when two of them caught hold of my bridle, one on each side, and the third, presenting his musket, told me I must go back to Ali.

When the human mind has for some time been fluctuating between hope and despair, tortured with anxiety, and hurried from one extreme to another, it affords a sort of gloomy relief to know the worst that can possibly happen; such was my situation. An indifference about life, and all its enjoyments, had completely benumbed my faculties, and I rode back with the Moors with apparent unconcern. But a change took place much sooner than I had any reason to expect. In passing through some thick bushes, one of the Moors ordered me to untie my bundle, and show them the contents. Having examined the different articles, they found nothing worth taking except my cloak, which they considered as a very valuable acquisition; and one of them pulling it from me, wrapped it about himself. This cloak had been of great use to me; it served to cover me from the rains in the day, and to protect me from the mosquitoes in the night; I therefore earnestly begged him to return it, and followed him some little way to obtain it, but, without paying any attention to my request, he and one of his companions rode off with their prize. When I attempted to follow them the third, who had remained with me, struck my horse over the head, and presenting his musket, told me I should proceed no farther.

I now perceived that these men had not been sent by any authority to apprehend me, but had pursued me solely in the view to rob and plunder me. Turning my horse's head, therefore, once more towards the east, and observing the Moor follow the track of his confederates, I congratulated myself on having escaped with my life, though in great distress, from such a horde of barbarians.

I was no sooner out of sight of the Moor, than I struck into the woods, to prevent being pursued, and kept pushing on with all possible speed, until I found myself near some high rocks, which I remembered to have seen in my former route from Queira to Deena; and directing my ccurse a little to the northward, I fortunately fell in with the path.

It is impossible to describe the joy that arose in my mind when I looked around and concluded that I was out of danger. I felt like one recovered from sickness; I breathed freer; I found unusual lightness in my limbs; even the desert looked pleasant, and I dreaded nothing so much as falling in with some wandering parties of Moors, who might convey me back to the land of thieves and murderers from which I had just escaped.

I soon became sensible, however, that my situation was very deplorable, for I had no means of procuring food, nor prospect of finding water. About ten o'clock, perceiving a herd of goats feeding close to the road, I took a circuitous route to avoid being seen, and continued travelling through the wilderness, directing my course, by compass, nearly east-south-east, in order to reach as soon as possible some town or village of the kingdom of Bambarra.

A little after noon, when the burning heat of the sun was reflected with double violence from the hot sand, and the distant ridges of the hills, seen through the ascending vapour, seemed to wave and fluctuate like the unsettled sea, I became faint with thirst, and climbed a tree in hopes of seeing distant smoke, or some other appearance of a human habitation, but in vain; nothing appeared all around but thick underwood, and hillocks of white sand.

About four o'clock I came suddenly upon a large herd of goats, and pulling my horse into a bush, I watched to observe if the keepers were Moors or Negroes. In a little time I perceived two Moorish boys, and with some difficulty persuaded them to approach me. They informed me that the herd belonged to Ali, and that they were going to Deena, where the water was more plentiful, and where they intended to stay until the rain had filled the pools in the Desert. They showed me their empty water-skins, and told me that they had seen no water in the woods. This account afforded me but little consolation; however, it was in vain to repine, and I pushed on as fast as possible, in hopes of reaching some wateringplace in the course of the night. My thirst was by this time become insufferable; my mouth was parched and inflamed; a sudden dimness would frequently come over my eyes, with other symptoms of fainting; and my horse being very much fatigued, I began seriously to apprehend that I should perish of thirst. To relieve the burning pain in my mouth and throat, I chewed the leaves of different shrubs, but found them all bitter, and of no service.

A little before sunset, having reached the top of a gentle rising, I climbed a high tree, from the topmost branches of which I cast a melancholy look over the barren wilderness, but without discovering the most distant trace of a human dwelling. The same dismal uniformity of shrubs and sand everywhere presented itself, and the horizon was as level and uninterrupted as that of the sea.

Descending from the tree, I found my horse devouring the stubble and brushwood with great avidity; and as I was now too faint to attempt walking, and my horse too much fatigued to carry me, I thought it but an act of humanity, and perhaps the last I should ever have it in my power to perform, to take off his bridle and let him shift for himself; in doing which I was suddenly affected with sickness and giddiness, and falling upon the sand, felt as if the hour of death was fast approaching. "Here then (thought I), after a short but ineffectual struggle, terminate all my hopes of being useful in my day and generation; here must the short span of my life come to an end." I cast (as I believed) a last look on the surrounding scene, and whilst I reflected on the awful change that was about to take place, this world, with its enjoyments, seemed to vanish from my recollection. Nature, however, at length resumed its functions; and on recovering my senses, I found myself stretched upon the sand, with the bridle still in my hand, and the sun just sinking behind the trees. I now summoned all my resolution, and determined to make another effort to prolong my existence. And as the evening was somewhat cool, I resolved to travel as far as my limbs would carry me, in hopes of reaching (my only resource) a watering-place. With this view, I put the bridle on my horse, and driving him before me, went slowly along for about an hour, when I perceived some lightning from the north-east, a most delightful sight, for it promised rain. The darkness and lightning increased very rapidly, and in less than an hour I heard the wind roaring among the bushes. I had already opened my mouth to receive the refreshing drops which I expected; but I was instantly covered with a cloud of sand, driven with such force by the wind, as to give a very disagreeable sensation to my face and arms, and I was obliged to mount my horse, and stop under a bush to prevent being suffocated. The sand continued to fly in amazing quantities for near an hour, after which I again set forward, and travelled with difficulty until ten o'clock. About this time I was agreeably surprised by some very vivid flashes of lightning, followed by a few heavy drops of rain. In a time the sand ceased to fly, and I alighted and spread out all my clean clothes to collect the rain, which at length I saw would certainly fall. For more than an hour it rained plentifully, and I quenched my thirst by wringing and sucking my clothes.

There being no moon, it was remarkably dark, so that I was obliged to lead my horse, and direct my way by the compass, which the lightning enabled me to observe. In this manner I travelled, with tolerable expedition, until past midnight; when the lightning becoming more distant, I was under the necessity of groping along, to the no small danger of my hands and eyes. About two o'clock my horse started at something, and looking round, I was not a little surprised to see a light at a short distance among the trees, and supposing it to be a town, I groped along the sand in hopes of finding corn-stalks, cotton, or other appearances of cultivation, but found none. As I approached, I perceived a number of other lights in different places, and began to suspect that I had fallen upon a party of Moors. However, in my present situation, I was resolved to see who they were, if I could do it with safety. I accordingly led my horse cautiously towards the light, and heard by the lowing of the cattle, and the clamorous tongues of the herdsmen, that it was a watering-place, and most likely belonged to the Moors. Delightful as the sound of the human voice was to me, I resolved once more to strike into the woods, and rather run the risk of perishing of hunger than trust myself again in their hands; but being still thirsty, and dreading the approach of the burning day, I thought it prudent to search for the wells, which I expected to find at no great distance. In this pursuit, I inadvertently approached so near to one of the tents as to be perceived by a woman, who immediately screamed out. Two people came running to her assistance from some of the neighbouring tents, and passed so very near to me that I thought I was discovered, and hastened again into the woods.

About a mile from this place I heard a loud and confused noise somewhere to the right of my course, and in a short time was happy to find it was the croaking of frogs, which was heavenly music to my ears. I followed the sound, and at daybreak arrived at some shallow muddy pools, so full of frogs that it was difficult to discern the water. The noise they made frightened my horse, and I was obliged to keep them quiet by beating the water with a branch until he had drank. Having here quenched my thirst, I ascended a tree, and the morning being calm, I soon perceived the smoke of the watering place which I had passed in the night; and observed another pillar of smoke east-south-east, distant twelve or fourteen miles. Towards this I directed my route, and reached the cultivated ground a little before eleven o'clock, where, seeing a number of Negroes at work planting corn, I inquired the name of the town, and was informed that it was a Foulah village, belonging to Ali, called Shrilla. I had now some doubts about entering it; but my horse being very much fatigued, and the day growing hot, not to mention the pangs of hunger which began to assail me, I resolved to venture, and accordingly rode up to the Dooty's house, where I was unfortunately denied admittance, and could not obtain even a handful of corn either for myself or horse. Turning from this inhospitable door, I rode slowly out of the town, and perceiving some low scattered huts without the walls, I directed my route towards them; knowing that in Africa, as well as in Europe, hospitality does not always prefer the highest dwellings. At the door of one of these huts, an old motherly-looking woman sat, spinning cotton; I made signs to her that I was hungry, and inquired if she had any victuals with her in the hut. She immediately laid down her distaff, and desired me, in Arabic, to come in. When I had seated myself upon the floor, she set before me a dish of kouskous, that had been left the preceding night, of which I made a tolerable meal; and in return for this kindness, I gave her one of my pocket handkerchiefs; begging at the same time, a little corn for my horse, which she readily brought me.

Overcome with joy at so unexpected a deliverance, I lifted up my eyes to heaven, and whilst my heart swelled with gratitude, I returned thanks to that gracious and bountiful Being, whose power had supported me under so many dangers, and had now spread for me a table in the wilderness.

Whilst my horse was feeding, the people began to assemble, and one of them whispered something to my hostess which very much excited her surprise. Though I was not well acquainted with the Foulah language, I soon discovered that some of the men wished to apprehend and carry me back to Ali, in hopes, I suppose, of receiving a reward. I therefore tied up the corn; and lest any one should suspect I had ran away from the Moors, I took a northerly direction, and went cheerfully along, driving my horse before me; followed by all the boys and girls of the town. When I had travelled about two miles, and got quit of all my troublesome attendants, I struck again into the woods and took shelter under a large tree, where I found it necessary to rest myself; a bundle of twigs serving me for a bed, and my saddle for a pillow.

I was awakened about two o'clock by three Foulahs, who, taking me for a Moor, pointed to the sun, and told me it was time to pray. Without entering into conversation with them, I saddled my horse and continued my journey. I travelled over a level, but more fertile country than I had seen for some time, until sunset, when, coming to a path that took a southerly direction, I followed it until midnight, at which time I arrived at a small pool of rain-water, and the wood being open, I determined to rest by it for the night. Having given my horse the remainder of the corn, I made my bed as formerly; but the mosquitoes and flies from the pool prevented sleep for some time, and I was twice disturbed in the night by wild beasts, which came very near, and whose howlings kept the horse in continual terror.

July 4th. At daybreak I pursued my course through the woods as formerly; saw numbers of antelopes, wild hogs, and ostriches; but the soil was more hilly, and not so fertile as I had found it the preceding day. About eleven o'clock I ascended an eminence, where I climbed a tree, and discovered, at about eight miles' distance, an open part of the country, with several red spots, which I concluded were cultivated land; and directing my course that way, came to the precincts of a watering-place about one o'clock. From the appearance of the place, I judged it to belong to the Foulahs, and was hopeful that I should meet a better reception than I had experienced at Shrilla. In this I was not deceived; for one of the shepherds invited me to come into his tent, and partake of some dates. This was one of those low Foulah tents in which there is room just sufficient to sit upright, and in which the family, the furniture, etc., seem huddled together like so many articles in a chest. When I had crept upon my hands and knees into this humble habitation, I found that it contained a woman and three children, who, together with the shepherd and myself, completely occupied the floor. A dish of boiled corn and dates was produced, and the master of the family, as is customary in this part of the country, first tasted himself, and then desired me to follow his example. Whilst I was eating, the children kept their eyes fixed upon me; and no sooner did the shepherd pronounce the word *Nazarani*, than they began to cry, and their mother crept slowly towards the door, out of which she sprang like a greyhound, and was instantly followed by her children, so frightened were they at the very name of a Christian, that no entreaties could induce them to approach the tent. Here I purchased some corn for my horse in exchange for some brass buttons; and having thanked the shepherd for his hospitality, struck again into the woods. At sunset, I came to a road that took the direction for Bambarra, and resolved to follow it for the night; but about eight o'clock hearing some people coming from the southward, I thought it prudent to hide myself among some thick bushes near the road. As these thickets are generally full of wild beasts, I found my situation rather unpleasant; sitting in the dark, holding my horse by the nose with both hands, to prevent him from neighing, and equally afraid of the natives without, and the wild beasts within. My fears, however, were soon dissipated, for the people, after looking round the thicket, and perceiving nothing, went away; and I hastened to the more open parts of the wood, where I pursued my journey E.S.E. until midnight, when the joyful cry of frogs induced me once more to deviate a little from my route, in order to quench my thirst. Having accomplished this from a large pool of rainwater, I sought for an open place, with a single tree in the midst, under which I made my bed for the night. I was disturbed by some wolves towards morning, which induced me to set forward a little before day; and having passed a small village called Wassalita, I came about ten o'clock (July 5th) to a Negro town called Wawra, which properly belongs to Kaarta, but was at this time tributary to Mansong, King of Bambarra.

Wawra is a small town surrounded with high walls, and inhabited by a mixture of Mandingoes and Foulahs. The inhabitants employ themselves chiefly in cultivating corn, which they exchange with the Moors for salt. Here, being in security from the Moors, and very much fatigued, I resolved to rest myself, and meeting with a hearty welcome from the Dooty, whose name was Flancharee, I laid myself down upon a bullock's hide, and slept sounly for about two hours. The curiosity of the people would not allow me to sleep any longer. They had seen my saddle and bridle, and were assembled in great number to learn who I was, and whence I came. Some were of opinion that I was an Arab; others insisted that I was some Moorish Sultan; and they continued to debate the matter with such warmth, that the noise awoke me. The Dooty (who had formerly been at Gambia) at last interposed in my behalf, and assured them that I was certainly a white man; but he was convinced from my appearance that I was a very poor one.

In the course of the day, several women, hearing that I was going to Sego, came and begged me to inquire of Mansong, the king, what was become of their children. One woman in particular, told me that her son's name was Mamadee; that he was no heathen, but prayed to God morning and evening, and had been taken from her about three years ago, by Mansong's army: since which she had never heard of him. She said she often dreamed about him; and begged me, if I should see him, either in Bambarra, or in my own country, to tell him that his mother and sister were still alive. In the afternoon the Dooty examined the contents of the leather bag, in which I had packed up my clothes; but finding nothing that was worth taking, he returned it, and told me to depart in the morning.

July 6th. It rained very much in the night, and at daylight I departed, in company with a Negro, who was going to a town called Dingyee for Corn; but we had not proceeded above a mile, before the ass upon which he rode kicked him off, and he returned, leaving me to prosecute the journey by myself.

I reached Dingyee about noon; but the Dooty and most of the inhabitants had gone into the fields to cultivate corn. An old Foulah, observing me wandering about the town, desired me to come to his hut, where I was well entertained; and the Dooty, when he returned, sent me some victuals for myself and corn for my horse.

July 7th. In the morning, when I was about to depart, my landlord, with a great deal of diffidence, begged me to give him a lock of my hair. He had been told, he said, that white men's hair made a saphie, that would give to the possessor all the knowledge of white men. I had never before heard of so simple a mode of education, but instantly complied with the request; and my landlord's thirst for learning was such that, with cutting and pulling, he cropped one side of my head pretty closely; and would have done the same with the other, had I not signified my disapprobation by putting on my hat, and assuring him that I wished to reserve some of this precious merchandise for a future occasion.

I reached a small town called Wassiboo about twelve o'clock, where I was obliged to stop until an opportunity should offer of procuring a guide to Satilé, which is distant a very long day's journey, through woods without any beaten track. I accordingly took up my residence of the Dooty's house, where I staid four days; during which time I amused myself by going to the fields with the family to plant corn. Cultivation is carried on here on a very extensive scale; and, as the natives themselves express it, "hunger is never known." In cultivating the soil, the men and women work together. They use a large sharp hoe, much superior to that used in Gambia; but they are obliged, for fear of the Moors, to carry their arms with them to the field. The master, with the handle of his spear, marks the field into regular plats, one of which is assigned to every three slaves.

On the evening of the 11th, eight of the fugitive Kaartans arrived at Wassiboo. They had found it impossible to live under the tyrannical government of the Moors, and were now going to transfer their allegiance to the King of Bambarra. They offered to take me along with them as far as Satilé, and I accepted the offer.

July 12th. At daybreak we set out, and travelled with uncommon expedition until sunset: we stopped only twice in the course of the day, once at a watering-place in the woods, and another time at the ruins of a town, formerly belonging to Daisy,[1] called *Illa-Compe* (the corn town). When we arrived in the neighbourhood of Satilé the people who were employed in the cornfields, seeing so many horsemen, took us for a party of Moors, and ran screaming away from us. The whole town was instantly alarmed, and the slaves were seen in every direction driving the cattle and horses towards the town. It was in vain that one of our company galloped up to undeceive them: it only frightened them the more; and when we arrived at the town we found the gates shut and the people all under arms. After a long parley we were permitted to enter; and as there was every appearance of a heavy tornado the Dooty allowed us to sleep in his baloon, and gave us each a bullock's hide for a bed.

July 13th. Early in the morning we again set forward. The roads were wet and slippery; but the country was very beautiful, abounding with rivulets, which were increased by the rain into rapid streams. About ten o'clock we came to the ruins of a village, which had been destroyed by war about six months before; and in order to prevent any town from being built there in future, the large Bentang tree, under which the natives spent the day, had been burned down, the wells filled up, and everything that could make the spot desirable completely destroyed.

About noon my horse was so much fatigued that I could not keep up with my

[1] King of Kaarta.

companions; I therefore dismounted, and desired them to ride on, telling them that I would follow as soon as my horse had rested a little. But I found them unwilling to leave me. The lions, they said, were very numerous in those parts, and though they might not so readily attack a body of people, they would soon find out an individual. It was therefore agreed that one of the company should stay with me to assist in driving my horse, while the others passed on to Galloo to procure lodgings, and collect grass for the horses before night. Accompanied by this worthy Negro, I drove my horse before me, until about four o'clock, when we came in sight of Galloo, a considerable town, standing in a fertile and beautiful valley surrounded with high rocks.

As my companions had thoughts of settling in this neighbourhood, they had a fine sheep given them by the Dooty; and I was fortunate enough to procure plenty of corn for my horse. Here they blow upon elephants' teeth when they announce evening prayers, in the same manner as at Kemmoo.

Early next morning (July 14th), having first returned many thanks to our landlord for his hospitality, while my fellow-travellers offered up their prayers that he might never want, we set forward, and about three o'clock arrived at Moorja, a large town, famous for its trade in salt, which the Moors bring here in great quantities to exchange for corn and cotton cloth. As most of the people here are Mahommedans, it is not allowed to the Kafirs to drink beer, which they call *Neo-dollo* (corn spirit), except in certain houses. In one of these I saw about twenty people sitting round large vessels of this beer with the greatest conviviality, many of them in a state of intoxication. As corn in plentiful, the inhabitants are very liberal to strangers. I believe we had as much corn and milk sent us by different people as would have been sufficient for three times our number; and though we remained here two days, we experienced no diminution of their hospitality.

On the morning of the 16th we again set forward, accompanied by a coffle of fourteen asses, loaded with salt, bound for Sansanding. The road was particularly romantic, between two rocky hills; but the Moors sometimes lie in wait here to plunder strangers. As soon as we had reached the open country, the master of the salt coffle thanked us for having staid with him so long, and now desired us to ride on. The sun was almost set before we reached Datliboo. In the evening we had a most tremendous tornado. The house in which we lodged being flat-roofed, admitted the rain in streams. The floor was soon ankle deep, the fire extinguished, and we were left to pass the night upon some bundles of firewood that happened to lie in a corner.

July 17th. We departed from Datliboo, and about ten o'clock passed a large coffle returning from Sego, with corn hoes, mats, and other household utensils. At five o'clock we came to a large village, where we intended to pass the night, but the Dooty would not receive us. When we departed from this place my horse was so much fatigued that I was under the necessity of driving him, and it was dark before we reached Fanimboo, a small village; the Dooty of which no sooner heard that I was a white man than he brought out three old muskets and was much disappointed when he was told that I could not repair them.

July 18th. We continued our journey; but, owing to a light supper the preceding night, we felt ourselves rather hungry this morning, and endeavoured to procure some corn at a village, but without success. The towns were now more numerous, and the land that is not employed in cultivation affords excellent pasturage for large herds of cattle; but owing to the great concourse of people daily going to and returning from Sego, the inhabitants are less hospitable to strangers.

My horse becoming weaker and weaker every day, was now of very little service to me; I was obliged to drive him before me for the greater part of the day, and did not reach Geosorro until eight o'clock in the evening. I found my companions wrangling with the Dooty, who had absolutely refused to give or sell them any provisions; and as none of us had tasted victuals for the last twenty-four hours, we were by no means disposed to fast another day, if we could help it. But finding our entreaties without effect, and being very much fatigued, I fell asleep, from which I was awakened, about midnight, with the joyful information, "kinnenata" (the victuals is come). This made the remainder of the night pass away pleasantly; and at daybreak, July 19th, we resumed our journey, proposing to stop at village called Doolinkeaboo, for the night following. My fellow-travellers, having better horses than myself, soon left me, and I was walking barefoot, driving my horse, when I was met by a coffle of slaves, about seventy in number, coming from Sego. They were tied together by their necks with thongs of a bullock's hide, twisted like a rope; seven slaves upon a thong, and a man with a musket between every seven. Many of the slaves were ill-conditioned, and a great number of them women. In the rear came Sidi Mahomed's servant, whom I remembered to have seen at the camp of Benowm; he presently knew me, and told me that these slaves were going to Morocco, by the way of Ludamar, and the Great Desert.

In the afternoon, as I approached Doolinkeaboo, I met about twenty Moors on horseback, the owners of the slaves I had seen in the morning; they were well armed with muskets, and were very inquisitive concerning me, but not so rude as their countrymen generally are. From them I learned that Sidi

Mahomed was not at Sego, but had gone to Kancaba for gold dust.

When I arrived at Doolinkeaboo, I was informed that my fellow-travellers had gone on, but my horse was so much fatigued that I could not possibly proceed after them. The Dooty of the town, at my request, gave me a draught of water, which is generally looked upon as an earnest of greater hospitality; and I had no doubt of making up for the toils of the day by a good supper and a sound sleep; unfortunately I had neither one nor the other. The night was rainy and tempestuous, and the Dooty limited his hospitality to the draught of water.

July 20th. In the morning I endeavoured, both by entreaties and threats, to procure some victuals from the Dooty, but in vain. I even begged some corn from one of his female slaves, as she was washing it at the well, and had the mortification to be refused. However, when the Dooty was gone to the fields, his wife sent me a handful of meal, which I mixed with water, and drank for breakfast. About eight o'clock I departed from Doolinkeaboo, and at noon stopped a few minutes at a large korree, where I had some milk given me by the Foulahs. And hearing that two Negroes were going from thence to Sego, I was happy to have their company, and we set out immediately. About four o'clock we stopped at a small village, where one of the Negroes met with an acquaintance, who invited us to a sort of public entertainment, which was conducted with more than common propriety. A dish made of sour milk and meal, called *Sinkatoo*, and beer made from their corn, was distributed with great liberality, and the women were admitted into the society—a circumstance I had never before observed in Africa. There was no compulsion, every one was at liberty to drink as he pleased; they nodded to each other when about to drink, and on setting down the calabash, commonly said *berka* (thank you). Both men and women appeared to be somewhat intoxicated, but they were far from being quarrelsome.

Departing from thence, we passed several large villages, where I was constantly taken for a Moor, and became the subject of much merriment to the Bambarrans; who seeing me drive my horse before me, laughed heartily at my appearance. He has been at Mecca, says one, you may see that by his clothes; another asked me if my horse was sick, a third wished to purchase it, etc.; so that I believe the very slaves were ashamed to be seen in my company. Just before it was dark, we took up our lodging for the night at a small village, where I procured some victuals for myself, and some corn for my horse, at the moderate price of a button, and was told that I should see the Niger (which the Negroes called Jolliba, or *the great water*) early the next day. The lions are here very numerous; the gates are shut a little after sunset, and nobody allowed to go out. The thoughts of seeing the Niger in the morning, and the troublesome buzzing of mosquitoes, prevented me from shutting my eyes during the night; and I had saddled my horse and was in readiness before daylight; but, on account of the wild beasts, we were obliged to wait until the people were stirring, and the gates opened. This happened to be a market-day at Sego, and the roads were everywhere filled with people carrying different articles to sell. We passed four large villages, and at eight o'clock saw the smoke over Sego.

As we approached the town, I was fortunate enough to overtake the fugitive Kaartans, to whose kindness I had been so much indebted in my journey through Bambarra. They readily agreed to introduce me to the king; and we rode together through some marshy ground, where, as I was anxiously looking around for the river, one of them called out, *geo affili* (see the water), and looking forwards, I saw with infinite pleasure the great object of my mission—the long sought for majestic Niger, glittering to the morning sun, as broad as the Thames at Westminster, and flowing slowly *to the eastward*. I hastened to the brink, and, having drank of the water, lifted up my fervent thanks in prayer to the Great Ruler of all things, for having thus far crowned my endeavours with success.

The circumstance of the Niger's flowing towards the east and its collateral points did not, however, excite my surprise; for although I had left Europe in great hesitation on this subject, and rather believed that it ran in the contrary direction, I had made such frequent inquiries during my progress, concerning this river, and received from Negroes, of different nations, such clear and decisive assurances that its general course was *towards the rising sun*, as scarce left any doubt on my mind; and more especially as I knew that Major Houghton had collected similar information in the same manner.

I waited more than two hours without having an opportunity of crossing the river; during which time, the people who had crossed, carried information to Mansong, the king, that a white man was waiting for a passage, and was coming to see him. He immediately sent over one of his chief men, who informed me that the king could not possibly see me, until he knew what had brought me into his country; and that I must not presume to cross the river without the king's permission. He therefore advised me to lodge at a distant village, to which he pointed, for the night; and said that in the morning he would give me further instructions how to conduct myself. This was very discouraging. However, as there was no remedy, I set off for the village; where I found, to my great mortification, that no person would admit me into his house. I was regarded with astonishment and fear, and was obliged to sit all day without victuals, in the shade of a tree; and the night threatened to be very uncomfortable, for the wind rose, and there was great appearance of a heavy rain; and the wild beasts are so very numerous in the neighbourhood, that I should have been under the necessity of climbing up the tree, and resting among the branches. About sunset, however, as I was preparing to pass the night in this manner, and had turned my horse loose that he might graze at liberty, a woman, returning from the labours of the field, stopped to observe me, and perceiving that I was weary and dejected, inquired into my situation, which I briefly explained to her; whereupon, with looks of great compassion, she took up my saddle and bridle, and told me to follow her. Having conducted me into her hut, she lighted up a lamp, spread a mat on the floor, and told me I might remain there for the night. Finding that I was very hungry, she said she would procure me something to eat. She accordingly went out, and returned in a short time with a very fine fish; which having caused to be half broiled upon some embers, she gave me for supper. The rites of hospitality being thus performed towards a stranger in distress, my worthy benefactress (pointing to the mat, and telling me I might sleep there without apprehension) called to the female part of her family, who had stood gazing on me all the while in fixed astonishment, to resume their task of spinning cotton; in which they continued to employ themselves great part of the night. They lightened their labours by songs, one of which was composed extempore; for I was myself the subject of it. It was sung by one of the young women, the rest joining in a sort of chorus. The air was sweet and plaintive, and the words, literally translated, were these: "The winds roared, and the rains fell. The poor white man, faint and weary, came and sat under our tree. He has no mother to bring him milk; no wife to grind his corn." *Chorus:* "Let us pity the white man; no mother has he," etc., etc.

ACROSS THE KALAHARI DESERT [1]

(1849)

DAVID LIVINGSTONE

(1813-73)

In trying to benefit the tribes living under the Boers of the Cashan mountains, I twice performed a journey of about three hundred miles to the eastward of Kolobeng. Sechele [2] had become so obnoxious to the Boers, that, though anxious to accompany me in my journey, he dared not trust himself

[1] From *Missionary Travels and Researches in South Africa* (1857).
[2] Chief of the Bakwains.

among them. This did not arise from the crime of cattle-stealing; for that crime, so common among the Caffres, was never charged against his tribe, nor, indeed, against any Bechuana tribe. It is, in fact, unknown in the country, except during actual warfare. His independence and love of the English were his only faults. In my last journey there, of about two hundred miles, on parting at the river Marikwe he gave me two servants, "to be," as he said, "his arms to serve me," and expressed regret that he could not come himself. "Suppose we went north," I said, "would you come?" This was the first time I had thought of crossing the Desert to Lake Ngami.

The conduct of the Boers, who had sent a letter designed to procure my removal out of the country, became more fully developed on this than on any former occasion. When I spoke to Mr Hendrick Potgeiter of the danger of hindering the Gospel of Christ among these poor savages, he became greatly excited, and called one of his followers to answer me. He threatened to attack any tribe that might receive a native teacher, yet he promised to use his influence to prevent those under him from throwing obstacles in our way. I could perceive plainly that nothing more could be done in that direction, so I commenced collecting all the information I could about the desert, with the intention of crossing it if possible. Sekomi, the chief of the Bamangwato, was acquainted with a route which he kept carefully to himself, because the Lake country abounded in ivory, and he drew large quantities thence periodically at but small cost to himself.

Sechele, who valued highly everything European, and was always fully alive to his own interest, was naturally anxious to get a share of that inviting field.

Sechele, by my advice, sent men to Sekomi, asking leave for me to pass along his path, accompanying the request with the present of an ox. Sekomi's mother, who possesses great influence over him, refused permission, because she had not been propitiated. This produced a fresh message; and the most honourable man in the Bakwain tribe, next to Sechele, was sent with an ox for both Sekomi and his mother. This too, was met by refusal. It was said, "The Matabele, the mortal enemies of the Bechuanas, are in the direction of the lake, and, should they kill the white man, we shall incur great blame from all his nation."

The exact position of the Lake Ngami had, for half a century at least, been correctly pointed out by the natives, who had visited it when rains were more copious in the Desert than in more recent times, and many attempts had been made to reach it by passing through the Desert in the direction indicated; but it was found impossible, even for Griquas, who, having some Bushman blood in them, may be supposed more capable of enduring thirst than Europeans. It was clear, then, that our only chance of success was by going round, instead of through, the Desert. The best time for the attempt would have been about the end of the rainy season, in March or April, for then we should have been likely to meet with pools of rain-water, which always dry up during the rainless winter. I communicated my intention to an African traveller, Colonel Steele, then *aide-de-camp* to the Marquis of Tweedale, at Madras, and he made it known to two other gentlemen, whose friendship we had gained during their African travel—namely, Major Vardon, and Mr Oswell. All of these gentlemen were so enamoured with African hunting and African discovery, that the two former must have envied the latter his good fortune in being able to leave India to undertake afresh the pleasures and pains of desert life. I believe Mr Oswell came from his high position, at a very considerable pecuniary sacrifice, and with no other end in view but to extend the boundaries of geographical knowledge. Before I knew of his coming I had arranged that the payment for the guides furnished by Sechele should be the loan of my waggon, to bring back whatever ivory he might obtain from the chief at the lake. When at last Mr Oswell came, bringing Mr Murray with him, he undertook to defray the entire expenses of the guides, and fully executed his generous intention.

Sechele himself would have come with us, but, fearing that the much-talked-of assault of the Boers might take place during our absence, and blame be attached to me for taking him away, I dissuaded him against it by saying that he knew Mr Oswell "would be as determined as himself to get through the Desert."

Before narrating the incidents of this journey, I may give some account of the great Kalahari Desert, in order that the reader may understand in some degree the nature of the difficulties we had to encounter.

The space from the Orange River in the south. lat. 29°, to Lake Ngami in the north, and from about 24° east long. to near the west coast, has been called a desert simply because it contains no running water, and very little water in wells. It is by no means destitute of vegetation and inhabitants, for it is covered with grass and a great variety of creeping plants; besides which there are large patches of bushes and even trees. It is remarkably flat, but intersected in different parts by the beds of ancient rivers; and prodigious herds of certain antelopes, which required little or no water, roam over the trackless plains. The inhabitants, Bushmen and Bakalahari, prey on the game and on the countless rodentia and small species of the feline race which subsist on these. In general the soil is light-coloured soft sand, nearly pure silica. The beds of the ancient rivers contain much alluvial soil; and as that is baked hard by the burning sun, rain-water stands in pools in some of them for several months in the year.

The quantity of grass which grows on this remarkable region is astonishing, even to those who are familiar with India. It usually rises in tufts with bare spaces between, or the intervals are occupied by creeping plants, which, having their roots buried far beneath the soil, feel little the effects of the scorching sun. The number of these which have tuberous roots is very great; and their structure is intended to supply nutriment and moisture when during the long droughts they can be obtained nowhere else. Here we have an example of a plant, not generally tuber-bearing, becoming so under circumstances where that appendage is necessary to act as a reservoir for preserving its life; and the same thing occurs in Angola to a species of grape-bearing vine, which is so furnished for the same purpose. The plant to which I at present refer is one of the cucurbitaceæ which bears a small scarlet-coloured eatable cucumber. Another plant, named Leroshúa, is a blessing to the inhabitants of the Desert. We see a small plant with linear leaves, and a stalk not thicker than a crow's quill; on digging down a foot or eighteen inches beneath, we come to a tuber, often as large as the head of a young child; when the rind is removed, we find it to be a mass of cellular tissue, filled with fluid much like that in a young turnip. Owing to the depth beneath the soil at which it is found, it is generally deliciously cool and refreshing.

But the most surprising plant of the Desert is the "Kengwe" or "Kēme" *(Cucumis caffer)*, the water-melon. In years when more than the usual quantity of rain falls, vast tracts of the country are literally covered with these melons; this was the case annually when the fall of rain was greater than it is now, and the Bakwains sent trading parties every year to the lake. It happens commonly once every ten or eleven years, and for the last three times its occurrence has coincided with an extraordinarily wet season. Then animals of every sort and name, including man, rejoice in the rich supply. The elephant, true lord of the forest, revels in this fruit, and so do the different species of rhinoceros, although naturally so diverse in their choice of pasture. The various kinds of antelopes feed on them with equal avidity, and lions, hayænas, jackals, and mice all seem to know and appreciate the common blessing.

The human inhabitants of this tract of country consist of Bushmen and Bakalahari. The former are probably the aborigines of the southern portion of the continent, the latter the remnants of the first emigration of Bechuanas. The Bushmen live in the Desert from choice, the Bakalahari from compulsion, and both possess an intense love of liberty. The Bushmen are exceptions in language, race, habits, and appearance. They are the only real nomads in the country; they never cultivate the soil nor rear any domestic animal, save wretched dogs. They are so intimately acquainted with the habits of the game, that they follow them in their migrations, and prey upon them from place to place, and thus prove as complete a check upon their inordinate increase as the other carnivora. The chief subsistence of the Bushmen is the flesh of game, but that is eked out by what the women collect of roots and beans, and fruits of the Desert. Those who inhabit the hot, sandy plains of the Desert possess generally thin wiry forms capable of great exertion and of severe privations. Many are of low stature, though not dwarfish; the specimens brought to Europe have been selected, like costermongers' dogs, on account of their extreme ugliness; consequently English ideas of the whole tribe are formed in the same way as if the ugliest specimens of the English were exhibited in Africa as characteristic of the entire British nation. That they are like baboons is in some degree true, just as these and other simiæ are in some points frightfully human.

The Bakalahari are traditionally reported to be the oldest of the Bechuana tribes, and they are said to have possessed enormous herds of the large horned cattle mentioned by Bruce, until they were despoiled of them and driven into the Desert by a fresh migration of their own nation. Living ever since on the same plains with the Bushmen, subjected to the same influences of climate, enduring the same thirst, and subsisting on similar food for centuries, they seem to supply a standing proof that locality is not always sufficient of itself to account for difference in races. The Bakalahari retain in undying vigour the Bechuana love for agriculture and domestic animals. They hoe their gardens annually, though often all they can hope for is a supply of melons and pumpkins. And they carefully rear small herds of goats, though I have seen them lift water for them out of small wells with a bit of ostrich eggshell, or by spoonfuls. They generally attach themselves to influential men in the different Bechuana tribes living adjacent to their desert home, in order to obtain supplies of spears, knives, tobacco, and dogs, in exchange for the skins of the animals they may kill.

Such was the Desert which we were now preparing to cross—a region formerly of terror to the Bechuanas from the numbers of serpents which infested it and fed on the different kinds of mice, and from the intense thirst which these people often endured when their water-vessels were insufficient for the distances to be travelled over before reaching the wells.

Just before the arrival of my companions, a party of the people of the lake came to Kolobeng, stating that they were sent by Lechulatebe, the chief, to ask me to visit that country. They brought such flaming accounts of the quantities of ivory to be found there (cattlepens made of elephants' tusks of enormous size, etc.) that the guides of the Bakwains were quite as eager to succeed in reaching the lake as any one of us could desire. This was fortunate, as we knew the way the strangers had come was impassable for waggons.

Messrs Oswell and Murray came at the end of May, and we all made a fair start for the unknown region on the 1st of June, 1849. Proceeding northwards, and passing through a range of tree-covered hills to Shokuane, formerly the residence of the Bakwains, we soon after entered on the high road to the Bamangwato, which lies generally in the bed of an ancient river or wady that must formerly have flowed N. to S. The adjacent country is perfectly flat, but covered with open forest and bush, with abundance of grass; the trees generally are a kind of acacia called "Monáto," which appears a little to the south of this region, and is common as far as Angola. A large caterpillar, called "Nato," feeds by night on the leaves of these trees, and comes down by day to bury itself at the root in the sand in order to escape the piercing rays of the sun. The people dig for it there, and are fond of it when roasted, on account of its pleasant vegetable taste. When about to pass into the chrysalis state it buries itself in the soil, and is sometimes sought for as food even then. If left undisturbed, it comes forth as a beautiful butterfly; the transmutation was sometimes employed by me with good effect, when speaking with the natives, as in illustration of our own great change and resurrection.

The soil is sandy, and there are here and there indications that at spots which now afford no water whatever there were formerly wells and cattle-stations.

Boatlanáma, our next station, is a lovely spot in the otherwise dry region. The wells from which we had to lift out the water for our cattle are deep, but they were well filled. A few villages of Bakalahari were found near them, and great numbers of pallahs, springbucks, guinea-fowl, and small monkeys.

Lopépe came next. This place afforded another proof of the desiccation of the country. The first time I passed it, Lopépe was a large pool with a stream flowing out of it to the south; now it was with difficulty we could get our cattle watered, by digging down in the bottom of a well.

At Mashüe—where we found a never-failing supply of pure water in a sandstone rocky hollow—we left the road to the Bamangwato hills, and struck away to the north into the Desert. Having watered the cattle at a well called Lobotáni, about N.W. of Bamangwato, we next proceeded to a real Kalahari fountain, called Serotli. The country around is covered with bushes and trees of a kind of leguminosæ, with lilac flowers. The soil is soft white sand, very trying to the strength of the oxen, as the wheels sink into it over the felloes and drag heavily. At Serotli we found only a few hollows like those made by the buffalo and rhinoceros when they roll themselves in the mud. In a corner of one of these there appeared water, which would have been quickly lapped up by our dogs, had we not driven them away. And yet this was all the apparent supply for some eighty oxen, twenty horses, and about a score of men. Our guide, Ramotóbi, who had spent his youth in the Desert, declared that, though appearances were against us, there was plenty of water at hand. We had our misgivings, for the spades were soon produced; but our guides, despising such new-fangled aid, began in good earnest to scrape out the sand with their hands. The only water we had any promise of for the next seventy miles—that is, for a journey of three days with the waggons—was to be got here. By the aid of both spades and fingers two of the holes were cleared out, so as to form pits six feet deep and about as many broad. Our guides were specially earnest in their injunctions to us not to break through the hard stratum of sand at the bottom, because they knew, if it were broken through, "the water would go away." They are quite correct, for the water seems to lie on this flooring of incipient sandstone. The value of the advice was proved in the case of an Englishman whose wits were none of the brightest, who, disregarding it, dug through the sandy stratum in the wells at Mohotluáni: the water immediately flowed away downwards, and the well became useless. When we came to the stratum we found that the water flowed in on all sides close to the line where the soft sand came into contact with it. Allowing it to collect, we had enough for the horses that evening; but as there was not sufficient for the oxen, we sent them back to Lobotáni, where, after thirsting four full days (ninety-six hours), they got a good supply. The horses were kept by us as necessary to procure game for the sustenance of our numerous party. Next morning we found the water had flowed in faster than at first, as it invariably does in these reservoirs, owing to the passages widening by the flow. Large quantities of the sand come into the well with the water, and in the course of a few days the supply, which may be equal to the wants of a few men only, becomes sufficient for oxen as well.

In the evening of our second day at Serotli a hyæna, appearing suddenly among the grass, succeeded in raising a panic among our cattle. This false mode of attack is the plan which this cowardly animal always adopts. His courage resembles closely that of a turkey-cock. He will bite, if an animal is running away; but if the animal stand still, so does he. Seventeen of our draught oxen ran away, and in their flight went right into the hands of Sekomi, whom, from his being unfriendly to our success, we had no particular wish to see. Cattle-stealing, such as in the circumstances might have occurred in Caffraria, is here unknown; so Sekomi sent back our oxen, and a message strongly dissuading us against attempting the Desert. "Where are you going? You will be killed by the sun and thirst, and then all the white men will blame me for not saving you." This was backed by a private message from his mother. "Why do you pass me? I always made the people collect to hear the word that you have got. What guilt have I, that you pass without looking at me?" We replied by assuring the messengers that the white men would attribute our deaths to our own stupidity and "hard-headedness" (tlogo, e thata) "as we did not intend to allow our companions and guides to return till they had put us into our graves." We sent a handsome present to Sekomi, and a promise that, if he allowed the Bakalahari to keep the wells open for us, we would repeat the gift on our return.

After exhausting all his eloquence in fruitless attempts to persuade us to return, the under-chief, who headed the party of Sekomi's messengers, inquired, "Who is taking them?" Looking round, he exclaimed, with a face expressive of the most unfeigned disgust, "It is Ramotobi!" Our guide belonged to Sekomi's tribe, but had fled to Sechele; as fugitives in this country are always well received, and may even afterwards visit the tribe from which they have escaped, Ramotobi was in no danger, though doing that which he knew to be directly opposed to the interests of his own chief and tribe.

All around Serotli the country is perfectly flat, and composed of soft white sand. There is a peculiar glare of bright sunlight from a cloudless sky over the whole scene; and one clump of trees and bushes, with open spaces between, looks so exactly like another, that if you leave the wells, and walk a quarter of a mile in any direction, it is difficult to return. Oswell and Murray went out on one occasion to get an eland, and were accompanied by one of the Bakalahari. The perfect sameness of the country caused even this son of the Desert to lose his way; a most puzzling conversation forthwith ensured between them and their guide. One of the most common pharases of the people is *Kia itumėla*, I thank you, or I am pleased; and the gentleman were both quite familiar with it, and with the word *metse*, water. But there is a word very similar in sound, *Kia timėla*, I am wandering; its perfect is *Ki timėtse*, I have wandered. The party had been roaming about, perfectly lost, till the sun went down; and, through their mistaking the verb "wander" for "to be pleased" and "water," the colloquy went on at intervals during the whole bitterly cold night in somewhat the following style:

"Where are the waggons?"

Real answer: "I don't know. I have wandered. I never wandered before. I am quite lost."

Supposed answer: "I don't know. I want water. I am glad, I am quite pleased. I am thankful to you."

"Take us to the waggons, and you will get plenty of water."

Real answer (looking vacantly around): "How did I wander? Perhaps the well is there, perhaps not. I don't know. I have wandered."

Supposed answer: "Something about thanks; he says he is pleased, and mentions water again." The guide's vacant stare, while trying to remember, is thought to indicate mental imbecility, and the repeated thanks were supposed to indicate a wish to deprecate their wrath.

"Well, Livingstone *has* played us a pretty trick, giving us in charge of an idiot, Catch us trusting him again. What can this fellow mean by his thanks and talk about water? O, you born fool! take us to the waggons, and you will get both meat and water. Wouldn't a thrashing bring him to his senses again?"

"No, no, for then he will run away, and we shall be worse off than we are now."

The hunters regained the waggons next day by their own sagacity, which becomes wonderfully quickened by a sojourn in the Desert; and we enjoyed a hearty laugh on the explanation of their midnight colloquies.

The water having at last flowed into the wells we had dug, in sufficient quantity to allow a good drink to all our cattle, we departed from Serotli in the afternoon; but as the sun even in winter, which it now was, is always very powerful by day, the waggons were dragged but slowly through the deep heavy sand, and we advanced only six miles before sunset. We could only travel in the mornings and evenings, as a single day in the hot sun and heavy sand would have knocked up the oxen. Next day we passed Pepacheu (white tufa), a hollow lined with tufa, in which water sometimes stands, but it was now dry; and at night our trocheamer showed that we had made but twenty-five miles from Serotli.

Ramotobi was angry at the slowness of our progress, and told us that, as the next water was three days in front, if we travelled so slowly we should never get there at all. The utmost endeavours of the servants, cracking their whips, screaming and beating, got only nineteen miles out of the poor beasts. We had thus proceeded forty-four miles from Serotli; and the oxen were more exhausted by the soft nature of the country, and the thirst, than if they had travelled double the distance over a hard road containing supplies of water: we had, as far as we could judge, still thirty miles more of the same dry work before us. At this season the grass becomes so dry as to crumble to powder in the hands; so the poor beasts stood wearily chewing, without taking a single fresh mouthful, and lowing painfully at the smell of water in our vessels in the waggons. We were all determined to succeed; so we endeavoured to save the horses by sending them forward with the guide, as a means of making a desperate effort in case the oxen should fail. Murray went forward with them, while Oswell and I remained to bring the waggons on their trail as far as the cattle could drag them, intending then to send the oxen forward too.

The horses walked quickly away from us; but on the morning of the third day, when we imagined the steeds must be near the water, we discovered them just alongside the waggons. The guide, having come across the fresh footprints of some Bushmen who had gone in an opposite direction to that which we wished to go, turned aside to follow them. An antelope had been ensnared in one of the Bushmen's pitfalls. Murray followed Ramotobi most trustingly along the Bushmen's spoor, though that led them away from the water we were in search of; witnessed the operation of slaughtering, skinning, and cutting up the antelope; and then, after a hard day's toil, found himself close upon the waggons! The knowledge still retained by Ramotobi of the trackless waste of scrub, through which we were now passing, seemed admirable. For sixty or seventy miles beyond Serotli, one clump of bushes and trees seemed exactly like another; but, as we walked together this morning, he remarked, "When we come to that hollow we shall light upon the highway of Sekomi; and beyond that again lies the river Mokóko"; which, though we passed along it, I could not perceive to be a river-bed at all.

After breakfast some of the men, who had gone forward on a little path with some footprints of water-loving animals upon it, returned with the joyful tidings of *metse*, water, exhibiting the mud on their knees in confirmation of the news being true. It does one's heart good to see the thirsty oxen rush into a pool of delicious rain-water, as this was. In they dash until the water is deep enough to be nearly level with their throat, and then they stand drawing slowly in the long refreshing mouthfuls, until their formerly collapsed sides distend as if they would burst. So much do they imbibe, that a sudden jerk, when they come out on the bank, makes some of the water run out again from their mouths; but as they have been days without food too, they very soon commence to graze, and of grass there is always abundance everywhere. This pool was called Mathuluáni; and thankful we were to have obtained so welcome a supply of water.

After giving the cattle a rest at this spot, we proceeded down the dry bed of the river Mokóko. The name refers to the water-bearing stratum before alluded to; and in this ancient bed it bears enough of water to admit of permanent wells in several parts of it. We had now the assurance from Ramotobi that we should suffer no more from thirst. Twice we found rain-water in the Mokóko before we reached Mokokonyáni, where the water, generally below ground elsewhere, comes to the surface in a bed of tufa. The adjacent country is all covered with low, thorny scrub, with grass, and here and there clumps of the 'wait-a-bit thorn,' or *Acacia detinens*.

At Lotlakáni (a little reed), another spring three miles farther down, we met with the first Palmyra trees which we had seen in South Africa; they were twenty-six in number.

The ancient Mokóko must have been joined by other rivers below this, for it becomes very broad, and spreads out into a large lake, of which the lake we were now in search of formed but a very small part. We observed that, wherever an ant-eater had made his hole, shells were thrown out with the earth, identical with those now alive in the lake.

When we left the Mokóko Ramotobi seemed, for the first time, to be at a loss as to which direction to take. He had passed only once away to the west of the Mokóko, the scenes of his boyhood. Mr Oswell, while riding in front of the waggons, happened to spy a Bushwoman running away in a bent position, in order to escape observation. Thinking it to be a lion, he galloped up to her. She thought herself captured, and began to deliver up her poor little property, consisting of a few traps made of cords; but, when I explained that we only wanted water, and would pay her if she led us to it, she consented to conduct us to a spring. It was then late in the afternoon, but she walked briskly before our horses for eight miles, and showed us the water of Nchokotsa. After leading us to the water she wished to go away home, if indeed she had any—she had fled from a party of her countrymen, and was now living far from all others with her husband—but as it was now dark we wished her to remain. As she believed herself still a captive we thought she might slip away by night, so, in order that she should not go away with the impression that we were dishonest, we gave her a piece of meat and a good large bunch of beads; at the sight of the latter she burst into a merry laugh, and remained without suspicion.

At Nchokotsa we came upon the first of a great number of saltpans, covered with an efflorescence of lime, probably the nitrate. A thick belt of mopane-trees (a *Bauhinia*) hides this salt-pan, which is twenty miles in circumference, entirely from the view of a person coming from the south-east; and, at the time the pan burst upon our view, the setting sun was casting a beautiful blue haze over the white incrustations, making the whole look exactly like a lake. Oswell threw his hat up in the air at the sight, and shouted out a huzza which made the poor Bushwoman and the Bakwains think him mad. I was a little behind him, and was as completely deceived by it as he; but as we had agreed to allow each other to behold the lake at the same instant, I felt a little chagrined that he had, unintentionally, got the first glance. We had no idea that the long-looked-for lake was still more than three hundred miles distant. One reason of our mistake was that the river Zouga was often spoken of by the same name as the lake—viz., Noka ea Batletli ("river of the Batletli").

The mirage on these salinas was marvellous. It is never, I believe, seen in perfection, except over such saline incrustations. Here not a particle of imagination was necessary for realizing the exact picture of large collections of water; the waves danced along above, and the shadows of the trees were vividly reflected beneath the surface in such an admirable manner that the loose cattle, whose thirst had not been slaked sufficiently by the very brackish water of Nchokotsa, with the horses, dogs, and even the Hottentots, ran off towards the deceitful pools. A herd of zebras in the mirage looked so exactly like elephants, that Oswell began to saddle a horse in order to hunt them; but a sort of break in the haze dispelled the illusion. Looking to the west and north-west from Nchokotsa, we could see columns of black smoke, exactly like those from a steam-engine, rising to the clouds, and were assured that these arose from the burning reeds of the Noka ea Batletli.

On the 4th of July we went forward on horseback towards what we supposed to be the lake, and again and again did we seem to see it; but at last we came to the veritable water of the Zouga, and found it to be a river running to the N.E. A village of Bakurutse lay on the opposite bank; these live among Batletli, a tribe having a click in their language, and who were found by Sebituane to possess large herds of the great horned cattle. They seem allied to the Hottentot family. Mr Oswell, in trying to cross the river, got his horse bogged in the swampy bank. Two Bakwains and I managed to get over by wading beside a fishing-weir. The people were friendly, and informed us that this water came out of the Ngami. This news gladdened all our hearts, for we now felt certain of reaching our goal. We might, they said, be a moon on the way; but we had the river Zouga at our feet, and by following it we should at last reach the broad water.

Next day, when we were quite disposed to be friendly with every one, two of the Bamangwato, who had been sent on before us by Sekomi to drive away all the Bushmen and Bakalahari from our path, so that they should not assist or guide us, came and sat down by our fire. We had seen their footsteps fresh in the way, and they had watched our slow movements forward, and wondered to see how we, without any Bushmen, found our way to the waters. This was the first time they had seen Ramotobi. "You have reached the river now," said they; and we, quite disposed to laugh at having won the game, felt no ill-will to anyone. They seemed to feel no enmity to us either; but after an apparently friendly conversation proceeded to fulfil to the last the instructions of their chief. Ascending the Zouga in our front, they circulated the report that our object was to plunder all the tribes living on the river and lake; but when they had got half-way up the river, the principal man sickened of fever, turned back some distance, and died. His death had a good effect, for the villagers connected it with the injury he was attempting to do to us. They all saw through Sekomi's reasons for wishing us to fail in our attempt; and though they came to us at first armed, kind and fair treatment soon produced perfect confidence.

When we had gone up the bank of this beautiful river about ninety-six miles from the point where we first struck it, and understood that we were still a considerable distance from the Ngami, we left all the oxen and waggons, except Mr Oswell's, which was the smallest, and one team, at Ngabisáne, in the hope that they would be recruited for the home journey, while we made a push for the lake. The Bechuana chief of the Lake region, who had sent men to Sechele, now sent orders to all the people on the river to assist us, and we were received by the Bakóba, whose language clearly shows that they bear an affinity to the tribes in the north. They call themselves Bayeèye—*i.e.*, men; but the Bechuanas call them Bakóba, which contains somewhat of the idea of slaves. They have never been known to fight, and, indeed, have a tradition that their fore-fathers, in their first essays at war, made their bows of the Palma-Christi; and, when these broke, gave up fighting altogether. They have invariably submitted to the rule of every horde which has overrun the countries adjacent to the rivers on which they specially love to dwell. They are thus the Quakers of the body politic in Africa.

The canoes of these inland sailors are truly primitive craft: they are hollowed out of the trunks of single trees by means of iron adzes; and, if the tree has a bend, so has the canoe. I liked the frank and manly bearing of these men, and, instead of sitting in the waggon, preferred a seat in one of the canoes. I found they regarded their rude vessels as an Arab does his camel. They have always fires in them, and prefer sleeping in them while on a journey to spending the night on shore. "On land you have lions"—say they—"serpents, hyænas, and your enemies; but in your canoe, behind a bank of reed, nothing can harm you." Their submissive disposition leads to their villages being frequently visited by hungry strangers. We had a pot on the fire in the canoe by the way, and when we drew near the villages devoured the contents. When fully satisfied ourselves I found we could all look upon any intruders with perfect complacency, and show the pot in proof of having devoured the last morsel.

While ascending in this way the beautifully wooded river we came to a large stream flowing into it. This was the river Tamunak'le. I inquired whence it came. "Oh, from a country full of rivers—so many no one can tell their number—and full of large trees!" This was the first confirmation of statements I had heard from the Bakwains who had been with Sebituane, that the country beyond was not "the large sandy plateau" of the philosophers. The prospect of a highway capable of being traversed by boats to an entirely unexplored and very populous region, grew from that time forward stronger and stronger in my mind; so much so, that, when we actually came to the lake, this idea occupied such a large portion of my mental vision that the actual discovery seemed of but little importance.

Twelve days after our departure from the waggons at Ngabisane we came to the north-east end of Lake Ngami; and on the 1st of August, 1849, we went down together to the broad part, and, for the first time, this fine-looking sheet of water was beheld by Europeans. The direction of the lake seemed to be N.N.E. and S.S.W. by compass. The southern portion is said to bend round to the west, and to receive the Teoughe from the north at its north-west extremity. We could detect no horizon where we stood looking S.S.W.; nor could we form any idea of the extent of the lake except from the reports of the inhabitants of the district; and, as they professed to go round it in three days, allowing twenty-five miles a-day would make it seventy-five, or less than seventy geographical miles in circumference. Other guesses have been made since as to its circumference, ranging between seventy and one hundred miles. It is shallow, for I subsequently saw a native punting his canoe over seven or eight miles of the north-east end; it can never, therefore, be of much value as a commercial highway. In fact, during the months preceding the annual supply of water from the north, the lake is so shallow that it is with difficulty cattle can approach the water through the boggy, reedy banks. These are low on all sides, but on the west there is a space devoid of trees, showing that the waters have retired thence at no very ancient date. This is another of the proofs of desiccation met with so abundantly throughout the whole country. A number of dead trees lie on this space, some of them embedded in the mud, right in the water. We were informed by the Bayeíye, who live on the lake, that, when the annual inundation begins, not only trees of great size, but antelopes, as the spring-buck and tsessebe (*Acronotus lunata*), are swept down by its rushing waters; the trees are gradually driven by the winds to the opposite side, and become embedded in mud.

The water of the lake is perfectly fresh when full, but brackish when low; and that coming down the Tamunak'le we found to be so clear, cold, and soft, the higher we ascended, that the idea of melting snow was suggested to our minds. We found this region, with regard to that from which we had come, to be clearly a hollow, the lowest point being Lake Kumadau; the point of the ebullition of water, as shown by one of Newman's barometric thermometers, was only between 207½° and 206°, giving an elevation of not much more than two thousand feet above the level of the sea. We had descended above two thousand feet in coming to it from Kolobeng.

PILGRIMAGE TO MECCAH [1]

(1853)

SIR RICHARD BURTON

(1821-90)

AT half-past five A.M. on Tuesday, the 6th of September, we arose refreshed by the cool, comfortable night, and loaded the camels. We travelled towards the south-east, and entered a country destitute of the low ranges of hill, which from Al-Madinah south-wards had bounded the horizon. After a two miles' march our camels climbed up a precipitous ridge, and then descended into a broad gravel plain. From ten to eleven A.M. our course lay southerly over a high tableland, and we afterwards traversed, for five hours and a half, a plain which bore signs of standing water. This day's march was peculiarly Arabia. It was a desert peopled only with echoes—a place of death for what little there is to die in it—a wilderness where, to use my companion's phrase, there is nothing but He.[2] Nature scalped, flayed, discovered all her skeleton to the gazer's eye. The horizon was a sea of mirage; gigantic sand-columns whirled over the plain; and on both sides of our road were huge piles of bare rock, standing detached upon the surface of sand and clay. I remarked one block which could not measure fewer than thirty feet in height. Through these scenes we travelled till about half-past four P.M., when the guns suddenly roared a halt. There was not a trace of human habitation

[1] From *Pilgrimage to Al-Madinah and Meccah.*

[2] *La Siwa Hu—i.e.*, where there is none but Allah.

around us: Shaykh Mas'ud correctly guessed the cause of our detention at the inhospitable "halting-place of the Mutayr" (Badawin). "Cook your bread and boil your coffee," said the old man; "the camels will rest for a while, and the gun will sound at nightfall."

We had passed over about eighteen miles of ground; and our present direction was south-west twenty degrees of Al-Sufayna.

At half-past ten that evening we heard the signal for departure, and, as the moon was still young, we prepared for a hard night's work. We took a south-westerly course through what is called Wa'ar—rough ground covered with thicket. Darkness fell upon us like a pall. The camels tripped and stumbled, tossing their litters like cockboats in a short sea; at times the Shugdufs were well nigh torn off their backs. When we came to a ridge worse than usual, old Mas'ud would seize my camel's halter, and, accompanied by his son and nephew bearing lights, encourage the animals with gesture and voice. It was a strange, wild scene. The black, basaltic field was dotted with the huge and doubtful forms of spongy-footed camels with silent tread, looming like phantoms in the midnight air; the hot wind moaned, and whirled from the torches flakes and sheets of flame and fiery smoke, whilst ever and anon a swift-travelling Takht-rawan, drawn by mules, and surrounded by runners bearing gigantic mashals or cressets, threw a passing glow of red light upon the dark road and the dusky multitude. On this occasion the rule was "every man for himself." Each pressed forward into the best path, thinking only of preceding his neighbour. The Syrians, amongst whom our little party had become entangled, proved most unpleasant companions: they often stopped the way, insisting upon the right to precedence. On one occasion a horseman had the audacity to untie the halter of my dromedary, and thus to cast us adrift, as it were, in order to make room for some excluded friend. I seized my sword; but Shaykh Abdullah stayed my hand, and addressed the intruder in terms sufficiently violent to make him slink away. Nor was this the only occasion on which my companion was successful with the Syrians. He would begin with a mild "Move a little, O my father!" followed, if fruitless, by "Out of the way, O Father of Syria!" and if still ineffectual, advancing to a "Begone, O he!" This ranged between civility and sternness. If without effect it was supported by revilings to the "Abusers of the Salt," the "Yazid," the "Offspring of Shimr." Another remark which I made about my companion's conduct well illustrates the difference between the Eastern and the Western man. When traversing a dangerous place Shaykh Abdullah the European attended to his camel with loud cries of "Hai! Hai!" and an occasional switching. Shaykh Abdullah the Asiatic commended himself to Allah by repeated ejaculations of "Yá Sátir! Yá Sattár!"

The morning of Wednesday (September 7th) broke as we entered a wide plain. In many places were signs of water: lines of basalt here and there seamed the surface, and wide sheets of the tufaceous gypsum called by the Arabs *Sabkhah* shone like mirrors set in the russet framework of the flat. After our harassing night, day came on with a sad feeling of oppression, greatly increased by the unnatural glare:

> In vain the sight, dejected to the ground,
> Stoop'd for relief: thence hot ascending streams
> And keen reflection pain'd.

We were disappointed in our expectations of water, which usually abounds near this station, as its name, *Al-Ghadir*, denotes. At ten A.M. we pitched the tent in the first convenient spot, and we lost no time in stretching our cramped limbs upon the bosom of mother Earth. From the halting-place of the Mutayr to Al-Ghadir is a march of about twenty miles, and the direction south-west twenty-one degrees.

In our anxiety to rest we had strayed from the Damascus caravan amongst the mountains of Shammar. Our Shaykh Mas'ud manifestly did not like the company; for shortly after three P.M. he insisted upon our striking the tent and rejoining the Hajj, which lay encamped about two miles distant in the western part of the basin. We loaded, therefore, and half an hour before sunset found ourselves in more congenial society. To my great disappointment, a stir was observable in the Caravan. I at once understood that another night-march was in store for us.

At six P.M. we again mounted, and turned towards the eastern plain. A heavy shower was falling upon the western hills, whence came damp and dangerous blasts. Between nine P.M. and the dawn of the next day we had a repetition of the last night's scenes, over a road so rugged and dangerous, that I wondered how men could prefer to travel in the darkness. But the camels of Damascus were now worn out with fatigue; they could not endure the sun, and our time was too precious for a halt. My night was spent perched upon the front bar of my Shugduf, encouraging the dromedary; and that we had not one fall excited my extreme astonishment. At five A.M. (Thursday, 8th September) we entered a wide plain thickly clothed with the usual thorny trees, in whose strong grasp many a Shugduf lost its covering, and not a few were dragged with their screaming inmates to the ground. About five hours afterwards we crossed a high ridge, and saw below us the camp of the Caravan, not more than two miles distant.

At eleven A.M. we had reached our station. It is about twentyfour miles from Al-Ghadir, and its direction is south-east ten degrees. It is called Al-Birkat (the Tank), from a large and now ruinous cistern built of hewn stone by the Caliph Harun. The land belongs to the Utaybah Badawin, the bravest and most ferocious tribe in Al-Hijaz; and the citizens denote their dread of these banditti by asserting that to increase their courage they drink their enemy's blood. My companions shook their heads when questioned upon the subject, and prayed that we might not become too well acquainted with them—an ill-omened speech!

The Pasha allowed us a rest of five hours at Al-Birkat: we spent them in my tent which was crowded with Shaykh Abdullah's friends. To requite me for this inconvenience, he prepared for me an excellent water-pipe, a cup of coffee, which, untainted by cloves and by cinnamon, would have been delicious, and a dish of dry fruits. As we were now nearing the Holy City, all the Meccans were busy canvassing for lodgers and offering their services to pilgrims.

At four P.M. we left Al-Birkat, and travelled eastwards over rolling ground thickly wooded. There was a network of footpaths through the thickets, and clouds obscured the moon; the consequence was inevitable loss of way. About two A.M. we began ascending hills in a south-westerly direction, and presently we fell into the bed of a large rock-girt Fiumara, which runs from east to west. At six A.M. (Sept. 9th) we left the Fiumara, and, turning to the west, we arrived about an hour afterwards at the station. Al-Zaribah, "the valley," is an undulating plain amongst high granite hills. In many parts it was faintly green; water was close to the surface, and rain stood upon the ground. During the night we had travelled about twenty-three miles, and our present station was south-east 56° from our last.

Having pitched the tent and eaten and slept, we prepared to perform the ceremony of *Al-Ihram* (assuming the pilgrim-garb), as Al-Zaribah is the Mikat, or the appointed place. Between the noonday and the afternoon prayers a barber attended to shave our heads, cut our nails and trim our mustachios. Then, having bathed and perfumed ourselves—the latter is a questionable point—we donned the attire, which is nothing but two new cotton cloths, each six feet long by three and a half broad, white, with narrow red stripes and fringes: in fact, the costume called *Al-Eddeh*, in the baths at Cairo. One of these sheets, technically termed the *Rida*, is thrown over the back, and, exposing the arm and shoulder, is knotted at the right side in the style *Wishah*. The *Izar* is wrapped round the loins from waist to knee, and, knotted or tucked in at the middle, supports itself. Our heads were bare, and nothing was allowed upon the instep.

After the toilette, we were placed with our faces in the direction of Meccah, and ordered to say aloud, "I vow this Ihram of Hajj (the pilgrimage) and the Umrah (the Little Pilgrimage) to Allah Almighty!" Having thus performed a two-bow prayer, we repeated without rising from the sitting position, these words, "O Allah! verily I purpose the Hajj and the Umrah, then enable me to accomplish that two, and accept them both of me, and make both blessed to me!" Followed the *Talbiyat* or exclaiming:

Here I am! O Allah! here am I—
No partner hast Thou, here am I;
Varrily the praise and the grace are Thine,
and the empire—
No partner has Thou, here am I!

And we were warned to repeat these words as often as possible, until the conclusion of the ceremonies. Then Shaykh Abdullah, who acted as director of our consciences, bade us be good pilgrims, avoiding quarrels, immorality, bad language, and light conversation. We must so reverence life that we should avoid killing game, causing an animal to fly, and even pointing it out for destruction; nor should we scratch ourselves, save with the open palm, lest vermin be destroyed, or a hair uprooted by the nail. We were to respect the sanctuary by sparing the trees, and not to pluck a single blade of grass.

At three P.M. we left Al-Zaribah, travelling towards the south-west, and a wondrously picturesque scene met the eye. Crowds hurried along, habited in the pilgrim-garb, whose whiteness contrasted strangely with their black skins; their newly shaven heads glistening in the sun, and their long black hair streaming in the wind. The rocks rang with shouts of *Labbayk! Labbayk!* At a pass we fell in with the Wahhabis, accompanying the Baghdad Caravan, screaming "Here am I"; and, guided by a large loud kettledrum, they followed in double file the camel of a standard-bearer, whose green flag bore in huge white letters the formula of the Moslem creed. They were wild-looking mountaineers, dark and fierce, with hair twisted into thin Dalik or plaits: each was armed with a long spear, a matchlock, or a dagger. They were seated upon coarse wooden saddles, without cushions or stirrups, a fine saddle-cloth alone denoting a chief. The women emulated the men; they either guided their own dromedaries, or, sitting in pillion, they clung to their husbands; veils they disdained, and their countenances certainly belonged not to a "soft sex." These Wahhabis were by no means pleasant companions. Most of them were followed by spare dromedaries, either unladen or carrying water-skins, fodder, fuel, and other necessaries for the march. The beasts delighted in dashing furiously through the file, which being lashed together, head and tail, was thrown each time into the greatest confusion. And whenever we were observed smoking we were cursed aloud for Infidels and Idolaters.

Looking back at Al-Zaribah, soon after our departure, I saw a heavy nimbus settle upon the hill-tops, a sheet of rain being stretched between it and the plain. The low grumbling of thunder sounded joyfully in our ears. We hoped for a shower, but were disappointed by a dust-storm, which ended with a few heavy drops. There arose a report that the Badawin had attacked a party of Meccans with stones, and the news caused men to look exceeding grave.

At five P.M. we entered the wide bed of the Fiumara, down which we were to travel all night. Here the country falls rapidly towards the sea, as the increasing heat of the air, the direction of the watercourses, and signs of violence in the torrent-bed show.

At about half-past five P.M. we entered a suspicious-looking place. On the right was a stony buttress, along whose base the stream, when there is one, swings; and to this depression was our road limited by the rocks and thorn trees which filled the other half of the channel. The left side was a precipice, grim and barren, but not so abrupt as its brother. Opposite us the way seemed barred by piles of hills, crest rising above crest into the far blue distance. Day still smiled upon the upper peaks, but the lower slopes and the Fiumara bed were already curtained with grey sombre shade.

A damp seemed to fall upon our spirits as we approached this Valley Perilous. I remarked that the voices of the women and children sank into silence, and the loud *Labbayk* of the pilgrims were gradually stilled. Whilst still speculating upon the cause of this phenomenon, it became apparent. A small curl of the smoke, like a lady's ringlet, on the summit of the right-hand precipice, caught my eye; and simultaneous with the echoing crack of the matchlock, a high-trotting dromedary in front of me rolled over upon the sands—a bullet had split its heart—throwing the rider a goodly somersault of five or six yards.

Ensued terrible confusion; women screamed, children cried, and men vociferated, each one striving with might and main to urge his animal out of the place of death. But the road being narrow, they only managed to jam the vehicles in a solid immovable mass. At every matchlock shot, a shudder ran through the huge body, as when the surgeon's scalpel touches some more sensitive nerve. The Irregular horsemen, perfectly useless, galloped up and down over the stones, shouting to and ordering one another. The Pasha of the army had his carpet spread at the foot of the left-hand precipice, and debated over his pipe with the officers what ought to be done. No good genius whispered, "Crown the heights."

Then it was that the conduct of the Wahhabis found favour in my eyes. They came up, galloping their camels—

Torrents less rapid, and less rash—

with their elf-locks tossing in the wind, and their flaring matches casting a strange lurid light over their features. Taking up a position, one body began to fire upon the Utaybah robbers, whilst two or three hundred, dismounting, swarmed up the hill under the guidance of the Sharif Zayd. I had remarked this nobleman at Al-Madinah as a model specimen of the pure Arab. Like all Sharifs, he is celebrated for bravery, and has killed many with his own hand. When urged at Al-Zaribah to ride into Meccah, he swore that he would not leave the Caravan till in sight of the walls; and, fortunately for the pilgrims, he kept his word. Presently the firing was heard far in our rear, the robbers having fled. The head of the column advanced, and the dense body of pilgrims opened out. Our forced halt was now exchanged for a flight. It required much management to steer our Desert-craft clear of danger; but Shaykh Mas'ud was equal to the occasion. That many were not, was evident by the boxes and baggage that strewed the shingles. I had no means of ascertaining the number of men killed and wounded; reports were contradictory, and exaggeration unanimous. The robbers were said to be a hundred and fifty in number; their object was plunder, and they would eat the shot camels. But their principal ambition was the boast, "We, the Utaybah, on such and such a night, stopped the Sultan's Mahmil one whole hour in the Pass."

As we advanced, our escort took care to fire every large dry Asclepias, to disperse the shades which buried us. Again the scene became wondrous wild. On either side were ribbed precipices, dark, angry, and towering above, till their summits mingled with the glooms of night; and between them formidable looked the chasm, down which our host hurried with shouts and discharge of matchlocks. The torch-smoke and the night-fires of flaming Asclepias formed a canopy, sable above and livid red below; it hung over our heads like a sheet, and divided the cliffs into two equal parts. Here the fire flashed fiercely from a tall thorn, that crackled and shot up showers of sparks into the air; there it died away in lurid gleams, which lit up a truly Stygian scene. As usual, however, the picturesque had its inconvenience. There was no path. Rocks, stone-banks, and trees obstructed our passage. The camels now blind in darkness, then dazzled by a flood of light, stumbled frequently; in some places slipping down a steep descent, in others sliding over a sheet of mud. I passed that night crying, "Hai! Hai!" switching the camel, and fruitless endeavouring to fustigate Mas'ud's nephew, who resolutely slept upon the water-bags. During the hours of darkness we made four or five halts, when we boiled coffee and smoked pipes; but man and beasts were beginning to suffer from a deadly fatigue.

Dawn (Saturday, Sept. 10th) found us still travelling down the Fiumara, which here is about a hundred yards broad. We then turned northward, and sighted Al-Mazik, more generally known as Wady Laymun, the Valley of the Limes. On the right bank of the Fiumara stood the Maccan Sharif's state pavilion, green and gold: it was surrounded by his attendants, and he had prepared to receive the Pasha of the Caravan. We advanced half a mile, and encamped temporarily in a hill-girt bulge of the Fiumara bed.Shaykh Mas'ud allowed us only four hours' halt; he wished to precede the main body. After breaking our fast joyously upon limes, pomegranates, and fresh dates, we sallied forth to admire the beauties of the place. We are once more on classic ground—the ground of the ancient Arab poets—and this Wady, celebrated for the purity of its air, has from remote ages been a favourite resort of the Maccans. Nothing can be more soothing to the brain than the dark green foliage of the limes and pomegranates; and from the base of the southern hill bursts a bubbling stream, whose

Chiare, fresche e dolci acque

flow through the gardens, filling them with the most delicious of melodies, the gladdest sound which Nature in these regions knows.

Exactly at noon Mas'ud seized the halter of the foremost camel, and we started down the Fiumara. Troops of Badawi girls looked over the orchard walls laughingly, and children came out to offer us fresh fruit and sweet water. At two P.M., travelling south-west, we arrived at a point where the torrent-bed turns to the right: and, quitting it, we climbed with difficulty over a steep ridge of granite. Before three o'clock we entered a hill-girt plain, which my companions called "Sola." In some places were clumps of trees, and scattered villages warned us that we were approaching a city. Far to the left rose the blue peaks of Taif, and the mountain road, a white thread upon the nearer heights, was pointed out to me. Here I first saw the tree, or rather shrub, which bears the balm of Gilead, erst so celebrated for its tonic and stomachic properties. I told Shaykh Mas'ud to break off a twig, which he did heedlessly. The act was witnessed by our party with a roar of laughter; and the astounded Shaykh was warned that he had become subject to an atoning sacrifice. Of course he denounced me as the instigator, and I could not fairly refuse assistance.

At four P.M. we came to a steep and rocky pass, up which we toiled with difficulty. The face of the country was rising once more, and again presented the aspect of numerous small basins divided and surrounded by hills. As we jogged on we were passed by the cavalcade of no less a personage than the Sharif of Meccah.

We halted as evening approached, and strained our eyes, but all in vain, to catch sight of Meccah, which lies in a winding valley. By Shaykh Abdullah's direction I recited, after the usual devotions, the following prayer:

"O Allah! verily this is Thy Safeguard (*Amn*) and Thy Sanctuary (*Harim*)! Into it whoso entereth becometh safe (*Amin*). So deny (*Harim*) my Flesh and Blood, my Bones and Skin, to Hell-fire. O Allah! save me from Thy Wrath on the Day when Thy Servants shall be raised from the Dead. I conjure Thee by this that Thou art Allah, besides whom is none (Thou only) the Merciful, the Compassionate. And have Mercy upon our Lord Mohammed, and upon the Progeny of our Lord Mohammed, and upon his Followers, One and All!" This was concluded with the "Talbiyat," and with an especial prayer for myself.

We again mounted, and night completed our disappointment. About one A.M. I was aroused by general excitement. "Meccah! Meccah!" cried some voices; "The Sanctuary! O the Sanctuary!" exclaimed others; and all burst into loud "*Labbayk*," not unfrequently broken by sobs. I looked out from my litter, and saw by the light of the southern stars the dim outlines of a large city, a shade darker than the surrounding plain. We were passing over the last ridge by a cutting called the Saniyat Kuda'a, the winding place of the cut. The "winding path" is flanked on both sides by watch-towers, which command the Darb al-Ma'ala or road leading from the north into Meccah. Thence we passed into the Ma'abidah (northern suburb) where the Sharif's Palace is built. After this, on the left hand, came the deserted abode of the Sharif bin Aun, now said to be a "haunted house." Opposite it lies the Jannat al-Ma'ala, the holy cemetery of Meccah. Thence, turning to the right, we entered the Sulaymaniyah or Afghan quarter. Here the boy Mohammed, being an inhabitant of the Shamiyah or Syrian ward, thought proper to display some apprehension. The two are on bad terms; children never meet without exchanging volleys of stones, and men fight furiously with quarterstaves.

At the Sulaymaniyah we turned off the main road into a by-way, and ascended by narrow lanes the rough heights of Jabal Hindi, upon which stands a small, whitewashed, and crenellated building called a fort. Thence descending, we threaded dark streets, in places crowded with rude cots and dusky figures, and finally at two A.M. we found ourselves at the door of the boy Mohammed's house.

The boy Mohammed left me in the street, and having at last persuaded the sleepy and tired Indian porter, by violent kicks and testy answers to twenty cautious queries, to swing open the huge gate of his fortress, he rushed upstairs to embrace his mother. After a minute I heard the *Zaghritah, Lululú*, or shrill cry which in these lands welcomes the wanderer home; the sound so gladdening to the returner sent a chill to the stranger's heart.

Presently the youth returned. His manner had changed from a boisterous and jaunty demeanour to one of grave and attentive courtesy—I had become his guest. He led me into the gloomy hall, seated me upon a large carpeted Mastabah, or platform, and told his *bara Miyan* (great Sir), the Hindustani porter, to bring a light. Meanwhile a certain shuffling of slippered feet above informed my hungry ears that the *Kabirah*, the mistress of the house, was intent on hospitable thoughts. When the camels were unloaded, appeared a dish of fine vermicelli, browned and powdered with loaf-sugar. The boy Mohammed, I, and Shaykh Nur, lost no time in exerting our right hands; and truly, after our hungry journey, we found the *Kunafah* delicious. After the meal we procured cots from a neighbouring coffee-house, and we lay down, weary, and anxious to snatch an hour or two of repose. At dawn we were expected to perform our *Twaf al-Kudum, or* "Circumambulation of Arrival," at the Harim.

Scarcely had the first smile of morning beamed upon the rugged head of the eastern hill, Abu Kubays, when we arose, bathed, and proceeded in our pilgrim-garb to the Sanctuary. We entered by the Bab al-Ziyadah, or principal northern door, descended two long flights of steps, traversed the cloister, and stood in sight of the Bayt Allah.

There at last it lay, the bourn of my long and weary Pilgrimage, realising the plans and hopes of many and many a year. The mirage medium of Fancy invested the huge catafalque and its gloomy pall with peculiar charms. There were no giant fragments of hoar antiquity as in Egypt, no remains of graceful and harmonious beauty as in Greece and Italy, no barbarous gorgeousness as in the buildings of India; yet the view was strange, unique—and how few have looked upon the celebrated shrine! I may truly say that, of all the worshippers who clung weeping to the curtain, or who pressed their beating hearts to the stone, none felt for the moment a deeper emotion than did the Haji from the far-north. It was as if the poetical legends of the Arab spoke truth, and that the waving wings of angels, not the sweet breeze of morning, were agitating and swelling the black covering of the shrine.

WHERE THE NILE IS BORN [1]

(1861-62)

J. H. SPEKE

(1827-64)

[In 1858, exploring the African lakes under the leadership of Richard Burton, Speke had come upon a great lake which he named the Victoria Nyanza. This he believed to be the source of the Nile. Though Burton would not credit it, Speke had the support of the Royal Geographical Society, and two years later set out to prove his theory. By October 1861 he reached the south-west corner of Victoria Nyanza; crossed the Kagera on January 16, 1862; and on February 19 came to the capital of Uganda. Here, for some months, further journey was prevented by King Mtésa.]

JUNE 29th. To have two strings to my bow, and press our departure as hotly as possible, I sent first Frij off with Nasib to the queen, conveying, as a parting present, a block-tin brush-box, a watch without a key, two sixpenny pocket-handkerchiefs, and a white towel, with an intimation that we were going, as the king had expressed his desire of sending us to Gani. Her Majesty accepted the present, finding fault with the watch for not ticking like the king's, and would not believe her son Mtésa had been so hasty in giving us leave to depart, as she had not been consulted on the subject yet. Setting off to attend the king at his appointed time, I found the Kamraviona already there, with a large Court attendance, patiently awaiting his Majesty's advent. As we were all waiting on, I took a rise out of the Kamraviona by telling him I wanted a thousand men to march with me through Kidi to Gani. Surprised at the extent of my requisition, he wished to know if my purpose was fighting. I made him a present of the great principle that power commands respect, and it was to prevent my chance of fighting that we required so formidable an escort. His reply was that he would tell the king; and he immediately rose and walked away home.

K'yengo and the representatives of Usüi and Karagűé now arrived by order of the king to bid farewell, and received the slaves and cattle lately captured. As I was very hungry, I set off home to breakfast. Just as I had gone, the provoking king inquired after me, and so brought me back again, though I never saw him the whole day. K'yengo, however, was very communicative. He said he was present when Sunna, with all the forces he could muster, tried to take the very countries I now proposed to travel through; but, though in person exciting his army to victory, he could make nothing of it. He advised

[1] From *Journal of the Discovery of the Source of the Nile* (1863).

my returning to Karagŭé, when Rŭmanika would give me an escort through Nkolé to Unyoro; but finding that did not suit my views, as I swore I would never retrace one step, he proposed my going by boat to Unyoro, following down the Nile.

This, of course, was exactly what I wanted; but how could King Mtésa, after the rebuff he had received from Kamrasi, be induced to consent to it. My intention, I said, was to try the king on the Usoga and Kidi route first, then on the Masai route to Zanzibar, affecting perfect indifference about Kamrasi; and all those failing—which, of course, they would—I would ask for Unyoro as a last and only resource. Still I could not see the king to open my heart to him, and therefore felt quite nonplussed. "Oh," says K'yengo, "the reason why you do not see him is merely because he is ashamed to show his face, having made so many fair promises to you which he knows he can never carry out: bide your time, and all will be well," At 4 P.M., as no hope of seeing the king was left, all retired.

June 30th. Unexpectedly, and for reasons only known to himself, the king sent us a cow and load of butter, which had been asked for many days ago. The new moon seen last night kept the king engaged at home, paying his devotions with his magic horns or fetishes. The spirit of this religion—if such it can be called—is not so much adoration of a Being supreme and beneficent, as a tax to certain malignant furies—a propitiation, in fact, to prevent them bringing evil on the land, and to insure a fruitful harvest. It was rather ominous that hail fell with violence, and lightning burnt down one of the palace huts, while the king was in the midst of his propitiatory devotions.

July 1st. As Bombay was ordered to the palace to instruct the king in the art of casting bullets, I primed him well to plead for the road, and he reported to me the results, thus: First, he asked one thousand men to go through Kidi. This the king said was impracticable, as the Waganda had tried it so often before without success. Then, as that could not be managed, what would the king devise himself? Bana only proposed the Usoga and Kidi route because he thought it would be to the advantage of Uganda. "Oh," says the king cunningly, "if Bana merely wishes to see Usoga he can do so, and I will send a suitable escort, but no more." To this Bombay replied, "Bana never could return; he would sooner do anything then return—even penetrate the Masai to Zanzibar, or go through Unyoro"; to which the king, ashamed of his impotence, hung down his head and walked away.

In the meanwhile, and whilst this was going on at the king's palace, I went with Grant,[1] by appointment, to see the queen. As usual, she kept us waiting

[1] Speke's only European companion, Captain J. A. Grant.

some time, then appeared sitting by an open gate, and invited us, together with many Wakungŭ and Wasumbŭa, to approach. Very lavish with stale, sour *pombé*, she gave us all some, saving the Wasumbŭa, whom she addressed very angrily, asking what they wanted, as they have been months in the country. These poor creatures, in a desponding mood, defended themselves by saying, which was quite true, that they had left their homes in Sorombo to visit her and to trade. They had, since their arrival in the country, been daily in attendance at her palace, but never had the good fortune to see her excepting on such lucky occasions as brought the Wazungŭ (white men) here, when she opened her gates to them, but otherwise kept them shut. The queen retorted, "And what have you brought me, pray? Where is it? Until I touch it you will neither see me nor obtain permission to trade. Uganda is no place for idle vagabonds." We then asked for a private interview, when, a few drops of rain falling, the queen walked away, and we had orders to wait a little. During this time two boys were birched by the queen's orders, and an officer was sent out to inquire why the watch we had given her did not go. This was easily explained. It had no key; and, never losing sight of the main object, we took advantage of the opportunity to add, that if she did not approve of it, we could easily exchange it for another on arrival at Gani, provided she would send an officer with us.

The queen, squatting within her hut, now ordered both Grant and myself to sit outside and receive a present of five eggs and one cock each, saying coaxingly, "These are for my children." Then, taking out the presents, she learned the way of wearing her watch with a tape guard round her neck, reposing the instrument in her bare bosom, and of opening and shutting it, which so pleased her, that she declared it quite satisfactory. The key was quite a minor consideration, for she could show it to her attendants just as well without one. The towel and handkerchief were also very beautiful, but what use could they be put to? "Oh, your Majesty, to wipe the mouth after drinking *pombé*." "Of course," is the reply,—"excellent; I won't use a *mŭqgŭ* napkin any more, but have one of these placed on my cup when it is brought to drink, and wipe my mouth with it afterwards. But what does Bana want?" "The road to Gani," says Bombay for me. "The king won't see him when he goes to the palace, so now he comes here, trusting your superior influence and good-nature will be more practicable." "Oh!" says her Majesty, "Bana does not know the fact of the case. My son has tried all the roads without success, and how he is ashamed to meet Bana face to face." "Then what is to be done, your Majesty?" "Bana must go back to Karagŭé and wait for a year, until my son is crowned, when he will make friends with the surrounding chiefs, and the roads will be opened." "But Bana says he will not retrace one step; he would sooner lose his life." "Oh, that's nonsense! he must not be headstrong; but before anything more can be said I will send a message to my son, and Bana can then go with Kaddŭ, K'yengo, and Viarŭngi, and tell all they have to say to Mtésa tomorrow, and the following day return to me, when everything will be concluded." We all now left but Kaddŭ and some of the queen's officers, who waited for the message to her son about us. To judge from Kaddŭ, it must have been very different from what she led us to expect, as, on joining us, he said there was not the smallest chance of our getting the road we required, for the queen was so decided about it no further argument would be listened to.

July 2nd. Three goats were stolen, and suspicion falling on the king's cooks, who are expert foragers, we sent to the Kamraviona, and asked him to order out the Mganga; but his only reply was, that he often loses goats in the same way. He sent us one of his own for present purposes, and gave thirty baskets of potatoes to my men. As the king held a Court, and broke it up before 8 A.M., and no one would go there for fear of his not appearing again, I waited till the evening for Bombay, Kaddŭ, K'yengo, and Viarŭngi, when, finding them drunk, I went myself, fired a gun, and was admitted to where the king was hunting guinea-fowl. On seeing me, he took me affectionately by the hand, and, as we walked along together, he asked me what I wanted, showed me the house which was burnt down, and promised to settle the road question in the morning.

July 3rd. With Kaddŭ, K'yengo, and Viarŭngi all in attendance, we went to the palace, where there was a large assemblage prepared for a levee, and fired a gun, which brought the king out in state. The Sakibobo, or provincial governor, arrived with a body of soldiers armed with sticks, made a speech, and danced at the head of his men, all pointing sticks upwards, and singing fidelity to their king.

The king then turned to me, and said, "I have come out to listen to your request of last night. What is it you do want?" I said, "To open the country to the north, that an uninterrupted line of commerce might exist between England and this country by means of the Nile. I might go round by Nkolé" (K'yengo looked daggers at me); "but that is out of the way, and not suitable to the purpose." The queen's deputation was now ordered to draw near, and questioned in a whisper. As K'yengo was supposed to know all about me, and spoke fluently both in Kiganda and Kisŭahili, he had to speak first; but K'yengo, to everybody's surprise, said, "One white man wishes to go to Kamrasi's, whilst the other wishes to return through Unyamŭézi." This announcement made the king reflect; for he had been privately primed by his mother's attendants that we both wished to go to Gani, and therefore shrewdly inquired if Rŭmanika knew we wished to visit Kamrasi, and whether he was aware we should attempt the passage north from Uganda. "Oh, yes! of course Bana wrote to Bana Mdogo" (the little master) "as soon as he arrived in Uganda, and told him and Rŭmanika all about it." "Wrote! what does that mean?" and I was called upon to explain. Mtésa, then seeing a flaw in K'yengo's statements, called him a story-teller, ordered him and his party away, and bade me draw near.

The moment of triumph had come at last, and suddenly the road was granted! The king presently let us see the motive by which he had been influenced. He said he did not like having to send to Rumanika for everything: he wanted his visitors to come to him direct; moreover, Rumanika had sent him a message to the effect that we were not to be shown anything out of Uganda, and when we had done with it were to be returned to him. Rŭmanika, indeed! who cared about Rŭmanika? Was not Mtésa the king of the country, to do as he liked? and we all laughed. Then the king, swelling with pride, asked me whom I liked best—Rŭmanika or himself—an awkward question, which I disposed of by saying that I liked Rŭmanika very much because he spoke well, and was very communicative; but I also liked Mtésa, because his habits were much like my own—fond of shooting and roaming about; whilst he had learned so many things from my teaching, I must ever feel a yearning towards him.

With much satisfaction I felt that my business was now done; for Budja was appointed to escort us to Unyoro, and Jumba to prepare us boats, that we might go all the way to Kamrasi's by water.

To keep the king up to the mark, and seal our passage, in the evening I took a Lancaster rifle, with ammunition, and the iron chair he formerly asked for, as a parting present, to the palace, but did not find him, as he had gone out shooting with his brothers.

July 4th. Grant and I now called together on the king to present the rifle, chair, and ammunition, as we could not thank him in words sufficiently for the favour he had done us in granting the road through Unyoro. I said the parting gift was not half as much as I should like to have been able to give; but we hoped, on reaching Gani, to send Petherick up to him with everything that he could desire. We regretted we had no more powder or shot, as what was intended, and actually placed out expressly to be presented on this occasion, was stolen. The king, turning the subject adroitly, asked me how many cows and women I would like, holding his hand up with spread fingers, and desiring me to count by hundreds; but the reply was five cows and goats would be enough, for we wished to travel lightly in boats, starting from the Murchison Creek. Women were declined on such grounds as would seem rational to him. But if the king would clothe my naked men with me *mbŭgŭ* (bark cloth) each, and give a small tusk each to nine Wanyamŭézi porters, who desired to return to their home, the obligation would be great.

Everything was granted without the slightest hesitation; and then the king, turning to me, said, "Well, Bana, so you really wish to go?" "Yes, for I have not seen my home for four years and upwards"—reckoning five months to the year, Uganda fashion. "And you can give no stimulants?" "No." "Then you will send me some from Gani—brandy if you like; it makes people sleep sound, and gives them strength." Next we went to the queen to bid her farewell, but did not see her.

On returning home I found half my men in a state of mutiny. They had been on their own account to beg for the women and cows which had been refused, saying, If Bana does not want them we do, for we have been starved here ever since we came, and when we go for food get broken heads; we will not serve with Bana any longer; but as he goes north, we will return to Karagŭé and Unyanyembé. Bombay, however, told them they never had fed so well in all their lives as they had in Uganda, counting from fifty to sixty cows killed, and *pombé* and plantains every day, whenever they took the trouble to forage; and for their broken heads they invariably received a compensation in women; so that Bana had reason to regret every day spent in asking for food for them at the palace—a favour which none but his men received, but which they had not, as they might have done, turned to good effect by changing the system of plundering for food in Uganda.

July 5th. By the king's order we attended at the palace early. The gun obtained us as all a speedy admittance, when the king opened conversation by saying, "Well, Bana, so you really are going?" "Yes; I have enjoyed your hospitality for a long time, and now wish to return to my home." "What provision do you want?" I said, five cows and five goats, as we shan't be long in Uganda; and it is not the custom of our country, when we go visiting, to carry anything away with us. The king then said, "Well, I wish to give you much, but you won't have it"; when Budja spoke out, saying, "Bana does not know the country he has to travel through; there is nothing but jungle and famine on the way, and he must have cows"; on which the king ordered us sixty cows, fourteen goats, ten loads of butter, a load of coffee and tobacco, one hundred sheets of *mbŭgŭ*, as clothes for my men, at a suggestion of Bombay's, as all my cloth had been expended even before I left Karagŭé.

This magnificent order created a pause, which K'yengo took advantage of by producing a little bundle of peculiarly shaped sticks and a lump of earth—all of which have their own particular magical powers, as K'yengo described to the king's satisfaction. After this Viarŭngi pleaded the cause of my mutinous followers, till I shook my finger angrily at him before the king, rebuked him for intermeddling in other people's affairs, and told my own story, which gained the sympathy of the king, and induced him to say, "Supposing they desert Bana, what road do they expect to get?" Maula was now appointed to go with Rozaro to Karagŭé for the powder and other things promised yesterday, while Viarŭngi and all his party, though exceedingly anxious to get away, had orders to remain here prisoners as a surety for the things arriving. Further, Kaddŭ and two other Wakungŭ received orders to go to Usŭi with two tusks of ivory to purchase gunpowder, caps, and flints, failing which they would proceed to Unyanyembé, and even to Zanzibar, for the king must not be disappointed, and failure would cost them their lives.

Not another word was said, and away the two parties went, with no more arrangement than a set of geese—Maŭla without a letter, and Kaddŭ without any provision for the way, as if all the world belonged to Mtésa, and he could help himself from any man's garden that he liked, no matter where he was. In the evening my men made a humble petition for their discharge, even if I did not pay them, producing a hundred reasons for wishing to leave me, but none which would stand a moment's argument: the fact was, they were afraid of the road to Unyoro, thinking I had not sufficient ammunition.

July 6th. I visited the king, and asked leave for boats to go at once; but the fleet admiral put a veto on this by making out that dangerous shallows exist between the Murchison Creek and the Kira district station, so that the boats of one place never visit the other; and further, if we went to Kira, we should find impracticable cataracts to the Urondogani boat-station; our better plan would therefore be, to deposit our property at the Urondogani station, and walk by land up the river, if a sight of the falls at the mouth of the lake was of such material consequence to us.

Of course this man carried everything his own way, for there was nobody able to contradict him, and we could not afford time to visit Usoga first, lest by the delay we might lose an opportunity of communicating with Petherick. Grant now took a portrait of Mtésa by royal permission, the king sitting as quietly as his impatient nature would permit. Then at home the Wanyamŭézi porters received their tusks of ivory, weighing from 16 to 50 lb. each, and took a note besides on Rŭmanika each for twenty fundo of beads, barring one Bogŭé man, who, having lent a cloth to the expedition some months previously, thought it would not be paid to him, and therefore seized a sword as security; the consequence was, his tusk was seized until the sword was returned, and he was dismissed minus his beads, for having so misconducted himself. The impudent fellow then said, "It will be well for Bana if he succeeds in getting the road through Unyoro; for, should he fail, I will stand in his path at Bogŭé."

July 7th. Early in the morning the king bade us come to him to say farewell. Wishing to leave behind a favourable impression I instantly complied. On the breast of my coat I suspended the necklace the queen had given me, as well as his knife, and my medals. I talked with him in as friendly and flattering a manner as I could, dwelling on his shooting, the pleasant cruising on the lake, and our sundry picnics, as well as the grand prospect there was now of opening the country to trade, by which his guns, the best in the world, would be fed with powder—and other small matters of a like nature—to which he replied with great feeling and good taste. We then all rose with an English bow, placing the hand on the heart whilst saying *adieu*; and there was a complete uniformity in the ceremonial, for whatever I did, Mtésa, in an instant, mimicked with the instinct of a monkey.

We had, however, scarcely quitted the palace gate before the king issued himself, with his attendants and his brothers leading, and women bringing up the rear; here K'yengo and all the Wazinza joined in the procession with ourselves, they kneeling and clapping their hands after the fashion of their own country. Budja just then made me feel very anxious, by pointing out the position of Urondogani as I thought, too far north. I called the king's attention to it, and in a moment he said he would speak to Budja in such a manner that would leave no doubts in my mind, for he liked me much, and desired to please me in all things. As the procession now drew to our camp, and Mtésa expressed a wish to have a final look at my men, I ordered them to turn out with their arms and n'yanzig for the many favours they had received. Mtésa, much pleased, complimented them on their goodly appearance, remarking that with such a force I would have no difficulty in reaching Gani, and exhorted them to follow me through fire and water; them exchanging adieus again he walked ahead in gigantic strides up the hill, the pretty favourite of his harem, Lŭbŭga—beckoning and waving with her little hands, and crying, "Bana! Bana!"—trotting after him conspicuous among the rest, though all showed a little feeling at the severance. We saw them no more.

July 7th to 11th. With Budja appointed as the general director, a lieutenant of the Sakibobo's to furnish us with sixty cows in his division at the first halting-place, and Kasoro (Mr Cat), a lieutenant of Jumba's, to provide the boats at Urondogani, we started at 1 P.M. on the journey northwards. The Wangŭana still grumbled, swearing they would carry no loads, as they got no rations, and threatening to shoot us if we pressed them, forgetting that their food had been paid for to the king in rifles, chronometers, and other articles, costing about 2000 dollars; and, what was more to the point, that all the ammunition was in our hands. A judicious threat of the stick, however, put things right, and on we marched five successive days to Kari—as the place was afterwards named, in consequence of the tragedy mentioned below—the whole distance accomplished being thirty miles from the capital, through a fine hilly country, with jungles and rich cultivation alternating. The second march, after crossing the Katawana river with its many branches flowing northeast into the huge rush-drain of Lŭajerri, carried us beyond the influence of the higher hills, and away from the huge grasses that characterise the southern boundary of Uganda bordering on the lake.

Each day's march to Kari was directed much in the same manner. After a certain number of hours' travelling, Budja appointed some village of residence for the night, avoiding those which belonged to the queen, lest any rows should take place in them, which would create disagreeable consequences with the king, and preferring those the heads of which had been lately seized by the orders of the king. Nevertheless, wherever we went, the villagers forsook their homes, and left their houses, property, and gardens an easy prey to the thieving propensities of the escort. To put a stop to this vile practice was now beyond my power; the king allowed it, and his men were the first in every house, taking goats, fowls, skins, *mbŭgŭs*, cowries, beads, drums, spears, tobacco, *pombé*—in short, everything they could lay their hands on—in the most ruthless manner. It was a perfect marauding campaign for them all, and all alike were soon laden with as much as they could carry.

A halt of some days had become necessary at Kari to collect the cows given by the king; and, as it is one of his most extensive pasture-grounds, I strolled with my rifle (11th) to see what new animals could be found; but no sooner did I wound a zebra than messengers came running after me to say Kari, one of my men, had been murdered by the villagers three miles off; and such was the fact. He, with others of my men, had been induced to go plundering, with a few boys of the Waganda escort, to a certain village of potters, as pots were required by Budja for making plantain-wine, the first thing ever thought of when a camp is formed. On nearing the place, however, the women of the village, who were the only people visible, instead of running away, as our braves expected, commenced hullalooing, and brought out their husbands. Flight was now the only thought of our men, and all would have escaped had

Kari not been slow and his musket empty. The potters overtook him, and, as he pointed his gun, which they considered a magic-horn, they speared him to death, and then fled at once. Our survivors were not long in bringing the news into camp, when a party went out, and in the evening brought in the man's corpse and everything belonging to him, for nothing had been taken.

July 12th. To enable me at my leisure to trace up the Nile to its exit from the lake, and then go on with the journey as quickly as possible, I wished the cattle to be collected and taken by Budja and some of my men with the heavy baggage overland to Kamrasi's. Another reason for doing so was, that I thought it advisable Kamrasi should be forewarned that we were coming by the water route, lest we should be suspected and stopped as spies by his officers on the river, or regarded as enemies, which would provoke a fight. Budja, however, objected to move until a report of Kari's murder had been forwarded to the king, lest the people, getting bumptious, should try the same trick again; and Kasoro said he would not go up the river as he had received no orders to do so.

In this fix I ordered a march back to the palace, mentioning the king's last words, and should have gone, had not Budja ordered Kasoro to go with me. A page then arrived from the king to ask after Bana's health, carrying the Whitworth rifle as his master's card, and begging for a heavy double-barrelled gun to be sent him from Gani. I called this lad to witness the agreement I had made with Budja, and told him, if Kasoro satisfied me, I would return by him, in addition to the heavy gun, a Massey's patent log. I had taken it for the navigation of the lake, and it was now of no further use to me, but, being an instrument of complicated structure, it would be a valuable addition to the king's museum of magic charms. I added I should like the king to send me the robes of honour and spears he had once promised me, in order that I might, on reaching England, be able to show my countrymen a specimen of the manufactures of his country. The men who were with Kari were now sent to the palace, under accusation of having led him into ambush, and a complaint was made against the villagers, which we waited the reply to. As Budja forbade it, no men would follow me out shooting, saying the villagers were out surrounding our camp, and threatening destruction on any one who dared show his face; for this was not the high road to Uganda, and therefore no one had a right to turn them out of their houses and pillage their gardens.

July 13th. Budja lost two cows given to his party last night, and seeing ours securely tied by their legs to trees, asked by what spells we had secured them; and would not believe our assurance that the ropes that bound them were all the medicines we knew of. One of the queen's sisters, hearing of Kari's murder, came on a visit to condole with us, bringing a pot of *pombé*, for which she received some beads. On being asked how many sisters the queen had, for we could not help suspecting some imposition, she replied she was the only one, till assured ten other ladies had presented themselves as the queen's sisters before, when she changed her tone, and said, "That is true, I am not the only one; but if I had told you the truth I might have lost my head." This was a significant expression of the danger of telling court secrets.

I suspected that there must be a considerable quantity of game in this district, as stake-nets and other traps were found in all the huts, as well as numbers of small antelope hoofs spitted on pipe-sticks—an ornament which is counted the special badge of the sportsman in this part of Africa. Despite, therefore, of the warnings of Budja, I strolled again with my rifle, and saw pallah, small plovers, and green antelopes with straight horns, called *mpéo*, the skin of which makes a favourite apron for the Mabandwa.

July 14th. I met to-day a Mhŭma cowherd in my strolls with the rifle, and asked him if he knew where the game lay. The unmannerly creature, standing among a thousand of the sleekest cattle, gruffishly replied, "What can I know of any other animals than cows?" and went on with his work, as if nothing in the world could interest him but his cattle-tending. I shot a doe leucotis, called here *nsunnŭ*, the first one seen upon the journey.

July 15th. In the morning, when our men went for water to the springs, some Waganda in ambush threw a spear at them, and this time caught a Tartar, for the "horns" as they called their guns, were loaded, and two of them received short-wounds. In the evening, whilst we were returning from shooting, a party of Waganda, also lying in the bush, called out to know what we were about; saying, "Is it not enough that you have turned us out of our homes and plantations, leaving us to live like animals in the wilderness?" and when told we were only searching for sport, would not believe that our motive was any other than hostility to themselves.

At night one of Budja's men returned from the palace, to say the king was highly pleased with the measures adopted by his Wakungŭ, in prosecution of Kari's affair. He hoped now as we had cows to eat, there would be no necessity for wandering for food, but all would keep together "in one garden." At present no notice would be taken of the murderers, as all the culprits would have fled far away in their fright to escape chastisement. But when a little time had elapsed, and all would appear to have been forgotten, officers would be sent and the miscreants apprehended, for it was impossible to suppose anybody could be ignorant of the white men being the guests of the king, considering they had lived at the palace so long. The king took this opportunity again to remind me that he wanted a heavy solid double gun, such as would last him all his life; and intimated that in a few days the arms and robes of honour were to be sent.

July 16th. Most of the cows for ourselves and the guides—for the king gave them also a present, ten each—were driven into camp. We also got 50 lb. of butter, the remainder to be picked up on the way. I strolled with the gun, and shot two zebras, to be sent to the king, as, by the constitution of Uganda, he alone can keep their royal skins.

July 17th. We had to halt again, as the guides had lost most of their cows, so I strolled with my rifle and shot a ndjezza doe, the first I had ever seen. It is a brown animal, a little smaller than leucotis, and frequents much the same kind of ground.

July 18th. We had still to wait another day for Budja's cows, when, as it appeared all-important to communicate quickly with Petherick, and as Grant's leg was considered too weak for travelling fast, we took counsel together, and altered our plans. I arranged that Grant should go to Kamrasi's direct with the property, cattle, and women, taking my letters and a map for immediate despatch to Petherick at Gani, whilst I should go up the river to its source or exit from the lake, and come down again navigating as far as practicable.

At night the Waganda startled us by setting fire to the huts our men were sleeping in, but providentially did more damage to themselves than to us, for one sword only was buried in the fire, whilst their own huts, intended to be vacated in the morning, were burnt to the ground. To fortify ourselves against another invasion, we cut down all their plantains to make a boma or fence.

We started all together on our respective journeys; but, after the third mile, Grant turned west, to join the highroad to Kamrasi's, whilst I went east for Urondogani, crossing the Luajerri, a huge rush-drain three miles broad, fordable nearly to the right bank, where we had to ferry in boats, and the cows to be swum over with men holding on to their tails. It was larger than the Katonga, and more tedious to cross, for it took no less than four hours, mosquitoes in myriads biting our bare backs and legs all the while. The Lŭajerri is said to rise in the lake and fall into the Nile, due south of our crossing-point. On the right bank wild buffalo are described to be as numerous as cows, but we did not see any, though the country is covered with a most inviting jungle for sport, with intermediate lays of fine grazing grass. Such is the nature of the country all the way to Urondogani, except in some favoured spots, kept as tidily as in any part of Uganda, where plantains grow in the utmost luxuriance. From want of guides, and misguided by the exclusive ill-natured Wahŭma who were here in great numbers tending their king's cattle, we lost our way continually, so that we did not reach the boatstation until the morning of the 21st.

Here at last I stood on the brink of the Nile; most beautiful was the scene, nothing could surpass it! It was the very perfection of the kind of effect aimed at in a highly kept park; with a magnificent stream from 600 to 700 yards wide, dotted with islets and rocks, the former occupied by fishermen's huts, the latter by sterns and crocodiles basking in the sun—flowing between fine high grassy banks, with rich trees and plantains in the background, where herds of the nsunnŭ and hartebeest could be seen grazing, while the hippopotami were snorting in the water, and florikan and guinea-fowl rising at our feet. Unfortunately, the chief district officer, Mlondo, was from home, but we took possession of his huts—clean, extensive, and tidily kept—facing the river, and felt as if a residence here would do one good. Delays and subterfuges, however, soon came to damp our spirits. The acting officer was sent for, and asked for the boats; they were all scattered, and could not be collected for a day or two; but, even if they were at hand, no boat ever went up or down the river. The chief was away and would be sent for, as the king often changed his orders, and, after, all., might not mean what had been said. The district belonged to the Sakibobo, and no representative of his had come here. These excuses, of course, would not satisfy us. The boats must be collected, seven, if there are not ten, for we must try them, and come to some understanding about them, before we march up stream, when, if the officer values his life, he will let us have them, and acknowledge Karoso as the king's representative, otherwise a complaint will be sent to the palace, for we won't stand trifling.

We were now confronting Usoga, country which may be said to be the very counterpart of Uganda in its richness and beauty. Here the people use such huge iron-headed spears with short handles, that, on seeing one to-day, my people remarked that they were better fitted for digging potatoes than piercing men. Elephants, as we had seen by their devastations during the last two marches, were very numerous in this neighbourhood. Till lately, a party from Unyoro, ivory-hunting, had driven them away. Lions were also described as very numerous and destructive to human life. Antelopes were common in the jungle, and the hippopotami, though frequenters of the plantain-garden and constantly heard, were seldom seen on land in consequence of their unsteady habits.

The king's page again came, begging I would not forget the gun and stimulants, and bringing with him the things I asked for—two spears, one shield, one dirk, two leopard-cat skins, and two sheets of small antelope skins. I told my men they ought to shave their heads, and bathe in the holy river, the cradle of Moses—the waters of which, sweetened with sugar, men carry all the way from Egypt to Mecca, and sell to the pilgrims. But Bombay, who is a philosopher of the Epicurean school, said, "We don't look on those things in the same fanciful manner that you do; we are contented with all the commonplaces of life, and look for nothing beyond the present. If things don't go well, it is God's will; and if they do go well, that is His will also."

July 22nd. The acting chief brought a present of one cow, one goat, and *pombé*, with a mob of his courtiers to pay his respects. He promised that the seven boats, which are all the station could muster, would be ready next day, and in the meanwhile a number of men would conduct me to the shooting-ground. He asked to be shown the books of birds and animals, and no sooner saw some specimens of Wolf's handiwork, than, in utter surprise, he exclaimed, "I know how these are done; a bird was caught and stamped upon the paper," using action to his words, and showing what he meant, while all his followers n'yanzigged for the favour of the exhibition.

In the evening I strolled in the antelope parks, enjoying the scenery and the sport excessively. A noble buck nsunnŭ, standing by himself, was the first thing seen on this side, though a herd of hartebeests were grazing on the Usoga banks. One bullet rolled my fine friend over, but the rabble looking on no sooner saw the hit than they rushed upon him and drove him off, for he was only wounded. A chase ensued, and he was tracked by his blood when a pongo (bush boc) was started and divided the party. It also brought me to another single buck nsunnŭ, which was floored at once, and left to be carried home by some of my men in company with the Waganda, while I went on, shot a third nsunnŭ buck, and tracked him by his blood till dark, for the bullet had pierced his lungs and passed out on the other side. Failing to find him on the way home, I shot, besides florikan, and guinea-chicks, a wonderful goat-sucker, remarkable for the exceeding length of some of its feathers floating out far beyond the rest in both wings. Returning home, I found the men who had charge of the dead buck all in a state of excitement; they no sooner removed his carcass, than two lions came out of the jungle and lapped his blood. All the Waganda ran away at once; but my braves feared my anger more than the lions, and came off safely with the buck on their shoulders.

July 23rd. Three boats arrived, like those used on the Murchison Creek, and when I demanded the rest, as well as a decisive answer about going to Kamrasi's, the acting Mkungŭ said he was afraid accidents might happen, and he would not take me. Nothing would frighten this pig-headed creature into compliance, though I told him I had arranged with the king to make the Nile the channel of communication with England. I therefore applied to him for guides to conduct me up the river, and ordered Bombay and Kasoro to obtain fresh orders from the king, as all future Wazungŭ, coming to Uganda to visit or trade, would prefer the passage by the river. I shot another buck in the evening, as the Waganda love their skins, and also a load of guinea-fowl—three, four, and five at a shot—as Kasoro and his boys prefer them to anything.

July 24th. The acting officer absconded, but another man came in his place, and offered to take us on the way up the river tomorrow, humbugging Kasoro into the belief that his road to the palace would branch off from the first stage, though in reality it was here. The Mkungŭ's women brought *pombé*, and spent the day gazing at us, till, in the evening, when I took up my rifle, one ran after Bana to see him shoot, and followed like a man; but the only sport she got was on an ant-hill, where she fixed herself some time, popping into her mouth and devouring the white ants as fast as they emanated from their cells—for, disdaining does, I missed the only *pongo* buck I got a shot at in my anxiety to show the fair one what she came for.

I marched up the left bank of the Nile at a considerable distance from the water, to the Isamba Rapids, passing through rich jungle and plantain-gardens. Nango, an old friend, and district officer of the place, first refreshed us with a dish of plantain-squash and dried fish, with *pombé*. He told us he is often threatened by elephants, but he sedulously keeps them off with charms; for if they ever tasted a plantain they would never leave the garden until they had cleared it out. He then took us to see the nearest falls of the Nile—extremely beautiful, but very confined. The water ran deep between its banks, which were covered with fine grass, soft cloudy acacias, and festoons of lilac convolvuli; whilst here and there, where the land had slipped above the rapids, bared places of red earth could be seen, like that of Devonshire; there, too, the waters, impeded by a natural dam, looked like a huge mill-pond, sullen and dark, in which two crocodiles, laving about, were looking out for prey. From the high banks we looked down upon a line of sloping wooded islets lying across the stream, which divide its waters, and, by interrupting them, cause at once dam and rapids. The whole was more fairy-like, wild, and romantic than—I must confess that my thoughts took that shape—anything I ever saw outside of a theatre. It was exactly the sort of place, in fact, where, bridged across from one side-slip to the other, on a moonlight night, brigands would assemble to enact some dreadful tragedy.

Even the Wangŭana seemed spellbound at the novel beauty of the sight, and no one thought of moving till hunger warned us night was setting in, and we had better look out for lodgings.

Start again, and after drinking *pombé* with Nango, when we heard that three Wakungŭ had been seized at Kari, in consequence of the murder, the march was commenced, but soon after stopped by the mischievous machinations of our guide, who pretended it was too late in the day to cross the jungles on ahead, either by the road to the source or the palace, and therefore would not move till the morning; then, leaving us, on the pretext of business, he vanished, and was never seen again. A small black fly, with thick shoulders and bullet head, infests the place, and torments the naked arms and legs of the people with its sharp stings to an extent that must render life miserable to them.

After a long struggling march, plodding through huge grasses and jungle, we reached a district which I cannot otherwise describe than by calling it a "Church Estate." It is dedicated in some mysterious manner to Lŭbari (Almighty), and although the king appeared to have authority over some of the inhabitants of it, yet others had apparently a sacred character, exempting them from the civil power, and he had no right to dispose of the land itself. In this territory there are small villages only at every fifth mile, for there is no road, and the lands run high again, whilst, from want of a guide, we often lost the track.

At last, with a good push for it, crossing hills and threading huge grasses, as well as extensive village plantations lately devastated by elephants—they had eaten all that was eatable, and what would not serve for food they had destroyed with their trunks, not one plantain or one hut being left entire—we arrived at the extreme end of the journey, the farthest point ever visited by the expedition on the same parallel of latitude as King Mtésa's palace, and just forty miles east of it.

We were well rewarded; for the "stones," as the Waganda call the falls, was by far the most interesting sight I had seen in Africa. Everybody ran to see them at once, though the march had been long and fatiguing, and even my sketch-block was called into play. Though beautiful the scene was not exactly what I expected; for the broad surface of the lake was shut out from view by a spur of hill, and the falls, about 12 feet deep, and 400 to 500 feet broad, were broken by rocks. Still it was a sight that attracted one to it for hours—the roar of the waters, the thousands of passenger-fish, leaping at the falls with all their might; the Wasoga and Waganda fishermen coming out in boats and taking post on all the rocks with rod and hook, hippopotami and crocodiles lying sleepily on the water, the ferry at work above the falls, and cattle driven down to drink at the margin of the lake—made, in all, with the pretty nature of the country—small hills, grassy-topped, with trees in the folds, and gardens on the lower slopes—as interesting a picture as one could wish to see.

The expedition had now performed its functions. I saw that old father Nile without any doubt rises in the Victoria N'yanza, and, as I had foretold, that lake is the great source of the holy river which cradled the first expounder of our religious belief.

HOW A MAN AND A DONKEY CAME TO CHEYLARD [1]

(1878)

ROBERT LOUIS STEVENSON

(1850-94)

It was two o'clock in the afternoon before I got my journal written up and my knapsack repaired, for I was determined to carry my knapsack in future and have no more ado with baskets; and half an hour afterwards I set out for Le Cheylard l'Évêque, a place on the borders of the forest of Mercoire. A man, I was told, should walk there in an hour and a half; and I thought it scarce too ambitious to suppose that a man encumbered with a donkey might cover the same distance in four hours.

All the way up the long hill from Langogne it rained and hailed alternately; the wind kept freshening steadily, although slowly; plentiful hurrying clouds—some dragging veils of straight rain-shower, others massed and luminous as though promising snow—careered out of the north and followed me along my way. I was soon out of the cultivated basin of the Allier, and away from the ploughing oxen, and such-like sights of the country. Moor, heathery marsh, tracts of rock and pines, woods of birch all jewelled with the autumn yellow, here and there a few naked cottages and bleak fields,—these were the characters of the country. Hill and valley followed valley and hill; the little green and stony cattle-tracks wandered in and out of one another, split into three or four, died away in marshy hollows, and began again sporadically on hillsides or at the borders of a wood.

There was no direct road to Cheylard, and it was no easy affair to make a passage in this uneven country and through this intermittent labyrinth of tracks. It must have been about four when I struck Sagnerousse, and went on

[1] From *Travels with a Donkey in the Cévennes.*

my way rejoicing in a sure point of departure. Two hours afterwards, the dusk rapidly falling, in a lull of the wind, I issued from a fir-wood where I had long been wandering, and found, not the looked-for village, but another marish bottom among rough-and-tumble hills. For some time past I had heard the ringing of cattle-bells ahead; and now, as I came out of the skirts of the wood, I saw near upon a dozen cows and perhaps as many more black figures, which I conjectured to be children, although the mist had almost unrecognizably exaggerated their forms. These were all silently following each other round and round in a circle, now taking hands, now breaking up with chains and reverences. A dance of children appeals to very innocent and lively thoughts; but, at night-fall on the marshes, the thing was eerie and fantastic to behold. Even I, who am well enough read in Herbert Spencer, felt a sort of silence fall for an instant on my mind. The next I was pricking Modestine forward, and guiding her like an unruly ship through the open. In a path, she went doggedly ahead of her own accord, as before a fair wind; but once on the turf or among heather, and the brute became demented. The tendency of lost travellers to go round in a circle was developed in her to the degree of passion, and it took all the steering I had in me to keep even a decently straight course through a single field.

While I was thus desperately tacking through the bog, children and cattle began to disperse, until only a pair of girls remained behind. From these I sought direction on my path. The peasantry in general were but little disposed to counsel a wayfarer. One old devil simply retired into his house, and barricaded the door on my approach; and I might beat and shout myself hoarse, he turned a deaf ear. Another, having given me a direction which, as I found afterwards, I had misunderstood, complacently watched me going wrong without adding a sign. He did not care a stalk of parsley if I wandered all night upon the hills! As for these two girls, they were a pair of impudent sly sluts, with not a thought but mischief. One put out her tongue at me, the other bade me follow the cows, and they both giggled and jogged each other's elbows. The Beast of Gévaudan ate about a hundred children of this district; I began to think of him with sympathy.

Leaving the girls, I pushed on through the bog, and got into another wood and upon a well-marked road. It grew darker and darker. Modestine, suddenly beginning to smell mischief, bettered the pace of her own accord, and from that time forward gave me no trouble. It was the first sign of intelligence I had occasion to remark in her. At the same time, the wind freshened into half a gale, and another heavy discharge of rain came flying up out of the north. At the other side of the wood I sighted some red windows in the dusk. This was the hamlet of Fouzilhic; three houses on a hillside, near a wood of birches. Here I found a delightful old man, who came a little way with me in the rain to put me safely on the road for Cheylard. He would hear of no reward, but shook his hands above his head almost as if in menace, and refused volubly and shrilly, in unmitigated *patois*.

All seemed right at last. My thoughts began to turn upon dinner and a fireside, and my heart was agreeably softened in my bosom. Alas, and I was on the brink of new and greater miseries. Suddenly, at a single swoop, the night fell. I have been abroad in many a black night, but never in a blacker. A glimmer of rocks, a glimmer of the track where it was well beaten, a certain fleecy density, or night within night, for a tree—this was all that I could discriminate. The sky was simply darkness overhead; even the flying clouds pursued their way invisibly to human eyesight. I could not distinguish my hand at arm's-length from the track, nor my goad, at the same distance, from the meadows or the sky.

Soon the road that I was following split, after the fashion of the country, into three or four in a piece of rocky meadow. Since Modestine had shown such a fancy for beaten roads, I tried her instinct in this predicament. But the instinct of an ass is what might be expected from the name; in half a minute she was clambering round and round among some boulders, as lost a donkey as you would wish to see. I should have camped long before had I been properly provided; but as this was to be so short a stage, I had brought no wine, no bread for myself, and little over a pound for my lady friend. Add to this, that I and Modestine were both handsomely wetted by the showers. But now, if I could have found some water, I should have camped at once in spite of all. Water, however, being entirely absent, except in the form of rain, I determined to return to Fouzilhic, and ask a guide a little farther on my way—"a little farther lend thy guiding hand."

The thing was easy to decide, hard to accomplish. In this sensible roaring blackness I was sure of nothing but the direction of the wind. To this I set my face. The road had disappeared, and I went across country, now in marshy opens, now baffled by walls unscalable to Modestine, until I came once more in sight of some red windows. This time they were differently disposed. It was not Fouzilhic, but Fouzilhac, a hamlet little distant from the other in space, but worlds away in the spirit of its inhabitants. I tied Modestine to a gate, and groped forward, stumbling among rocks, plunging mid-leg in bog, until I gained the entrance of the village. In the first lighted house there was a woman who would not open to me. She could do nothing, she cried to me through the door, being alone and lame; but if I would apply at the next house, there was a man who could help me if he had a mind.

They came to the next door in force, a man, two women, and a girl, and brought a pair of lanterns to examine the wayfarer. The man was not ill-looking, but had a shifty smile. He leaned against the doorpost, and heard me state my case. All I asked was a guide as far as Cheylard.

"*C'est que, voyez-vous, il fait noir,*" said he.

I told him that was just my reason for requiring help.

"I understand that," said he, looking uncomfortable; "*mais—c'est—de la peine.*"

I was willing to pay, I said. He shook his head. I rose as high as ten francs; but he continued to shake his head.

"Name your own price, then," said I.

"*Ce n'est pas ça,*" he said at length, and with evident difficulty; "but I am not going to cross the door—*mais je ne sortirai pas de la porte.*"

I grew a little warm, and asked him what he proposed that I should do.

"Where are you going beyond Cheylard?" he asked by way of answer.

"That is no affair of yours," I returned, for I was not going to indulge his bestial curiosity; "it changes nothing in my present predicament."

"*C'est vrai, ça,*" he acknowledged with a laugh; "*oui, c'est vrai. Et d'où venez-vous?*"

A better man than I might have felt nettled.

"Oh," said I, "I am not going to answer any of your questions, so you may spare yourself the trouble of putting them. I am late enough already; I want help. If you will not guide me yourself, at least help me to find someone else who will."

"Hold on," he cried suddenly. "Was it not you who passed in the meadow while it was still day?"

"Yes, yes," said the girl, whom I had not hitherto recognized; "it was monsieur; I told him to follow the cows."

"As for you, mademoiselle," said I, "you are a *farceuse.*"

"And," added the man, "what the devil have you done to be still here?"

What the devil, indeed! But there I was.

"The great thing," said I, "is to make an end of it"; and once more proposed that he should help me to find a guide.

"*C'est que,*" he said again, "*c'est que—il fait noir.*"

"Very well," said I; "take one of your lanterns."

"No," he cried, drawing a thought backward, and again intrenching himself behind one of his former phrases; "I will not cross the door."

I looked at him. I saw unaffected terror struggling on his face with unaffected shame; he was smiling pitifully and wetting his lip with his tongue, like a detected schoolboy. I drew a brief picture of my state, and asked him what I was to do.

"I don't know," he said; "I will not cross the door."

Here was the Beast of Gévaudan, and no mistake.

"Sir," said I, with my most commanding manners, "you are a coward."

And with that I turned my back upon the family party, who hastened to retire within their fortifications; and the famous door was closed again, but not till I had overheard the sound of laughter. *Filia barbara pater barbarior.* Let me say it in the plural: the Beasts of Gévaudan.

The lanterns had somewhat dazzled me, and I ploughed distressfully among stones and rubbish-heaps. All the other houses in the village were both dark and silent; and though I knocked at here and there a door, my knocking was unanswered. It was a bad business; I gave up Fouzilhac with my curses. The rain had stopped, and the wind, which still kept rising, began to dry my coat and trousers. "Very well," thought I, "water or no water, I must camp." But the first thing was to return to Modestine. I am pretty sure I was twenty minutes groping for my lady in the dark; and if it had not been for the unkindly services of the bog, into which I once more stumbled, I might have still been groping for her at the dawn. My next business was to gain the shelter of a wood, for the wind was cold as well as boisterous. How, in this well-wooded district, I should have been so long in finding one, is another of the insoluble mysteries of this day's adventures; but I will take my oath that I put near an hour to the discovery.

At last black trees began to show upon my left, and, suddenly crossing the road, made a cave of unmitigated blackness right in front. I call it a cave without exaggeration; to pass below that arch of leaves was like entering a dungeon. I felt about until my hand encountered a stout branch, and to this I tied Modestine, a haggard, drenched, desponding donkey. Then I lowered my pack, laid it along the wall on the margin of the road, and unbuckled the straps. I knew well enough where the lantern was; but where were the candles? I groped and groped among the tumbled articles, and, while I was thus groping, suddenly I touched the spirit-lamp. Salvation! This would serve my turn as well. The wind roared unwearyingly among the trees; I could hear the boughs tossing and the leaves churning through half a mile of forest; yet the scene of my encampment was not only as black as the pit, but admirably sheltered. At the second match the wick caught flame. The light was both livid and shifting; but it cut me off from the universe, and doubled the darkness of the surrounding night.

I tied Modestine more conveniently for herself, and broke up half the black bread for her supper, reserving the other half against the morning. Then I gathered what I should want within reach, took off my wet boots and gaiters, which I wrapped in my waterproof, arranged my knapsack for a pillow under the flap of my sleeping bag, insinuated my limbs into the interior, and buckled myself in like a *bambino.* I opened a tin of Bologna sausage and broke a cake of chocolate, and that was all I had to eat. It may sound offensive, but I ate them together, bite by bite, by way of bread and meat. All I had to wash down this revolting mixture was neat brandy; a revolting beverage in itself. But I was rare and hungry; ate well, and smoked one of the best cigarettes in my experience. Then I put a stone in my straw hat, pulled the flap of my fur cap over my neck and eyes, put my revolver ready to my hand, and snuggled well down among the sheepskins.

I questioned at first if I were sleepy, for I felt my heart beating faster than usual, as if with an agreeable excitement to which my mind remained a stranger. But as soon as my eyelids touched, that subtle glue leaped between them, and they would no more come separate. The wind among the trees was my lullaby. Sometimes it sounded for minutes together with a steady, even rush, not rising nor abating; and again it would swell and burst like a great crashing breaker, and the trees would patter me all over with big drops from the rain of the afternoon. Night after night, in my own bedroom in the country, I have given ear to this perturbing concert of the wind among the woods; but whether it was a difference in the trees, or the lie of the ground, or because I was myself outside and in the midst of it, the fact remains that the wind sang to a different tune among these woods of Gévaudan. I hearkened and hearkened; and meanwhile sleep took gradual possession of my body and subdued my thoughts and senses; but still my last waking effort was to listen and distinguish, and my last conscious state was one of wonder at the foreign clamour in my ears.

Twice in the course of the dark hours—once when a stone galled me underneath the sack, and again when the poor patient Modestine, growing angry, pawed and stamped upon the road—I was recalled for a brief while to consciousness, and saw a star or two overhead, and the lace-like edge of the foliage against the sky. When I awoke for the third time (Wednesday, September 25th), the world was flooded with a blue light, the mother of the dawn. I saw the leaves labouring in the wind and the ribbon of the road; and, on turning my head, there was Modestine tied to a beech, and standing half across the path in an attitude of inimitable patience. I closed my eyes again, and set to thinking over the experience of the night. I was surprised to find how easy and pleasant it had been, even in this tempestuous weather. The stone which annoyed me would not have been there, had I not been forced to camp blindfold in the opaque night; and I had felt no other inconvenience, except when my feet encountered the lantern or the second volume of Peyrat's *Pastors of the Desert* among the mixed contents of my sleeping-bag; nay, more, I had felt not a touch of cold, and awakened with unusually lightsome and clear sensations.

With that, I shook myself, got once more into my boots and gaiters, and, breaking up the rest of the bread for Modestine, strolled about to see in what part of the world I had awakened. Ulysses, left on Ithaca, and with a mind unsettled by the goddess, was not more pleasantly astray. I have been after an adventure all my life, a pure dispassionate adventure, such as befell early and heroic voyagers; and thus to be found by morning in a random woodside nook in Gévaudan—not knowing north from south, as strange to my surroundings as the first man upon the earth, an inland castaway—was to find a fraction of my daydreams realized. I was on the skirts of a little wood of birch, sprinkled with a few beeches; behind, it adjoined another wood of fir; and in front, it broke up and went down in open order into a shallow and meadowy dale. All around there were bare hilltops, some near, some far away, as the perspective closed or opened, but none apparently much higher than the rest. The wind huddled the trees. The golden specks of autumn in the birches tossed shiveringly. Overhead the sky was full of strings and shreds of vapour, flying, vanishing, reappearing, and turning about an axis like tumblers, as the wind hounded them through heaven. It was wild weather and famishing cold. I ate some chocolate, swallowed a mouthful of brandy, and smoked a cigarette before the cold should have time to disable my fingers. And by the time I had got all this done, and had made my pack and bound it on the pack-saddle, the day was tiptoe on the threshold of the east. We had not gone many steps along the lane before the sun, still invisible to me, sent a glow of gold over some cloud mountains that lay ranged along the eastern sky.

The wind had us on the stern, and hurried us bitingly forward. I buttoned myself into my coat, and walked on in a pleasant frame of mind with all men, when suddenly, at a corner, there was Fouzilhic once more in front of me. Nor only that, but there was the old gentleman who had escorted me so far the night before, running out of his house at sight of me, with hands upraised in horror.

"My poor boy!" he cried, "what does this mean?"

I told him what had happened. He beat his old hands like clappers in a mill, to think how lightly he had let me go; but when he heard of the man of Fouzilhac anger and depression seized upon his mind.

"This time, at least," said he, "there shall be no mistake."

And he limped along, for he was very rheumatic, for about half a mile, and until I was almost within sight of Cheylard, the destination I had hunted for so long.

IN DARKEST AFRICA [1]

(1887)

SIR H. M. STANLEY

(1841-1904)

[*Emin Pasha, Governor of the equatorial province of the Sudan, having been isolated by the Mahdist rising of 1881-85, Stanley in 1887 led an expedition to his relief. On June 15 he reached Yambuya; there he left his rearguard, and on the 28th set out with the advance guard.*]

An African road generally is a foot-track tramped by travel to exceeding smoothness and hardness as of asphalt when the season is dry. It is only twelve inches wide from the habit of the natives to travel in single file one after another. When such a track is old it resembles a winding and shallow gutter, the centre has been trodden oftener than the sides—rain-water has rushed along and scoured it out somewhat—the sides of the path have been raised by humus and dust, the feet of many passengers have brushed twigs and stones and pressed the dust aside. A straight path would be shorter than the usual one formed by native travel by a third in every mile on an average. This is something like what we hoped to meet in defiling out of the gate of the entrenched camp at Yambuya, because during four preceding expeditions into Africa we had never failed to follow such a track for hundreds of miles. Yambuya consisted of a series of villages. Their inhabitants must have neighbours to the Eastward as well as to the Southward or Westward. Why not?

We marched out of the gate, company after company in single file. Each with its flag, its trumpeter or drummer, each with its detail of supernumeraries, with fifty picked men as advance guard to handle the bill-hook and axe, to cut saplings, 'blaze,' or peel a portion of the bark of a tree a hand's-breadth, to sever the leaves and slash at the rattan, to remove all obtrusive branches that might interfere with the free passage of the hundreds of loaded porters,

[1] From *In Darkest Africa.*

to cut trees to lay across streams for their passage, to form zeribas or bomas of bush and branch around the hutted camp at the end of the day's travel. The advance guard are to find a path, or, if none can be found, to choose the thinnest portions of the jungle and tunnel through without delay, for it is most fatiguing to stand in a heated atmosphere with a weighty load on the head. If no thinner jungle can be found, then through anything, however impenetrable it may appear; they must be brisk—"chap-chap"—as we say, or an ominous murmur will rise from the impatient carriers behind. They must be clever and intelligent in wood-craft; a green-horn, or as we call him 'goee-goee,' must drop his bill-hook, and take the bale or box. Three hundred weary fellows are not to be trifled with, they must be brave also—quick to repel assault—arrows are poisonous, spears are deadly—their eyes must be quick to search the gloom and shade, with sense alert to recognition, and ready to act on the moment. Dawdlers and goee-goees are unbearable; they must be young, lithe, springly—my 300 behind me have no regard for the ancient or the corpulent—they would be smothered with chaff and suffocated with banter. Scores of voices would cry out, "Wherein lies this fellow's merit? It is all in his stomach? Nay, it is in his wooden back—tut—his head is too big for a scout. He has clearly been used to hoeing. What does the field-hand want on the Continent? You may see he is only a Banian slave! Nay, he is only a Consul's freed man! Bosh! he is a mission boy!" Their bitter tongues pierce like swords through the armour of stupidity, and the bill-hooks with trenchant edges are wielded most manfully, and the bright keen axes flash and sever the saplings, or slice a broad strip of bark from a tree, and the bush is pierced, and the jungle gapes open, and fast on their heels continuously close presses the mile-long caravan.

This is to be the order, and this the method of the march, and I have stood observing the files pass by until the last of the rear-guard is out of the camp, and the Major and Jameson and the garrison next crowd out to exchange the farewell.

"Now, Major, my dear fellow, we are in for it. Neck or nothing! Remember your promise, and we shall meet before many months."

"I vow to goodness. I shall be after you sharp. Let me once get those fellows from Bolobo and nothing shall stop me."

"Well, then, God bless you—keep a stout heart—and Jameson—old man—the same to you."

Captain Nelson, who heard all this, stepped up in his turn to take a parting grasp, and I strode on to the front, while the Captain placed himself at the head of the rear-guard.

The column had halted at the end of the villages or rather the road that Nelson the other day had commenced.

"Which is the way, guide?" I asked to probably the proudest soul in the column—for it is a most exalted position to be at the head of the line. He was in a Greekish costume, with a Greekish helmet *à la* Achilles.

"This, running towards the sunrise," he replied.

"How many hours to the next village?"

"God alone knows," he answered.

"Know ye not one village or country beyond here?"

"Not one; how should I?" he asked.

This amounted to what the wisest of us knew.

"Well, then, set on in the name of God, and God be ever with us. Cling to any track that leads by the river until we find a road."

"Bismillah!" echoed the pioneers, the Nubian trumpets blew the signal of "move on" and shortly the head of the column disappeared into the thick bush beyond the utmost bounds of the clearings of Yambuya.

This was on the 28th day of June, and until the 5th of December, for 160 days, we marched through the forest, bush and jungle, without ever having seen a bit of greensward of the size of a cottage chamber floor. Nothing but miles and miles, endless miles of forest, in various stages of growth and various degrees of altitude, according to the ages of the trees, with varying thickness of undergrowth according to the character of the trees which afforded thicker or slighter shade: . . . an absolutely unknown region opened to the gaze and knowledge of civilized man for the first time since the waters disappeared and were gathered into the seas, and the earth became dry land. . . . With the temperature of 86° in the shade we travelled along a path very infrequently employed, which wound under dark depths of bush. It was a slow process, interrupted every few minutes by the tangle. The bill-hooks and axes, plied by fifty men, were constantly in requisition; the creepers were slashed remorselessly, lengths of track one hundred yards or so were as fair as similar extents were difficult.

At noon we looked round the elbow of the Aruwimi, which is in view of Yambuya, and saw above, about four miles, another rapid with its glancing waters as it waved in rollers in the sunshine; the rapids of Yambuya were a little below us. Beneath the upper rapids quite a fleet of canoes hovered about it. There was much movement and stir, owing, of course, to the alarm that the Yambuyas had communicated to their neighbours. At 4 P.M. we observed that the point we had gazed at abreast of the rapids consisted of islands. These were now being crowded with the women and children of Yankondé, whom as yet we had not seen. About a hundred canoes formed in the stream crowded with native warriors, and followed the movements of the column as it appeared and disappeared in the light and into the shadows, jeering, mocking, and teasing.

The head of the column arrived at the foot of a broad cleared road, twenty feet wide and three hundred yards long, and at the farther end probably three hundred natives of the town of Yankondé stood gesticulating, shouting, with drawn bows in their hands. In all my experience of Africa I had seen nothing of this kind. The pioneers halted, reflecting, and remarking somewhat after this manner: "What does this mean? The pagans have carved a broad highway out of the bush to their town for us, and yet there they are at the other end, ready for a fight! It is a trap, lads, of some kind, so look sharp."

With the bush they had cut they had banked and blocked all passage to the forest of either side of the road for some distance. But, with fifty pairs of sharp eyes searching around above and below, we were not long in finding that this apparent highway through the bush bristled with skewers six inches long sharpened at both ends, which were driven into the ground half their length, and slightly covered with green leaves so carelessly thrown over them that we had thought at first these strewn leaves were simply the effect of clearing bush.

Forming two lines of twelve men across the road, the first line was ordered to pick out the skewers, the second line was ordered to cover the workers with their weapons, and at the first arrow shower to fire. A dozen scouts were sent on either flank of the road to make their way into the village through the woods. We had scarcely advanced twenty yards along the cleared way before volumes of smoke broke out of the town, and a little cloud of arrows came towards us, but falling short. A volley was returned, the skewers were fast being picked out, and an advance was steadily made until we reached the village at the same time that the scouts rushed out of the underwood, and as all the pioneers were pushed forward the firing was pretty lively, under cover of which the caravan pressed through the burning town to a village at its eastern extremity, as yet unfired. . . .

It was nearly 9 P.M. before the rear-guard entered camp. Throughout the night the usual tactics were resorted to by the savages to create alarm and disturbance, such as vertically dropping assegais and arrows heavily tipped with poison, with sudden cries, whoops, howls, menaces, simultaneous blasts of horn-blowing from different quarters, as though a general attack was about to be made. Strangers unacquainted with the craftiness of these forest satyrs might be pardoned for imagining that daylight only was required for our complete extermination. Some of these tactics I knew before in younger days, but there was still something to be gleaned from the craft of these pure pagans. The camp was surrounded by sentries, and the only orders given were to keep strict silence and sharpen their eyesight. . . .

We wandered about for ten minutes or so looking for a track next morning, and at last discovered one leading through a vast square mileage of manioc fields, and at the little village of Bahunga, four miles S.E. of Yankondé, we gladly rested, our object being not to rush at first setting out after a long river voyage, but to accustom the people little by little to the long journey before them.

On the 30th we lit on a path which connected a series of fourteen villages, each separate and in line, surrounded by their respective fields, luxuriant with crops of manioc, or, as some call it, the cassava. We did not fail to observe, however, that some disaster had occurred many months before, judging from the traces. The villages we passed through were mostly newly built, in the sharp, conical—candle-extinguisher—or rather four-angled spiry type; burnt poles, ruins of the former villages, marked the sites of former dwellings. Here and there were blazings on trees, and then I knew that Arabs and Manyuema must have visited here—probably Tippu-Tib's brother.

The following day our march was through a similar series of villages, twelve in number, with a common, well-trodden track running from one to another. In this distance sections of the primeval forest separated each village; along the track were pitfalls for some kind of large forest game, or bow-traps fixed for small animals, such as rabbits, squirrels, rats, small monkeys. In the neighbourhood of each village the skewers were plentiful in the ground, but as yet no hurt had been received from them.

Another serious inconvenience of forest travel was experienced on this day. Every fifty yards or so a great tree, its diameter breast high, lay prostrate across the path over which the donkeys had to be assisted with a frequency that was becoming decidedly annoying. Between twenty and fifty of these had to be climbed over by hundreds of men, not all of whom were equally expert at this novel travelling, and these obstructions by the delays thus occasioned began to be complained of as very serious impediments. The main approaches to the many villages were studded with these poisoned skewers, which made every one except the booted whites tread most gingerly. Nor could the Europeans be altogether indifferent, for, slightly leaning, the skewer was quite capable of piercing the thickest bootleather and burying the splinters of its head deep in the foot—an agony of so dreadful a nature that was worth the trouble of guarding against.

At 3 P.M. we camped near some pools overhung by water-lilies far removed from a village, having had three wounded during the traverse through the settlements.

This morning, about three hours before dawn, the camp was wakened by howls, and loud and continued horn-blowing. These were shortly after hushed, and the voices of two men were heard so clear and distinct that many like myself attempted to pierce the intense darkness in the vain effort to see these midnight orators.

The first Speaker said, "Hey, strangers, where are you going?"

The Parasite echoed, "Where are you going?"

Speaker. This country has no welcome for you.

Parasite. No welcome for you.

Speaker. All men will be against you.

Parasite. Against you.

Speaker. And you will be surely slain.

Parasite. Surely slain.

Speaker. Ah-ah-ah-ah-ah-aah.

Parasite. Ah-ah-aaah.

Speaker. Ooh-ooh-ooh-ooh-ooooh.

Parasite. Ooh-ooh-ooooooh.

This parasite was such a palpable parasite, with such a sense of humour—that it raised such a chorus of laughter so sudden, startling, and abrupt, that scared speaker and parasite away in precipitate haste.

At dawn of the 2nd, feeling somewhat uneasy at the fact that the track which brought us to these pools was not made by man but by elephants, and feeling certain that the people had made no provision of food beyond the day, I sent 200 men back to the villages to procure each a load of manioc. By the manner these men performed this duty, the reflection came into my mind that they had little or no reasoning faculties, and that not a half of the 389 people then in the camp would emerge out of Africa. They were now brimful of life and vitality—their rifles were perfect, their accoutrements were new, and each possessed 10 rounds of cartridges. With a little care for their own selves and a small portion of prudence, there was no reason why they should not nearly all emerge safe and sound, but they were so crude, stolid, unreasoning, that orders and instructions were unheeded, except when under actual supervision, and, to supervise them effectually, I should require 100 English officers of similar intelligence and devotion to the four then with me. In the meantime they will lose their lives for trifles which a little sense would avoid, and until some frightful calamity overtakes them I shall never be able thoroughly to impress on their minds that to lose life foolishly is a crime.

A party of scouts were also sent ahead along the track to observe its general direction, and, about the same time that the foragers returned, the scouts returned, having captured six natives in the forest. They belonged to a tribe called the Babali, and were of a light chocolate in hue, and were found forming traps for game.

As we endeavoured to draw from them some information respecting the country to which the track led, they said, "We have but one heart. Don't you have two," which meant, Do not speak so fairly to us if you mean any harm to us, and like all natives they asserted strongly that they did not eat human meat, but that the custom was practised by the Babanda, Babali, Babukwa tribes, occupying the bank of the Aruwimi above Yankondé. . . .

After distributing the manioc, with an injunction to boil the roots three times in different waters, we resumed the march at 1 P.M. and camped at 4 o'clock.

The next day we left the track and struck through the huge towering forest and jungly undergrowth by compass. My position in this column was the third from the leader, so that I could direct the course. In order to keep a steady movement, even if slow, I had to instruct the cutters that each man as he walked should choose an obstructing Iliané, or obstrusive branch of bush, and give one sharp cut and pass on—the two head men were confining themselves to an effective and broad 'blaze' on the trees, every ten yards or so, for the benefit of the column, and, as the rear party would not follow us for perhaps two months, we were very particular that these 'blazes' should be quite a hand's-breadth peel of bark.

Naturally penetrating a trackless wild for the first time the march was at a funereal pace, in some places at the rate of 400 yards an hour, in other more open portions, that is of less undergrowth, we could travel at the rate of half, three-quarters, and even a mile per hour—so that from 6.30 A.M. to 11 A.M. when we halted for lunch and rest, and from 12.30 P.M. to 3 o'clock or 4 P.M. in from six to seven hours per day, we could make a march of about five miles. On the usual African track seen in other regions we could have gone from fourteen to eighteen miles during the same time. Therefore our object was to keep by settlements, not only to be assured of food, but in the hope of utilizing the native roads. We shall see later how we fared.

At 4 P.M. of this day we were still on the march, having passed through a wilderness of creeks, mud, thick scum-faced quagmires green with duck-weed into which we sank knee-deep, and the stench exhaled from the fetid slough was most sickening. We had just emerged out of this baneful stretch of marshy ground, intersected by lazy creeks and shallow long stream-shaped pools, when the forest became suddenly darkened, so dark that I could scarcely read the compass, and a distant murmur increasing into loud soughing and wrestling and tossing of branches and groaning of mighty trees warned us of the approach of a tempest. As the ground round about was most uninviting, we had to press on through the increasing gloom, and then, as the rain began to drip, we commenced to form camp. The tents were hastily pitched over the short scrubby bush, while bill-hooks crashed and axes rang, clearing a space for the camp. The rain was cold and heavily dripped, and every drop, large as a dollar on their cotton clothes, sent a shiver through the men. The thunder roared above, the lightning flashed a vivid light of fire through the darkness, and still the weary hungry caravan filed in until 9 o'clock. The rain was so heavy that fires could not be lit, and until three in the morning we sat huddled and crouching amid the cold, damp, and reeking exhalations and minute spray. Then bonfires were kindled, and around these scores of flaming pyramids the people sat, to be warmed into hilarious animation, to roast the bitter manioc, and to still the gnawing pain of their stomachs.

On the 4th we struck N. by E., and in an hour heard natives singing in concert afar off. We sent scouts ahead to ascertain what it meant. We presently heard firing which seemed to approach nearer. We mustered the men in the nearest company, stacked goods and deployed them as skirmishers. Then messengers came and reported that the scouts had struck the river, and, as they were looking upon it, a canoe advanced into view with its crew standing with drawn bows and fixed arrows, which were flown at them at once, and compelled the scouts to fire. We then resumed the march, and at 8 A.M. we were on the river again in time to see a line of native canoes disappearing round a bend on the opposite bank, and one canoe abandoned tied to the bank with a goat.

Observing that the river was calm and free from rapids, and desirous of saving the people from as much labour as circumstances would offer, the steel boat sections were brought up to the bank, and Mr Jephson, whose company had special charge of the *Advance*, commenced to fit the sections together. In an hour the forty-four burdens, which the vessel formed, had been attached together and fitted to their respective places and launched. As the boat weighed forty-four loads and had a capacity of fifty loads, and at least ten sick, we could then release ninety-eight people from the fatigue of bearing loads and carrying Lieutenant Stairs, who was still very ill. Mr Jephson and crew were despatched across river and the goat secured.

As the *Advance* was in the river, it was necessary for the column to cling to the bank, not only for the protection of the boat, but to be able to utilize the stream for lessening labour. Want of regular food, lack of variety, and its poor nutritive qualities, coupled with the urgency which drove us on, requiring long marches and their resulting fatigue, would soon diminish the strength of the stoutest. A due regard for the people therefore must be shown, and every means available for their assistance must be employed. Therefore, the boat keeping pace with the column, we travelled up-stream until 3 P.M. and camped.

On the 5th the boat and column moved up, as on the day previous, and made six-and-half miles. The river continued to be from 500 to 800 yards wide. The bank was a trifle more open than in the interior, though frequently it was impossible to move before an impenetrable mass of jungle had been tunnelled to allow our passage under the vault of close network of branch and climber, cane, and reed above. At 2.30 we reached the village of Bukanda. We had come across no track, but had simply burst out of the bush and a somewhat young forest with a clearing. In the middle of the clearing by the river side was the village. This fact made me think, and it suggested that if tracks were not discoverable by land, and as the people were not known to posses the power of aerial locomotion, that communication was maintained by water.

We had reason to rejoice at the discovery of a village, for since the 2nd the caravan subsisted on such tubers of manioc as each man took with him on that date. Had another day passed without meeting with a clearing we should have suffered from hunger.

It was evening before the boat appeared, the passage of rapids, and an adventure with a flotilla of eleven canoes had detained her. The canoes had been abandoned in consequence, and the commander of the boat had secured them to an island. One was reported to be a capacious hollow log, capable of carrying nearly as much as the boat. Since the river was the highway of the natives, we should be wise to employ the stream, by which we should save our men, and carry our sick as well as a reserve of food. For we had been narrowly brought to the verge of want on the last day, and we were utter strangers in a strange land, groping our way through darkness. The boat was sent back with an extra crew to secure the canoe and paddle her up to our camp.

Of course Bukanda had been abandoned long before we reached it—the village of cone huts was at our disposal—the field of manioc also. This custom also was unlike anything I had seen in Africa before. Previously the natives may have retired with their women, but the males had remained with spear and target, representing ownership. Here the very fowls had taken to flight. It was clearly a region unsuitable for the study of ethnology.

At noon of the 6th we defiled out of Bukanda refurnished with provisions, and two hours later were in camp in uninhabited space.

ACROSS THE SYRIAN DESERT [1]

(1911)

GERTRUDE BELL

(1868-1926)

DUMEIR

February 9th [*1911*]

WE'RE, off. And now I must tell you the course of the negotiations which preceded this journey. First as you know I went to the sons of Abdul Kadir and they called up Sheikh Muhammad Bassam and asked him to help me. I called on him the following evening. He said it was too early, the desert camels had not come in to Damascus, there was not a dulul (riding camel) to be had and I must send out to a village a few hours away and buy. This was discouraging, as I could not hope to get them for less than £ 15 apiece. I wanted five, and I should probably have to sell them for an old song at Hit. Next day Fattuh went down into the bazaar and came back with the news that he and Bassam between them had found an owner of camels ready to hire for £ 7 apiece. It was dear, but I closed with the offer. All the arrangements were made and I dispatched the caravan by the Palmyra road. Then followed misfortune. The snow closed down upon us, the desert post did not come in for three weeks, and till it came we were without a guide. Then Bassam invented another scheme. The old sheikh of Kubeisa near Hit (you know the place) was in Damascus and wanted to return home; he would journey with us and guide us. So all was settled again.

But the sheikh Muhammad en Nawan made continuous delays; we were helpless, for we could not cross the Syrian desert without a guide and still the post did not come in. The snow in the desert had been without parallel. At last Muhammad en Nawan was ready. I sent off my camels to Dumeir yesterday (it is the frontier village of the desert) and went myself to sleep at the English hospital, whence it was easier to slip off unobserved. For I am supposed to be travelling by Palmyra and Deir with four zaptiehs. This morning Fattuh and I drove here, it took us four hours, and the sheikh came on his dulul. The whole party is assembled in the house of a native of Kubeisa, I am lodged in

[1] From *The Letters of Gertrude Bell.*

a large, windowless room spread with felts, a camel is stabled at my door and over the way Fattuh is cooking my dinner. One has to put on clogs to walk across the yard, so inconceivably muddy it is, and in the village one can't walk at all, one must ride. I got in about one and lunched, after which I mounted my mare and went out to see some ruins a mile or two away. It was a big Roman fortified camp. And beyond it the desert stretched away to the horizon. That is where we go to-morrow. It's too heavenly to be back in all this again, Roman forts and Arab tents and the wide desert. . . . We have got for a guide the last desert postmen who came in three days ago, having been delayed nine days by the snow. His name is Ali.

SYRIAN DESERT
February 10th

There is in Dumeir a very beautiful temple, rather like one of the temples at Baalbek. As soon as the sun was up I went out and took some photographs of it, but I was ready long before one camels were loaded; the first day's packing is always a long business. Finally we got off soon after nine, a party of fifteen, myself, the sheikh, Fattuh, Ali and my four camel men, and the other seven merchants who are going across to the Euphrates to buy sheep. In half an hour we passed the little Turkish guard house which is the last outpost of civilisation and plunged into the wilderness. Our road lay before us over a flat expanse bounded to the N. by the range of barren hills that trend away to the N.E. and divide us from the Palmyran desert, and to the S. by a number of distant tells, volcanic I should think. I rode my mare all day, for I can come and go more easily upon her, but when we get into the heart of the desert I shall ride a camel. It's less tiring. Three hours from Dumeir we came to some water pools, which are dry in summer, and here we filled our skins, for where we are camping there is no water. There was a keen wind, rising sometimes into a violent storm which brought gusts of hail upon us, but fortunately it was behind us so that it did not do us much harm. Late in the afternoon another hailstorn broke over us and clearing away left the distant hills white with snow. We had come to a place where there was a little scrub which would serve as firewood, and here we camped under the lee of some rising ground. Our companions have three big Arab tents, open in front, and we our two English tents, and oddly enough we are quite warm in spite of the rain and cold wind. I don't know why it is that one seldom feels cold in the desert; perhaps because of the absence of damp. The stony, sandy ground never becomes muddy. A little grass is beginning to grow and as you look over the wide expanse in front of you it is almost green. The old sheikh is lamenting that we are not in a house in Damsacus (but I think one's first camp in the Hamar is worth a street full of houses). "By the head of your father!" he said, "how can you leave the garden of the world and come out into this wilderness?" Perhaps it does require explanation.

February 11th

But to-day's experiences will not serve to justify my attitude. When I went to bed a hurricane was blowing. I woke from time to time and heard the good Fattuh hammering in the tent pegs, and wondered if any tent would stand up in that gale and also what was going to happen next. About an hour before dawn Fattuh called me and asked whether I was cold. I woke in surprise and putting my hand out felt the waterproof valise that covered me wet with snow. "It is like the sea," cried Fattuh. Therefore I lighted a candle and saw that it had drifted into my tent a foot deep. I dug down, found my boots and hat and put them under the Wolsey valise; I had gone to bed as I stood, and put all my extra clothing under the valise for warmth, so that nothing had come to harm. At dawn Fattuh dragged out the waterproof sheet that covers the ground and with it most of the snow. The snow was lying in great drifts where the wind had blown it, it was banked up against our tents and those of the Arabs and every hour or so the wind brought a fresh storm upon us. We cleared it out of our tents and settled down to a day as little uncomfortable as we could manage to make it. . . .

February 12th

We have got into smooth waters at last. You can imagine what I felt like when I looked out of my tent before dawn and saw a clear sky and the snow almost vanished. But the cold! Everything in my tent was frozen stiff—yesterday's damp skirt was like a board, my gloves like iron, my sponges—well, I'll draw a veil over my sponges—I did not use them much. . . . I spent an hour trudging backwards and forwards over the forzen desert trying to pretend I was warm while the camels were loaded. The frozen tents took a world of time to pack—with frozen fingers too. We were off soon after eight, but for the first hour the wet desert was like a sheet of glass and the camels slipped about and fell down with much groaning and moaning. They are singularly unfitted to cope with emergencies. For the next hour we plodded over a slippery melting surface, for which they are scarcely better suited, then suddenly we got out of the snow zone and all was well. It got on to my camel and rode her for the rest of the day. She is the most charming of animals. You ride a camel with only a halter which you mostly tie loosely round the peak of your saddle. A tap with your camel switch on one side of her neck or the other tells her the direction you want her to go, a touch with your heels sends her on, but when you wish her to sit down you have to hit her lightly and often on the neck saying at the same time: "Kh kh kh kh," that's as near as I can spell it. The big soft saddle, the *shedad*, is so easy and comfortable that you never tire. You Ioll about and eat your lunch and observe the landscape through your glasses: you might almost sleep. So we swung on through an absolutely flat plain till past five, when we came to a shallow valley with low banks on either side, and here we camped. The name of the place is Aitha, there is a full moon and it is absolutely still except for the sound of the pounding of coffee beans in the tents of my travelling companions. I could desire nothing pleasanter.

February 13th

We were off soon after six. The sun rose gloriously half an hour later and we began to unfreeze. It is very cold riding on a camel, I don't know why unless it has to do with her extreme height. We rode on talking cheerfully of our various adventures till after ten which is the time when my companions lunch, so I lunch too. The camels were going rather languidly for they were thirsty, not having drunk since they left Damascus. They won't drink when it is very cold. But our guide, Ali, promised us some pools ahead, good water, he said. When we got there we found that some Arabs had camped not far off and nothing remained of the pools but trampled mud. . . . So we had to go searching round for another pool and at last we found one about a mile away with a very little water in it, but enough for the riding camels, my mare and our water skins. It is exceedingly muddy however. We got into camp about four not far from some Arab tents. . . . It is a wonderfully interesting experience this. Last night they all sat up half the night because my mare pricked her ears and they thought she heard robbers. They ran up the banks and cried out, "Don't come near! we have soldiers with us and camels." It seemed to me when I heard of it (I was asleep at the time) a very open deceit, but it seems to have served the purpose for the thief retired. As we rode this morning Ali detected hoof marks on the hard ground and was satisfied that it was the mare of our enemy.

February 14th

What I accuse them of is not that they choose to live differently from us: for my part I like that; but that they do their own job so very badly. . . . Everybody in the desert knows that camels frequently stray away while feeding, yet it occurs to no one to put a man to watch over them. No, when we get into camp they are just turned off to feed where they like and go where they will. Consequently yesterday at dusk four of our baggage camels were missing and a riding camel belonging to one of the Damascene sheep merchants and everyone had to turn out to look for them. I could not do anything so I did not bother and while I was dining the sheikh looked in and said our camels had come back—let us thank God! It is certain that no one else could claim any credit. But the riding camel was not to be found, nor had she come back when I was ready to start at 4.30 this morning. We decided to wait till dawn and that being two hours off and the temperature 30° I went to bed again and to sleep. At dawn there was no news of her, so we started, leaving word with some Arabs where we were gone. She has not yet appeared, nor do I think she will. I was very sorry for the merchant, who now goes afoot, and very much bored by the delay. For we can't make it up at the other end because the camels have to eat for at least two hours before sunset. They eat shik; so does my little mare, she being a native of the desert. At ten o'clock we came to some big water pools, carefully hollowed out "in the first days," said Ali, with the earth banked up high round them, but now half-filled with mud and the banks broken. Still they hold a good deal a water in the winter and the inhabitants of the desert for miles around were driving their sheep and camels there to drink. We too filled our water skins. We got into camp at three, near some Arab tents. The sheikh, a charming old man, has just paid us a long visit. We sat round Muhammad's coffee fire and talked. It was all the more cheerful because the temperature is now 46°—a blessed change from 26°. My sponges have unfrozen for the first time. We have got up into the high, flat plain which is the true Hamad, the Smooth, and the horizon from my tent door is as round as the horizon of the sea. The sharp, dry air is wonderfully delicious: I think every day of the Syrian desert must prolong your life by two years. Sheikh Muhammad had confided to me that he had three wives, one in Damascus, one in Kubeisa, and one in Bagdad, but the last he has not seen for twenty-three years. "She has grown old, oh lady—by the truth of God! and she never bore but one daughter."

February 15th

We were off at five this morning in bitter frost. Can you picture the singular beauty of these moonlit departures! the frail Arab tents falling one by one, leaving the camp-fires blazing into the night; the dark masses of the kneeling camels; the shrouded figures binding up the loads, shaking the ice from the water skins, or crouched over the hearth for a moment's warmth before mounting. "Yallah, yallah, oh, children!" cries the old sheikh, knocking the ashes out of his narghileh. "Are we ready?" So we set out across the dim wilderness, Sheikh Muhammad leading on his white dulul. The sky ahead reddens, and fades, the moon pales and in sudden splendour the sun rushes up over the rim of the world. To see with the eyes is good, but while I wonder and rejoice to look upon this primeval existence, it does not seem to be a new thing; it is familiar, it is a part of inherited memory. After an hour and a half of marching we came to the pool of Khafiyeh, and since there is no water for three days ahead we had to fill all our empty skins. But the pool was a sheet of ice, the water skins were frozen and needed careful handling—for if you unfold them they crack and break—and we lighted fire and set to work to thaw them and ourselves. I sent the slow baggage camels on, and with much labour we softened the skins and contrived to fill them. The sun was now up and a more barren prospect than it revealed you cannot imagine. The Hamad stretched in front of us, flat and almost absolutely bare; for several hours we rode over a wilderness of flints on which nothing grew. It was also the coldest day we have had, for the keen frosty wind blew straight into our faces. We stopped once to wait for the baggage camels and warmed ourselves at a bonfire meanwhile, and again we stopped for half an hour to lunch. We watched our shadows catch us up and march ahead of us as the sun sank westward and the three o'clock we pitched camp in the stony waste. Yet I can only tell you that we have spent a very pleasant day. The old sheikh never stops talking, bless him, he orders us all about when we pitch and break up camp, but as Fattuh and I know much more about the pitching of our tents than he does, we pay no attention. "Oh Fattuh," said I this evening when he had given us endless advice, "do you pity the wife in Bagdad?" "Effendim," said Fattuh, "she must be exceedingly at rest." Still, for my part I should be sorry not to see Sheikh Muhammad for twenty-three years.

February 16th

After I had gone to bed last night I heard Ali shouting to all whom it might concern: "We are English soldiers! English soldiers!" But there was no one to hear and the desert would have received with equal indifference the information that we were Roman legionaries. We came to the end of the inhospitable. Hamad to-day, and the desert is once more diversified by a slight rise and fall of the ground. It is still entirely waterless, so waterless that in the spring when the grass grows thick the Arabs cannot camp here. All along our way there is proof of former water storage—I should think Early Moslem, marking the Abbassid post road. The pools have been dug out and banked up, but they are now full of earth and there is very little water in them.

We are camped to-night in what is called a valley. It takes a practised eye to distinguish the valley from the mountain, the one is so shallow and the other so low. The valleys are often two miles wide and you can distinguish them best by the fact that there are generally more "trees" in them than on the heights. I have made great friends with one of the sheep merchants. His name is Muhiyyed Din. He is coming back in the spring over this road with his lambs. They eat as they go and travel four hours a day. "It must be a dull job," said I. "Eh wallah!" he replied, "but if the spring grass is good the master of the lambs rejoices to see them grow fat." He travels over the whole desert, here and in Mesopotamia, buying sheep and camels; to Nejd too, and to Egypt, and he tells me delightful tales of his adventures. What with one thing and another the eight or nine hours of camel riding a day are never dull. But Truth of God! the cold!

February 17th

We were running short of water this morning. The water difficulty has been enhanced by the cold. The standing pools are exceedingly shallow so that when there is an inch of ice over them little remains but mud; what the water is like that you scrape up under these conditions I leave to the imagination. Besides the mud it has a sharp acrid taste of skins after forty-eight hours in them—not unhealthy I believe, but neither is it pleasant. So it happened that we had to cut down rather to the south to-day instead of going to the well of Kara which we could not have reached this evening. Sheikh Muhammad was much agitated at this programme. He expected to find the camps of the tribes whom he knew at and near the well, and he feared that by coming to the south of them we might find ourselves upon the path of a possible raiding party of Arabs whom he did not know coming up from the south. Ali tried to reassure him, saying that the chances were against raiding parties (good, please God!) and that we were relying upon God. But the Sheikh was not to be comforted. "Life of God! what is this talk! To God is the command! we are in the Shamuyyeh where no one is safe—Face of God!" He is master of a wonderful variety of pious ejaculations. So we rode for an hour or two (until we forgot about it) carefully scanning the horizon for ghazus; it was just as well that we had this to occupy us, for the whole day's march was over ground as flat as a board. It had been excruciatingly cold in the early morning—but about midday the wind shifted round to the south and we began to feel the warmth of the sun. For the first time we shed our fur coats, and the lizards came out of their holes. Also the horizon was decorated with fantastic mirage which greatly added to the enjoyment of looking for ghazus. An almost imperceptible rise in the ground would from afar stand up above the solid earth as if it were the high back of a camel. We saw tents with men beside them pitched on the edge of mirage lakes and when at last we actually did come to a stretch of shallow water, it was a long time before I could believe that it was not imaginary. I saw how the atmospheric delusion worked by watching some gazelles. They galloped away over the plain just like ordinary gazelles, but when they came to the mirage they suddenly got up on to stilts and looked the size of camels. It is excessively bewildering to be deprived of the use of one's eyes in this way. We had a ten hours' march to reach the water by which we are camped. It lies in a wide shallow basin of mud, most of it is dried up, but a few pools remain in the deeper parts. The Arabs use some sort of white chalky stone—is it chalk?—to precipitate the mud. We have got some with us. We boil the water, powder the chalk and put it in and it takes nearly all the mud down to the bottom. Then we pour off the water.

February 18th

We were pursued all day by a mad wind which ended by bringing a shower of sleet upon us while we were getting into camp. In consequence of the inclemency of the weather I had the greatest difficulty in getting the sheikh and the camel drivers to leave their tents and they were still sitting over the coffee fire when we and the Damascene merchants were ready to start. Inspired of God I pulled out their tent pegs and brought their roof about their ears—to the great joy of all except those who were sitting under it. So we got off half an hour before dawn and after about an hour's riding dropped down off the smooth plain into an endless succession of hills and deep valleys—when I say *deep* they are about 200 feet deep and they all run north into the hollow plain of Kara. I much prefer this sort of country to the endless flat and it is quite interesting sitting a camel down a stony descent. The unspeakable devilish wind was fortunately behind us—Callupon the Prophet! but it did blow!

February 20th

We marched yesterday thirteen and a half hours without getting anywhere. We set off at five in a delicious still night with a temperature of 36—it felt quite balmy. The sun rose clear and beautiful as we passed through the gates of our valley into a wide low plain—we were to reach the Wady Hauran, which is the father of all valleys in this desert, in ten hours, and the little ruin of Muheiwir in half an hour more and there was to be plentiful clear water.

We were in good spirits, as you may imagine; the Sheikh sang songs of Nejd and Ali instructed me in all the desert roads. We rode on and on. At two o'clock I asked Ali whether it were two hours to Muheiwir? "More," said he. "Three?" said I. "Oh, lady, more." "Four?" I asked with a little sinking of heart. "Wallahi, not so much." We rode on over low hills and hollow plains. At five we dropped into the second of the valleys el Ud. By this time Fattuh and I were on ahead and Ali was anxiously scanning the landscape from every high rock. The Sheikh had sat down to smoke a narghileh while the baggage camels came up. "My lady," said Fattuh, "I do not think we shall reach water to-night." And the whole supply of water which we had was about a cupful in my flask. We went on for another half-hour down the valley and finally, in concert with Ali, selected a spot for a camp. It was waterless, but, said he, the water was not more than two hours off: he would take skins and fetch some, and meantime the starving camels would eat trees. But when the others came up, the Father of Camels, Abdullah, he from whom we hired our beasts, protested that he must have water to mix the camel meal that night (they eat a kind of dough), and rather against our better judgment we went on. We rode an hour farther, by which time it was pitch dark. Then Muhiyyed Din came up to me and said that if by chance we were to meet a ghazu in the dark night it might go ill with us. That there was reason in this was admitted by all; we dumped down where we stood, in spite of the darkness Fattuh had my tent up before you could wink, while I hobbled my mare and hunted among the camel loads for my bed. No one else put up a tent; they drew the camels together and under the shelter they gave made a fire of what trees they could find. Fattuh and I divided the water in my flask into two parts; with half we made some tea which he and I shared over some tinned meat and some bread; the other half we kept for the next morning when I shared it with the sheikh. We were none of us thirsty really; this weather does not make you thirsty. But my poor little mare had not drunk for two days, and she whinnied to everyone she saw. The last thing I heard before I went to sleep was the good Fattuh reasoning with her. "There is no water," he was saying. "There is none. Ma fi, ma fi." Soon after five he woke me up. I put on my boots, drank the tea he brought (having sent half to the poor old sheikh, who had passed the night under the lee of his camel) and went out into a cheerless daybreak. The sky was heavy with low-hanging clouds, the thermometer stood at 34, as we mounted our camels a faint and rather dismal glow in the east told us that the sun was rising. It was as well that we had not tried to reach water the night before. We rode to-day for six and a half hours before we got to rain pools in the Wady Hauran, and an hour more to Muheiwir and a couple of good wells in the valley bed. For the first four hours our way lay across barren levels; after a time we saw innumerable camels pasturing near the bare horizon and realized that we must be nearing the valley: there is no water anywhere but in the Hauran and all the tents of the Deleim are gathered near it. Then we began to descend through dry and stony water-courses and at midday found ourselves at the bottom of the great valley, and marched along the edge of a river of stones with a few rain pools lying in it. So we came to Muheiwir which is a small ruined fort, and here we found two men of the Deleim with a flock of sheep—the first men we have seen for four days. Their camp is about three miles away. Under the ruined fort there are some deep springs in the bed of the stream and by them we camped, feeling that we needed a few hours' rest after all our exertions. The sheikh had lighted his coffee fire while I was taking a first cursory view of the ruin. "Oh, lady," he cried, "honour us!" I sat down and drank a cup of coffee. "Where," said he, looking at me critically, "where is thy face in Damascus, and where thy face here?" And I am bound to say that his remark was not without justification. But after ten days of frost and wind and sun what would you have? The clouds have all cleared away—sun and water and ruins, the heart of man can desire no more. The sheikh salutes you.

February 21st

We got off at four this morning and made a twelve hours' stage. It was freezing a little when we started, the moon rode high upon the shoulder of the Scorpion and was not strong enough to extinguish him—this waning moon has done us great service. It took us two hours to climb up out of the Wady Hauran. I was talking to Muhiyyed Din when the sheikh came up, and said "Oh, lady, speech before dawn is not good." He was afraid of raising some hidden foe. Reckless courage is not his characteristic. We have camped under a low bank, selecting carefully the east side of it so that our camp fires can be seen only by the friendly Deleim to the east of us. We are nowhere to-night—just out in the open wilderness which has come to feel so homelike. Four of the sheep merchants left us yesterday hearing that the sheikhs with whom they deal were camped near at hand, for each man deals every year with the same sheikh. If you could see the western sky with the evening star burning in it, you would give thanks—as I do.

February 22nd

An hour's ride from our camp this morning brought us to the small desert fortress of Amej. . . . But Muhiyyed Din and the other sheep merchants found that their sheikhs were close at hand and we parted with much regret and a plentiful exchange of blessings. So we rode on till at four o'clock we reached the fortress of Khubbaz and here we have camped beneath the walls where Fattuh and I camped two years ago. It feels almost like returning home. It blew all day; I must own that the desert would be nicer if it were not so plagued with wind. The sheikh and Ali and one of the camel drivers sang trios for part of the afternoon to beguile the way. I have written down some of the sheikh's songs. They are not by him, however, but by the most famous of modern desert poets, the late Emir of Nejd.

February 23rd

The morning came grey and cheerless with an occasional scud of rain. We set off about six and took the familiar path across barren watercourses to Ain Zaza. The rain fell upon us and made heavy and sticky going, but it cleared before we reached the Ain and we lunched there and waited for the baggage camels till eleven. Kubeisa was only an hour and a half away, and it being so early I determined to refuse all the sheikh's pressing invitations that we should spend the night with him, and push on to Hit, three and a half hours farther. The baggage camels were informed of the change of plan and Fattuh and I rode on in high spirits at the thought of rejoining our caravan that evening. For you remember the caravan which we despatched from Damascus was to wait for us at Hit. But before we reached Kubeisa the rain came down again in torrents. Now the ground here is what the Arabs called *sabkha*, soft, crumbly salt marsh, sandy when it is dry and ready at a moment's notice to turn into a world of glutinous paste. This is what it did, and since camels cannot walk in mud I was presently aware of a stupendous downfall and found myself and my camel prostrate in the sticky glue. It feels like the end of the universe when your camel falls down. However we both rolled up unhurt and made the best of our way to the gates of Kubeisa. And here another misfortune awaited us. The rain was still falling, heavily, Abdullah, Father of Camels, declared that his beasts could not go on to Hit across a road all sabkha, and even Fattuh admitted that, tired and hungry as they were, it would be impossible. So in great triumph and with much praising of God, the sheikh conducted us to his house where I was seized by a pack of beautiful and very inquisitive women ("They are shameless!" said Fattuh indignantly) and conducted into the pitch-dark room on the ground floor which is the living-room. But the sheikh rescued me and took me upstairs to the reception room on the roof. Everyone we met fell on his neck and greeted him with a kiss on either cheek, and no sooner were we seated upstairs and a bonfire of trees lighted in the middle of the room, than all the worthies of Kubeisa began to assemble to greet him and hear the news. At the end they numbered at least fifty. Now this was the room in which I was supposed to eat and sleep—there was no other. I took Fattuh aside—or rather outside, for the room was packed to overflowing—and said "The night will be troublesome." Fattuh knitted his brows and without a word strode down the stairs. I returned to the company and when the room grew to smoky with trees and tobacco sat outside talking to the sheikh's charming son, Namân. The rain had stopped. My old acquaintances in Kubeisa had all been up to salute me and I sat by the fire and listened to the talk and prayed that Fattuh might find some means of escape. He was as resourceful as usual. After a couple of hours he returned and said, "With your permission, oh, Muhammad. We are ready." He had found a couple of camels and a donkey and we were off. So we took a most affectionate leave of the sheikh and left him to his narghileh. Half the town of Kubeisa, the female half, followed us through the streets, and we turned our faces to Hit. The two camels carried our diminished loads, Fattuh rode the donkey (it was so small that his feet touched the ground and he presently abandoned it in favour of one of the baggage camels and sent it back) and I was supposed to ride my mare. But she had a sore heel, poor little thing, and kept stumbling in the mud, so I walked most of the way. We left at 2.30 and had two and a half hours before sunset. The first part of our way was hard and dry; presently we saw the smoke of the Hit pitch fires upon the horizon and when we had passed between some low hills, there was the great mound of Hit and its single minaret in front of us. There remained an hour and a half of journey, the sun had set and our road was all sabkha. The camels slipped and slithered and tumbled down: "Their legs are like soap," explained the camel boy. If the rain had fallen again we should have been done. But it kept off till just as we reached Hit. The mound still loomed through the night and we could just see enough to keep more or less to our road—less rather than more—but not enough to make out whether stone or mud or sulphur pools lay in front of us. So we three great travellers, Fattuh, the mare and I, came into Hit, wet and weary, trudging through the dark, and looking, I make no doubt, like so many vagabonds, and thus ingloriously ended our fine adventure. The khan stands outside the town; the khanji is an old friend. "Ya Abud!" shouted Fattuh, "the caravan, our caravan, is it here?" "Kinship and welcome and may the earth be wide to you! They are here!" The muleteers hurried out, seized my bridle, seized my hand in theirs and laid it upon their forehead. All was safe and well, we and they and the animals and the packs. Praise God! there is no other but He. The khanji brought me tea, and various friends came to call, I dined and washed and went to bed.

And so you see, we have crossed the Syrian Desert as easily as if it had been the Sultan's highroad, and we have made many friends and seen the ruins we went out to see, and over and above all I have conceived quite a new theory about the mediæval roads through the desert which I will prove some day by another journey.

FORESTALLED [1]

(1911)

ROBERT FALCON SCOTT

(1868-1912)

[*It was in November 1911 that Scott and his companions left their winter quarters at Cape Evans for the final attempt to reach the South Pole. By December 5 they were at Camp 30.*]

TUESDAY, *December 5.*—Camp 30. Noon. We awoke this morning to a raging, howling blizzaard. . . . The ponies—heads, tails, legs, and all parts not protected by their rugs—are covered with ice; the animals are standing deep in snow, the sledges are almost covered, and huge drifts above the tents. We have had breakfast, rebuilt the walls, and are now again in our bags. One cannot see the next tent, let alone the land. What on earth does such weather mean at this time of year? It is more than our share of ill-fortune, I think, but the luck may turn yet. . . .

Wednesday, December 6.—Camp 30. Noon. Miserable, utterly miserable. We have camped in the "Slough of Despond." The tempest rages with unabated violence. . . . The snow is steadily climbing higher about walls, ponies, tents, and sledges. The ponies look utterly desolate. Oh! but this is too crushing, and we are only 12 miles from the Glacier. A hopeless feeling descends on one and is hard to fight off. . . .

Thursday, December 7.—Camp 30. The storm continues and the situation is now serious. One small feed remains for the ponies after to-day, so that we must either march to-morrow or sacrifice the animals. That is not the worst; with the help of the dogs we could get on, without doubt. The serious part is that we have this morning started our Summit rations—that is to say, the food calculated from the Glacier depot has been begun. The first supporting party can only go on a fortnight from this date and so forth. The storm shows no sign of abatement. . . .

Friday, December 8.—Camp 30. Hoped against hope for better condi-

[1] From *Scott's Last Expedition.*

tions, to wake to the mournfullest snow and wind as usual. We had breakfast at 10, and at noon the wind dropped. We set about digging out the sledges, no light task. We then shifted our tent sites. All tents had been reduced to the smallest volume by the gradual pressure of snow. The old sites are deep pits with hollowed-in wet centres. The resetting of the tents has at least given us comfort, especially since the wind has dropped. About 4 the sky showed signs of breaking, the sun and a few patches of land could be dimly discerned. . . . Alas! as I write the sun has disappeared and snow is again falling. Our case is growing desperate. . . . Wilson thinks the ponies finished, but Oates thinks they will get another march in spite of the surface, *if it comes to-morrow*. If it should not, we must kill the ponies to-morrow and get on as best we can with the men on ski and the dogs. But one wonders what the dogs can do on such a surface. . . .

Saturday, December 9.—Camp 31. I turned out two or three times in the night to find the weather slowly improving; at 5.30 we all got up, and at 8 got away with the ponies—a most painful day. The tremendous snowfall . . . had made the surface intolerably soft, and after the first hour there was no glide. We pressed on the poor halfrationed animals, but could get none to lead for more than a few minutes; following, the animals would do fairly well. . . . The situation was saved by P.O. Evans, who put the last pair of snow-shoes on Snatcher. From this he went on without much pressing, the other ponies followed, and one by one were worn out. . . . We went on all day without lunch. . . . By 8 P.M. we had reached within a mile or so of the slope ascending to the gap which Shackleton called the Gateway. I had hoped to be through the Gateway with the ponies still in hand at a very much earlier date, and but for the devastating storm we should have been. . . .

At 8 p.m. the ponies were quite done, one and all. They came on painfully slowly a few hundred yards at a time. By this time I was hauling ahead, a ridiculously light load, and yet finding the pulling heavy enough. We camped, and the ponies have been shot. Poor beasts! they have done wonderfully well considering the terrible circumstances under which they worked, but yet it is hard to have to kill them so early. The dogs are going well in spite of the surface. . . .

Wednesday, December 20.—Camp 42. 6500 feet about. Just got off our best half march—10 miles 1150 yards (geo.), over 12 miles stat. With an afternoon to follow we should do well to-day. . . . Turning this book [1] seems to have brought luck. . . .

[1] Scott had been writing on one side of each page of his journal; now he reversed the book and wrote on the other sides.

I have just told off the people to return to-morrow night: Atkinson, Wright, Cherry-Garrard, and Keohane. All are disappointed—poor Wright rather bitterly, I fear. I dreaded this necessity of choosing—nothing could be more heartrending. I calculated our programme to start from 85° 10' with 12 units of food and eight men. We ought to be in this position to-morrow night, less one day's food. . . .

Friday, December 22.—Camp 44, about 7100 feet. . . . This, the third stage of our journey, is opening with good promise. We made our depot this morning, then said an affecting farewell to the returning party, who have taken things very well, dear, good fellows as they are. . . .

Wednesday, January 3 [1912].—Height: Lunch, 10,110; Night, 10,180. Camp 56. . . . Within 150 miles of our goal. Last night I decided to reorganise, and this morning told off Teddy Evans, Lashly, and Crean to return. They are disappointed, but take it well; . . . we proceed as a five-man unit to-morrow. We have 5½ units of food—practically over a month's allowance for five people—it ought to see us through. . . .

Thursday, January 4.—We were naturally late getting away this morning, the sledge having to be repacked and arrangements completed for separation of parties. . . . Teddy Evans is terribly disappointed, but has taken it very well and behaved like a man. Poor old Crean wept, and even Lashly was affected. I was glad to find their sledge is a mere nothing to them, and thus, no doubt, they will make a quick journey back. . . .

Saturday, January 6.—Height 10,470. T.—22.3°. Obstacles arising—last night we got amongst sastrugi—they increased in height this morning and now we are in the midst of a sea of fish-hook waves. . . We took off our ski after the first 1½ hours and pulled on foot. It is terribly heavy in places, and, to add to our trouble, every sastrugus is covered with a beard of sharp branching crystals. We have covered 6½ miles, but we cannot keep up our average if this sort of surface continues. . . .

Wednesday, January 10.—Camp 62. T.—11°. Last depot 88° 29' S.; 159° 33' E.; Var. 180°. Terrible hard march in the morning; only covered 5.1 miles (geo.). Decided to leave depot at lunch camp. Built cairn and left one week's food together with sundry articles of clothing. We are down as close as we can go in the latter. We go forward with eighteen days' food. Yesterday I should have said certain to see us through, but now the surface is beyond words, and if it continues we shall have the greatest difficulty to keep our march long enough. . . . Only 85 miles (geo.) from the Pole, but it's going to be a stiff pull *both ways* apparently; still we do make progress, which is something. . . .

Sunday, January 14.—Camp 66. Lunch T.—18°, Night T.—15°. Sun showing mistily through overcast sky all day. Bright southerly wind with very low drift. In consequence the surface was a little better, and we came along very steadily 6.3 miles in the morning, and 5.5 in the afternoon, but the steering was awfully difficult and trying; very often I could see nothing, and Bowers on my shoulders directed me. . . . Meanwhile we are less than 40 miles from the Pole. . . . Oates seems to be feeling the cold and fatigue more than the rest of us, but we are all very fit. It is a critical time, but we ought to pull through. . . . Oh! for a few finedays! So close it seems and only the weather to baulk us. . . .

Tuesday, January 16.—Camp 68. Height 9760. T.—23.5°. The worst has happened, or nearly the worst. We marched well in the morning and covered 7½ miles. Noon sight showed us in Lat. 89° 42' S., and we started off in high spirits in the afternoon, feeling that to-morrow would see us at our destination. About the second hour of the march Bowers' sharp eyes detected what he thought was a cairn; he was uneasy about it, but argued that it must be a sastrugus. Half an hour later he detected a black speck ahead. Soon we knew that this could not be a natural snow feature. We marched on, found that it was a black flag tied to a sledge bearer; near by the remains of a camp; sledge tracks and ski tracks going and coming and the clear trace of dogs' paws—many dogs. This told us the whole story. The Norwegians have forestalled us and are first at the Pole. It is a terrible disappointment, and I am very sorry for my loyal companions. Many thoughts come and much discussion have we had. To-morrow we must march on to the Pole and then hasten home with all the speed we can compass. All the daydreams must go; it will be a wearisome return. . . .

Wednesday, January 17.—Camp 69. T.—22° at start Night–21°. The Pole. Yes, but under very different circumstances from those expected. We have had a horrible day—add to our disappointment a head wind 4 to 5, with a temperature—22°, and companions labouring on with cold feet and hands.

We started at 7.30, none of us having slept much after the shock of our discovery. We followed the Norwegian sledge tracks for some way; as far as we make out there are only two men. In about three miles we passed two small cairns. Then the weather overcast and the tracks being increasingly drifted up and obviously going too far to the west, we decided to make straight for the Pole according to our calculations. At 12.30 Evans had such cold hands we camped for lunch—an excellent "week-end one." We had marched 7.4 miles. Lat. sight gave 89° 53' 37". We started out and did 6½ miles due south. To-night little Bowers is laying himself out to get sights in terrible difficult circumstances; the wind is blowing hard, T.—21°, and there is that curious damp, cold feeling in the air which chills one to the bone in no time. We have been descending again, I think, but there looks to be a rise ahead; otherwise there is very little that is different from the awful monotony of past days. Great God! this is an awful place and terrible enough for us to have laboured to it without the reward of priority. Well, it is something to have got here, and the wind may be our friend to-morrow. . . .

Thursday morning, January 18.—Decided after summing up all observations that we were 3.5 miles away from the Pole—one mile beyond it and 3 to the right. More or less in this direction Bowers saw a cairn or tent.

We have just arrived at this tent, 2 miles from our camp, therefore about 1½ miles from the Pole. In the tent we find a record of five Norwegians having been here, as follows:

Roald Amundsen.
Olav Olavson Bjaaland.
Hilmer Hanssen.
Sverre H. Hassel.
Oscar Wisting.
16 Dec., 1911

The tent is fine—a small compact affair supported by a single bamboo. A note from Amundsen, which I keep, asks me to forward a letter to King Haakon! . . .

Left a note to say I had visited the tent with companions. Bowers photographing and Wilson sketching. Since lunch we have marched 6.2 miles S.S.E. by compass (*i.e.*, northwards). Sights at lunch gave us ½ to ¾ of a mile from the Pole, so we call it the Pole Camp. (Temp. Lunch—21°). We built a cairn, put up our poor slighted Union Jack, and photographed ourselves—mighty cold work all of it—less than ½ a mile south we saw stuck up an old underrunner of a sledge. This we commandeered as a yard for a floorcloth sail. I imagine it was intended to mark the exact spot of the Pole as near as the Norwegians could fix it. (Height 9500.) A note attached talked of the tent as being 2 miles from the Pole. Wilson keeps the note. There is no doubt that our predecessors have made thoroughly sure of their mark and fully carried out their programme. I think the Pole is about 9500 feet in height; this is remarkable, considering that in Lat. 88° we were about 10,500.

We carried the Union Jack about ¾ of a mile north with us and left it on a piece of stick as near as we could fix it. I fancy the Norwegians arrived at the Pole on the 15th Dec. and left on the 17th, ahead of a date quoted by me in London as ideal—viz., Dec. 22. . . . Well, we have turned our back now on the goal of our ambition and must face our 800 miles of solid dragging—and goodbye to most of the daydreams!

Wednesday, January 24.—Lunch Temp.—8°. Things beginning to look a little serious. A strong wind at he start has developed into a full blizzard at lunch, and we have had to get into our sleeping-bags. It was a bad march, but we covered 7 miles. . . . At 12.30 the sun coming ahead made it impossible to see the tracks further, and we had to stop. By this time the gale was at its height and we had the dickens of a time getting up the tent, cold fingers all round. We are only 7 miles from our depot, but I made sure we should be there to-night. This is the second full gale since we left the Pole. I don't like the look of it. In the weather breaking up? If so, God help us, with the tremendous summit journey and scant food. Wilson and Bowers are my stand-by. I don't like the easy way in which Oates and Evans get frostbitten.

Thursday, January 25.—Temp. Lunch—11°, Temp. night—16°. Thank God we found our Half Degree Depot. After lying in our bags yesterday afternoon and all night, we debated breakfast; decided to have it later and go without lunch. At the time the gale seemed as bad as ever, but during breakfast the sun showed and there was light enough to see the old track. It was a long and terribly cold job digging out our sledge and breaking camp, but we got through and on the march without sail, all pulling. . .

We are not without ailments: Oates suffers from a very cold foot; Evans' fingers and nose are in a bad state, and to-night Wilson is suffering tortures from his eyes. Bowers and I are the only members of the party without troubles just at present. . . .

Saturday, January 27.—. . . The forenoon march was over the belt of storm-tossed sastrugi; it looked like a rough sea. Wilson and I pulled in front on ski, the remainder on foot. It was very tricky work following the track, which pretty constantly disappeared, and in fact only showed itself by faint signs anywhere—a foot or two of raised sledge-track, a dozen yards of the trail of the sledgemeter wheel, or a spatter of hard snow-flicks where feet had trodden. . . . We are slowly getting more hungry, and it would be an advantage to have a little more food, especially for lunch. It we get to the next depot in a few marches (it is now less than 60 miles and we have a full week's food) we ought to be able to open out a little, but we can't look for a real feed till we get to the pony food depot. A long way to go, and, by Jove, this is tremendous labour. . . .

Sunday, February 11.—R. 25. Lunch Temp. – 6.5°, Supper – 3.5°. The worst day we have had during the trip and greatly owing to our own fault. We started on a wretched surface with light S.W. wind, sail set, and pulling on ski—horrible light, which made everything look fantastic. As we went on light got worse, and suddenly we found ourselves in pressure. Then came the fatal decision to steer east. We went on for 6 hours, hoping to do a good distance, which, in fact, I suppose we did, but for the last hour or two we pressed on into a regular trap. Getting on to a good surface we did not reduce our lunch meal, and thought all going well, but half an hour after lunch we got into the worst ice mess I have ever been in. For three hours we plunged on on ski, first thinking we were too much to the right, then too much to the left; meanwhile the disturbance got worse and my spirits received a very rude shock. There were times when it seemed almost impossible to find a way out of the awful turmoil in which we found ourselves. At length, arguing that there must be a way on our left, we plunged in that direction. It got worse, harder, more icy and crevassed. We could not manage our ski and pulled on foot, falling into crevasses every minute—most luckily no bad accident. At length we saw a smoother slope towards the land, pushed for it, but knew it was a woefully long way from us. The turmoil changed in character, irregular crevassed surface giving way to huge chasms, closely packed and most difficult to cross. It was very heavy work, but we had grown desperate. We won through at 10 P.M. and I write after 12 hours on the march. I *think* we are on or about the right track now, but we are still a good number of miles from the depot, so we reduced rations to-night. . . .

Saturday, February 17.—A very terrible day. Evans looked a little better after a good sleep, and declared, as he always did, that he was quite well. He started in his place on the traces, but half an hour later worked his ski shoes adrift, and had to leave the sledge. The surface was awful, the soft, recently-fallen snow clogging the ski and runners at every step, the sledge groaning, the sky overcast, and the land hazy. We stopped after about one hour, and Evans camp up again, but very slowly. Half an hour later he dropped out again on the same plea. He asked Bowers to lend him a piece of string. I cautioned him to come on as quickly as he could, and he answered cheerfully as I thought. We had to push on, and the remainder of us were forced to pull very hard, sweating heavily. Abreast the Mountain Rock we stopped, and seeing Evans a long way astern, I camped for lunch. There was no alarm at first, and we prepared tea and our own meal, consuming the latter. After lunch, and Evans still not appearing, we looked out, to see him still afar off. By this time we were alarmed, and all four started back on ski. I was first to reach the poor man and shocked at his appearance; he was on his knees with clothing disarranged, hands uncovered and frostbitten, and a wild look in his eyes. Asked what was the matter, he replied with a slow speech that he did't know, but thought he must have fainted. We got him on his feet, but after two or three steps he sank down again. He showed every sign of complete collapse. Wilson, Bowers and I went back for the sledge, whilst Oates remained with him. When we returned he was practically unconscious, and when we got him into the tent quite comatose. He died quietly at 12.30 A.M. . . .

Monday, March 5.Lunch. Regret to say going from bad to worse. We got a slant of wind yesterday afternoon, and going on 5 hours we converted our wretched morning run of 3½ miles into something over 9. We went to bed on a cup of cocoa and pemmican solid with the chill off. (R. 47.) The result is telling on all, but mainly on Oates, whose feet are in a wretched condition. . . . We started march on tea and pemmican as last night—we pretend to prefer the pemmican this way. Marched for 5 hours this morning over a slightly better surface covered with high moundy sastrugi. Sledge capsized twice; we pulled on foot, covering about 5½ miles. We are two pony marches and 4 miles about from our depot. Our fuel dreadfully low and the poor Soldier nearly done. It is pathetic enough because we can do nothing for him. . . .

Sunday, March 11.—Titus Oates is very near the end, one feels.What we or he will do, God only knows. We discussed the matter after breakfast; he is a brave fine fellow and understands the situation, but he practically asked for advice. Nothing could be said but to urge him to march as long as he could. . . .

Friday, March 16 or Saturday 17.—Lost track of dates, but think the last correct. Tragedy all along the line. At lunch, the day before yesterday, poor Titus Oates said he couldn't go on; he proposed we should leave him in his sleeping-bag. That we could not do, and induced him to come on, on the afternoon march. In spite of its awful nature for him he struggled on and we made a few miles. At night he was worse and we knew the end had come.

Should this be found I want these facts recorded. Oates' last thoughts were of his Mother, but immediately before he took pride in thinking that his regiment would be pleased with the bold way in which he met his death. We can testify to his bravery. He has borne intense suffering for weeks without complaint, and to the very last was able and willing to discuss outside subjects. He did not—would not—give up hope to the very end. He was a brave soul. This was the end. He slept through the night before last, hoping not to wake; but he woke in the morning— yesterday. It was blowing a blizzard. He said, "I am just going outside and may be some time." He went out into the blizzard and we have not seen him since. . . .

I can only write at lunch and then only occasionally. The cold is intense,–40° at midday. My companions are unendingly cheerful, but we are all on the verge of serious frostbites, and though we constantly talk of fetching through I don't think any one of us believes it in his heart. . . .

Sunday, March 18.—My right foot has gone, nearly all the toes—two days ago I was proud possessor of best feet. . . . Bowers takes first place in condition, but there is not much to choose after all.The others are still confident of getting through—or pretend to be—I don't know! . . .

Wednesday, March 21.—Got within 11 miles of depot Monday night; had to lay up all yesterday in severe blizzard. To-day forlorn hope, Wilson and Bowers going to depot for fuel.

Thursday, March 22 and 23.—Blizzard bad as ever—Wilson and Bowers unable to start—to-morrow last chance—no fuel and only one or two of food left—must be near the end. . . .

Thursday, March 29.—Since the 21st we have had a continuous gale from W.S.W. and S.W. We had fuel to make two cups of tea a piece and bare food for two days on the 20th. Every day we have been ready to start for our depot 11 *miles* away, but outside the door of the tent it remains a scene of whirling drift. I do not think we can hope for any better things now. We shall stick it out to the end, but we are getting weaker, of course, and the end cannot be far.

It seems a pity, but I do not think I can write more.

R. Scott

For God's sake look after our people.

THE EPIC OF MOUNT EVEREST [1]

(1924)

Sir Francis Younghusband

(1863-)

The great moment had now arrived. Twice the climbers had been rebuffed by snow and cold and wind. For the third time they now returned to the assault. And this time the weather was almost perfect. They themselves were exhausted and reduced in numbers; but the blizzards were over; day after day the mountain stood out sharp and clear; and the climbers were eager to seize the last opportunity before the monsoon should break, smother the whole mountain in snow, and make climbing impossible.

Being human, each climber would naturally have wished that he himself might be in the first of the successive pairs of climbers which would carry out

[1] From *The Epic of Mount Everest.*

the assault. The mountain might be carried at the first assault and the other pairs not have a chance. Or, even if the first pair failed, the monsoon or some tempest might prevent more than one pair making an attempt. The odds were on the first pair. And Norton as the leader might very well have put himself in the first pair. But . . . he had chivalrously stood down. Not his own personal fame, but the success of the whole Expedition was the one and only thing he had in mind. . . . Every little act that would contribute towards success was to be done. Every little act that might foil success was to be shunned. So now it was to be Mallory and Geoffrey Bruce, who at the moment seemed to be palpably the strongest of the climbers, who were to make the first assault and it was hoped gain the great prize.

They set off from Camp III on June 1st, taking with them nine of the "Tigers." The weather was again perfect and they were full of hope. On their way to the North Col they fixed the rope ladder on the ice wall below the chimney in the crevasse so as to make things easier for laden porters. And on arrival at Camp IV they found Odell and Irvine already established there prepared to fulfil the function of supporters, attend to the comfort of exhausted climbers after an assault, have warm meals ready, and succour returning parties of porters.

On June 2nd Mallory and Geoffrey Bruce with their nine porters set out for the real assault on the mountain. They hoped to establish Camp V the first day, Camp VI the second, and be on the summit the third. And it was not an unreasonable hope, for the weather conditions remained perfect, the sky was clear and there were no signs yet of the monsoon. Alas! in the Himalaya a bright sun and a clear sky as a rule mean wind. Between the heated plains and the icy peaks strong currents of air are set in motion. And no sooner had Mallory's party got outside the shelter of the ice blocks on the North Col than they were struck with the full blast of the raging air sweeping on the mountain from the north-west. The party was provided with windproof clothing, but it was of no more avail than are 'waterproofs' against tropical rain. The wind tore through windproof garments, through woollen garments, through the very flesh, right into the bones. It penetrated everythig. And it not only penerated: it exerted pressure. Laden porters could scarely keep their foothold against it. . . . Through this tearing wind the party had to make their way up the steep rocky Face Edge of Everest.

Camp V was to have been established on the east or sheltered side of the ridge at about 25,300 feet. But at about 25,000 feet the porters became exhausted. (It is well again to remind ourselves that before the Everest Expedition 24,600 feet was the highest altitude attained by any man, even unladen.) Only four porters were game. The remainder had deposited their loads, unable to come on. Mallory had to stop, therefore, and organize a camp, white Geoffrey Bruce and the sturdy Lobsang went back twice and carried up the missing loads on their own backs. It was a gallant effort for Lobsang, because he had already carried his own load up; and for Bruce, because he had not, like the porters, been accustomed all his life to carrying loads on mountains—or anywhere else.

"Two fragile little tentlets perched on an almost precipitous slope," in Norton's words, now were dignified with the style and title of Camp V. Five porters, according to plan, were returned to the North Col supporting Camp and three of the best were kept to carry on one more tent to form a camp 2000 feet higher.

The next morning, June 3rd, Mallory and Bruce should have set out for the summit. But even over-night they had not been hopeful of the men. The wind had entered not only their bones, but their hearts. It had chiled all the spirit in them. And next morning neither Bruce nor Mallory could make anything of them. One was ready to go on. The other two professed themselves sick. Geoffrey Bruce, like his older cousin, General Bruce, has a great way with these hillmen. But nothing even he could do could stir them. Moreover, Bruce himself was suffering the penalty of carrying those loads on the previous day, and his heart was strained. There was nothing for it but to return to the North Col. The first attempt, upon which the Expedition had counted so much, had failed.

Now as Mallory and Bruce were leaving Camp V downward, Norton and Somervell, timed to follow them a day behind, were leaving camp IV upward. And the parties met in between the two camps. The sight of Mallory coming back was a nasty blow to Norton. It meant one less chance of reaching the summit. It *might* mean also that no porters at all would be able to carry a camp any higher than 25,000 feet, and this would mean an end of every chance. It was a bad look-out. However, while Mallory and Bruce pursued their way downward to the North Col, there to be welcomed and refreshed by Odell and Irvine . . . Norton and Somervell proceeded upward. They too experienced the biting Everest wind. But they were able to reach Camp V and there they kept four of their porters in the hopes that on the morrow they would be willing to carry one tent to about the 27,000 feet level. These four porters had to sleep in one of the tents fixed by Mallory, while the two climbers slept in the other. Norton and Somevell found the floor of their tent had been well-levelled by their predecessors and, after making a good meal of pemmican and 'bully' beef, coffee and biscuits, they spent a fair night, sleeping at least half of it—and this latter is an important point, for it had formerly been supposed that sleep at so high an altitude would be impossible.

The crux, however, was whether the porters would or would not go on the next day.... On the following morning the two climbers rose at five o'clock to tackle the problem, and the next few hours were one of the great turning-points in the history of Everest exploration. It these porters, as well as Mallory's, proved to be unfit or unwilling to go on not only would the Expedition end in failure, but any future expedition would be discouraged: they would almost take it for granted that porters could not carry loads beyond 25,000 feet.

If we are to understand what men are like at five o'clock in the morning on the face of Mound Everst we must recall what bees are like on a cold autumn morning. Ordinarily these busy little beings are full of life and activity. Now they can scarcely move; they are numbed; they have neither energy nor intelligence; the spring of being is almost gone out of them. The porters were just like that, and probably Norton himself was not very much livelier. When he got down to the men's tent groans were the only answer he got to his questions. But he then did a very wise thing. He induced them to cook and eat a meal, and he went back and had some breakfast himself. . . .

All having fed, Norton addressed himself to the task. The struggle which now ensued between him and the four porters was essentially a struggle of spirit. All that organization could do had been done. Thought could do not more. It was simply a question whether spirit could be induced to drive the body any further. And this depended not so much upon will power as upon imagination. And here again Norton showed wisdom. He appealed to the imagination. . . . There was no holding a pistol to their heads; no physical force; no threats; nor even bribing by money. He simply painted for the porters a picture of themselves covered with honour and glory and receiving praises from every one; and he told them how their names would be inscribed in letters of gold in the book which would be written to describe their achievement if only they would carry loads to 27,000 feet. It was a master-stroke. The appeal was made straight to their manhood. "Show yourselves men and you will be honoured by men," was in effect what Norton said. . . . To their everlasting honour the porters now responded. Three, at least, did; the other was really too ill. Their names my readers should turn into gold as they read them. The are:

NAPBOO YISHAY
LHAKPA CHEDI
SEMCHUMBI

The critical point had been turned and an advance instead of a retreat was made. And once they were off the men went well—though Semchumbi, through suffering from a blow on the knee, went somewhat lame and had to be shepherded by Somervell, who was himself feeling his throat very badly, and had constantly to stop and cough. The easy scree of the first day's climb became looser as they climbed higher, and energy as well as temper suffered, says Somervell, in the weary plod from 25,000 to 26,800 feet, when the scree give place to sloping slabs covered with small stones, which render footing precarious. And halts were needed to help them to keep breathing sufficiently to meet their bodily needs. But the weather continued fine and the wind was markedly less severe than on the day before. As they passed the highest point which they and Mallory had reached in 1922—and which was, of course, by a long way the record height man had then reached—their spirits rose. They were going to camp higher still. And given another clear day and good conditions what might they not achieve!

So they progressed till about 1.30, when it was evident that the gallant Semchumbi could go no farther. A narrow cleft in the rocks facing north and affording the suggestion—it was little more—of some shelter from the north-west wind was selected. Norton set the two leading porters to scrape and pile the loose stones forming the floor of the cleft into the usual platform for a tent. On it the tiny tent for the two climbers was pitched; and this was Camp VI, 26,800 feet. A tent had been set at an altitude no less than 11,000 feet higher than the summit of Mont Blanc. . . .

The diminutive 'camp' having been pitched, the three porters were dispatched back to the North Col camp. They had played their part heroically and established for ever the all-important point that a tent *can* be pitched within climbable distance of the summit. And now the climbers were left alone to do *their* part.

But before they actually commenced the climb a night had to be spent in the camp and a second very important point had to be cleared up. Could men *sleep* at nearly 27,000 feet? By the next morning that question also had been answered—and answered favourably. Norton entered in his diary for that day, "Spent the best night since I left Camp I.". . .

The day which would determine failure or success had come. Before the sun set on June 4th Norton and Somervell, or one of them, would either stand on the summit of Mount Everest or have to withdraw, once more baffled. The weather conditions were as good as they could ever be. The day was nearly windless and brilliantly fine. Alas! now that the weather was favourable the men were exhausted. They were not the men they might have been if they could have started fresh from Camp I, and come leisurely up the glacier gradually acclimatizing themselves on the way and leaving all the gruelling spade-work to be done by others. Norton always did hold, before the Expedition left England, that more climbers were required. And more climbers would have been sent if the susceptibilities of the Tibetan Government had not to be considered. Four more climbers would have meant many more transport animals for one thing. And the Tibetan Government were already suspicious of the size of these annual expeditions. . . .

Norton and Somervell started at 6.45 and struck off to the right in a slanting direction south-westward along the North Face towards the summit, which was about a mile distant as the crow files and 2200 feet above them. They might have struck upward and got on to the top of the Ridge and followed it along, but they preferred to keep under its shelter. It might have been too windy on the top. The drawback to this course was that at the start, when they most wanted the sun, they were in shade. They trudged slowly up a broad rocky shoulder making for a patch of sunlight. And at length, panting, puffing, and sometimes slipping back on the scree, and so compelled to stop to regain breath, they attained the sunlight and began to get warm.

They crossed the snowy patch with Norton gallantly chipping steps in front, and about an hour from camp reached the bottom edge of the broad yellow band of rock which is such a conspicuous feature in distant views of the mountain. It is about a thousand feet in thickness and afforded the climbers a safe and easy route as they traversed it diagonally, for it is made up of a series of broad ledges, some ten feet or more wide, running parallel to its general direction and sufficiently broken up to afford easy access from one ledge to the next.

The going was good. The day was perfect. But by the time they reached the 27,500 feet level they were feeling in distress. Norton says he felt it bitterly cold, and he shivered so violently as he sat in the sun during one of their numerous halts that he suspected the approach of malaria. . . . To see if he really had malaria he took his pulse, and to his surprise found it about sixty-four, which was only about twenty above his normally very slow pulse.

Besides this feeling of cold Norton also at the time was beginning to experience trouble with his eyes. He was seeing double, and in a difficult step was sometimes in doubt where to put his feet.

Somervell too was in trouble. For some weeks he had suffered in the throat. And now the process of breathing in the intensely cold dry air, which caught the back of the larynx, had a disastrous effect on his already very bad sore throat. He had constantly to stop and cough.

The altitude was also beginning to tell upon both of them. About 27,500 feet there was an almost sudden change, says Somervell. A little lower down they could walk comfortably, taking three or four breaths for each step, but now seven, eight, or ten complete respirations were necessary for each single step forward. Even at this slow rate of progress they had to indulge in a rest for a minute or two every twenty or thirty yards. . . .

About midday, when they were at about the 28,000 feet level, they were getting near the limit of endurance. They were just below the top edge of the yellow band and nearing the big couloir or gully which runs vertically down the mountain and cuts off the base of the final pyramid from the great North-east Ridge. Here Somervell finally succumbed to his throat trouble. As it was, he nearly died of it, and if he had gone farther he certainly would have succumbed. Telling Norton that he would only hinder him if he went on, he suggested that Norton that he would only hinder him if he went on, he suggested that Norton should climb the mountain by himself; and he then settled down on a sunny ledge to watch him do it.

But Norton himself was not far from the end of his tether, and could only struggle on a little farther. He followed the actual top edge of the band, which led at a very slightly uphill angle into and across the big couloir. But to reach the latter he had to turn the end of two pronounced buttresses which ran down the face of the mountain. Here the going became a great deal worse. The slope below him was very steep, the foothold ledges narrowed to a few inches in width. And as he approached the shelter of the big couloir their was a lot of powdery snow which concealed the precarious footholds. The whole face of the mountain was composed of slabs like the tiles on a roof, and all sloped at much and same angle as tiles. He had twice to retrace his steps and follow a different band of strata. And the couloir itself was filled with powdery snow into which he sank to the knee, and even to the waist, and which yet was not of a consistency to support him in the event of a slip.

Beyond the couloir the going got steadily worse. He found himself stepping from tile to tile, as it were, each tile sloping smoothly and steadily downwards, and he began to feel that he was too much dependent on the mere friction of a boot-nail. It was not exactly diffcult going, reports Norton, but it was a dangerous place for a single unroped climber, as one slip would in all probability have sent him to the bottom of the mountain.

The strain of climbing so carefully was not beginning to tell upon Norton, and he was getting exhausted. In addition, his eye trouble was becoming worse, and was a severe handicap. He had perhaps 200 feet more of the nasty going to surmount before he emerged on to the north face of the final pyramid, to safety and an easy route to the summit. But it was now 1p.m. His rate of progress was too slow—he had ascended only about 100 feet in a distance of perhaps 300 yards since he left Somervell—and their was no chance of his being able to climb the remaining 876 feet if he was to return in safety. So he turned back at an altitude which was subsequently fixed by theodolite observation at 28,126 feet.

Norton as well as Somervell had to give up when within only about three hours' climb of the summit. There it was, not half a mile away, but one after another they had to turn back. . . .

We now come back to Mallory. Fury raged in his soul as he was forced to return from Camp V. Fury not against the individual porters who could not be brought to go farther, but against the whole set of circumstances which thus compelled him to go back at the very moment when the weather at last was favourable. But Mallory was in no mind to be finally thwarted. He would recoil but to spring higher. He was absolutely possessed with the idea of climbing Mount Everest. Climbing Everest was no incident in his life. He had made it his whole life. . . . And to get him away from Everest before Everest itself had hurled him back you would have had to pull him up by the very roots of his being.

With fresh plans kindling within him he passed on from Camp IV straight through on the same day to Camp III, there to examine the possibilities of an ascent with oxygen. Mallory never was a real enthusiast for oxygen. But, if it were the only way of getting up Mount Everest, use it he would. Neither was Irvine an oxygen enthusiast, and privately he told Odell that he would rather get to the final pyramid without oxygen than to the top with it—a sentiment with which most of us will assuredly agree. And so probably would Mallory. But had this to consider—that Norton and Somervell would be doing the very utmost that the present Expedition could do *without* oxygen. And, if they did not succeed, then one last attempt should be made—this time *with* oxygen. He therefore, as was his wont, threw his whole soul into the arrangements for an oxygen attempt. And he chose for his companion Irvine, not Odell, because Irvine had faith in the use of oxygen, which Odell had not. . . .

In the light of subsequent experience we may doubt the wisdom of using oxygen on this attempt. The heavy apparatus was a colossal handicap. And it afterwards proved that acclimatization had much greater effect than was then supposed. Oddell, who had acclimatized slowly, afterwards climbed twice to 27,000 feet—once with a 20-lb. oxygen apparatus on his back, though he did not use the oxygen after 26,000 feet, finding it did him little good. If Mallory had taken Odell and had made the final attempt without oxygen it is quite legitimate to suppose that the summit might have been reached. For Odell had not gone through the trying experience of the rescue which Norton, Somervell, and Mallory had;[1] and he was probably by now quite fit to reach the summit. And, exhausted as Mallory was from the effects of the rescue, yet with a fit and experienced climber beside him, with the knowledge that 28,100 feet had already actually been reached—always a great aid to endeavour—and with his spirit to spur him on, he might have kept up with Odell to the end. Or Odell and Irvine without using oxygen might have succeeded; for neither had Irvine been strained by the rescue exertions.

All this is conjecture, though. And at the time that Mallory was making his preparations he did not know that Norton had reached 28,100 feet, or how wonderfully Odell was acclimatizing. All he knew was that, so far, Odell had *not* been acclimatzing so well as the rest. And therefore the best chance of reaching the summit seemed to be by using oxygen.

On June 3rd Mallory and Geoffrey Bruce had arrived back at Camp III straight from Camp V, and together they now examined into the possibilities of collecting sufficient porters capable of carrying up oxygen supplies to Camp VI. The men had improved in health as the result of rest and fine weather; and by dint of strong, personal persuasion Bruce was just able to get together sufficient men. And while these negotiations were proceeding Irvine was occupied in getting the oxygen apparatus into efficient working order. . . .

Arrangements were completed on June 3rd, and on the next day Mallory and Irvine climbed up to the North Col again with the new porters. The two climbers used oxygen and covered the distance in the fast time of two and a half hours. They were well pleased with the result, but Odell was more sceptical. Irvine's throat was already suffering much from the cold dry air, and Odell thinks that the discomfort was palpably aggravated by the use of oxygen.

Here on the North Col the new climbling party and the support were assembled. This Camp IV had, indeed, become a kind of advanced mountain base for the actual assaults on the mountain. Odell has given a description of it. Its peculiarity was that it was pitched on snow and not on rock, like the others, even the highest, no rock being available. Perched on an ice-ledge it had four tents: two for sahibs and two for porters. The ledge was a shelf of névé with a greatest breadth of about 30 feet. And a high wall of ice which rose above it on the western side gave comforting protection from the chilly

[1] The rescue, on May 24th, of four porters stranded on the North Col.

winds which constantly blow from that direction. . . .

Into this camp on the same day, June 4th, that Mallory and Irvine arrived up from Camp III, Norton and Somervell returned form their great climb. They had come straight back from their highest point, without halting at Camps V and VI. Somervell had as nearly as possible collapsed altogether in a choking fit. And Norton that night became totally blind from snow-blindness. They were disappointed—and naturally so—as has already been said. But to be disappointed because you have reached *only* 28,100 feet is surely a remarkable confirmation of Einstein's theory of relativity! Only recently men who had reached an altitude as high as this camp to which Norton and Somervell and now *descended* 5000 feet were looked upon as heroes.

However, there was the fact that they had not got to the *top*, and here was Mallory, with steam at high pressure, ready to make one last desperate effort. Norton entirely agreed with this decision, and was "full of admiration for the indomitable spirit of the man, determined, in spite of his already excessive exertions, not to admit defeat while any chance remained." And such was Mallory's will power and nervous energy that he seemed to Norton entirely adequate to the task. All Norton differed with him about was as to taking Irvine as his companion. Irvine was suffering from throat trouble and was not the experienced climber that Odell was. Moreover, Odell though he had acclimatized slowely was beginning to show that he was a climber of unequalled endurance and toughness. But, as Mallory had completed his plans, Norton, very rightly, made no attempt at that late stage to interfere with them.

Mallory halted one day, June 5th, in camp with Norton, now in great pain from his snow-blindness. And on the 6th he set out with Irvine and four porters. Who can tell his feelings? Certainly he well knew the dangers, and he set out in no rash, foolhardy spirit. This was his third expedition to Mount Everest; at the end of the first he had written that the highest of mountains is capable of "a severity so awful and so fatal that the wiser sort of men do well to think and tremble even on the threshold of their high endeavour"; and on both the second and third Expeditions he had experienced to the full the severity of Everest.

He knew the dangers before him and was prepared to meet them. But he was a man of vision and imagination as well as daring. He could see all that success meant. Everest was the embodiment of the physical forces of the world. Against it he had to pit the spirit of man. He could see the joy in the faces of his comrades if he succeeded. He could imagine the thrill his success would cause among all fellow-mountaineers; the credit it would bring to England; the interest all over the world; the name it would bring him; the enduring satisfaction to himself that he had made his life worth while. All this must have been in his mind. He had known the sheer exhilaration of the struggle in his minor climbs among the Alps. And now on mighty Everest exhilaration would be truned into exaltation—not at the time, perhaps, but later on assuredly. Perhaps he never exactly formulated it, yet in his mind must have been present the idea of "all or nothing." Of the two alternatives, to turn back a third time or to die, the latter was for Mallory probably the easier. The agony of the first would be more than he as a man, as a mountaineer, and as an artist, could endure.

Irvine, younger and less experienced than Mallory, would not be so acutely aware of the risks. On the other hand, he would not so vididly visualize all that success would mean. But Odell has recorded that he was no less determined than Mallory upon going "all out." It had been his ambition to have "a shot at the summit." And now that the chance had come he welcomed it "almost with boyish enthusiasm."

In this frame of mind the pair set out on the morning of June 6th. The sightless Norton could only press their hands and pathetically wish them good luck. Odell and Hazard (who had come up from Camp III as Somervell had gone down) had prepared them a meal of fried sardines with biscuits and plenty of hot tea and chocolate, and at 8.40 they started. Their personal loads consisted of the modified oxygen apparatus with two cylinders only and a few other small items, such as wraps and a food ration for the day, in all about 25 lb. The eight porters with them carried provisions, bedding, and additional oxygen cylinders, but no oxygen apparatus for their own use.

The morning was brilliant. It clouded over in the afternoon and a little snow fell in the evening; but this was not serious and four of Mallory's porters returned in the evening from Camp V with a note saying there was no wind there and that things looked hopeful. The next morning, the 7th, Mallory's party moved on to Camp VI, while Odell came up in support to Camp V. It would have been better of course if he could have gone with them and so made a party of three. Three is the ideal number for a mountain party. But the tiny tents held only two climbers. There were not sufficient porters to carry a second tent. And he could only follow a day behind, acting as a kind of support.

Mallory made Camp VI all right with his four porters. And this fact is another evidence of the value of Norton and Somervell's work. Through *their* having got porters up to this camp, 26,800 feet, the second lot of porters with

Mallory went there almost as a matter of course. And from there they were sent back with a note form Mallory to Odell saying the weather was perfect for the job, but that the oxygen apparatus was a nasty load for climbing.

That evening as Odell from Camp V looked out of his tent the weather was most promising; and he thought of the hopeful feelings with which Mallory and Irvine would go to sleep. Success would seem to be at last within their grasp.

Of what happened after that we know little. Owing to some defect in the oxygen apparatus which required adjustment, or from some other cause, their start must have been late, for when Odell, following in the rear, caught sight of them it was 12.50 P.M. and they were then only at the second rock step which, according to Mallory's schedule, they should have reached at 8 A.M. at latest. And the day had not turned out so fine as the previous evening had promised. There was much mist about the mountain. It might have been finer up where Mallory and Irvine were, for Odell, looking up from below, did notice that the upper part of the mist was luminous. But there was sufficient cloud about to prevent Odell from keeping in touch with the two climbers; and through the drifting mists he had only a single glimpse of them again.

As he reached the top of a little craig, at about 26,000 feet, there was a sudden clearing above him. The clouds parted. The whole summit ridge and the final pyramid was unveiled. And far away on a snow slope he noticed a tiny object moving and approach the rock step. A second object followed. And then the first climbed to the top of the step. As he stood intently watching this dramatic appearance the scene became enveloped in cloud once more. And this was the last that was ever seen of Mallory and Irvine. Beyond that all is mystery.

CANADA

IN SEARCH OF THE PACIFIC[1]

(1793)

SIR ALEXANDER MACKENZIE

(1755-1820)

THE month of April being now past, in the early part of which I was most busily employed in trading with the Indians, I ordered our old canoes to be repaired with bark, and added four new ones to them, when with the furs and provisions I had purchased, six canoes were loaded and dispatched on the 8th of May for Fort Chepewyan. I had, however, retained six of the men who agreed to accompany me on my projected voyage of discovery. I also engaged my hunters, and closed the business of the year for the company by writing my public and private dispatches.

Having ascertained, by various observations, the latitude of this place to be 56.9 North, and longitude 117.35.15 West:—on the 9th day of May (1793) the canoe was put into the water: her dimensions were twenty-five feet long within, exclusive of the curves of stem and stern, twenty-six inches hold, and four feet nine inches beam. At the same time she was so light, that two men could carry her on a good road three or four miles without resting. In this slender vessel, we shipped provisions, goods for presents, arms, ammunition, and baggage, to the weight of three thousand pounds, and an equipage of ten people—viz., Alexander Mackay, Joseph Landry, Charles Ducette, François Beaulieux, Baptist Bisson, François Courtois and Jacques Beauchamp, with two Indians as hunters and interpreters. With these persons I embarked at seven in the evening. My winter interpreter, with another person, whom I left here to take care of the fort, and supply the natives with ammunition during the summer, shed tears on the reflection of those dangers which we might encounter in our expedition, while my own people offered up their prayers that we might return in safety from it.

We began our voyage with a course south by west against a strong current one mile and three quarters, south-west by south one mile, and landed before eight on an island for the night.

The weather was clear and pleasant, though there was a keenness in the air, and at a quarter past three in the morning we continued our voyage. The canoe being strained from its having been very heavily laden, became so leaky that we were obliged to land, unload and gum it. As this circumstance took place

[1] From *Journal of a Voyage thgrough the North-west Continent of America* (1801).

about twelve, I had an opportunity of taking an altitude, which made our latitude 55.58.48.

May 11. The weather was overcast. With a strong wind ahead, we embarked at four in the morning, and left all the fresh meat behind us, but the portion which had been assigned to the kettle; the canoe being already too heavily laden. Our course was west-south-west one mile, where a small river flowed in from the east, named *Quiscatina Sepy*, or River with the High Banks; we found a chief of the Beaver Indians on an hunting-party. I remained, however, in my canoe, lest the friends of my hunters might discourage them from proceeding on the voyage. We therefore continued our course, but several Indians kept company with us, running along the bank and conversing with my people, who were so attentive to them that they drove the canoe on a stony flat, so that we were under the necessity of landing to repair the damages.

Some of the Indians passed the night with us, and I was informed by them that, according to our mode of proceeding, we should, in ten days, get as far as the rocky mountains. I inquired, with some anxiety, after an old man who had already given me an account of the country beyond the limits of his tribe, and was very much disappointed at being informed that he had not been seen for upwards of a moon. . . .

May 19. It rained very hard in the early part of the night, but the weather became clear towards the morning, when we embarked at our usual hour. The last Indians whom we saw had informed us that at the first mountain there was a considerable succession of rapids, cascades, and falls, which they never attempted to ascend; and where they always passed over land the length of a day's march. My men imagined that the carrying-place was at a small distance below us, as a path appeared to ascend an hill, where there were several lodges of the last year's construction. The account which had been given me of the rapids was perfectly correct: though by crossing to the other side, I must acknowledge with some risk, in such an heavy-laden canoe, the river appeared to me to be practicable, as far as we could see: the traverse therefore was attempted, and proved successful. We now towed the canoe along an island, and proceeded without any considerable difficulty till we reached the extremity of it, when the line could be no longer employed, and in endeavouring to clear the point of the island, the canoe was driven with such violence on a stony shore, as to receive considerable injury. We now employed every exertion in our power to repair the breach that had been made, as well as to dry such articles of our loading as more immediately required it: we then transported the whole across the point, when we reloaded and continued our course about three quarters of a mile. We could now proceed no farther on this side of the water, and the traverse was rendered extremely dangerous not only from the strength of the current, but by the cascades just below us, which, if we had got among them, would have involved us and the canoe in one common destruction. We had no other alternative than to return by the same course we came, or to hazard the traverse, the river on this side being bounded by a range of steep, overhanging rocks, beneath which the current was driven on with resistless impetuosity from the cascades. Here are several islands of solid rock, covered with a small portion of verdure, which have been worn away by the constant force of the current presenting, as it were, so many large tables. By crossing from one to the other of these islands we came at length to the main traverse, on which we ventured, and were successful in our passage. Mr Mackay and the Indians, who observed our manœuvres from the top of a rock, were in continual alarm for our safety, with which their own, indeed, may be said to have been nearly connected: however, the dangers we encountered were very much augmented by the heavy loading of the canoe.

When we had effected our passage, the current on the west side was almost equally violent with that from whence we had just escaped, but the craggy bank being somewhat lower, we were enabled, with a line of sixty fathoms, to tow the canoe, till we came to the foot of the most rapid cascade we had hitherto seen. Here we unloaded, and carried every thing over a rocky point of an hundred and twenty paces. When the canoe was reloaded I ascended the bank, which was so elevated that the men, who were coming up a strong point could not hear me, though I called to them with the utmost strength of my voice, to lighten the canoe of part of its lading. And here I could not but reflect, with infinite anxiety, on the hazard of my enterprise: one false step of those who were attached to the line, or the breaking of the line itself, would have at once consigned the canoe, and every thing it contained, to instant destruction; it, however, ascended the rapid in perfect security. . . .

May 20. We continued our toilsome and perilous progress, and as we proceeded the rapidity of the current increased, so that in the distance of two miles we were obliged to unload four times, and carry every thing but the canoe: indeed, in many places it was with the utmost difficulty that we could prevent her from being dashed to pieces against the rocks by the violence of the eddies. At five we had proceeded to where the river was one continuous rapid. Here we again took every thing out of the canoe, in order to tow her up with the line, though the rocks were so shelving as greatly to increase the toil and hazard of that operation. At length, however, the agitation of the water was so great that a wave striking on the bow of the canoe broke the line, and filled us with inexpressible dismay, as it appeared impossible that the vessel could escape from being dashed to pieces, and those who were in her from perishing. Another wave, however, more propitious than the former, drove her out of the tumbling water, so that the men were enabled to bring her ashore, and though she had been carried over rocks by these swells which left them naked a moment after, the canoe had received no material injury. The men were, however, in such a state from their late alarm, that it would not only have been unavailing but imprudent to have proposed any further progress at present, particularly as the river above us, as far as we could see, was one white sheet of foaming water.

That the discouragements, difficulties, and dangers, which had hitherto attended the progress of our enterprize, should have excited a wish in several of those who were engaged in it to discontinue the pursuit, might be naturally expected; and indeed it began to be muttered on all sides that there was no alternative but to return.

Instead of paying any attention to these murmurs, I desired those who had uttered them to exert themselves in gaining an ascent of the hill, and encamp there for the night. In the mean time I set off with one of the Indians, and though I continued my examination of the river almost as long as there was any light to assist me, I could see no end of the rapids and cascades: I was therefore perfectly satisfied, that it would be impracticable to proceed any farther by water. . . .

May 21. No alternative was left us; nor did any means of proceeding present themselves to us, but the passage of the mountain over which we were to carry the canoe as well as the baggage. As this was a very alarming enterprize, I dispatched Mr Mackay with three men and the two Indians to proceed in a straight course from the top of the mountain, and to keep the line of the river till they should find it navigable. If it should be their opinion, that there was no practicable passage in that direction, two of them were instructed to return in order to make their report; while the others were to go in search of the Indian carrying-place.

At sun-set Mr Mackay returned with one of the men, and in about two hours was followed by the others. They had penetrated thick woods, ascended hills and sunk into valleys, till they got beyond the rapids, which, according to their calculation, was a distance of three leagues. The two parties returned by different routes, but they both agreed, that with all its difficulties, and they were of a very alarming nature, the outward course was that which must be preferred. Unpromising, however, as the account of their expedition appeared, it did not sink them into a state of discouragement; and a kettle of wild rice, sweetened with sugar, which had been prepared for their return, with their usual regale of rum, soon renewed that courage which disdained all obstacles that threatened our progress: and they went to rest, with a full determination to surmount them on the morrow. I sat up, in the hope of getting an observation of Jupiter and his first satellite, but the cloudy weather prevented my obtaining it.

May 22. At break of day we entered on the extraordinary journey which was to occupy the remaining part of it. The men began, without delay, to cut a road up the mountain, and as the trees were but of small growth, I ordered them to fell those which they found convenient, in such a manner, that they might fall parallel with the road, but, at the same time, not separate them entirely from the stumps, so that they might form a kind of railing on either side. The baggage was now brought from the waterside to our encampment. This was likewise from the steep shelving of the rocks, a very perilous undertaking, as one false step of any of the people employed in it, would have been instantly followed by falling headlong into the water. When this important object was attained, the whole of the party proceeded with no small degree of apprehension, to fetch the canoe, which, in a short time, was also brought to the encampment; and, as soon as we had recovered from our fatigue, we advanced with it up the mountain, having the line doubled and fastened successively as we went on to the stumps; while a man at the end of it, hauled it round a tree, holding it on and shifting it as we proceeded; so that we may be said, with strict truth, to have warped the canoe up the mountain: indeed by a general and most laborious exertion, we got everything to the summit by two in the afternoon. At noon, the latitude was 56.0.47 North. At five, I sent the men to cut the road onwards, which they effected for about a mile, when they returned. . . .

May 23. The weather was clear at four this morning, when the men began to carry. I joined Mr Mackay and the two Indians in the labour of cutting a road. The ground continued rising gently till noon, when it began to decline; but though on such an elevated situation, we could see but little, as mountains of a still higher elevation and covered with snow, were seen far above us in every direction. In the afternoon the ground became very uneven; hills and deep defiles alternately presented themselves to us. Our progress, however, exceeded my expectation, and it was not till four in the afternoon that the carriers overtook us. At five, in a state of fatigue that may be more readily conceived than expressed, we encamped near a rivulet or spring that issued from beneath a large mass of ice and snow.

Our toilsome journey of this day I compute at about three miles; along the first of which the land is covered with plenty of wood, consisting of large trees, encumbered with little underwood, through which it was by no means difficult to open a road, by following a well-beaten elk path: for the two succeeding miles we found the country overspread with the trunks of trees, laid low by fire some years ago; among which large copses had sprung up of a close growth, and intermixed with briars, so as to render the passage through them painful and tedious. . . .

May 24. We continued our very laborious journey, which led us down some steep hills, and through a wood of tall pines. After much toil and trouble in bearing the canoe through the difficult passages which we encountered, at four in the afternoon we arrived at the river, some hundred yards above the rapids or falls, with all our baggage. I compute the distance of this day's progress to be about four miles; indeed, I should have measured the whole of the way if I had not been obliged to engage personally in the labour of making the road. . . .

June 5. This morning we found our canoe and baggage in the water, which had continued rising during the night. We then gummed the canoe, as we arrived at too late an hour to perform that operation on the preceding evening. This necessary business being completed, we traversed to the North shore, where I disembarked with Mr Mackay, and the hunters, in order to ascend an adjacent mountain, with the hope of obtaining a view of the interior part of the country. I directed my people to proceed with all possible diligence, and that, if they met with any accident, or found my return necessary, they should fire two guns. They also understood, that when they should hear the same signal from me, they were to answer, and wait for me, if I were behind them.

When we had ascended to the summit of the hill we found that it extended onwards in an even, level country; so that, encumbered as we were with the thick wood, no distant view could be obtained; I therefore climbed a very lofty tree, from whose top I discerned on the right a ridge of mountains covered with snow, bearing about north-west; from thence another ridge of high land, whereon no snow was visible, stretched towards the south; between which and the snowy hills on the east side, there appeared to be an opening, which we determined to be the course of the river.

Having obtained all the satisfaction that the nature of the place would admit, we proceeded forward to overtake the canoe, and after a warm walk came down upon the river, when we discharged our pieces twice, but received no answering signal. I was of the opinion, that the canoe was before us, while the Indians entertained an opposite notion. I, however, crossed another point of land, and came again to the waterside about ten. Here we had a long view of the river, which circumstance excited in my mind some doubts of my former sentiments. We repeated our signals, but without any return; and as every moment now increased my anxiety, I left Mr Mackay and one of the Indians at this spot to make a large fire, and send branches adrift down the current as notices of our situation, if the canoe was behind us; and proceeded with the other Indian across a very long point, where the river makes a considerable bend, in order that I might be satisfied if the canoe was ahead. About twelve we arrived once more at the river, and the discharge of our pieces was as unsuccessful as it had hitherto been. The water rushed before us with uncommon velocity; and we also tried the experiment of sending fresh branches down it. To add to the disagreeableness of our situation, the gnats and musquitoes appeared in swarms to torment us. When we returned to our companions, we found that they had not been contented with remaining in the position where I had left them, but had been three or four miles down the river, but were come back to their station, without having made any discovery of the people on the water.

Various very unpleasing conjectures at once perplexed and distressed us: the Indians, who are inclined to magnify evils of any and every kind, had at once consigned the canoe and every one on board it to the bottom; and were already settling a plan to return upon a raft, as well as calculating the number of nights that would be required to reach their home. As for myself, it will be easily believed, that my mind was in a state of extreme agitation; and the imprudence of my conduct in leaving the people, in such a situation of danger and toilsome exertion, added a very painful mortification to the severe apprehensions I already suffered: it was an act of indiscretion which might have put an end to the voyage that I had so much at heart, and compelled me at length to submit to the scheme which my hunters had already formed for our return.

At half-past six in the evening, Mr Mackay and the Cancre set off to proceed down the river, as far as they could before the night came on, and to continue their journey in the morning to the place where we had encamped the preceding evening. I also proposed to make my excursion upwards; and, if we both failed of success in meeting the canoe, it was agreed that we should return to the place where we now separated.

In this situation we had wherewithal to drink in plenty, but with solid food we were totally unprovided. We had not seen even a partridge throughout the day, and the tracks of reindeer that we had discovered, were of an old date. We were, however, preparing to make a bed of the branches of trees, where we should have had no other canopy than that afforded us by the heavens, when we heard a shot, and soon after another, which was the notice agreed upon, if Mr Mackay and the Indian should see the canoe: that fortunate circumstance was also confirmed by a return of the signal from the people. I was, however, so fatigued from the heat and exercise of the day, as well as incommoded from drinking so much cold water, that I did not wish to remove till the following morning; but the Indian made such bitter complaints of the cold and hunger which he suffered, that I complied with his solicitations to depart; and it was almost dark when we reached the canoe, barefooted, and drenched with rain. . . .

June 12. The weather was cloudy and raw, and as the circumstances of this day's voyage had compelled us to be frequently in the water, which was cold as ice, we were almost in a benumbed state. Some of the people who had gone ashore to lighten the canoe, experienced great difficulty in reaching us, from the rugged state of the country; it was, indeed, almost dark when they arrived. We had no sooner landed than I sent two men down the river to bring me some account of its circumstances, that I might form a judgment of the difficulties which might await us on the morrow; and they brought back a fearful detail of rapid current, fallen trees, and large stones. At this place our guide manifested evident symptoms of discontent: he had been very much alarmed in going down some of the rapids with us, and expressed an anxiety to return. He shewed us a mountain, at no great distance, which he represented as being on the other side of a river, into which this empties itself.

June 13. At an early hour of this morning the men began to cut a road, in order to carry the canoe and lading beyond the rapid; and by seven they were ready. That business was soon effected, and the canoe reladen, to proceed with the current which ran with great rapidity. In order to lighten her, it was my intention to walk with some of the people; but those in the boat with great earnestness requested me to embark, declaring, at the same time, that, if they perished, I should perish with them. I did not then imagine in how short a period their apprehension would be justified. We accordingly pushed off, and had proceeded but a very short way when the canoe struck, and notwithstanding all our exertions, the violence of the current was so great as to drive her sideways down the river, and break her by the first bar, when I instantly jumped into the water, and the men followed my example; but before we could set her straight, or stop her, we came to deeper water, so that we were obliged to re-embark with the utmost precipitation. One of the men who was not sufficiently active, was left to get on shore in the best manner in his power. We had hardly regained our situations when we drove against a rock which shattered the stern of the canoe in such a manner, that it held only by the gunwales, so that the steersman could no longer keep his place. The violence of this stroke drove us to the opposite side of the river, which is but narrow, when the bow met with the same fate as the stern. At this moment the foreman seized on some branches of a small tree in the hope of bringing up the canoe, but such was their elasticity that, in a manner not easily described, he was jerked on shore in an instant, and with a degree of violence that threatened his distruction. But we had no time to turn from our own situation to enquire what had befallen him; for, in a few moments, we came across a cascade which broke several large holes in the bottom of the canoe, and started all the bars, except one behind the scooping seat. If this accident, however, had not happened, the vessel must have been irretrievably overset. The wreck becoming flat on the water, we all jumped out, while the steersman, who had been compelled to abandon his place, and had not recovered from his fright, called out to his companions to save themselves. My peremptory commands superseded the effects of his fear, and they all held fast to the wreck; to which fortunate resolution we owed our safety, as we should otherwise have been dashed against the rocks by the force of the water, or driven over the cascades. In this condition we were forced several hundred yards, and every yard on the verge of destruction; but, at length, we most fortunately arrived in shallow water and a small eddy, where we were enabled to make a stand, from the weight of the canoe resting on the stones, rather than from any exertions of our exhausted strength. For though our efforts were short, they were pushed to the utmost, as life or death depended on them. This alarming scene, with all its terrors and dangers, occupied only a few minutes; and in the present suspension of it, we called to the people on shore to come to our assistance, and they immediately obeyed the summons. The foreman, however, was the first with us; he had escaped unhurt from the extraordinary jerk with which he was thrown out of the boat, and just as we were beginning to take our effects out of the water, he appeared to give his assistance. The Indians, when they saw our deplorable situation, instead of making the least effort to help us, sat down and gave vent to their tears. I was on the outside of the canoe, where I remained till everything was got on shore, in a state of great pain from the extreme cold of the water; so that at length, it was with difficulty I could stand, from the benumbed state of my limbs.

The loss was considerable and important, for it consisted of our whole stock of balls, and some of our furniture; but these considerations were forgotten in the impressions of our miraculous escape. Our first enquiry was after the absent man, whom in the first moment of danger, we had left to get on shore, and in a short time his appearance removed our anxiety. We had, however, sustained no personal injury of consequence, and my bruises seemed to be in the greater proportion.

All the different articles were now spread out to dry. The powder had fortunately received no damage, and all my instruments had escaped. Indeed, when my people began to recover from their alarm and to enjoy a sense of safety, some of them, if not all, were by no means sorry for our late misfortune, from the hope that it must put a period to our voyage, particularly as we were without a canoe, and all the bullets sunk in the river. It did not, indeed, seem possible to them that we could proceed under these circumstances. I listened, however, to the observations that were made on the occasion without replying to them, till their panic was dispelled, and they had got themselves warm and comfortable, with an hearty meal, and rum enough to raise their spirits. . . .

June 22. At six in the morning we proceeded on our voyage, with two of the Indians, one of them in a small pointed canoe, made after the fashion of the Esquimaux, and the other in our own.

Our courses were south-south-east a mile and an half, south-east half a mile, south by east four miles and an half, south-east by south half a mile, south by west half a mile, south-east by east one mile, south-south-west a mile and an half, south by east one mile and a quarter. The country, on the right, presented a very beautiful appearance: it rose at first rather abruptly to the height of twenty-five feet, when the precipice was succeeded by an inclined plain to the foot of another steep; which was followed by another extent of gently rising ground: these objects, which were shaded with groves of fir, presenting themselves alternately to a considerable distance.

We now landed near a house, the roof of which alone appeared above ground; but it was deserted by its inhabitants who had been alarmed at our approach.

From this place we steered east by north half a mile, south by east three-quarters of a mile, and south by west a mile and an half, when we landed again on seeing some of the natives on the high ground, whose appearance was more wild and ferocious than any whom we had yet seen. Indeed I was under some apprehension that our guides, who went to conciliate them to us, would have fallen a prey to their savage fury. At length, however, they were persuaded to entertain a more favourable opinion of us, and they approached us one after another, to the number of sixteen men, and several women. I shook hands with them all, and desired my interpreters to explain that salutation as a token of friendship. They immediately invited us to pass the night at their lodges, which were at no great distance, and promised, at the same time, that they would, in the morning, send two men to introduce us to the next nation, who were very numerous, and ill-disposed towards strangers.

Among the men I found a Rocky Mountain Indian, who had been with them for some time. As he was understood by my interpreters, and was himself well acquainted with the language of the strangers, I possessed the means of obtaining every information respecting the country, which it might be in their power to afford me. I stated to these people the objects of my voyage, and the very great advantages which they would receive from my successful termination of it. They expressed themselves very much satisfied at my communications, and assured me that they would not deceive me respecting the subject of my enquiry. An old man also, who appeared to possess the character of a chief, declared his wish to see me return to his land, and that his two young daughters should then be at my disposal. I now proceeded to request the native, whom I had particularly selected, to commence his information, by drawing a sketch of the country upon a large piece of bark, and he immediately entered on the work, frequently appealing to, and sometimes asking the advice of, those around him. He described the river as running to the east of south, receiving many rivers, and every six or eight leagues encumbered with falls and rapids, some of which were very dangerous, and six of them impracticable. The carrying-places he represented as of great length, and passing over hills and mountains. He depicted the lands of three other tribes, in succession, who spoke different languages. Beyond them he knew nothing either of the river or country, only that it was still a long way to the sea; and that, as he had heard, there was a lake, before they reached the water, which the natives did not drink. As far as his knowledge of the river extended, the country on either side was level, in many places without wood, and abounding in red deer, and some of a small fallow kind. Few of the natives, he said, would come to the banks for some time; but that at a certain season they would arrive there in great numbers, to fish. They now procured iron, brass, copper, and trinkets, from the westward; but formerly these articles were obtained from the lower parts of the river, though in small quantities. A knife was produced which had been brought from that quarter. The blade was ten inches long, and an inch and an half broad, but with a very blunted edge. The handle was of horn. We understood that this instrument had been obtained from white men, long before they had heard that any came to the westward. One very old man observed, that as long as he could remember, he was told of white people to the southward; and that he had heard, though he did not vouch for the truth of the report, that one of them had made an attempt to come up the river, and was destroyed.

These people describe the distance across the country as very short to the western ocean; and, according to my own idea, it cannot be above five or six degrees. They assured us that the road was not difficult, as they avoided the mountains, keeping along the low lands between them, many parts of which are entirely free from wood. According to their account, this way is so often travelled by them, that their path is visible throughout the whole journey, which lies along small lakes and rivers. It occupied them, they said, no more than six nights, to go to where they meet the people who barter iron, brass, copper, beads, etc., with them, for dressed leather, and beaver, bear, lynx, fox, and marten skins. They had been informed by those whom they meet to trade with, that the white people, from whom these articles are obtained, were building houses at the distance of three days, or two nights journey from the place where they met last fall. With this route they all appeared to be well acquainted.

My people had listened with great attention to the relation which had been given me, and it seemed to be their opinion, that it would be absolute madness to attempt a passage through so many savage and barbarous nations. My situation may, indeed, be more easily conceived than expressed: I had no more than thirty days provision remaining, exclusive of such supplies as I might obtain from the natives, and the toil of our hunters, which, however, was so precarious as to be matter of little dependence: besides, our ammunition would soon be exhausted, particularly our ball, of which we had not more than an hundred and fifty, and about thirty pounds weight of shot, which, indeed, might be converted into bullets, though with great waste.

The more I heard of the river, the more I was convinced it could not empty itself into the ocean to the North of what is called the River of the West, so that with its windings, the distance must be very great. Such being the discouraging circumstances of my situation, which were now heightened by the discontents of my people, I could not but be alarmed at the idea of attempting to get to the discharge of such a rapid river, especially when I reflected on the tardy progress of my return up it, even if I should meet with no obstruction from the natives; a circumstance not very probable, from the numbers of them which would then be on the river; and whom I could have no opportunity of conciliating in my passage down, for the reasons which have been already mentioned. At all events, I must give up every expectation of returning this season to Athabasca. Such were my reflections at this period; but instead of continuing to indulge them, I determined to proceed with resolution, and set future events at defiance. . . .

[*A determination which brought him on July 19 "within sight of a narrow arm of the sea," and a day later "ten half-starved men in a leaky vessel" were riding the waters of the Pacific. The night of the 21st they slept upon a rock, and next morning Mackenzie "mixed up some vermilion in melted grease, and inscribed in large characters on the south-east face of the rock this brief memorial: 'Alexander Mackenzie, from Canada, by land, the twenty-second of July, one thousand seven hundred and ninety-three.' "*]

TO THE COUNTRY OF THE CROW INDIANS[1]

FRANÇOIS ANTOINE LAROCQUE

(*fl.* 1805)

AT my arrival at Rivière Fort de la Bosse I prepared for going on a voyage of discovery to the Rocky Mountains and set off on the 2nd June with two men, having each of us two horses, one of which was laden with goods to facilitate an intercourse with the Indians we might happen to see on our road. Mr Charles McKenzie and Mr Lassana set out with me to go and pass the summer at the Missouri, and having to parsue the same road we Kept Company as far as the B.B.[2] village.

Mr McKenzie with the other men set of about two in the afternoon, but I having [been] so very busy that I had not as yet been able to write my letters to my friends remained and wrote letters and settled some little business of my own. After sunset we supped and bidding farewell to Mr Chabelly[3] and Henry and to all the people, departed, everyone being affected at our departure, thinking it more than probable that I should not return with my men, and I confess I left the fort with a heavy heart, but riding at a good rate I soon got chearful again, and thought of nothing but the [means] of ensuring success to my undertaking. . . .

Monday 3rd. I sat of early in the morning and stopped at 12 to refresh our horses, and encamped at night at River la Sorie, where we had not been two hours encamped when three, and after many other Assiniboins rushed in upon us, a few endeavouring to take our horses, but seeing our guns and running to them we made them depart. . . . There were 40 tents of them not 10 acres from us. . . . I gave 1 fm.[4] tobacco to their Chief to make his young men smoke and engage them to remain peaceable. . . .

Thinking it hower not prudent to pass the night so close to them, we

[1] From *The Journal of Larocque*, Publications of the Canadian Archieves, No. 3.
[2] Big Bellies, called by the French *Gros Ventres*.
[3] Charles Chaboillez.
[4] Fathom, the tobacco being made in the form of a rope.

saddled our horses and departed. . . . We walked all night to come out of their reach for they are the worst cunning horse-thieves that ever I . . . heard of. . . .

Tuesday 4th. We proceeded on our journey early in the morning having very fine weather all day, and at night encamped on the banks of the River la Sourie at a place called Green River. . . .

Wednesday 5th. We followed the Green River till eleven o'clock when we arrived at the woods, where being an appearance of rainy weather we encamped. There was no Buffalo in sight. At 12 it began to rain and continued hard and uninterruptedly until next morning. Here we saw plenty of wild fowls, Ducks, Bustards, Geese, Swans, etc., and killed a number of them. . . .

Friday 7th. The weather continued cloudy, but the sun appearing now and then we hoped for fair weather, . . . but as yesterday it began to rain at 12, at two we found some wood on some sandy hills in the plains where we stopped to cook our goods, being completely trenched [drenched]. There being no water on the sandhills, we raised a Bark of Elm tree and putting one end in a Kettle, the other end a little higher, all the water that fell on the Bark ran into the kettle; . . . we also made a tent with bark and passed the night comfortably enough. . . .

Sunday 9th. . . . at 1 o'clock in the afternoon we arrived on the Bank of the River la Sourie. The water being amazing high we made a raft to cross our things over the River and the horses swam over. . . .

Monday 10th. slept in the Mandan plain, saw plenty of buffaloes all along, but did not dare to fire at them, being on the enemies lands in Sioux. . . .

Tuesday 11th. At 8 in the morning I saw the banks of the Missoury, at 12 arrived at the River Bourbeuse, when we. . . unloaded our horses and crossed the property on our shoulders there being not more than 2 feet of water, but we sunk up to our middle in mud, the horses bemired themselves in crossing and it was with difficulty we got them over the bank. . . . We intended to get the villages to-day but being overtaken by a Shower of rain we encamped in a coulé at the Serpent lodge, being a winter village of the B. Belly's at the Elbow of the River, where I passed part of last winter. . . .

Wednesday 12th. I arrived at 9 o'clock in the morning on the banks of the Missoury, fired a few shots to inform the indians of our being there and in a few hours many came over with Canoes to cross us and our things. Lafrance proceeded to the Mandans, but I and my men with Mr McKenzie crossed here at the B.Belly's and entered into dift lodges, gave my men each a small equipment of Knives, Tobacco and ammunition to give the landlords. . . .

Friday 14th. The indians here are exceedingly troublesome to sell their horses to us, the prise that we usually pay them for a horse can purchase two from the Rocky Mountain Indians[1] who are expected dayly. . . . I told them that the purpose of our coming was not to purchase horses either from them or the Rocky Mountains, that we came for Skins and Robes and that for that purpose one of us was to pass the summer with them and one at the Mandans; that I and two men were sent by the white people's Chief to smoke a pipe of peace and amity with the Rocky Mountain Indians and to accompany them to their lands to examine them and see if there were Beavers as is reported and to engage them to hunt it, that we would not purchase a horse from none, therefore that their best plan would be to dress Buffalo Robes, so as to have ammunition to trade with the Rocky Mountain Indians.

They pretend to be in fear of the surrounding nations, that is Assineboines, Sioux, Cheyennes, and Ricaras, so as to have an excuse for not trading their guns with the Rocky Mountain Indians, and likewise to prevent us. . . .

Saturday 15th. I was sent for by one of the Chiefs who asked me what I intended to do with the pipe stem I had brought, upon my telling him that it was for the Rocky Mountain Indians he made a long harangue to dissuade me from going there, saying that I would be obliged to winter there on account of the length of the way, that the Cayennes and Ricaras were enemies and constantly on the Road, and that it was probable we should be killed by them. He gave the worst character possible to the Rocky Mountain Indians, saying they were thieves and liars . . . to all which I answered that my Chief had sent me to go, and that I would or die. . . .

Thursday 20th. I was again teased by some of the Chief to purchase horses and was told the Big Bellys had two hearts and that they [did] not know whether they would allow me to go to the Rocky Mountains, and in the course of a long harangue they made use of all their art to induce me not to go, representing the journey as dangerous to the last degree and that the Rocky Mountains would not come, for they were afraid of the Ricaras and Assiniboines, to all of which I could make no answer but by signs, as there was no one present that could speak to them properly, one of my men of the name of Souci spoke the Sioux language, but there was no one there that understood that language. About [noon] two of the young B.B. that had been sent to meet the Rocky Mountains arrived, they left the Rocky Mountain Indians in the morning and they will be here in 3 or 4 days. . . .

Friday 21st. I went to see the Borgne, enquired of him what he and the Big Bellys thought of our going to the Rocky Mountains and whether they have

[1] Or Crows.

a mind to prevent us. He answered to my wish, that the Rocky Mountains were good people, that they had plenty of Beaver on their hands, and that his adopted son, one of the Chiefs of the Rocky Mountains and the greater would take care of us, for that he would strongly recommend to him to put the white people in his heart and watch over them. . . . He is the only Chief that speaks so, but as he has the most authority of any I hope by his means we will pass. . . .

Sunday 23rd. Three men and one woman arrived from the Rocky Mountains about noon, the others are near at hand and would have arrived to-day but for rain which fell in the evening.

In the evening I went to see the Brother of the Borgne, where I found two Rocky Mountain Indians, one of whom was the Chief of whom the Borgne had spoken to me. I smoked with them for some time when the Borgne told them that I was going with them and spoke very much in our favor. They appeared to be very well pleased. . . .

Tuesday 25th. About one in the afternoon the Rocky Mountain Indians arrived, they encamped at a little distance from the village with the warriors, to the number of 645, passed through the village on horseback with their shields and other warlike implements. . . .

Thursday 27th. Assembled the Chiefs of the different Bands of the Rock Mountains and made them a present of

2	Large Axes	16	large Knives
2	Small Axes	12	Small do
8	Ivory Combs	2	lbs. Vermillion
10	Wampum Shells	8	doz. Rings
8	fire steels and Flint	4	papers co'd Glasses
4	cassetête	4	Doz. Awls
6	Masses B.C.[1] Beads	1½	lb. Blue Beads
4	f. Tobacco	2	Doz. do
8	Cock feathers	1000	balls and powder

Made them smoke in a stem which I told them was that of the Chief of the White people who was desirous of making them his Children. . . . That I and two men were going with them to see their lands, . . . that our Chief sent them those goods that lay before them, to make them listen to what we were now telling them, that he expected they would treat all white people as their Brethren for that we were in peace and friendship with the Red skinned people and did not go about to get a scalp . . . and if they behaved well towards

[1] Probably Blue Canton.

us and kill Beavers, Otters, and Bears, they would have white people on the lands in a few year, who would winter with them and supply them with all their wants, and I told them many other things which I thought was necessary and closed the Harangue by making them smoke the Medicine Pipe. . . .

Saturday 29th. Saddled our horses and left the B. Belly village. We remained about half an hour in the Rocky Mountain Camp where they threw down their tents and all sat of. . . . We marched along the Knife River. . . .

Wednesday, July 3rd. We continued our journey for about 4 hours through a very hilly country and encamped at the foot of a very high Hill on the top of which I ascended, but could see at no considerable distance, another range of hills surrounding this on all sides. I lost my spy-glass in coming down. . . .

Tuesday 9th. From the Big Belly village to the place I lost my spy-glass the country was very hilly, from that to this place it was much more upon a level though not entirely so. The plains produce plenty of fine grass. In the course of this days journey . . . Buffalo were seen in amazing numbers, we camped on the side of a small Creek running West into the lesser Missouri. . . .

Saturday 13th. We set of at 9 through hilly and barren Country, in crossing two small Creeks, and arrived at 12 on the bank of lesser Missouri. We crossed it and encamped on its border about 2 miles higher. The River is here about 3/4 of an acre in breadth from bank to bank but there is very little water running, the bed appearing dry in many places. . . . A few days ago a child being sick I gave him a few drops of Turlington balsam which eased him immediately of his cholic. This cure gave me such a reputation of being a great phisician that I am plagered to cure every distemper in the camp. A man came to-day to me desiring me to act the man mid wife to his wife. . . .

Saturday 27th. We arrived at noon at the Powder River after 6 hours ride by course West by South for about 20 miles. The Powder River is here about 3/4 of an acre in breadth, its waters middling deep, but it appears to have risen lately as a quantity of leaves and wood are drifting on it. . . . There are Beaver dams all along the river . . . the plains on the western side of the river were covered with Buffaloes and the bottoms full of Elk and Jumping deers and Bears which last are mostly yellow and very fierce. It is amazing how very barren the ground is between this and the lesser Missouri. . . . Our horses were nearly starved. The current . . . is very strong and the water so muddy as to be hardly drinkable. The Indians say it is always so, and that is the reason they call it Powder River. . . .

Sunday, August 4th. We did not rise the Camp till late in the evening. In the morning we ascended the hills of the River and saw the Rocky Mountains not at a very great distance with Spy Glass, its cliffs and hollows could be easily observed with the wood interspersed among the Rocks. . . .

Tuesday 6th. We rose the Camp at 7 and proceeded upwards along the pine River in a S. Western direction for 12 miles, having the Rocky Mountains a head and in sight all day. . . . The Indians often inquire when I intend to depart. They appear to wish me to be off. I have 23 Beaver skins which they think a great deal, and more than we have occasion for. They thought that upon seeing the Rocky Mountains we would immediately depart as they cannot emmagine what I intend to see in them. It is hard to make them understand by signs only, especially in this case for they do not want to understand. . . .

Sunday 11th. They are undetermined in what course to proceed from this place, they have sent a party of young men along the Mountains Westerly, and are to wait here until they return. They often enquire with anxious expectation of our departure when I intend to leave them and to-day they were more troublesome than usual. What I have seen of their lands hitherto has not given me the satisfaction I look for [in] Beavers. I told them that I would remain with them 20 or 30 days more. That I wished very much to see the River aux Roches Jaunes[1] and the place they usually inhabit, otherwise that I would be unable to return and bring them their wants. They saw it was true, but to remove the objection of my not knowing their lands a few of them assembled and draughted on a dressed skin I believe a very good map of their Country and they showed me the place where at different season they were to be found. The only reason I think they have in wishing my departure is their haste to get what goods I still have. . . .

Tuesday 13th. We sat of at half after 8 in the morning following a West Course along the Mountain, through Creeks and hills such as I never saw before, it being impossible to climb these hills with Loaded Horses, we were obliged to go round them about the middle of their height from whence we were in imminent danger of rolling down, being so steep that one side of the horses rubbed against the side of the hill. One false step of the horse would certainly have been fatal to himself and rider. . . . We encamped at 12 on the banks of a small branch of the Tongue River, whose water was very clear and cold as Ice. . . .

Thursday 15th. Fine clear weather. I traded 8 Beavers and purchased a horse for which I paid a gun, 200 balls, one flanel Robe, one shirt, one half axe, one battle do. one bow iron, one comb, one But Knife, one small do. 2

[1] The Yellowstone.

Wampoon hair pipes, 2 axes, one Wampoon shell, 40 B. Blue Beads, 2 Mass Barley Corn do, and one fm. W.S. Red Stroud.[1]. . .

Monday 19th. Since we are close to the mountains many women have deserted with their lovers to their fine tents that are across the mountain. . . . Harangues were twice made to rise the Camp, and counter orders were given before the tents were thrown down. The reason of this is that the wife of the Spotted Crow, who regulates our movements, has deserted, [and] he is for going one way while the Chief of the other bands is for following our old course. . . .

Thursday 22nd. Water frose the thickness of paper last night in horsetracks. I was called to a Council in the Chiefs Brothers tent Lodge, where the Spotted Crow resigned his employment of regulating our marches, an other old man took the office upon himself and told me that he intended to pursue their old course to the River aux Roches Jaune. . . .

Saturday 24th. This morning we were allarmed by the report that three Indians had been seen on the first hill of the mountain and that three Buffaloes were in motion and that two shots had been heard towards the large Horn River. Thirty men saddled their horses and immediately went off to see what was the matter while all the other Kept in readiness to follow if necessary. In a few hours some came back and told us that they had seen 35 on foot walking on the banks of one of the branches of the Large Horn River. In less time than the Courier Could well tell his news no one remained in the Camp, but a few old men and women, all the rest scampered off in pursuit. I went along with them, we did not all Set off together nor could we all Keep together, as some horses were slower than other, but the foremost stopped galloping on a hill, and continued on with a small trot as people came up. They did the dance when the Chief arrived, he and his band or part of it galloped twice before the main body of the people, who still continued their trot, intersecting the line of their course, while one of his friends, I suppose his aide de Camp, harangued. They were all dressed in their best Cloths. Many of them were followed by their wives who carried their arms, and who were to deliver them at the time of Battle. . . . Ahead of us were some young men on different hills making signs with their Robes which way we were to go. As soon as all the Chiefs were come up and had made their harangue, every one set off the way he liked best and pursued according to his own judgement. The Country is very hilly and full of large Creeks whose banks are Rocks, so that the pursued had the advantage of being able to get into places where it was impossible to go with horses and hide themselves. All

[1] Blanket made at Stroud, in Gloucestershire.

escaped but two of the foremost, who being scouts of the party, had advanced nearer to us than the others and had not discovered us, they were surrounded after a long race but Killed and scalped in a twinkling. . . .

Sunday 25th. The Scalp dance was danced all night and the scalps carried in procession through the day.

Monday 26th. . . . at noon . . . we sat off. . . . We encamped in the mountain 9 miles distant from our last encampment by a small Creek in which there was little running water, but an amazing number of Beaver Dams. I counted 6 in about 2 points of the River but most of them appeared to be old Dams. The young men paraded all day with the scalps tied to their horses bridles singing and keeping time with the Drum and Sheskequois or Rattle. . . .

Sunday, September 8th. I sat off early this morning with two Indians to visit the River aux Roches Jaunes and the adjacent part. I intended to return from this place as the Indians will take a very round about road to go there. We were not half way when we fell in with Buffaloes, my guides were so bent upon hunting that they did not guide me where I wanted, and we returned at night to the tents with meat, but with rain, as it rained from noon till night. . . .

Tuesday 10th. We rose the Camp at 9 and took a N. West Course to the River aux Roches Jaunes where we arrived at two in the afternoon. . . . This is a fine large River in which there is a strong current, but the Indians say there are no falls. Fordable places are not easily found although I believe the water to be at its lowest. . . .

Wednesday 11th. 5 Big Bellys arrived and came into our lodge, being the Chief Lodge. They brought words of peace from their nation and say they Come to trade horses. They were well received by the Indians and presents of different articles were made them. They told me they had traded last winter with Mr Donald whom they made Known to me as crooked arm. I went round the Island in which we are encamped, it is about 5 miles in circumference and thickly wooded in some places all along the North Side of the Island. The Beaver has cut down about 50 feet of the wood. . . .

Saturday 14th. Having now full filled the instructions I received from Mr Chaboillez, which were to examine the lands of the Crow Indians and see if there is Beaver as was reported, and I to invite them to hunt it, I now prepared to depart. I assembled the Chiefs in Council, and after having smoked a few pipes, I informed them that I was setting off, that I was well pleased with them and their behaviour towards me, and that I would return to them next fall. I desired them to kill Beavers and Bears all winter, for that I would come and trade with them and bring them their wants. I added many reasons to show them that it was their interest to hunt Beavers, and then proceeded to settle the manners of Knowing one another next fall, and how I am to find them which is as follows. Upon my arrival at the Island, if I do not find them I am to go to the Mountain called Amanchabé Chije and then light 4 dift fires on 4 successive days, and they will Come to us (for it is very high and the fire can be seen at a great distance) in number 4 and not more, if more than four come to us we are to act upon the defensive for it will be other Indians. If we light less than 3 fires, they will not come to us, but think it is enemies. . . . I have 122 Beavers 4 Bears and two otters, which I traded not so much for their value (for they are all summer skins) as to show them that I set some value on the Beavers and our property. The presents I made them I thought were sufficient to gain their good will in which I think I succeeded. . . .

We departed about noon, 2 Chiefs accompanied us about 8 miles, we stopped and smoked a parting pipe, they embrased us, we shook hands and parted, they followed us about one mile, at a distance, gradually lessening their steps till we were almost out of sight, and Crying or pretending to Cry, they then turned their backs and went home. At parting they promised that none of their young men would follow us, they took heaven and earth to witness to attest their sincerity in what they had told us, and that they had opened their ears to my words and would do as I desired them, they made me sweare by the same that I would return and that I told them no false words (and certainly I had no intention of breaking my oath nor have I still . . .).

AUSTRALIA

BY WAY OF MOUNT HOPELESS[1]

(1860-61)

WILLIAM JOHN WILLS

(1834-61)

[*On August 21, 1860, an expedition for the exploration of the Australian interior had left Melbourne under the leadership of a Robert O'Hara Burke. On November 11 Burke reached Cooper's Creek, in Queensland. Here he waited over a month for his third officer, Wright, whom he had sent back for further supplies. As Wright did not come Burke, with Wills, King, and Gray, pushed on, leaving the Cooper's Creek depot in charge of Brahe. By February 4, 1861, Burke and his comrades succeeded in reaching the Gulf of Carpentaria, and on the 26th turned back, looking always for the supplies Wright was to bring. On April 16 Gray died, and when at last the others, worn out by famine and hardship, reached the depot they found it deserted.*]

April, 1861.

THE advance party of the V.E.E., consisting of Burke, Wills, and King (Gray being dead), having returned from Carpentaria, on the 21st April, 1861, in an exhausted and weak state, and finding that the depot party left at Cooper's Creek had started for the Darling with their horses and camels fresh and in good condition, deemed it useless to attempt to overtake them, having only two camels, both done up, and being so weak themselves as to be unable to walk more than four or five miles a day. Finding also that the provisions left at the depot for them would scarcely take them to Menindie, they started down Cooper's Creek for Adelaide, *via* Mount Hopeless, on the morning of 23rd April, 1861, intending to follow as nearly as possible the route taken by Gregory. By so doing they hoped to be able to recruit themselves and the camels whilst sauntering slowly down the creek, and to have sufficient provisions left to take them comfortably, or at least without risk, to some station in South Australia.

Tuesday, 23rd April, 1861. Having collected together all the odds and ends that seemed likely to be of use to us, in addition to provisions left in the plant, we started at 9.15 A.M., keeping down the southern bank of the creek; we only went about five miles, and camped at 11.30 on a billibong, where the feed was pretty good. We find the change of diet already making a great improvement in our spirits and strength. The weather is delightful, days agreeably warm, but the nights very chilly. The latter is more noticeable from

[1] From *A Successful Exploration through the Interior of Australia* (1863).

our deficiency in clothing, the depot party having taken all the reserve things back with them to the Darling.—To Camp No. 1.

Wednesday, 24th April, 1861. As we were about to start this morning, some blacks came by, from whom we were fortunate enough to get about twelve pounds of fish for a few pieces of straps and some matches, etc. This is a great treat for us, as well as a valuable addition to our rations. We started at 8.15 P.M. on our way down the creek, the blacks going in the opposite direction.—To Camp No. 2.

Thursday, 25th April, 1861. Awoke at five o'clock after a most refreshing night's rest—the sky was beautifully clear, and the air rather chilly. We had scarcely finished breakfast, when our friends the blacks, from whom we obtained the fish, made their appearance with a few more, and seemed inclined to go with us and keep up the supply. We gave them some sugar, with which they were greatly pleased—they are by far the most well-behaved blacks we have seen on Cooper's Creek. We did not get away from the camp until 9.30 A.M., continuing our course down the most southern branch of the creek, which keeps a general south-west course.—To Camp No. 3. The waterhole at this camp is a very fine one, being several miles long. The water-fowl are numerous, but rather shy, not nearly so much so, however, as those on the creeks between here and Carpentaria.

Friday, 26th April, 1861. We loaded the camels by moonlight this morning, and started at a quarter to six: striking off to the south of the creek, we soon got on a native path which leaves the creek just below the stony ground, and takes a course nearly west across a piece of open country. Leaving the path on our right at a distance of three miles, we turned up a small creek, which passes down between some sandhills, and, finding a nice patch of feed for the camels at a waterhole, we halted at 7.15 for breakfast. We started again at 9.50 A.M., continuing our westerly course along the path: we crossed to the south of the watercourse above the water, and proceeded over the most splendid salt-bush country that one could wish to see, bounded on the left by sandhills, whilst to the right the peculiar-looking flat-topped sandstone ranges form an extensive amphitheatre, through the far side of the arena of which may be traced the dark line of creek timber. At twelve o'clock we camped in the bed of the creek at Camp No. [3], our last camp on the road down from the Gulf, having taken four days to do what we then did in one. This comparative rest and the change in diet have also worked wonders, however; the leg-tied feeling is now entirely gone, and I believe that in less than a week we shall be fit to undergo any fatigue whatever. The camels are improving, and seem capable of doing all that we are likely to require of them.—To Camp No. 4.

Saturday, 27th April, 1861. We started at six o'clock, and, following the native path, which at about a mile from our camp takes a southerly direction, we soon came to the high sandy alluvial deposit which separates the creek at this point from the stony rises. Here we struck off from the path, keeping well to the south of the creek, in order that we might mess in a branch of it that took a southerly direction. At 9.20 we came in on the creek again where it runs due south, and halted for breakfast at a fine waterhole with fine fresh feed for the camels. Here we remained until noon, when we moved on again, and camped at one o'clock on a general course, having been throughout the morning S.W. eight miles.

Sunday, 28th April, 1861. Morning fine and calm, but rather chilly. Started at 4.45 A.M., following down the bed of a creek in a westerly direction by moonlight. Our stage was, however, very short for about a mile—one of the camels (Landa) got bogged by the side of a waterhole, and although we tried every means in our power, we found it impossible to get him out. All the ground beneath the surface was a bottomless quicksand, through which the beast sank too rapidly for us to get bushes of timber fairly beneath him; and being of a very sluggish stupid nature he could never be got to make sufficiently strenuous efforts towards extricating himself. In the evening, as a last chance, we let the water in from the creek, so as to buoy him up and at the same time soften the ground about his legs; but it was of no avail. The brute lay quietly in it, as if he quite enjoyed his position.—To Camp No. 6.

Monday, 29th April, 1861. Finding Landa still in the hole, we made a few attempts at extricating him, and then shot him, and after breakfast commenced cutting off what flesh we could get at for jerking.

Tuesday, 30th April, 1861. Remained here to-day for the purpose of drying the meat, for which process the weather is not very favourable.

Wednesday, 1st May, 1861. Started at 8.40, having loaded our only camel, Rajah, with the most necessary and useful articles, and packed up a small swag each, of bedding and clothing for our own shoulders. We kept on the right bank of the creek for about a mile, and then crossed over at a native camp to the left, where we got on a path running due west, the creek having turned to the north. Following the path we crossed an open plain, and then some sand ridges, whence we saw the creek straight ahead of us running nearly south again: the path took us to the southernmost point of the bend in a distance of about two and a half miles from where we had crossed the creek, thereby saving us from three to four miles, as it cannot be less than six miles round by the creek.—To Camp No. 7.

Thursday, 2nd May, 1861. Breakfasted by moonlight and started at 6.30.

Following down the left bank of the creek in a westerly direction, we came at a distance of six miles on a lot of natives who were camped on the bed of a creek. They seemed to have just breakfasted, and were most liberal in their presentations of fish and cake. We could only return the compliment by some fish-hooks and sugar. About a mile farther on we came to a separation of the creek, where what looked like the main branch turned towards the south. This channel we followed, not however without some misgivings as to its character, which were soon increased by the small and unfavourable appearance that the creek assumed. On our continuing along it a little farther it began to improve and widened out with fine waterholes of considerable depth. The banks were very steep, and a belt of scrub lined it on either side. This made it very inconvenient for travelling, especially as the bed of the creek was full of water for a considerable distance. At eleven A.M. we halted, until 1.30 P.M., and then moved on again, taking a S.S.W. course for about two miles, when at the end of a very long waterhole it breaks into billibongs, which continue splitting into sandy channels until they are all lost in the earthy soil of a box forest. Seeing little chance of water ahead, we turned back to the end of the long waterhole and camped for the night. On our way back Rajah showed signs of being done up. He had been trembling greatly all the morning. On this account his load was further lightened to the amount of a few pounds by the doing away with the sugar, ginger, tea, cocoa, and two or three tin plates.—To Camp No. 8.

Friday, 3rd May, 1861. Started at seven A.M., striking off in a northerly direction for the main creek.

Saturday, 4th May, 1861. Rajah was so stiff this morning as to be scarcely able to get up with his load. Started to return down the creek at 6.45, and halted for breakfast at 9 A.M., at the same spot as we breakfasted at yesterday. Proceeding from there down the creek we soon found a repetition of the features that were exhibited by the creek examined on Thursday. At a mile and a half we came to the last waterhole, and below that the channel became more sandy and shallow, and continued to send off billibongs to the south and west, slightly changing its course each time until it disappeared altogether in a north-westerly direction. Leaving King with the camel, we went on a mile or two to see if we could find water; and being unsuccessful we were obliged to return to where we had breakfasted as being the best place for feed and water.

Sunday, 5th May, 1861. Started by myself to reconnoitre the country in a southerly direction, leaving Mr Bruke and King with the camel at Camp No. 10. Travelled S.W. by S. for two hours, following the course of the most southerly billibongs; found the earthy soil becoming more loose and cracked up, and the box track gradually disappearing. Changed course to west for a high sand ridge, which I reached in one hour and a half, and continuing in the same direction to one still higher, obtained from it a good view of the surrounding country. To the north were the extensive box forests bounding the creek on either side. To the east earthy plains intersected by watercourses and lines of timber, and bounded in the distance by sand ridges. To the south the projection of the sand ridge partially intercepted the view; the rest was composed of earthy plains, apparently clothed with chrysanthemums. To the westward another but smaller plain was bounded also by high sand ridges running nearly parallel with the one on which I was standing.

This dreary prospect offering no encouragement to proceed, I returned to Camp 10 by a more direct and better route than I had come.

Monday, 6th May, 1861. Moved up the creek again to Camp No. 9, at the junction, to breakfast, and remained the day there. The present state of things is not calculated to raise our spirits much; the rations are rapidly diminishing; our clothing, especially the boots, are all going to pieces, and we have not the materials for repairing them properly; the camel is completely done up and can scarcely get along, although he has the best of feed and is resting half his time. I suppose this will end in our having to live like the blacks for a few months.

Tuesday, 7th May, 1861. Breakfasted at daylight; but when about to start found that the camel would not rise even without any load on his back. After making every attempt to get him up, we were obliged to leave him to himself.

Mr Burke and I started down the creek to reconnoitre; at about eleven miles we came to some blacks fishing; they gave us some half a dozen fish each, for luncheon, and intimated that if we would go to their camp we should have some more and some bread. I tore in two a piece of macintosh stuff that I had, and Mr Burke gave one piece and I the other. We then went on to their camp about three miles farther. On our arrival they led us to a spot to camp on, and soon afterwards brought a lot of fish, and a kind of bread which they call nardoo. The lighting a fire with matches delights them, but they do not care about having them. In the evening various members of the tribe came down with lumps of nardoo and handfuls of fish, until we were positively unable to eat any more. They also gave us some stuff they call bedgery or pedgery; it has a highly intoxicating effect when chewed even in small quantities. It appears to be the dried stems and leaves of some shrub.

Wednesday, 8th May, 1861. Left the blacks' camp at 7.30, Mr Bruke returning to the junction, whilst I proceeded to trace down the creek. This I found a shorter task than I had expected, for it soon showed signs of running out, and at the same time kept considerably to the north of west. There were several fine waterholes within about four miles of the camp I had left, but not a drop all the way beyond that, a distance of seven miles. Finding that the creek turned greatly towards the north, I returned to the blacks' encampment, and as I was about to pass they invited me to stay; I did so, and was even more hospitably entertained than before.

Thursday, 9th May, 1861. Parted from my friends, the blacks, at 7.30, and started for Camp No. 9.

Friday, 10th May, 1861. Mr Bruke and King employed in jerking the camel's flesh, whilst I went to look for the nardoo seed for making bread: in this I was unsuccessful, not being able to find a single tree of it in the neighbourhood of the camp. I, however, tried boiling the large kind of bean which the blacks call padlu; they boil easily, and when shelled are very sweet, much resembling in taste the French chestnut; they are to be found in large quantities nearly everywhere.

Saturday, 11th May, 1861. To-day Mr Burke and King started down the creek to the blacks' camp, determined to ascertain all particulars about the nardoo. I have now my turn at the meat jerking, and must devise some means for trapping the birds and rats, which is a pleasant prospect after our dashing trip to Carpentaria, having to hang about Cooper's Creek, living like the blacks.

Sunday, 12th May, 1861. Mr Burke and King returned this morning having been unsuccessful in their search for the blacks, who it seems have moved over to the other branch of the creek.

Tuesday, 14th May, 1861. Mr Burke and King gone up the creek to look for blacks with four days' provisions. Self employed in preparing for a final start on their return.

This evening Mr Burke and King returned, having been some considerable distance up the creek and found no blacks. It is now settled that we plant the things, and all start together the day after to-morrow.

Wednesday, 15th, 1861. Planting the things and preparing to leave the creek for Mount Hopeless.

Thursday, 16th, 1861. Having completed our planting, etc., started up the creek for the second blacks' camp, a distance of about eight miles: finding our loads rather too heavy we made a small plant here of such articles as could best be spared.

Nardoo, Friday, 17th May, 1861. Started this morning on a blacks' path, leaving the creek on our left, our intention being to keep a south-easterly direction until we should cut some likely looking creek, and then to follow it down. On approaching the foot of the first sandhill, King caught sight in the flat of some nardoo seeds, and we soon found that the flat was covered with them. This discovery caused somewhat of a revolution in our feelings, for we considered that with the knowledge of this plant we were in a position to support ourselves, even if we were destined to remain on the creek and wait for assistance from town.

Friday, 24th May, 1861. Started with King to celebrate the Queen's birthday by fetching from Nardoo Creek what is now to us the staff of life; returned at a little after two P.M. with a fair supply, but find the collecting of the seed a slower and more troublesome process than could be desired.

Monday, 27th May, 1861. Started up the creek this morning for the depot, in order to deposit journals and a record of the state of affairs here. On reaching the sandhills below where Landa was bogged, I passed some blacks on a flat collecting nardoo seed. Never saw such an abundance of the seed before. The ground in some parts was quite black with it. There were only two or three gins[1] and children, and they directed me on, as if to their camp, in the direction I was before going; but I had not gone far over the first sandhill when I was overtaken by about twenty blacks, bent on taking me back to their camp, and promising any quantity of nardoo and fish. On my going with them, one carried the shovel, and another insisted on taking my swag in such a friendly manner that I could not refuse them. They were greatly amused with the various little things I had with me. In the evening they supplied me with abundance of nardoo and fish, and one of the old men, Poko Tinnamira, shared his gunyah with me.

Tuesday, 28th May, 1861. Left the blacks' camp, and proceeded up the creek; obtained some mussels near where Landa died, and halted for breakfast. Still feel very unwell.

Wednesday, 29th. Started at seven A.M., and went on to the duckholes, where we breakfasted coming down. Halted there at 9.30 A.M. for a feed, and then moved on. At the stones saw a lot of crows quarrelling about something near the water; found it to be a large fish, of which they had eaten a considerable portion. As it was quite fresh and good, I decided the quarrel by taking it with me. It proved a most valuable addition to my otherwise scanty supper of nardoo porridge. This evening I camped very comfortably in a mia-mia, about eleven miles from the depot. The night was very cold, although not entirely cloudless.

Thursday, 30th May, 1861. Reached the depot this morning at eleven A.M.;

[1] Native women.

no traces of anyone except blacks having been here since we left. Deposited some journals and a notice of our present condition. Started back in the afternoon, and camped at the first waterhole. Last night, being cloudy, was unusually warm and pleasant.

Friday, 31st May, 1861. Decamped at 7.30 A.M., having first breakfasted; passed between the sandhills at nine A.M., and reached the blanket mia-mias at 10.40 A.M.; from there proceeded on to the rocks, where I arrived at 1.30 P.M., having delayed about half an hour on the road in gathering some portulac. It had been a fine morning, but the sky now became overcast, and threatened to set in for steady rain; and as I felt very weak and tired, I only moved on about a mile further, and camped in a sheltered gully under some bushes.

Saturday, 1st June, 1861. Started at 7.45 A.M.; passed the duckholes at ten A.M. and my second camp up, at two P.M., having rested in the meantime about forty-five minutes. Thought to have reached the blacks' camp, or at least where Landa was bogged, but found myself altogether too weak and exhausted; in fact, had extreme difficulty in getting across the numerous little gullies, and was at last obliged to camp from sheer fatigue.

Sunday, 2nd June, 1861. Started at half-past six, thinking to breakfast at the blacks' camp below Landa's grave. Found myself very much fagged, and did not arrive at their camp until ten A.M., and then found myself disappointed as to a good breakfast, the camp being deserted. Having rested awhile and eaten a few fishbones, I moved down the creek, hoping by a late march to be able to reach our own camp; but I soon found, from my extreme weakness, that that would be out of the question. A certain amount of good luck, however, still stuck to me, for on going along by a large waterhole I was so fortunate as to find a large fish, about a pound and a half in weight, which was just being choked by another which it had tried to swallow, but which had stuck in its throat. I soon had a fire lit, and both of the fish cooked and eaten: the large one was in good condition. Moving on again after my late breakfast, I passed Camp No. 67 of the journey to Carpentaria, and camped for the night under some polygonum bushes.

Monday, 3rd June, 1861. Started at seven o'clock, and keeping on the south bank of the creek was rather encouraged at about three miles by the sound of numerous crows ahead; presently fancied I could see smoke, and was shortly afterwards set at my ease by hearing a cooey from Pitchery, who stood on the opposite bank, and directed me round the lower end of the waterhole, continually repeating his assurance of abundance of fish and bread. Having with some considerable difficulty managed to ascend the sandy path that led to the camp, I was conducted by the chief to a fire where a large pile of fish were just being cooked in the most approved style. These I imagined to be for the general consumption of the half-dozen natives gathered around, but it turned out that they had already had their breakfast. I was expected to dispose of this lot—a task which, to my own astonishment, I soon accomplished, keeping two or three blacks pretty steadily at work extracting the bones for me. The fish being disposed of, next came a supply of nardoo cake and water until I was so full as to be unable to eat any more; when Pitchery, allowing me a short time to recover myself, fetched a large bowl of the raw nardoo flour mixed to a thin paste, a most insinuating article, and one that they appear to esteem a great delicacy. I was then invited to stop the night there, but this I declined, and proceeded on my way home.

Tuesday, 4th June, 1861. Started for the blacks' camp intending to test the practicability of living with them, and to see what I could learn as to their ways and manners.

Wednesday, 5th June, 1861. Remained with the blacks. Light rain during the greater part of the night, and more or less throughout the day in showers. Wind blowing in squalls from south.

Thursday, 6th June, 1861. Returned to our own camp: found that Mr Burke and King had been well supplied with fish by the blacks. Made preparation for shifting our camp nearer theirs on the morrow.

Friday, 7th June, 1861. Started in the afternoon for the blacks' camp with such things as we could take; found ourselves all very weak in spite of the abundant supply of fish that we have lately had. I myself, could scarcely get along, although carrying the lightest swag, only about thirty pounds. Found that the blacks had decamped, so determined on proceeding to-morrow up to the next camp, near the nardoo field.

Saturday, 8th June, 1861. With the greatest fatigue and difficulty we reached the nardoo camp. No blacks, greatly to our disappointment; took possession of their best mia-mia and rested for the remainder of the day.

Sunday, 9th June, 1861. King and I proceeded to collect nardoo, leaving Mr Burke at home.

Monday, 10th Jund, 1861. Mr Burke and King collecting nardoo; self at home too weak to go out; was fortunate enough to shoot a crow.

Tuesday, 11th June, 1861. King out for nardoo; Mr Burke up the creek to look for the blacks.

Wednesday, 12th June, 1861. King out collecting nardoo; Mr Burke and I at home pounding and cleaning. I still feel myself, if anything, weaker in the legs, although the nardoo appears to be more thoroughly digested.

Thursday, 13th June , 1861. Mr Burke and King out for nardoo; self weaker than ever; scarcely able to go to the waterhole for water.

Friday, 14th June, 1861. Night alternately clear and cloudy; no wind; beautifully mild for the time of year; in the morning some heavy clouds on the horizon. King out for nardoo; brought in a good supply. Mr Burke and I at home, pounding and cleaning seed. I feel weaker than ever, and both Mr B. and King are beginning to feel very unsteady in the legs.

Saturday, 15th June, 1861. Night clear, calm, and cold; morning very fine, with a light breath of air from N.E. King out for nardoo; brought in a fine supply. Mr Burke and I pounding and cleaning; he finds himself getting very weak, and I am not a bit stronger.

Sunday, 16th June, 1861. We finished up the remains of the camel Rajah yesterday, for dinner; King was fortunate enough to shoot a crow this morning.

The rain kept all hands in, pounding and cleaning seed during the morning. The weather cleared up towards the middle of the day, and a brisk breeze sprang up in the south, lasting till near sunset, but rather irregular in its force. Distant thunder was audible to westward and southward frequently during the afternoon.

Monday, 17th June, 1861. Night very boisterous and stormy; northerly wind blowing in squalls, and heavy showers of rain, with thunder in the north and west. King out in the afternoon for nardoo.

Tuesday, 18th June, 1861. Exceedingly cold night; sky clear, slight breeze, very chilly and changeable; very heavy dew, warmer towards noon.

Wednesday, 19th June, 1861. About eight o'clock a strong southerly wind sprung up, which enabled King to blow the dust out of our nardoo seed, but made me too weak to render him any assistance.

Thursday, 20th June, 1861. Night and morning very cold, sky clear. I am completely reduced by the effects of the cold and starvation. King gone out for nardoo; Mr Burke at home pounding seed; he finds himself getting very weak in the legs. King holds out by far the best; the food seems to agree with him pretty well.

Finding the sun come out pretty warm towards noon, I took a sponging all over; but it seemed to do little good beyond the cleaning effects, for my weakness is so great that I could not do it with proper expedition.

I cannot understand this nardoo at all—it certainly will not agree with me in any form; we are now reduced to it alone, and we manage to consume from four to five pounds per day between us; it appears to be quite indigestible, and cannot possibly be sufficiently nutritious to sustain life by itself.

Friday, 21st June, 1861. Last night was cold and clear, winding up with a strong wind from N.E. in the morning. I feel much weaker than ever and can scarcely crawl out of the mia-mia. Unless relief comes in some form or other, I cannot possibly last more than a fortnight.

It is a great consolation, at least, in this position of ours, to know that we have done all we could, and that our deaths will rather be the result of the mismanagement of others than of any rash acts of our own. Had we come to grief elsewhere, we could only have blamed ourselves; but here we are returned to Cooper's Creek, where we had every reason to look for provisions and clothing; and yet we have to die of starvation, in spite of the explicit instructions given by Mr Burke—"That the depot party should await our return"; and the strong recommendation to the Committee "that we should be followed up by a party from Menindie."

Saturday, 22nd June, 1861. There were a few drops of rain during the night, and in the morning, about nine A.M., there was every prospect of more rain until towards noon, when the sky cleared up for a time.

Mr Burke and King are out for nardoo; the former returned much fatigued. I am so weak to-day as to be unable to get on my feet.

Sunday, 23rd June, 1861. All hands at home. I am so weak as to be incapable of crawling out of the mia-mia. King holds out well, but Mr Burke finds himself weaker every day.

Monday, 24th June, 1861. A fearful night. At about an hour before sunset, a southerly gale sprung up and continued throughout the greater portion of the night; the cold was intense, and it seemed as if one would be shrivelled up. Towards morning it fortunately lulled a little, but a strong cold breeze continued till near sunset, after which it became perfectly calm.

King went out for nardoo in spite of the wind, and came in with a good load; but he himself terribly cut up. He says that he can no longer keep up the work, and as he and Mr Burke are both getting rapidly weaker, we have but a slight chance of anything but starvation, unless we can get hold of some blacks.

Tuesday, 25th June, 1861. Night calm, clear, and intensely cold, especially towards morning. Near daybreak, King reported seeing a moon in the east, with a haze of light stretching up from it; he declared it to be quite as large as the moon, and not dim at the edges. I am so weak that any attempt to get a sight of it was out of the question; but I think it must have been Venus in the Zodiacal Light that he saw, with a corona around her.

26th. Mr Burke and King remain at home cleaning and pounding seed; they are both getting weaker every day; the cold plays the deuce with us, from the small amount of clothing we have: my wardrobe consists of a wide-awake, a merino shirt, a regatta shirt without sleeves, the remains of a pair of flannel trousers, two pairs of socks in rags, and a waistcoat, of which I have managed to keep the pockets together. The others are no better off. Besides these, we have between us, for bedding, two small camel pads, some horsehair, two or three little bits of rag, and pieces of oilcloth saved from the fire.

The day turned out nice and warm.

Wednesday, 27th June, 1861. Mr Burke and King are preparing to go up the creek in search of the blacks; they will leave me some nardoo, wood, and water, with which I must do the best I can until they return. *I think this is almost our only chance.* I feel myself, if anything, rather better, but I cannot say stronger: the nardoo is beginning to agree better with me; but without some change I see little chance for any of us. They have both shown great hesitation and reluctance with regard to leaving me, and have repeatedly desired my candid opinion in the matter. I could only repeat, however, that I considered it our only chance, for I could not last long on the nardoo, even if a supply could be kept up.

Friday, 29th June, 1861. Clear, cold night, slight breeze from the east, day beautifully warm and pleasant. Mr Burke suffers greatly from the cold and is getting extremely weak; he and King start to-morrow up the creek to look for the blacks; it is the only chance we have of being saved from starvation. I am weaker than ever, although I have a good appetite and relish the nardoo much; but it seems to give us no nutriment, and the birds here are so shy as not to be got at. Even if we got a good supply of fish, I doubt whether we could do much work on them and the nardoo alone. Nothing now but the greatest good luck can save any of us; and as for myself I may live four or five days if the weather continues warm. My pulse is at forty-eight, and very weak, and my legs and arms are nearly skin and bone. I can only look out, like Mr Micawber, "for *something to turn up*"; starvation on nardoo is by no means very unpleasant, but for the weakness one feels, and the utter inability to move one's self; for as far as appetite is concerned, it gives the greatest satisfaction.

(*Signed*) W.J. WILLS

[*Burke died two days after leaving Wills; King, returning to Wills, found him lying dead in his gunyah. He himself managed to find the natives, with whom, three months later, the search-party found him.*]

UNITED STATES

THE STORY OF POCAHONTAS[1]

As told in a Letter to James the First's Queen by Captain John Smith (1579-1631)

MOST ADMIRED QUEENE,

The love I beare my God, my King and Countrie, hath so of emboldened mee in the worst of extreme dangers, that now honestie doth constraine mee [to] presume thus farre beyond myselfe, [as] to present your Majestie [with] this short discourse.

Some ten yeeres agoe, being in Virginia, and taken prisoner by the power of Powhatan their chiefe King, I received from this great Salvage exceeding great courtesie, especially from his sonne, Nantaquans, the most manliest, comeliest, boldest spirit I ever saw in a Salvage, and his sister Pocahontas, the Kings most deare and welbeloved daughter, being but a childe of twelve or thirteene yeeres of age, whose compassionate pitifull heart, of my desperate estate, gave me much cause to respect her. I being the first Christian this proud King and his grim attendants ever saw, and thus inthralled in their barbarous power, I cannot say I felt the least occasion of want that was in the power of those, my mortall foes, to prevent, notwithstanding all their threats.

After some six weeks fatting amongst those Salvage Courtiers, at the minute of my Execution, she hazarded the beating out of her owne braines to save mine; and not only that, but so prevailed with her father, that I was safely conducted to James Towne, where I found about eight and thirtie miserable, poore and sicke creatures to keepe possession of all those large territories of Virginia: such was the weaknesse of this poore Commonwealth as, had the Salvages not fed us, we directly had starved. And this reliefe, most gracious Queene, was commonly brought us by this Lady Pocahontas: notwithstanding all these passages when inconstant Fortune turned our peace to warre, this tender Virgin would still not spare to dare to visit us, and by her our jarres have beene oft appeased and our wants still supplyed. Were it the policie of her father thus to imploy her, or the ordinance of God thus to make her his instrument, or her extraordinarie affection to our Nation, I know not: but of this I am sure—when her father, with the utmost of his policie and power, sought to surprize mee, [1] having but eighteene with mee, the darke night could not affright her from comming through the irkesome woods, and

[1] From *The Travels of Captain John Smith.*

with watered eies gave me intelligence, with her best advice [how] to escape his furie; which had hee knowne, hee had surely slaine her.

James Towne, with her wild traine, she as freely frequented as her fathers habitation, and during the time of two or three yeeres, she next, under God, was still the instrument to preserve this Colonie from death, famine and utter confusion, which, if in those times had once beene dissolved, Virginia might have lain as it was at our first arrivall to this day.

Since then, this businesse having beene turned and varied by many accidents, it is most certaine [that] after a long and troublesome warre, after my departure, betwixt her father and our Colonie—all which time shee was not heard of—about two yeeres after, shee herselfe was taken prisoner, being so detained neere two yeeres, and, at last, rejecting her barbarous condition, was maried to an English Gentleman with whom at this present she is in England; the first Christian ever of that Nation, the first Virginian ever spake English, or had a childe in mariage by an Englishman, a matter surely, if my meaning bee truly considered and well understood, worthy a Princes understanding.

Thus, most gracious Lady, I have related to your Majestie, what, at your best leisure, our approved Histories will account you at large, and however this might bee presented [to] you from a more worthy pen, it cannot from a more honest heart, [for] as yet I never begged any thing of the state or any; and it is my want of abilitie, and her exceeding desert; your birth, meanes and authoritie; her birth, vertue, want and simplicitie, doth make mee thus bold, humbly to beseech your Majestie to take this knowledge of her, though it be from one so unworthy as my selfe, her husbands estate not being able to make her fit to attend your Majestie. If she should not be well received, seeing this Kingdome may rightly have a Kingdome by her meanes, her present love to us might turne to such scorne and furie as to divert all this good to the worst of evill; where [as] finding so great a Queene should doe her some honour would so ravish her with content as endeare her dearest bloud to effect that [which] your Majestie and all the Kings honest subjects most earnestly desire. And so I humbly kisse your gracious hands.

Hearing she was at Branford with divers of my friends, I went to see her. After a modest salutation, without any word, she turned about, as not seeming well contented. But not long after, she began to talke and remembred mee well what courtesies shee had done; saying:

"You did promise Powhatan what was yours should bee his, and he the like to you. You called him father, being in his land a stranger, and by the same reason so must I doe you."

Which though I would have excused, I durst not allow of that title, because she was a Kings daughter. With a well set countenance she said:

"Were you not afraid to come into my fathers Countrie, and caused feare in him and all his people but mee, and feare you here I should call you father. I tell you then I will, and you shall call mee childe, and so I will bee for ever and ever your Countrieman. They did tell us alwaies you were dead, and I knew no other till I came to Plimoth; yet Powhatan did command Uttamatomakkin to seeke you, and know the truth, because your Countriemen will lie much."

This Salvage, one of Powhatans Councell, being an understanding fellow, the King purposely sent him, as they say, to number the people here and informe him well what wee were and our state. Arriving at Plimoth, according to his directions, he got a long sticke, whereon by notches hee did thinke to have kept the number of all the men hee could see, but hee was quickly wearie of that taske. Comming to London, where by chance I met him, having renewed our acquaintance, he told mee Powhatan did bid him to finde me out, to shew him our God, the King, Queene and Prince, I so much had told them of. Concerning God, I told him the best I could; the King, I heard he had seene, and the rest hee should see when he would. He denied ever to have seene the King, till by circumstances he was satisfied he had. Then he replyed very sadly:

"You gave Powhatan a white Dog, which Powhatan fed as himselfe, but your King gave me nothing, and I am better than your white Dog."

The small time I staid in London, divers Courtiers and others, my acquaintances, hath gone with mee to see her, that did thinke God had a great hand in her conversion, and they have seene many English Ladies worse favoured, proportioned and behavioured: and it pleased both the King and Queenes Majestie honourably to esteeme her, accompanied with that honourable Lady, the Lady De la Ware, and that honourable Lord, her husband, and divers other persons of good qualities, both publikely at the maskes and otherwise, to her great satisfaction and content: which, doubtlesse, she would have deserved, had she lived to arrive in Virginia.

[*In 1617 "the Lady Pocahontas, alias Rebecca, with her husband and others, in the good ship called the 'George' " was about to sail for Virginia, when "it pleased God at Gravesend to take this young Ladie to his mercie, where shee made not more sorrow for her unexpected death, than joy to the beholders, to heare and see her make so religious and godly an end. Her little childe Thomas Rolfe, therefore, was left at Plimoth with Sir Lewis Stukly, that desired the keeping of it."*]

BY HORSE FROM BOSTON TO NEW HAVEN[1]

(1704)

SARAH KNIGHT

MONDAY, Octb'r ye second, 1704—About three o'clock afternoon, I begun my Journey from Boston to New-Haven; being about two Hundred Mile. My Kinsman, Capt. Robert Luist, waited on me as farr as Dedham, where I was to meet ye Western post.

Tuesday, October ye third, about 8 in the morning, I with the Post proceeded forward without observing any thing remarkable; And about two, afternoon, Arrived at the Post's second stage, where the western Post mett him and exchanged Letters. Here, having called for something to eat, ye woman bro't in a Twisted thing like a cable, but something whiter; and laying it on the bord, tugg'd for life to bring it into capacity to spread; wch having wth great pains accomplished, shee serv'd in a dish of Pork and Cabage, I suppose the remains of Dinner. The sause was of a deep Purple, wch I tho't was boil'd in her dye Kettle; the bread was Indian, and every thing on the Table service Agreeable to these. I, being hungry gott a little down; but my stomach was soon cloy'd, and what cabbage I swallowed serv'd me for a Cudd the whole day after.

Having here discharged the Ordinary for self and Guide, (as I understood was the custom) About Three afternoon went on with my Third Guide, who Rode very hard; and having crossed Providence Ferry, we come to a River wch they Generally Ride thro'. But I dare not venture; so the Post got a Ladd and Cannoo to carry me to tother side, and hee rid thro' and Led my hors. The Cannoo was very smal and shallow, so that when we were in she seem'd redy to take in water, which greatly terrified mee, and caused me to be very circumspect, sitting with my hands fast on each side, my eyes stedy, not daring so much as to lodg my tongue a hair's breadth more on one side of my mouth then tother, nor so much as think on Lott's wife, for a wry thought would have oversett our wherey: But was soon put out of this pain, by feeling the Cannoo on Shore, wch I as soon almost saluted with my feet; and Rewarding my sculler, again mounted and made the best of our way forwards. The Rode here was very even and ye day pleasant, it being now near Sunsett. But the Post told mee we had neer 14 miles to Ride to the next Stage, (where we were to Lodg). I askt him of the rest of the Rode, foreseeing wee must travail in the night. Hee told mee there was a bad River we were to Ride thro', wch was so very firce a hors could sometimes hardly stem it: But it was

[1] From *The Journal of Madame Knight* (1704).

but narrow, and wee should soon be over. I can't express The concern of mind this relation sett me in: no thoughts but those of the dang'ros River could entertain my Imagination, and they were as formidable as varios, still Tormenting me with blackest Ideas of my Approching fate—Sometimes seeing my self drowning, other whiles drowned, and at the best like a holy Sister Just come out of a Spiritual Bath in dripping Garments.

Now was the Glorious Luminary, wth his swift Coursers, arrived at his Stage, leaving poor me wth the rest of this part of the lower world in darkness, with which *wee* were soon Surrounded, the only Glimering we now had was from the spangled Skies, Whose Imperfect Reflections rendered every Object formidable. Each lifeless Trunk, with its shatter'd Limbs, appear'd an Armed Enymie; and every little stump like a Ravenous devourer. Nor could I so much as discern my Guide, when at any distance, which added to the terror.

Thus, absolutely lost in Thought, and dying with the very thoughts of drowning, I come up wth the Post, who I did not see till even with his Hors: he told mee he stopt for mee: and wee Rode on Very Deliberatly a few paces, when we entred a Thickett of Trees and Shrubbs, and I perceived by the Hors's going, we were on the descent of a Hill, wch, as wee come neerer the bottom, 'twas totaly dark wth the Trees that surrounded it. But I knew by the Going of the Hors wee had entred the water, wch my Guide told mee was the hazzardos River he had told me off; and hee, Riding up close to my Side, Bid me not fear—we should be over Imediatly. I now ralyed all the Courage I was mistriss of, Knowing that I must either Venture my fate of drowning, or be left like ye Children in the wood. So, as the Post bid me, I gave Reins to my Nagg; and sitting as stedy as Just before in the Cannoo, in a few minutes got safe to the other side, which hee told me was the Narragansett country.

Here Wee found great difficult in Travailing, the way being very narrow, and on each side the Trees and bushes gave us very unpleasant welcomes wth their Branches and bow's, wch wee could not avoid, it being so exceeding dark. My Guide, as before so now, putt on harder than I, wth my weary bones, could follow; so left mee and the way beehind him. Now Returned my distressed aprehensions of the place where I was: the dolesome woods, my Company next to none, Going I knew not whither, and encompased wth Terrifying darkness: The least of which was enough to startle a more Masculine courage. Added to which the Reflections, as in the afternoon of ye day that my Call was very Questionable, wch till then I had not so Prudently as I ought considered. Now, coming to ye foot of a hill, I found great difficulty in ascending; But being got to the Top, was there amply recompenced with the friendly Appearance of the Kind Conductress of the night, Just then Advancing above the Horisontall Line. The Rapture wch the Sight of that fair Planett produced in mee, caus'd mee, for the Moment, to forgett my present wearyness and past toils; and Inspir'd me for most of the remaining way with very divirting tho'ts, some of which, with the other Occurances of the day, I reserved to note down when I should come to my Stage.

From hence wee kept on, with more ease yn before: the way being smooth and even, the night warm and serene, and the Tall and thick Trees at a distance, especially wn the moon glar'd light through the branches, fill'd my Imagination wth the pleasant delusion of a Sumpteous citty, fill'd wth famous Buildings and churches, wth their spiring steeples, Balconies, Galleries and I know not what: Granduers wch I had heard of, and wch the stories of foreign countries had given me the Idea of.

Being thus agreably entertain'd without a thou't of any thing but thoughts themselves, I on a sudden was Rous'd from these pleasing Imaginations, by the Post's sounding his horn, which assured mee hee was arrived at the Stage, where we were to Lodg; and that musick was then most musickall and agreeable to mee.

Being come to mr Havens', I was very civilly Received, and courteously entertained, in a clean comfortable House; and the Good woman was very active in helping off my Riding clothes, and then ask't what I would eat. I told her I had some Chocolett, if shee would prepare it; which with the help of some Milk, and a little clean brass Kettle, she soon effected to my satisfaction. I then betook me to my Appartment, wch was a little Room parted from the Kitchen by a single bord partition; where, after I had noted the Occurrances of the past day, I went to bed, which, tho' pretty hard, Yet neet and handsome.

ACROSS THE ALLEGHANYS[1]

(1753)

GEORGE WASHINGTON

(1732-99)

[*Intelligence having been received that the French were making encroachments on British territory beyond the Alleghany Mountains, Governor Dinwiddie resolved to send a commission to demand their designs. On October 31, 1753, he dispatched the officer he had chosen, Major George Washington, then aged twenty-one.*]

[1] From "Journal of a Tour over the Alleghany Mountains" (1753-54), as given in *The Life of George Washington*, by Jared Sparks (1839).

I WAS commissioned and appointed by the Hon. Robert Dinwiddie, Esq., Governor of Virginia, to visit and deliver a letter to the commandant of the French forces on the Ohio, and set out on the intended journey on the same day; the next I arrived at Fredericksburg, and engaged Mr Jacob Vanbraam to be my French interpreter, and proceeded with him to Alexandria, where we provided necessaries. From thence we went to Winchester, and got baggage, horses, etc., and from thence we pursued the new road to Will's Creek, where we arrived on the 14th of November.

Here I engaged Mr Gist to pilot us out, and also hired four others as servitors, Barnaby Currin, and John M'Quire, Indian traders, Henry Steward and William Jenkins; and in company with those persons, left the inhabitants the next day.

The excessive rains and vast quantity of snow which had fallen prevented our reaching Mr Frazier's, an Indian trader, at the mouth of Turtle Creek, on Monongahela River, until Thursday, the 22nd. We were informed here that expresses had been sent a few days before to the traders down the river, to acquaint them with the French general's death, and the return of the major part of the French army into winter quarters.

The waters were quite impassable without swimming our horses, which obliged us to get the loan of a canoe from Frazier, and to send Barnaby Currin and Henry Steward down the Monongahela, with our baggage, to meet us at the Fork of the Ohio, about ten miles; there to cross the Allegany.

As I got down before the canoe I spent some time in viewing the rivers, and the land in the Fork, which I think extremely well situated for a fort, as it has the absolute command of both rivers. The land at the point is twenty or twenty-five feet above the common surface of the water; and a considerable bottom of flat, welltimbered land all around it, very convenient for building. The rivers are each a quarter of a mile or more across, and run here very nearly at right angles, Allegany bearing north-east, and Monongahela south-east. The former of these two is a very rapid and swift running river, the other deep and still, without any perceptible fall.

About two miles from this, on the south-east side of the river, at the place where the Ohio Company intended to erect a fort, lives Shingiss, King of the Delawares. We called upon him, to invite him to counsel at the Logstown.

Shingiss attended us to the Logstown, where we arrived between sunsetting and dark, the twenty-fifth day after I left Williamsburg. We travelled over some extremely good and bad land to get to this place.

As soon as I came into town, I went to Monacatoocha (as the Half-King was out at his hunting-cabin on Little Beaver Creek, about fifteen miles off), and informed him by John Davidson, my Indian interpreter, that I was sent a messenger to the French generanl, and was ordered to call upon the sachems of the Six Nations to acquaint them with it. I gave him a string of wampum and a twist of tobacco, and desired him to send for the Half-King, which he promised to do by a runner in the morning, and for other sachems. I invited him and the other great men present to my tent, where they stayed about an hour, and returned.

According to the best observations I could make, Mr Gist's new settlement (which we passed by) bears about west-north-west seventy miles from Will's Creek; Shannopins, or the Fork, north by west, or north-north-west, about fifty miles from that; and from thence to the Logstown the course is nearly west about eighteen or twenty miles; so that the whole distance, as we went and computed it, is at least one hundred and thirty-five or one hundred and forty miles from our back inhabitants.

25th. Came to town, four of ten Frenchmen who had deserted from a company at the Kuskuskas, which lies at the mouth of the river. I got the following account from them. They were sent from New Orleans with a hundred men, and eight canoe loads of provisions to this place, where they expected to have met the same number of men from the forts on this side of Lake Erie, to convoy them and the stores up, who were not arrived when they ran off.

I inquired into the situation of the French on the Mississippi, their numbers, and what forts they had built. They informed me that there were four small forts between New Orleans and the Black Islands, garrisoned with about thirty or forty men, and a few small pieces in each. That at New Orleans, which is near the mouth of the Mississippi, there are thirty-five companies of forty men each, with a pretty strong fort mounting eight carriage guns; and at the Black Islands there are several companies, and a fort with six guns. The Black Islands are about a hundred and thirty leagues above the mouth of the Ohio, which is about three hundred and fifty above New Orleans. They also acquainted me that there was a small palisadoed fort on the Ohio, at the mouth of the Obaish, about sixty leagues from the Mississippi. The Obaish heads near the west end of Lake Erie, and affords the communication between the French on the Mississippi and those on the lakes. These deserters came up from the lower Shannoah town with one Brown, an Indian trader, and were going to Philadelphia.

About three o'clock this evening the Half-King came to town. I went up and invited him, with Davidson, privately, to my tent, and desired him to relate some of the particulars of his journey to the French commandant, and of his reception there; also, to give me an account of the ways and distance. He told me that the nearest and levelest way was now impassable, by reason of many large, miry savannas; that we must be obliged to go by Venango, and should not get to the near fort in less than five or six nights' sleep, good travelling. When he went to the fort, he said he was received in a very stern manner by the late commander, who asked him very abruptly what he had come about, and to declare his business, which he said he did in the following speech:

"Fathers, I am come to tell you your own speeches, what your own mouths have declared. Fathers, you, in former days, set a silver basin before us, wherein there was the leg of a beaver, and desired all the nations to come and eat of it, to eat in peace and plenty, and not to be churlish to one another; and that if any such person should be found to be a disturber I here lay down by the edge of the dish a rod, which you must scourge them with; and if your father should get foolish, in my old days, I desire you may use it upon me as well as others.

"Now, fathers, it is you who are the disturbers of this land, by coming and building your towns, and by taking it away unknown to us, and by force.

"Fathers, we kindled a fire a long time ago at a place called Montreal, where we desired you to stay, and not to come and intrude upon our land. I now desire you may dispatch to that place for be it known to you, fathers, that this is our land, and not yours.

"Fathers, I desire you may hear me in civilness; if not, we must handle that rod which was laid down for the use of the obstreperous. If you had come in a peaceable manner, like our brothers the English, we would not have been against your trading with us as they do; but to come, fathers, and build houses upon our land, and to take it by force, is what we cannot submit to.

"Fathers, both you and the English are white, we live in a country between; therefore, the land belongs to neither one nor the other. But the Great Being above allowed it to be a place of residence for us; so, fathers, I desire you to withdraw, as I have done our brothers the English; for I will keep you at arm's length. I lay this down as a trial for both, to see which will have the greatest regard to it, and that side we will stand by, and make equal sharers with us. Our brothers, the English, have heard this, and I come now to tell it to you; for I am not afraid to discharge you off this land."

This, he said, was the substance of what he spoke to the general, who made this reply:

"Now, my child, I have heard your speech; you spoke first, but it is my time to speak now. Where is my wampum that you took away with the marks of towns on it? This wampum I do not know, which you have discharged me off the land with; but you need not put yourself to the trouble of speaking, for I will not hear you. I am not afraid of flies or musquitoes, for Indians are such as those; I tell you down that river I will go, and build upon it, according to my command. If the river was blocked up, I have forces sufficient to burst it open, and tread under my feet all that stand in opposition, together with their alliances; for my force is as the sand upon the sea shore; therefore, here is your wampum; I sling it at you. Child, you talk foolish; you say this land belongs to you, but there is not the black of my nail yours. I saw that land sooner than you did; before the Shannoahs and you were at war. Lead was the man who went down and took possession of that river. It is my land, and I will have it, let who will stand up for, or say against it. I will buy and sell with the English [mockingly]. If people will be ruled by me, they may expect kindness, but not else."

The Half-King told me he had inquired of the general after two Englishmen who were made prisoners, and received this answer:

"Child, you think it a very great hardship that I made prisoners of those two people at Venango. Don't you concern yourself with it; we took and carried them to Canada, to get intelligence of what the English were doing in Virginia."

He informed me that they had built two forts, one on Lake Erie, and another on French Creek, near a small lake, about fifteen miles asunder, and a large wagon-road between. He gave me a plan of them of his own drawing.

26th. We met in council at the long-house about nine o'clock, where I spoke to them as follows:

"Brothers, I have called you together in council, by order of your brother, the Governor of Virginia, to acquaint you that I am sent with all possible dispatch to visit and deliver a letter to the French commandant, of very great importance to your brothers the English; and I dare say to you, their friends and allies.

"I was desired, brothers, by your brother, the Governor, to call upon you, the sachems of the nations, to inform you of it, and to ask your advice and assistance to proceed the nearest and best road to the French. You see, brothers, I have gotten thus far on my journey.

"His Honour likewise desired me to apply to you for some of your young men to conduct and provide provisions for us on our way, and be a safeguard against those French Indians who have taken up the hatchet against us. I have spoken thus particularly to you, brothers, because his Honour, our Governor, treats you as good friends and allies, and holds you in great esteem. To confirm what I have said, I give you this string of wampum."

After they had considered for some time on the above discourse, the Half-King got up and spoke:

"Now, my brother, in regard to what my brother the Governor has desired of me, I return you this answer:

"I rely upon you as a brother ought to do, as you say we are brothers, and one people. We shall put heart in hand and speak to our fathers, the French, concerning the speech they made to me; and you may depend that we will endeavour to be your guard.

"Brother, as you have asked my advice, I hope you will be ruled by it, and stay until I can provide a company to go with you. The French speech-belt is not here; I have to go for it to my hunting-cabin. Likewise, the people whom I have ordered in are not yet come, and cannot until the third night from this; until which time, brother, I must beg you to stay.

"I intend to send the guard of Mongoes, Shannoahs, and Delawares, that our brothers may see the love and loyalty we bear them."

As I had orders to make all possible dispatch, and waiting here was very contrary to my inclination, I thanked him in the most suitable manner I could, and told him that my business required the greatest expedition, and would not admit of that delay. He was not well pleased that I should offer to go before the time he had appointed, and told me that he could not consent to our going without a guard, for fear some accident should befall us, and draw a reflection upon him. Besides, said he, this is a matter of no small moment, and must not be entered into without due consideration; for I intend to deliver up the French speech-belt, and make the Shannoahs and Delawares do the same. And accordingly he gave orders to King Shingiss, who was present, to attend on Wednesday night with the wampum; and two men of their nation to be in readiness to set out with us the next morning. As I found it was impossible to get off without affronting them in the most egregious manner, I consented to stay.

I gave them back a string of wampum which I met with at Mr Frazier's, and which they sent with a speech to his Honour the Governor, to inform him that three nations of French Indians—namely, Chippewas, Ottowas, and Orundaks, had taken up the hatchet against the English; and desired them to repeat it over again. But this they postponed doing until they met in full council with the Shannoah and Delaware chiefs.

27th. Runners were dispatched very early for the Shannoah chiefs. The Half-King set out himself to fetch the French speechbelt from his hunting cabin.

28th. He returned this evening, and came with Monacatoocha and two other sachems to my tent, and begged (as they had complied with his Honour the Governor's request, in providing men, etc.) to know on what business we were going to the French. This was a question I had all along expected, and had provided as satisfactory answers as I could; which allayed their curiosity a little.

Monacatoocha informed me that an Indian from Venango brought news a few days ago that the French had called all the Mingoes, Delawares, etc., together at that place; and told them that they intended to have been down the river this fall, but the waters were growing cold, and the winter advancing, which obliged them to go into quarters; but that they might assuredly expect them in the spring with a far greater number; and desired that they might be quite passive, and not intermeddle unless they had a mind to draw all their force upon them; for that they expected to fight the English three years (as they supposed there would be some attempts made to stop them), in which time they should conquer. But that if they should prove equally strong, they and the English would join to cut them all off, and divide the land between them; that though they had lost their general and some few of their soldiers, yet there were men enough to reinforce them, and make them masters of the Ohio.

This speech, he said, was delivered to them by one Captain Joncaire, their interpreter-in-chief, living at Venango, and a man of note in the army.

29th. The Half-King and Monacatoocha came very early, and begged me to stay one day more; for notwithstanding they had used all the diligence in their power, the Shannoah chiefs had not brought the wampum they ordered, but would certainly be in to-night; if not, they would delay me no longer, but would send it after us as soon as they arrived. When I found them so pressing in their request, and knew that the returning of wampum was the abolishing of agreements, and giving this up was shaking off all dependence upon the French, I consented to stay, as I believed an offence offered at this crisis might be attended with greater ill consequence than another day's delay. They also informed me that Shingiss could not get in his men, and was prevented from coming himself by his wife's sickness (I believe by fear of the French), but that the wampum of that nation was lodged with Kustalogo, one of their chiefs, at Venango.

In the evening, late, they came again, and acquainted me that the Shannoahs were not yet arrived, but that it should not retard the prosecution of our journey. He delivered in my hearing the speech that was to be made to the French by Jeskakake, one of their old chiefs, which was giving up the belt the late commandant had asked for, and repeating nearly the same speech he himself had done before.

He also delivered a string of wampum to this chief, which was sent by King Shingiss, to be given to Kustalogo, with orders to repair to the French, and deliver up the wampum.

He likewise gave a very large string of black and white wampum, which was to be sent up immediately to the Six Nations, if the French refused to quit the land at this warning, which was the third and last time, and was the right of this Jeskakake to deliver.

30th. Last night, the great men assembled at their council house, to consult further about this journey, and who were to go; the result of which was, that only three of their chiefs, with one of their best hunters, should be our convoy. The reason they gave for not sending more, after what had been proposed at council the 26th, was, that a greater number might give the French suspicions of some bad design, and cause them to be treated rudely; but I rather think they could not get their hunters in.

We set out about nine o'clock with the Half-King, Jeskakake, White Thunder, and the Hunter; and travelled on the road to Venango, where we arrived the 4th of December, without anything remarkable happening but a continued series of bad weather.

This is an old Indian town, situated at the mouth of French Creek, on the Ohio; and lies near north about sixty miles from the Logstown, but more than seventy the way we were obliged to go.

We found the French colours hoisted at a house from which they had driven Mr John Frazier, an English subject. I immediately repaired to it, to know where the commander resided. There were three officers, one of whom, Captain Joncaire, informed me that he had the command of the Ohio; but that there was a general officer at the near fort, where he advised me to apply for an answer. He invited us to sup with them, and treated us with the greatest complaisance.

The wine, as they dosed themselves pretty plentifully with it, soon banished the restraint which at first appeared in their conversation, and gave a licence to their tongues to reveal their sentiments more freely.

They told me that it was their absolute design to take possession of the Ohio, and by G—— they would do it; for that, although they were sensible the English could raise two men for their one, yet they knew their motions were too slow and dilatory to prevent any undertaking of theirs. They pretend to have an undoubted right to the river from a discovery made by one La Salle, sixty years ago; and the rise of this expedition is, to prevent our settling on the river or waters of it, as they heard of some families moving out in order thereto. From the best intelligence I could get, there have been fifteen hundred men on this side Ontario Lake. But upon the death of the general, all were recalled, to about six or seven hundred, who were left to garrison four forts, one hundred and fifty, or thereabouts, in each. The first of them is on French Creek, near a small lake, about sixty miles from Venango, near north northwest; the next lies on Lake Erie, where the greater part of their stores are kept, about fifteen miles from the other; from this it is one hundred and twenty miles to the carrying-place, at the Falls of Lake Erie, where there is a small fort, at which they lodge their goods in bringing them from Montreal, the place from whence all their stores are brought. The next fort lies about twenty miles from this, on Ontario Lake. Between this fort and Montreal, there are three others, the first of which is nearly opposite to the English fort Oswego. From the fort on Lake Erie to Montreal is about six hundred miles, which, they say, requires no more (if good weather) than four weeks' voyage, if they go in barks or large vessels, so that they may cross the lake; but if they come in canoes, it will require five or six weeks, for they are obliged to keep under the shore.

December 5th. Rained excessively all day, which prevented our travelling. Captain Joncaire sent for the Half-King, as he had but just heard that he came with me. He affected to be much concerned that I did not make free to bring them in before. I excused it in the best manner of which I was capable, and told him, I did not think their company agreeable, as I had heard him say a good deal in dispraise of Indians in general; but another motive prevented me from bringing them into his company; I knew that he was an interpreter, and a person of very great influence among the Indians, and had lately used all possible means to draw them over to his interest; therefore I was desirous of giving him no opportunity that could be avoided.

When they came in there was great pleasure expressed at seeing them. He wondered how they could be so near without coming to visit him, made several trifling presents, and applied liquor so fast that they were soon rendered incapable of the business they came about, notwithstanding the caution which was given.

6th. The Half-King came to my tent quite sober, and insisted very much that I should stay and hear what he had to say to the French. I fain would have prevented him from speaking anything until he came to the commandant, but could not prevail. He told me that at this place a council-fire was kindled, where all their business with these people was to be transacted, and that the management of the Indian affairs was left solely to Monsieur Joncaire. As I was desirous of knowing the issue of this, I agreed to stay; but sent our horses a little way up French Creek, to raft over and encamp, which I knew would make it near night.

About ten o'clock they met in council. The King spoke much the same as he had before done to the general; and offered the French speech-belt which had before been demanded, with the marks of four towns on it, which Monsieur Joncaire refused to receive, but desired him to carry it to the fort to the commander.

7th. Monsieur La Force, commissary of the French stores, and three other soldiers, came over to accompany us up. We found it extremely difficult to get the Indians off to-day, as every stratagem had been used to prevent their going up with me. I had last night left John Davidson (the Indian interpreter), whom I brought with me from town, and strictly charged him not to be out of their company, as I could not get them over to my tent; for they had some business with Kustalogo chiefly to know why he did not deliver up the French speech-belt which he had in keeping; but I was obliged to send Mr Gist over to-day to fetch them, which he did with great persuasion.

At twelve o'clock, we set out for the fort, and were prevented arriving there until the 11th by excessive rains, snows, and bad travelling through many mires and swamps; these we were obliged to pass to avoid crossing the creek, which was impassable, either by fording or rafting, the water was so high and rapid.

We passed over much good land since we left Venango, and through several extensive and very rich meadows, one of which, I believe, was nearly four miles in length, and considerably wide in some places.

12th. I prepared early to wait upon the commander, and was received and conducted to him by the second officer in command. I acquainted him with my business, and offered my commission and letter; both of which he desired me to keep until the arrival of Monsieur Reparti, captain of the next fort, who was sent for and expected every hour.

This commander is a knight of the military order of St Louis, and named Legardeur de St Pierre. He is an elderly gentleman, and has much the air of a soldier. He was sent over to take the command immediately upon the death of the late general, and arrived here about seven days before me.

At two o'clock the gentleman who was sent for arrived, when I offered the letter, etc., again, which they received, and adjourned into a private apartment for the captain to translate, who understood a little English. After he had done it the commander desired I would walk in and bring my interpreter to peruse and correct it; which I did.

13th. The chief officers retired to hold a council of war, which gave me an opportunity of taking the dimensions of the fort, and making what observations I could.

It is situated on the south or west fork of French Creek, near the water; and is almost surrounded by the creek, and a small branch of it, which form a kind of island. Four houses compose the sides. The bastions are made of piles driven into the ground, standing more than twelve feet above it, and sharp at top, with portholes cut for cannon, and loopholes for the small arms to fire through. There are eight six-pounds pieces mounted in each bastion, and one piece of four pounds before the gate. In the bastions are a guard-house, chapel, doctor's lodging, and the commander's private store; round which are laid platforms for the cannon and men to stand on. There are several barracks without the fort, for the soldiers' dwellings, covered, some with bark and some with boards made chiefly of logs. There are also several other houses, such as stables, smith's shop, etc.

I could get no certain account of the number of men here; but, according to the best judgment I could form, there are a hundred, exclusive of officers, of whom there are many. I also gave orders to the people who were with me to take an exact account of the canoes, which were hauled up to convey their forces down in the spring. This they did, and told fifty of birch bark, and a hundred and seventy of pine; besides many others, which were blocked out, in readiness for being made.

14th. As the snow increased very fast, and our horses daily became weaker, I sent them off unloaded, under the care of Barnaby Currin and two others, to make all convenient dispatch to Venango, and there to wait our arrival, if there was a prospect of the river's freezing; if not, then to continue down to Shannopin's Town, at the Fork of the Ohio, and there to wait until we came to cross the Allegany, intending myself to go down by water, as I had the offer of a canoe or two.

As I found many plots concerted to retard the Indians' business, and prevent their returning with me, I endeavoured all that lay in my power to frustrate their schemes, and hurried them on to execute their intended design. They accordingly pressed for admittance this evening, which at length was granted them, privately, to the commander and one or two other officers. The Half-King told me that he offered the wampum to the commander, who evaded taking it, and made many fair promises of love and friendship; said he wanted to live in peace, and trade amicably with them, as a proof of which, he would send some goods immediately down to the Logstown for them. But I rather think the design of that is to bring away all our straggling traders they meet with, as I privately understand they intended to carry an officer with them. And what rather confirms this opinion, I was inquiring of the commander by what authority he had made prisoners of several of our English subjects. He told me that the country belonged to them; that no Englishman had a right to trade upon those waters; and that he had orders to make every person prisoner who attempted it on the Ohio, or the waters of it.

This evening I received an answer to his Honour the Governor's letter from the commandant.

15th. The commandant ordered a plentiful store of liquor and provision to be put on board our canoes, and appeared to be extremely complaisant, though he was exerting every artifice which he could invent to set our Indians at variance with us, to prevent their going until after our departure; presents, rewards, and everything which could be suggested by him or his officers. I cannot say that ever in my life I suffered so much anxiety as I did in this affair. I saw that every stratagem which the most fruitful brain could invent was practised to win the Half-King to their interest; and that leaving him there was giving them the opportunity they aimed at. I went to the Half-King and pressed him in the strongest terms to go; he told me that the commandant would not discharge him until the morning. I then went to the commandant, and desired him to do their business, and complained of ill treatment; for keeping them, as they were part of my company, was detaining me. This he promised not to do, but to forward my journey as much as he could. He protested he did not keep them, but was ignorant of the cause of their stay; though I soon found it out. He had promised them a present of guns, if they would wait until the morning. As I was very much pressed by the Indians to wait this day for them, I consented, on a promise that nothing should hinder them in the morning.

16th. The French were not slack in their inventions to keep the Indians this day also. But as they were obliged, according to promise, to give the present, they then endeavoured to try the power of liquor, which I doubt not would have prevailed at any other time than this; but I urged and insisted with the King so closely upon his word that he refrained, and set off with us as he had engaged.

We had a tedious and very fatiguing passage down the creek. Several times we had liked to have been staved against rocks; and many times were obliged all hands to get out and remain in the water half an hour or more, getting over the shoals. At one place, the ice had lodged and made it impassable by water; we were therefore obliged to carry our canoe across the neck of land, a quarter of a mile over. We did not reach Venango until the 22nd, where we met with our horses.

This creek is extremely crooked. I dare say the distance between the fort and Venango cannot be less than one hundred and thirty miles, to follow the meanders.

23rd. When I got things ready to set off, I sent for the Half-King to know whether he intended to go with us or by water. He told me that White Thunder had hurt himself much, and was sick and unable to walk; therefore he was obliged to carry him down in a canoe. As I found he intended to stay here a day or two, and knew that Monsieur Joncaire would employ every scheme to set him against the English, as he had before done, I told him I hoped he would guard against his flattery, and let no fine speeches influence him in their favour. He desired I might not be concerned, for he knew the French too well for anything to engage him in their favour; and that though he could not go down with us, he yet would endeavour to meet at the Fork with Joseph Campbell, to deliver a speech for me to carry to his Honour the Governor. He told me he would order the Young Hunter to attend us, and get provisions, etc., if wanted.

Our horses were now so weak and feeble, and the baggage so heavy (as we were obliged to provide all the necessaries which the journey would require), that we doubted much their performing it. Therefore, myself and others, except the drivers, who were obliged to ride, gave up our horses for packs, to assist along with the baggage. I put myself in an Indian walking dress, and continued with them three days, until I found there was no probability of their getting home in any reasonable time. The horses became less able to travel every day; the cold increased very fast; and the roads were becoming much worse by a deep snow, continually freezing; therefore, as I was uneasy to get back to make report of my proceedings to his Honour the Governor, I determined to prosecute my journey the nearest way through the woods on foot.

Accordingly, I left Mr Vanbraam in charge of our baggage, with money and directions to provide necessaries from place to place for themselves and horses, and to make the most convenient dispatch in travelling.

I took my necessary papers, pulled off my clothes, and tied myself up in a watch-coat. Then, with gun in hand and pack on my back, in which were my papers and provisions, I set out with Mr Gist, fitted in the same manner, on Wednesday, the 26th. The day following, just after we had passed a place called Murdering Town (where we intended to quit the path and steer across the country for Shannopin's Town), we fell in with a party of French Indians, who had lain in wait for us. One of them fired at Mr Gist or me, not fifteen steps off, but fortunately missed. We took this fellow into custody, and kept him till about nine o'clock at night, then let him go, and walked all the remaining part of the night without making any stop, that we might get the start so far as to be out of the reach of their pursuit the next day, since we were well assured they would follow our track as soon as it was light. The next day we continued travelling until quite dark, and got to the river about two miles above Shannopin's. We expected to have found the river frozen, but it was not, only about fifty yards from each shore. The ice, I suppose, had broken up above, for it was driving in vast quantities.

There was no way for getting over but on a raft, which we set about with but one poor hatchet, and finished just after sun-setting. This was a whole day's work; we next got it launched, then went on board of it and set off; but before we were half way over, we were jammed in the ice in such a manner that we expected every moment our raft to sink, and ourselves to perish. I put out my setting-pole to try to stop the raft, that the ice might pass by, when the rapidity of the stream threw it with so much violence against the pole that it jerked me out into ten feet of water; but I fortunately saved myself by catching hold of one of the raft logs. Notwithstanding all our efforts, we could not get to either shore, but were obliged, as we were near an island, to quit our raft and make to it.

The cold was so extremely severe that Mr Gist had all his fingers and some of his toes frozen; and the water was shut up so hard that we found no difficulty in getting off the island on the ice in the morning, and went to Mr Frazier's. We met here with twenty warriors, who were going to the southward to war; but coming to a place on the head of the Great Kenhawa, where they found seven people killed and scalped (all but one woman with very light hair), they turned about and ran back, for fear the inhabitants should rise and take them as the authors of the murder. They report that the bodies were lying about the house, and some of them much torn and eaten by the hogs. By the marks which were left, they say they were French Indians of the Ottoway nation who did it.

As we intended to take horses here, and it required some time to find them, I went up about three miles to the mouth of Youghiogany, to visit Queen Aliquippa, who had expressed great concern that we passed her in going to the fort. I made her a present of a watchcoat and a bottle of rum, which latter was thought much the better present of the two.

Tuesday, the Ist of January, we left Mr Frazier's house, and arrived at Mr Gist's, at Monongahela, the 2nd, where I bought a horse and saddle. The 6th, we met seventeen horses loaded with materials and stores for a fort at the

Fork of the Ohio, and the day after, some families going out to settle. This day we arrived at Will's Creek, after as fatiguing a journey as it is possible to conceive, rendered so by excessive bad weather. From the Ist day of December to the 15th, there was but one day on which it did not rain or snow incessantly; and throughout the whole journey we met with nothing but one continued series of cold, wet weather, which occasioned very uncomfortable lodgings, especially after we had quitted our tent, which was some screen from the inclemency of it.

On the 11th I got to Belvoir, where I stopped one day to take necessary rest, and then set out and arrived in Williamsburg the 16th, when I waited upon his Honour the Governor, with the letter I had brought from the French commandant, and to give an account of the success of my proceedings. This I beg leave to do by offering the foregoing narrative, as it contains the most remarkable occurrences which happened in my journey.

I hope what has been said will be sufficient to make your Honour satisfied with my conduct, for that was my aim in undertaking the journey, and chief study throughout the prosecution of it.

"TO SETTLE THE WILDERNESS"[1]

(1769)

DANIEL BOON

(1734-1820)

IT was on the 1st of May, 1769, that I resigned my domestic happiness, and left my family and peaceful habitation on the Yadkin river, in North Carolina, to wander through the wilderness of America, in quest of the country of Kentucky, in company with John Finley, John Stuart, Joseph Holden, James Monay and William Cool.

On the 7th June, after travelling in a western direction, we found ourselves on Red river, where John Finley had formerly been trading with the Indians, and from the top of an eminence, saw with pleasure the beautiful level of Kentucky. For some time we had experienced the most uncomfortable weather. We now encamped, made a shelter to defend us from the inclement season, and began to hunt and reconnoitre the country. We found abundance of wild beasts in this vast forest. The buffaloes were more numerous than cattle on their settlements, browsing on the leaves of the cane, or crossing the herbage on these extensive plains. We saw hundreds in a drove, and the

[1] From *Life and Adventures of Colonel Daniel Boon* (1823).

numbers about the salt springs were amazing. In this forest, the habitation of beasts of every American kind, we hunted with great success until December.

On the 22nd December, John Stuart and I had a pleasant ramble; but fortune changed the day at the close of it. We passed through a great forest, in which stood myriads of trees, some gay with blossoms, others rich with fruits. Nature was here a series of wonders and a fund of delight. Here she displayed her ingenuity and industry in a variety of flowers and fruits, beautifully coloured, elegantly shaped, and charmingly flavoured; and we were favoured with numberless animals presenting themselves perpetually to our view. In the decline of the day, near Kentucky river, as we ascended the brow of a small hill, a number of Indians rushed out of a cane brake and made us prisoners. The Indians plundered us and kept us in confinement seven days. During this we discovered no uneasiness or desire to escape, which made them less suspicious; but in the dead of night, as we lay by a large fire in a thick cane brake, when sleep had locked up their senses, my situation not disposing me to rest, I gently awoke my companion. We seized this favourable opportunity and departed, directing our course toward our old camp, but found it plundered and our company destroyed and dispersed.

About this time, as my brother with another adventurer who came to explore the country shortly after us, was wandering through the forest, they accidentally found our camp. Notwithstanding our unfortunate circumstances, and our dangerous situation, surrounded with hostile savages, our meeting fortunately in the wilderness gave us the most sensible satisfaction.

Soon after this, my companion in captivity, John Stuart, was killed by the savages, and the man who came with my brother (while on a private excursion) was soon after attacked and killed by the wolves. We were now in a dangerous and helpless situation, exposed daily to perils and death, among savages and wild beasts, not a white man in the country but ourselves.

Although many hundred miles from our families in the howling wilderness, we did not continue in a state of indolence, but hunted every day, and prepared a little cottage to defend us from the winter. On the 1st of May, 1770, my brother returned home for a new recruit of horses and ammunition, leaving me alone, without bread, salt or sugar, or even a horse or a dog. I passed a few days uncomfortably—the idea of a beloved wife and family, and their anxiety on my account, would have disposed me to melancholy if I had further indulged the thought.

One day I undertook a tour through the country, when the diversity of beauties of nature I met with in this charming season expelled every gloomy thought. Just at the close of the day, the gentle gales ceased; profound calm ensued; not a breath shook the tremulous leaf. I had gained the summit of a commanding ridge, and looking around with astonishing delight beheld the ample plains and beauteous tracks below. On one hand I surveyed the famous Ohio rolling in silent dignity, and marking the western boundary of Kentucky with inconceivable grandeur. At a vast distance I beheld the mountains lift their venerable brows and penetrate the clouds. All things were still. I kindled a fire near a fountain of sweet water, and feasted on the line [*sic*] of a buck which I had killed a few hours before. The shades of night soon overspread the hemisphere, and the earth seemed to gasp after the hovering moisture. At a distance I frequently heard the hideous yells of savages. My excursion had fatigued my body and amused my mind. I laid me down to sleep, and awoke not until the sun had chased away the night. I continued this tour, and in a few days explored a considerable part of the country, each day equally pleasing as the first; after which I returned to my old camp, which had not been disturbed in my absence. I did not confine my lodging to it, but often reposed in thick cane brakes to avoid the savages, who I believe frequently visited my camp, but fortunately for me, in my absence. No populous city, with all its varieties of commerce and stately structures, could afford so much pleasure to my mind as the beauties of nature I found in this country.

Until the 27th July I spent my time in an uninterrupted scene of sylvan pleasures, when my brother, to my great felicity, met me, according to appointment, at our old camp. Soon after we left the place and proceeded to Cumberland river, reconnoitring that part of the country, and giving names to the different rivers.

In March 1771 I returned home to my family, being determined to bring them as soon as possible, at the risk of my life and fortune, to reside in Kentucky, which I esteemed a second Paradise.

On my return I found my family in happy circumstances. I sold my farm on the Yadkin and what goods we could not carry with us, and on the 25th September, 1773, we took leave of our friends and proceeded on our journey to Kentucky, in company with five more families, and forty men that joined us in Powell's Valley, which is 150 miles from the new settled parts of Kentucky; but this promising beginning was soon overcast with a cloud of adversity.

On the 10th October the rear of our company was attacked by a party of Indians, who killed six and wounded one man. Of these my oldest son was one that fell in the action. Though we repulsed the enemy, yet this unhappy affair scattered our cattle and brought us into extreme difficulty—we returned forty miles to the settlement on Clench river. We had passed over two mountains, Powel's and Walden's, and were approaching Cumberland mountain, when this adverse fortune overtook us. These mountains are in the wilderness, in passing from the old settlements in Virginia to Kentucky, are ranged in a southwest and northeast direction, are of great length and breadth, and not far distant from each other. Over them nature hath formed passes less difficult than might be expected from the view of such huge piles. The aspect of these cliffs are so wild and horrid, that it is impossible to behold them without horror.

Until the 6th June, 1774, I remained with my family on the Clench, until I and another person were solicited by Governor Dunmore of Virginia, to conduct a number of surveyors to the falls of Ohio. This was a tour of 800 miles, and took us sixty-two days.

On my return Gov. Dunmore gave me the command of three garrisons during the campaign against the Shawanese. In March 1775, at the solicitation of a number of gentlemen of North Carolina, I attended their treaty at Wataga with the Cherokee Indians, to purchase the lands on the south side of Kentucky river. After this, I undertook to mark out a road in the best passage from the settlements through the wilderness to Kentucky.

Having collected a number of enterprising men well armed, I soon began this work—we proceeded until we came within fifteen miles of where Boonsborough now stands, where the Indians attacked us, and killed two and wounded two more of our party. This was on the 22nd March, 1775—two days after we were again attacked by them, when we had two more killed and three wounded. After this we proceeded on to Kentucky river without opposition.

On the 1st April we began to erect the fort of Boonsborough, at a salt lick, sixty yards from the river on the south side. On the 4th the Indians killed one of our men. On the 14th June, having completed the fort, I returned to my family on the Clench, and whom I soon after removed to the fort—my wife and daughter were supposed to be the first white women that ever stood upon the banks of Kentucky river.

On the 24th December an Indian killed one of our men and wounded another; and on the 15th July, 1776, they took my daughter prisoner—I immediately pursued them with eight men, and on the 16th overtook and engaged them; I killed two of them and recovered my daughter.

The Indians having divided themselves into several parties, attacked in one day all our infant settlement and forts, doing a great deal of damage—the husbandmen were ambushed and unexpectedly attacked while toiling in the fields. They continued this kind of warfare until the 15th April, 1777, when nearly 100 of them attacked the village of Boonsborough, and killed a number of its inhabitants. On the 19th Col. Logan's fort was attacked by 200 Indians—there were only thirteen men in the fort, of whom the enemy killed two and wounded one.

On the 20th August Col. Bowman arrived with 100 men from Virginia, with which additional force we had almost daily skirmishes with the Indians, who began now to learn the superiority of the 'long knife, as they termed the Virginians; being out-generalled in almost every action. Our affairs began now to wear a better aspect, the Indians no longer daring to face us in open field, but sought private opportunities to destroy us.

On the 7th February, 1778, while on a hunting expedition alone, I met a party of 102 Indians and two Frenchmen, marching to attack Boonsborough—they pursued and took me prisoner, and conveyed me to Old Chelicothe, the principal Indian town on little Miami, where we arrived on the 18th February, after an uncomfortable journey. On the 10th March I was conducted to Detroit, and while there was treated with great humanity by Governor Hamilton, the British commander at that port, and Intendant for Indian affairs.

The Indians had such an affection for me, that they refused 100*l.* sterling offered them by the Governor if they would consent to leave me with him, that he might be enabled to liberate me on my parole. Several English gentlemen then at Detroit, sensible of my adverse fortune, and touched with sympathy, generously offered to supply my wants, which I declined with many thanks, adding that I never expected it would be in my power to recompense such unmerited generosity.

On the 10th April the Indians returned with me to Old Chelicothe, where we arrived on the 25th. This was a long and fatiguing march, although through an exceeding fertile country, remarkable for springs and streams of water. At Chelicothe I spent my time as comfortable as I could expect; was adopted according to their custom, into a family where I became a son, and had a great share in the affection of my new parents, brothers, sisters and friends. I was exceedingly familiar and friendly with them, always appearing as cheerful and contented as possible, and they put great confidence in me. I often went a-hunting with them, and frequently gained their applause for my activity at our shooting matches. I was careful not to exceed many of them in shooting, for no people are more envious than they in this sport. I could observe in their countenances and gestures the greatest expressions of joy when they exceeded me, and when the reverse happened, of envy. The Shawanese king took great notice of me, and treated me with profound respect and entire friendship, often entrusting me to hunt at my liberty. I frequently returned with the spoils of the woods, and as often presented some of what I had taken to him, expressive of duty to my sovereign. My food and lodging was in common with them, not so good indeed as I could desire, but necessity made every thing acceptable.

I now began to mediate an escape, and carefully avoided giving suspicion. I continued at Chelicothe until the first day of June, when I was taken to the salt springs on Sciotha, and there employed ten days in the manufacturing of salt. During this time I hunted with my Indian masters, and found the land for a great extent about this river to exceed the soil of Kentucky.

On my return to Chelicothe 150 of the choicest Indian warriors were ready to march against Boonsborough; they were painted and armed in a frightful manner. This alarmed me, and I determined to escape.

On the 16th June, before sun-rise, I went off secretly, and reached Boonsborough on the 20th, a journey of 160 miles, during which I had only one meal. I found our fortress in a bad state, but we immediately repaired our flanks, gates, posterns, and formed double bastions, which we completed in ten days. One of my fellow prisoners escaped after me, brought advice that on account of my flight, the Indians had put off their expedition for three weeks.

About August 1st, I set out with 19 men to surprise Point Creek Town on Sciotha, within four miles of which we fell in with 40 Indians, going against Boonsborough:—we attacked them and they soon gave way without any loss on our part—the enemy had one killed and two wounded—we took three horses and all their baggage.

About this time I returned to Kentucky with my family; for during my captivity my wife, thinking me killed by the Indians, had transported my family and goods on horses through the wilderness, amidst many dangers, to her father's house in North Carolina.

On the 6th of October, 1780, soon after my settling again at Boonsborough, I went with my brother to the Blue Licks, and on our return, he was shot by a party of Indians. They followed me by the scent of a dog, which I shot and escaped. The severity of the winter caused great distress in Kentucky, the enemy during the summer having destroyed most of the corn. The inhabitants lived chiefly on Buffaloe's flesh.

In spring, 1782, the Indians harassed us. In May they ravished, killed, and scalped a woman and her two daughters near Ashton's station, and took a negro prisoner. August 8th two boys were carried off from Major Hoy's station. Our affairs became more and more alarming. The savages infested the country and destroyed the woods as opportunity presented.

August 18th Colonels Todd and Trigg, Major Harland and myself, speedily collected 176 men well armed, and pursued the savages. They had marched beyond the Blue Licks, to a remarkable bend of the main fork of Licking River, about 43 miles from Lexington, where we overtook them on the 19th. The savages, observing us, gave way, and we, ignorant of their numbers, passed the river. When they saw our proceedings (having accordingly the advantage in situation) they formed their line of battle from one end of the Licking to the other, about a mile from the Blue Licks. The engagement was close and warm for about fifteen minutes, when we, being overpowered by numbers, were obliged to retreat, with the loss of 67 men, 7 of whom were taken prisoners. The brave and much lamented Colonels Todd and Trigg, Major Harland, and my second son were among the dead.

When General Clark, at the falls of Ohio, heard of our disaster he ordered an expedition to pursue the savages. We overtook them within two miles of their towns, and we should have obtained a great victory had not some of them met us when about two hundred poles from their camp. The savages fled in the utmost disorder, and evacuated all their towns. We burned to ashes Old Chelicothe, Peccaway, New Chelicothe, and Wills Town; entirely destroyed their corn and other fruits; and spread desolation through their country.

In October a party atacked Crab Orchard, and one of them being a good way before the others, boldly entered a house, in which were only a woman and her children and a negro man. The savage used no violence, but attempted to carry off the negro, who happily proved too strong for him, and threw him on the ground, and in the struggle the woman cut off his head with an axe, whilst her little daughter shut the door. The savages instantly came up and applied their tomahawks to the door, when the mother putting an old rusty gun barrel through the crevices, the savages immediately went off.

From that time till the happy return of peace between the United States and Great Britain, the Indians did us no mischief. Soon after this the Indians desired peace.

Two darling sons and a brother I have lost by savage hands, which have also taken from me 40 valuable horses and abundance of cattle. Many dark and sleepless nights have I spent, separated from the cheerful society of men, scorched by the summer's sun, and pinched by the winter's cold, an instrument ordained to settle the wilderness.

DANIEL BOON

Fayette, County Kentucky

CAPTAIN BENJAMIN BONNEVILLE, PIONEER[1]

(1832)

WASHINGTON IRVING

(1783-1859)

[*Captain Benjamin Bonneville (c. 1795-1878), being desirous of exploring the Rocky Mountains, obtained leave of absence from his regiment in 1831. He was away so long that he was considered to be dead, and his name was struck off the army list. How Irving met him and came to write his adventures is best told in Irving's own words.*]

PROLOGUE

IT was in the autumn of 1835, at the country seat of Mr John Jacob Astor, at Hellgate, that I first met with Captain Bonneville. He was then just returned from a residence of upwards of three years among the mountains, and was on his way to report himself at headquarters, in the hopes of being reinstated in the service. From all that I could learn, his wanderings in the wilderness, though they had gratified his curiosity and his love of adventure, had not much benefited his fortunes. Like Corporal Trim in his campaigns, he had "satisfied the sentiment," and that was all.

There was something in the whole appearance of the captain that prepossessed me in his favour. He was of the middle size, well made and well set; and a military frock of foreign cut, that had seen service, gave him a look of compactness. His countenance was frank, open, and engaging; well-browned by the sun, and had something of a French expression. He had a pleasant black eye, a high forehead, and, while he kept his hat on, the look of a man in the jocund prime of his days; but the moment his head was uncovered, a bald crown gained him credit for a few more years than he was really entitled to.

Being extremely curious, at the time, about everything connected with the far west, I addressed numerous questions to him. They drew from him a number of extremely striking details, which were given with mingled modesty and frankness; and in a gentleness of manner, and a soft tone of voice, that contrasted singularly with the wild and often startling nature of his themes. It was difficult to conceive the mild, quiet-looking personage before you, the actual hero of the stirring scenes related.

In the course of three or four months, happening to be at the city of Washington, I again came upon the captain, who was attending the slow adjustment of his affairs with the War Department. I found him quartered

[1] From *Adventures of Captain Bonneville* (1837).

with a worthy brother in arms, a major in the army. Here he was writing at a table, covered with maps and papers, in the centre of a large barrack-room, fancifully decorated with Indian arms, and trophies, and war dresses, and the skins of various wild animals, and hung round with pictures of Indian games and ceremonies, and scenes of war and hunting. In a word, the captain was beguiling the tediousness of attendance at Court by an attempt at authorship; and was rewriting and extending his travelling notes, and making maps of the regions he had explored. As he sat at the table, in this curious apartment, with his high bald head of somewhat foreign cast, he reminded me of some of those antique pictures of authors that I have seen in old Spanish volumes.

The result of his labours was a mass of manuscript, which he subsequently put at my disposal, to fit it for publication, and bring it before the world.

It was on the first of May, 1832, that Captain Bonneville took his departure from the frontier post of Fort Osage, on the Missouri. He had enlisted a party of one hundred and ten men, most of whom had been in the Indian country, and some of whom were experienced hunters and trappers. Fort Osage, and other places on the borders of the western wilderness, abound with characters of the kind, ready for any expedition.

The ordinary mode of transportation in these great inland expeditions of the fur traders is on mules and pack-horses; but Captain Bonneville substituted waggons. Though he was to travel through a trackless wilderness, yet the greater part of his route would lie across open plains, destitute of forests, and where wheel carriages can pass in every direction. The chief difficulty occurs in passing the deep ravines cut through the prairies by streams and winter torrents. Here it is often necessary to dig a road down the banks, and to make bridges for the waggons.

In transporting his baggage in vehicles of this kind, Captain Bonneville thought he would save the great delay caused every morning by packing the horses, and the labour of unpacking in the evening. Fewer horses also would be required, and less risk incurred of their wandering away, or being frightened or carried off by the Indians. The waggons, also, would be more easily defended, and might form a kind of fortification in case of attack in the open prairies. A train of twenty waggons, drawn by oxen, or by four mules or horses each, and laden with merchandise, ammunition, and provisions, were disposed in two columns in the centre of the party, which was equally divided, into a van and a rear guard.

As sub-leaders or lieutenants in his expedition, Captain Bonneville had made choice of Mr I. R. Walker and Mr M. S. Cerré. The former was a native of Tennessee, about six feet high, strong-built, dark-complexioned, brave in spirit, though mild in manners. He had resided for many years in Missouri, on the frontier; had been among the earliest adventurers to Santa Fé, where he went to trap beaver, and was taken by the Spaniards. Being liberated, he engaged with the Spaniards and Sioux Indians in a war against the Pawnees; then returned to Missouri, and had acted by turns as sheriff, trader, trapper, until he was enlisted as a leader by Captain Bonneville. Cerré, his other leader, had likewise been in expeditions to Santa Fé, in which he had endured much hardship. He was of the middle size, light-complexioned, and though but about twenty-five years of age, was considered an experienced Indian trader.

It was a great object with Captain Bonneville to get to the mountains before the summer heats and summer flies should render the travelling across the prairies distressing; and before the annual assemblages of people connected with the fur trade should have broken up, and dispersed to the hunting grounds.

The two rival associations, the American Fur Company and the Rocky Mountain Fur Company, had their several places of rendezvous for the present year at no great distance apart, in Pierre's Hole, a deep valley in the heart of the mountains, and thither Captain Bonneville intended to shape his course.

It is not easy to do justice to the exulting feelings of the worthy captain, at finding himself at the head of a stout band of hunters, trappers, and woodmen; fairly launched on the broad prairies, with his face to the boundless west. The tamest inhabitant of cities, the veriest spoilt child of civilization, feels his heart dilate and his pulse beat high, on finding himself on horseback in the glorious wilderness; what then must be the excitement of one whose imagination had been stimulated by a residence on the frontier, and to whom the wilderness was a region of romance!

His hardy followers partook of his excitement. Most of them had already experienced the wild freedom of savage life, and looked forward to a renewal of past scenes of adventure and exploit. Their very appearance and equipment exhibited a piebald mixture, half civilized and half savage. Many of them looked more like Indians than white men, in their garbs and accoutrements, and their very horses were caparisoned in barbaric style, with fantastic trappings. The outset of a band of adventurers on one of these expeditions is always animated and joyous.

The welkin rang with their shouts and yelps, after the manner of the savages; and with boisterous jokes and light-hearted laughter. As they passed the straggling hamlets and solitary cabins that fringe the skirts of the frontiers, they would startle their inmates by Indian yells and war-whoops, or regale them with grotesque feats of Indian horsemanship, well suited to their half savage appearance. Most of these abodes were inhabited by men who had themselves been in similar expeditions: they welcomed the travellers, therefore, as brother trappers, treated them with a hunter's hospitality, and cheered them with an honest God speed at parting. . . .

On the 6th of May the travellers passed the last border habitation, and bade a long farewell to the ease and security of civilization. The buoyant and clamorous spirits with which they had commenced their march gradually subsided as they entered upon its difficulties. They found the prairies saturated with the heavy cold rains, prevalent in certain seasons of the year in this part of the country. The waggon wheels sank deep in the mire, the horses were often to the fetlock, and both steed and rider were completely jaded by the evening of the 12th, when they reached the Kansas River; a fine stream about three hundred yards wide, entering the Missouri from the south. Though fordable in almost every part at the end of summer and during the autumn, yet it was necessary to construct a raft for the transportation of the waggons and effects.

All this was done in the course of the following day, and by evening the whole party arrived at the agency of the Kansas tribe. This was under the superintendence of General Clarke, brother of the celebrated traveller of the same name, who, with Lewis, made the first expedition down the waters of the Columbia. He was living like a patriarch, surrounded by labourers and interpreters, all snugly housed, and provided with excellent farms.

The Kansas resemble the Osages in features, dress, and language: they raise corn and hunt the buffalo, ranging the Kansas river, and its tributary streams; at the time of the captain's visit, they were at war with the Pawnees of the Nebraska, or Platte river.

The unusual sight of a train of waggons caused quite a sensation among these savages, who thronged about the caravan, examining every thing minutely, and asking a thousand questions: exhibiting a degree of excitability, and a lively curiosity, totally opposite to that apathy with which their race is so often reproached.

The personage who most attracted the captain's attention at this place was "White Plume," the Kansas chief, and they soon became good friends. White Plume (we are pleased with his chivalrous *soubriquet*) inhabited a large stone house, built for him by order of the American Government: but the establishment had not been carried out in correspondent style. It might be palace without, but it was wigwam within; so that, between the stateliness of his mansion, and the squalidness of his furniture, the gallant White Plume presented some such whimsical incongruity as we see in the gala equipments of an Indian chief, on a treaty-making embassy at Washington, who has been generously decked out in cocked hat and military coat, in contrast to his breech-clout and leather leggings; being grand officer at top and ragged Indian at bottom.

White Plume was so taken with the courtesy of the captain and pleased with one or two presents received from him, that he accompanied him a day's journey on his march, and passed a night in his camp, on the margin of a small stream.

The method of encamping generally observed by the captain was as follows: The twenty waggons were disposed in a square, at the distance of thirty-three feet from each other. In every interval there was a mess stationed; and each mess had its fire, where the men cooked, ate, gossiped, and slept. The horses were placed in the centre of the square, with a guard stationed over them at night.

The horses were 'side lined,' as it is termed: that is to say, the fore and hind foot on the same side of the animal were tied together, so as to be within eighteen inches of each other. A horse thus fettered is for a time sadly embarrassed, but soon becomes sufficiently accustomed to the restraint to move about slowly. It prevents his wandering, and his being easily carried off at night by lurking Indians. When a horse that is 'foot free' is tied to one thus secured, the latter forms, as it were, a pivot, round which the other runs and curvets, in case of alarm.

The encampment of which we are speaking presented a striking scene. The various mess-fires were surrounded by picturesque groups, standing, sitting, and reclining; some busied in cooking, others in cleaning their weapons: while the frequent laugh told that the rough joke or merry story was going on. In the middle of the camp, before the principal lodge, sat the two chieftains, Captain Bonneville and White Plume, in soldier-like communion. The latter was squatted on his buffalo robe, his strong features and red skin glaring in the broad light of a blazing fire, while he recounted astounding tales of the bloody exploits of his tribe and himself, in their wars with the Pawnees; for there are no old soldiers more given to long campaigning stories than Indian 'braves.'

From the middle to the end of May Captain Bonneville pursued a western course, over vast undulating plains, destitute of tree or shrub, rendered miry by occasional rain, and cut up by deep water courses, where they had to dig roads for their waggons down the soft crumbling banks, and to throw bridges across the streams. The weather had attained the summer heat; the thermometer standing about fifty-seven degrees in the morning early, but rising to about ninety degrees at noon. The incessant breezes, however, which sweep these vast plains, render the heat endurable.

Game was scanty, and they had to eke out their scanty fare with wild roots and vegetables, such as the Indian potato, the wild onion, and the prairie tomato, and they met with quantities of 'red root,' from which the hunters make a very palatable beverage. The only human being that crossed their path was a Kansas warrior, returning from some solitary expedition of bravado, or revenge, bearing a Pawnee scalp as a trophy.

The country gradually rose as they proceeded westward, and their route took them over high ridges, commanding wide and beautiful prospects. The vast plain was studded on the west with innumerable hills of conical shape, such as are seen north of the Arkansas river. These hills have their summits apparently cut off about the same elevation, so as to leave flat surfaces at top. It is conjectured by some that the whole country may originally have been of the altitude of these tabular hills; but through some process of nature may have sunk to its present level; these insulated eminences being protected by broad foundations of solid rock.

On the 2nd of June, they arrived on the main stream of the Nebraska or Platte river; twenty-five miles below the head of the Great Island.

Keeping up along the course of this river for several days, they were obliged, from the scarcity of game, to put themselves upon short allowance, and, occasionally, to kill a steer. They bore their daily labours and privations, however, with great good humour, taking their tone, in all probability, from the buoyant spirit of their leader.

"If the weather was inclement," says the captain, "we watched the clouds, and hoped for a sight of the blue sky and the merry sun. If food was scanty, we regaled ourselves with the hope of soon falling in with herds of buffalo, and having nothing to do but slay and eat."

On the 11th of June they came to the fork in the Nebraska, where it divides itself into two equal and beautiful streams. One of these branches rises in the west south-west, near the head waters of the Arkansas. Up the course of this branch, as Captain Bonneville was well aware, lay the route to the Camanche and Kioway Indians, and to the northern Mexican settlements; of the other branch he knew nothing. Its sources might lie among wild and inaccessible cliffs, and tumble and foam down rugged defiles and over craggy precipices; but its direction was in the true course, and up this stream he determined to prosecute his route to the Rocky mountains. Finding it impossible, from quicksands and other dangerous impediments, to cross the river in this neighbourhood, he kept up along the south fork for two days, merely seeking a safe fording place.

At length he encamped, caused the bodies of the waggons to be dislodged from the wheels, covered with buffalo-hides, and besmeared with a compound of tallow and ashes; thus forming rude boats. In these they ferried their effects across the stream, which was six hundred yards wide, with a swift and strong current. Three men were in each boat, to manage it; others waded across, pushing the barks before them. Thus all crossed in safety. A march of nine miles took them over high rolling prairies to the north fork; their eyes being regaled with the welcome sight of herds of buffalo at a distance, some careering the plain, others grazing and reposing in the natural meadows.

Skirting along the north fork for a day or two, excessively annoyed by musquitoes and buffalo gnats, they reached, in the evening of the 17th, a small but beautiful grove, from which issued the confused notes of singing birds, the first they had heard since crossing the boundary of Missouri. After so many days of weary travelling, through a naked, monotonous and silent country, it was delightful once more to hear the song of the bird, and to behold the verdure of the grove. It was a beautiful sunset, and a sight of the glowing rays, mantling the tree-tops and rustling branches, seemed to gladden every heart. They pitched their camp in the grove, kindled their fires, partook merrily of their rude fare, and resigned themselves to the sweetest sleep they had enjoyed since their outset upon the prairies.

The country now became rugged and broken. High bluffs advanced upon the river, and forced the travellers occasionally to leave its banks and wind their course into the interior. In one of the wild and solitary passes they were startled by the trail of four or five pedestrians, whom they supposed to be spies from some predatory camp of either Arickara or Crow Indians. This obliged them to redouble their vigilance at night, and to keep especial watch upon their horses.

In these rugged and elevated regions they began to see the blacktailed deer, a species larger than the ordinary kind, and chiefly found in rocky and mountainous countries. They had reached also a great buffalo range; Captain Bonneville ascended a high bluff, commanding an extensive view of the surrounding plains. As far as his eye could reach, the country seemed absolutely blackened by innumerable herds. No language, he says, could convey an adequate idea of the vast living mass thus presented to his eye. He remarked that the bulls and cows generally congregated in separate herds.

On the 21st they encamped amidst high and beetling cliffs of indurated clay and sandstone, bearing the semblance of towers, castles, churches, and fortified cities. At a distance it was scarcely possible to persuade oneself that the works of art were not mingled with these fantastic freaks of nature.

Amidst this wild and striking scenery Captain Bonneville, for the first time, beheld flocks of the ahsahta, or bighorn, an animal which frequents these cliffs in great numbers. They accord with the nature of such scenery, and add much to its romantic effect; bounding like goats from crag to crag, often trooping along the lofty shelves of the mountains, under the guidance of some venerable patriarch, with horns twisted lower than his muzzle, and sometimes peering over the edge of a precipice, so high that they appear scarce bigger than crows.

When on the march Captain Bonneville always sent some of his best hunters in advance to reconnoitre the country, as well as to look out for game. On the 24th of May, as the caravan was slowly journeying up the banks of the Nebraska, the hunters came galloping back, weaving their caps, and giving the alarm cry, "Indians! Indians!"

The captain immediately ordered a halt: the hunters now came up and announced that a large war-party of Crow Indians were just above, on the river. The captain knew the character of these savages; one of the most roving, warlike, crafty, and predatory tribes of the mountains; horse-stealers of the first order, and easily provoked to acts of sanguinary violence. Orders were accordingly given to prepare for action, and every one promptly took the post that had been assigned him, in the general order of the march, in all cases of warlike emergency.

Every thing being put in battle array, the captain took the lead of his little band, and moved on slowly and warily. In a little while he beheld the Crow warriors emerging from among the bluffs. There were about sixty of them; fine martiai-looking fellows, painted and arrayed for war, and mounted on horses decked out with all kinds of wild trappings. They came prancing along in gallant style, with many wild and dexterous evolutions, for none can surpass them in horsemanship; and their bright colours, and flaunting and fantastic embellishments, glaring and sparkling in the morning sunshine, gave them really a striking appearance.

Their mode of approach, to one not acquainted with the tactics and ceremonies of this rude chivalry of the wilderness, had an air of direct hostility. They came galloping forward in a body as if about to make a furious charge, but, when close at hand, opened to the right and left, and wheeled in wild circles round the travellers, whooping and yelling like maniacs.

This done, their mock fury sank into a calm, and the chief approaching the captain, who had remained warily drawn up, though informed of the pacific nature of the manœuvre, extended to him the hand of friendship. The pipe of peace was smoked, and now all was good fellowship.

The Crows were in pursuit of a band of Cheyennes, who had attacked their village in the night and killed one of their people. They had already been five-and-twenty days on the track of the marauders, and were determined not to return home until they had sated their revenge.

A few days previously, some of their scouts, who were ranging the country at a distance from the main body, had discovered the party of Captain Bonneville. They had dogged it for a time in secret, astonished at the long train of waggons and oxen, and especially struck with the sight of a cow and calf, quietly following the caravan; supposing them to be some kind of tame buffalo. Having satisfied their curiosity, they had carried back to their chief intelligence of all that they had seen. He had, in consequence, diverged from his pursuit of vengeance to behold the wonders described to him.

"Now that we have met you," said he to Captain Bonneville, "and have seen these marvels with our own eyes, our hearts are glad." In fact, nothing could exceed the curiosity evinced by these people as to the objects before them. Waggons had never been seen by them before, and they examined them with the greatest minuteness; but the calf was the peculiar object of their admiration. They watched it with intense interest as it licked the hands accustomed to feed it, and were struck with the mild expression of its countenance, and its perfect docility.

At the request of the Crow chieftain the two parties encamped together, and passed the residue of the day in company. The chief, of course, had his scalps to show and his battles to recount. The Blackfoot is the hereditary enemy of the Crow, towards whom hostility is like a cherished principle of religion; for every tribe, besides its casual antagonists, has some enduring foe with whom there can be no permanent reconciliation. The Crows and Blackfeet, upon the whole, are enemies worthy of each other.

The present party of Crows, however, evinced nothing of the invidious character for which they are renowned. During the day and night that they were encamped in company with the travellers, their conduct was friendly in the extreme. They were, in fact, quite irksome in their attentions, and had a caressing manner at times quite importunate. It was not until after separation on the following morning, that the captain and his men ascertained the secret of all this loving kindness. In the course of their fraternal caresses, the Crows had contrived to empty the pockets of their white brothers; to abstract the very buttons from their coats, and, above all, to make free with their hunting knives.

By equal altitudes of the sun, taken at this last encampment, Captain Bonneville ascertained his latitude to be 41° 47' north. The thermometer, at six o'clock in the morning, stood at fifty-nine degrees; at two o'clock P.M., at ninety-two degrees; and at six o'clock in the evening, at seventy degrees.

The Black Hills, or Mountains, now began to be seen at a distance, printing the horizon with their rugged and broken outlines; and threatening to oppose a difficult barrier in the way of the travellers.

On the 26th of May, the travellers encamped at Laramie's fork, a clear and beautiful stream, rising in the west-south-west, maintaining an average width of twenty yards, and winding through broad meadows abounding in currants and gooseberries, and adorned with groves and clumps of trees.

By an observation of Jupiter's satellites, with a Dolland reflecting telescope, Captain Bonneville ascertained the longitude to be 102° 57' west of Greenwich.

For some days past Captain Bonneville had been made sensible of the great elevation of country into which he was gradually ascending, by the effect of the dryness and rarefaction of the atmosphere upon his waggons. The woodwork shrunk; the paint-boxes of the wheels were continually working out, and it was necessary to support the spokes by stout props to prevent their falling asunder.

The travellers were now entering one of those great steppes of the far west, where the prevalent aridity of the atmosphere renders the country unfit for cultivation. In these regions, there is a fresh sweet growth of grass in the spring, but it is scanty and short, and parches up in the course of the summer, so that there is none for the hunters to set fire to in the autumn. It is a common observation, that "above the forks of the Platte the grass does not burn."

In the course of a day or two more, the travellers entered that wild and broken tract of the Crow country called the Black Hills, and here their journey became toilsome in the extreme. Rugged steeps and deep ravines incessantly obstructed their progress, so that a great part of the day was spent in the painful toil of digging through banks, filling up ravines, forcing the waggons up the most forbidding ascents, or swinging them with ropes down the face of dangerous precipices. The shoes of their horses were worn out, and their feet injured by the rugged and stony roads. The travellers were annoyed also by frequent but brief storms, which would come hurrying over the hills, or through the mountain defiles, rage with great fury for a short time, and then pass off, leaving every thing calm and serene again.

For several nights the camp had been infested by vagabond Indian dogs, prowling about in quest of food. They were about the size of a large pointer;

with ears short and erect, and a long bushy tail—altogether they bore a striking resemblance to a wolf. These skulking visitors would keep about the purlieus of the camp until daylight; when, on the first stir of life among the sleepers, they would scamper off until they reached some rising ground, where they would take their seats, and keep a sharp and hungry watch upon every movement. The moment the travellers were fairly on the march, and the camp was abandoned, these starveling hangers-on would hasten to the deserted fires, to seize upon the half-picked bones, the offals and garbage that lay about; and, having made a hasty meal, with many a snap and snarl and growl, would follow leisurely on the trail of the caravan. Many attempts were made to coax or catch them, but in vain. Their quick and suspicious eyes caught the slightest sinister movement, and they turned and scampered off.

At length one was taken. He was terribly alarmed, and crouched and trembled as if expecting instant death. Soothed, however, by caresses, he began after a time to gather confidence and wag his tail, and at length was brought to follow close at the heels of his captors; still, however, darting around furtive and suspicious glances, and evincing a disposition to scamper off upon the least alarm.

On the first of July, the band of Crow warriors again crossed their path. They came in vaunting and vainglorious style; displaying five Cheyenne scalps, the trophies of their vengeance. They were now bound homewards, to appease the manes of their comrade by these proofs that his death had been revenged, and intended to have scalp-dances and other triumphant rejoicings. Captain Bonneville and his men, however, were by no means disposed to renew their confiding intimacy with these crafty savages, and above all, took care to avoid their pilfering caresses. They remarked one precaution of the Crows with respect to their horses; to protect their hoofs from the sharp and jagged rocks among which they had to pass, they had covered them with shoes constructed of buffalo hide.

The route of the travellers lay generally along the course of the Nebraska or Platte; but occasionally, where steep promontories advanced to the margin of the stream, they were obliged to make inland circuits. One of these took them through a bold and stern country, bordered by a range of low mountains, running east and west. Every thing around bore traces of some fearful convulsion of nature in times long past. Hitherto the various strata of rock had exhibited a gentle elevation towards the south-west, but here every thing appeared to have been subverted, and thrown out of place. In many places there were heavy beds of white sandstone resting upon red. Immense strata of rocks jutted up into crags and cliffs; and sometimes formed perpendicular walls and overhanging precipices.

An air of sterility prevailed over these savage wastes. The valleys were destitute of herbage, and scantily clothed with a stunted species of wormwood, generally known among traders and trappers by the name of sage. From an elevated point of their march through this region, the travellers caught a beautiful view of the Powder River Mountains away to the north, stretching along the very verge of the horizon, and seeming, from the snow with which they were mantled, to be a chain of small white clouds, connecting sky and earth.

Though the thermometer at midday ranged from eighty to ninety, and even sometimes rose to ninety-three degrees, yet occasional spots of snow were to be seen on the tops of the low mountains, among which the travellers were journeying; proofs of the great elevation of the whole region.

The Nebraska, in its passage through the Black Hills, is confined to a much narrower channel than that through which it flows, in the plains below; but it is deeper and clearer, and rushes with a stronger current. The scenery, also, is more varied and beautiful. Sometimes it glides rapidly, but smoothly, through a picturesque valley, between wooded banks; then forcing its way into the bosom of rugged mountains, it rushes impetuously through narrow defiles, roaring and foaming down rocks and rapids, until it is again soothed to rest in some peaceful valley.

On the 12th of July Captain Bonneville abandoned the main stream of the Nebraska, which was continually shouldered by rugged promontories, and making a bend to the south-west for a couple of days, part of the time over plains of loose sand, encamped on the 14th, on the banks of the Sweet Water, a stream about twenty yards in breadth, and four or five feet deep, flowing between low banks over a sandy soil, and forming one of the forks or upper branches of the Nebraska.

Up this stream they now shaped their course for several successive days, tending, generally, to the west. The soil was light and sandy; the country much diversified. Frequently the plains were studded with isolated blocks of rock, sometimes in the shape of a half globe, and from three to four hundred feet high. These singular masses had occasionally a very imposing, and even sublime appearance, rising from the midst of a savage and lonely landscape.

As the travellers continued to advance, they became more and more sensible of the elevation of the country. The hills around were more generally capped with snow. The men complained of cramps and colics, sore lips and mouths, and violent headaches. The woodwork of the waggons also shrunk so much, that it was with difficulty the wheels were kept from falling to pieces. The country bordering upon the river was frequently gashed with deep ravines, or traversed by high bluffs, to avoid which the travellers were obliged to make wide circuits through the plains. In the course of these, they came upon immense herds of buffalo, which kept scouring off in the van, like a retreating army.

It was on the 20th of July that Captain Bonneville first came in sight of the grand region of his hopes and anticipations, the Rocky Mountains. He had been making a bend to the south, to avoid some obstacles along the river, and had attained a high, rocky ridge, when a magnificent prospect burst upon his sight. To the west rose the Wind River Mountains, with their bleached and snowy summits towering into the clouds. These stretched far to the north-north-west, until they melted away into what appeared to be faint clouds, but which the experienced eyes of the veteran hunters of the party recognised for the rugged mountains of the Yellowstone; at the feet of which extended the wild Crow country, a perilous, though profitable region for the trapper.

To the south-west the eye ranged over an immense extent of wilderness, with what appeared to be a snowy vapour resting upon its horizon. This, however, was pointed out as another branch of the Great Chippewyan, or Rocky, chain; being the Eutaw Mountains, at whose basis the wandering tribe of hunters of the same name pitch their tents.

We can imagine the enthusiasm of the worthy captain when he beheld the vast and mountainous scene of his adventurous enterprise thus suddenly unveiled before him. We can imagine with what feelings of awe and admiration he must have contemplated the Wind River sierra, or bed of mountains; that great fountain head, from whose springs, and lakes, and melted snows, some of those mighty rivers take their rise, which wander over hundreds of miles of varied country and clime, and find their way to the opposite waves of the Atlantic and the Pacific.

The Wind River Mountains are, in fact, among the most remarkable of the whole Rocky chain; and would appear to be among the loftiest. They form, as it were, a great bed of mountains, about eighty miles in length, and from twenty to thirty in breadth; with rugged peaks, covered with eternal snows, and deep, narrow valleys, full of springs, and brooks, and rock-bound lakes. From this great treasury of waters issue forth limpid streams, that, augmenting as they descend, become main tributaries of the Missouri, on the one side, and the Columbia, on the other; and give rise to the Seeds-ke-dee Agie, or Green river, the great Colorado of the west, that empties its current into the Gulf of California.

The Wind River Mountains are notorious in hunters' and trappers' stories;

their rugged defiles, and the rough tracts about their neighbourhood, having been lurking places for the predatory hordes of the mountains, and scenes of rough encounter with Crows and Blackfeet. It was to the west of these mountains, in the valley of the Seeds-ke-dee Agie, or Green river, that Captain Bonneville intended to make a halt, for the purpose of giving repose to his people and his horses, after their weary journeying; and of collecting information as to his future course. This Green River valley, and its immediate neighbourhood, as we have already observed, formed the main point of rendezvous, for the present year, of the rival fur companies, and the motley populace, civilized and savage, connected with them. Several days of rugged travel, however, yet remained for the captain and his men before they should encamp in this desired resting place.

On the 21st of July, as they were pursuing their course through one of the meadows of the Sweet Water, they beheld a horse grazing at a little distance. He showed no alarm at their approach, but suffered himself quietly to be taken, evincing a perfect state of tameness. The scouts of the party were instantly on the look out for the owners of this animal; lest some dangerous band of savages might be lurking in the vicinity. After a narrow search, they discovered the trail of an Indian party, which had evidently passed through that neighbourhood but recently. The horse was accordingly taken possession of, as an estray; but a more vigilant watch than usual was kept round the camp at nights, lest his former owners should be upon the prowl.

The travellers had now attained so high an elevation that on the 23rd of July, at daybreak, there was considerable ice in the waterbuckets, and the thermometer stood at twenty-two degrees. The rarety of the atmosphere continued to affect the woodwork of the waggons, and the wheels were incessantly falling to pieces. A remedy was at length devised. The tire of each wheel was taken off; a band of wood was nailed round the exterior of the felloes, the tire was then made red-hot, replaced round the wheel, and suddenly cooled with water. By this means, the whole was bound together with great compactness.

On the 24th the travellers took final leave of the Sweet Water, and keeping westwardly over a low and very rocky ridge, one of the most southern spurs of the Wind River Mountains, they encamped, after a march of seven hours and a half, on the banks of a small clear stream, running to the south, in which they caught a number of fine trout.

The sight of these fish was hailed with pleasure, as a sign that they had reached the waters which flow into the Pacific; for it is only on the western streams of the Rocky Mountains that trout are to be taken. The stream on which they had thus encamped, proved, in effect, to the tributary to the Seeds-ke-dee Agie, or Green river, into which it flowed, at some distance to the south.

Captain Bonneville now considered himself as having fairly passed the crest of the Rocky Mountains; and felt some degree of exultation in being the first individual that had crossed, north of the settled provinces of Mexico, from the waters of the Atlantic to those of the Pacific, with waggons.

ON THE OREGON TRAIL[1]

(1846)

FRANCIS PARKMAN

(1823-93)

I. *With the Emigrants*

We were now at the end of our solitary journeyings along the St Joseph trail. On the evening of the twenty-third of May we encamped near its junction with the old legitimate trail of the Oregon emigrants. We had ridden long that afternoon, trying in vain to find wood and water, until at length we saw the sunset sky reflected from a pool encircled by bushes and rocks. The water lay in the bottom of a hollow, the smooth prairie gracefully rising in ocean-like swells on every side. We pitched our tents by it; not however before the keen eye of Henry Chatillon had discerned some unusual object upon the faintly defined outline of the distant swell. But in the moist, hazy atmosphere of the evening nothing could be clearly distinguished. As we lay around the fire after supper a low and distant sound, strange enough amid the loneliness of the prairie, reached our ears—peals of laughter, and the faint voices of men and women. For eight days we had not encountered a human being, and this singular warning of their vicinity had an effect extremely impressive.

About dark a sallow-faced fellow descended the hill on horseback, and, splashing through the pool, rode up to the tents. He was enveloped in a huge cloak, and his broad felt hat was weeping about his ears with the drizzling moisture of the evening. Another followed, a stout, square-built, intelligent-looking man, who announced himself as leader of an emigrant party, encamped a mile in advance of us. About twenty wagons, he said, were with him; the rest of his party were on the other side of the Big Blue, waiting for a woman who was in the pains of child-birth, and quarrelling meanwhile among themselves.

[1] From *The Oregon Trail.*

These were the first emigrants that we had overtaken, although we had found abundant and melancholy traces of their progress throughout the course of the journey. Sometimes we passed the grave of one who had sickened and died on the way. The earth was usually torn up, and covered thickly with wolf-tracks. Some had escaped this violation. One morning, a piece of plank, standing upright on the summit of a grassy hill, attracted our notice, and, riding up to it, we found the following words very roughly traced upon it, apparently with a red-hot piece of iron:

MARY ELLIS

Died May 7th, 1845,
aged Two Months

Such tokens were of common occurrence.

We were late in breaking up our camp on the following morning, and scarcely had we ridden a mile when we saw, far in advance of us, drawn against the horizon, a line of objects stretching at regular intervals along the level edge of the prairie. An intervening swell soon hid them from sight, until, ascending it a quarter of an hour after, we saw close before us the emigrant caravan, with its heavy white wagons creeping on in slow procession, and a large drove of cattle following behind. Half a dozen yellow-visaged Missourians, mounted on horseback, were cursing and shouting among them, their lank, angular proportions enveloped in brown homespun, evidently cut and adjusted by the hands of a domestic female tailor. As we approached, they called out to us: "How are ye, boys? Are ye for Oregon or California?"

As we pushed rapidly by the wagons children's faces were thrust out from the white coverings to look at us; while the care-worn, thin-featured matron, or the buxom girl, seated in front, suspended the knitting on which most of them were engaged to stare at us with wondering curiosity. By the side of each wagon stalked the proprietor, urging on his patient oxen, who shouldered heavily along, inch by inch, on their interminable journey. It was easy to see that fear and dissension prevailed among them; some of the men—but these, with one exception, were bachelors—looked wistfully upon us as we rode lightly and swiftly by, and then impatiently at their own lumbering wagons and heavy-gaited oxen. Others were unwilling to advance at all, until the party they had left behind should have rejoined them. Many were murmuring against the leader they had chosen, and wished to depose him; and this discontent was fomented by some ambitious spirits, who had hopes of succeeding in his place. The women were divided between regrets for the homes they had left and fear of the deserts and savages before them.

We soon left them far behind, and hoped that we had taken a final leave; but our companions' wagon stuck so long in a deep muddy ditch that before it was extricated the van of the emigrant caravan appeared again, descending a ridge close at hand. Wagon after wagon plunged through the mud, and as it was nearly noon, and the place promised shade and water, we saw with satisfaction that they were resolved to encamp. Soon the wagons were wheeled into a circle: the cattle were grazing over the meadow, and the men, with sour, sullen faces, were looking about for wood and water. They seemed to meet but indifferent success. As we left the ground, I saw a tall, slouching fellow, with the nasal accent of 'down East,' contemplating the contents of his tin cup, which he had just filled with water.

"Look here, you," said he; "it's chock-full of animals!"

The cup, as he held it out, exhibited, in fact, an extraordinary variety and profusion of animal and vegetable life.

Riding up the little hill, and looking back on the meadow, we could easily see that all was not right in the camp of the emigrants. The men were crowded together, and an angry discussion seemed to be going forward. R—— was missing from his wonted place in the line, and the Captain told us that he had remained behind to get his horse shod by a blacksmith attached to the emigrant party. Something whispered in our ears that mischief was on foot; we kept on, however, and, coming soon to a stream of tolerable water, we stopped to rest and dine. Still the absentee lingered behind. At last, at the distance of a mile, he and his horse suddenly appeared, sharply defined against the sky, on the summit of a hill; and close behind a huge white object rose slowly into view.

"What is that blockhead bringing with him now?"

A moment dispelled the mystery. Slowly and solemnly, one behind the other, four long trains of oxen and four emigrant wagons rolled over the crest of the hill and gravely descended, while R—— rode in state in the van. It seems that during the process of shoeing the horse, the smothered dissensions among the emigrants suddenly broke into open rupture. Some insisted on pushing forward, some on remaining where they were, and some on going back. Kearsley, their captain, threw up his command in disgust. "And now, boys," said he, "if any of you are for going ahead, just you come along with me."

Four wagons, with ten men, one woman, and one small child, made up the force of the 'go-ahead' faction, and R——, with his usual proclivity toward mischief, invited them to join our party. Fear of the Indians—for I can conceive no other motive—must have induced him to court so burdensome an alliance. At all events, the proceeding was a cool one. The men who joined us, it is true, were all that could be desired; rude, indeed, in manners, but frank, manly, and intelligent. To tell them we could not travel with them was out of the question. I merely reminded Kearsley that if his oxen could not keep up with our mules he must expect to be left behind, as we could not consent to be further delayed on the journey; but he immediately replied that his oxen "*should* keep up; and if they couldn't, why, he allowed, he'd find out how to make 'em."

On the next day, as it chanced, our English companions broke the axle-tree of their wagon, and down came the whole cumbrous machine, lumbering into the bed of a brook. Here was a day's work cut out for us. Meanwhile our emigrant associates kept on their way, and so vigorously did they urge forward their powerful oxen, that, what with the broken axle-tree and other mishaps, it was full a week before we overtook them; when at length we discovered them, one afternoon, crawling quietly along the sandy brink of the Platte. But meanwhile various incidents occurred to ourselves.

It was probable that at this stage of our journey the Pawnees would attempt to rob us. We began therefore to stand guard in turn, dividing the night into three watches, and appointing two men for each. Deslauriers and I held guard together. We did not march with military precision to and fro before the tents: our discipline was by no means so strict. We wrapped ourselves in our blankets, and sat down by the fire; and Deslauriers, combining his culinary functions with his duties as sentinel, employed himself in boiling the head of an antelope for our breakfast. Yet we were models of vigilance in comparison with some of the party; for the ordinary practice of the guard was to lay his rifle on the ground, and, enveloping his nose in his blanket, meditate on his mistress, or whatever subject best pleased him. This is all well enough when among Indians who do not habitually proceed further in their hostility than robbing travellers of their horses and mules, though, indeed, a Pawnee's forbearance is not always to be trusted; but in certain regions further to the west, the guard must beware how he exposes his person to the light of the fire, lest some keen-eyed skulking marksman should let fly a bullet or an arrow from the darkness.

Among various tales that circulated around our campfire was one told by Boisverd, and not inappropriate here. He was trapping with several companions on the skirts of the Blackfoot country. The man on guard, knowing that it behoved him to put forth his utmost precaution, kept aloof from the firelight, and sat watching intently on all sides. At length he was aware of a dark, crouching figure, stealing noiselessly into the circle of the light. He hastily cocked his rifle, but the sharp click of the lock caught the ear of the Blackfoot, whose senses were all on the alert. Raising his arrow, already fitted to the string, he shot it in the direction of the sound. So sure was his aim, that he drove it through the throat of the unfortunate guard, and then, with a loud yell, bounded from the camp.

As I looked at the partner of my watch, puffing and blowing over his fire, it occurred to me that he might not prove the most efficient auxiliary in time of trouble.

"Deslauriers," said I, "would you run away if the Pawnees should fire at us?"

"*Ah! oui, oui, monsieur!*" he replied very decisively.

At this instant a whimsical variety of voices—barks, howls, yelps, and whines—all mingled together, sounded from the prairie, not far off, as if a conclave of wolves of every age and sex were assembled there. Deslauriers looked up from his work with a laugh, and began to imitate this medley of sounds with a ludicrous accuracy. At this they were repeated with redoubled emphasis, the musician being apparently indignant at the successful efforts of a rival. They all proceeded from the throat of one little wolf, not larger than a spaniel, seated by himself at some distance. He was of the species called the prairie-wolf: a grim-visaged, but harmless little brute, whose worst propensity is creeping among horses and gnawing the ropes of raw hide by which they are picketed around the camp. Other beasts roam the prairies, far more formidable in aspect and in character. These are the large white and grey wolves, whose deep howl we heard at intervals from far and near.

At last I fell into a doze, and, awaking from it, found Deslauriers fast asleep. Scandalized by this breach of discipline, I was about to stimulate his vigilance by stirring him with the stock of my rifle; but, compassion prevailing, I determined to let him sleep a while, and then arouse him to administer a suitable reproof for such forgetfulness of duty. Now and then I walked the rounds among the silent horses, to see that all was right. The night was chill, damp, and dark, the dank grass bending under the icy dewdrops. At the distance of a rod or two the tents were invisible, and nothing could be seen but the obscure figures of the horses, deeply breathing, and restlessly starting as they slept, or still slowly champing the grass. Far off, beyond the black outline of the prairie, there was a ruddy light, gradually increasing, like the glow of a conflagration; until at length the broad disk of the moon, blood-red, and vastly magnified by the vapors, rose slowly upon the darkness, flecked by one or two little clouds, and as the light poured over the gloomy plain, a fierce and stern howl, close at hand, seemed to greet it as an unwelcome intruder. There was something impressive and awful in the place and the hour; for I and the beasts were all that had consciousness for many a league around.

II. *—and the Redskins*

On the following day the heights closed around us, and the passage of the mountains began in earnest. Before the village left its 'camping-ground' I set forward in company with the Eagle Feather, a man of powerful frame, but with a bad and sinister face. His son, a light-limbed boy, rode with us, and another Indian, named The Panther, was also of the party. Leaving the village out of sight behind us, we rode together up a rocky defile. After a while, however, the Eagle Feather discovered in the distance some appearance of game, and set off with his son in pursuit of it, while I went forward with The Panther. This was a mere *nom de guerre*; for, like many Indians, he concealed his real name out of some superstitious notion. He was a noble-looking fellow. As he suffered his ornamented buffalo-robe to fall in folds about his loins, his stately and graceful figure was fully displayed; and while he sat his horse in an easy attitude, the long feathers of the prairie-cock fluttering from the crown of his head, he seemed the very model of a wild prairie-rider. He had not the same features with those of other Indians. Unless his face greatly belied him, he was free from the jealousy, suspicion, and malignant cunning of his people. For the most part, a civilized white man can discover very few points of sympathy between his own nature and that of an Indian. With every disposition to do justice to their good qualities, he must be conscious that an impassable gulf lies between him and his red brethren. Nay, so alien to himself do they appear, that, after breathing the air of the prairie for a few months or weeks, he begins to look upon them as a troublesome and dangerous species of wild beast. Yet, in the countenance of The Panther, I gladly read that there were at least some points of sympathy between him and me. We were excellent friends, and as we rode forward together through rocky passages, deep dells, and little barren plains, he occupied himself very zealously in teaching me the Dahcotah language. After a while, we came to a grassy recess, where some gooseberry-bushes were growing at the foot of a rock: and these offered such temptation to my companion, that he gave over his instructions, and stopped so long to gather the fruit, that before we were in motion again the van of the village came in view. An old woman appeared, leading down her pack-horse among the rocks above. Savage after savage followed, and the little dell was soon crowded with the throng.

That morning's march was one not to be forgotten. It led us through a sublime waste, a wilderness of mountains and pine-forests, over which the spirit of loneliness and silence seemed brooding. Above and below, little could be seen but the same dark green foliage. It overspread the valleys, and enveloped the mountains, from the black rocks that crowned their summits to the streams that circled around their base. I rode to the top of a hill whence I could look down on the savage procession as it passed beneath my feet, and, far on the left, could see its thin and broken line, visible only at intervals, stretching away for miles among the mountains. On the farthest ridge, horsemen were still descending like mere specks in the distance.

I remained on the hill until all had passed, and then descending followed after them. A little farther on I found a very small meadow, set deeply among steep mountains; and here the whole village had encamped. The little spot was crowded with the confused and disorderly host. Some of the lodges were already set up, or the squaws perhaps were busy in drawing the heavy coverings of skins over the bare poles. Others were as yet mere skeletons, while others still, poles, covering, and all, lay scattered in disorder on the ground among buffalo-robes, bales of meat, domestic utensils, harness, and weapons. Squaws were screaming to one another, horses rearing and plunging, dogs yelping, eager to be disburdened of their loads, while the fluttering of feathers and the gleam of savage ornaments added liveliness to the scene. The small children ran about amid the crowd, while many of the boys were scrambling among the overhanging rocks, and standing with their little bows in their hands, looking down upon the restless throng. In contrast with the general confusion, a circle of old men and warriors sat in the midst, smoking in profound indifference and tranquillity. The disorder at length subsided. The horses were driven away to feed along the adjacent valley, and the camp assumed an air of listless repose. It was scarcely past noon; a vast white canopy of smoke from a burning forest to the eastward overhung the place, and partially obscured the rays of the sun; yet the heat was almost insupportable. The lodges stood crowded together without order in the narrow space. Each was a hot-house, within which the lazy proprietor lay sleeping. The camp was silent as death. Nothing stirred except now and then an old woman passing from lodge to lodge. The girls and young men sat together in groups, under the pine-trees upon the surrounding heights. The dogs lay panting on the ground, too languid even to growl at the white man. At the entrance of the meadow, there was a cold spring among the rocks, completely overshadowed by tall trees and dense undergrowth. In this cool and shady retreat a number of girls were assembled, sitting together on rocks and fallen logs, discussing the latest gossip of the village, or laughing and throwing water with their hands at the intruding Meneaska. The minutes seemed lengthened into hours. I lay for a long time under a tree studying the Ogillallah tongue, with the aid of my friend The Panther. When we were both tired of this, I lay down by the side of a deep, clear pool, formed by the water of the spring. A shoal of little fishes of about a pin's length were playing in it, sporting together, as it seemed, very amicably; but on closer observation, I saw that they were engaged in cannibal warfare among themselves. Now and then one of the smallest would fall a victim, and immediately disappear down the maw of his conqueror. Every moment, however, the tyrant of the pool, a goggle-eyed monster about three inches long, would slowly emerge with quivering fins and tail from under the shelving bank. The small fry at this would suspend their hostilities, and scatter in a panic at the appearance of overwhelming force.

"Soft-hearted philanthropists," thought I, "may sigh long for their peaceful millennium; for, from minnows to men, life is incessant war."

Evening approached at last; the crests of the mountains were still bright in sunshine, while our deep glen was completely shadowed. I left the camp, and climbed a neighbouring hill. The sun was still glaring through the stiff pines on the ridge of the western mountain. In a moment he was gone, and, as the landscape darkened, I turned again towards the village. As I descended the howling of wolves and the barking of foxes came up out of the dim woods from far and near. The camp was glowing with a multitude of fires, and alive with dusky naked figures, whose tall shadows flitted, weird and ghostlike, among the surrounding crags.

I found a circle of smokers seated in their usual place; that is, on the ground before the lodge of a certain warrior, who seemed to be generally known for his social qualities. I sat down to smoke a parting pipe with my savage friends. That day was the first of August, on which I had promised to meet Shaw at Fort Laramie. The fort was less than two days' journey distant, and that my friend need not suffer anxiety on my account, I resolved to push forward as rapidly as possible to the place of meeting. I went to look after the Hail-Storm, and, having found him, I offered him a handful of hawks'-bells and a paper of vermilion, on condition that he would guide me in the morning through the mountains.

The Hail-Storm ejaculated "*How!*" and accepted the gift. Nothing more was said on either side; the matter was settled, and I lay down to sleep in Kongra-Tonga's lodge.

Long before daylight, Raymond shook me bv the shoulder.

"Everything is ready," he said.

I went out. The morning was chill, damp, and dark; and the whole camp seemed asleep. The Hail-Storm sat on horseback before the lodge, and my mare Pauline and the mule which Raymond rode were picketed near it. We saddled and made our other arrangements for the journey, but before these were completed the camp began to stir, and the lodge-coverings fluttered and rustled as the squaws pulled them down in preparation for departure. Just as the light began to appear, we left the ground, passing up through a narrow opening among the rocks which led eastward out of the meadow. Gaining the top of this passage, I turned and sat looking back upon the camp, dimly visible in the grey light of morning. All was alive with the bustle of preparation. I turned away, half unwilling to take a final leave of my savage associates. We passed among rocks and pine-trees so dark, that for a while we could scarcely see our way. The country in front was wild and broken, half hill, half plain, partly open and partly covered with woods of pine and oak. Barriers of lofty mountains encompassed it; the woods were fresh and cool in the early morning, the peaks of the mountains were wreathed with mist, and sluggish vapours were entangled among the forests upon their sides. At length the black pinnacle of the tallest mountain was tipped with gold by the rising sun. The Hail-Storm, who rode in front, gave a low exclamation. Some large animal leaped up from among the bushes, and an elk, as I thought, his horns thrown back over his neck, darted past us across the open space, and bounded like a mad thing away among the adjoining pines. Raymond was soon out of his saddle, but before he could fire, the animal was full two hundred yards distant. The ball struck its mark, though much too low for mortal effect. The elk, however, wheeled in his flight, and ran at full speed among the trees, nearly at right angles to his former course. I fired and broke his shoulder; still he moved on, limping down into a neighbouring woody hollow, whither the young Indian followed and killed him. When we reached the spot, we discovered him to be no elk, but a black-tailed deer, an animal nearly twice as large as the common deer, and quite unknown in the east. The reports of the rifles had reached the ears of the Indians, and several of them came to the spot. Leaving the hide of the deer to the Hail-Storm, we hung as much of the meat as we wanted behind our saddles, left the rest to the Indians, and resumed our journey. Meanwhile the village was on its way, and had gone so far that to get in advance of it was impossible. We directed our course so as to strike its line of march at the nearest point. In a short time, through the dark trunks of the pines, we could see the figures of the Indians as they passed. Once more we were among them. They were moving with even more than their usual precipitation, crowded together in a narrow pass between rocks and old pine-trees. We were on the eastern descent of the mountain, and soon came to a rough and difficult defile, leading down a very steep declivity. The whole swarm poured down together, filling the rocky passage-way like some turbulent mountain stream. The mountains before us were on fire, and had been so for weeks. The view in front was obscured by a vast dim sea of smoke, while on either hand rose the tall cliffs, bearing aloft their crests of pines, and the sharp pinnacles and broken ridges of the mountains beyond were faintly traceable as through a veil. The scene in itself was grand and imposing, but with the savage multitude, the armed warriors, the naked children, the gaily apparelled girls, pouring impetuously down the heights, it would have formed a noble subject for a painter, and only the pen of a Scott could have done it justice in description.

We passed over a burnt track where the ground was hot beneath the horses' feet, and between the blazing sides of two mountains. Before long we had descended to a softer region, where we found a succession of little valleys watered by a stream, along the borders of which grew abundance of wild gooseberries and currants, and the children and many of the men straggled from the line of march to gather them as we passed along. Descending still farther, the view changed rapidly. The burning mountains were behind us, and through the open valleys in front we could see the prairie, stretching like an ocean beyond the sight. After passing through a line of trees that skirted the brook, the Indians field out upon the plains. I was thirsty and knelt down by the little stream to drink. As I mounted again, I very carelessly left my rifle among the grass, and my thoughts being otherwise absorbed, I rode for some distance before discovering its absence. I lost no time in turning about and galloping back in search of it. Passing the line of Indians, I watched every warrior as he rode by me at a canter, and at length discovered my rifle in the hands of one of them, who, on my approaching to claim it, immediately gave it up. Having no other means of acknowledging the obligation, I took off one of my spurs and gave it to him. He was greatly delighted, looking upon it as a distinguished mark of favour, and immediately held out his foot for me to buckle it on. As soon as I had done so, he struck it with all his force into the side of his horse, which gave a violent leap. The Indian laughed and spurred harder than before. At this the horse shot away like an arrow, amid the screams and laughter of the squaws, and the ejaculations of the men, who exclaimed: "Washtay!—Good!" at the potent effect of my gift. The Indian had no saddle, and nothing in place of a bridle except a leather string tied round the horse's jaw. The animal was of course wholly uncontrollable, and stretched away at full speed over the prairie, till he and his rider vanished behind a distant swell. I never saw the man again, but I presume no harm came to him. An Indian on horseback has more lives than a cat.

The village encamped on the scorching prairie, close to the foot of the mountains. The heat was most intense and penetrating. The coverings of the lodgings were raised a foot or more from the ground, in order to procure some circulation of air; and Reynal thought proper to lay aside his trapper's dress of buckskin and assume the very scanty costume of an Indian. Thus elegantly attired, he stretched himself in his lodge on a buffalo-robe, alternately cursing the heat, and puffing at the pipe which he and I passed between us. There was present also a select circle of Indian friends and relatives. A small boiled puppy was served up as a parting feast, to which was added, by way of dessert, a wooden bowl of gooseberries from the mountains.

"Look there," said Reynal, pointing out of the opening of his lodge; "do you see that line of buttes about fifteen miles off? Well, now do you see that farthest one, with the white speck on the face of it? Do you think you ever saw it before?"

"It looks to me," said I, "like the hill that we were camped under when we were on Laramie Creek, six or eight weeks ago."

"You've hit it," answered Reynal.

"Go and bring in the animals, Raymond," said I; "we'll camp there to-night, and start for the fort in the morning."

The mare and the mule were soon before the lodge. We saddled them, and in the meantime a number of Indians collected about us. The virtues of Pauline, my strong, fleet, and hardy little mare, were well known in camp, and several of the visitors were mounted upon good horses which they had brought me as presents. I promptly declined their offers, since accepting them would have involved the necessity of transferring Pauline into their barbarous hands. We took leave of Reynal, but not of the Indians, who are accustomed to dispense with such superfluous ceremonies. Leaving the camp, we rode straight over the prairie towards the white-faced bluff, whose pale ridges swelled gently against the horizon, like a cloud. An Indian went with us, whose name I forget, though the ugliness of his face and the ghastly width of his mouth dwell vividly in my recollection. The antelope were numerous, but we did not heed them. We rode directly towards our destination, over the arid plains and barren hills; until, late in the afternoon, half spent with heat, thirst, and fatigue, we saw a gladdening sight; the long line of trees and the deep gulf that mark the course of Laramie Creek. Passing through the growth of huge dilapidated old cotton-wood trees that bordered the creek, we rode across to the other side. The rapid and foaming waters were filled with fish playing and splashing in the shallows. As we gained the farther bank, our horses turned eagerly to drink, and we, kneeling on the sand, followed their example. We had not gone for before the scene began to grow familiar.

"We are getting near home, Raymond," said I.

There stood the big tree under which we had encamped so long; there were the white cliffs that used to look down upon our tent when it stood at the bend of the creek; there was the meadow in which our horses had grazed for weeks, and a little farther on, the prairie-dog village where I had beguiled many a languid hour in shooting the unfortunate inhabitants.

"We are going to catch it now," said Raymond, turning his broad face up towards the sky.

In truth the cliffs and the meadow, the stream and the groves, were darkening fast. Black masses of cloud were swelling up in the south, and the thunder was growling ominously.

"We will camp there," I said, pointing to a dense grove of trees lower down the stream. Raymond and I turned towards it, but the Indian stopped and called earnestly after us. When we demanded what was the matter, he said, that the ghosts of two warriors were always among those trees, and that if we slept there, they would scream and throw stones at us all night, and perhaps steal our horses before morning. Thinking it as well to humour him, we left behind us the haunt of these extraordinary ghosts, and passed on towards Chugwater, riding at full gallop, for the big drops began to patter down. Soon we came in sight of the popular saplings that grew about the mouth of the little stream. We leaped to the ground, threw off our saddles, turned our horses loose, and drawing our knives began to slash among the bushes to cut twigs and branches for making a shelter against the rain. Bending down the taller saplings as they grew, we piled the young shoots upon them, and thus made a convenient pent-house; but our labour was needless. The storm scarcely touched us. Half a mile on our right the rain was pouring down like a cataract, and the thunder roared over the prairie like a battery of cannon; while we by good fortune received only a few heavy drops from the skirt of the passing cloud. The weather cleared and the sun set gloriously. Sitting close under our leafy canopy, we proceeded to discuss a substantial meal of *wasna* which Weah-Washtay had given me. The Indian had brought with him his pipe and a bag of *shong-sasha*; so before lying down to sleep, we sat for some time smoking together. First, however, our wide-mouthed friend had taken the precaution of carefully examining the neighbourhood. He reported that eight men, counting them on his fingers, had been encamped there not long before—Bisonette, Paul Dorion, Antoine Le Rouge, Richardson, and four others, whose names he could not tell. All this proved strictly correct. By what instinct he had arrived at such accurate conclusions, I am utterly at a loss to divine.

It was still quite dark when I awoke and called Raymond. The Indian was already gone, having chosen to go on before us to the fort. Setting out after him, we rode for some time in complete darkness, and when the sun at length rose, glowing like a fiery ball of copper, we were within ten miles of the fort. At length, from the summit of a sandy bluff we could see Fort Laramie, miles before us, standing by the side of the stream, like a little grey speck, in the midst of the boundless desolation. I stopped my horse, and sat for a moment looking down upon it. It seemed to me the very centre of comfort and civilization. We were not long in approaching it, for we rode at speed the greater part of the way. Laramie Creek still intervened between us and the friendly walls. Entering the water at the point where we had struck upon the bank, we raised our feet to the saddle behind us, and thus kneeling as it were on horseback, passed dry-shod through the swift current.

FRANCE

SEEKING HOLY PLACES[1]

St Silvia of Aquitania

(*c.* 385)

MEANWHILE, as we walked, we arrived at a certain place, where the mountains between which we were passing opened themselves out and formed a great valley, very flat and extremely beautiful; and beyond the valley appeared Sinai, the holy Mount of God.[2] This spot where the mountains opened themselves out is united with the place where are the Graves of Lust. And when we came there those holy guides, who were with us, bade us, saying: "It is a custom that prayer be offered by those who come hither, when first from this place the Mount of God is seen." So then did we. Now, from thence to the Mount of God is perhaps four miles altogether through that valley which I have described as great.

For that valley is very great indeed, lying under the side of the Mount of God; it is perhaps—as far as we could judge from looking at it and as they told us—sixteen miles in length. In breadth they called it four miles. We had to cross this valley in order to arrive at the mount. This is that same great and flat valley in which the children of Israel waited during the days when holy Moses went up into the Mount of God, where he was for forty days and forty nights. This is the valley in which the calf was made; the spot is shown to this day, for a great stone stands fixed in the very place. This, then, is the valley at the head of which was the place where holy Moses was when he fed the flocks of his father-in-law, where God spake to him from the Burning Bush. Now, our route was first to ascend the Mount of God at the side from which we were approaching, because the ascent here was easier; and then to descend to the head of the valley where the Bush was, this being the easier way of descent from the Mount of God. And so it seemed good to us that having seen all things which we desired, descending from the Mount of God, we should come to where the Bush is, and thence retrace our way through the middle of the valley, throughout its length, with the men of God, who showed us each place in the valley mentioned in Scripture.

So then we did. Then, going from that place where we had offered up prayer as we came from Faran, our route was to cross through the middle of

[1] From *The Pilgrimage of S. Silvia of Aquitania*, translated by J.H. Bernard (Palestine Pilgrims' Text Society), 1891.

[2] Silvia's manuscript begins thus abruptly with her approach to Mount Sinai, the first part having been lost.

the head of the valley, and so wind round to the Mount of God. The mountain itself seems to be single, in the form of a ring; but when you enter the ring [you see that] there are several, the whole range being called the Mount of God. That special one at whose summit is the place where the majesty of God descended, as it is written, is in the centre of all. And although all which form the ring are so lofty as I think I never saw before, yet that central one on which the majesty of God descended is so much higher than the others, that when we had arrived at it, all those mountains which we had previously thought lofty were below us as if they were very little hills. And this is truly an admirable thing, and, as I think, not without the grace of God, that although that central one specially called Sinai, on which the majesty of God descended, is higher than all the others, yet it cannot be seen until you come to its very foot, though before you actually are on it. For after you have accomplished your purpose, and have descended, you see it from the other side, which you could not do before you are on it. This I learnt from the report of the brethren before we arrived at the Mount of God, and after I had arrived there I perceived it to be so for myself.

It was late on the Sabbath when we came to the mountain, and arriving at a certain monastery, the kindly monks who lived there entertained us, showing us all kindliness; for there is a church there with a priest. There we stayed that night, and then early on the Lord's day we began to ascend the mountains one by one with the priest and the monks who lived there. These mountains are ascended with infinite labour, because you do not go up gradually by a spiral path (as we say, "like a snail shell"), but you go straight up as if up the face of a wall, and you must go straight down each mountain until you arrive at the foot of that central one which is strictly called Sinai. And so, Christ our God commanding us, we were encouraged by the prayers of the holy men who accompanied us; and although the labour was great—for I had to ascend on foot, because the ascent could not be made in a chair—yet I did not feel it. To that extent the labour was not felt, because I saw that the desire which I had was being fulfilled by the command of God. At the fourth hour we arrived at that peak of Sinai, the holy Mount of God, where the law was given—*i.e.*, at that place where the majesty of God descended on the day when the mountain smoked. In that place there is now a church—not a large one, because the place itself, the summit of the mountain, is not large; but the church has in itself a large measure of grace.

When therefore, by God's command, we had arrived at the summit, and come to the door of the church, the priest who was appointed to the church, coming out of his cell, met us, a blameless old man, a monk from early youth, and (as they say here) an *ascetic*; in short, a man quite worthy of the place. The other priests met us also, as well as all the monks who lived there by the mountain; that is, all of them who were not prevented by age or infirmity. But on the very summit of the central mountain no one lives permanently; nothing is there but the church and the cave where holy Moses was. Here the whole passage having been read from the book of Moses, and the oblation made in due order, we communicated; and as I was passing out of the church the priests gave us gifts of blessing from the place; that is, gifts of the fruits grown in the mountain. For although the holy mount of Sinai itself is all rocky, so that it has not a bush on it, yet down near the foot of the mountains—either the central one or those which form the ring—there is a little plot of ground; here the holy monks diligently plant shrubs and lay out orchards and fields; and hard by they place their own cells, so that they may get, as if from the soil of the mountain itself, some fruit which they may seem to have cultivated with their own hands. So, then, after we had communicated and the holy men had given us these gifts of blessing, and we had come out of the door of the church, I began to ask them to show us the several localities. Thereupon the holy men deigned to show us each place. For they showed us the famous cave where holy Moses was when for the second time he went up to the Mount of God to receive the tables [of the law] again after he had broken the first on account of the sin of the people; and the other places also which we desired to see or which they knew better they deigned to show us. But I would have you to know, ladies, venerable sisters, that from the place where we were standing—that is, in the enclosure of the church wall, on the summit of the central mountain—those mountains which we had at first ascended with difficulty were like little hills in comparison with that central one on which we were standing. And yet they were so enormous that I should think I had never seen higher, did not this central one overtop them by so much. Egypt and Palestine and the Red Sea and the Parthenian Sea, which leads to Alexandria, also the boundless territories of the Saracens, we saw below us, hard though it is to believe: all which things those holy men pointed out to us.

Having satisfied every desire with which we had made haste to ascend, we began now to descend from the summit of the Mount of God to another mountain which is joined to it; the place is called Horeb, and there is a church there. This is that Horeb where was the holy prophet Elijah when he fled from the face of King Ahab, where God spake to him saying, "What doest thou here, Elijah?" as it is written in the books of Kings. For the cave where holy Elijah hid is shown to this day before the door of the church which is there;

the stone altar is also shown which holy Elijah built that he might offer sacrifice to God. All which things the holy men deigned to show us. There we offered an oblation and an earnest prayer, and the passage from the book of Kings was read; for we always especially desired that when we came to any place the corresponding passage from the book should be read. There having made an oblation, we went on to another place not far off, which the priests and monks pointed out—viz., that place where holy Aaron had stood with the seventy elders when holy Moses received from the Lord the law for the children of Israel. There, although the place is not roofed in, there is a huge rock having a circular flat surface on which, it is said, these holy persons stood. And in the middle there is a sort of altar made with stones. The passage from the book of Moses was read, and one psalm said which was appropriate to the place; and then, having offered a prayer, we descended.

Now, it began to be about the eighth hour, and we had yet three miles to go before we should have gone through the mountains we had entered upon late the day before; but we had to go out at a different side from that by which we had entered, as I said above, because it was necessary to walk over all the holy places and to see the cells that were there, and so to go out at the head of that above-mentioned valley lying under the Mount of God. It was furthermore necessary to go out at the head of the valley, because there were there many cells of holy men and a church where the Bush is; this bush is alive to the present day, and sends forth shoots. So having descended the Mount of God, we arrived at the Bush about the tenth hour. This is the Bush I spoke of above, from which God spake to Moses in the fire, which is in the place where there are many cells and the church at the head of the valley. Before the church there is a very pleasant garden with abundance of good water, in which garden the Bush is. The place is shown near where holy Moses stood when God said to him, "Loose the latchet of thy shoe," etc. When we came to this place it was the tenth hour, and because it was so late we could not make an oblation; but prayer was offered in the church, and also in the garden at the Bush; also the passage was read from the book of Moses as usual, and so, as it was late, we took a light meal there in the garden before the Bush with the holy men. So there we stayed, and rising early on the next day, we asked the priests that the oblation should be made, which was done accordingly.

Now, our way was to go through that central valley, throughout its length—*i.e.*, the valley where, as I said before, the children of Israel stayed while Moses ascended and descended the Mount of God. The holy men used to show us each place as we came to it throughout the valley.... As we went we saw from the opposite side the summit of the mountain, which looks down over the whole valley; from which place holy Moses saw the children of Israel dancing at the time when they made the calf. They also showed a huge rock at the place where holy Moses descended with Joshua, the son of Nun, on which rock he, being angry, brake the tables which he was carrying. They also showed their dwelling-places throughout the valley, of which the foundations appear to this day, of circular form, made with stone: they also showed the place where holy Moses, when he returned from the Mount, bade the children of Israel run "from gate to gate. . . ." They showed also that place where it rained manna and quails. In fine, everything recorded in the holy books of Moses as having been done in that place, to wit, the valley which I said lies under the Mount of God, holy Sinai, was shown to us; of all which things it is superfluous to write in detail, not only because such great things could not be retained [in the memory], but because when it pleases you to read the holy books of Moses you will see more quickly all the things that were there done.

But, as I was saying, this is the valley where the Passover was celebrated, the first year being completed of the journeying of the children of Israel from the land of Egypt;. . . . there they tarried until the tabernacle should be made, and . . . the place was shown to us where Moses at the first constructed the tabernacle. . . . We saw also in the far end of the valley the Graves of Lust, at that spot where we came back again to our road—*i.e.,* where, going out of the great valley, we re-entered the path between the mountains above mentioned by which we had come. On that day we met with those other very holy monks who, by reason of age or infirmity, were unable to be present in the Mount of God to make an oblation; however, they deigned to receive us very kindly when we arrived at their cells. So we saw all the holy places which we desired, and also all the places which the children of Israel had touched in going to or returning from the Mount of God; and having also seen holy men who lived there in the name of God, we returned to Faran. And although I ought always to thank God in everything (not to speak of these so great benefits which. He has vouchsafed to confer on me, unworthy and undeserving, that I should walk through all these places, benefits unmeried indeed), yet I am not even able sufficiently to thank all those holy men who deigned with willing mind to receive my insignificant self in their monasteries, or to guide me through all the places which I was always seeking in accordance with the Holy Scriptures. Many indeed of these holy men who lived in or round about the Mount of God deigned to guide us back to Faran; they were, however, of stronger frame.

Now, when we had arrived at Faran, which is distant thirty-five miles from the Mount of God, we had to stay there two days to recruit our strength. Then rising early on the third day, we came at length to the station—that is, to the desert of Faran—where we had halted on our way [to Sinai], as I said above. Thence on the next day making a circuit, and going yet a little way between the mountains, we arrived at the station which is over the sea—*i.e.*, in the place where there is an exit from among the mountains, and the path begins to the quite near the sea; near the sea to this extent, that at one moment the waves come up to the feet of the animals, and at another moment path through the desert is 100, 200, or sometimes more than 500, paces from the sea: the road there is not inland, but the deserts are quite sandy. The people of Faran, who were accustomed to travel about there with their camels, place landmarks here and there, and, attending to these, they march by day. At night the camels take note of them. In short, the people of Faran from habit travel by night in that place more quickly and surely than other men could travel on a highroad. So on our return journey we came out from among the mountains at that spot where we had entered originally, and thus we wound round to the sea. The children of Israel also, returning to Sinai, the Mount of God, returned by the way that they had gone to that very place where we came out from among the mountains, and finally approached the Red Sea. Thence our return journey was by the route that we had taken going; and the children of Israel made their march from the very same place, as it is written in the books of holy Moses. We returned to Clesma by the same route and the same stations which we had gone by: when we got to Clesma we had to recruit for a while, for we had stoutly made our way through the sandy soil of the desert.

THE REDISCOVERY OF THE MISSISSIPPI[1]

(1673)

FATHER JACQUES MARQUETTE

(1637-75)

THE day of the Immaculate Conception of the blessed Virgin, whom I had always invoked since I have been in this Ottawa country, to obtain of God the grace to be able to visit the nations on the river Missisipi, was indentically that on which M. Jollyet arrived with orders of the Comte de Frontenac, our governor, and M. Talon, our intendant, to make this discovery with me. I was the more enraptured at this good news, as I saw my designs on the point of

[1] From *Discovery and Exploration of the Mississippi Valley,* by J. G. Shea (1852).

being accomplished, and myself in the happy necessity of exposing my life for the salvation of all these nations, and particularly for the ilinois, who had, when I was at Lapointe du St Esprit, very earnestly entreated me to carry the word of God to their country.

We were not long in preparing our outfit, although we were embarking on a voyage the duration of which we could not foresee. Indian corn, with some dried meat, was our whole stock of provisions. With this we set out in two bark canoes, M. Jollyet, myself, and five men, firmly resolved to do all and suffer all for so glorious an enterprise.

It was on the 17th of May, 1673, that we started from the mission of St. Ignatius at Michilimakinac, where I then was. Our joy at being chosen for this expedition roused our courage, and sweetened the labour of rowing from morning till night. As we were going to seek unknown countries, we took all possible precautions, that, if our enterprise was hazardous, it should not be foolhardy: for this reason we gathered all possible information from Indians who had frequented those parts, and even from their accounts traced a map of all the new country, marking down the rivers on which we were to sail, the names of the nations and places through which we were to pass, the course of the great river, and what direction we should take when we got to it.

Above all, I put our voyage under the protection of the Blessed Virgin Immaculate, promising her, that if she did us the grace to discover the great river, I would give it the name of Conception; and that I would also give that name to the first mission which I should establish among these new nations, as I have actually done among the Ilinois.

With all these precautions we made our paddles play merrily over a part of Lake Huron and that of the Ilinois into the bay of the Fetid.

The first nation that we met was that of the Wild Oats, I entered their river to visit them, as we have preached the gospel to these tribes for some years past, so that there are many good Christians among them.

I informed these people of the Wild Oats of my design of going to discover distant regions to instruct them in the mysteries of our Holy Religion; they were very much surprised, and did their best to dissuade me. The told me, that I would meet nations that never spare strangers, but tomahawk them without any provocation; that the war which had broken out among various nations on our route exposed us to another evident danger—that of being killed by the war-parties which are constantly in the field; that the Great River is very dangerous, unless the difficult parts are known; that it was full of frightful monsters who swallowed up men and canoes together; that there is even a demon there who can be heard from afar, who stops the passage and engulfs all who dare approach; lastly, that the heat is so excessive in those countries, that it would infallibly cause our death.

I thanked them for their kind advice, but assured them that I could not follow it, as the salvation of souls was concerned; that for them I should be too happy to lay down my life; that I made light of their pretended demon, that we would defend ourselves well enough against the river-monsters; and, besides, we should be on our guard to avoid the other dangers with which they threatened us. After having made them pray and given them some instruction, I left them, and, embarking in our conoes, we soon after reached the extremity of the Bay of the Fetid, where our Fathers labour sucessfully in the conversion of these tribes, having baptized more than two thousand since they have been there.

We left this bay to enter a river emptying into it. It is very beautiful at its mouth, and flows gently; it is full of bustards, duck, teal, and other birds, attracted by the wild oats of which they are very fond; but when you have advanced a little up this river, it becomes very difficult, both on account of the currents and of the sharp rocks which cut the canoes and the feet of those who are obliged to drag them, especially when the water is low. For all that we passed the rapids safely, and as we approached Machkoutens, the Fire nation, I had the curiosity to drink the mineral waters of the river which is not far from this town. I also took time to examine an herb, the virtue of which an Indian who possessed the secret, had, with many ceremonies, made known to Father Alloues. Its root is useful against the bite of serpents, the Almighty having been pleased to give this remedy against a poison very common in the country. I put some into my canoe to examine it at leisure, while we kept on our way toward Maskoutens, where we arrived on the 7th of June.

Here we are then at Maskoutens. This word in Algonquin, may mean Fire nation, and that is the name given to them. This is the limit of the discoveries made by the French, for they have not yet passed beyond it.

This town is made up of three nations gathered here, Miamis, Maskoutens, and Kikabous. The first are more civil, liberal, and better made; they wear two long ear-locks, which give them a good appearance; they have the name of being warriors and seldom send out war parties in vain; they are very docile, listen quietly to what you tell them, and showed themselves so eager to hear Father Allouez when he was instructing them, that they gave him little rest, even at night. The Maskoutens and Kikabous are ruder and more like peasants, compared to the others.

When I visited them, I was extremely consoled to see a beautiful cross planted in the midst of the town, adorned with several white skins, red belts, bows and arrows, which these good people had offered to the Great Manitou (such is the name they give to God) to thank him for having had pity on them during the winter, giving them plenty of game when they were in greatest dread of famine.

No sooner had we arrived than M. Jollyet and I assembled the sachems; he told them that he was sent by our governor to discover new countries, and I, by the Almighty, to illumine them with the light of the gospel; that the Sovereign Master of our lives wished to be known by all nations, and that to obey his will, I did not fear death, to which I exposed myself in such dangerous voyages; that we needed two guides to put us on our way, these, making them a present, we begged them to grant us. This they did very civilly, and even proceeded to speak to us by a present, which was a mat to serve us as a bed on our voyage.

The next day, which was the tenth of June, two Miamis whom they had given us as guides, embarked with us, in the sight of a great crowd, who could not wonder enough to see seven Frenchmen alone in two canoes, dare to undertake so strange and so hazardous an expedition.

We knew that there was, three leagues from Maskoutens, a river emptying into the Missisipi; we knew too, that the point of the compass we were to hold to reach it, was the west-south-west; but the way is so cut up by marshes and little lakes, that it is easy to go astray, especially as the river leading to it is so covered with wild oats, that you can hardly discover the channel. Hence, we had good need of our two guides, who led us safely to a portage of twentyseven hundred paces, and helped us to transport our canoes to enter this river, after which they returned, leaving us alone in an unknown country, in the hands of Providence.

We now leave the waters which flow to Quebec, a distance of four or five hundred leagues, to follow those which will henceforth lead us into strange lands. Before embarking, we all began together a new devotion to the Blessed Virgin Immaculate, which we practised every day, addressing her particular prayers to put under her protection both our persons and the success of our voyage. Then after having encouraged one another, we got into our canoes, The river on which we embarked is called Meskousing; it is very broad, with a sandy bottom, forming many shallows, which render navigation very difficult. It is full of vine-clad islets. On the banks appear fertile lands diversified with wood, prairie, and hill. Here you find oaks, walnut, white-wood, and another kind of tree with branches armed with long thorns. we saw no small game of fish, but deer and moose in considerable numbers.

Our route was south-west, and after sailing about thirty leagues, we perceived a place which had all the appearances of an iron-mine, and in fact, one of our party who had seen some before, averred that the one we had found was very good and very rich. It is covered with three feet of good earth, very near a chain of rock, whose base is covered with fine timber. After forty leagues on this same route, we reached the mouth of our river, and finding ourselves at 42½° N., we safely entered the Missisipi on the 17th of June, with a joy that I can not express.

Here then we are on this renowned river, of which I have endeavoured to remark attentively all the peculiarities. The Missisipi river has its source in several lakes in the country of the nations to the north; it is narrow at the mouth of the Miskousing; its current, which runs south, is slow and gentle; on the right is a considerable chain of very high mountains, and on the left fine lands; it is in many places studded with islands. On sounding, we have found ten fathoms of water. Its breadth is very unequal: it is sometimes three-quarters of a league, and sometimes narrows into three *arpents* (220 yards). We gently follow its course, which bears south and south-east till the forty-second degree. Here we perceive that the whole face is changed; there is now almost no wood or mountain, the islands are more beautiful and covered with finer trees; we see nothing but deer and moose, bustards and wingless swans, for they shed their plumes in this country. From time to time we meet monstrous fish, one of which struck so violently against our canoe, that I took it for a large tree about to knock us to pieces. Another time we perceived on the water a monster with the head of a tiger, a pointed snout like a wild-cat's a beard and ears erect, a grayish head and neck all black.

Having descended as for as 41° 28', following the same direction we find that turkeys have taken the place of game, and the pisikious, or wild cattle, that of other beasts. We call them wild cattle, because they are like our domestic cattle; they are not longer, but almost as big again, and more corpulent; our men having killed one, three of us had considerable trouble in moving it. The head is very large, the forehead flat and a foot and a half broad between the horns, which are exactly like those of our cattle, except that they are black and much larger. Under the neck there is a kind of large crop hanging down, and on the back a pretty high hump. The whole head, the neck, and part of the shoulders, are covered with a great mane like a horse's; it is a crest a foot long, which renders them hideous, and falling over their eyes, prevents their seeing before them. The rest of the body is coverd with a coarse curly hair like the wool of our sheep, but much stronger and thicker. It falls in summer, and the skin is then as soft as velvet. At this time the

Indians employ the skins to make beautiful robes, which they paint of various colours.

We advanced constantly, but as we did not know where we were going, having already made more than a hundred leagues without having discovered anything but beasts and birds, we kept well on our guard. Accordingly we make only a little fire on the shore at night to prepare our meal, and after supper keep as far off from it as possible, passing the night in our canoes, which we anchor in the river pretty far from the bank. Even this did not prevent one of us being always as a sentinel for fear of a surprise.

Proceeding south and south-southwest, we find ourselves at 41° north; then at 40° and some minutes, partly by south-east and partly by south-west, after having advanced more than sixty leagues since entering the river, without discovering anything.

At last, on the 25th of June, we perceived footprints of men by the waterside, and a beaten path entering a beautiful prairie. We stopped to examine it, and concluding that it was a path leading to some Indian village, we resolved to go and reconnoitre; we accordingly left our two canoes in charge of our people, cautioning them strictly to beware of a surprise; then M. Jollyet and I undertook this rather hazardous discovery for two single men, who thus put themselves at the discretion of an unknown and barbarous people. We followed the little path in silence, and having advanced about two leagues, we discovered a village on the banks of the river, and two others on a hill, half a league from the former. Then, indeed, we recommended ourselves to God, with all our hearts; and, having implored his help, we passed on undiscovered, and came so near that we even heard the Indians talking. We then deemed it time to announce ourselves, as we did by a cry, which we raised with all our strength, and then halted without advancing any further. At this cry the Indians rushed out of their cabins, and having probably recognised us as French, especially seeing a black gown, or at least having no reason to distrust us, seeing we were but two, and had made known our coming, they deputed four old men to come and speak with us. Two carried tobacco-pipes, well-adorned, and trimmed with many kinds of feathers. They marched slowly, lifting their pipes toward the sun, as if offering them to him to smoke, but yet without uttering a single word. They were a long time coming the little way from the village to us. Having reached us at last, they stopped to consider us attentively. I now took courage, seeing these ceremonies, which are used by them only with friends, and still more on seeing them covered with stuffs, which made me judge them to be allies. I, therefore, spoke to them first, and asked them, who they were; they answered that they were Ilinois and, in token of peace, they presented their pipes to smoke. They then invited us to their village where all the tribe awaited us with impatience.

At the door of the cabin in which we were to be received, was an old man awaiting us in a very remarkable posture; which is their usual ceremony in receiving strangers. This man was standing, perfectly naked, with his hands stretched out and raised toward the sun, as if he wished to screen himself from its rays, which nevertheless passed through his fingers to his face. When we came near him, he paid us this compliment: "How beautiful is the sun, O Frenchman, when thou comest to visit us! All our town awaits thee, and thou shalt enter all our cabins in peace." He then took us into his, where there was a crowd of people, who devoured us with their eyes, but kept a profound silence. We heard, however, these words occasionally addressed to us: "Well done, brothers, to visit us!"

As soon as we had taken our places, they showed us the usual civility of the country, which is to present the calumet. You must not refuse it, unless you would pass for an enemy, or at least for being impolite. It is, however, enough to pretend to smoke. While all the old men smoked after us to honour us, some came to invite us on behalf of the great sachem of all the Ilinois to proceed to his town, where he wished to hold a council with us. We went with a good retinue, for all the people who had never seen a Frenchman among them could not tire looking at us: they threw themselves on the grass by the wayside, they ran ahead, then turned and walked back to see us again. All this was done without noise, and with marks of a great respect entertained for us.

Having arrived at the great sachem's town, we espied him at his cabin-door, between two old men, all three standing naked, with their calumet turned to the sun. He harangued us in few words, to congratulate us on our arrival, and then presented us his calumet and made us smoke; at the same time we entered his cabin, where we received all their usual greetings. Seeing all assembled and in silence, I spoke to them by four presents which I made: by the first, I said that we marched in peace to visit the nations on the river to the sea: by the second, I declared to them that God their Creator had pity on them, since, after their having been so long ignorant of him, he wished to become known to all nations; that I was sent on his behalf with this design; that it was for them to acknowledge and obey him: by the third, that the great chief of the French informed them that he spread peace everywhere, and had overcome the Iroquois. Lastly, by the fourth, we begged them to give us all the information they had of the sea, and of the nations through which we should have to pass to reach it.

When I had finished my speech the sachem rose, and, laying his hand on the head of a little slave, whom he was about to give us, spoke thus: "I thank thee, Blackgown, and thee, Frenchman," addressing M. Jollyet, "for taking so much pains to come and visit us; never has the earth been so beautiful, nor the sun so bright, as to-day; never has our river been so calm, nor so free from rocks, which your canoes have removed as they passed; never has our tobacco had so fine a flavour, nor our corn appeared so beautiful as we behold it to-day. Here is my son, that I give thee, that thou mayest know my heart. I pray thee to take pity on me and all my nation. Thou knowest the Great Spirit who has made us all; thou speakest to him and hearest his word: ask him to give me life and health, and come and dwell with us, that we may know him."

We slept in the sachem's cabin, and the next day took leave of him, promising to pass back through his town in four moons.

[*In spite of the fact that he returned from his first voyage much weakened by dysentery, Father Marquette set out upon a second, in the November of 1674. On April 8 he reached once again the town of the Ilionis, where he was received "as an angel from heaven," and, having founded the mission of the Immaculate Conception, continued his journey. The following extract is from a contemporary "Relation."*]

After the Ilinois had taken leave of the father, filled with a great idea of the Gospel, he continued his voyage, and soon after reached the Ilinois lake,[1] on which he had nearly a hundred leagues to make by an unkown route, because he was obliged to take the southern [eastern] side of the lake, having gone thither by the northern [western]. His strength, however, failed so much, that his men despaired of being able to carry him alive to their journey's end; for, in fact, he became so weak and exhausted, that he could no longer help himself, nor even stir, and had to be handled and carried like a child.

He nevertheless maintained in this state an admirable equanimity, joy and gentleness, consoling his beloved companions, and encouraging them to suffer courageously all the hardships of the way, assuring them that our Lord would not forsake them when he was gone. During this navigation he began to prepare more particularly for death, passing his time in colloquies with our Lord, with His holy mother, with his angel-guardian, or with all heaven. He was often heard pronouncing these words: "I believe that my Redeemer liveth," or "Mary, mother of grace, mother of God, remember me." Besides a spiritual reading made for him every day, he toward the close asked them to read him his meditation on the preparation for death, which he carried about him: he recited his breviary every day; an although he was so low, that

[1] Lake Michigan.

both sight and strength had greatly failed, he did not omit it till the last day of his life, when his companions induced him to cease, as it was shortening his days.

A week before his death, he had the precaution to bless some holy water, to serve him during the rest of his illness, in his agony, and at his burial, and he instructed his companions how to use it.

The eve of his death, which was a Friday, he told them, all radiant with joy, that it would take place on the morrow. During the whole day he conversed with them about the manner of his burial, the way in which he should be laid out, the place to be selected for his interment; he told them how to arrange his hands, feet, and face, and directed them to raise a cross over his grave. He even went so far as to enjoin them, only three hours before he expired, to take his chapel-bell, as soon as he was dead, and ring it while they carried him to the grave. Of all this he spoke so calmly and collectedly, that you would have thought that he spoke of the death and burial of another, and not of his own.

Thus did he speak with them as they sailed along the lake, till, perceiving the mouth of a river, with an eminence on the bank which he thought suited for his burial, he told them that it was the place of his last repose. They wished, however, to pass on, as the weather permitted it, and the day was not far advanced; but God raised a contrary wind, which obliged them to return and enter the river pointed out by Father Marquette.

They then carried him ashore, kindled a little fire, and raised for him a wretched bark cabin, where they laid him as little uncomfortably as they could; but they were so overcome by sadness that, as they afterward said, they did not know what they were doing.

The father, being thus stretched on the shore, like St Francis Xavier, as he had always so ardently desired, and left alone amid those forests—for his companions were engaged in unloading—he had leisure to repeat all the acts in which he had employed himself during the preceding days.

When his dear companions afterward came up, all dejected, he consoled them, and gave them hopes that God would take care of them after his death in those new and unknown countries; he gave them his last instructions, thanked them for all the charity they had shown him during the voyage, bagged their pardon for the trouble he had given them, and directed them also to ask pardon in his name of all our fathers and brothers in the Ottawa country, and then disposed them to receive the sacrament of penance, which he administered to them for the last time; he also gave them a paper on which he had written all his faults since his last confession, to be given to his superior, to oblige him to pray more earnestly for him. In fine, he promised not to forget them in heaven, and as he was very kind-hearted, and knew them to be worn out with the toil of the preceding days, he bade them go and take a little rest, assuring them that his hour was not yet so near, but that he would wake them when it was time, as in fact he did, two or three hours after, calling them when about to enter his agony.

When they came near he embraced them for the last time, while they melted in tears at his feet; he then asked for the holy water and his reliquary, and taking off his crucifix which he wore around his neck, he placed it in the hands of one, asking him to hold it constantly opposite him, raised before his eyes; then feeling that he had but a little time to live, he made a last effort, clasped his hands, and with his eyes fixed sweetly on his crucifix, he pronounced aloud his profession of faith, and thanked the Divine Majesty for the immense grace he did him in allowing him to die in the Society of Jesus; to die in it as a missionary of Jesus Christ, and above all to die in it, as he had always asked, in a wretched cabin, amid the forests, destitute of all human aid.

On this he became silent, conversing inwardly with God; yet from time to time words escaped him; *"Sustinuit anima mea in verba ejus,"* or *"Mater Dei, memento mei,"* which were the last words he uttered before entering on his agony, which was very calm and gentle.

He had prayed his companions to remind him, when they saw him about to expire, to pronounce frequently the names of Jesus and Mary. When he could not do it himself, they did it for him; and when they thought him about to pass, one cried aloud Jesus Maria, which he several times repeated distinctly, and then, as if at those sacred names something had appeared to him, he suddenly raised his eyes above his crucifix, fixing them apparently on some object which he seemed to regard with pleasure, and thus with a countenance all radiant with smiles, he expired without a struggle, as gently as if he had sunk into a quiet sleep.

His two poor companions after, shedding many tears over his body, and having laid it out as he had directed, carried it devoutly to the grave, ringing the bell according to his injunction, and raised a large cross near it to serve as a mark for passers-by.

THREE HUNDRED MILES TO OAXACA[1]

Nicolas Joseph Thiery de Menonville

(Botanist to King Louis XVI)

[*Bent upon "naturalizing the nopal and cochineal insect in the French colonies"—the cultivation of the cochineal being then the monopoly of the Spanish—M. de Menonville had left France in January 1977 for Havanah. From Havanah he went to Vera Cruz, "pretending to be actuated by that volatility and inconstancy of disposition, oftentimes . . . ascribed to Frenchmen, and which occasionally is so favourable a cover to deep designs." Learning that the cochineal of Oaxaca yielded the finest colour, he managed to get a passport for Orizaba, "to the licence in which" he "meant to give the trifling extention of sixty leagues"—namely, to Guaxaca [Oaxaca]. But the night before his departure the passport was suddenly recalled, on the ground that "the secrets of the rich culture of the country" were not for strangers' eyes, and he was ordered to quit Mexico.*]

I repaired to my lodging, deadly sick at heart: I walked backwards and forwards, now threw myself on a seat, and now into my cot, swinging it from one side to the other with such violence as to risk breaking my head against the ceiling; not the least ray of comfort beamed on my mind; in vain did I exclaim to myself aloud, Be calm, thou mad man! poor intemperate fool, take pity on thy intellects! Art thou not yet at Vera Cruz? has thou not reached this distance on thy road? and dost thou not still remain? Oh! yes, retorted anguish, but thou art ordered hence, thou must go, and empty-handed. Thy plan of four years' standing, even in the very port, now falls to wreck.

I passed the whole morning a prey to such tormenting reflections, and under the greatest agitation, swallowing three quarts of lemonade, but without the least appetite for food; no, the smallest morsel would certainly have choked me.

At length, tired and overcome by the weight of so much affliction, my mind made a last effort for relief; by dint of perpetual repetition—thou art still at Vera Cruz—the fundamental point of a desperate project presented itself to my ideas; I calculated, that as no appointed time was fixed for my departure, and as there was no ship in the port which would sail for three weeks to come, I might in a fortnight's time complete a stolen journey. Thou absolutely must, said I to myself, penetrate into the interior, though destitute of passport, must bear away the fleece for which thou hast sailed, despite of

[1] From Pinkerton's *Voyages and Travels.*

all the dragons in the way. Inflamed by this idea, the very apprehension of being unable to realise it threw me into a cold sweat. I now thought of nothing but developing my plan, and digesting its detail.

Everything tended to strengthen me in my last resolves, though I reflected upon many obstacles I should have to encounter.

In the first place, nothing less than a miracle, on a road over which so many pikemen were dispersed for the purpose of arresting deserters and strangers, could guard me from being asked by some one or other of them for my passport.

In the second place, my dress was not that of a Spaniard, and this inconvenience neither time nor my means allowed of my remedying.

Thirdly, I spoke the Spanish language very indifferently.

In the fourth place, I was almost entirely ignorant of the road, and it was only by the merest chance and nicest management I was enabled to learn by what gate I had to leave the town.

Finally, it was necessary I should set out on foot, in a climate where I should have much to encounter from the season of the year, and the sands through which I had to travel. I must also go unprovided with linen, provision, change of dress, and books, and without instruments to reap the possible result of my excursion, in encreasing our knowledge of natural history.

The plan I framed for remedying these inconveniences was as follows: I shall travel on foot, said I to myself, as a botanical physician resident at Vera Cruz, in search of simples; I shall assume the appearance of taking a walk rather than being on a journey, shall lodge only in the poorest huts of the Indians, and in places away from the highroad, pretending to have lost my way; I shall avoid all towns, hamlets and villages, where possible, and where not, pass through them by night; I shall declare myself a Catalan from the frontiers of France, which will explain the reason of my speaking French well, and the Spanish but indifferently; I shall always go neatly drest, wear some trinkets, affect a good-humoured and free disposition, and pay liberally for all I take. With all these precautions I must indeed be unlucky if I should be taken for a foreigner or a deserter.

In fine, after some little provision against the most urgent wants, for example, a broad brimmed hat, a net for the hair, a rosary, an indispensable article, etc.; and after setting aside about three hundred gourds in quadruples, I fixed upon the Friday night following for my departure.

It was about nine o'clock when, after carefully locking up all my effects, I departed, as if merely to take a walk.

I soon reached the rampart, scaled it, and bade adieu to the city.

For a long time I travelled briskly along through the sands, under favour of the light afforded by the stars; but a violent wind effacing all traces of the road, and the sky being overclouded, I found myself wandering I knew not whither, at the distance of more than a league from the town: undecided, I went first one way then another, to the crowing of cocks, and observed the rising of smoke, but all in vain. Though I had twenty times before travelled over these spots, night, by enveloping all objects with the same shadowy veil, disfigured the rallying points which otherwise might have struck my memory. I climbed large mounts of sand, some firm, and others moveable, until I was utterly exhausted. At length anxiety, combined with fatigue, made me determine on re-entering the city; but now was the embarrassment to find it, for I no longer distinguished its fires: at length I saw one at the distance of three hundred toises, I ran thither, it was the cabin of a free negro whom I had seen before in my neighbourhood. I told him I had lost my way in returning from Medelina; he directed me on the right road, and I was exceedingly surprized at finding myself a quarter of league north of the city, while I imagined myself in the west. I immediately scaled the rampart, and returned to my home, terribly fatigued, and still more vexed at my bad beginning.

However, after changing my linen I threw myself into my hammock, and enjoyed a sleep as sweet as it was necessary. The next day, at three in the morning, I left home a second time, and again scaled the ramparts, this time with some risk of breaking my neck; behold now Don Quixote in the country.

I used every precaution not to miss the road; but directing my steps too much towards the north, I again strayed from my way, and was lost nearly an hour in the sands; however, recognizing in the heavens the ear of corn of the constellation Virgo, and Mars, and Saturn, which were already in the east, I directed my steps west ward till daybreak: at four I overheard the country people going to market, and, guided by their voice, kept on a parallel with the road, but about a hundred fathoms distant, to avoid being seen. At length, by dawn of day, the road taking through a forest, I was obliged to enter it, but I took the precaution to slacken my pace as often as I distinguished any Indians, negroes, or Spaniards; after they had passed I made up for lost time. At five o'clock I had cleared the forest, and was two leagues and a half from Vera Cruz: here the road divided, and occasioned a new embarrassment. Perceiving a muleteer with a train of a hundred and twenty mules advancing, I put questions to him with caution, and learnt that he came from Guaxaca, by the road of Monte Calabaça, which he pointed out to me, observing at the same time, that he passed it the day before. After this, Very good, said I to myself, to-night I shall sleep at Calabaça.

[*That night, however, he got no farther than a hut near the river 'Jamapa.'*]

The host was a shephered: him I conjured, as well as the hostess, *por amor de Dios* to give me drink and food: this they did with all diligence. I drank successively a quart of water, two quarts of milk, and as many of lemonade, and devoured the wing and thigh of a turkey, with three fresh-laid eggs, before I answered the least question. The shepherd asked me if I was a Spaniard (Castillano). I answered, I was a physician of Catalonia. I judged as much, said he, from your gait; you Europeans take longer strides than we Creoles. Thus do those who are most nearly connected with nature observe her with keenest eye. As the shepherd seemed to me rather curious and discerning, I paid him, and complaining of a dreadful headache, threw myself on a hurdle made of branches, where I fell asleep. Four reals which I gave my host earned me at least four thousand benedictions. I slept so tranquilly that I did not wake until three the next morning.

At length I reached mount Calabaça by five in the evening, much fatigued. The apprehension of losing my way, and of not readily finding any other resting place, made me determine on halting here. I expected to have found it a village: it was but a rancho, the farmer, a Spaniard, or at least of mixed breed, was civil but grave, and of rather, as he seemed to me, a harsh character. I accosted him and entreated shelter: he granted my request, admonishing me beforehand that he kept no inn, and had neither bread, nor meat, not wine, nor brandy, but to what he had I was heartily welcome. I begged of him half a dozen eggs, which I ate with tortillas. My host, who appeared to me to be an old soldier, and who, as I afterwards learnt, was really one of those pikemen whom I so much dreaded, seemed a wily old fox, at least by the questions he put me; but as I had undoubtedly every resemblance of a physician, he could but give me credit for my tale. Notwithstanding this pertinaciously refused me a horse for the next day, for I thought myself now far enough from Vera Cruz to venture this indulgence: I was however forced to forgo it. I offered to pay him for his supper, but he refused to take any recompense. Upon this I gave four reals to his wife or mistress; for though he had a number of children I could not learn from him whether or no he was married. My liberality earned me for the night the enjoyment of an old cloak, which had once been blue, but which from service had become grey. In this I wrapped myself, and laid me down on a mat on the floor of a neighbouring penthouse: but for this kindness I risked to have died of cold for scarcely had I left the door of the hut before one of those dreadful storms of rain fell which are termed at St Domingo avelasses, and of which the drops are as large, and fall with as loud a sound as the most formidable hailstones of Europe. The noise they made was frightful: the rain driven by the wind penetrated the branches and leaves which covered the penthouse, and ran through as from so many spouts: in an instant the whole of the interior was drenched: one would have thought a waterspout had burst over the place. The weather caused me the most mournful reflections. In a country intersected by torrents and rivers, if this storm should only be the precursor of others, how should I be able to travel, especially on my return with the booty I hoped to gain? Could even the best horse in the world carry me safe among the rocks and trees which are almost always brought down the ravines after such storms? These reflections were very far from comfortable; but having planned every thing for the best, I had no other reliance than on Providence: with this conclusion I covered my head with the cloak, and enjoyed a profound sleep till four the next morning.

The melancholy ideas which had afflicted me the evening before vanished with the shades of night: a clear and serene sky, a cool morning, the prospect of the mountains of Orissava, from which I was now but twenty leagues distant: their branch, which advanced forward about eight leagues like a steep and inaccessible rampart along the whole contour of the plain, delighted me, and instilled fresh courage in my breast.

By eleven in the morning I had travelled eight leagues without eating, and without drinking any thing but a little lemonade, which I procured of two Indians who were building a hut, and who were the only rational beings I met with. I now found myself at the foot of the first chain of mountains, but the steep and almost perpendicular declivity before me, the projecting rocks of which were discernible through the hanging woods, formed only a portion of the obstacles which nature, not satisfied with this bulwark, has opposed to the entrance into Mexico. In advance of these steeps, and at the very foot of them, she has formed an enormous fosse, at the bottom of which runs a river ten fathoms broad, of such rapid, such violent current that it has dug itself a bed, through ten strata of different kind of stone, of eighty feet deep; over this bed it winds its course like a serpent amid the sands, almost without a murmur, but foaming, and with the rapidity of lightning: on throwing a pebble into the river, I judged the depth of it to be fifteen feet: when from a wretched bridge made of half rotton bavens, by which this river is crossed one looks down on the torrent below, the head turns dizzy.

Half a league lower down is another river, which empties itself into this, called the Rio de la Punta. I found at the end of the bridge by which it is passed a Spaniard who received toll; as he had neither bread nor wine, I resolved on proceeding to dine at San Lorenzo, though the distance was full three leagues. The toll-gatherer warned me, *de las aguas* (the coming rain), I heeded him not, but had cause to repent: a heavy shower quickly brought me back, and subjected me to his jeers. On its ceasing I resumed my road. At length I came to a ravine, the bed of a torrent, a hundred and fifty fathoms broad, and forty feet deep. I fancied before me the enormous skeleton of some extinct river, if such an expression be permitted, the only one I could fancy adequate to depicting the gigantic ideas enforced on my imagination by the singular spectacle of the rocks, the immense trunks of trees, the enormous stones of all colours, rounded by long and violent friction, which were piled on each other in confusion in the chasm . . . . how mightily powerful then must have been the vast and inconceivable volume of water that thus could have made the sport of weights and bulks like these! Scarcely, though the bed was dry, was I enabled to pass these obstruction to my way.

At length I arrived, excessively fatigued, at San Lorenzo. The inn here is for a Spanish inn a charming one, and to me was truly so. The mistress was civil, and I was served with diligence. I had four fresh eggs, a chicken, and some excellent bread, together with some tent wine. Immediately after I departed, resolved on reaching Villa Cordova that day, but scarcely had I left the churchyard, where I had been to examine at leisure its plumeriæ (frangipaniers), with purple-coloured, rosy, and yellow flowers, and thirty feet high, before the rain again began to fall. I took shelter under an Indian hut, when at the instant a negro passed me with three horses. I asked him to let me have one of his horses, and he agreed to conduct me as far as to his village, two leagues beyond, but the name of which I forget. I jumped on horseback, upon this, without either books, spur, or cloak: the negro, in order to shelter me from the rain, contrived to cover my head with a mat, which hung down before and behind like a Dalmatian mantle: never was Robinson Crusoe more grotesquely apparelled.

[*Thus he came to 'Cordova,' and on the following day to Orizaba.*]

At dawn next day I pondered on the means of learning distinctly the route and distance to Guaxaca. After long meditation I entered a convent of Carmelites, where I begged to speak with the prior: I was no doubt thought to assume above my sphere in such a request, and the sub-prior came to me. Judging from his round and jolly countenance, I deemed him a person in whom I might confide. I therefore told him, as in secret, that being a physician and botanist, my occupation was the study of natural history and plants; that for three years I had been on my travels in view of perfecting myself in this branch of science; that during a tempest I had made a vow to go on foot to Nsra. Snra. de la Soledad, in Guaxaca, which till now I had faithfully executed, but that, feeling myself exhausted with fatigue, and pressed for time in order to return for embarkation, I was solicitous of learning whether such a favourable interpretation of my vow could be admitted, as would allow my completing the residue of my pilgrimage on foot, in presenting, as was but reasonable, for the indulgence of deviating from the letter of my vow, certain pious offerings and alms. After a learned discussion on this point, my Carmelite was of opinion that I certainly might, by means to prayers and alms, acquit myself towards our Lady of the Solitude: taking him at his word, I drew from my purse four medios d'oro, and begged of him to take upon himself the offering I wished to make: this he refused, affirming the sum to be thrice too large. In vain did I insist: I could not prevail on him to accept any thing, which not a little disconcerted me, as I hoped by dint of bribery to obtain from him the information which I needed: nevertheless, I did not lose all hope from the civility he shewed me: he even presented me to four other fathers, shewed me the house, the garden, and was in raptures at the description I afforded him of different plants, of which the community was wholly ignorant. At length I was on the point of losing my sub-prior, when I bethought me of enquiring whether there was not a convent of Carmelites at Guaxaca, and how far that city might be distant: this time my good monk fell into the snare. Anxious to appear well informed on what I enquired, he afforded me an itinerary so minutely detailed, league by league, and village after village, that the general of an army might have trusted to it for the plan of a march, as I had full means afterwards of ascertaining. Highly charmed, after a route of forty leagues, in which I had, as it were, been obliged to feel my way, at meeting with a perfect and unsuspected guide, I departed, loaded with civility.

[*Following the good Carmelite's itinerary, he came at length to 'Aquiotepec.'*]

I departed (from Aquiotepec) at eleven in the morning, after taking some refreshments: it was necessary in order to pass the mountain, at the foot of which Aquiotepec is situate, to ascend by a path only two feet broad, cut in the side of the rock. Let the reader figure to himself two hundred steps of this tremendous staircase, from each of which a precipice was visible below, six hundred yards deep, in which with horrid crash Rio Grande forced its way, and then conceive the dread which froze my faculties; I trembled in every limb, my head turned dizzy, and I was obliged to alight, and lead my horse behind me; I held him by the bridle, but without looking back, and constantly ready, in case of the least false step, to leave my hold, and let him drink alone of the water of that stream, which would for him have been the river of oblivion. Oftentimes at a slippery spot, there was merely the branch of a tree, laid on insecure stones, to hinder the passenger from rolling into this frightful abyss; beyond, it was requisite to make a turn in a very narrow passage, where the body of a horse could only pass by twisting; I know not how the poor animal contrived, though one might freely venture a wager he had done so a hundred times.

By three o'clock I found myself on the crest of this mountain; spite of its elevation, as nothing is great but by comparison, it seemed but a hillock by side of those mountains I saw on my left: we travelled on this crest the space of three hours. I found here some new species of cactus with flat and rampant leaves, and an aloe with crenelled leaves, dentated at the edge with thorns. I was now enabled to enjoy at leisure one of the most beautiful prospects in nature; behind me, still were distinctly visible the environs of Tecuacan; in front the two prominences of La Corta, a mountain six leagues from Guaxaca; Rio Grande ran on my right between frightful steeps; finally, on the left, an immense country consisting of hills and gorges covered with wood, extended between me and the mountains on which San Juan del Ré was situate, and terminated with an insensible slope towards Tecuacan.

I began to be fatigued and weary of so long a route, when an opening shewed me the end of my toils, at least for this day. This was Quicattan, which we discovered two leagues before us, in a tolerably handsome gorge; we descended into it by a road somewhat less bad than that of the ascent; but the aspect it presented was not less horrible: it was a perpendicular chasm of eight hundred yards, by a breadth of thrice that number, seemingly occasioned by a mountain which had been swallowed up in this spot, and the fragments and ruins of which strewed around Quicattan formed so many eminences.

But how much was the pleasure of beholding Quicattan interrupted by the appearance of a *garita*, which seemed to forbid my entrance. How to pass without being stopt, interrogated, and delayed by these wretched guards! These were the continually renascent subject of my fears; to sleep on my horse, to counterfeit sickness, these were slender stratagems now worn thread bare, and which I felt no inclination to repeat: I chose a plan more simple, founded on the little consideration these kind of people had inspired me with, as despicable here as elsewhere. On getting near them, I descended my horse in a bold and determinded manner, and my gold cane hanging at my button hole, and my diamond ring on my finger, entered the garita without ceremony, and pulling out some gold before the tobacco guards, related to them the embarrassment I was under for want of change. I mingled the statement with a thousand incidents relating to my dread of thieves, and the unevenness of the road; finishing with begging change for some medio d'oros, or doubloons. Such prattle no doubt made them so silent, they never put a single question to me: on the contrary I met with civility from them, approaching even to meanness, and they gave me change for as much as I wanted. I then thanked and left them, inviting the chief of the guard, in a manner a superior accosts one beneath him, to pay me a visit at the *cafa reale.*

I returned to supper; and in the interval arrived the officer of the tobacco guard, from whom I learnt whatever I would by means of a few glasses of brandy. The rogue was perfectly well acquainted with the whole country from Panama to Acapulco, and from Carthagena to Vera Cruz: he talked fluently on politics, declaimed against the government; and in case of need, assuredly was open to seduction.

The casero introduced to me likewise another traveller, in an honest Franciscan friar, about to preach at Guatemala. I enquired if he was inclined to accompany me in the morning; and he consented, provided I would wait until he had celebrated mass: this being agreed upon, I retired to rest, and he to supper.

The next day we set off at five in the morning, and arrived, after a smart ride of a league and a half, at the passage of Rio Grande. Rain had fallen in the mountains; another day's rain would have rendered the river impracticable. Here it is much wider than at Aquiotepec, its breadth not being less than four hundred yards, and the sides, consequently, much less precipitous. An Indian, beckoned to from the opposite side, came and took the leading horses by the bridle, and, perfectly naked, conducted us over the river; for our part, we were in the water up to the saddle bow, and he to the breast; and this took place so leisurely that I had full opportunity of noticing all the danger. The current was so rapid that it confounded me. I was obliged to steady myself by the pommel, my legs on the horse's rump, and my breast on its neck. The animal itself trembled, and advanced not a step without first feeling his way, on account of the enormous rounded stones at the bottom. At length we got through, and my fellow traveller, breathless with fear, and not less pale than myself, remarked in good French, that if we had been drowned without having first gone to mass, the people would not have failed to ascribe our death to a failure of devotion. I laughed heartily at the fancy, and seeing whom I had to deal with by this sally, I was no longer under any constraint with him: he was indeed one of the pleasantest fellows, for a monk, I ever met with; and with this a man of sense, one who had seen the world, lively, and inquisitive as much as becomes a man; finally he was highly engaging, obliging, and unceremonious. We arrived at an early hour at Don Dominquillo, where, thanks to the good father, who took with him a well supplied larder, we made an excellent dinner.

Don Dominquillo is situate at the confluence of the Rio Grande and the Rio de las Vueltas, or the Turns, so denominated from its frequent windings. As we were saddling our horses in order to depart, we heard a horn, and immediately after saw a Spaniard, dressed in blue turned up with red, with a large silver plate, in form of a shield, on his side, and a small horn of the same metal depending from a cord which passed over the shoulder; he was a courier. As a specimen of his diligence, he left Tecuacan the day before, and reckoned on reaching Guaxaca on the morrow by six in the morning. I held discourse with him for a few minutes; he seemed inquisitive, but I readily concealed from him my designs: he took a different road to ours, over the mountains, in order to avoid crossing the rivers, no doubt from apprehension of being stopt by their course.

As for us, we passed through the gorge in which flows the river de las Vueltas: this gorge is in places a hundred paces broad, at others scarcely a dozen yards: in order to go in a direct line through the windings of this gorge, it is necessary to cross the river seventy times: my fellow travellers reckoned the number; the muleteer by means of small pebbles, and the monk by the beads of his rosary, and their accounts tallied; for my part, after the twentieth time I was tired of counting, and was so much fatigued that I could willingly have halted midway in order to take a nap.

At length, the garge enlargening to a quarter of a league, we left the windings of the river, and arrived at Atletlauca. I felt unpleasantly from having my feet so frequently wetted, and retired to rest without supper, in spite of the solicitations of my fellow traveller: tormented by the gnats, I rose the next morning by three, and wakened everybody: it was so cold that we were obliged to make a fire. We made a hearty breakfast from the store of the good father, and about four o'clock we departed, and four leagues from Atletlauca, after having crossed the river of Turns seven or eight times, we distinguished Galiatitlan: charming hamlet! no, never shall I forget thee. I no longer wonder at the anxiety I felt that morning to set off, the impatience I experienced to arrive: these were, doubtless, forebodings of my good fortune. Not mines nor metallic wealth dost thou enjoy, perhaps, but thou first presented me with the object of my prayers and researches: yes, thou art the most lovely of hamlets!

At Galiatitlan it was that, for the first time in my life, I saw the cochineal alive on the nopal by which it is nourished: I even trembled with ecstacy: the day before, my capuchin, who was very well acquainted with the country, on detailing its riches and cultivation, had mentioned to me cochineal. I merely expressed to him a desire of having some in my possession, that I might the better be enabled to describe it; but when he told me it was likewise to be found at Los Cues, which I had passed through, I was vexed with myself exceedingly, at missing the opportunity I had had of finding it sooner, and at less expence.

Still I had nothing wherewith to reproach myself, for how was I to have known there was cochineal at Los Cues? After all, I had no cause to repent my going so far in search of it, as my extra journies afforded me the opportunity of seeing more of it, of speaking of it more largely, of procuring excellent vanilla, and finally, of meeting with more safe means of transporting and preserving all my treasures.

To return to my dear cochineal. On arriving at Galiatitlan, I saw a garden full of nopals, and had no doubt I should there find the precious insect I was so desirous to examine. I therefore leapt from my horse, under pretence of altering my stirrup leathers, entered the grounds of the Indian proprietor, began a conversation with him, and enquired to what use he put those plants? He answered, "to cultivate *la grana*." I seemed astonished, and begged to see the cochineal; but my surprize was real when he brought it me, for instead of the red insect I expected, there appeared one covered with a white powder. I was tormented with the doubts I entertained, and to resolve them bethought me of crushing one on white paper; and what was the result? It yielded the truly royal purple hue. Intoxicated with joy and admiration, I hastily left my Indian, throwing him two reals for his pains, and galloped at full speed after my companion. At last, said I to myself, I have seen this insect, have held it in my hands, I shall undoubtedly meet with it again, as I am now in the country where it is cultivated: the Indians assuredly will sell it me; and I thus shall be able to bear off my prize, the object and end of all my ardent wishes!

Still certain reflections mixed gall with my delight: I could not hide from myself the difficulty I should have to bring to a safe haven an animal so light, so pliable, to easy to crush; an animal which, once separated from the plant, could never settle on it again: the shocks of a horse, a journey of a hundred leagues by land, could I hope with these to preserve it? and the enormous plants on which I saw the insect, was it possible for me to transport them? how was I to hide them? and what a case must it not require to contain a tree eight feet high, by a diameter of five or six.

[*Another fourteen leagues and he was in Oaxaca, entering it on foot, "with the appearance of a person who had recently left it for a walk." Here he bought boxes—"so well made that better could not have been produced in any workshop in Paris"—in which to pack his dear cochineal, and, delighted with the success that has thus far attended him, imagined himself in a dream, "from which I dreaded to awake."*]

In this state I walked through the streets without well knowing whither I went; at length I found myself in one of the suburbs called de las Vueltas, or the Turnings, a name distinctive of the gardens of this country, where it is considered beauty to intersect them by walls and partitions, which occasion so many windings and recesses in the same inclosure. Among others were some plantations of nopals. In some I saw men employed lopping off the branches, in others planting; at length I distinguished one which appeared to me magnificent and so thickly loaded with cochineal, that not a single leaf could be taken from the nopal without crushing a thousand of the insects. In order to take a survey at leisure, I entered into a garden, parted from the plantation only by a hedge, under pretence of buying flowers. The first objects in this garden which excited my attention, was a violet-coloured aster, as large as those grown with us, but produced on a shrub resembling our elder-tree; what, however, engrossed almost the whole of my attention and thoughts was the beautiful plantation of nopals, and while the bouquet I had ordered was being gathered, I satiated my eyes with the spectacle before me. The noples were thickly planted at about four feet distance, in lines six feet apart. I learnt that this nopal ground belonged to a negro who was not there at that time. I fed myself with hopes of buying of him both the nopal and some of the insects. . . .

The plan I had arranged, to purchase some nopals and cochineal on the succeeding day, occasioned me to wake very early in the morning: I was up therefore by three o'clock, and taking with me two Indian servants belonging to the inn, each with a large basket and towels, I repaired to the plantation of nopals I had seen the day before.

I left the servants at the gate on entering, and myself took charge of their baskets. The negro owner was scarcely awake, He came towards me with a simple, modest, and civil air, quite different from what is usual among people of his stamp in the kingdom of Mexico. I informed him that being a physician, I wanted, for the purpose of making an ointment for the gout, a few leaves of the nopal, with the cochineal upon them, which I begged him to sell me, as the case was urgent; telling him I was willing to pay for them whatever he might require: he permitted me to take as much as I pleased. I did not require twice bidding, but immediately selected eight of the handsomest branches, each two feet long, and consisting of seven or eight leaves in length, but so perfectly covered with cochineals, as to be quite white with them. I cut them off myself, placed them in the best possible manner in the baskets, and covered them with the towels. I then enquired what they were worth. He protested they were well worth two reals: I readily believed him: I, who would not have held them dear at as many quadruples; but, that I might not render him aware of how good a bargain I reckoned upon having made, I merely gave him a dollar, telling him I had no change, and begging him to keep the remainder to drink my health with. The good old negro rubbed his eyes, fancying himself still asleep; and while he overwhelmed me with gratitude, I called in my Indians, loaded them with the two baskets and made off with the rapidity of lightning.

My heart beat in a manner that beggars description: it seemed to me as if I was bearing away the golden fleece, but, at the same time, as if the furious dragon, placed over it as a guard, was following close at my heels; all the way along I kept humming the famous line, *At length I have it in my power*, and should willingly have sung it aloud, but for fear of being overheard. I arrived at my inn out of breath, and slipped in unperceived, and without having met with a single person in the streets. The dawn was opening, but nobody yet had risen in the house. I shut myself up in my room, and then packed my dear nopals, with inexpressible satisfaction, and in the tenderest manner imaginable, in two of my small boxes, taking the precaution to lay them two at top, and two at bottom, separating them by the partition, and sticks of a dry and pliant wood. Whatever my future fortune may be, said I to myself, I have now completed the end of my journey; I may now set off. Yes, even directly; but no; vanilla, which I had been told could be obtained no nearer than at a distance of twenty leagues hence, vanilla comes as it were of itself to invite my taking it: let us effect this second conquest.

[*He effected it next day, and by four in the morning of the day following set out on his homeward journey. We will join him at 'San Sebastiano'.*]

At San Sebastiano I swallowed two new-laid eggs, and immediately set off again with excellent horses: the one I rode, however, was difficult to manage, and had no bridle, a circumstance to which I failed to pay attention on setting out, or till I had left the village: every thing, however, went on well until I reached Santo Antonio: thrice had I alighted to collect seeds from plants, and thrice had I again quietly mounted; but the fourth time, the restive beast rising on its hind legs, struck at me on the stomach with the fore ones, and with such force as to fell me to the ground; not content, he spurned again his hind-legs at me, and galloped away at full speed. For an instant I thought all was over with me, and far as the little power of reflection allowed, which remained with me, I was anxious only for my dear cochineal. I dreaded lest it would yet remain buried in Mexico, and be for ever lost to my country: the thought went near to kill me; however, resuming after a few instants, the faculty of breathing, and my stomach by degrees recovering its tone, I gathered that I did not immediately need extreme unction. Collecting strength, I rose, though with great difficulty, and drew as a conclusion from the incident that a botanist should travel on foot. I took no trouble about the horse. It carried away not any of my property, and should I have recovered, I should not have mounted him again.

The next day I took care to be provided with gentler horses, and more complete furniture, and by ten o'clock arrived in sight of Tecuacan. I was anxious to pass round Tecuacan, as I had done on my way coming; but with all my baggage this was not practicable, and the topith, in short, flatly refused: it was necessary therefore I should travel through it: the town appeared to me a desert, and I compared it to those enchanted cities the work of genii, when a magician of the most formidable kind, in my eyes, made his appearance before me, no other than a stout, sharking customs officer, mounted on an excellent horse, his saddle bow beset, both in front and behind, with pistols. The redoubted champion advancing, summoned me, in the King's name, to return to the custom house.

I was in a dreadful state, though it must be allowed, that at times danger affords resources which are gathered merely from its presence. On reaching the customs house I instantly determined on my plan: composing my countenance, therefore, I entered with an easy air. I found two Spaniards in the office, one of whom, the director, lessened my choler by the affable and prepossessing manner in which he received me. I told him that I was a botanist, that I had been employed in collecting medicinal plants throughout the whole province, with which my trunks were full, and that I had with me nothing else. I added, moreover, that I begged they would satisfy themselves on this head, and proceed through the examination as speedily as possible, as I was solicitous or reaching Vera Cruz for the purpose of going on ship board.

The director said that this was enough, and entered into the most friendly conversation with me; however, I notwithstanding caused my boxes to be opened, although against his inclination, for the purpose of satisfying him, and out of bravado towards his deputy, who appeared to be inquisitive and suspicious. On looking over the cases, in which, among a variety of herbs and roots, with which he was altogether unacquainted, was the vanilla which was equally unknown to him; he shrugged up his shoulders, and smiled. I opened others which contained cochineal, covered and mingled with other plants: *aqui sta grana*—this is cochineal, said he, apparently with surprise, but at the same time with an air of indifference, which argued nothing displeasing. In my notice of his observation, I seemed equally indifferent. He afterwards noticed the double bottoms, and fancied for an instant he had caught his bird, signifying as much by a glance, which at the same time seemed to hint that he could shut his eyes occasionally to what he could not see without injuring; but, rendered bold by the assurance I had acquired, that no objection would be taken to my cochineal, I raised the bottoms, partitions, and the pieces of wood, which separated the plants, when my nopals were distinguished among other plants, carefully folded in fine white paper. What are these nopals for, this cochineal? For an unguent. For what malady? The gout. Ah ah! do but see, exclaimed he then, laughed heartily as he pointed out among my collection the nuts of the most common fruits of the country, and seeds even of its most despised herbs.

The director now obliged me to shut all my cases; before I did this, I picked up even the smallest leaves which had fallen, but with so much care, that they could entertain not the slightest doubt of my placing on them a value, far greater than on the cochineal: they could not indeed help admiring to see a Frenchman come from such a distance to collect some of the meanest herbs of the country; and frankly confessed, that no Spaniard could be found possessed of equal resolution. By accident a mirror happened to hang before me, and seeing myself in it, dirty and with my clothes torn, I could not but feel amazement and high gratification at the little difficulty I had hitherto met with. In France, taken for a highwayman, I should have been stopped by the police: in Mexico I was not even asked for my passport.

[*Chapulco, Aquulsingo, Orissava, Villa de Cordova, La Punta, Calabaça—where his "old fox of a host" was "much astonished at seeing me, whom he had observed going on foot, return on horseback"—the Rio de Jamapa—all were passed in safety, until at length—*]

We arrived at Vera Cruz, at the gate of Orissava, before daybreak. I was in a condition so little fit to be seen that I thought it best to go and change my dress before I entered the city. Leaving, therefore, the Indian to take care of my trunks, I scaled the walls, entered my lodgings, where I found every thing as I had left it; dressed myself in a decent manner, and repaired to the gate of Orissava, which was then opening. I was a little surprised and somewhat terrified at not finding there my horses; but I learnt that, there being no officers at that gate, they had been taken to that of Mexico. I ran through the town thither, and reached it at the instant of their making their approach. The guards wished to send me to the customs house, which did not open before eight o'clock: I instantly felt all the inconvenience consequent on traversing the city, and exposing my prize to the looks of every one, and shuddered at the thought; I therefore saw no better expedient of disembarrassing myself than tickling the natural vanity of the Spaniards. What, said I to the chief clerk, do you then so soon forget the French physician? and is it possible you could wish to make him kick his heels in attendance like a footman, for the space of four hours? Besides, are you such novices? Cannot you yourselves make the requisite examination? You cannot be such geese but know your business, and how to act without advice. Do but look; what I bring is nothing but herbs, nothing but botanical collections; and as I spoke I opened my boxes. They were not disposed to take the trouble of examining more than two, and the only things to which my good folks took exception were the sticks which supported my nopals: they fancied these must needs be some precious wood, and enquired its name of me. I found it no difficult matter to invent one, and I obtained my dismission. *Vay usted con Dios*, Pass in God's name, was all they said. I did not require twice bidding, but soon reached my own home.

There was nobody yet up in the house, not a soul stirring in the street, and every thing was placed secure in my apartment without a single person observing me.

I had now attained my wishes, and my satisfaction was extreme; my expedition was complete, and in the short space of twenty days, the half of one of which had been uselessly spent. I had also stopped two days at Guaxaca; so that I had travelled in sixteen days two hundred and forty leagues, of which forty I had journeyed on foot, over roads so bad as often to be almost impassable, under a burning sun, in a wretched country, without reasources, and among people of whose language I was ignorant; in a country, in short, where I was destitute of a protector, or any connections, and where every public officer from his station ought to be inimical to me; to have effected, under such circumstances, so long and tiresome a journey, without illness, and without accident, was a matter so extraordinary, so lucky, that I scarcely was able to persuade myself of its reality.

A VISIT TO LADY HESTER STANHOPE[1]

(1832)

ALPHONSE DE LAMARTINE

(1790-1869)

LADY HESTER STANHOPE, the niece of Mr Pitt, after the death of her uncle, left England, and travelled through Europe. Young, beautiful, and rich, she was welcomed everywhere with the cordiality and respect which her rank, fortune, wit, and beauty were calculated to secure her; but she constantly refused to unite her lot to that of her most worthy suitors, and, after some years passed in the chief capitals of Europe, she embarked with a numerous suite for Constantinople. The motives of this expatriation have never been known; some have attributed it to the death of a young English general, killed at that period in Spain, and whom a never-ending sorrow for his fate brought perpetually to the mind of Lady Hester; others to the pure love of adventure, which the enterprising and courageous character of this young lady seemed to evince. Whatever it was, she departed. She passed some years at Constantinople, and at length embarked for Syria in an English vessel, which also bore the greater part of her treasures, and immense sums in jewels, and presents of all kinds.

A tempest assailed the ship in the Gulf of Macri, upon the coast of Caramania, opposite the Isle of Rhodes. It struck upon a rock some miles from the shore. The vessel was shattered to pieces in a few seconds, and the treasures of Lady Stanhope (sic) were buried in the waves. She herself escaped death with difficulty, and was borne, on a remnant of the wreck, to a small desert island, where she passed twenty-four hours without food or assistance. At last, some fishermen of Marmoriza, who were searching for the spoils of the shipwreck, discovered her, and conducted her to Rhodes, where she made herself known to the English consul. This deplorable disaster did not diminish her courage. She went to Malta, and thence to England. She collected the residue of her fortune; she sold, at a sacrifice, part of her lands, embarked her riches, and presents adapted to the countries she purposed visiting, a second time on board a vessel, and put to sea. The voyage was fortunate, and she landed at Latakia, the ancient Laodicea, upon the coast of Syria, between Tripolis and Alexandretta. She established herself in the environs, learnt Arabic, surrounded herself with all the persons who could facilitate her intercourse with the Arab, Druze, and Maronite populations of the country, and prepared, as I was then doing myself, for travels of discovery

[1] From *Travels in the East* (1839).

into the least accessible parts of Arabia, Mesopotamia, and the Desert.

When she had rendered herself familiar with the language, costumes, manners, and usages of the country, she organized numerous caravan, loaded camels with rich presents for the Arabs, and traversed all the districts of Syria. She sojourned at Jerusalem, Damascus. Aleppo, Koms, Balbek, and Palmyra. It was in this last station that the numerous tribes of wandering Arabs, who had facilitated her approach to these ruins, collected around her tent to the number of forty or fifty thousand, and, enraptured with her beauty, grace, and magnificence, proclaimed her Queen of Palmyra, and delivered to her patents, by which it was stipulated, that every European, protected by her, might come in full security to visit the desert and the ruins of Balbek and Palmyra, provided that he engaged to pay a tribute of one thousand piastres. This treaty still exists, and would be faithfully executed by the Arabs, if positive proof were given of the protection of Lady Hester.

On her return from Palmyra, she was, however, about to be carried off by a numerous tribe of other Arabs, who were at enmity with those of Palmyra. She was apprised in time by one of her people, and owed her safety, and that of her caravan, to a forced march at night, and to the swiftness of her horses, which cleared an incredible extent of desert in twenty-four hours. She returned to Damascus, where she resided some months, under the protection of the Turkish pacha, to whom the Porte had especially recommended her.

After a wandering life in all the countries of the East, Lady Hester Stanhope settled at last in an almost inaccessible solitude, upon one of the mountains of Lebanon, near Saïde, the ancient Sidon. The Pacha of Acre, Abdallah-Pacha, who entertained for her a profound respect, and an absolute devotion, ceded to her the ruins of a convent, and the village of Digioun, peopled by the Druzes. She built there several houses, surrounded by an outer wall, like our fortifications of the Middle Ages. She formed a charming garden by artificial means, in the manner of the Turks—a garden of flowers and fruits, vineyards, kiosks enriched with arabesque sculpture and paintings; water flowing in marble channels, water spouting in the midst of the kiosks, avenues of oranges, figs, and citrons. There Lady Hester lived several years in a luxury altogether oriental, accompanied by a great number of European or Arab dragomans, by a numerous suite of women and black slaves, and maintaining amicable and even political relations with the Porte, Abdallah-Pacha, the Emir Beschir, sovereign of Lebanon, and, above all, with the Arab scheiks of the deserts of Syria and Bagdad.

Her fortune, still considerable, was diminished by the derangement her affairs suffered from her absence, and she found herself reduced to thirty or forty thousand francs of income, which was, however, sufficient in this country for the establishment she is obliged to keep up. But the persons who had accompanied her from Europe died or removed; the friendship of the Arabs, which it is necessary to sustain by unceasing presents and imposing illusions, cooled, the intercourse became less frequent, and Lady Hester fell into the complete isolation in which I found her; but in this state the heroic cast of her character was displayed by all the energy and constancy of courage. She never thought of retracing her steps; the world and the past caused her no regret; she flinched not under abandonment, misfortune, or the prospect of an old age amidst oblivion. She remained alone where she is yet, without books, journals, letters from Europe, friends, or even servants attached to her person, surrounded only by some negresses and black children, and a few Arab peasants to cultivate her garden, to take care of the horses, and to protect her personal safety. It is generally believed in the country, and my communications with her induce me likewise to believe, that the super-natural vigour of her mind and resolution is sustained not only by her strength of character, but also by exalted religious ideas, in which the mysticism of Europe is mingled with certain Oriental superstitions, and especially with the ravings of astrology. Whatever it may be, Lady [Hester] Stanhope has a great renown in the East, and excites the astonishment of Europe. Finding myself so near her, I desired to see her; her choice of solitude and meditation had so much apparent sympathy with my own inclinations, that I felt glad in the idea of ascertaining in what we coincided. But nothing is more difficult for an European than to gain admission to her; she refuses any communication with English travellers, with women, or with the membes of her own family. I had, therefore, little hope of being introduced to her, and I had no letter of recommendation; knowing, however, that she preserved some distant relations with the Arabs of Palestine and Mesopotamia, and that a protection from her hand, addressed to these tribes, might be of the very greatest utility to me in my future travels, I resolved to send her, by an Arab, the following letter:

MY LADY,

A traveller like yourself, a stranger like you, in the East, and an imitator of you, in my search after the contemplation of its territories, its ruins, and the great works of God, I have just arrived in Syria, with my family. I should reckon that day amongst the most interesting of my journey, on which I should become acquainted with a woman, who is herself one of the wonders of this East which I come to visit.

If you will do me the favour of receiving me, be pleased to name the day which will be convenient to you, and let me know if I must come alone, or if I may bring with me some of the friends who accompany me, and who will attach no less value than myself to the honour of being presented to you.

Let not this request, my lady, in any degree constrain you, from politeness, to grant me what is offensive to your habits of complete seclusion. I understand too well myself the value of liberty. and the charm of solitude, not to appreciate your refusal, and to respect its motives.

Accept, etc.

I had not long to wait for an answer: the 30th, at three o'clock in the afternoon, the equerry of Lady [Hestor] Stanhope, who is at the same time her physician, arrived at my house with orders to accompany me to Digioun, the residence of this extraordinary woman.

We started at four o'clock. I was accompanied by Doctor Leonardi, M. de Parseval, a domestic, and a guide. We were all on horseback. I passed through, about half an hour from Beirout, a wood of magnificent firs, originally planted by the Emir Fakardin upon an elevated promontory, the view from which extends to the right, over the stormy sea of Syria, and to the left over the magnificent valley of Lebanon—an admirable landscape, in which the choicest of Western vegetation, the vine, fig-tree, mulberry, and pyramidal poplar, are united with the lofty columns of Eastern palms, the broad leaves of which shake in the wind like bunches of feathers. A few paces beyond, we enter into a sort of desert of red sand, raised into immense moving masses like the waves of the ocean. There was a brisk wind this evening, and it ploughed up the sand, raised it aloft, and scooped out hollows, as it makes the breakers of the sea lash and roar. This spectacle was new and sad, as an insight into the true and vast desert which I was soon to enter upon. No mark of men or animals was visible on this turbulent scene; we were guided only by the bellowing of the waves on the one side, and by the transparent ridges of Lebanon on the other. We soon recovered a sort of road or path, strewed with enormous angular blocks of stone. This road, which follows the sea even into Egypt, conducted us to a ruined house the remnant of an old fortified tower, where we passed the gloomy hours of the night, stretched upon a mat of rushes, and covered up with our mantles. As soon as the moon had risen we got on horseback again. It was one of those nights in which the sky is resplendent with stars, in which the most perfect serenity appears to reign in those vast ethereal regions we contemplate from below, but in which nature immediately around us seems to groan and torture herself into violent convulsions. The desolate aspect of the coast for some leagues added to this painful impression. We had left behind us, with the twilight, the beautiful shady slopes, the verdant valleys of Lebanon. Savage hills, strewed from top to bottom with black, white, and grey stones, the relics of earthquakes, arose close beside us; to our left and to our right, the sea, agitated since the morning by a growling tempest, rolled its heavy and threatening waves, which we saw as they came from afar, by the shadow which they cast before them, and broke upon the beach with the noise of thunder, throwing their thick and bubbling froth upon the ridge of damp sand we were travelling on, bathing each time the feet of our horses, and threatening to drag us back with it. A moon as brilliant as a winter sun shed sufficient light upon the sea to discover to us its fury, and not sufficient clearness upon our route to satisfy our eyes as to the perils of the road. A glimmering light shortly broke on the top of the mountains of Lebanon, with the white or sombre fog of morning, and spread over all this scene a false and pale tint which was neither day nor night, which had neither the splendour of the one nor the serenity of the other; an hour painful to the eye and to the thought, a contest fo two opposing principles of which nature often presents the afflicting image, and which we more often find in our own hearts.

At seven in the morning, under a sun already oppressive, we quitted Saïde, the ancient Sidon, which sits upon the waves as a glorious memento of a past dominion, and we climbed the slatey, naked, and broken hills, which, rising insensibly from stage to stage, led us to the solitude that we sought in vain to forestall with our eyes. Each peak as we cleared it disclosed to us one more elevated, which we had to wind round or climb up; the mountains were linked with mountains, like the rings of a chain, leaving between them only deep ravines, dry, scorched, and scattered with blocks of greyish rock. These mountains are completely bare of vegetation and of soil. They are the skeletons of hills which the waters and the winds have gnawed for ages. It was not there that I expected to find the residence of a female who had visited the world, and who had had the universe to select from. At length, from the top of one of these rocks, my eyes fell upon a deeper and broader valley, closed in on all sides by mountains more majestic, but not less sterile. In the middle of this valley, the hill of Digioun, like the base of a large tower, took root, and mounting in circular layers of rock, grew attenuated as it approached the summit, and formed an esplanade of some hundred fathoms broad, covered with a beautiful lively green vegetation. A white wall, flanked by a kiosk at one of its angles, encircled this verdant spot. This was the abode of Lady Hester. We reached it at midday. The house is not what we call by the same name in Europe, it is not even what is called a house in Asia; it is a confused and strange aggregation of ten or twelve little houses, each containing but one or two chambers on the ground floor, without windows, and separated from one another by small courts or gardens—an assemblage very similar in aspect to those poor convents which we meet with in Italy or Spain upon high mountains, belonging to the mendicant orders. According to her custom, Lady [Hester] Stanhope was not to be seen until three or four o'clock in the afternoon. We were each conducted into a sort of narrow cell, dark, and without furniture. We were served with breakfast, and we threw ourselves on a divan, whilst waiting for the rising of the invisible hostess of this romantic habitation. I fell asleep. At three o'clock they came and knocked at my door, to announce to me that she expected me. I passed through a court, a garden, an open kiosk with hangings of jessamine, then two or three gloomy corridors, and I was introduced by a little negro child, six or eight years old, into the cabinet of Lady Hester.

So profound an obscurity reigned that I had great difficulty in distinguishing the noble, grave, mild, and majestic features of the white form, which in Oriental costume rose from the divan, and came forward stretching out her hand. Lady Hester appears to be fifty years old; she has those features which years cannot alter. The freshness, colour, and grace of youth are gone; but when the beauty is in the figure itself, in the chasteness of the outlines, in the dignity, majesty, and expression of a male or female face, it changes at the different epochs of life, but it does not pass away. Such is the beauty of Lady Hester. She had upon her head a white turban, on her forehead a little fillet of purple wool falling on each side of the head upon the shoulders. A long shawl of yellow cashmere, and an immense Turkish robe of white silk, with hanging sleeves, covered her person in simple and majestic folds, and it was only in the opening which this first tunic left upon her breast that a second robe of Persian flowered stuff, reaching to the neck, and fastened by a clasp of pearls, could be perceived. Yellow Turkish boots, embroidered with silk, completed this beautiful Oriental costume, which she wore with the freedom and gracefulness of a person who has never worn any other since her infancy.

"You have come a long way to see a hermit," she said to me; "you are welcome; I receive few strangers, scarcely one or two in a year; but your letter pleased me, and I desired to know a person who loved, like me, God, nature, and solitude. Something besides, told me that our stars were friendly, and that we should agree well together. I see with pleasure that my presentiment has not deceived me; and your features which I now see, and the very noise of your steps whilst you were traversing the corridor, have sufficiently informed me respecting you to prevent my repenting of having resolved to see you. Let us sit down and converse. We are already friends."

"How!" said I to her; "do you honour so quickly with the name of friends, my lady, a man whose name and life are completely unknown to you? You are ignorant who I am."

"True," replied she; "I know neither who you are according to the world, nor what you have done whilst living amongst men; but I know already what you are before God. Do not take me for a foot, as the world often calls me; but I cannot resist the inclination to speak to you with an open heart. There is a science, lost at present in your Europe, a science which was born in the East, where it has never perished, and where it yet survives. I possess it. I read in the stars. We are all children of some one of those celestial fires which preside at our birth, and whose fortunate or malignant influence is written in our eyes, on our foreheads, in our features, in the lines of our hand, in the form of our foot, in our gesture, and in our gait. I have only seen you a few minutes, and yet I know you as if I had lived an age with you. Do you wish that I open to you yourself? Do you wish that I predict your destiny?"

"Pray avoid doing so, my lady," answered I, smiling; "I do not deny what I am ignorant of; I will not affirm, that in visible and invisible nature in which every thing is held, every thing enchained, beings of an inferior order, like man, may not be under the influence of superior beings, like stars or angels; but I have no need of their revelation to know myself—corruption, infirmity, and woe! And as to the secrets of my future destiny, I should consider it a profanation of the Divinity, who conceals them from me, if I sought them from a creature. In regard to the future, I believe only in God, free-will, and virtue."

"Never mind," said she to me, "believe what you please; as to me, I see evidently that you are born under the influence of very happy, potent, and benevolent stars. You will soon return to Europe; Europe is done; France alone has a grand mission yet to accomplish; you will participate in it; I do not at present know how, but I can tell you this evening, if you desire it, when I have consulted your stars. I do not yet know the names of all; I see more than three; I distinguish four, perhaps five, and, who knows, more yet? One of them is certainly Mercury, who gives clearness and emphasis to the intellect and to the power of expression; you ought to be a poet—that is evident from your eyes and the higher part of your face; lower, you are under the empire of quite distinct, almost opposing stars, in which there is an influence of energy and action. There is the sun also," continued she, with a start, "in the leaning of your head, and in the manner you throw it on your left shoulder. You may thank God: there are few men who are born under more than one star, few whose star is happy, still fewer whose star, when favourable, is not counterbalanced by the malignant influence of an opposing star. You, on the contrary, have several, and all are in harmony to serve you, and to act in concert for your advantage. What is your name?"

I told it to her.

"I had never heard of it!" she exclaimed in the accent of truth.

"See, my lady, what glory is! I have composed some verses in my life which have made my name be re-echoed a million of times in the literary circles of Europe; but this echo is too weak to traverse your sea and mountains, and here I am quite a new man, a man completely unknown, with a name never pronounced! I am only the more flattered by the kindness you have showered upon me; I owe it only to you and myself."

"Yes," said she, "poet or not, I esteem you, and I place hopes in you; we shall see each other again, be assured! You will return to the West, but you will not be long in returning to the East; it is your country."

"It is, at least," said I, "the country of my imagination."

"Do not laugh," she resumed, "it is your actual country—it is the country of your fathers. I am now certain of it; look at your foot!"

"I see there," said I, "nothing but the dust of your roads which covers it, and which would make me blush in a salon of old Europe."

"That's nothing," continued she; "it is not that. Look at your foot. I had not myself taken notice of it before. See; the instep is very high, and between your heel and toes, when your foot is on the ground, there is a sufficient elevation to let water pass without wetting you. It is the Arab's foot; it is the foot of the East; you are a son of these climates, and we draw near the day on which we shall each return to the land of our fathers. We shall see each other again."

A black slave now entered, and prostrating herself before her, bowing her forehead to the ground, and placing her hands upon her head, spoke to her some words in Arabic.

"Go," said she to me; "dinner is served; be quick and return; I am going to concern myself about you, and to see more distinctly through the confusion of my ideas as to your person and your future. As for me, I never eat with anyone; I live too abstemiously; bread, and some fruits, as I feel hungry, are sufficient; I cannot put a guest upon my diet."

I was conducted beneath a bower of jessamine and laurel-rose, at the gate of the garden. The table was set for M. de Parseval and me; we dined with great dispatch, but she did not even wait for our rising from table, but sent Leonardi to tell me she was waiting for me. I hastened to her; I found her smoking a long Eastern pipe; she ordered one to be brought to me. I was already accustomed to see the most elegant and beautiful women smoking in the East; I no longer felt anything shocking in the graceful and careless attitude, nor in the odoriferous smoke escaping in light curls from the lips of a handsome woman, and interrupting the conversation without stifling it. We conversed a long time, and always on the favourite subject, the sole and mysterious theme of this extraordinary woman, the modern enchantress, recalling the famous magicians of antiquity—the Circe of the deserts. It appeared to me that the religious doctrines of Lady Hester were a clever though confused mixture of the different religions in the midst of which she had condemned herself to live; mysterious as the Druzes, whose mystic secret she, of all the world, perhaps, alone knew; resigned as the Moslem, and like him a fatalist; with the Jew, expecting the Messiah; and with the Christian, professing the worship of Christ and the practice of his charity and morality. Add to this, the fantastic colouring and supernatural dreams of an imagination tinctured with oriental extravagance, and heated by solitude and meditation, the impressions, perhaps, of the Arabic astrologers, and you will have an idea of this compound of the sublime and ridiculous, which it is more convenient to stigmatise as madness than to analyse and comprehend. No! this woman is not mad. Madness, which displays itself in the eyes, so as never to be mistaken, is not expressed in her wild and straight look; madness, which is always betrayed in conversation by the interruptions it gives to the chain of discourse by sudden, disordered, and eccentric bursts, is not perceptible in the elevated, mystic, and obscure, though sustained, connected, and powerful conversation of Lady Hester. If I were called upon to decide, I should rather say it was the voluntary and studied madness of one who knows what she is about, and who has her own reasons for appearing insane. The sway, founded on admiration, which her genius has exercised, and still exercises, over the Arab population which surrounds her mountains, proves sufficiently that this affected madness is but a means. To the men of this land of prodigies, to these men of rocks and deserts, whose imagination is more vivid and wreathed in mist than the horizon of their sands or seas, the words of Mahomet or Lady Hester Stanhope are necessary! They require the knowledge of the stars, prophecies, miracles, the second sight of genius! Lady Hester has comprehended this from the extent of her truly superior intellect. Then, perhaps, like all others gifted with powerful intellectual faculties, she has concluded by deceiving herself, and by becoming the first neophyte of the symbol she had elevated for others. Such is the effect this woman produced upon me.

After having smoked several pipes, and drunk several cups of coffee, which the black slaves brought every quarter of an hour, she said to me,

"Come, I will lead you into a sanctuary where I allow nothing profane to enter—my garden."

We descended to it by some steps, and, in a positive enchantment, I followed her through one the most beautiful Turkish gardens which I had yet seen in the East. There were arbours of vine where the light was dulled, but on the verdant arches of which glittered the grapes of the promised land, like myriads of lustres; kiosks (summer-houses), where the sculptured arabesques were entwined in jessamine and the climbing canes of Asia; canals, in which an artificial water came murmuring for a league of distance, and spouted up through marble jets; alleys, lined with all the fruit-trees of England, Europe, and these beautiful climates; plots of green sward, sprinkled with shrubs in flower, and marble compartments surrounding the shoots of flowers new to my eyes. Such was her garden. We rested in several of the kiosks with which it was ornamented; and never did the inexhaustible conversation of Lady Hester lose the mystic tone or the elevation of style which it had assumed in the morning.

"Since destiny," said she to me at the close, "has sent you here, and so astonishing a sympathy in our stars permits me to confide to you what I conceal from the profane—come, and I will let your eyes behold a prodigy of nature, the destination of which is known only to myself and my scholars; the prophecies of the East had many ages ago announced it, and you will judge yourself if these prophecies are accomplished." She opened a door of the garden, which introduced us to a small inner court, where I perceived two magnificent Arabian mares, of pure race and of rare symmetry. "Approach and look at this bay mare," said she; "see if nature has not accomplished in her all that is written touching the mare which is to carry the Messiah—'She shall be born ready saddled.'"

I saw, in fact, upon this fine animal, a sport of nature sufficiently uncommon to serve as a delusion for vulgar credulity amongst a half barbarous people; the mare had, from a defect in the shoulders, a cavity so broad and deep, and so much in the form of a Turkish saddle, that it might be said with truth, she was born ready saddled; and even to the stirrups, she could be easily mounted without the aid of an artificial saddle. The mare, a splendid animal in other respects, appeared used to the admiration and respect which Lady (Hester) Stanhope and her slaves testified for her, and to have a presentiment of the dignity of her future mission; no person had ever mounted her, and two Arab grooms attended and watched her, without losing her a moment out of sight. Another white mare, and, in my opinion, infinitely more beautiful, partook, with the Messiah's mare, the respect and attentions of Lady Hester. No one had ever mounted her either. Lady Hester did not tell me, but she left me to infer, that although the destiny of the white mare was less sanctified, she had likewise one of great mystery and importance; and I thought I understood that Lady Hester reserved her for herself, on the day when she should make her entry, by the side of the

Messiah, into the reconquered Jerusalem. After having caused the two animals to be promenaded for some time upon a green plot, outside the enclosure of the fortress, and admiring their suppleness and grace, we returned; and I renewed to her my request, that she would at length allow me to present to her M. de Parseval, my friend and fellow-traveller, who had followed me, in spite of myself, to her house, and who had been vainly waiting since the morning for a favour of which she was so chary. She consented at last, and we all three returned into the little salon which I have already described, to pass the evening or the night. Coffee and pipes reappeared in oriental profusion, and the room was soon filled with such a cloud of smoke, that the figure of her ladyship was visible only through an atmosphere similar to that of a magical invocation. She conversed with the same vigour, grace, and abundance, but with infinitely less of the supernatural, upon subjects not so sacred for her, as she had exhibited with me when alone throughout the day.

The night thus wore away in the free discussion, without any affectation on the part of Lady Hester, of all the subjects which hazard calls up, and brings into conversation. I found that no chord was wanting in her high and strong intellect, and that every key that was touched gave out a just, full, and powerful sound, except perhaps the metaphysical chord, which too much stretching and solitude had rendered false, or elevated to a diapason too high for mortal intelligence. We separated, with a sincere regret on my part, and an obliging reluctance testified on hers.

"No farewells," said she to me; "we shall often meet againt in this journey, and more often yet in other journeys, of which you have not formed any project. Go to repose, and recollect that you leave a friend in the solitudes of Lebanon."

OF A JOURNEY TO MALAGA AND OF WHAT HAPPENED THERE [1]

(1844)

THÉOPHILE GAUTIER

(1811-72)

A PIECE of news, well calculated to throw a whole Spanish town into a state of commotion, had suddenly been bruited about Granada, to the great delight of the *aficionados*. The new circus at Malaga was at last finished, after having cost the contractor five million reals. In order to inaugurate in

[1] From *Wanderings in Spain* (1853), an anonymous translation of *Voyage en Espagne* (1845).

solemnly, by exploits worthy of the palmy days of the art, the great Montes de Chielana—Montes, the first *espada* of Spain, the brilliant successor of Romero and Pepe Illo—had been engaged with his quadrille, and was to appear in the ring three days consecutively. We had already been present at several bull-fights, but we had not been fortunate enough to see Montes, who was prevented by his political opinion from making his appearance in the circus at Madrid; and to quit Spain without having seen Montes would be something as barbarous and savage as to leave Paris without having witnessed the performance of Mademoiselle Rachel. Although, had we taken the direct road, we ought to have proceeded at once to Cordova, we could not resist this temptation, and we resolved, in spite of the difficulties of the journey and the short time at our diposal, to make a little excursion to Malaga.

There is no diligence from Granada to Malaga, and the only means of transport are the *galeras* or mules: we chose the latter as bing surer and quicker, for we were under the necessity of taking the cross-roads through the Alpurjas, in order to arrive even on the very day of the fight.

Our friends in Granada recommended us a *cosario* (conductor of a convoy) named Lanza, a good-looking honest fellow, and very intimate with the brigands. This fact would certainly not tell much in his favour in France, but on the other side of the Pyrenees the case is different. The muleteers and conductors of the *galeras* know the robbers and make bargains with them; for so much a head, or so much for the whole convoy, according to the terms agreed upon, they obtain a free passage, and are never attacked. These arrangements are observed by both parties with the most scrupulous probity, if I may use the word, and if it is not too much out of place when talking of transactions of this description. When the chief of the gang infesting a peculiar track takes advantage of the *indulto*, or, for some reason or other, cedes his business and customers to any one else, he never neglects presenting officially to his successor those *cosarios* who pay him "black mail" in order that they may not be molested by mistake. By this system, travellers are sure of not being pillaged, while the robbers avoid the risk of making an attack and meeting with a degree of resistance which is often accompanied with danger to them; so that the arrangement is advantageous to both parties.

One night, between Alhama and Velez, our *cosario* had dropped to sleep upon the neck of his mule, in the rear of the convoy, when suddenly he was awakened by shrill cries, and saw a number of *trabtcos* glistening at the roadside. There was no doubt about the matter; the convoy was attacked. In the greatest state of surprise, he threw himself from his mule, and averting the muzzles of the blunderbusses with his hand, declared who he was.

"Ah! we beg your pardon, Señor Lanza," said the brigands, quite confused at their mistake, "but we did not recognise you. We are honest men, totally incapable of so indelicate a proceeding as to molest you. We have too much honour to deprive you of even so mush as a single cigar."

If you do not travel with a man who is known along the road, it is absolutely necessary to be accompanied by a numerous escort, armed to the teeth, and which cost a great deal, besides offering less security, for the *escopeteros* are generally retired robbers.

It is the custom in Andalusia, when a person travels on horseback, and goes to the bull-fights, to put on the national costume. Accordingly our little caravan was rather picturesque, and made a very good appearance as it left Granada. Seizing with delight this opportunity of disguising myself out of Carnival time, and quitting, for a short space, my horrible French attire, I donned my a *majo's* costume, consisting of a peaked hat, embroidered jacket, velvet waistcoat, with filigree buttons, red silk sash, webbed breeches, and gaiters open at the calf. My travelling companion wore his dress of green velvet and Cordova leather. Some of the others wore *monteras*, black jackets and breeches decorated with silk trimmings of the same colour, and yellow cravats and sashes. Lanza was remarkable for the magnificence of his silver buttons, made of pillared dollars, soldered to a shank, and the floss-silk embroideries of his second jacket, which he wore hanging from his shoulder like a hussar's pelisse.

The mule that had been assigned to me was close-shaved halfway up his body, so that I was enabled to study his muscular development with as much ease as if he had been flayed. The saddle was composed of two variegated horse-cloths, put on double, in order to soften as much as possible the projecting vertebræ, and the sloping shape of the animal's backbone. On each side hung down, in the guise of stirrups, two kinds of wooden troughs, rather resembling our ratraps. The head-trappings were so loaded with rosettes, tufts and other gewgaws, that it was almost impossible to distinguish the capricous brute's sour crabbed profile through the mass of ornament fluttering about it.

Whenever they travel, Spaniards resume their ancient originality, and eschew the imitation of anything foreign. The national characteristics reappear in all their pristine vigour, in these convoys through the mountains—convoys which cannot differ much from the caravans through the desert. The roughness of the roads, that are scarcely marked out, the grand savage aspects of the various places you pass through, the picturesque costume of the *arrieros,* and the strange trappings of the mules, horses and asses, marching along in files, all transport you a thousand miles away from civilised life. Travelling becomes a reality, an action in which you take a part. In a diligence a man is no longer a man, he is but an inert object, a bale of goods, and does not much differ from his portmanteau. He is thrown from one place to the other, and might as well stop at home. The pleasure of travelling consists in the obstacles, the fatigue, and even the danger. What charm can any one find in an excursion, when he is always sure of reaching his destination, of having horses ready waiting for him, a soft bed, an excellent supper, and all the ease and comfort which he can enjoy in his own home! One of the great misfortunes of modern life is the want of any sudden surprise, and the absence of all adventures. Everything is so well arranged, so admirably combined, so plainly labelled, that chance is an utter impossibility; if we go on progressing, in this fashion, towards perfection for another century, every man will be able to foresee everything that will happend to him from the day of his birth to the day of his death. Human will will be completely annihilated. There will be no more crimes, no more virtues, no more characters, no more orginality. It will be impossible to distinguished a Russian from a Spaniard, an Englishman from a Chinese, or a Frenchman from an American. People will not even be able to recognise one another, for every one will be alike. An intense feeling of *ennui* will then take possession of the universe, and suicide will decimate the population of the globe, for the principal spirng of life, namely, curiosity, will have been destroyed for ever.

A journey in Spain is still a perilous and romantic affair. You must risk your life, and possess courage, patience and strengh. You are exposed to danger at every step you take. Privations of all kinds, the absence of the most indispensable articles, the wretched state of the roads, that would offer insurmountable difficulties to any but an Andalusian muleteer, the most horrible heat, with the sun darting its rays upon you as if it were about to split your skull, are the most trifling inconveniences. Besides all this, there are the *factions*, the robbers, and the innkeepers, all ready to plunder and ill-treat you, and who regulate their honesty by the number of carbines that accompany you. Peril encircles you, follows you, goes before you, is all around you. You hear nothing but terrible and mysterious stories discussed in a low, terrified tone. Yesterday the bandits supped in the very *posada* at which you alight. A caravan has been attacked and carried off into the mountains by the brigands, in the hope that their prisoners will be ransomed. Pallilos is lying in ambush at such and such a spot, which you will have to pass. Without doubt there is a good deal of exaggeration in all this, but however incredulous you may be, you cannot avoid believing something of it, when, at each turn of the road, you perceive wooden crosses with inscriptions of this kind: *Aqui mataron a un hombre, Aqui murio de maupairada.*

We had left Granada in the evening, and were to travel all night. It was not long before the moon rose, frosting with silver the precipitious rocks exposed to her beams. These rocks threw their long strange shadows over the road we were following, and produced some very singular optical effects. We heard in the distance, like the notes of an harmonica, the tinkling of the asses' beles, for the asses had been sent on beforehand with our luggage, or some *mozo de mulas* singing some amorous coupletes with that guttural tone and peculiar, far-sounding pitch of voice, so poetical when heard at night and in the mountains. The song was delightful; and the reader will perhaps thank us for giving two stanzas, which were probably improvised, and which, from their graceful quaintness, have ever since remained engraved on our memory:

Son tus labios dos cortinas	Thy lips are two curtains
De terciopelo carmesi;	Of crimson velvet;
Entre cortina y cortina	Between curtain and curtain,
Niña, dime que se.	Dear girl, say to me, "Yes."
Atame con un cabello	Fasten me with a hair
A los bancos de tu cama,	To the frame of your couch;
Aunque el cabello se rompa	Even if the hair should snap,
Segura esta que no me vaya.	Be sure that I would not leave you.

We soon passed, Cacin, where we forded a pretty little torrent some inches deep. The clear water glittered on the sand like the scales on the belly of a bleak, and then streamed down the steep mountainside like an avalanche of silver spangles.

Beyond Cacin, the road becomes most wretchedly bad. Our mules sunk up to their girths in the stones, while they had a shower of sparks round each of their hoofs. We had to ascend and descend, to pass along the edges of precipiaes and to proceed in all sorts of zigzags and diagonals, for we had entered those inaccessible solitudes, those savage and precipitous mountain chains, the Alpujarras, whence the Moors, so runs the report, could never the completely expelled, and where some thousands of their descendants live concealed at the present day.

At a turn in the road, we experienced a very tolerable amount of alarm. We perceived, by the light of the moon, seven strapping fellows, draped in long mantles, with peaked hats on their heads, and *trabuchos* on their shoulders, standing motionless in the middle of the way. The adventure we had so long panted for was about to be realised in the most romantic manner possible. Unfortunately, the banditti saluted us politely with a respectful *Vayan Ustedes con Dios.* They were the very reverse of robbers, being Miquelets, that is to say, gendarmes! Oh, what a cruel disappointment was this for two enthusiastic young traveller, who would willingly have lost their luggage for the sake of an adventure.

We were to stop for the night at a little town called Alhama, perched like an eagle's nest upon the top of a mountain peak. Nothing can be more picturesque than the sharp angle which the road conducting to this eyrie is obliged to make, in order to adapt itself to the unevenness of the ground. We reached our destination about two in the morning, half dead with hunger and thirst, and worn out with fatigue. We quenched our thirst by means of three or four jars of water, and appeased our hunger by a tomato omelette, which, considering it was Spanish one, did not contain too many feathers. A stony kind of mattress, bearing a strong family likeness to a sack of walnuts, was given us for a couch. At the expiration of two minutes, I was buried in that peculiar sleep attributed to the Just, and my companion relgiously followed my example. The day surprised us in the same attitudes, as motionless as lumps of lead.

I went down into the kitchen to implore them to give me some food, and , thanks to my eloquence, obtained some cutlets, a fowl fried in oil, and half of a watermelon, besides for dessert, some Barbary figs, whose prickly skin the landlady took off very dexterously. The watermelon did us a great deal of good; the rosy pulp contained inside its green rind has a most delightfully cool and thirst-assuaging look. Scarcely have you bitten it, before you are inundated up to your elbows with a very agreeably flavoured and slightly sweet juice, which bears no sort of resemblance to that of our cantaloups. We really stood in need of this refreshing fruit to moderate the burning effects of the peppers and spices with which all Spanish dishes are seasoned. We were on fire internally and roasted externally; the heat was atrocious. We lay down upon the brick floor of our room, on which the forms of our bodies were marked by pools of perspiration. The only method we could discover for rendering the place, comparatively speaking, a little cool was by closely shutting all the doors and windows, and remaining in complete darkness.

In spite of this Indian temperature, however, I boldly threw my jacket over my shoulder, and went out to take a turn in the streets of Alhama. The sky was as white as metal in a state of fusion: the paving stones glistened as if they had been waxed and polished; the whitewashed walls presented a micaceous scintillating appearance, while the pitiless blinding sunshine penetrated into every hole and corner. The shutters and doors were cracking with heat, the gasping soil was full of yawning fissures, and the branches of the vines writhed like green wood when thrown into the fire; while, in addition to all this, there was the reflection of the neighbouring rocks, which cast back the rays of light even hotter than they were before. To complete my torture, I had got on very thin shoes, through which the pavement burnt the soles of my feet. There was not a breath of air, not so much wind as would have ruffled a feather. It is impossible to conceive anything more dull, more melancholy, or more savage.

I wandered at hazard through the solitary streets, whose chalkcoloured walls, pierced by a few windows, scattered far appart, and closed by means of wooden shutters, gave them a completely African appearance, until, I will not say without meeting a human being, but absolutely without seeing a living creature, I reached the great square, which is exceedingly picturesque and quaint. It is crossed by the stone arches of an aqueduct, and consists simply of a level space cleared away on the bare rock itself, which has grooves cut in it to prevent persons from slipping. The whole of one side overlooks the abyss, at the bottom of which peep out, from the midst of clumps of trees, several mills that are turned by a torrent which foams so violently that it resembles a quantity of soapsuds.

The hour fixed upon for our departure was approaching, and I returned to the *posada* wet through with perspiration, just as if I had been out in a heavy shower of rain, but satisfied at having done my duty as a traveller, although you might have boiled eggs by the mere heat of the atmosphere.

Our caravan again set out, proceeding through most abominable but highly picturesque roads, where no other creature but a mule could have stood without falling. I had thrown the bridle on the neck of mine, thinking that he was better qualified to direct his steps than I was, and leaving him all the responsibility of passing the dangerous points. I had already had several very animated discussions with him, in order to induce him to walk beside the mule of my companion, but I was at last convinced of the inutility of my efforts. I bow, in all submission, to the truth of the saying *As obstinate as a mule.* Give a mule the spur and it will stand still; touch it with a whip, it will lie down; pull it up, and it will start off at full gallop: in the mountains, a mule is really intractable; it feels its importance and takes a most unfair advantage of it. Very often, right in the middle of the road, a mule will suddenly stop, raise its head, stretch out its neck, draw back its lips, so as to expose its gums and long teeth, and indulge in a series of the most horrible inarticulate sighs, convulsive sobs, and frightful clucking, resembling the shrieks of a child who is being murdered. During the time it is indulging in this system of vocalisation you might kill it, without being able to make it move one step.

Our path now lay through a veritable Campo Santo. The crosses erected where murders had been committed became frightfully numerous: in the situations that were favourable to this kind of thing, we sometimes counted more than three or four crosses in less than a hundred paces; we were no longer on a road, but in a cemetery. I must own, however, that if it were the custom in France to perpetuate the memory of violent deaths by the erection of crosses, there would be quite as many of them in certain streets of Paris as there are on the road from Granada to Velez-Malaga. The dates of a great number of these sinister monuments are already very old; it is very certain, however, that they keep the traveller's mind actively employed, rendering him attentive to the slightest noise, causing him to look very carefully about him, and hindering any feeling of *ennui.* At every turn of the road, he says to himself, if he sees a rock that looks at all suspicious, or a mysterious cluster of trees: "There is some vagabond concealed behind there, who is in the act of taking aim, and is on the point of making me the pretext for another cross destined to edify the travellers of future generations who may happen to pass by the spot."

When we emerged from the defiles, the crosses became somewhat less frequent. Our road now lay along the bases of stern, grand mountains, whose summits were cut off by immense archipelagos of mist. The country was a complete desert, with no other habitations save the reed hut of some *aguador,* or vendor of brandy. This brandy is colourless, and is drunk out of long glasses filled up with water, which causes it to turn white exactly as eau-de-Cologne would.

The weather was heavy had stormy, and the heat suffocating: a few large drops of water, the only ones that had fallen for a space of four months, from the implacable sky of lapis-lazuli, spotted the parched sand, and made it resemble a panthers skin; however, there was no shower after all, and the canopy of heaven resumed its immutable serenity. The sky was so constantly blue during my stay in Spain, that I find the following notice in my pocket book: "Saw a white cloud," as if such an object was worthy of being especially recorded. We inhabitants of the north are so accustomed to behold the heavens covered with clouds, constantly varying in form and colour, and with which the wind builds mountains, islands and palaces, that it soon destroys again to build elsewhere, that we cannot form any conception of the feeling of profound melancholy caused by this azure tint, as uniform as eternity itself, and which is always hanging over one's head. In a little village which we traversed, all the population were standing outside their houses in order to enjoy the rain, just as we should go in doors to avoid it.

The night had set in without any twilight, almost in an instant, as is the case in warm climates, and we were not very far from Velez-Malaga, where we intended sleeping. The mountain-steeps begain to be less abrupt, and gradually subsided in small stony plains, traversed by streams fifteen or twenty feet broad, and one foot deep; their banks were covered with gigantic reeds. The funeral crosses again became more numerous than ever, and their white colour caused them to stand out distinctly from the blue mist of night. We counted three of them in the distance of twenty paces, but the fact is, that the spot presents a most lonely appearance and is admirably adapted for an ambuscade.

It was eleven o'clock when we entered Velez-Malaga; the windows were joyfully lighted up, and the streets re-echoed with songs and the sounds of guitars. The young maidens seated in the balconies were singing verses which the *novios* accompanied from the street below, and each stanza was followed by laughter, shouts and applause, which I thought would never end. Other groups were dancing the cachucha, the fandango, and the jalo, at the corners of the streets. The guitars emitted a dull hum like that of bees, the castagnettes rattled merrily, and all was music an delight. It would almost appear as if the most important business of a Spaniard's life were pleasure; he gives himself up to it, heart and soul, with admirable ease and frankness. No nation in the world appears to know less of misfortune than the Spaniards, and a stranger travelling through the Peninsula can scarcely believe that the state of political affairs can be so serious, or that he is traversing a country which for ten years has been ravaged and laid waste by civil war.

Our supper was extremely frugal; all the servants, both male and female, were gone out to dance, so that we had to content ourselves with a simple *gaspacho*. In France a dog with the least pretensions to a good education would refuse to compromise himself by putting his nose into such a mixture; but it is the favourite dish of the Andalusians, and the most lovely women do not hesitate of an evening to swallow large messes of this diabolical soup. By a providential chance we had, to enable us to wash down this meagre repast, a large decanter of excellent dry white Malaga, which we conscientiously finsihed to the last pearly drop, and which restored our strength, that was completely exhausted by a ride of nine hours, over the most improbable roads, and in a temperature like that of a lime-kiln.

At three o'clock the conveyance set out once more upon its march. The sky looked lowering; a warm mist hung over the horizon, and the humidity of the air warned us that we were approaching the sea, which soon afterwards appeared in the extreme distance like a streak of hard blue. A few fleecy flacks of foam were visible here and there, while the waves came and died way in regular volumes upon the sand, which was as fine as boxwood sawdust. High cliffs rose upon our right. At one moment the rocks separated and left us a free passage, and at the next day barricaded the road, and obliged us to wind slowly round them. It is not often that Spanish roads proceed in a right line; it would be so difficult a task to overcome the various obstacles, that it is far better to go round than to surmount them. The famous motto, *Linea recta brevissima*, would in Spain be completely false.

The rising sun dispersed the mist as if it had been so much smoke; the sky and the sea recommenced their azure struggle, in which it is impossible to say which of the two is victorious; the cliffs resumed their varied tints of reddish-brown, shot-colour, amethyst, and burnt topaz; the sand began once again to rise in small thin clouds, and the water to glisten in the intensity of the sunshine. Far, far away, almost on the line of the horizon, the sails of five fishing-boats palpitated in the wind like the wings of a dove.

The declivities now became less steep; from time to time, a little house appeared, as white as lump-sugar, with a flat roof and a kind of peristyle formed by a vine clustering over trellis-work, supported at each end by a square pillar, and in the middle by a massive pylone that presented quite an Egyptian appearance. The *aguardiente* stores became more numerous; they were still built of reeds, but they were more natty, and boasted of white-washed counters daubed with a few streaks of red. The road, which was now distinctly marked out, began to be lined on each side with a line of cactus and aloes-trees, broken now and then by gardens and houses, before which women were mending nets, and children, completely naked, playing about. On seeing us pass by on our mules, they cried out, "*Toro! Toro!*" taking us on account for our *majo* costume, for proprietors of *ganaderias*, or for the *toreros* belonging to the quadrille directed by Montes.

Carts drawn by oxen and strings of asses now followed at shorter intervals, and the bustle which invariably marks the neighbourhood of a large town became every moment more apparent. On all sides, convoys of mules, carrying persons who were on their way to witness the opening of the circus, made their appearance: we met a great number in the mountains coming from a distance of thirty or forty leagues. The *aficionados* are as superior, by their passionate and furious love of their favourite amusement, to our dilettanti, as the interest excited by a bull-fight is superior to that produced by the representation of an opera: nothing stops them; neither the heat nor the difficulty or danger of the journey; provided they reach thier destination and obtain a place near the *barrera,* from which they can pat the bull on the back, they consider themselves amply repaid for whatever fatigue they may have undergone. What tragic or comic author can boast of possessing such powers of attraction?

It is impossible to conceive anything more picturesque and strange than the environs of Malaga. You appear to the transported to Africa: the dazzling whiteness of the houses, the deep indigo colour of the sea, and the overpowering intensity of the sun, all combine to keep up the illusion. On each side of the road are numbers of enormous aloes-trees, bristling up and waving their leafy cutlasses, and gigantic cactuses with their green broad foliage and missshapen trunks writhing hideously like monstrous boa-constrictors, or resembling the backbones of so many stranded whales; while here and there a palmtree shoots up like a column displaying its green capital by the side of some tree of European parentage, which seems surprised at such a neighbour, and alarmed at seeing the formidable vegetation of Africa crawling at its feet.

An elegant white tower now stood out upon the blue sky behind; it was the Malaga lighthouse; we had reached our destination. It was about eight o'clock in the morning; the town was already alive and stirring: the sailors were passing and repassing, loading and unloading the vessels anchored in the port, and displaying a degree of animation which was something uncommon in a Spanish town; the women, with their heads and figures enveloped in large scarlet shawls, which suited their Moorish faces most marvellously, were walking quickly along, and dragging after them some brat, who was entirely naked, or who had only got on a shirt. The men, with their cloaks thrown round them, or their jackets cast over their shoulders, hurried on their way; and it is a curious fact, that all this crowd was proceeding in the same direction—that is, towards the *Plaza de Toros.*

We put up at the *parador* of the Three Kings, which, comparatively speaking, is a very comfortable establishment, shaded by a fine vine whose tendrils clustered round the ironwork of the balcony, and adorned with a large room, where the landlady sat enthroned behind a counter, loaded with porcelain, somewhat after the fashion of the Parisian *cafés.* A very beautiful servant-girl, a charming specimen of the lovely women for which Malaga is celebrated all through Spain, showed us to our rooms, and threw us, for a few minutes, into a state of desperate anxiety, by informing us that all the places in the circus were already taken, and that we should have great difficulty in procuring any. Fortunately, our *cosario,* Lanza, got us two *asientos de preferencia* (numbered seats); it is true that they were exposed to the sun, but we did not care for that. We had long since sacrificed the freshness of our complexion, and were not particular about our bistre-coloured yellow faces becoming a trifle more sunburnt.

The performances were to begin at five o'clock, but we were advised to be at the circus at about one, as the corridors would be choked up by the crowd at an early hour, and prevent us from reaching our places, although they were numbered and reserved. We swallowed our breakfast, therefore, as quickly as we could, and set out towards the *Plaza de Toros,* preceded by our guide Antonio, a tall, thin fellow, whose waist was tied in most atrociously by a borad red sash, increasing still more his natural meagreness, which he pleasantly attributed to the fact of his having been crossed in love.

The streets were swarming with an immense multitude, which became more and more dense as we approached the circus; the *aguadors*, the vendors of iced *cebada*, of paper fans, and parasols and of cigars, as well as the *calessin* drivers, were creating a frightful uproar: a confused rumour floated over the town like a fog of noise.

After twisting and turning about, for a considerable time, in the narrow, complicated streets of Malaga, we at last arrived before the building, whose exterior offers nothing remarkable. A detachment of troops had considerable difficulty in keeping back the crowd, which would otherwise have invaded the Circus; although it was not more than one o'clock, at the latest, the seats wer all occupied from top to bottom, and it was only by a free use of our elbows, and the interchange of a profusion of invectives, that we succeeded in reaching our stalls.

The Circus at Malaga is really antique in size, and will contain twelve or fifteen thousand spectators in its vast funnel-like interior, of which the arena forms the bottom, while the acroteria rises to the height of a five-storied house. It gives you a notion of what the Roman amphitheatres must have been, as well as those terrible spectacles where men were opposed to wild beasts, under the eyes of a whole nation.

It is impossible to conceive any sight more strange and more splendid than that of these immense rows of seats occupied by an impatient crowd, endeavouring to while away the hours they had to wait by all kinds of jokes and *andaluzados* of the most piquant originality. The number of persons in modern costume was very limited; those who were dressed in this manner were greeted with shouts of laughter, cries and hisses; this imporved the general appearance of the audience very much; the vivid-coloured jackets and sashes, the scarlet drapery of the women, and the green and jonquil fans prevented the crowd from presenting that black, lugubrious aspect which always distinguishes it in France, where the sombre tints predominate.

There was a great number of women present, and I remarked very many pretty ones among them. Never did more gentle, Madonnalike faces, more silken eyelashes, or more gentle smiles ever watch over a sleeping child. The various chances of the bull's death are attentively observed by pale, lovely beings, of whom an elegiac poet would be glad to make an Elvira. The merit of the different rusts is discussed by mouths so pretty that you would fain hear them talk of nothing but love. Beacuse they behold unmoved scenes of carnage which would cause our sensitive Parisian beauties to faint, it must not be inferred that they are cruel and deficient in tenderness of soul; in spite of their presence at such sights, they are good, simple-minded, and full of compassion for the unfortunate. But custom is everything; the sanguinary side of a bull-fight, which is what strikes foreigners the most forcibly, is exactly that which least interests Spaniards, who devote their whole attention to the importance of the different blows and the amount of address displayed by the *toreros*, who do not run so great a risk as might at first be imagined.

It was not more than two o'clock, ard the sun inundated with a deluge of fire all the seats on the side we were placed. How we envied those favoured individuals who were revelling in the bath of shade thrown over them by the upper boxes! After riding thirty leagues in the mountains, the fact of remaining the whole day exposed to an African sun, with the thermometer at thirty-eight, is rather creditable on the part of a wretched critic, who, on this occasion, and paid for his place and did not wish to lose.it.

The *asientos de sombra* (places in the shade) hurled all kinds of sarcasms at us; they sent us the water-merchants, to prevent us from catching fire; they begged permission to light their cigars at our fiery noses, and kindly offered us a little oil in order that we might be properly fried. We answered as successfully as our means would allow, and when the shade, shifting as the day advanced, delivered up one of our tormentors to the rays of the sun, the event was celebrated by shouts of laughter and an endless tumult of applause.

Thanks to some jars full of water, some dozen oranges, and two fans in constant movement, we managed not to catch fire, and we were not quite roasted, nor struck by apoplexy when the musicians took possession of the places set apart for them, and the picket of cavalry proceeded to clear the arena for a whole host of *muchachos* and *mozos*, who, by some inexplicable process, found places among the general mass of spectators, although, mathematically speaking, there was not room for one more; under certain circumstances, however, a crowd is marvellously elastic.

An immense sigh of satisfaction proceeded from the fifteen thousand breasts that were now relieved from the irksome necessity of waiting any longer. The members of the *Ayuntamiento* were greeted with frantic applause, and on their entering their box, the orchestra struck up the national airs—*yo que soy Contrabandista* and the march of *Riego*—the whole assemblage singing them at the same time, clapping their hands, and stamping their feet.

At five o'clock precisely the gates of the arena were thrown open, and the actors in the drama about to be presented proceeded in procession round the circus. At the head were the three *picadores*, Antonio Sanchez and Jose Trigo, both from Seville, and Francisco Briones, from Puerto Real, with their hand upon their hip and their lance upon their foot, as grave as Roman conquerors going in triumph to the Capitol. On the saddles of their horses was the name of the proprietor of the circus, Antonio Maria Alvarez, formed with giltheaded nails. After them came the *capeadores* or *chulos*, with their cocked hats and gaudy-coloured mantles; while the *banderilleros*, dressed like Figaro, followed close behind. In the rear of the *cortège*, in majestic isolation, marched the two *matadores—the swords*, as they are styled in Spain—Montes de Chiclana and Jose Parra de Madrid. Montes was always accompanied by his own faithful quadrille, a very important thing for the safety of the combatants; for in these times of political dissensions it often happens that the Christino *toreros* will not assist the Carlist *toreros* when in danger, and *vice versa*. The procession was significantly terminated by the team of mules destined to remove the dead bulls and horses.

The conflict was about to commence. The Alguacil, dressed in everyday costume, and whose duty it was to carry the keys of the *toril* to the groom of the circus, had a spirited horse, which he managed very awkwardly, prefacing the tragedy with rather an amusing farce. He first lost his hat, and then his stirrups. His trousers, which had no straps, were rucked up as far as his knees in the most grotesque fashion, and, in consequence of the door having been maliciously opened for the bull's entrance, before the alguacil had had time to quit the circus, his fright was increased to a fearful pitch, rendering him still more ridiculous by the contortions he threw himself into on his steed. He was not, however, unhorsed, to the great disappointment of the vulgar; the bull, dazzled by the torrents of light which inundated the arena, did not instantly perceive him, but allowed him to escape without injury. It was therefore in the midst of an immense Homeric and Olympian fit of laughter that the fight began, but silence was soon restored, the bull having ripped up the horse of the first *picador*, and thrown the second.

All our attention was engrossed by Montes, whose name is popular all through Spain, and whose feats of daring form the subject of a thousand wonderful stories. Montes was born at Chiclana, in the neighbourhood of Cadiz. He is from forty to forty-three years of age, and rather above the middle size. He has a serious cast of countenance, a deliberate, measured walk, and a pale olive complexion, with nothing remarkable about him save the mobility of his eyes, which appear to be the only part of his impassible face endowed with life; he seems to be more supple than robust, and owes his success more to his coolness, the justness of his glance, and his profound study, of the art, than to his muscular force. At the very first step a bull takes in the arena, Montes can tell whether he is short or long sighted, whether he is *clear* or *dark*; that is to say, whether he attacks frankly or has recourse to stratagem, whether he is *de muchas piernas* or *aplomado*, light or heavy, and whether he will shut his eyes to execute the *cogida* or keep them open. Thanks to these observations, made with the rapidity of thought, Montes is always enabled to vary his mode of defence as circumstances require. However, as he carries his cool temerity to the greatest possible lengths, he has during his career received a considerable number of thrusts, as the scar down his cheek proves, and on several occasions he has been borne out of the circus grievously wounded.

On this occasion, he wore an extremely elegant and magnificent suit of apple-green silk embroidered with silver, for Montes is a rich man, and, if he still continues to appear in the arena, it is from a love of the art, and the want of strong emotions; his fortune amounts to more than 50,000 duros, which is a considerable sum for him to possess, if we consider what the *matadores* have to pay for their dress, a complete suit costing from 1500 to 2000 francs, and also the perpetual journeys they are always making, accompanied by their quadrille, from one town to another.

Montes is not like other *espadas*, contented with despatching a bull when the signal of his death is given. He is always on the watch, he directs the combat, and comes to the succour of the *picadores* and *chulos* in peril. More than one *torero* owes his life to Montes' intervention. One bull, that would not allow his attention to be diverted by the cloaks that the *chulos* were waving before him, had ripped up the belly of a horse that he had thrown down, and was endeavouring to do the same to the rider, who was protected by the carcass of his steed. Montes seized the savage beast by the tail, and in the midst of the frantic applause of the whole assembly, caused him to waltz round several times, to his infinite disgust; thus allowing time for the *picador* to be carried off. Sometimes he will place himself motionless before the bull, with his arms crossed on his breast, and his eye fixed, and the monster will suddenly stop short, subjugated by his opponent's look, which is as bright, as sharp and as cold as the blade of a sword. A feat of this description is followed by shouts, bellowings, vociferations, stamping of feet, and thunders of bravoes, of which it is impossible to form any idea; a feeling of delirium seizes every one present, a general giddiness causes the fifteen thousand spectators intoxicated with *aguardiente*, sunshine, and blood to reel upon their seats; handkerchiefs are waved, and hats thrown up into the air, while Montes alone, calm in the midst of this multitude, enjoys in silence the profound feeling of joy which he restrains within his own breast, merely bowing slightly like a man who is capable of performing many other feats of the same description. I can easily understand a man risking his life every minute for applause like this; it is not dear at the price. O ye singers with golden throats, ye fairy-footed *danseuses*, ye actors of all descriptions, ye emperors and ye poets, ye who fancy that you have excited a people's enthusiasm, you never heard Montes applauded!

Sometimes the spectators themselves beg him to execute one of those daring feats in which he is always successful. A pretty-girl says to him, as she blows him a kiss, "Come Señor Montes, come, Paquirro" (which is his Christian name), "I know how gallant you are; do some trifle, *una cosita*, for a lady." Whereupon Montes leaps over the bull, placing his hand on the animal's neck as he does so, or else, shaking his cape before the animal's muzzle, by a rapid movement, wraps it round him so as to form an elegant piece of drapery with irreproachable folds; he then springs on one side, and lets the bull, who is unable to stop himself, pass by.

The manner in which Montes kills the bull is remarkable for its precision, certainty, and ease: with him all idea of danger ceases; he is so collected and so completely master of himself, he appears so sure of success, that the combat seems no longer to be serious, and, perhaps, loses somewhat of its exciting nature. It is impossible to fear for his life; he strikes the bull where he likes, when he likes, and how he likes. The chances of the conflict become somewhat too unequal; a less skillful *matador* will sometimes produce a more startling effect by the risks and danger which he incurs. This will, perhaps, appear to be a piece of refined barbarity; but *aficionados* and all those persons who have been present at a bull-fight, and felt interested in favour of some particularly courageous, frank bull, will most certainly share our sentiments. A circumstance which happened on the last day of the performances will prove the truth of our assertion as surely as it proved, rather harshly, to Montes, how strictly impartial a Spanish public is both towards man and beast.

A magnificent black bull had just been let loose in the arena. The quick, decided manner in which he issued from the *toril* caused all the connoisseurs present to conceive the highest opinion of him. He possessed all the qualities requisite for a fighting bull; his horns were long, sharp, and well curved; his clean-made, slim, and nervous legs showed his extreme agility, while his broad dewlap and well-developed flanks gave proof of an immense amount of strength; indeed, he was called the Napoleon of the herd, that being the only name capable of conveying a suitable idea of his incontestable superiority. Without hesitating a single instant, he rushed at the *picador* stationed near the *tablas*, overthrew him, together with his horse, who was killed on the spot, and then attacked the second *picador*, who was not more fortunate, and whom the assistants had scarcely time to help over the barrier, severely bruised and injured by his fall. In less than a quarter of an hour six horses lay ripped open on the ground; the *chulos* only shook their coloured capes at a very long distance off, without losing sight of the barrier, over which they leaped immediately Napoleon gave signs of approaching. Montes himself appeared troubled, and on one occasion had actually placed his foot on the ledge of the *tablas*, ready to jump over to the other side, in case he was too closely pressed; a thing he had not done during the two preceding days. The delight of the spectators was made manifest by the most noisy exclamations, and the most flattering compliments for the bull were heard from every mouth. He shortly afterwards performed a new feat of strength, which wound up the enthusiasm to its highest possible pitch.

A *sobre-saliente* (double) *de picador*—for the two principal ones were too much injured to appear again—was awaiting, lance in rest, the attack of the terrible Napoleon; the latter, without paying any attention to the wound he received in the shoulder, caught the horse under the belly, and, with one movement of his head, caused him to fall with his forelegs on the top of the *tablas*; then, raising his hind-quarters by a second movement, sent him and his master completely over the barrier into the corridor of refuge which runs all round the arena.

So great an exploit caused thunders of applause. The bull was master of the field, galloping about victoriously, and amusing himself in default of any other adversaries by tossing into the air the dead bodies of the horses he had already gored. The supply of victims was exhausted, and there were no more horses in the stables of the circus to mount the *picadores*. The *banderilleros* were seated astride upon the *tablas*, not daring to harass with their darts, ornamented with paper, so redoubtable an adversary, whose rage most certainly stood in no need of artificial excitement. The spectators became impatient at this pause in the proceedings, and vociferated, "*Las banderillas! las banderillas! Fuego al alcade.*" To the stake with the alcade for not giving the necessary order! At last, at a sign from the director of the games, one *banderillero* detached himself from the rest, and planted two darts in the neck of the furious animal, immediately retreating as speedily as possible, but yet not quickly enough, as the bull's horn grazed his arm, and tore up his sleeve. On seeing this, and in spite of the hooting and vociferations of the public, the alcade gave the death order, and made a sign to Montes to take his *muleta* and his sword, contrary to all the rules of Tauromachy, which require that a bull shall have received at least four pairs of *banderillas* before being delivered up to the sword of the *matador*.

Instead of advancing, according to his usual custom into the middle of the arena, Montes posted himself at the distance of some twenty paces from the barrier, in order to have a place of refuge in case of failure. He was very pale, and, without indulging in any of those sportive acts and tricks of courage which have procured him the admiration of all Spain, he displayed the scarlet *muleta*, and called the bull, who required no pressing to come up to him. Montes made two or three passes with his *muleta*, holding his sword horizontally on a level with the monster's eyes; suddenly the bull fell down, as if struck by lightning, and after giving one convulsive start, expired. The sword had pierced his forehead and entered his brain, contrary to the rules of the art, which require the *matador* to pass his arm between the horns of the animal, and stab him between the nape of the neck and the shoulders, thereby augmenting the danger of the man, but giving some chance to his four-footed adversary.

When the public understood the blow, for all this had passed with the rapidity of thought, one universal shout of indignation rose from the *tendidos* to the *palcos*; a storm of abuse and hisses, accompanied by the most incredible tumult, burst forth on all sides. "Butcher, assassin, brigand, thief, galley-slave, headsman!" were the gentlest terms employed. "*A centa Montes*! To the stake with Montes! To the dogs with Montes! Death to the alcade!" were the cries which were everywhere heard. Never did I behold such a degree of fury, and I blush to own that I shared in it myself. Mere vociferations, however, did not long suffice; the crowd commenced throwing at the poor wretch fans, hats, sticks, jars full of water, and pieces of the benches torn up for the purpose. There was still one more bull to kill, but his death took place unperceived, in the midst of the horrible tumult. It was Jose Para, the second *espada*, who despatched the bull, with two very skillful thrusts. As for Montes, he was livid; his face turned green with rage, and his teeth made the blood start from his white lips, although he displayed great calmness, and leant with affected gracefulness on the hilt of his sword, the point of which, reddened against the rules, he had wiped in the sand.

On what does popularity depend! On the first and second days of the performance no person would ever have conceived it possible that so sure an artist, one so certain of his public as Montes, could be punished with such severity for an infraction of the rules, which was, doubtless, called for by the most imperious necessity, on account of the extraordinary agility, strength, and fury of the animal. When the fight was concluded he got into a calessin, followed by his quadrille, and swearing by all that he held sacred that he would never put his foot in Malaga again. I do not know whether he has kept his word, and remembered the insults of the last day longer than the triumphs and applause of the two preceding ones. At present I am of opinion that the public of Malaga was unjust towards the great Montes de Chiclana, all whose blows had been superbly aimed, and who, in every case of danger, had displayed heroic coolness and admirable address, so much so, indeed, that the delighted audience had made him a present of all the bulls he killed, and allowed him to cut off an ear of each, to show that they were his property, and could not be claimed either by the hospital or the proprietor of the circus.

We returned to our *parador*, giddy, intoxicated, and saturated with violent emotion, hearing nothing, as we passed along the streets, but the praises of the bull, and imprecations against Montes.

ITALY

HOW FRIAR JOHN OF PIAN DE CARPINE JOURNEYED TO THE COURT OF KUYUK KHAN [1]

As related by Friar Benedict the Pole

(1245)

In the year of Our Lord one thousand two hundred and forty-five Friar John of the order of Minor Friars, and of Pian de Carpine, despatched by the Lord Pope to the Tartars in company with another friar, left Lyons, in France, where the Pope was, on Easter day (16th April), and having arrived in Poland he took at Breslau a third friar of the same order, Benedict by name, a Pole by nationality, to be the companion of his labour and tribulations and to act as his interpreter. Through the assistance of Conrad, Duke of the Poles, they reached Kiew, a city of Ruscia, now under the dominion of the Tartars. The headman of the city gave them an escort for a distance of six days thence to the first camp of the Tartars, near the border of Comania.

When the chiefs of this camp heard that they were envoys of the Pope they asked for and received presents from them. Friars John and Benedict having by their order left behind the third friar, who was too feeble, also their horses and the servants they had brought with them, set out for a second camp on the Tartars' own horses and with pack-animals provided by them; and so, after changing horses at several camps, they came on the third day to the chief of an army of eight thousand men, and his attendants, having asked for and received presents, conducted them to their chief Curoniza. He questioned them as to the motive of their journey and the nature of their business. This having been stated, he gave them three of his Tartars, who got them supplied with horses and food from on army to another, till finally they came to a prince, Bati by name, who is one of the greatest princes of the Tartars, and the same that ravaged Ungaria.

On the route thither they crossed the rivers called Nepere and Don. They spent five weeks and more on the road, to wit, from the Sunday, *Invocavit*,[2] to the Thursday, *Cenæ Domini*,[3] on which day they reached Bati, finding him beside the great river Ethil, which the Ruscians call Volga, and which is

1 From *The Journey of William of Rubruck to the Eastern Parts of the World (1253-55), with Two Accounts of the Earlier Journey of John of Pian de Carpine, translated* from the Latin and edited by William Woodville Rockhill (Hakluyt Society, 1900, Second Series, No. IV).

2 The first Sunday in Lent (February 26, 1246).

3 Holy Thursday (April 5, 1246).

believed to be the Tanais. The attendants of Bati having asked for and received presents, consisting of forty beaver-skins and eighty badger-skins, these presents were carried between two consecrated fires; and the Friars were obliged to follow the presents, for it is a custom among the Tartars to purify ambassadors and gifts by fire. Beyond the fires there was a cart with a golden statue of the Emperor, which it is likewise customary to worship. But the Friars refusing positively to worship it, were nevertheless obliged to bow their heads before it. Bati, having heard the letter of the Pope, and examined every word of it, sent them after five days—that is to say, on the Tuesday after Easter—together with his letters which he gave to one of their own Tartar guides, to the son of the great Emperor, which son's name is Cuyuc Kan, in the fatherland of the Tartars.

Leaving therefore Prince Bati, the Friars, having wrapped their legs with bandages, so as to be able to bear the fatigue of riding, left Comania behind after two weeks. In this country they found a great deal of wormwood, for this country was once called Pontus, and Ovidius says of Pontus:

Tristia per vacous horrent absinthia campos,

While the Friars were travelling through Comania they had on their right the country of the Saxi, whom we believe to be Goths, and who are Christians; after them the Gazars, who are Christians. In this country is the rich city of Ornarum, which was captured by the Tartars by means of inundations of water. After that the Circasses, and they are Christians; after that the Georgians, and they too are Christians. Prior to that, while in Ruscia, they had the Morduans on their left, and they are pagans, and for the most part they shave the backs of their heads. After them were the Bylers, and they are pagans; and after that the Bascards, who are the ancient Ungari; then the Cynocephales, who have dogs' heads; and then the Parocitæ, who have a small narrow mouth, who can masticate nothing, but who live on liquids and sustain themselves on the odours of meats and fruits.

On the border of Comania they crossed a river called Jaiac, and there begins the country of the Kangitæ. They travelled through this for twenty days, and they found few people there, but many swamps and vast salt marshes and salt rivers, which we take to be the Mæotide swamps. For eight days they went through a vast desert, barren and sandy. After the country of the Kangitæ they came to Turkya, where they for the first time found a big city called Janckynt, and they travelled for about ten days in this Turkya. Now, Turkya professes the religion of Machomet. After Turkya they entered a country called Kara-Kytai, which meaneth

Black Kytai; and these people are pagans, and they found no town there. These were once the masters of the Tartars. After that they entered the country of the Tartars on the feast of Mary Magdalen.[1]

They found the Emperor in that country in a great tent which is called Syra-Orda,[2] and here they remained for four months, and they were present at the election of Cuyuc Kan, their Emperor. And the same Friar Benedict the Pole told us orally that he and the other friar saw there about five thousand great and mighty men, who on the first day of the election of the king, all appeared dressed in baldakin; but neither on that day nor on the next, when they appeared in white samites, did they reach an agreement. But on the third day, when they wore red samites, they came to an agreement and made the election. This same friar declared also that about three thousand envoys, coming from different parts of the world, were present at that same court with messages, letter, tribute or presents of divers kinds and in great numbers. These same friars, who were counted among them, had to put on, as of necessity bound, baldakin over their gowns, for no ambassador may appear in the presence of the chosen and crowned sovereign unless he be properly dressed.

Having been taken into the Syra-Orda—that is to say, the tent of the Emperor—they saw him there crowned and gorgeous in splendid attire seated on a raised dais, richly ornamented with gold and silver, and above it was trellis-work, and around the edge four separate flights of steps led up to the platform. Three of these flights were in front of the dais; by the middle one the Emperor alone goes up or comes down, by the two side ones the nobles and others pass, but by the fourth, which is behind the Emperor, his mother, his wife, and his relatives ascend. The Syra-Orda had three openings in guise of doors; the middle one, which far exceeded the others in size, was always left without any guard, the King alone entering by it. And if anyone else should have entered by it, he would have been without a doubt put to death. The two other side doors were closed with silk hangings, and had very rigid guards, who watched them in arms, and through these everyone else passed with sings of reverence for fear of the established punishment.

On the third day the letter of the Lord Pope was carefully listened to and gone over through the medium of officials and interpreters. After that the Friars were sent to the mother of the Emperor, whom they found in another locality, seated in like fashion, in a large and most beautiful tent. After

[1] Friar John, who was at this time about sixty-five years of age, had thus ridden something like three thousand miles in one hundred and six days.

[2] Yellow Pavilion.

receiving them with great courtesy and friendliness, she sent them back to her son. While they were stopping there, they used frequently to have with them some of the Georgians living among the Tartars. They are quite respected by the Tartars, because they are a strong and warlike people. They are called Georgians because Saint George aids them in their fights; and he is their patron and they honour him above all other saints. They use the Greek idiom in their Holy Scriptures, and they have crosses over their tents and carts. The customs of the Greeks are observed in divine service among the Tartars.

The business on which the Friars had come having been settled, they took their leave of the Emperor, carrying back with them letters of his signed with his seal to the Lord Pope; and they went their way back, travelling westward with the ambassadors of the soldan of Babylon, who after accompanying them for fifteen days then left them and turned southward. The Friars continued on their journey westward, and after passing the Rhine at Cologne, got back to the Lord Pope in Lyons, and presented to him the letters of the Emperor of the Tartars.

MARCO POLO EPITOMIZES HIS GREAT TRAVELS AND TELLS OF THE SPIRITS OF THE DESERT [1]

Marco Polo

(*c.* 1254–*c.* 1324)

I

At the time when Baldwin II was Emperor of Constantinople, where a magistrate representing the Doge of Venice then resided, and in the year of Our Lord 1250, Nicolò Polo, the father of Marco, and Maffeo, the brother of Nicolò, respectable and well-informed men, embarked in a ship of their own, with a rich and varied cargo of merchandise, and reached Constantinople in safety. After mature deliberation on the subject of their proceedings it was determined, as the measure most likely to improve their trading capital, that they should prosecute their voyage into the Euxine or Black Sea. With this view they made purchases of many fine and costly jewels, and taking their departure from Constantinople, navigated that sea to a port named Soldaria, from whence they travelled on horseback many days until they reached the court of a powerful chief of the Western Tartars, named Barka, who dwelt in the cities of Bolgara and Assara, and had the reputation

[1] From *The Travels of Marco Polo, the Venetian.*

of being one of the most liberal and civilized princes hitherto known amongst the tribes of Tartary. He expressed much satisfaction at the arrival of these travellers, and received them with marks of distinction. In return for which courtesy, when they had laid before him the jewels they brought with them, and perceived that their beauty pleased him, they presented them for his acceptance. The liberality of this conduct on the part of the two brothers struck him with admiration; and being unwilling that they should surpass him in generosity, he not only directed double the value of the jewels to be paid to them, but made them in addition several rich presents.

The brothers having resided a year in the dominions of this prince, they became desirous of revisiting their native country, but were impeded by the sudden breaking out of a war between him and another chief, named Alaù, who ruled over the Eastern Tartars. In a fierce and very sanguinary battle that ensued between their respective armies, Alaù was victorious, in consequence of which, the roads being rendered unsafe for travellers, the brothers could not attempt to return by the way they came; and it was recommended to them, as the only practicable mode of reaching Constantinople, to proceed in an easterly direction, by an unfrequented route, so as to skirt the limits of Barka's territories. Accordingly they made their way to a town named Oukaka, situated on the confines of the kingdom of the Western Tartars. Leaving that place, and advancing still further, they crossed the Tigris, one of the four rivers of Paradise, and came to a desert, the extent of which was seventeen days' journey, wherein they found neither town, castle, nor any substantial building, but only Tartars with their herds, dwelling in tents on the plain. Having passed this tract, they arrived at length at a well-built city called Bokhara, in a province of that name, belonging to the dominions of Persia, and the noblest city of that kingdom, but governed by a prince whose name was Barak. Here, from inability to proceed further, they remained three years.

It happened while these brothers were in Bokhara, that a person of consequence and gifted with eminent talents made his appearance there. He was proceeding as ambassador from Alaù before mentioned, to the Grand Khan, supreme chief of all the Tartars, named Kublaï, whose residence was at the extremity of the continent, in a direction between north-east and east. Not having ever before had an opportunity, although he wished it, of seeing any natives of Italy, he was gratified in a high degree at meeting and conversing with these brothers, who had now become proficients in the Tartar language; and after associating with them for several days, and finding their manners agreeable to him, he proposed to them that they should accompany him to the presence of the Great Khan, who would be pleased by their appearance at his court, which had not hitherto been visited by any person from their country; adding assurances that they would be honourably received, and recompensed with many gifts. Convinced as they were that their endeavours to return homeward would expose them to the most imminent risks, they agreed to this proposal, and recommending themselves to the protection of the Almighty, they set out on their journey in the suite of the ambassador, attended by several Christian servants whom they had brought with them from Venice. The course they took at first was between the north-east and north, and an entire year was consumed before they were enabled to reach the imperial residence, in consequence of the extraordinary delays occasioned by the snows and the swelling of the rivers, which obliged them to halt until the former had melted and the floods had subsided.

Being introduced to the presence of the Grand Khan, Kublaï, the travellers were received by him with the condescension and affability that belonged to his character, and as they were the first Latins who had made their appearance in that country, they were entertained with feasts and honoured with other marks of distinction. Entering graciously into conversation with them, he made earnest enquiries on the subject of the western parts of the world, of the emperor of the Romans, and of other Christian kings and princes. He wished to be informed of their relative consequence, the extent of their possessions, the manner in which justice was administered in their several kingdoms and principalities, how they conducted themselves in warfare, and above all he questioned them particularly respecting the pope, the affairs of the church, and the religious worship and doctrine of the Christians. Being well instructed and discreet men, they gave appropriate answers upon all these points, and as they were perfectly acquainted with the Tartar (Moghul) language, they expressed themselves always in becoming terms; insomuch that the Grand Khan, holding them in high estimation, frequently commanded their attendance.

When he had obtained all the information that the two brothers communicated with so much good sense he expressed himself well satisfied, and having formed in his mind the design of employing them as his ambassadors to the Pope, after consulting with his ministers on the subject, he proposed to them, with many kind entreaties, that they should accompany one of his officers, named Khogatal, on a mission to the see of Rome. His object, he told them, was to make a request to his holiness that he would send to him a hundred men of learning, thoroughly acquainted with the principles of the Christian religion, as well as with the seven arts, and qualified to prove to the learned of his dominions, by just and fair argument, that the faith professed by Christians is superior to, and founded upon more evident truth than, any other; that the gods of the Tartars and the idols worshipped in their houses were only evil spirits, and that they and the people of the East in general were under an error in reverencing them as divinities. He moreover signified his pleasure that upon their return they should bring with them, from Jerusalem, some of the holy oil from the lamp which is kept burning over the sepulchre of our Lord Jesus Christ, whom he professed to hold in veneration and to consider as the true God. Having heard these commands addressed to them by the Grand Khan, they humbly prostrated themselves before him, declaring their willingness and instant readiness to perform, to the utmost of their ability, whatever might be the royal will. Upon which he caused letters, in the Tartarian language, to be written in his name to the Pope of Rome, and these he delivered into their hands. He likewise gave orders that they should be furnished with a golden tablet displaying the imperial cipher, according to the usage established by his majesty; in virtue of which the person bearing it, together with his whole suite, are safely conveyed and escorted from station to station by the governors of all places within the imperial dominions, and are entitled, during the time of their residing in any city, castle, town, or village, to a supply of provisions, and everything necessary for their accommodation.

Being thus honourably commissioned they took their leave of the Grand Khan, and set out on their journey, but had not proceeded more than twenty days when the officer, named Khogatal, their companion, fell dangerously ill, in the city named Alau. In this dilemma it was determined, upon consulting all who were present, and with the approbation of the man himself, that they should leave him behind. In the prosecution of their journey they derived essential benefit from being provided with the royal tablet, which procured them attention in every place through which they passed. Their expenses were defrayed, and escorts were furnished. But notwithstanding these advantages, so great were the natural difficulties they had to encounter, from the extreme cold, the snow, the ice, and the flooding of the rivers, that their progress was unavoidably tedious, and three years elapsed before they were enabled to reach a sea-port town in the lesser Armenia, named Laiassus. Departing from thence by sea they arrived at Acre in the month of April 1269, and there learned, with extreme concern, that Pope Clement the Fourth was recently dead. A legate whom he had appointed, named M. Tebaldo de' Vesconti di Piacenza, was at this time resident in Acre, and to him they gave an account of what they had in command from the Grand Khan of Tartary. He advised them by all means to wait the election of another Pope, and when that should take place to proceed with the objects of their embassy. Approving of this counsel, they determined upon employing the interval in a visit to their families in Venice. They accordingly embarked at Acre in a ship bound to Negropont, and from thence went on to Venice, where Nicolò Polo found that his wife, whom he had left with child at his departure, was dead, after having been delivered of a son, who received the name of Marco, and was now of the age of nineteen years.

In the meantime the election of a Pope was retarded by so many obstacles that they remained two years in Venice, continually expecting its accomplishment; when at length, becoming apprehensive that the Grand Khan might be displeased at their delay, or might suppose it was not their intention to revisit his country, they judged it expedient to return to Acre; and on this occasion they took with them young Marco Polo. Under the sanction of the legate they made a visit to Jerusalem, and there provided themselves with some of the oil belonging to the lamp of the holy sepulchre, conformably to the directions of the Grand Khan. As soon as they were furnished with his letters addressed to that prince, bearing testimony to the fidelity with which they had endeavoured to execute his commission, and explaining to him that the Pope of the Christian Church had not as yet been chosen, they proceeded to the before-mentioned port of Laiassus. Scarcely, however, had they taken their departure when the legate received messengers from Italy, despatched by the college of cardinals, announcing his own elevation to the papal chair; and he thereupon assumed the name of Gregory the Tenth. Considering that he was now in a situation that enabled him fully to satisfy the wishes of the Tartar sovereign, he hastened to transmit letters to the King of Armenia, communicating to him the event of his election, and requesting, in case the two ambassadors who were on their way to the Court of the Grand Khan should not have already quitted his dominions, that he would give directions for their immediate return. These letters found them still in Armenia, and with great alacrity they obeyed the summons to repair once more to Acre; for which purpose the king furnished them with an armed galley; sending at the same time an ambassador from himself, to offer his congratulations to the sovereign pontiff.

Upon their arrival his Holiness received them in a distinguished manner, and immediately despatched them with letters papal, accompanied by two friars of the order of Preachers, who happened to be on the spot; men of letters and of science, as well as profound theologians, One of them was named Fra Nicolò da Vicenza, and the other, Fra Guielmo da Tripoli. To them he gave licence and authority to ordain priests, to consecrate bishops, and to grant absolution as fully as he could do in his own person. He also charged them with valuable presents, and among these, several handsome vases of crystal, to be delivered to the Grand Khan in his name, and along with his benediction. Having taken leave, they again steered their course to the port of Laiassus, where they landed, and from thence proceeded into the country of Armenia. Here they received intelligence that the soldan of Babylonia, named Bundokdari, had invaded the Armenian territory with a numerous army, and had overrun and laid waste the country to a great extent. Terrified at these accounts, and apprehensive for their lives, the two friars determined not to proceed further, and delivering over to the Venetians the letters and presents entrusted to them by the Pope, they placed themselves under the protection of the Master of the Knights Templars, and with him returned directly to the coast. Nicolò, Maffeo, and Marco, however, undismayed by perils or difficulties (to which they had long been inured), passed the borders of Armenia, and prosecuted their journey. After crossing deserts of several days' march, and passing many dangerous defiles, they advanced so far, in a direction between north-east and north, that at length they gained information of the Grand Khan, who then had his residence in a large and magnificent city named Cle-men-fu. Their whole journey to this place occupied no less than three years and a half; but during the winter months, their progress had been inconsiderable. The Grand Khan having notice of their approach whilst still remote, and being aware how much they must have suffered from fatigue, sent forward to meet them at the distance of forty days' journey, and gave orders to prepare in every place through which they were to pass whatever might be requisite to their comfort. By these means, and through the blessing of God, they were conveyed in safety to the royal Court.

Upon their arrival they were honourably and graciously received by the Grand Khan, in a full assembly of his principal officers. When they drew nigh to his person they paid their respects by prostrating themselves on the floor. He immediately commanded them to rise, and to relate to him the circumstances of their travels, with all that had taken place in their negotiations with his Holiness the Pope. To their narrative, which they gave in the regular order of events and delivered in perspicuous language, he listened with attentive silence. The letters and the presents from Pope Gregory were then laid before him, and, upon hearing the former read, he bestowed much commendation on the fidelity, the zeal, and the diligence of his ambassadors; and, receiving with due reverence the oil from the holy sepulchre, he gave directions that it should be preserved with religious care. Upon his observing Marco Polo, and inquiring who he was, Nicolò made answer, "This is your servant and my son"; upon which the Grand Khan replied, "He is welcome, and it pleases me much," and he caused him to be enrolled amongst his attendants of honour. And on account of their return he made a great feast and rejoicing; and as long as the said brothers and Marco remained in the Court of the Grand Khan they were honoured even above his own courtiers. Marco was held in high estimation and respect by all belonging to the Court. He learnt in a short time and adopted the manners of the Tartars, and acquired a proficiency in four different languages, which he became qualified to read and write. Finding him thus accomplished, his master was desirous of putting his talents for business to the proof, and sent him on an important concern of state to a city named Karazan, situated at the distance of six months' journey from the imperial residence; on which occasion he conducted himself with so much wisdom and prudence in the management of the affairs entrusted to him, that his services became highly acceptable. On his part, perceiving that the Grand Khan took a pleasure in hearing accounts of whatever was new to him respecting the customs and manners of people, and the peculiar circumstances of distant countries, he endeavoured, wherever he went, to obtain correct information on these subjects, and made notes of all he saw and heard, in order to gratify the curiosity of his master. In short, during seventeen years that he continued in his service, he rendered himself so useful that he was employed on confidential missions to every part of the empire and its dependencies; and sometimes also he travelled on his own private account, but always with the consent, and sanctioned by the authority, of the Grand Khan. Under such circumstances it was that Marco Polo had the opportunity of acquiring a knowledge, either by his own observation, or what he collected from others, of so many things, until his time unknown, respecting the eastern parts of the world, and which he diligently and regularly committed to writing. And by this means he obtained so much honour that he provoked the jealousy of the other officers of the Court.

Our Venetians having now resided many years at the imperial Court, and in that time having realized considerable wealth, in jewels of value and in gold, felt a strong desire to revisit their native country, and, however honoured and caressed by the sovereign, this sentiment was ever predominant in their minds. It became the more decidedly their object, when they reflected on the very advanced age of the Grand Khan, whose death, if it should happen previously to their departure, might deprive them of that public assistance by which alone they could expect to surmount the innumerable difficulties of so long a journey, and reach their homes in safety; which on the contrary, in his lifetime, and through his favour, they might reasonably hope to accomplish. Nicolò Polo accordingly took an opportunity one day, when he observed him to be more than usually cheerful, of throwing himself at his feet, and soliciting on behalf of himself and his family to be indulged with his Majesty's gracious permission for their departure. But far from showing himself disposed to comply with the request, he appeared hurt at the application, and asked what motive they could have for wishing to expose themselves to all the inconveniences and hazards of a journey in which they might probably lose their lives. If gain, he said, was their object, he was ready to give them the double of whatever they possessed, and to gratify them with honours to the extent of their desires; but that, from the regard he bore to them, he must positively refuse their petition.

It happened, about this period, that a queen named Bolgana, the wife of Arghun, sovereign of India, died, and as her last request (which she likewise left in a testamentary writing) conjured her husband that no one might succeed to her place on his throne and in his affections who was not a descendant of her own family, now settled under the dominion of the Grand Khan, in the country of Kathay. Desirous of complying with this solemn entreaty, Arghun deputed three of his nobles, discreet men, whose names were Ulatai, Apusca, and Goza, attended by a numerous retinue, as his ambassadors to the Grand Khan, with a request that he might receive at his hands a maiden to wife from among the relatives of his deceased queen. The application was taken in good part, and under the directions of his Majesty choice was made of a damsel aged seventeen, extremely handsome and accomplished, whose name was Kogatin, and of whom the ambassadors, upon her being shown to them, highly approved. When everything was arranged for their departure, and a numerous suite of attendants appointed, to do honour to the future consort of King Arghun, they received from the Grand Khan a gracious dismissal, and set out on their return by the way they came. Having travelled for eight months, their further progress was obstructed and the roads shut up against them, by fresh wars that had broken out amongst the Tartar princes. Much against their inclinations, therefore, they were constrained to adopt the measure of returning to the Court of the Grand Khan, to whom they stated the interruption they had met with.

About the time of their reappearance Marco Polo happened to arrive from a voyage he had made, with a few vessels under his orders, to some parts of the East Indies, and reported to the Grand Khan the intelligence he brought respecting the countries he had visited, with the circumstances of his own navigation, which, he said, was performed in those seas with the utmost safety. This latter observation having reached the ears of the three ambassadors, who were extremely anxious to return to their own country, from whence they had now been absent three years, they presently sought a conference with our Venetians, whom they found equally desirous of revisiting their home; and it was settled between them that the former, accompanied by their young queen, should obtain an audience of the Grand Khan, and represent to him with what convenience and security they might effect their return by sea, to the dominions of their master; whilst the voyage would be attended with less expense than the journey by land, and be performed in a shorter time; according to the experience of Marco Polo, who had lately sailed in those parts. Should his Majesty incline to give his consent to their adopting that mode of conveyance they were then to urge him to suffer the three Europeans, as beings persons well skilled in the practice of navigation, to accompany them until they should reach the territory of King Arghun. The Grand Khan upon receiving this application showed by his countenance that it was exceedingly displeasing to him, averse as he was to parting with the Venetians. Feeling, nevertheless, that he could not with propriety do otherwise than consent, he yielded to their entreaty. Had it not been that he found himself constrained by the importance and urgency of this peculiar case they would never otherwise have obtained permission to withdraw themselves from his service. He sent for them, however, and addressed them with much kindness and condescension, assuring them of his regard, and requiring from them a promise that when they should have resided some time in Europe and with their own family they would return to him once more. With this object in view he caused them to be furnished with the golden tablet (or royal *chop*), which contained his order for their having free and safe conduct through every part of his dominions, with the needful supplies for themselves and their attendants. He likewise gave them authority to act in the capacity of his ambassadors to the Pope, the Kings of France and Spain, and the other Christian princes.

At the same time preparations were made for the equipment of fourteen ships, each having four masts, and capable of being navigated with nine sails, the construction and rigging of which would admit of ample description; but, to avoid prolixity, it is omitted. Among these vessels there were at least four or five that had crews of two hundred and fifty or two hundred and sixty men. On them were embarked the ambassadors, having the queen under their protection, together with Nicolò, Maffeo, and Marco Polo, when they had first taken their leave of the Grand Khan, who presented them with many rubies and other handsome jewels of great value. He also gave directions that the ships should be furnished with stores and provisions for two years.

After a navigation of about three months, they arrived at an island which lay in a southerly direction, named Java, where they saw various objects worthy of attention, of which notice shall be taken in the sequel of the work. Taking their departure from thence, they employed eighteen months in the Indian seas before they were enabled to reach the place of their destination in the territory of king Arghun; and here it may be proper to mention, that between the day of their sailing and that of their arrival, they lost by deaths, of the crews of the vessels and others who were embarked, about six hundred persons; and of the three ambassadors, only one, whose name was Goza, survived the voyage; whilst of all the ladies and female attendants one only died.

Upon landing they were informed that king Arghun had died some time before, and that the government of the country was then administered, on behalf of his son, who was still a youth, by a person of the name of Ki-akato. From him they desired to receive instructions as to the manner in which they were to dispose of the princess, whom, by the orders of the late king, they had conducted thither. His answer was, that they ought to present the lady to Kasan, the son of Arghun, who was then at a place on the borders of Persia, which has its denomination from the Arbor secco, where an army of sixty thousand men was assembled for the purpose of guarding certain passes against the irruption of the enemy. This they proceeded to carry into execution, and having effected it, they returned to the residence of Ki-akato, because the road they were afterwards to take lay in that direction. Here, however, they reposed themselves for the space of nine months. When they took their leave he furnished them with four golden tablets, each of them a cubit in length, five inches wide, and weighing three or four marks of gold. Their inscription began with invoking the blessing of the Almighty upon the Grand Khan, that his name might be held in reverence for many years, and denouncing the punishment of death and confiscation of goods to all who should refuse obedience to the mandate. It then proceeded to direct that the three ambassadors, as his representatives, should be treated throughout his dominions with due honour, that their expenses should be defrayed, and that they should be provided with the necessary escorts. All this was fully complied with, and from many places they were protected by bodies of two hundred horse; nor could this have been dispensed with, as the government of Ki-akato was unpopular, and the people were disposed to commit insults and proceed to outrages, which they would not have dared to attempt under the rule of their proper sovereign. In the course of their journey our travellers received intelligence of the Grand Khan (Kublaï) having departed this life;

which entirely put an end to all prospect of their revisiting those regions. Pursuing, therefore, their intended route, they at length reached the city of Trebizond, from whence they proceeded to Constantinople, then to Negropont, and finally to Venice, at which place, in the enjoyment of health and abundant riches, they safely arrived in the year 1295. On this occasion they offered up their thanks to God, who had now been pleased to relieve them from such great fatigues, after having preserved them from innumerable perils.

II

The town of Lop is situated towards the north-east, near the commencement of the great desert, which is called the Desert of Lop. It belongs to the dominions of the Grand Khan, and the inhabitants are of the Mahometan religion. Travellers who intend to cross the desert usually halt for a considerable time at this place, as well to repose from their fatigues as to make the necessary preparations for their further journey. For this purpose they load a number of stout asses and camels with provisions and with their merchandise. Should the former be consumed before they have completed the passage, they kill and eat the cattle of both kinds; but camels are commonly here employed in preference to asses, because they carry heavy burthens and are fed with a small quantity of provender. The stock of provisions should be laid in for a month, that time being required for crossing the desert in the narrowest part. To travel it in the direction of its length would prove a vain attempt, as little less than a year must be consumed, and to convey stores for such a period would be found impracticable. During these thirty days the journey is invariably over either sandy plains or barren mountains; but at the end of each day's march you stop at a place where water is procurable; not indeed in sufficient quantity for large numbers, but enough to supply a hundred persons, together with their beasts of burthen. At three or four of these halting-places the water is salt and bitter, but at the others, amounting to about twenty, it is sweet and good. In this tract neither beasts nor birds are met with, because there is no kind of food for them.

It is asserted as a well-known fact that this desert is the abode of many evil spirits, which amuse travellers to their destruction with most extraordinary illusions. If, during the daytime, any persons remain behind on the road, either when overtaken by sleep or detained by their natural occasions, until the caravan has passed a hill and is no longer in sight, they unexpectedly hear themselves called to by their names, and in a tone of voice to which they are accustomed. Supposing the call to proceed from their companions, they are led away by it from the direct road, and not knowing in what direction to advance, are left to perish. In the night-time they are persuaded they hear the march of a large cavalcade on one side or the other of the road, and concluding the noise to be that of the footsteps of their party, they direct theirs to the quarter from whence it seems to proceed; but upon the breaking of day, find they have been misled and drawn into a situation of danger. Sometimes likewise during the day these spirits assume the appearance of their travelling companions, who address them by name and endeavour to conduct them out of the proper road. It is said also that some persons, in their course across the desert, have seen what appeared to them to be a body of armed men advancing towards them, and apprehensive of being attacked and plundered have taken to flight. Losing by this means the right path, and ignorant of the direction they should take to regain it, they have perished miserably of hunger. Marvellous indeed, and almost passing belief, are the stories related of these spirits of the desert, which are said at times to fill the air with the sounds of all kinds of musical instruments, and also of drums and the clash of arms; obliging the travellers to close their line of march and to proceed in more compact order. They find it necessary also to take the precaution before they repose for the night, to fix an advanced signal, pointing out the course they are afterwards to hold, as well as to attach a bell to each of the beasts of burthen for the purpose of their being more easily kept from straggling. Such are the excessive troubles and dangers that must unavoidably be encountered in the passage of this desert.

OF VARIOUS DANGERS ENCOUNTERED IN A JOURNEY TO PARIS[1]

Benvenuto Cellini

(1500–71)

I HAD at this time formed a resolution to set out for France, as well because I perceived that the Pope's favour was withdrawn from me, on account of the ill offices of slanderers, who misrepresented my services, as for fear that those enemies of mine, who had most power and influence, might still do me some great injury; for these reasons I was desirous to remove to some other country, and see whether fortune would there prove more favourable to me. Having determined to set out the next morning, I bid my faithful Felice enjoy all I had as his own till my return: and in case I should never come back, my intention was that the whole should devolve to him.

[1] From *Memoirs*, translated by Thomas Roscoe.

Happening at this time to have a Perugian journeyman, who assisted me in making a piece of work for the Pope, I paid him off, and dismissed him my service: the poor man intreated me to let him go with me, offering to bear his own expenses: he observed to me, moreover, that if I should happen to be employed for any time by the king of France, it was proper I should have Italians in my service, especially such as I knew, and were most likely to be of use to me. In a word, he had so persuasive a tongue, that I agreed to carry him with me upon his own terms.

Ascanio happening to be present at this conversation, said to me, with tears in his eyes:

"When you took me again into your service I intended it should be for life, and now I am resolved it shall."

I made answer that should not be upon any account. The poor lad was then preparing to follow me on foot. When I perceived that he had formed such a resolution I hired a horse for him likewise, and, having put my portmanteau behind him, took with me a good deal more baggage than I should otherwise have done.

Leaving Rome, I bent my course to Florence, from whence I travelled to Bologna, Venice, and Padua: upon my arrival at the last city, my friend, Albertaccio del Bene, carried me to his own house from the inn at which I had put up. The day following I went to pay my respects to Signor Pietro Bembo, who was not yet made a cardinal. He gave me the kindest reception I had ever met with; and said to Albertaccio:

"I am resolved that Benvenuto shall stay here with all his company, if they were a hundred in number; so determine to stay here with him, for I will not restore him to you upon any account."

Thus I stayed to enjoy the conversation of that excellent person. He had caused an apartment to be prepared for me, which would have been too magnificent even for a cardinal, and insisted upon my sitting constantly next to him at table; he then intimated to me, in the most modest terms he could think of, that it would be highly agreeable to him if I were to draw his likeness; there was, luckily for me, nothing that I desired more; so having put some pieces of the whitest alabaster into a little box, I began the work, applying the first day or two hours without ceasing. I made so fine a sketch of the head that my illustrious friend was astonished at it; for though he was a person of immense literature, and had an uncommon genius for poetry, he had not the least knowledge of my business; for which reason he thought that I had finished the figure when I had hardly begun it; insomuch that I could not make him sensible that it required a considerable time to bring it to perfection. At last I formed a resolution to take my own time about it, and finish it in the completest manner I could; but as he wore a short beard; according to the Venetian fashion, I found it a very difficult matter to make a head to please myself. I, however, finished it at last, and it appeared to me to be one of the most complete pieces I had ever produced. He appeared to be in the utmost astonishment; for he took it for granted, that as I had made it of wax in two hours, I could make it of steel in ten: but when he saw that it was not possible for me to do it in two hundred, and that I was upon the point of taking my leave of him, in order to set out for France, he was greatly concerned, and begged I would make him a reverse for his medal, and that the devise should be the horse Pegasus, in the midst of a garland of myrtle. This I did in about three hours, and it was finished in an admirable taste; he was highly pleased with it, and said:

"Such a horse as this, appears to be a work ten times more considerable than that little head, upon which you bestowed so much pains; I cannot possibly account for this."

He then begged and prayed of me to make it for him in steel, and said:

"For God's sake oblige me; you can do it very soon, if you will."

I promised him that though it did not suit me to make it there I would do it for him without fail at the first place I happened to fix my residence. Whilst this conversation passed between us, I went to bargain for three horses, which I had occasion for on my journey to France. My illustrious host, who had great interest in Padua, secretly befriended me on the occasion; insomuch that when I was going to pay for the horses, for which I had agreed to give fifty ducats, the owner of them said to me:

"In consideration of your merit, sir, I make you a present of the three horses."

I answered: "It is not you that make me the present; and I do not choose to receive it of him that does, because I have not earned it by my services."

The good man told me, that if I did not take those horses, I could not get any others in Padua, but should be under a necessity of walking. I thereupon went to the munificent Signor Pietro, who affected to know nothing at all of the matter, but loaded me with caresses, and used his utmost persuasions to prevail upon me to stay at Padua. I, who would by no means hear of this, and was determined to perform the journey at any rate, found myself obliged to accept of the three horses, and with them instantly set out for France.

I took the road through the Grisons, for it was unsafe to travel any other way on account of the war. We passed the two great mountains of Alba and Merlina (it was then the eighth of May, and they were covered with snow notwithstanding) at the utmost hazard of our lives. When we had travelled over them, we stopped at a little town, which, as nearly as I can remember, is called Valestat, and there took up our quarters. In the night there arrived a courier from Florence, whose name was Burbacca. I had heard this courier spoken of as a man of character, and clever at his business, but did not know that he had then forfeited that reputation by his knavery. As soon as he saw me at the inn, he called to me by my name, and said that he was going about some business of importance in Lyons, and begged I would be so good as to lend him a little money to defray the expense of his journey. I answered that I could not lend him money, but if he would travel in my company, I would bear his charges as far as Lyons. The rogue then fell a-crying, and counterfeited great concern, telling me, that when a poor courier, who was about business of importance to the nation, happened to be in want of cash, it was the part of a man like me to assist him. He told me at the same time, that he was charged with things of great value belonging to Signor Filippo Strozzi; and as he had a casket with a leather cover, he whispered me very softly, that there were jewels to the amount of many thousand ducats in it, together with letters of the utmost consequence from Signor Filippo Strozzi. I thereupon desired him to let me fasten the jewels somewhere about his body, which would be running less hazard than carrying them in the casket; at the same time he might leave the casket, worth, perhaps, ten crowns, to me, and I would assist him as far as five-and-twenty. The fellow made answer, that he would travel with me in that manner, since he had no other remedy, for it would do him no honour to leave the casket; and so we were both agreed.

Setting out betimes in the morning, we arrived at a place situated between Valestat and Vezza, where there is a lake fifteen miles long, upon which we were to sail to Vezza. When I saw the barks, I was terribly frightened, because they are made of very thin deal boards, neither well nailed together, nor even pitched; and if I had not seen four German gentlemen with their horses in one of them, I should never have ventured on board, but have turned back directly. I thought within myself at seeing the stupid security of these gentlemen, that the waters of the German lakes did not drown the passengers like those of Italy. My two young fellow-travellers said to me:

"Benvenuto, it is a dangerous thing to enter one of these barks with four horses."

My answer to them was:

"Don't you see, ye poor cowards, that those four gentlemen have entered one before you, and that they sail away merrily? If it were a lake of wine, I should fancy that they were rejoiced at the thoughts of being plunged into it;

but as it is a lake of water only, I take it for granted they have no more inclination to be drowned in it than ourselves."

This lake was fifteen miles long, and about three broad; the country, on one side, was a lofty mountain full of caverns, on the other it was level and covered with grass. When we had advanced about four miles, it began to grow stormy, insomuch that the watermen called to us for help, begging that we would assist them in rowing; and so we did for a time. I signified to them soon after, that their best way was to make the opposite shore: but they affirmed it to be impossible, because there was not a sufficient depth of water, so that the bark would be soon beaten to pieces in these shallows and we should all go to the bottom; they however still importuned us to lend them a hand, and were constantly calling out to each other for assistance. As I perceived them in such terror and jeopardy, having a sorrel horse on board, I put on its bridle, and held it in my left hand: the horse, by a kind of instinct and intelligence common to those animals, seemed to perceive my intent; for by turning his face towards the fresh grass, I wanted him to swim to the apposite shore, and carry me over upon his back. At the very same instant there poured in from that side a wave so large, that it almost overwhelmed the vessel. Ascanio then crying out, "Mercy! help me, dear father!" was going to throw himself upon me; but I clapped my hand to my dagger, and bid the rest follow the example I had set them, since by means of their horses they might save their lives, as I hoped to save mine; adding, "That I would kill the first who should offer to throw himself upon me."

In this manner we advanced several miles in the most imminent danger of our lives. When we had advanced about half way, we saw a piece of level ground, under the foot of a mountain, where we might get on shore and refresh ourselves. Here the four German gentlemen had landed. But upon our expressing a desire to go on shore, the watermen would not consent to it upon any account: I then said to my young men:

"Now is the time, my boys, to show your spirit; clap your hands to your swords, and compel them to land us."

We effected our purpose with great difficulty, as they made a long resistance; however, even after we had landed, we were obliged to climb a steep mountain for two miles, which was more difficult than going up a ladder of equal height. I was armed with a coat of mail, had heavy boots, with a fowling-piece in my hand, and it rained as hard as it could pour; those devils of Germans ascended at a surprising rate with their horses, while ours were quite unequal to the task, and ready to sink with the fatigue of climbing the rugged steep.

When we had mounted a good way, Ascanio's horse, which was a fine Hungarian courser, had got a little before Burbacca the courier, and the young man had given him his pike to carry. It happened, through the ruggedness of the road, that the horse slipped, and went staggering on in such a manner, being quite helpless, as to hit against the point of the rogue of a courier's pike, which he could not keep out of the way, and which transpierced the beast in the throat and killed it. My other young man, in attempting to help his brown nag, slipped towards the lake, and caught at a vine-branch which was exceedingly small. Upon this horse there was a cloak-bag, in which I had put all my money, with whatever else I had most valuable, to avoid being under a necessity of carrying it about me: I bid the youth endeavour to save his life, and never mind what became of the horse; the fall was of above a mile, and he would have tumbled headlong down into the lake. Exactly under this place our watermen had planted themselves, so that if the horse had fallen, it would have come souse down upon their heads. I was before all the rest, and stood to see the horse tumble, which seemed, without the least fear, to go headlong to perdition; whereupon I said to my young men:

"Be under no sort of concern, let us endeavour to preserve ourselves, and return thanks to God for all his mercies."

Burbacca told me he was not concerned for his own loss, but for mine. I asked him why he was sorry for my trifling loss, and not for his own, which was so considerable. He than answered in a passion:

"In such a case as this, and considering the terms we are upon, it is proper to tell the whole truth; I know that you had a good heap of ducats in the cloak-bag; as for my casket which I affirmed to be full of jewels and precious stones, it is all a story; there is nothing in it but a little caviar."

When I heard this I could not help laughing; the young fellows laughed also; as for Burbacca, he lamented and expressed great concern for my loss. The horse made an effort to relieve and extricate itself, when we had let it go, so that it was happily saved. Thus laughing and making ourselves merry, we again exerted our strength to ascend the steep mountain.

The four German gentlemen who had got to the summit of the craggy precipice before us, sent some peasants to our assistance. At last we arrived at the miserable inn, wet, tired, and hungry; we were received in the kindest manner by the people of the house, and met with most comfortable refreshment. The horse which had been so much hurt, was cured by means of certain herbs which the hedges are full of; and we were told that if we constantly applied those herbs to the wound, the beast would not only recover, but be of as much use to us as ever; accordingly we did as we were directed. Having thanked the gentlemen, and being well refreshed and recovered of our fatigue, we left the inn, and continued our journey, returning thanks to God for preserving us from so great and imminent a danger. We arrived at a village beyond Vezza, where we took up our quarters; here we heard the watch sing at all the hours of the night very agreeably; and as the houses in town were of wood, he was constantly bidding them take care of their fires. Burbacca, who had been greatly frightened in the day-time, was continually speaking and crying out in his dreams: "O God, I am drowning!" This was occasioned by his panic the day before, and by his having indulged the bottle too freely, and drinking with all the Germans; sometimes he hallooed out, "I am burning!" sometimes "I am drowning!" and sometimes he thought himself in hell suffering punishment for his sins. This night passed away so agreeably, that all our anxiety and trouble were converted into laughter and merriment.

Having risen very early next morning, we proceeded on our journey, and went to dine at a very agreeable place called Lucca; where we met with the best of treatment; we then took guides to conduct us to a town called Zurich. The guide who attended me passed over a dike which was overflowed, so that the stupid creature slipped, and both the horse and he tumbled into the water. I, who was behind, having that instant stopped my horse, staid awhile to see him rise; and behold, the fellow, as if nothing at all had happened, fell a-singing again, and made signs to me to go on. I thereupon turned to the right, and, breaking through certain hedges, served as a guide to Burbacca and my young men. The guide fell a-scolding, telling me, in the German language, that if the country people saw me they would put them to death. We travelled on and escaped this second danger. Our next stage was Zürich, a fine city, which may be compared to a jewel for lustre, and there we staid a day to rest ourselves; we left it early in the morning, and arrived at another handsome town called Solothurn; from thence we proceeded to Lausanne, Geneva, and Lyons: we stopped four days at this last city, having travelled thither very merrily, singing and laughing all the way. I enjoyed myself highly in the company of some of my friends, was reimbursed the expenses I had been at, and, at the expiration of four days, set out for Paris. This part of our journey was exceedingly agreeable; except only that when we came as far as Palesse, a gang of freebooters made an attempt to assassinate us, and with great difficulty we escaped them. From thence we continued our journey to Paris, without meeting any ill accident, and travelling on in uninterrupted mirth, arrived safely at that metropolis.

RAMESES II SETS OUT FOR ENGLAND [1]

(1816)

GIOVANNI BATTISTA BELZONI

(1778–1823)

[Born in Padua, Belzoni came in 1803 to London, where with his wife he became eventually a performer of feats of strength at Astley's Circus. His next feat was to invent a hydraulic machine and take it out to Egypt in the hope of regulating the waters of the Nile. Failing to win over Mohammed Ali to his scheme, he determined on a journey up the Nile. Whereupon he was asked by the British Consul, Henry Salt, if he would undertake the bringing down from Thebes of the colossal bust of Rameses II, then known as Young Memnon. Belzoni, "undertaking the enterprise cheerfully," set out from Boolak on June 30, 1816, his "implements for the operation" being only " a few poles and ropes of palm leaves." And on July 22 he and Mrs Belzoni—who was "determined to accompany me—saw for the first time the ruins of great Thebes."]

On the 22nd we saw for the first time the ruins of great Thebes, and landed at Luxor. It is absolutely impossible to imagine the scene displayed. It appeared to me like entering a city of giants, who, after a long conflict, were all destroyed, leaving the ruins of their various temples as the only proofs of their former existence. The temple of Luxor presents to the traveller at once one of the most splendid groups of Egyptian grandeur. The extensive propylæon, with the two obelisks, and colossal statues in the front; the thick groups of enormous columns; the variety of apartments and the sanctuary it contains; the beautiful ornaments which adorn every part of the walls and columns, the battles on the propylæon . . . cause in the astonished traveller an oblivion of all that he has seen before. If his attention be attracted to the north side of Thebes by the towering remains that project a great height above the wood of palm trees, he will gradually enter that forest-like assemblage of ruins of temples, columns, obelisks, colossi, sphynxes, portals, and an endless number of other astonishing objects, that will convince him at once of the impossibility of a description.

On the west side of the Nile, still the traveller finds himself among wonders. The temples of Gournou, Memnonium, and Medinet Aboo attest the extent of the great city on this side. The unrivalled colossal figures in the plains of Thebes, the number of tombs excavated in the rocks, those in the great valley of the kings, with their paintings, sculptures, mummies, sar-

[1] From *Narrative of the Operations and Recent Discoveries . . . in Egypt and Nubia* (1822).

cophagi, figures, etc., are all objects worthy of the admiration of the traveller; who will not fail to wonder how a nation, which was once so great as to erect these stupendous edifices, could so far fall into oblivion, that even their language and writing are totally unknown to us.

After having taken a cursory view of Luxor and Carnak, to which my curiosity led me on my landing, I crossed the Nile to the west, and proceeding straight to the Memnonium, I had to pass before the two colossal figures in the plain. I need not say that I was struck with wonder. They are mutilated indeed, but their enormous size strikes the mind with admiration. The next object that met my view was the Memnonium. It stands elevated above the plain, which is usually inundated by the Nile. The water reaches quite to the propylæon; and though this is considerably lower than the temple, I beg leave to observe, that it may be considered as one of the proofs that the bed of the Nile has risen considerably higher since the Memnonium was erected; for it is not to be supposed that the Egyptians built the propylæon, which is the entrance to the temple, so low as not to be able to enter it when the water was at its height. The groups of columns of that temple, and the views of the numerous tombs excavated in the high rock behind it, present a strange appearance. On my approaching these ruins, I was surprised at the sight of the great colossus of Memnon, or Sesostris, or Osymandias, or Phamenoph, or perhaps some other King of Egypt; for such are the various opinions of its origin, and so many names have been given to it, that at last it has no name at all. I can but say that it must have been one of the most venerated statues of the Egyptians; for it would have required more labour to convey such a mass of granite from Assouan to Thebes, than to transport the obelisk commonly known under the appellation of Pompey's Pillar to Alexandria.

As I entered these ruins my first thought was to examine the colossal bust I had to take away. I found it near the remains of its body and chair, with its face upwards, and apparently smiling on me, at the thought of being taken to England. I must say, that my expectations were exceeded by its beauty, but not by its size. I observed that it must have been absolutely the same statue as is mentioned by Norden, lying in his time with its face downwards, which must have been the cause of its preservation. I will not venture to assert who separated the bust from the rest of the body by an explosion, or by whom the bust has been turned face upwards. The place where it lay was nearly in a line with the side of the main gateway into the temple; and, as there is another colossal head near it, there may have been one on each side of the doorway, as they are to be seen at Luxor and Carnak.

All the implements brought from Cairo to the Memnonium consisted of fourteen poles, eight of which were employed in making a sort of car to lay the bust on, four ropes of palm leaves, and four rollers, without tackle of any sort. I selected a place in the porticoes; and, as our boat was too far off to go to sleep in it every night, I had all our things brought on shore, and made a dwelling house of the Memnonium. A small hut was formed of stones, and we were handsomely lodged. Mrs Belzoni had by this time accustomed herself to travel, and was equally indifferent with myself about accommodations. I examined the road by which I was to take the bust to the Nile. As it appeared that the season of the inundation was advancing very fast, all the lands which extend from the Memnonium to the waterside would have been covered in one month's time; and the way at the foot of the mountain was very uneven, and in some parts ran over the ground to which the water reached, so that, unless the bust was drawn over those places before the inundation commenced, it would become impossible to effect it after, till the next summer; a delay which might have occasioned even still more difficulties than I had to encounter at that time; for I have reason to assert, that an intrigue was going on to prevent the removal of the head.

On the 24th of July I went to the Cacheff of Erments to obtain an order to the Caimakan of Gournou and Agalta, to procure for me eighty Arabs, to assist in the removal of the young Memnon. He received me with that invariable politeness which is peculiar to the Turks, even when they do not mean in the slightest degree to comply with your wishes, and which often deceives a traveller, who only *en passant* takes coffee, smokes his pipe, and goes away.

I presented the firman from the Defterdar at Siout. He received it reverently, and promised to do every thing in his power to get the Arabs to work; but observed that, at the present season, they were all occupied, and it would be better to wait till after the inundation of the Nile. I remarked, that I had seen a great many Arabs about the villages, who appeared perfectly idle, and who would be glad to gain something by being employed.

"You are mistaken," he replied, "for they would sooner starve than undertake a task so arduous as yours; since, to remove that stone, they must be helped by Mahomet, or they will never stir it the thickness of a thumb. Now, at the rise of the Nile, the Arabs of these banks are quite unoccupied, and that is the best time to employ them for such purposes."

The next objection was the Ramadan, which was just beginning; and the third, that he could not spare any Arabs, as they must work in the fields for the Bashaw, whose work could not be interrupted. I saw plainly, that I should have to encounter many difficulties, but I was determined to persist; and I told him, I should collect men myself, accompanied by my Janizary; and that all the Arabs I might find idle and willing to come, I should engage, according to the firman I had received from the Bashaw.

"To-morrow," he then replied, "I will send my brother to see if any men can be got."

The morning arrived, but no men appeared. I waited patiently till nine o'clock, and then mounted a camel and went again to Erments. I gave my interpreter some powder and about two pounds of raw coffee, to be produced when I should ask for them. I found the Cacheff occupied in giving directions to build a tomb for a Mahometan saint; but it was of no use to complain. I told him, therefore, that I came to drink coffee with him, and smoke a pipe. He was pleased, and we sat together on the divan. I pretended to be quite unconcerned about the removal of the colossus; and at a proper time I presented the powder and the coffee to him, with which he was much gratified. I then repeated to him that, if he would obtain men for me, it would be much to his advantage. He promised again that on the next morning I should have the assistance I wanted.

At last, on the 27th, he sent me a few men, but by no means sufficient for my purpose; yet, when others saw them at work, by permission, they were easily persuaded to join the party. I arranged my men in a row, and agreed to give them thirty paras a day, which is equal to fourpence halfpenny English money, with which they were much pleased, as it was more by one-half than they were accustomed to receive for their daily labour in the fields. The carpenter had made the car, and the first operation was to endeavour to place the bust on it. The fellahs of Gournou, who were familiar with Caphany, as they named the colossus, were persuaded that it could never be moved from the spot where it lay; and when they saw it moved, they all set up a shout. Though it was the effect of their own efforts, it was the devil, they said, that did it; and as they saw me taking notes, they concluded that it was done by means of a charm. The mode I adopted to place it on the car was very simple, for work of no other description could be executed by these people, as their utmost sagacity reaches only to pulling a rope, or sitting on the extremity of a lever as a counterpoise. By means of four levers I raised the bust, so as to leave a vacancy under it, to introduce the car; and after it was slowly lodged on this I had the car raised in front, with the bust on it, so as to get one of the rollers underneath. I then had the same operation performed at the back, and the colossus was ready to be pulled up. I caused it to be well secured on the car, and the ropes so placed that the power might be divided. I stationed men with levers to each side of the car, to assist occasionally, if the colossus should be inclined to turn to either side. In this manner I kept it safe from falling. Lastly, I placed men in the front, distributing them equally at the four ropes, while others were ready to change the rollers alternately. Thus I succeeded in getting it removed the distance of several yards from its original place.

According to my instructions, I sent an Arab to Cairo with the intelligence that the bust had begun its journey towards England.

On the 28th we recommenced work. The Arabs came pretty early, as they preferred to work in the morning, and rest in the middle of the day from twelve to two. This day we removed the bust out of the ruins of the Memnonium. To make room for it to pass, we had to break the bases of two columns. It was advanced about fifty yards out of the temple. In the evening I was very poorly: I went to rest, but my stomach refused any aliment. I began to be persuaded, that there is a great difference between travelling in a boat, with all that is wanted in it, and at leisure, and the undertaking of an operation which required great exertions in directing a body of men, who in point of skill are no better than beasts, and to be exposed to the burning sun of that country from morning till night.

On the next day, the 29th, I found it impossible to stand on my legs, and postponed the work to the day following. I had all our household furniture, beds, kitchen pottery, and provisions put on a camel, and returned to the boat, in hopes that the air might be cool at night; but I remained very ill the whole day, my stomach refusing to take almost anything.

On the 30th we continued the work, and the colossus advanced a hundred and fifty yards towards the Nile. I was a little better in the morning, but worse again in the evening.

On the 31st I was again a little better, but could not proceed, as the road became so sandy that the colossus sunk into the ground. I was therefore under the necessity of taking a long turn of above three hundred yards, to a new road. In the evening of this day I was much better.

On the 1st of August we still improved in our success, as we this day proceeded above three hundred yards. I was obliged to keep several men employed in making the road before us, as we went on with the head.

On the 2nd the head advanced farther; and I was in great hopes of passing a part of the land, to which the inundation would extend, previous to the water reaching that spot.

On the 3rd we went on extremely well, and advanced nearly four hundred yards. We had a bad road on the 4th, but still we proceeded a good way. On the 5th we entered the land I was so anxious to pass over, for fear the water should reach it and arrest our course; and I was happy to think that the next day would bring us out of danger. Accordingly I went to the place early in the morning, and to my great surprise found no one there except the guards and the carpenter, who informed me that the Caimakan had given orders to the Fellahs not to work for the Christian dogs any longer. I sent for him, to know the reason of this new proceeding; but he was gone to Luxor. I took the Janizary with me, and crossed the water to Luxor. I there found the Caimakan, who would give me no reason for his proceeding but saucy answers; and the more I attempted to bring him into good humour by smooth words and promises, the more insolent he became. My patience was great, and I was determined that day to carry it to its utmost length: but there is a certain point which, if exceeded, these people do not understand; and, in a country where respect is paid only to the strongest, advantage will always be taken of the weak: consequently if a man carry his policy beyond that point they mistake him for a coward; he is despised, and will have the more difficulties to encounter.

This was the case on the present occasion: my patience was mistaken; and this man, after having said all that he could against my nation, and those who protected me, was so much encouraged by my forbearance, that he attempted to put his hands on me, which I resisted. He then became more violent, and drew his sword, though he had a brace of pistols in his belt. There was no time to be lost. I instantly seized and disarmed him, placed my hands on his stomach and made him sensible of my superiority, at least in point of strength, by keeping him firm in a corner of the room. The pistols and sword, which I had thrown to the ground, were taken up by my Janizary; and after giving the fellow a good shaking, I took possession of them, and told him that I should send them to Cairo to show the Bashaw in what manner his orders were respected. He followed me towards the boat, and was no sooner out of the crowd that had assembled than he began to be quite humble, and talk of matters as if nothing had happened. He then told me, that the order he had given to the Fellahs not to work he had received from the Cacheff himself, and it could not be expected, that, being only a Caimakan, he could disobey his superior. I did not stop one instant, but ordered the boat to take me to Erments immediately.

[*The present of "a pair of fine English pistols" won from the Cacheff a new firman, with which Belzoni was back at Gournou before daylight.*]

Early on the morning of the 7th I sent for the Sheik of the Fellahs, and gave him the Cacheff's order. The men were ready in an hour after, and we continued the operation. The bust advanced this day considerably more than usual, owing to the men having rested on the preceding day: and on the 8th I had the pleasure of seeing it out of danger of being overtaken by the water.

On the 9th I was seized with such a giddiness in my head that I could not stand. The blood ran so copiously from my nose and mouth that I was unable to continue the operation: I therefore postponed it to the next day.

On the 10th and 11th we approached towards the river; and on the 12th, thank God! the young Memnon arrived on the bank of the Nile.

[*The next difficulty was to get a boat by which the "young Memnon" could descend the Nile. October had come before Belzoni could get even the promise of a vessel*].

I went to the house where all the owners of the boats were assembled, who at first were of one accord, that it was impossible to put the head on board the boat, alleging that it would break it to pieces if such a mass of stone were placed in it. They then strove to persuade me to leave the stone, as they were disposed to believe that there was no gold in it; and, if I took it, and found none after I had spent so much, I should lose all. Notwithstanding their simplicity, when I persuaded them than no accident would happen, and that I took all risks upon myself, they did not fail to ask me an enormous sum for the hire of the boat. I was in a dilemma, fearing that if I missed this boat I might lose the high water, which would have obliged me to wait till next year; and in a country like this, changing from one day to another its Government and way of thinking, I did not know what might happen. I therefore thought it best to secure myself from any future extortion, and give an enormous hire for the boat. This was three thousand piastres, equal to seventy-five pounds sterling, from that place to Cairo.

After all this was settled, and half the money paid down, the boat was to ascend the Nile as far as Assouan, to unload at that place, and to return immediately.

The time having elapsed, I was pleased to find the boat returned from Assouan, to take the colossal bust on board: but I was soon informed by the proprietor, that it was loaded with dates, and that he was come himself from Esne to return the money I had paid as earnest; for they could not think of taking that large stone into the boat, as it would crush it to pieces. All my persuasions were useless; and though I had a written agreement in my hands, they signified to me, that it was of no use, they never would take the stone on board.

My situation was far from pleasant, and I had no resource but to take the owner to Esne and lay the case before Khalil Bey, but even then I did not know how far he would interfere in compelling these people to keep to their agreement, as he had himself observed that he thought the stone would break the boat. This, however, was the only step I could take.

My vexation was great, thinking all my efforts and exertion in bringing the bust to the Nile were to no purpose, and that very probably it would never reach England, as the underhand machinations against it were so powerful. At that moment, however, a soldier arrived from Erments, acquainting me that the Cacheff was returned from Cairo; and he gave me at the same time a letter from him, with a present which he had sent of two small bottles of anchovies and two of olives. Strange as it may appear, it will be seen that the effects of a few salted little fish contributed the greatest share towards the removal of the colossus, which I had so much at heart, and which, in all probability, but for them, would not have been in the British Museum to this day. The letter contained a very gratifying invitation to a feast to be given by the Cacheff, and the present was in token of a friendly disposition towards me. I soon discovered the reason. The soldier acquainted me that the Cacheff was in a terrible rage with a certain correspondent and friend of his, a Frank, who for some time had raised his expectation of having some valuable presents sent him; but, instead of this, he received at last only a few bottles of insignificant fish, which may be had in plenty from the Nile, and a few olives not worth a pipe of tobacco. I took care that this should not be told to the owner of the boats; and, as it was arranged that we should go to Esne for the decision of the affair, I took them on board the little boat which I had hired, and we set off for that place, leaving the large one at Luxor.

On our arrival before Erments I begged the two owners of the boat to wait a little, as I had business with the Cacheff of the village. It was already an hour after sunset, and the village is about a mile from the Nile. I took my interpreter and Janizary with me, and set off alertly to my anchovy and olive man. I found him seated on a mat in the middle of a field, a stick fastened in the ground with a lantern attached to it, and all his attendants standing before him. On seeing me, he made a great parade of compliments; I suppose because he thought that, as he was disappointed of presents from one quarter, he would make the best market he could by trying the other. Pipes and coffee were brought as usual; and an offer was made me to send as many men as I liked to have to work, that I might take away the great head early the next morning, or anything else I pleased. Had I requested him to let me take the two large colossi of Thebes, Tommy and Dummy, as the Arabs call them, he would have had no objection to my putting them on board my little boat that night. I then introduced the affair of the boat, produced the written agreement I had drawn up at Esne with the two owners, and mentioned the money I had paid, which amounted to half the sum of what they were eventually to receive. He immediately said I need not go to Esne for the decision, the affair belonging to himself, as the boat was to be landed on a bank in his province. The two gentlemen from Esne were sent for, and when they heard that the cause was to be tried at Erments they were thunderstruck. They considered the boat lost to them, though I repeatedly told them that I would be answerable for any damage that might be incurred in the embarkation or landing; but it was all to no purpose. The Cacheff, however, insisted that they should keep their agreement with me; and still more to accommodate matters, as they were at a loss what to do with the dates, offered them his canja, which would contain as much as was necessary to be taken out of the boat, as I did not wish to unload it entirely.

Early on the 14th I went again to Gournou to begin the work, and was not a little surprised when I saw no Fellahs assembled. By one whom I met I was told that they were afraid, being ordered not to work for the English. I applied as before to the soldier, who sent a man to collect the Fellahs; but it was too late: they were all dispersed. Accordingly, I contented myself this day with only having the apparatus necessary to embark the head, conveyed over from Luxor. The Cacheff's boat from Erments arrived, and that at Luxor came also to Gournou to unload.

15th. The next day we collected, though not without trouble, a hundred and thirty men; and I began to make a causeway, by which to convey the head down to the riverside; for the bank was more than fifteen feet above the level of the water, which had retired at least a hundred feet from it.

Next morning a soldier came from the Cacheff to say that I was not to pay the Fellahs anything, as they were ordered to work for me for nothing as long as I required, and that he made me a present of their labour. I thanked him, but desired the soldier to tell him, at the same time, that it was not my custom to have the labour of men for nothing, nor would the consul of England accept of such a present. I this day finished the causeway down the bank, and had the head brought to the edge of the slope, ready to be embarked.

On the 17th of November I succeeded in my attempt, and the head of the younger Memnon was actually embarked. I cannot help observing that it was no easy undertaking to put a piece of granite of such bulk and weight on board a boat, that, if it received the weight on one side, would immediately upset; and this was to be done without the smallest help of any mechanical contrivance, even a single tackle, and only with four poles and ropes: the water was about eighteen feet below the bank where the head was to descend.

The causeway I had made gradually sloped to the edge of the water close to the boat, and with the four poles I formed a bridge from the bank into the centre of the boat, so that when the weight bore on the bridge, it pressed only on the centre of the boat. The bridge rested partly on the causeway, partly on the side of the boat, I put some mats well filled with straw. I necessarily stationed a few Arabs in the boat, and some at each side, with a lever of palm-wood, as I had nothing else. At the middle of the bridge I put a sack filled with sand, that, if the colossus should run too fast into the boat, it might be stopped. In the ground behind the colossus I had a piece of a plam-tree firmly planted, round which a rope was twisted, and then fastened to its car, to let it descend gradually. I set a lever at work on each side, and at the same time that the men in the boat were pulling, others were slackening the ropes, and others shifting the rollers as the colossus advanced.

Thus it descended gradually from the mainland to the causeway, when it sunk a good deal, as the causeway was made of fresh earth. This, however, I did not regret, as it was better it should be so, than that it should run too fast towards the water; for I had to consider, that, if this piece of antiquity should fall into the Nile, my return to Europe would not be very welcome, particularly to the antiquaries; though I have reason to believe that some among the great body of its scientific men would rather have seen it sunk in the Nile than where it is now deposited. However, it went smoothly on board. The Arabs, who were unanimously of opinion that it would go to the bottom of the river, or crush the boat, were all attention, as if anxious to know the result, as well as to learn how the operation was to be performed; and when the owner of the boat who considered it as consigned to perdition, witnessed my success, and saw the huge piece of stone, as he called it, safely on board, he came and squeezed me heartily by the hand.

"Thank Heaven!" I exclaimed, and I had reason to be thankful; for I will leave it to the judgment of any engineer, whether it would not be easier to embark a mass ten times larger on board a competent vessel, where all sorts of mechanical powers can be procured, instead of being destitute, as I was, of everything necessary.

The boat then crossed the water to Luxor, for what was to be taken in there, which was done in three days, and on the 21st we left Thebes on our return to Cairo.

I had just finished my business when I was again so afflicted with ophthalmia that for twelve days I kept myself shut up in the cabin of the boat, so that I can give no account of this voyage, till we reached Siout. I could then just peep at the light; but it gave me great pain whenever I attempted to open my eyes. At Siout I went to see the Deftardar Bey, to return him thanks for the firman he had given me when I ascended the Nile. I found him in his tent in the middle of a field of high clover, which had nearly reached its growth, and his horses were all out at grass. He was pleased to hear that I had succeeded in my undertaking, and requested to be remembered to the English consul, to whom he sent a letter by me.

Next morning we set off for Cairo, and reached it on the 15th of December, having been twenty-four days from Thebes. Thus I had been five months and a half in continual activity and exertion; but I must not let pass the unjust observation made by the ever voracious Count de Forbin, who asserted that I employed six months solely in taking the colossal bust on board the boat. It is true I was absent five months and a half from Cairo, and six months had elapsed before I reached Alexandria; but this time was not all devoted to the removal of the bust, as I employed only eighteen days in that operation and but a single day in embarking it.

At Cairo I found that the consul was gone to Alexandria, but had left with Mr Beechey, his secretary, instructions and letters for me. He requested that everything might be landed and lodged in the consulate except the bust. I could not conceive the reason of this distinction, as I thought that all the articles I collected were to go to the British Museum. However, I made no inquiry into the business, and everything was deposited as desired.

Having prepared for my departure for Alexandria, we left Boolak on the 3rd of January, 1817, and arrived in Raschid, or Rosetta, on the 10th. There I had to land the colossus, and embark it again on board a djerm; but as I had now some tackle of which I was destitute before, and proper people to work, I found it quite an easy operation. Besides, I took care to land it in a situation that was advantageous for embarking it again. Having done so, I set off on board the same djerm, with the bust, and was fortunate enough to reach Alexandria two hours after sunset of the same day, which was the fourth after our arrival in Rosetta. That very day above two hundred djerms came out of the Nile, some of which had been waiting for an opportunity of passing the bar above eighty days.

The next and final operation with respect to the bust, on my part, was to land it, and have it conveyed in safety to the Bashaw's magazine, there to await its embarkation for England. I had some difficulty in landing it, as the pier was much higher than the djerm, and the motion of the sea did not permit me to erect any bridge. I was so fortunate as to procure the crew of a British transport, which was there at the time; and with their help, with proper tackle, and a hundred men besides, it was landed safely.

SPAIN

"THE GOLDEN JOURNEY TO SAMARCAND" [1]

(1403)

RUY GONZALEZ DE CLAVIJO

(?-1412)

[*On Monday, May 22, 1403, Fray Alonzo Paez de Santa Maria, master of theology, Ruy Gonzalez de Clavijo, and Gomez de Salazar were sent by the "Lord Don Henry, by the grace of God King of Castille and Leon," as ambassadors to Tamerlane, the great Eastern conqueror. They went first from Cadiz to Constantinople, and thence to Trebizond, on through Armenia, Azerbijan, Irak, and Khorassan, arriving at Damghan, in "a wind so hot that it seemed as if it came out of hell," on July 17, 1404. Three days later they came to Vascal, and there we join them.*]

AND there they found a great knight called Ennacora, who was waiting for them by order of the lord, to do them honour. He came to see them at their lodging, and, as they were too unwell to dine with him, he sent them much meat and fruit. After they had dined, he sent to say that they should come to him, to a great palace, and that they should be clothed in the robes of the great lord. They replied that they could not walk, and that they trusted he would excuse them; but he sent again to ask them to come, and at last the master of theology went to him, and he dressed him in a robe, according to the custom; and it was usual when these robes were presented, to have grand feast, and afterwards to put on the robes; and then to touch the ground three times, with the knee, out of reverence for the great lord. This was done, and afterwards the knight sent horses to the ambassadors, and to their retinue. He also sent to say that they should proceed on their journey, as it was the command of the lord that they should follow him, as quickly as possible, both by day and night. They answered that they would prefer to rest for two days; but he replied that they must not stay any longer, for that, if the lord should know of it, it would cost him his life. The ambassadors were so ill that they were more dead than alive; so the knight caused soft pillows to be placed on the bows of their saddles, and so they departed. They travelled all night, and rested in a plain, near a deserted village.

On Monday they slept in some large buildings, which were erected by the road side, for travellers, as no people live in the country, for a distance of two

[1] From *Narrative of the Embassy of Ruy Gonzales de Clavijo to the Court of Timour at Samarcand*, translated and edited by Clements Markham (Hakluyt Society, No. 26 (1859)).

days journey, on account of the great heat, and the want of water. The water in the buildings was brought from a great distance, by pipes underground.

On Tuesday, the 22nd of July, they slept at a city called Jagaro, and the day was very hot. The city was in a plain, at the foot of a mountain without trees, and large pipes lead water from the mountain to the city. . . . In the previous winter there was much snow, and when the summer came it melted; and so much water came down the pipes that it ruined the castle and several houses. The road was very level, and there was not a single stone to be found on it; and the country was very hot, and with little water.

When they arrived they were given plenty of meat and fresh horses, and they set out again with the knight whom the great lord had sent, who provided them with food, and with all that they required; and gave them fresh horses every day, that they might travel faster. The lord had horses waiting at the end of each day's journey, at some places one hundred, and at others two hundred; and thus the posts were arranged, on the road, as far as Samarcand. Those whom the lord sent in any direction, or who were sent to him, went on these horses as fast as they could, day and night. He also had horses placed in deserts and uninhabited districts, as well as in places that were populous; and he caused great houses to be built in uninhabited places, where horses and provisions were supplied by the nearest towns and villages. Men were appointed to take care of these horses, who were called *Anchos*. Thus, when ambassadors or messengers arrive these men take their horses, take off their saddles, and place them on fresh horses, and one or two of these *Anchos* go with them, to take care of the horses; and when they reach another post they return with these horses. If any of the horses become tired on the road, and they meet another at any place, belonging to any other man, they take it in exchange for the tired horse. The custom is that when anyone rides on a road, if he is a lord, or merchant, or ambassador, he must give up his horse for the service of anyone who is going to the great lord, and if anyone refuses, it costs him his head, for such are the commands of Timour Beg. They even take horses from the troops, and the ambassadors often took horses from the troops, for themselves and their men; and, not only can those, who are going to the great lord, take the horses of such people, but they can even demand them from the son or the wife of the great lord himself. They told the ambassadors that even the eldest son of Timour Beg had been obliged to give up his horse to ambassadors who were going to the great lord.

Not only was this road thus supplied with post horses, but there were messengers on all the roads; so that news could come from every province in a few days. The lord is better pleased with him who travels a day a night for fifty leagues, and kills two horses, than with him who does the distance in three days.

The great lord, considering that the leagues were very long, in his empire of Samarcand, divided each league into two, and placed small pillars on the roads, to mark each league; ordering all his Zagatays to march twelve, or at least ten of these leagues, in each day's journey. They call these leagues *moles*, because these turrets, which he caused to be built at the end of each league, and these leagues, the lenth of which he regulated, are in a country which is called Mogolia. The ambassadors travelled in the country, and saw the pillars, and each of the leagues was equal to two leagues of Castille. . . .

The ambassadors left Jagaro on the day they arrived; and travelled all night, for, though they wished to rest, they were not permitted; and, although it was night, he heat was so great that it was quite wonderful, and there was a hot and burning wind.

On this night Gomez de Salazar, who had been ill, was nearly dying. There was no water on the road, during this day's journey, and they did not stop all night, except to give barley to the horses.

On Tuesday they travelled all day, without seeing any habitation whatever, until night, when they arrived at a city called Zabrain. This city is very large, and contains many fine houses and mosques; but most of them were deserted. When they had dined, they departed with fresh horses, and travelled all night. On Friday, near noon, they reached a deserted village, but the people brought them food, and all they required, from another village, distant about half a league. At the hour of vespers they set out again, and travelled all night, along a very level road.

On Saturday, the 26th of July, they arrived at a great city, which is called Nishapore. . . but Gomez de Salazar was left behind in a village, very ill, as he could not travel any longer. Five leagues before they reached the city, they met a knight who was marshal of the army of the lord, named Melialiorga. He was sent to them by the lord. He said that the lord had sent him to do them honour, and to provide them with all that they required. When he heard the Gomez de Salazar was left behind sick, he went back for him, and found him so weak that he could not stand. On the same night he caused a litter to be made, and, placing Gomez upon it, caused him to be carried on men's shoulders, to the city of Nishapore, where he was lodged in a good house, and attended by the best doctors; but it pleased God that the said Gomez should end his days at this place. . . .

On Sunday, the 27th of July, the ambassadors departed from this city, and slept near a deserted village. On Monday they slept at a large place, called Ferrior, and most of the inhabitants fled, from fear of the soldiers of the lord; for he had passed by, about twelve days before, and the troops which followed him had done much damage. They gave robes to the ambassadors at this place, which is very flat and very hot.

On Tuesday they slept in a great city called Hasegur, and departed again in the night. On Wednesday, the 30th of July, they came to a great city called Ojajan, where they were received with much honour, and were given food, and all that they required. In this city an order arrived from Shah Rokh Meerza, a son of Timour Beg, to invite the ambassadors to visit him at a city called Herat, which was a good thirty leagues off the road, on the right hand side, in the direction of India. He said that they should be received with great honour, and be supplied with all that they required. They consulted with the officer who accompanied them, and answered that the great lord had ordered that they should follow him as fast as possible, and that they trusted that he would, therefore, excuse them. This Shah Rokh Meerza was lord and emperor of this land of Khorassan.

On the same day the ambassadors reached the great city of Meshed were the grandson of the prophet Mohammed lies interred. He was the son of his daughter, and they say he is a saint. He lies buried in a great mosque, in a large tomb, which is covered with silver gilt. On account of his tomb, the city is crowded with pilgrims, who come here in great numbers every year. When the pilgrims arrive they dismount and kiss the ground, saying that they have reached a holy place. The ambassadors went to see the mosque; and afterwards, when in other lands people heard them say that they had been to this tomb, they kissed their clothes, saying that they had been near the holy Horazan. . . .

On Thursday, the last day of August, they came to a great city called Buelo, in the land of Khorassan. This city is in a very healthy situation, and was better peopled than any place between it and Sultanieh. They remained here a short time, to obtain barley and provisions, because they were about to cross a desert, fifty leagues in breadth. When they had eaten, they mounted fresh horses to cross the desert, and, departing in the evening, travelled all night.

On Friday they travelled all day and night, but could not reach any inhabited place. On Saturday, the 10th of August, at night, they reached a valley, covered with corn fields. A river ran through it, on the banks of which many Żagatay tents were pitched, belonging to the host of Timour Beg, with many sheep, horses and camels, as in this valley there was much grass.

When the ambassadors arrived they found a knight, who had been sent by the great lord to do them honour, and provide them with provisions, and to hurry them on their journey, as much as possible. The name of this knight was Mirabozar. He came to the ambassadors and said that he was sent to guide and assist them; and at this place the ambassadors exchanged the attendance of the first knight whom the lord had sent, for that of his Mirabozar; but the former still continued in their company, with his men, for the sake of food, and fodder for his beasts. The custom was that at any place where they arrived, whether it was a city or a village, they were supplied with much food, fruits, and fodder for horses, being three times as much as they wanted; and men were made to watch the property and horses of the ambassadors day and night, and if any were missing, the people of the place had to make up the loss. If the people when they arrived did not bring what was required they immediately received such a number of blows, with sticks and whips, that it was wonderful. The chiefs of the place were then sent for, and brought before these knights, the first thing they heard of being about blows and whippings. They received a wonderful number, and were told that they knew it to be the command of the great lord that, when ambassadors were on their way to him, they were to receive honour, and everything they required: that the said knights had arrived with these Frank ambassadors, and that they had not found anything ready for them: that the people should pay dearly for such neglect of the orders of the great lord; and that they would know, in future, what to expect when ambassadors arrived, if everything was not ready.

When they arrived at any city or village, the first thing which the followers of the knights, who accompanied the ambassadors, did, was to ask for the *reis* or chief of the place; and they took the first man they met in the street, and, with many blows, forced him to show them the house of the *reis*. The people who saw them coming, and knew they were troops of Timour Beg, ran away as if the devil was after them, and those who were behind their shops, selling merchandize, shut them up, and fled into their houses; and they said one to another. "*Elchee*," which means ambassador, and that, with the ambassadors, there would come a black day for them.

When they arrived at a village, the people brought out all the things that the ambassadors required. You must know that, from the time that they took leave of the son-in-law of the lord, the ambassadors and the ambassador of the Sultan of Babylon travelled in company; and these things were not only done for the ambassadors, but for every one who travelled with orders from the lord. They were to kill anyone who impeded the execution of his orders, and thus it was that the people were in marvellous terror of the lord and of his servants.

In these tents the knights caused much cooked meat to be placed before the ambassadors, together with rice, milk, cream, and melons, which are good and plentiful in this country.

The people of these tents have no other dwelling-place, and they wander over the plains, during both winter and summer. In summer they go to the banks of the rivers, and sow their corn, cotton, and melons, which I believe to be the best that can be found in the world. They also sow much millet, which they boil with their milk. In the winter they go to the warm districts. The lord, with all his host, wanders in the same way over the plains, winter and summer. His people do not march all together, but the lord, with his knights and friends, servants and women, go by one road, and the rest of the army by another, and so they pass their lives.

These people have many sheep, camels, and horses, and but few cows; and when the lord orders them to march with his army, they go with all that belongs to them, flocks and herds, women and children; and so they supply the host with flocks, especially with sheep, camels, and horses.

With these people the lord has performed many deeds, and conquered in many battles; for they are a people of great valour, excellent horsemen expert with the bow, and enured to hardships. If they have food, they eat; and if not, they suffer cold and heat, hunger and thirst, better than any people in the world. . . .

At dawn the ambassadors departed, with the knight who had been sent by the great lord, and travelled all night, and all next day, without seeing any habitation, except a large deserted building, where they rested, and procured barely for the horses. They were told that they were twelve leagues from any inhabited place. They departed, in the night, with good fresh horses, and travelled in the night, on account of the great heat, and during all this time they came to no water. The journey was so long that the horses were tired, and unable to move, being ready to perish of heat and thirst; the country was a sandy desert, and they were all in danger of dying of thirst.

A lad, belonging to the knight, had a horse which was a little fresher than the rest, and he went on as fast as he could, and arrived at a river, where he wet some shirts and other clothes, and returned with all haste; and those who could get a chance, drank the water, for they were ready to faint from heat and thirst. A little before sunset they reached a valley where there were some tents of the Zagatays, near a river they called Morghan. The journey which they made, during the last day and night, was twenty good leagues of Castille and more; and they rested here all night. On Tuesday they departed, and, after two leagues, arrived at a large building, which they call *caravanserai*, where there were Zagatays, guarding the horses of the lord.

They slept here, and at the hour of vespers departed with good horses, and travelled over great plains, where there were tents of the Zagatays; and they remained there all Wednesday.

On Thursday they departed, and took their siesta near a village, passing the night on the plain, near the banks of this river. On Friday they again started, and rested, at noon, by the tents of some Zagatays, departing in the afternoon, on fresh horses, and sleeping in the open air.

On Saturday, the 9th of August, they dined at a place called Salugar-sujassa, which once belonged to a great Caxis, whom they look upon as a saint. It was in a valley, near a river, and many channels of water passed through the place, which was well peopled, and full of gardens and beautiful vineyards.

This Caxis, the lord of this place, was dead, and he left two children. When Timour Beg passed through the place, about ten days before, he took these children with him, to bring them up, as the Caxis was of a noble family. The place was governed by the mother of these children, who received the ambassadors with much honour and gave them plenty of good, and all that they required, and dined with them. At night they departed on good horses, and travelled all night.

On Sunday they dined, and took their siesta, amongst some tents of the Zagatays, remaining there all day. On Monday they started very early, and slept in the plain; and at these tents they gave them meat and fruit, and all they required; and, notwithstanding that they belonged to the lord's army, they were obliged to provide all that the ambassadors wanted, and men to watch their horses day and night; and they had to give up their tents to the ambassadors. When they crossed any desert, these people had to supply meat, fodder, and water, at their own cost, though they wanted them for their own use.

On Tuesday, the 12th of August, they dined and took their siesta on a great plain, where there was a large building, and men watching the horses of the lord; and they mounted, and rode away from that place, at the hour of vespers.

At the hour of vespers they departed, and reached a city called Anchoy, of which one of the attendants of the ambassadors was a native. This city was beyond the land of Media, in a land called Tagiguinia, and the language of the people differed from the Persian. The men of the city received the ambassadors with much honour, and they remained there until Thursday, the 14th of August. They were well supplied with plenty of meat and wine; and were presented with a robe, and a horse. This city is in a plain, and is surrounded, for two leagues, by many gardens, vineyards and houses, with numerous channels of water.

On Thursday afternoon they departed, and slept amongst some tents of the Zagatays, in a plain, near the banks of a river. These Zagatays have received the privilege from the lord, to go where they like for pasture for their flocks and herds, as well in summer as in winter; and they serve the lord in his wars, whenever they are called for. They do not leave their women, children and flocks behind, when they go to the wars, but take them all with them. The women who have little children, when they travel, carry them in small cradles before them, on their horses, and they tie these cradles with broad bands, which they fasten round their waists; and thus they travel with their children, and ride as light as if they were without them. The poor people carry their children and tents on camels, and this way of travelling is very wearisome for the children, as the camels go very uneasily. Not only do these people, whom we met on the road, live in these plains; but there are a vast number of others, for, when we found some in any place, many others also appeared, in one part or another, and so we travelled amongst them. Near towns, and places where there was water and pasture, we met many of them, and they were so burnt by the sun that they looked as if they had come out of hell.

This country was very flat and very hot, and most of the troops who followed the lord travelled by night; and the ambassadors remained amongst these tents of the Zagatays until night. On Friday, at noon, they came to a village, where they dined and took their siesta. In the night they arrived at a great city, the name of which I have forgotten, but it was very large, and formerly it was walled, but now the wall is fallen, and most of the city is deserted, and in this city there were great edifices and mosques. The ambassadors were here presented with robes, and received with great honour.

On Saturday they departed on fresh horses, and slept amongst some tents of the Zagatays. On Sunday there was such a high wind that the men were obliged to dismount, and it was so hot that it felt like fire. The road led through sandy deserts, and the wind raised the sand in clouds, and concealed the road, so that they lost it many times during the day. The night sent for a man from the tents, to guide them, and it pleased God that they should find their way to a village called Alibed, where they took their siesta, and remained until the wind went down. In the night they slept at another village called Ux; but, as soon as the horses had eaten their barley, they set out again, and travelled all night, amongst small villages and fruit gardens.

On Monday, the 18th of August, they arrived at a city called Vacq, which is very large, and surrounded by a broad earthen wall, thirty paces across, but it is breached in many parts. This city had three divisions, and the first, between the first and second wall, was quite uninhabited, and much cotton was sown there. The second was inhabited; and the third was well peopled; and, though the other cities we had seen were without walls, this one was well provided with them. In this city the ambassadors were received with much honour, and were given meat and wine, and robes, and horses. On Tuesday they departed, and slept near a village, and on Wednesday they dined and took their siesta in a village, and passed the night in the open air.

On Thursday, the 21st of August, they reached a great river called the Viadme [Oxus], which is another of the rivers which flow from Paradise. It is a league in width, and flows through a very flat country, with great and wonderful force, and it is very muddy. It is lowest in winter, beacuse the waters are forzen in the mountains, and the snow does not melt: but in the month of April it begins to increase, and goes on increasing continually for four months; and this is because the summer melts the ice and snow. Last summer they said that it had swollen much more than usual; for it increased so much that the water reached a village, near the banks, and destroyed many houses, doing great damage.

This river descends from the mountains, flows through the plains of the territory of Samarcand, and the land of Tartary, and falls into the sea of Bakou. It separates the government of Samarcand from that of Khorassan.

The lord Timour Beg, as soon as he had gained the government of Samarcand, desired to pass over this great river, to conquer the land of Khorassan. He therefore caused a great bridge of timber to be made, supported by boats; and when his army had crossed, the bridge was destroyed; but, on his return to Samarcand, he ordered it to be made again, for the passage of himself and his host; and the ambassadors crossed over on this bridge; and they said that the lord had given an order to destroy the bridge, as soon as all his host had passed over. . . .

On the Thursday that the ambassadors reached this great river, they crossed to the other side, and, in the afternoon, they arrived at a great city called Termit, which once belonged to India the Less, but is now in the territory of Samarcand, having been conquered by Timour Beg, and from this place the empire of Samarcand begins. . . .

The custom which the lord causes to be observed at this great river is, that when he has passed from one side to the other, the people have to break the bridge, and afterwards no one can cross over; but there are boats in this river, which convey people from one side to the other, and no one is permitted to pass over in these boats, without showing a letter stating whence he comes, and whither he goes, even when he is a native of the land. When, however, anyone wishes to enter the land of Samarcand, this letter is not required. The lord has a great guard placed at these boats, who take heavy tolls from those who use them. This guard is also placed, because the lord has brought many captives into Samarcand, from the countries which he has conquered, to people the land, and enrich and ennoble it; so as to prevent them from escaping, and returning to their own land. Though, when the ambassadors passed, they found orphans, and women without support, in the land of Persia and Khorassan; yet the men had been taken by force, to people the land of Samarcand. One brought a cow, another and ass, another a sheep or goat; and they were fed, by the officers of the lord, on the road; and in this way the lord conveyed above one hundred thousand persons of the land of Samarcand.

This city of Termit, which the ambassadors had reached, was very large and populous, and it was without any wall. The city was surrounded by many gardens and streams of water. I cannot tell you more of this city, because we were very tired when we reached our lodging, except that we passed through populous streets and squares, where they sold many things. The ambassadors were received with much honour, and supplied with all that they required, and were presented with a silken robe. In this city a messenger arrived from the lord, who came to the ambassadors, and said that the lord saluted them, and desired to know how they had borne the journey, and how they had been treated, and whether they would soon arrive. When this messenger departed, they gave him a robe, and they also gave a Florentine robe to the knight who had been sent first, and who had come with them, the ambassador from the Sultan of Babylon doing the same. They also gave a horse to the second knight, whom the lord had sent; for such is the custom of all who come to the lord, to give something, and thus respect the custom of giving and taking presents. Their greatness is considered according to the number of presents they give, in honour of the lord, and such is the measure of the praise they receive.

On Friday, the 22nd of August, after dinner, the ambassadors departed, and slept on the plain, near some large houses. On Saturday they travelled over extensive plains, amongst many well peopled villages, and reached a village where they were supplied with all that they required. On Sunday they dined at some large buildings, where the lord is accustomed to stop, when he passes this way, and they were given much fruit and meat, wine and melons, and the melons were very good and large and abundant. The customs is to place the fruit before the ambassadors, on the ground.

On that day they departed, and slept on a plain, near the banks of a river. On Monday they dined at the foot of a high hill, where there was a handsome house, ornamented with very fine brickwork, and in it there were many ornamental patterns, painted in many colours. This hill is very high, and there is a pass leading up by a ravine, which looks as if it had been artificially cut, and the hills rise to a great height on either side, and the pass is smooth and very deep. In the centre of the pass there is a village, and the mountain rises to a great height behind. This pass is called the "Gates of Iron," and in all the mountain range there is no other pass, so that it guards the land of Samarcand, in the direction of India. These "Gates of Iron" produce a large revenue to the lord Timour Beg, for all merchants who come from India pass this way.

Timour Beg is also lord of the other "Gates of Iron," which are near Derbent, leading to the province of Tartary, and the city of Caffa, which are also in very lofty mountains, between Tartary and the land of Derbent, facing the sea of Bakou; and the people of Tartary are obliged to use that pass, when they go to Persia. The distance from the "Gates of Iron" at Derbent to those in the land of Samarcand is fifteen hundred leagues.

Say if a great lord, who is master of these "Gates of Iron," and of all the land that is between them, such as Timour Beg, is not a mighty prince! Derbent is a very large city, with a large territory. They call the "Gates of Iron" by the names of Derbent and Termit. At this house they made the ambassadors a present of a horse; and the horses of this country are much praised for their great spirit. These mountains of the "Gates of Iron" are without woods; and in former times they say that there were great gates, covered with iron, placed across the pass, so that no one could pass without an order.

On this day they departed, and slept in the open air, on the top of a hill. On the next day they dined and took their siesta near some tents of the Zagatays, on the banks of a river. In the afternoon they rode on, and slept on the top of a range of hills. They started again in the middle of the night, and dined next day at a village; and here an attendant of the Master Fray Alfonzo Paez, who had been ill, departed this life.

On Thursday, the 28th of August, at the hour of Mass, they arrived at the great city of Kesh, which is situated in a plain, traversed in every direction by channels of water, which irrigate many gardens. The surrounding country was flat, and they saw many villages, well watered pastures, and a very beautiful, bright and well peopled country. In these plains there were many corn fields, vineyards, cotton plantations, melon grounds, and groves of fruit-trees. The city was surrounded by a wall of earth, with a deep ditch, and drawbridges leading to the gates. The lord Timour Beg and his father were both natives of this city of Kesh.

In this city there are great mosques, and other edifices, especially a grand mosque which the lord Timour Beg has ordered to be built, for as yet it is not finished; within which the body of his father is interred. There is also another great chapel, which Timour Beg has ordered to be built, for his own body, and it was not finished. They say that when he was here, a month ago, he did not like this chapel, saying that the door was low, and ordering it to be raised, and they are now working at it. The first-born son of Timour Beg is also interred in this mosque, named Jehanghir. This mosque, with its chapels, was very rich, and beautifully ornamented in blue and gold, and within it there was a large court, with trees and ponds of water. In this mosque the lord gives twenty boiled sheep every day, for the souls of his father and son who lie buried there.

When the ambassadors arrived they were conducted to this mosque, and provided with much meat and fruit; and when they had dined they were taken to their lodging, in a great palace.

On Friday they were taken to see some great palaces which the lord has ordered to be built, and they say that they have been working at them every day for twenty years, and many workmen are still employed on them. These palaces had a long entrance, and a very high gateway. On each side there were arches of brick, covered with glazed tiles, and many patterns in various colours. These arches formed small recesses, without doors, and the ground was paved with glazed tiles. They are made for the attendants to sit in, when the lord is here.

In front of the first entrance there was another gateway, leading to a great courtyard paved with white stones, and surrounded by doorways of very rich workmanship. In the centre of the court there was a great pool of water, and this court was three hundred paces wide. The court led to the body of the building, by a very broad and lofty doorway, ornamented with gold and blue patterns on glazed tiles, richly and beautifully worked. On the top of this doorway there was the figure of a lion and a sun, which are the arms of the lord of Samarcand; and, though they say that Timour Beg ordered these palaces to be built, I believe that the former lord of Samarcand gave the order; because the sun and lion, which are here represented, are the arms of the lords of Samarcand; and those which Timour Beg bears, are three circles like O's, drawn in this manner ∵ and this is to signify that he is lord of the three parts of the world. . . .

The ambassadors were in this city of Kesh during the Thursday on which they arrived; and, having departed on Friday afternoon, they passed the night in a village. On Saturday, the 30th of August, they dined at a great house, which the lord had built, in a plain near the banks of a river, and in the midst of a large and very beautiful garden. They passed the night in a large village, which was a league from Samarcand, called Mecer. The knight who conducted them, now left the ambassadors, as on that they could easily reach the city of Samarcand; he said that he would announce their approach to the great lord, and that he would send a man to report their arrival; and that night the man was sent to report it to the great lord.

Next day, at dawn, he returned with an order from the great lord to the knight, that the ambassadors, and the ambassador of the Sultan of Babylon, who travelled with them, should be taken to a garden near the village, and remain there until he gave further orders. On Sunday, the 31st of August, at dawn, the ambassador were taken to this garden, which was surrounded by a mud wall, and might be about a league round. It contained a great number of fruit trees of all kinds, except citrons and limes; it was traversed by many channels of water, and a large stream flowed through the centre. These channels flowed amongst the trees, which were large and tall, and gave a pleasant shade. In the centre of the avenues formed by the trees, there were raised platforms, which traversed the whole garden. There was also a high mound of earth, made level on the top, and surrounded by wooden palings: and on this hill there were palaces, with chambers very richly ornamented with gold and blue, upon polished tiles. This hill was surrounded by a very deep ditch, full of water, into which the water poured down from a large pipe.

To ascend the hill there were two bridges, on opposite sides; and after the bridges were crossed, there were two doors, which opened upon flights of stairs leading up to the summit of the hill, where the palace stood. In this garden there were deer and many pheasants. Beyond the garden there was a great vineyard, as large as the garden, which was also surrounded by a mud wall, and all round the wall there were rows of tall trees, which looked very beautiful. They call this garden and palace *Talicia*, and in their own language *Calbet:* and in this garden the ambassadors were given much food, and all that they required. They had their tents pitched on the grass, near a stream of water, and there they remained.

On Thursday, the 4th of September, a noble who was related to the lord, came to the garden, and told the ambassadors that the lord was occupied with the business of some ambassadors from the emperor Tokatmish, and that, therefore, he could not see them yet: but, that they might not be impatient, he had sent some refreshments to them, and to the ambassador of the Sultan, that they might make merry for that day. They brought many sheep, cooked and dressed, and a roasted horse, with rice served up in various ways, and much fruit. When they had eaten they were presented with two horses, a robe, and a hat. The ambassadors were in this garden from Sunday, the 31st of August, to Monday, the 8th of September, when the lord sent for them; for it is the custom not to see any ambassador until five or six days are passed, and the more important the ambassador may be, the longer he has to wait.

On Monday, the 8th of September, the ambassadors departed from the garden where they had been lodged, and went to the city of Samarcand. The road went over a plain covered with gardens and houses and markets where they sold many things; and at three in the afternoon they came to a large garden and palace, outside the city, where the lord then was. When they arrived, they dismounted, and entered a building outside; where two knights came to them, and said that they were to give up those presents, which they brought for the lord, to certain men who would lay them before him, for such were the orders of the private Meerzas of the lord; so the ambassadors gave the presents to the two knights. They placed the presents in the arms of men who were to carry them respectfully before the lord, and the ambassador from the Sultan did the same with the presents which he brought.

The entrance to this garden was very broad and high, and beautifully adorned with glazed tiles in blue and gold. At this gate there were many porters, who guarded it, with maces in their hands. When the ambassadors entered they came to six elephants, with wooden castles on their backs, each of which had two banners, and there were men on the top of them. The ambassadors went forward, and found the men who had the presents well arranged on their arms, and they advanced with them in company with the two knights, who held them by the armpits, and the ambassador whom Timour Beg had sent to the King of Castille was with them; and those who saw him laughed at him, because he was dressed in the costume and fashion of Castille.

They conducted them to an aged knight, who was seated in an anteroom. He was a son of the sister of Timour Beg, and they bowed reverentially before him. They were then brought before some small boys, grandsons of the lord, who were seated in a chamber, and they also bowed before them. Here the letter, which they brought from the King to Timour Beg, was demanded, and they presented it to one of these boys, who took it. He was a son of Miran Meerza, the eldest son of the lord. The three boys then got up, and carried the letter to the lord; who desired that the ambassadors should be brought before him.

Timour Beg was seated in a portal, in front of the entrance of a beautiful palace; and he was sitting on the ground. Before him there was a fountain, which threw up the water very high, and in it there were some red apples. The lord was seated cross-legged, on silken embroidered carpets, amongst round pillows. He was dressed in a robe of silk, with a high white hat on his head, on the top of which there was a spinal ruby, with pearls and precious stones round it.

As soon as the ambassadors saw the lord they made a reverential bow, placing the knee on the ground, and crossing the arms on the breast; then they went forward and made another; and then a third, remaining with their knees on the ground. The lord ordered them to rise and come forward; and the knights who had held them until then let them go. Three Meerzas, who stood before the lord, and were his most intimate councillors, named Alodalmelec Meerza, Borundo Meerza, and Noor Eddin Meerza, then came and took the ambassadors by the arms, and led them forward until they stood together before the lord. This was done that the lord might see them better; for his eyesight was bad, being so old that the eyelids had fallen down entirely. He did not give them his hand to kiss, for it was not the custom for any great lord to kiss his hand; but he asked after the king, saying:

"How is my son the king? Is he in good health?"

When the ambassadors had answered Timour Beg turned to the knights who were seated around him, amongst whom were one of the sons of Tokatmish, the former Emperor of Tartary, several chiefs of the blood of the late Emperor of Samarcand, and others of the family of the lord himself, and said:

"Behold! here are the ambassadors sent by my son the King of Spain, who is the greatest king of the Franks, and lives at the end of the world. These Franks are truly a great people, and I will give my benediction to the King of Spain, my son. It would have sufficed if he had sent you to me with the letter, and without the presents, so well satisfied am I to hear of his health and prosperous state."

The letter which the king had sent was held before the lord, in the hand of his grandson; and the master of theology said, through his interpreter, that no one understood how to read the letter except himself, and that when his Highness wished to hear it he would read it. The lord then took the letter from the hand of his grandson and opened it, saying that he would hear it presently, and that he would send for the master and see him in private, when he might read it, and say what he desired.

The ambassadors were then taken to a room on the right hand side of the place where the lord sat; and the Meerzas, who held them by the arms, made them sit below an ambassador whom the Emperor Chayscan, Lord of Cathay, had sent to Timour Beg to demand the yearly tribute which was formerly paid. When the lord saw the ambassadors seated below the ambassador from the Lord of Cathay he sent to order that they should sit above him, and he below them. As soon as they were seated one of the Meerzas of the lord came and said to the ambassador of Cathay that the lord had ordered that those who were ambassadors from the King of Spain, his son and friend, should sit above him; and that he who was the ambassador from a thief and a bad man, his enemy, should sit below them; and from that time, at the feasts and entertainments given by the lord, they always sat in that order. . . .

As soon as these ambassadors, and many others, who had come from distant countries, were seated in order they brought much meat, boiled, roasted, and dressed in other ways, and roasted horses; and they placed these sheep and horses on very large round pieces of stamped leather. When the lord called for meat the people dragged it to him on these pieces of leather, so great was its weight; and as soon as it was within twenty paces of him the carvers came, who cut it up, kneeling on the leather. They cut it in pieces, and put the pieces in basins of gold and silver, earthenware and glass, and porcelain, which is very scarce and precious. The most honourable piece was a haunch of horse, with the loin, but without the leg, and they placed parts of it in ten cups of gold and silver. They also cut up the haunches of the sheep. They then put pieces of the tripes of the horses, about the size of a man's fist, into the cups, and entire sheep's heads, and in this way they made many dishes. When they had made sufficient they placed them in rows. Then some men came with soup, and they sprinkled salt over it, and put a little in each dish, as sauce; and they took some very thin cakes of corn, doubled them four times, and placed one over each cup or basin of meat.

As soon as this was done the Meerzas and courtiers of the lord took these basins, one holding each side, and one helping behind (for a single man could not lift them), and placed them before the lord, and the ambassadors, and the knights who were there; and the lord sent the ambassadors two basins, from those which were placed before him, as a mark of favour. When this food was taken away more was brought; and it is the custom to take this food, which is given to them, to their lodgings, and if they do not do so it is taken as an affront; and so much of this food was brought that it was quite wonderful.

When dinner was finished the men who bore the presents on their arms passed before the lord, and the same was done with the presents sent by the Sultan of Babylon; and three hundred horses were also brought before the lord, which had been presented that day. After this was done the ambassadors rose, and a knight was appointed to attend upon them, and to see that they were provided with all that they required. This knight, who was the chief porter of the lord, conducted the ambassadors, and the ambassador from the Sultan of Babylon, to a lodging near the place where the lord abode, in which there was a garden, and plenty of water.

When the ambassadors took leave of the lord he caused the presents which the king had sent to be brought, and received them with much complacency. He divided the scarlet cloth amongst his women, giving the largest share to his chief wife, named Caño, who was in this garden with him. The other presents brought by the ambassador from the Sultan, were not received, but returned to the men who had charge of them, who received them, and kept them for three days, when the lord ordered them to be brought again: because it is the custom not to receive a present until the third day. This house and garden, where the lord received the ambassadors, was called Dilkoosha, and in it there were many silken tents, and the lord remained there until the following Friday. . . .

[*The ambassadors left Samarcand on November 21, and " on Monday, the 24th day of the March, in the year of our Lord 1406,... reached the Court of their lord, the king of Castille, which they found in Alcala de Henares. Laus Deo."*]

MARCH TO HONDURAS[1]

(1524)

HERNAN CORTÉS

(1485-1547)

[*In the belief that the Pacific was the far-famed Indian Ocean, wherein "are scattered innumerable isles teeming with gold and pearls," Cortés had sent Cristoval de Olid to found a colony on the north shore of the Bay of Honduras. Arrived there, de Olid proved faithless to his chief, declaring that he himself would hold his conquest in the name of the Emperor. Whereupon Cortés dispatched his kinsman Francisco de las Casas to take de Olid prisoner. No tidings came from him, and on October 12, 1524, Cortés himself set out for Honduras, going not by sea, as the others had, but by land, through a country wholly unknown. In a letter to the Emperor Charles V he relates his experiences upon that marvellous march, some of which are here given.*]

[1] From *The Fifth Letter of Hernan Cortés to the Emperor Charles V*, translated by Don Pascual de Gayangos (Hakluyt Society, No. 40 (1868)).

MOST SACRED MAJESTY,

On the 23rd day of the month of October of the year 1525 past, I dispatched from the town of Trujillo, off the port and cape of Honduras, to the Hispaniola, a vessel, and in her a servant of mine, with orders to pass over to those kingdoms of Spain. The said servant was the bearer of letters, wherein I informed your Majesty of some events which had occurred at the gulf called Las Hibueras between the two captains I had sent thither and another captain named Gil Gonzalez, who went afterwards. And as I was unable at the time the said vessel and messenger departed, to give your Majesty any account of my journey and adventures, from the moment I left this great city of Tenuxtitlan[1] until I met with the people of those distant parts, it seemed to me important that your Highness should become acquainted with my doings... I will therefore narrate events plainly and to the best of my ability, because were I to attempt drawing them in their proper colouring, I am sure I could not do it, and, moreover, my narrative might perhaps be unintelligible to those for whom it is destined; and will relate only the principal and most remarkable incidents of the said journey, passing over in silence many others. . . .

Having taken my measures in the matters concerning Cristoval de Olid, as I wrote to your Majesty, I began to consider how long I had been inactive, and without undertaking things that might be of service to your Majesty; and although my arm was still sore and painful, I determined upon doing something useful. I therefore left this great city of Tenuxtitlan on the 12th day of October of the year 1524 last, followed by a few horse and foot, chosen among my own retainers and servants, and by some friends and connexions of mine. . . . I likewise took with me the principal among the natives of the land; and left the administration of justice and the government of the country in the hands of Alonso de Estrada and Rodrigo de Albornoz, the treasurer and accounting-master of your Majesty, conjointly with the licenciate Alonso de Zuazo. . . .

All this being accomplished, I set out with the said purpose from this city of Tenuxtitlan, and having reached Espiritu Santo, which is a town in the province of Coazacoalco,[2] distant one hundred and ten leagues from this city, whilst engaged in settling the internal affairs of the community, I dispatched messengers to Tabasco and Xiculango, informing the lords of those provinces of my intended journey, and ordering them to come and meet me, or send persons to whom I might communicate my instructions. . . . They did

[1] The old name for Mexico.
[2] Huazacoalco.

exactly as I told them; they received my messengers with due honour, and they sent me seven or eight worthy men duly authorised, as they are in the habit of doing on such occasions. Having inquired of these men the news of the land, I was told that on the sea-coast, beyond the region called Yucatan, towards the bay of the Asuncion, there were certain Spaniards who did them much harm, since, besides burning their villages and slaying their people—in consequence of which many places were deserted, and the inhabitants had fled to the mountains—they had been the cause of the total disappearance of trade, formerly very flourishing, on that coast. Some of them, who had been in those parts, described to me most of the villages of the coast, as far as the place of residence of Pedrarias Davila, who now governs those regions in your Majesty's name; and drew on a cloth a figure of the whole land, whereby I calculated that I could very well go over the greater part of it, and in particular over that portion of the country which was pointed out to me as the abode of the said Spaniards.

Thus instructed about the road which I was to take in order to carry out my plans, and bring the natives of the land to the knowledge of our holy Catholic faith, and your Majesty's service—certain as I was that on so long a journey I would have to traverse many different provinces and meet people of various races—being also curious to know whether the Spaniards mentioned to me were the same that I had sent under the captains Cristoval de Olid, Pedro de Alvarado, or Francisco de las Casas, I considered it useful to your Majesty's service to go thither in person, inasmuch as my journey being through regions and provinces hitherto unexplored, I would have ample opportunity of doing service to your Majesty, and putting the said countries by peaceful means under the imperial rule, as has since been done. . . .

There was then at anchor in the port of the said town of Espiritu Santo a large caravel, which had been sent to me from the town of Medellin, loaded with provisions. This I again filled with the stores I had brought with me, and, putting into it four pieces of artillery, as well as crossbows, muskets and other ammunition, directed the crew to sail for the island of Tabasco, and wait there for my commands. I also wrote to a servant of mine, who resides at the said town of Medellin, to load with provisions two other caravels and a large boat, then in the port, and send them to me. To Rodrigo de Paz, whom I left in charge of my house and property in this city of Tenuxtitlan, I gave instructions to remit to Medellin five or six thousand ounces of gold, to pay for the said provisions, and I even wrote to the treasurer begging him to advance me that money as I had none left in the hands of the aforesaid agent. All this was done according to my wishes: the caravels came as far as the river of

Tabasco, laden with provisions, though they proved to be of little use, because my route being far inland, neither the caravels, laden as they were, could go further up the river, nor could I send for them, owing to certain large morasses that lay between.

This matter of the provender to be dispatched by sea being thus settled, I began my journey, and marched along the coast until I reached a province called Çupilco,[1] about thirty-five leagues distant from the town of Espiritu Santo. On my road there, besides several morasses and water-streams, over all of which temporary bridges were thrown, I had to cross three very large rivers, one of them near a village called Tumalon, about nine leagues off the town of Espiritu Santo, the other at Agualulco, nine leagues farther on. These two were passed in canoes, the horses being led by the hand, and swimming across. The third river was so large and wide that it would have been impossible for the horses to swim across, and therefore I was obliged to look out for a more convenient spot up the stream, where I had a wooden bridge made for their passage and that of the men. It was a wonderful thing to behold, for the river measured at that spot nine hundred and thirty-four spans in width. . . .

From this province of Çupilco I was to proceed, according to the sketch or map given to me by the people of Tabasco and Xiculango, to another province called Çagoatan; but as the natives of those regions only travel by water, none could show me the land route, though they pointed out with their fingers that part of the map where the said province was supposed to be. I was therefore obliged to send in that direction some of my Spaniards and Indians to look out for a road, and, when found, to make it practicable for the rest of us, as our way was forcibly through very high mountains. It, however, pleased God Almighty that such a road was found, though hard and difficult in the extreme, not only on account of the said mountain-ridge to be traversed, but also of the many perilous marshes, over all of which, or the greater part, we had to throw bridges. . . .

At . . . Çagoatan we remained twenty days, incessantly occupied in finding out some road that might take us onwards; but the country around us was so full of morasses and lagoons, that we could not stir out of the place, and all our efforts proved in vain. Yet we were soon placed in such a state of jeopardy, through the exhaustion of our provisions, that we made up our minds to risk our lives in the attempt. Accordingly, having previously commended our souls to God our Creator, we threw a bridge over a morass three hundred paces in length; and on this bridge, which was formed by many

[1] Probably Tupilcos. It is, however, impossible to locate all the places Cortés mentions upon his march.

large pieces of timber, measuring thirty five or forty feet in length, crossed by others of similar dimensions, we passed the said morass, setting out immediately in search of that chain of mountains near to which stood, as we were told, the town of Chilapan. In the mean-while, I sent by another route a troop of horsemen and certain archers in the direction of the other village, called Acumba, and they were fortunate enough to find it that very day. Having swam through a river, or crossed it in two canoes which they found on its bank, they came suddenly upon the village, whose inhabitants took to flight. My men found inside plenty of provision, two Indians and some women, with whom they came to meet me. I slept that night in the fields.

On the next day God permitted that we should come to a country more open and dry, and less covered with swamps, so that, guided by the Indians taken at Acumba, we arrived the day after, at a very late hour, at the town of Chilapan, which we found completely burnt down, and its inhabitants all gone. . . .

I remained ten days at Chilapan, laying in provisions for the journey, and ordering certain excursions to be made in the neighbourhood, with a view to secure, if possible, some natives from whom I might learn the road; but with the exception of two, who were at first found hiding in the village, all our search was in vain. From these, however, I ascertained upon inquiry the road to Tepetitan, otherwise called Tamacastepeque; and, although they hardly knew their way thither, we were lucky enough, sometimes through their leading, and at others by our own device, to reach that place on the second day. We had to cross a very large river, called Chilapan, wherefrom the aforesaid town takes its name; which was done with great difficulty, owing to the depth of the waters and the rapidity of the current: we used rafts, there being no canoes at the place; and we lost a negro, who was drowned, and much luggage belonging to my Spaniards.

After this river, which we crossed at a place distant one league and a half from the said village of Chilapan, we had to pass, before reaching Tepetitan, several extensive and deep swamps or morasses, in all of which except one the horses sank deep to their knees, and sometimes to their ears. . . .

[*By way of Iztapan they came to Tatahuitalpan, to find it burnt down and deserted.*]

No sooner had we left the village of Tatahuitalpan than we came to a great morass, upwards of half a league in length, which we managed to pass, the Indians, our friends, having helped us by laying on our path great quantity of grass and branches of trees. After this we came to a very deep lagoon, over which we were compelled to throw a bridge for the passage of the heavy luggage and of the horses' saddles, the horses themselves swimming across it led by the hand. Immediately after this we came to another deep lagoon, extending for more than one league, and occasionally intersected by swamps, where our horses sank always knee-deep, and sometimes as far as the girdles; but the ground at the bottom being rather harder than usual, we passed it without accident, and arrived at the foot of a mountain covered with thick wood. We cut our way through this as well as we could for two consecutive days, until our guides declared that they had lost all traces of the road, and could proceed no further. The mountain was so high, and the forest so thick and impenetrable, that we could only see the spot where we placed our feet, or, looking upwards, the blue sky over our heads; and the trees were so tall and so close to each other that those who climbed up them to discover land could not see beyond a stone's throw.

As the Spaniards who had been sent forward with the guides to cut a path through the mountain communicated to me this painful information, I gave immediate orders that they should remain where they were, whilst I proceeded thither on foot that I might judge by myself of the gravity of the case. Having found upon inspection that the report was but too true, I made the people go back to a small morass which we had passed the day before, and where, on account of the water in it, there was some grass for the horses to eat, for they had not tasted anything for forty-eight hours. There we remained all that night greatly tormented by hunger, which was further increased by the little hope we had of arriving at a place of habitation. In this emergency, and seeing my people more dead than alive, I asked for a marine compass, which I was in the habit of carrying always with me, and which had often been of much use—though never so much as on that occasion—and recollecting the spot where the Indians had told me that the village stood, I found by calculation that, by marching in a north-eastern direction, we should come upon the village, or very near to it. I then ordered those who went forwards cutting the road to take that compass, and to guide themselves by it, which they did. And thus it pleased our Lord that my calculations turned out so true, that about the hour of vespers my men fell in with some idol-houses in the centre of the village. On hearing which the rest of my people felt so great a joy, that they all ran in that direction, without heeding a large swamp that stood in their way, and in which many horses sank so deep that they could not be extricated from it until the next day, God, however, permitting that we should not lose one of them. . . .

[*Leaving this village of Çagoatespan, Cortés crossed over a river, sending forward a band of pioneers to open the road before him.*]

In this way, after traversing for three consecutive days a mountainous district covered with thick wood, we came by a very narrow path to a large lagoon, measuring upwards of five hundred paces in width, and for the passage of which we tried in vain to find a place: it could never be found, neither up nor down, and our guides ended by declaring that unless we marched for twenty consecutive days in the direction of the mountains we should never be able to turn that lagoon.

I cannot well describe what were my disappointment and dismay on the receipt of such intelligence, for crossing that deep lagoon seemed a matter of utter impossibility, on account of its great width and of our not having boats. Even if we had had them for the men and heavy luggage, the horses would have found, in going in and out of it, most awful morasses, sprinkled with roots and stems of trees, and so shaped that, unless the beasts could fly over them, it was quite out of the question to attempt the crossing. Retracing our steps was equivalent to certain death, not only on account of the bad roads we had to go over, and the heavy rains that had lately fallen, but because we would find no food of any sort. It was, moreover, evident that the rivers had swollen since and carried away the bridges constructed by us; to make these again was entirely out of the question, for my people were exhausted by fatigue. . . .

I have already stated above the difficulties that stood in the way of our going on; the danger of retracing our steps was equally great; so that no man's intelligence, however powerful, could find means to extricate us from our position, if God, who is the true remedy and help in all afflictions, had not aided us. For when I was almost reduced to despair, I accidentally found a small canoe that had served for the passage of those Spaniards sent by me to inspect the road. I immediately took possession of it, and set about having the lagoon sounded, so as to ascertain the depth of its waters, which I found to be of at least four fathoms all the way. I than had some spears tied together and sunk into the water to see the quality of the soil, and it was found that besides the said depth of four fathoms, there were at least two more of mud and mire at the bottom. There was, therefore, no other alternative left us save the construction of a bridge, however difficult the undertaking might prove, owing to the depth of the waters. I immediately set about distributing among the people the work to be done and the timber to be cut. The beams or posts were to be from nine to ten fathoms in length, owing to the portion that was to remain above water. I gave orders that each Indian chief of those who followed our camp should, in proportion to the number of men he had under his orders, cut down and bring to the spot a certain number of trees of the required length, whilst I and my Spaniards, some of us on rafts and some in that canoe and in two more that were found afterwards, began to plant the posts in the bed of the river. But the work was so fatiguing, and so difficult at the same time, that all my men despaired of its ever being finished. Some even went so far as to privately express their opinion that it was far preferable to return now, than tarry until the men should be completely exhausted by fatigue and hunger; for the bridge could never be made fit for passage, and therefore, sooner or later, we should be compelled to abandon the undertaking and retrace our steps.

This opinion gained so much ground among my Spaniards, that they almost dared to utter it in my presence; upon which, seeing them so disheartened—and I confess they had good reasons to be so, the work I had undertaken being of such a nature that we could hardly expect to see it completed—knowing that we were without provisions, and that for some days our only food had been the roots of certain plants, I decided that they should no longer work at the bridge, intending to make it exclusively with the help of the Indians. I immediately sent for the chiefs of these, and having explained to them what our situation was, I told them that we must cross that river or perish in the attempt. That I begged, therefore, they would unite their efforts, and encourage their men to the construction of a solid bridge, for the river once crossed, we would soon come to a province called Aculan, where there was abundance of food, and where we might repose ourselves. . . . Besides which, I solemnly promised to them that upon our return to this great city of Tenuxtitlan, whereof most of them were natives, they would be most munificently rewarded by me in your Majesty's name. They agreed to work at it *viribus et poss*, and began at once to divide the task between them, and I must say that they worked so hard, and with such good will, that in less than four days they constructed a fine bridge, over which the whole of the men and horses passed. So solidly built it was, that I have no doubt it will stand for upwards of ten years without breaking—unless it is burnt down—being formed by upwards of one thousand beams, the smallest of which was as thick round as a man's body, and measured nine or ten fathoms in length, without counting a great quantity of lighter timber that was used as planks. And I can assure your Majesty that I do not believe there is a man in existence capable of explaining in a satisfactory manner the dexterity which these lords of Tenuxtitlan, and the Indians under them, displayed in constructing the said bridge; I can only say that it is the most wonderful thing that ever was seen.

All the men and horses once out of the lagoon, we came up, as it was feared, to a large morass, which lasted for three arrow throws, the most frightful thing that man ever saw, unsaddled horses sinking into it in such manner that at times their ears only could be seen; the more the poor beasts tried to get out of it, the deeper they sank into the mire, so that we soon lost all hope of saving any of them or even passing ourselves; yet by dint of perseverance and work we contrived to put under them certain bundles of grass, and light branches of trees, whereupon they might support themselves so as not to sink altogether, by which operation they were somewhat relieved. We were thus engaged going backwards and forwards to the assistance of our horses, when fortunately for us a narrow channel of water and mud was discovered, in which the beasts began at once to move and swim a little, so that with the help of God they all came out safe though so fatigued from the constant exertion that they could hardly stand on their feet. We all offered many thanks to our Supreme Lord for the immense favour received at his hands, for it is certain that without his merciful assistance we should all have perished on the spot, men and horses. . . .

[*Still pressing onward, Cortés came to the province of the Lord of Checan, where he was told that he would soon have to cross a chain of high and rocky mountains.*]

After traversing six leagues of level country we began to ascend the mountain pass, which is one of the most wonderful things in the world to behold; for were I to attempt its description, and picture to your Majesty its roughness, as well as the difficulties of every kind we had to surmount, I should utterly fail in the undertaking. I can, however, assure your Majesty that neither I nor those who are more eloquent could find words to give a proper idea of it; even if we did we could never be understood except by those who saw it with their own eyes, and experienced the fatigues and perils of the ascent. It will be sufficient to inform your Majesty that we were twelve days in making the eight leagues across the pass, and that we lost on this occasion no less than sixty-eight of our horses, that either fell down precipices or were ham-strung and disabled by their fall. The rest arrived so fatigued and hurt that scarcely one was of service to us, and three months passed before any of them were fit for riding. All the time we were ascending this awful pass it never ceased raining day and night, and yet the mountains we had to cross were so shaped, having no crevices wherein the rain might stop, that we had no water to drink, and were greatly tormented by thirst, most of our horses perishing through it. Indeed, had it not been for some which we were able to collect in copper kettles and other vessels, whilst encamping at night in huts made for that purpose, no man or horse could have escaped alive.

Whilst crossing this mountain pass a nephew of mine fell down and broke his leg in two or three places; and after this misfortune—which all of us deplored—we had the greatest difficulty to carry him over to the other side. . . .

But our dangers were not yet over. About one league before we came to the farms of Tenciz, . . . on the other side of those mountains, we were stopped by a large river, the waters of which were increased and swollen beyond measure by the late rains, so that it was impossible for us to cross it. The Spaniards sent in advance to explore, finding no passage, had gone up the stream and discovered the most wonderful ford that ever had been seen or heard of, for the river at that particular spot spreads for upwards of two-thirds of a league, owing to certain large rocks which impede its course. Between these rocks natural channels are formed, through which the water runs with great rapidity and force, there being no other possible outlet for the stream. By means of these rocks, which fortunately lay close enough to each other, we managed to pass that dangerous river, cutting down large trees, which we laid across, and holding fast by *bejucos* or pliable reeds thrown from one rock to another. Yet this mode of crossing was so dangerous that had one of us become giddy or lost his foot he must inevitably have perished. There were in the river more than twenty of these narrow channels, so that it took us two whole days to cross it. The horses swam across at a place lower down the river, where the current was not so strong; but although the distance to Tenciz was only one league, as I said before, they were nearly three days in doing it; indeed, most of them were so fatigued and broken down by their last march across the mountains, that my men were almost obliged to carry them on their shoulders, and even then they could not help themselves. . . . I arrived at Tenciz on the 15th day of May of 1525, the evening before Easter (Pascua de Resureccion), although most of my men—especially those who had horses to attend to—did not join me until three days after.

[*Cortés had thus been seven months upon the march. A few leagues farther on his guide fled in the night.*]

Seeing myself without a guide of any sort—through which our difficulties were likely to be increased twofold—I determined to send people in all directions, Spaniards as well as Indians, to spread over that province, and see what information they could gather. . . . They marched during eight consecutive days without meeting any living creature, save some women, who were of little use for our purpose, since they could neither show us the road, nor tell us about the lord of the land or his people. One of them, however, said she knew of a village called Chianteco, about two leagues further on, where I might find people able to give me the information I required, and news of the Spaniards. . . . I sent forthwith some of my men, and gave them that woman for a guide; but although the village was two good days' march through a deserted country and bad roads, the natives had previous notice of my coming, and not one of them could be secured to act as guide on the occasion.

Our Almighty Lord, however, permitted that whilst we were in a state of utmost despair, finding ourselves without a guide, and unable to use the compass, in the midst of mountains so intricate and rough that we had never seen the like of them before, with no other practicable road but the one on which we were, my men suddenly came upon a lad of about fifteen years of age, who, being interrogated, said he would guide us to certain habitations in Taniha, which was another of the provinces which I recollected that I had to pass. As according to the lad's report the habitations of Taniha were only two days' journey from the place in which we then were, I hastily repaired thither, and arrived two days after on the spot, when the out-runners of my little host succeeded in securing an old Indian, who guided us to the very villages of Taniha, situated two days' march beyond. At this latter place four Indians were taken prisoners, who, being interrogated by me, gave very positive information about the Spaniards in search of whom I came, declaring that they had actually seen them, and that they were at a place called Nito, distant only two day's march. . . .

I cannot describe to your Majesty my joy, and that of all my people, when the natives of Taniha gave us this news, seeing that we were so near the end of the perilous journey we had undertaken. . . . For, although there were still some pigs left of those I brought from Mexico, when we arrived at Taniha neither I nor my men had tasted any bread for eight consecutive days, our provision being entirely exhausted, our only food consisting of palmettos boiled with the meat, wnd without salt, and the cores of the palm-trees. Nor was food more abundant in these villages, of Taniha; for being situated so close to the settlements of the Spaniards, most of the inhabitants fearing a visit from them, had fled elsewhere, although, had they known the miserable plight in which I afterwards found my countrymen, they might have been secure against any inroad on their part.

The happy news received at this place made us, however, forget our past tribulations, and gave us courage to endure present miseries and troubles, especially that of hunger, against which we had to fight more resolutely than ever, for even those cores of palm-trees without salt, which, as I said before, constituted our principal aliment, could not be procured in sufficient quantity, for they had to be extracted from the stems of large and very high palm-trees, with such difficulty that two men had to work a whole day to procure that which they could eat in half in hour. . . .

[*At Nito Cortés found the starving remnant of the expedition commanded by Gil Gonzalez de Avila. Immediately he sent out to find food for all, but three expeditions returned empty-handed*]

I cannot express the feelings of horror and dismay that assailed me when I saw my hopes thus baffled for the third time, and calculated that not one of us could possibly escape death by starvation. But in this state of mind, and not knowing what to do, God Almighty, . . . was pleased to bring us help and assistance whence we did least expect it. For there happened to arrive in those very days a vessel from the islands with thirty men, exclusive of the crew, thirteen horses, seventy and odd pigs, besides twelve casks of salted meat, and thirteen loads of bread of the kind used in the islands. We all most earnestly thanked our God for the timely succour thus received, and having treated with the master, bought of him all those provisions, besides the vessel herself, for the sum of 4000 dollars.

Some time previous to the arrival of those Spaniards I had set about repairing a caravel which the people of that village had almost allowed to rot, and to build, with the pieces of other vessels that lay scattered here and there on the shore, a good-sized brigantine. When, therefore, this vessel from the islands arrived so unexpectedly among us, the caravel was completely finished and ready to take the sea; but I do believe that the brigantine's work could never have been done, had not a man come in that vessel's crew who, although not a carpenter himself, knew enough of that craft to help us in our work.

Some time after this, having sent parties of men in all directions by land, a path was discovered across mountains, distant eighteen leagues from the place where I then was, and leading to some habitations . . . known by the name of Leguela; [there] some Indians were taken, who told us that the place where Francisco de las Casas and Cristoval de Olid and Gil Gonzalez de Avila had resided, and whereat the said Cristoval de Olid died, was a town called Naco, . . . and therefore I gave orders to clear the road, and sent forward all my men, foot and horse, under one of my captains, keeping only with me the servants of my household, the sick and invalids, and a few more who preferred going by sea. I gave instructions to that captain and bade him . . . when at Naco . . . to send ten or twelve horsemen and as many crossbowmen to the bay and port of Saint Andrew, which is about twenty leagues from that place. In the meantime, I with the sick and wounded, and the rest of the army, would proceed thither by sea. . . .

The people gone, and the brigantine being made fit for sea, I thought of embarking in her and in the other vessels with the remainder of my people, but I found that, although we had salt meat enough, we had not sufficient bread, and that it was a very adventurous thing to put to sea without this article, especially with so many sick people as I had on board, for were we to encounter bad weather or contrary winds, we were sure to die of hunger, instead of finding remedy for our wants. But whilst I was considering what could best be done in such an emergency the master of that vessel that came from the islands . . . called upon me, and said that he himself had formed part of the expedition of Gil Gonzalez, . . . that he had two hundred men, one good brigantine, and four other vessels, and that . . . they had gone a good way up that river, and met with two great gulfs, the waters of which were sweet; and that all around those two gulfs there were several villages well stocked with food. That they had navigated to the very end of them, for a distance of fourteen leagues up the river, when all of a sudden the stream became so narrow and at the same time so impetuous and strong, that in six days they could only make four leagues, notwithstanding the waters were still very deep. That owing to that circumstance they had been unable to ascertain where the river led to; but that he believed it led to a country abounding in maize.

"But," he added, "you have not men enough to go on such a voyage of exploration; for when we were on that river eighty of us landed and entered a certain village without being seen, but soon after the natives returned in such force, and attacked us with such fury, that we had to take to our ships, and some of us were wounded."

Seeing, however, the extreme want in which my men were, and that it was far preferable to cross the land in search of food, however perilous of the route, . . . than to expose myself to the dangers of the sea without sufficient provisions, I determined at once to go up that river; for, besides finding food for the people under me, . . . it struck me that I might make some discovery whereby to be of service to your Majesty. I immediately mustered the force I had with me—that is, those who were still able to bear the fatigues of a march—and I found it to consist only of forty Spaniards, who, though not sufficiently strong for every kind of work, were nevertheless well enough to remain in guard of the ships whenever I might choose to land. With these forty Spaniards, and about fifty Indians who still remained out of those I brought from Mexico, I went on board the said brigantine . . . and with two other boats and four canoes set out in the direction of that river. . . .

[*Hardships and fighting followed in plenty, but the river expedition yielded a "most providential harvest," compensating "us for all our past troubles."*]

Our provisions being safely stowed in the ship and boats, I embarked with all the people of the division of Gil Gonzalez Leutville who were in that village, and those who still remained of my former army, and this being done I set sail . . . and steered for the harbour in the bay of St Andrew. I anchored near a point of land, where having landed all those who could make use of their legs, besides two horses that I had with me in the ship, ordered them to march to the said harbour . . . where the people of Naco were to be already waiting our arrival. . . .

I stayed there twenty days, seeing to what those settlers from Naco had better do, and looking for a convenient spot to found a city; for certainly that port is the best and the largest that can be found in all that coast of Tierra Firme, that is to say, from the Gulf of Pearls to Florida. God permitted that I should find one . . . and so, in your Majesty's name, I founded there a town, which I called the "Nativity of our Lady," because on that day the levelling of the ground commenced. . . .

When I heard . . . from the people who had lately come from Naco that the inhabitants of the village . . . had . . . fled to the mountains and refused to return . . . I took immediate measures to stop the evil, and gain, if possible, the confidence of the natives. I therefore wrote to the captain who there governed in my name, to try every means in his power to secure some of those Indians and send them under an escort to me. . . . The captain sent me a few, . . . taken in a foray he had made for the purpose,and whom I entertained and treated as well as I could, speaking to them myself by means of an interpreter, or through some of the principal Mexicans I had with me. They told them who I was and what I had done in their country, and how well they all had been treated by me since they became my friends, how, . . . on the contrary, those who were rebellious to your Majesty's authority I considered by enemies, and treated them as such, . . . and as they saw that the Indians of my suite seemed happy and well treated they had confidence in my words, and went away promising to persuade their chiefs and comrades. . . . And so they did; for a few days after this I received intelligence from the captain, saying that many Indian families belonging to the neighbouring villages . . . had peaceably returned to their dwellings, announcing that all the natives of that extensive province would soon do the same, having been informed who I was. . . . They ended by a prayer that I should . . . visit them. . . . This I would willingly have done had I not been obliged to proceed further on my march, in order to provide for certain matters, about which I will say something to your Majesty in the following chapter.

On my arrival, invincible Cæsar, at that village of Nito, where, as I said before, I found the people of Gil Gonzalez almost entirely forgotten and lost, I learned from them that Francisco de la Casas . . . had left at about sixty leagues lower down the coast, in a harbour called by the pilots Las Honduras, a certain number of Spaniards, who no doubt were still there. No sooner, therefore, did I arrive at that village of Saint Andrew (where in your Majesty's name the town called Natividad de Nuestra Señora has since been founded) than I began to consider which would be the best means of communicating with them; and so, whilst I attended to the said foundation and population, and gave my instructions to the captain and people at Naco as to what they were to do for the pacification of the Indians in that neighbourhood, I occupied myself about those people of Francisco de las Casas, sending thither, to Honduras, the vessel I had bought, with orders to ascertain whether they were still living. . . . The vessel came back, bringing on board the procurador and one of the regidores or aldermen of the town, who . . . begged me most earnestly, in the name of their fellow-citizens, to go and help them, as they were in the utmost distress. . . . Hearing the miserable plight to which those people were reduced, I again embarked with all the sick and wounded of my small army—though by that time some of them had died—it being my intention to send them from that place to the Islands and to New Spain, as I afterwards did. I took on board with me some of my own household servants, and gave orders besides that twenty horsemen and ten crossbowmen should go by land, having heard that the road to the village was good and practicable, though they would have to pass some rivers on their way thither.

Having met with contrary winds at sea, it took me full nine days to arrive at the port of Honduras, where I anchored; and having gone into a boat with two Franciscan friars, who had always accompanied me, besides the Spaniards of my suite, made quickly for the shore, where the people of the town were already expecting me. As the boat came near to the shore, all those people jumped into the water, and took me out of the boat in their arms, showing every sign of happiness and joy and my coming. . . .

Most invincible sovereign, may God our Lord preserve for many years the life, and increase the power, of your sacred Majesty. From this city of Tenuxtitlan, on the 3rd day of September of 1526.

HERNANDO CORTÉS

THE EXPEDITION OF GONZALO PIZARRO TO THE LAND OF CINNAMON [1]

(1539-42)

GARCILASSO INCA DE LA VEGA

IN the year 1539 the Marquis Don Francisco Pizarro, being in the city of Cuzco, received tidings that beyond the city of Quito, and beyond the limits of the empire formerly ruled by the Incas, there was a wide region where cinnamon grew; and he determined to send his brother, Gonzalo Pizarro, that he might conquer such another land as the Marquis himself had found, and become governor of it.

Having consulted with those in whom he could confide, the Marquis therefore handed over the government of Quito to his brother, in order that the people of that city might supply him with all things that he might require, for from thence he would have to make his entrance into the land of Cinnamon, which is east of the city of Quito.

With this object in view he sent for his brother, who was then in Charcas, arranging the affairs of that territory.

Gonzalo Pizarro soon arrived in Cuzco, and having arranged the projected conquest of the land of Cinnamon with this brother, the Marquis Don Francisco, he set out; thus accepting the adventure with a stout heart, regarding it as an opportunity of proving his valour, by deeds worthy of his former fame.

He levied more than two hundred soldiers in Cuzco, one hundred cavalry, and the rest infantry, at a cost of sixty thousand ducats; and marched to Quito, a distance of five hundred leagues, where Pedro de Puelles was governor. On the road he had encounters with the Indians, and was so hard pressed at Huanuco that his brother, the marquis, sent him assistance under Francisco de Chaves.

Freed from this danger, and from others of less importance, Gonzalo Pizarro reached Quito; and having shewn his commission from the marquis to Pedro de Puelles, the latter at once resigned the government. Gonzalo then made all the necessary preparations for the expedition, and added one hundred soldiers to his force, making a total of three hundred and forty; one hundred and fifty cavalry, and the rest infantry. He also took with him more than four thousand Indians, laden with arms, supplies, and all things requisite for the service, such as iron, hatchets, knives, ropes, hempen cords, and large

[1] From *Expeditions into the Valley of the Amazons,* translated by Clements Markham (Hakluyt Society, No. 24 (1859)).

nails; likewise nearly four thousand head of swine, and a flock of llamas, the latter carrying part of the luggage.

Gonzalo Pizarro left Pedro de Puelles in Quito as his deputy, and after having put the affairs of that city in order, he set out on Christmas Day, 1539. He marched with perfect success, and well supplied with provisions by the Indians, until he reached the limits of the ancient empire of the Incas. He then entered a province called Quijos.

As Francisco Lopez de Gomara and Agustin de Zarate agree well together, describing the occurrences nearly in the same words, and as I have heard many of those who were with Gonzalo Pizarro relate their adventures, I will describe the facts, sometimes making use of one authority, and sometimes of the other.

In this province of Quijos, which is north of Quito, many warlike Indians sallied forth against Gonzalo; but when they beheld the multitude of Spaniards and horses, they quickly retired, and were seen no more. A few days afterwards there was such an earthquake, that many houses, in the village where Gonzalo's party were resting, were thrown down. The earth opened in many places; there was lightning and thunder, insomuch that the Spaniards were much astonished; at the same time such torrents of rain fell, that they were surprised at the difference between that land and Peru. After suffering these inconveniences for forty or fifty days they commenced the passage of the snowy cordillera, where the snow fell in such quantities, and it was so cold, that many Indians were frozen to death because they were so lightly clad. The Spaniards, to escape from the cold and snow of that inclement region, left the swine and provisions behind them, intending to seek some Indian village. But things turned out contrary to their hopes, for, having passed the cordillera, they were much in want of provisions, as the land they came to was uninhabited. They made haste to pass through it, and arrived at a province and village called Sumaco, on the skirts of a volcano, where they obtained food. But, during two months, it did not cease to rain for a single day; so that the Spaniards received great injury, and much of their clothing became rotten.

In this province, called Sumaco, which is on the equinoctial line, or very near it, the trees, which they call cinnamon, grow, and of which the Spaniards were in search. They are very tall, with large leaves, like a laurel; and the fruit grows in clusters, and resembles an acorn. Many of these trees grow wild in the forests, and yield fruits; but they are not so good as those which the Indians get from the trees which they plant and cultivate for their own use, and for that of their neighbours, but not for the people of Peru. The latter never wish for any other condiment than their *uchu,* which the Spaniards call *aji,* and in Europe pepper.

In Sumaco and its neighbourhood the Spaniards found that the Indians went naked, without any clothes; the women having a little cloth in front for the sake of modesty. They go naked because the country is hot, and it rains so much that clothes would become rotten, as we have before said.

In Sumaco Gonzalo Pizarro left behind the greater part of his men; and taking with him the most active, he went in search of a road, if any could be found, to pass onwards; because all the country they had as yet traversed, which was nearly one hundred leagues, was dense forest, where in many parts they had to open a road by main force, and with the blows of hatchets. The Indians, whom they took as guides, deceived them, and led them through uninhabited wilds, where they suffered from hunger, and were obliged to feed on herbs, roots, and wild fruits.

Suffering these hardships, and others which can be more easily imagined than described, they arrived at a province called Cuca, where they found supplies. The chief received them well, and gave them food. Near this place a great river passess, which is supposed to be the largest of those streams, which unite to form that river which some call the Orellana, and others the Marañon.

Here they waited nearly two months for the Spaniards who were left at Sumaco. Having been joined by them, and recovered from their fatigue, they all proceeded together along the banks of that great river; but for more than fifty leagues they found neighter ford nor bridge by which they might pass over, for the river was so broad as not to admit either the one or the other.

At the end of this long journey, they came to a place where the river precipitates itself over a rock, more than two hundred feet high; and makes so great a noise, that the Spaniards heard it at a distance of six leagues before they arrived at it. They were astonished to see a thing so great and so strange; but much more did they wonder, forty for fifty leagues lower down, when they saw that the immense volume of water, contained in this river, was collected into a channel made by another enormous rock.

The channel is so narrow, that there are not more than twenty feet from one bank to the other; and the rock is so high, that from the top (where these Spaniards presently passed over) to the water was another two hundred feet, the same height as the fall. Certainly it is a marvellous thing that in that land should be found things so great and wonderful as those two rapids, and many others.

Gonzalo Pizarro and his captains, thinking that they might not find so easy a way of crossing the river again, to see what was on the other side, because all they had yet seen was a sterile and unprofitable land, bethought themselves of making a bridge over the chasm; but the Indians on the other side, though few in number, defended the pass bravely. The Spaniards were thus obliged to fight with them, a thing which they had not yet done with any Indians of that region. They fired their arquebusses, and killed a few, and the rest retired about two hundred paces, astonished at so strange a sight. They were terrified at the bravery and ferocity of that race, which they said brought lightning, rain, and thunder, to kill those who did not obey them. The Spaniards, seeing the passage clear, made a bridge of wood; and it must be considered what an undertaking it was to place the first beam across a chasm, at such a height above the water, that even to look down was an act of rashness. And so it proved to a Spaniard, who , wishing to look at the furious rush of water from the top of the rock, became giddy and fell in. On beholding the misfortune which had befallen their companion the others were more careful; and with much labour and difficulty placed the first beam, and with help of it, as many more as were necessary. Thus they made a bridge, by which men and horses safely passed over, They left it as it was, in case it should be necessary to return by it. They journeyed down the course of the river, through such dense forests, that it was necessary in many places to cut a road with hatchets.

Suffering these hardships, they reached a land called Guema, as poor and inhospitable as the most sterile of those they had passed; and they met few Indians, while even those, on seeing the Spaniards, entered the forests, and were seen no more.

The Spaniards, and their Indian followers, supported themselves on herbs and roots. Owing to hunger, and fatigue, and the heavy rains, many Spaniards and Indians fell sick and died; but, in spite of these disasters, they advanced many leagues, and arrived at another land, where they found Indians, a little more civilized than those they had seen before; who fed on maize bread, and dressed in cotton clothes. Gonzalo Pizarro then sent people in all directions, to see if they could find any open road, but all returned in a short time with the same story, that the land was covered with dense forest, full of lagoons and swamps, which could not be forded. On this acount they determined to build a brigantine, in which they might pass from one side of the river to the other, the river being nearly two leagues broad. They accordingly set up a forge for making nails, and burnt charcoal with grat trouble, because the heavy rains prevented the tinder from taking fire. They also made roofed huts to burn the wood in, and defend it from the rain. Some of the nails were made from the shoes of horses, which had been killed as food for the sick, and the rest of the iron they had brought with them. They now found it more valuable than gold.

Gonzalo Pizarro, as became so valiant a soldier, was the first to cut the wood, forge the iron, burn the charcoal, and employ himself in any other office, so as to give an example to the rest, that no one might have any excuse for not doing the same. For tar, for the brigantine, they used resin from the trees; for oakum, they had blankets and old shirts; and all were ready to give up their clothes, because they believed that the remedy for all their misfortunes would be the brigantine. Thus they completed and launched her, believing that on that day all their troubles would come to an end. But in a few days their hopes were destroyed, as we shall presently see.

They put all their gold on board the brigantine, amounting to more than one hundred thousand dollars, with many fine emeralds, also the iron, the forge, and everything else of value. They also sent the sick on board, who were unable to travel by land. Thus they started from this place, having journeyed already nearly two hundred leagues; and began the descent of the river, some by land, others on board the brigantine, never being far from each other, and every night they slept close together. They all advanced with much difficulty; for those on shore had to open the road in many places, by cutting with axes; while those on board had to labour hard to resist the current, so as not to get far from their comrades. When they could not make a road on one side of the river, owing to the dense nature of the forest, they passed to the other side in the brigantine, and four canoes. Having gone on in this way for more than two months, they met some Indians who told them by signs, and by means of some words understood by their own Indians, that ten days journey from the place where they then were, they would find an inhabited land; well supplied with provisions, and rich in gold, and all other things which they wanted. They also told them, by signs, that that land was on the banks of another great river which joined the one down which they were now travelling. The Spaniards rejoiced at this news. Gonzalo Pizarro selected, as captain of the brigantine, his lieutenant, Don Francisco de Orellana, with fifty soldiers; and ordered him to proceed to the place indicated by the Indians (which would be distant about eighty leagues); and having arrived at the point where the two rivers meet, to load the brigantine with provisions, and return up the river, to relieve the people, who were so afflicted with hunger, that each day there died several men, Spaniards as well as Indians. Of four thousand who started in this expedition, two thousand were already dead.

Francisco de Orellana continued his voyage, and in three days, without oar or sail, he navigated the eighty leagues, but did not find the supplies which had been promised; and he considered that if he should return with this news to Pizarro, he would not reach him within a year, on account of the strong current, though he had descended in three days; and that if he remained where he was, he would be of no use either to the one, or to the other. Not knowing how long Gonzalo Pizarro would take to reach the place, without consulting with anyone, he set sail, and prosecuted his voyage onwards, [1] intending to ignore Gonzalo, to reach Spain, and obtain that government for himself.

Many of his crew objected to this, suspecting his evil intentions; and they declared that it was not right to go beyond the orders of his captain-general, nor to desert him in his great necessity. A monk named Fray Gaspar de Carbajal, and a young cavalier named Hernan Sanchez de Vargas, a native of Badajos, whom the malcontents took for their chief, also dissented. Francisco de Orellana, however, appeased them for the time with fair speeches; though afterwards, when he had reduced them to obedience, he broke his word, and told the good monk that if he would not follow him he would leave him behind, like Hernan Sanchez de Vargas. That he might suffer a more cruel death, he did not kill Hernan Sanchez, but left him in that dreary place, surrounded on one side by the dense forest, on the other by a mighty river, so that he could neither escape by water nor land, and thus he would perish of hunger.

Francisco de Orellana continued his journey; and soon, to render his intention more clear, he renounced his obedience to Gonzalo Pizarro, and elected himself a captain of his Majesty, independent of anyone else. A foul deed (what else can such treason be called?) such as has been done by other worthies in the conquest of the New World; as captain Gonzales Hernandez de Oviedo y Valdes, Chronicler to his Catholic Majesty the Emperor Charles V, says in Book 17, Cap. 20, of his *General History of the Indies:* "those who did these things were paid in the same coin."

Francisco de Orellana, in descending the river, had some skirmishes with the Indians inhabiting that shore, who were very fierce, and in some parts the women came out to fight, with their husbands. On this account, and to make his voyage the more wonderful, he said that it was a land of Amazons, and besought his Majesty for a commission to conquer them. Further down the river they found more civilized Indians, who were friendly, and were astonished to see the brigantine, and such strange men. They made friends with them, and gave them food, as much as they wished. The Spaniards stayed with them some days; and then they sailed down to the sea, two

[1] And thus, by deserting his captain, discovered the course of the Amazon.

hundred leagues to the Isle of Trinidad, having suffered the hardships that have been described, and many great dangers on the river. In that island Orellana bought a ship, with which he went to Spain, and besought his Majesty to give him a commission to conquer that country, magnifying his discovery, by saying it was a land of gold and silver, and precious stones, and demonstrating his assertions by the fine show of these things, which he brought with him. His Majesty gave him power to conquer the land, and to govern it. Orellana then collected more than five hundred soldiers, many of them distinguished and noble cavaliers, with whom he embarked at San Lucar, and died at sea, his people dispersing in different directions. Thus his expedition met an end, in conformity with its evil beginning.

From it we will return to Gonzalo Pizarro, whom we left in great distress. He, having dispatched Orellana, with the brigantine, made ten or twelve canoes, and as many balsas, so as to be able to pass from one side of the river to the other, when they were impeded on land by dense forest, as they had been before. They journeyed on with the hope that their brigantine would soon succour them with food, to preserve them from the hunger which they suffered, for they had no other enemy in all their journey.

They arrived, at the end of two months, at the junction of the two great rivers, where they expected to find the brigantine, which they thought would be waiting for them with provisions, and which might not have been able to reach them before, on account of the strong current of the river. They found themselves deceived; and the hope of escaping from that hell, for such a land might be called by that name, was lost; (where they had passed through so many hardships and miseries, without remedy, or hope of escape.) They found, at the junction of the two great rivers, the good Hernan Sanchez de Vargas, who, with the constancy of a true gentleman, had insisted on being left behind, suffering hunger, and other hardships, to give Gonzalo Pizarro a complete account of what Francisco de Orellana had done against his captain-general, and against Hernan Sanchez himself, for having opposed his wicked intentions. The captains and soldiers were so grieved at being thus deceived of their hopes, and deprived of all relief, that they were ready to give way to despair.

Their general, although he felt the same grief as the rest, consoled and cheered them, saying that they should take heart, to bear like Spaniards these and even greater hardships, if greater there could be; that they had succeeded in being the conquerors of that empire, and should, therefore, behave like men chosen by Divine Providence for so great an enterprise. With this speech they were all refreshed, seeing the steadfastness of their captain-general.

They continued their journey, still along the banks of the great river, sometimes on one side, and sometimes on the other, as they were forced to pass from one side to the other. The work they had was incredible, to take the horses across on balsas, as they still had more than eighty, out of one hundred and fifty that they took from Quito. They also had nearly one thousand Indians, out of the four thousand they took from Peru; who served like sons to their masters, in these hardships and privations, searching for herbs and roots and wild fruits, frogs and serpents, and othe wretched food.

Suffering these miseries, they travelled down the river another hundred leagues, without finding any better land, nor any hope in advancing farther; for, from day to day they were worse off, without any chance of better times. These things having been considered by the general and his captains, they agreed to return to Quito (if it were possible), whence they had marched more than four hundred leagues.

But, as it was impossible to navigate up the river, on account of the strong current, they determined to take another road, and to return by the north of the river, because they had received notice that in that direction there were fewer lagoons and morasses. They plunged into the forest, opening a road with axes and bills.

Gonzalo Pizarro, and his party, struggled with many obstacles in the shape of mighty rivers, and morasses which they could not wade through. The forest were full of dense thorny foliage; and the trees were of great size. Gomara, in the end of his eighty-sixth chapter, describing the discovery made of that land by Vincente Yanez Pinçon after narrating what happened to the discoverer, finally speaks of the wonderful things which he saw, in these words: "The discoverers brought the bark of certain trees, which seemed to be cinnamon, and a skin of that animal which puts its young into its bosom; and they related, as a wonderful thing, that they saw a tree which sixteen men could not span round."

Besides these difficulties, Gonzalo Pizarro and his follwers had to contend against hunger, a cruel enemy both of men and beasts, which had destroyed so many of them in that uninhabitable land.

Gonzalo Pizarro intended to return to Peru, by leaving the river, and journeying by dense forests, no better than what he had passed before, where the road was formed by dint of strength of arms; feeding on herbs, roots, and wild fruits, and it was very little even of such food that they found, considering themselves lucky travellers to get any. Through the lagoons, morasses, and marshes, the worn out and sick people were carried on the backs of their comrades; and those who laboured most among them, were

Gonzalo Pizarro himself, and his captains, who thus gave fresh vigour to their followers to emulate their examples. Thus they went on for more than three hundred leagues, without escaping from the difficulties which have been mentioned, or lessening the labour which they had to endure: by which anyone can imagine how great were the hardships they endured in the four hundred leagues in going, and three hundred in returning; when their hunger was so great, that they were obliged to kill their horses: and previously they had eaten the greyhounds and mastiffs they had with them: and, as Gomara says in chap. 144, they even eat the Spaniards who died, according to the evil custom of the savages of those forests.

Many Indians perished from hunger, and Spaniards also, though the flesh of the horses was equally divided.

One of the greatest miseries which they suffered was the absence of salt, which in more than two hundred leagues, as Zarata says (Lib. IV, Cap. V) they did not find, and for want of which they were attacked by scurvy. On account of the constant waters from above and below, they were always wet; and their clothes rotted, so that they had to go naked. Shame obliged them to cover themselves with the leaves of trees, of which they made girdles to wind round their bodies. The excessive heat of the region made their nakedness bearable; but the thorns and matted underwood of those dense forests (which they had to cut by blows of their axes), cruelly tore them, and made them look as if they had been flayed.

The labour and want of food that Gonzalo Pizarro and his people suffered, was so great that four thousand Indians died of hunger, and among them was an Indian beloved by Gonzalo, whose death Gonzalo mourned as if he had been his own brother; two hundred and ten Spaniards also died, out of the three hundred and forty who started, without counting the fifty who followed Orellana. The eighty survivors, having passed the three hundred leagues of forest, reached a land more open, and less covered with water; where they found some game of different kinds, among which were deer. They killed what they could with slings, and with the arquebusses and the powder they had preserved. Of their skins they made short little coats, to cover their nakedness: thus on foot, without shoes, worn out and thin, so that they scarcely knew each other; they reached the borders of Quito.

They kissed the earth, giving thanks to God, who had delivered them from such great perils and hardships. Some began to eat with such will that it was necessary to stop them. Others were of a different constitution, and could not eat what they wished, because their stomachs, used to fasting and abstinence, would not receive what was given to them.

The city of Quito, which (on account of the wars of Don Diego de Almagro) was half depopulated, received notice of their condition, and those who remained sent clothes to Gonzalo Pizarro and his party.

They collected six suits of clothes, each man assisting with what he had, a cloak, a cap, a shirt, shoes or a hat; and thus they dressed Gonzalo and five others, it being impossible to clothe the rest.

A dozen horses were sent out, they had no more, as they had all been taken away, when the people went to serve his Majesty against Don Diego de Almagro. With the horses they sent much food; they would willingly have sent all the presents in the world; because Pizarro was the best beloved of any man in Peru, and had, by his own most noble qualities, endeared himself as much to strangers as to his own friends.

They chose a dozen of the principal people of the city to bring these gifts. These men went, and found Gonzalo Pizarro more than thirty leagues from the city; where they were met with much joy, and many tears, so that they could not determine of which of those two things there was most abundance. Gonzalo Pizarro and his party received the people from Quito with great joy; because, in their former misery, they had never hoped to reach this place. The citizens wept for grief to behold those who came, and to know that the missing had died of hunger. They consoled each other in thinking that there was no remedy for the past, and that tears availed little.

Gonzalo Pizarro, his captains and soldiers, received the gifts with joy; but seeing that there were only clothes and horses for the captains, they would neither dress nor mount, so that they might be on equal terms with their good soldiers: and thus they entered the city of Quito one morning, going to the church to hear mass, and to give thanks to God, for delivering them from such evils.

What follows, I heard from persons who were present. The twelve citizens who brought the presents to Gonzalo Pizarro, seeing that neither he nor his captains had either dressed themselves, or mounted the horses; and that they were determined to enter the city naked and barefooted; bethought themselves also of entering in the same plight, so as to share the honour, fame, and glory, that was merited by those who had passed through so many and such great hardships. Thus they entered all alike. Having heard mass, the citizens received Pizarro with all the welcome possible. This entrance took place in the beginning of June 1542, they having spent two years in the expedition.

OF WHAT BEFELL DON FERDINANDO DE SOTO, ADELANTADO OF THE LANDS OF FLORIDA[1]

(1540-42)

A Gentleman of Elvas

[*In the words of the Gentleman of Elvas, "Captaine Soto was the son of a squire of Xerez of Badajos. He went into the Spanish Indies, when Peter Arias of Avila [Pedrarias Davila] was Governor of the West Indies. And there he was without any thing else of his owne, save his sword and target: and for his good qualities and valour, Peter Arias made him captaine of a troope of horsemen, and by his commandement hee went with Fernando Pizarro to the conquest of Peru." With a fortune of 180,000 ducats he returned to Spain. Made by Charles V "Adelantado of the Lands of Florida," he landed at Espiritu Santo Bay in May 1539, and for nearly four years searched for gold. In 1541 he reached the Mississippi. Returning in the following year, disheartened and in "great dumps," he fell sick, "evil handled with fevers," and on the 21st of May died.*]

How he went through a Desert and fell into Great Distress

On Monday the 12 of April [1540] the Governour departed from Ocute: the cacique gave him two hundred Tamenes, to wit, Indians, to carrie burdens: he passed through a towne, the lord whereof was named Cofaqui, and came to a province of an Indian lord, called Patofa, who, because he was in peace with the lord of Ocute, and with the other bordering lords, had many daies before notice of the Governour, and desired to see him: he came to visit him, and made this speech following.

Mightie lord, now with good reason I will crave of fortune to requite this my so great prosperitie with some small adversitie; and I will count myself verie rich, seeing I have obtained that, which in this world I most desired, which is, to see, and be able to doe your lordship some service.... Where did this your countrie, which I doe governe, deserve to be visited of so soveraigne and so excellent a prince, whom all the rest of the world ought to obey and serve?... For mine owne part, from my very heart with reverence due to such a prince, I offer my selfe unto your lordship, and beseech you, that in reward of this my true good will, you will vouchsafe to make use of mine owne person, my countrie, and subjects.

[1] From *The Discovery and Conquest of Terra Florida by Don Ferdinando de So,* written by a Gentleman of Elvas, and translated out of the Portuguese by Richard Hakluyt. (Hakluyt Society, No. 9 (1851)).

The Governour answered him, that his offers and good will declared by the effect, did highly please him, whereof he would alwaies be mindfull to honour and favour him as his brother.

This countrie, from the first peaceable cacique unto the province of Patofa, which were fiftie leagues, is a fat countrie, beautifull, and very fruitfull, and very well watered, and full of good rivers. And from thence to the port de Spirito Santo, where we first arived in the land of Florida (which may be three hundred and fifty leagues, little more or lesse) is a barren land, and the most of it groves of wild pine trees, low and full of lakes, and in some places very hie and thicke groves, whither the Indians that were in armes fled, so that no man could find them, neither could any horses enter into them. . . .

In the towne of Patofa, the youth, which the Governour carried with him for an interpretour and a guide, began to fome at the mouth, and tumble on the ground, as one possessed with the divell. They said a gospel over him; and the fit left him. And he said that foure daies journie from thence toward the sunne rising was the province that he spake of. The Indians of Patofa said, that toward that part they knew no habitation; but that toward the northwest, they knew a province which was called Coça, a verie plentifull countrie, which had very great townes in it. The cacique told the Governour, that if he would go thither, he would give him guides and Indians for burdens; and if he would goe whither the youth spake of, that he would likewise give him those that he needed: and so, with loving words and offers of courtesie, they tooke their leaves the one of the other.

Hee gave him seven hundred Indian to beare burdens. He tooke maiz for foure daies journie. Hee travelled sixe daies by a path, which grew narrow more and more, till it was lost altogether. He went where the youth did lead him, and passed two rivers which were waded; each of them was two crossebow-shot over: the water came to the stirrops, and had so great a current, that it was needfull for the horsemen to stand one before another, that the footemen might passe above them leaning unto them. He came to another river of a greater current and largenes, which was passed with more trouble, because the horses did swim at the comming out about a lances length.

Having passed this river, the Governor came to a grove of pine trees, and threatened the youth, and made as though hee would have cast him to the dogges, because he had told him a lie, saying, it was but foure daies journie, and they had travelled nine, and every day seven or eight leagues; and the men by this time were growne wearie and weake, and the horses leane through the great scanting of the maiz. The youth said, that hee knew not where hee was. It saved him that he was not cast to the dogges, that there was never another whom John Ortiz[1] did understand. The Governour with them two, and with some horsemen and footemen, leaving the campe in a grove of pine trees, travelled that day five or six leagues to seek a way, and returned at night very comfortlesse, and without finding any signe of way or towne.

The next day there were sundrie opinions delivered, whether they should goe backe, or what they should doe: and because backward the countrie whereby they had passed was greatlie spoiled and destitute of maiz, and that which they brought with them was spent, and the men were very weake, and the horses likewise, they doubted much whether they might come to any place where they might helpe themselves.

And besides this, they were of opinion, that going in that sort out of order, that any Indians would presume to set upon them, so that with hunger, or with warre, they could not escape. The Governour determined to send horsemen from thence every way to seeke habitation; and the next day he sent foure captaines, every one a sundrie way with eight horsemen. At night they came againe, leading their horses, or driving them with a sticke before; for they were so wearie that they could not lead them; neither found they any way nor signe of habitation. The next day, the Governour sent other foure, with as many horsemen that could swim, to passe the ose[2] and rivers which they should find, and they had choice horses, the best that were in the campe. The captaines were Baltasar de Gallegos, which went up the river; and John Danusco, downe the river; Alfonso Romo, and John Rodriquez Lobillo went into the inward parts of the land.

The Governour brought with him into Florida thirteene sowes, and had by this time three hundred swine. He commanded every man should have halfe a pound of hog's flesh every day; and this hee did three or foure daies after the maiz was all spent. With this small quantitie of flesh, and some sodden hearbs, with much trouble the people were sustained. The Governour dismissed the Indians of Patofa, because hee had no food to give them; who desiring to accompanie and serve the Christians in their necessitie, making shew that it grieved them very much to returne, until they had left them in a peopled countrie, returned to their owne home.

John Danusco came on Sunday late in the evening, and brought newes that he had found a little towne twelve or thirteen leagues from thence; he brought a woman and a boy that he tooke there; with his comming and with those newes, the Governour and all the rest were so glad, that they seemed at that instant to have returned from death to life.

[1] The Interpreter.

[2] Ooze

Upon Monday, the twentie-sixe of Aprill, the Governour departed to go to the towne, which was called Aymay; and the Christians named it the towne of Relief. He left, where the camp had lien, at the foote of a pine tree, a letter buried, and letters carved in the barke of the pine, the contents whereof was this: *Dig here at the foot of this pine, and you shall find a letter*. And this he did, because when the captaines came, which were sent to seeke some habitation, they might see the letter, and know what was become of the Governour, and which way he was gone. There was no other way to the towne, but the markes that John Danusco left made upon the trees. The Governour, with some of them that had the best horses, came to it on the Monday. And all the rest inforcing themselves the best they could, some of them lodged within two leagues of the towne, some within three and foure, every one as he was able to goe, and his strength served him. There was found in the towne a storehouse full of the flowre of parched maiz; and some maiz, which was distributed by allowance.... Upon Wednesday came the captaines Baltasar de Gallegos, Alfonso Romo, and John Rodriquez Lobillo: for they had found the letter, and followed the way which the Governour had taken toward the towne....

How he came to the Great River[1]

And he travelled seven daies through a desert of many marishes and thicke woods; but it might all be travelled on horseback, except some lakes, which they swamme over. He came to a towne of the province of Quizquiz without being descried, and tooke all the people in it before they came out of their houses. The mother of the cacique was taken there; and he sent unto him by an Indian, that he should come to see him, and that he would give him his mother, and all the people which he had taken there. The cacique sent him answere againe, that his lordship should loose and send them to him, and that he would come to visit and serve him. The Governour, because his people for want of maiz were somewhat weake and wearie, and the horses also were leane, determined to accomplish his request, to see if hee could have peace with him, and so commanded to set free his mother and all the rest, and with loving words dismissed them, and sent them to him.

The next day, when the Governour expected the cacique, there came many Indians with their bowes and arrowes, with a purpose to set upon the Christians. The Governour had commanded all the horsemen to be armed, and on horsebacke, and in readines. When the Indians saw that they were

[1] The Mississippi, which de Soto was the first white man to cross.

readie, they staid a crossbow shot from the place where the Governour was, neere a brooke. And after halfe an hour that they had stood there stil, there came to the camp sixe principall Indians, and said, they came to see what people they were; and that long agoe they had been informed by their forefathers, that a white people should subdue them; and that therefore they would returne to their cacique, and bid him come presently to obey and serve the Governour: and after they had presented him with sixe or seven skinnes and mantles which they brought, they tooke their leave of him, and returned with the other, which waited for them by the brookes side. The cacique never came againe nor sent other message.

And because in the towne where the Governour lodged there was small store of maiz, he remooved to another halfe a league from Rio Grande, where they found plentie of maiz. And he went to see the river, and found that neere unto it was great store of timber to make barges, and good situation of ground to incampe in. Presently he remooved himselfe thither. They made houses, and pitched their campe in a plaine field a crossebow shot from the river. And thither was gathered all the maiz of the townes which they had latelie passed. They began presently to cut and hew down timber, and to saw plankes for barges. The Indians came presently down the river; they leaped on shore, and declared to the Governour, that they were subjects of a great lord, whose name was Aquixo, who was lord of many townes, and governed many people on the other side of the river, and came to tell him on his behalfe, that the next day he with all his men would come to see what it would please him to command him.

The next day with speed, the cacique came with two hundred canoes full of Indians with their bowes and arrowes, painted, and with great plumes of white feathers, and many other colours, with shields in their hands, wherewith they defended the rowers on both sides, and the men of warre stood from the head to the sterne, with their bowes and arrows in their hands. The canoe wherein the cacique was, had a tilt[1] over the sterne, and hee sate under the tilt; and so were other canoes of the principall Indians. And from under the tilt where the chiefe man sat, hee governed and commanded the other people. All joyned together, and came within a stones cast of the shore. From thence the cacique said to the Governour, which walked along the rivers side with others that waited on him, that he was come thither to visit, to honour, and to obey him; because he knew he was the greatest and mightiest lord on the earth: therefore he would see what he would command him to doe. The Governour yielded him thankes, and requested him to come on shore, that they might the

[1] Awning.

better communicate together. And without any answere to that point, hee sent him three canoes, wherein was great store of fish, and loaves made of the substance of prunes, like unto brickes. After he had received all, he thanked him, and prayed him againe to come on shore. And because the caciques purpose was, to see if with dissimulation he might doe some hurt, when they saw that the Governour and his men were in readinesse, they began to goe from the shore; and with a great crie, the crossebowmen which were ready, shot at them, and slue five or sixe of them. They retired with great order; none did leave his oare, though the next to him were slaine; and shielding themselves, they went farther off. Afterward they came many times and landed: and when any of us came toward them, they fled unto their canoes, which were verie pleasant to behold: for they were very great and well made, and had their tilts, plumes, paveses, and flagges, and with the multitude of people that were in them, they seemed to be a faire armie of gallies.

In thirtie daies space, while the Governour remained there, they made foure barges: in three of which hee commanded twelve horsemen to enter, in each of them foure; in a morning, three houres before day, men which hee trusted would land in despight of the Indians, and make sure the passage, or die, and some footemen being crossebowmen went with them, and rowers to set them on the other side. And in the other barge, he commanded John de Guzman to passe with the footmen, which was made captaine instead of Francisco Maldonado. And because the streame was swift, they went a quarter of a league up the river along the bancke, and crossing over, fell downe with the streame and landed right over against the camp. Two stones-cast before they came to land, the horsemen went out of the barges on horsebacke to a sandie plot of very hard and cleere ground, where all of them landed without any resistance. As soone as those that passed first were on land on the other side, the barges returned to the place where the Governour was: and within two houres after sunne-rising, all the people were over. The river was almost halfe a league broad. If a man stood still on the other side, it could not be discerned whether he were a man or no. The river was of great depth, and of a strong current; the water was alwaies muddie: there came downe the river continually many trees and timber, which the force of the water and streame brought downe. There was great store of fish in it of sundrie sorts, and the most of it differing from the freshwater fish of Spaine. . . .

And Sought a Sea that Could Not Be Found

Upon Monday the sixth of March 1542, the Governour departed from Autiamque to seeke Nilco, which the Indians said was neere the great river, with determination to come to the sea, and procure some succour of men and horses: for he had now but three hundred men of warre, and fortie horses, and some of them lame, which did nothing but helpe to make up the number: and for want of iron they had gone above a yeere unshod: and because they were used to it in the plaine countrie, it did them no great harme. John Oritz died in Autiamque; which grieved the Governour very much: because that without an interpretour hee feared to enter farre into the land, where he might be lost. From thence forward a youth that was taken in Cutifa-Chiqui did serve for interpretour, which had by that time learned somewhat of the Christians language. The death of John Ortiz was so great a mischiefe for the discovering inward, or going out of the land, that to learne of the Indians, that which in foure words hee declared, they needed a whole day with the youth; and most commonly hee understood quite contrarie that which was asked him: whereby it often happened that the way that they went one day, and sometimes two or three daies, they turned backe, and went astray through the wood here and there.

The Governour spent ten daies in travelling from Autiamque to a province called Ayays; and came to a towne that stood neere the river that passeth by Cayas and Autiamque. There hee commanded a barge to be made, wherewith he passed the river. When he had passed the river, there fell out such weather, that foure daies he could not travell for snow. As soone as it gave over snowing, he went three daies journey through a wildernesse, and a countrie so low, and so full of lakes and evill waies, that hee travelled one time a whole day in water, sometimes knee deepe, sometimes to the stirrup, and sometimes they swamme. . . .

Wednesday the 29 of March the Governour came to Nilco: he lodged with all his men in the cacique's towne . . . and within a league and halfe a league were other great townes, wherein was great store of maiz, of french beanes, of walnuts, and prunes. This was the best countrie that was seen in Florida. . . . And within fewe daies the Governour determined to goe to Guachoya, to learne there whether the sea were neere, or whether there were any habitation neere, where hee might relieve his companie, while the brigantines were making, which he meant to send to the land of the Christians.

And as soone as the Governour came to Guachoya, hee sent John Danusco, with as many men as could go in the canoes, up the river. For when they came downe from Nilco, they saw on the other side the river new cabins made. John Danusco went and brought the canoes loden with maiz, French beanes, prunes, and many loaves made of the substance of prunes. That day came an Indian to the Governour from the cacique of Guachoya, and said, that his lord would come the next day. The next day they saw many canoes come up the river, and on the other side of the great river they assembled together in the space of an houre; they consulted whether they should come or not; and at length concluded to come and crossed the river. In them came the cacique of Guachoya, and brought with him manie Indians, with great store of fish, dogges, deeres skinnes, and mantles. . . .

The Governour received him with much joy and gave him thankes. . . . He asked him whether hee had any notice of the sea? Hee answered, no; nor of any townes downe the river on that side: save that two leagues from thence was one towne of a principall Indian, a subject of his; and on the other side of the river, three daies journey from thence downe the river, was the province of Quigalta, which was the greatest lord that was in that countrie. The Governour thought that the cacique lied unto him, to rid him out of his owne townes, and sent John Danusco with eight horsemen downe the river to see what habitation there was, and to informe himselfe if there were any notice of the sea.

Hee travelled eight daies, and at his returne hee said, that in all that time he was not able to go above fourteen or fifteen leagues, because of the great creekes that came out of the river, and groves of canes, and thicke woods, that were along the bancks of the river, and that hee had found no habitation. The Governour fell into great dumps to see how hard it was to get to the sea; and worse, because his men and horses every day diminished, being without succour to sustaine themselves in the country; and with that thought he fell sick. But before he tooke to his bed, hee sent an Indian to the cacique of Quigalta, to tell him that hee was the childe of the sunne; and that all the way that hee came, all men obeyed and served him, that he requested him to accept of his friendship, and come unto him, for he would be very glad to see him; and in signe of love and obedience, to bring something with him of that which in his countrie was most esteemed.

The cacique answered by the same Indian:

That whereas he said he was the child of the sunne, if he would drie up the river he would beleeve him: and touching the rest, that hee was wont to visit none; but rather that all those of whom he had notice did visit him, served, obeyed and paid him tributes willingly or perforce: therefore, if hee desired to see him, it were best he should come thither that if hee came in peace, he would receive him with speciall good will; and if in warre, in like manner hee would attend him in the towne where he was; and that for him or any other hee would not shinke one foote backe.

By that time the Indian returned with this answere, the Governour had betaken himselfe to bed, being evill handled with fevers, and was much aggrieved that he was not in case to passe presently the river and to seeke him, to see if he could abate that pride of his, considering the river went now very strongly in those parts; for it was neere halfe a league broad and sixteen fathomes deep, and very furious, and ranne with a great current; and on both sides there were many Indians; and his power was not now so great but that hee had need to helpe himselfe rather by slights than by force. . . .

The Governour felt in himselfe that the houre approached wherein hee was to leave this present life, and called for the kings officers, captaines, and principall persons, to whom he made a speech, saying:

That now he was to goe to give an account before the presence of God of all his life past: and since it pleased Him to take him in such a time, that he His most unworthie servant did yeeld Him many thankes therefore; and desired all that were present and absent . . . that they would pray to God for him, that for His mercie He would forgive him his sinnes, and receive his soule into eternall glorie: and that they would quite and free him of the charge which hee had over them, and ought unto them all, and that they would pardon him for some wrongs which they might have received of him. And to avoid some division, which upon his death might fall out upon the choice of his successour, he requested them to elect a principall person, and able to governe, of whom all should like well; and when he was elected, they should sweare before him to obey him: and that he would thanke them very much in so doing; because the griefe that he had would somewhat be asswaged, and the paine that he felt, because he left them in so great confusion, to wit, in leaving them in a strange countrie, where they knew not where they were.

Baltasar de Gallegos answered him in the name of all the rest. And first of all comforting him, he set before his eies how short the life of this world was, and with how many troubles and miseries it is accompanied, and how God shewed him a singular favour which soonest left it: telling him many other things fit for such a time. . . . And touching the Governour which he commanded they should elect, he besought him, that it would please his lordship to name him which he thought fit, and him they would obey.

And presently he named Luys de Moscoso de Alvarado, his capitaine generall. And presently he was sworne by all that were present and elected for Governour.

The next day, being the 21 of May, 1542, departed out of this life, the valorous, virtuous, and valiant captaine, Don Fernando de Soto, Governour of Cuba, and Adelantado of Florida; whom fortune advanced, as it useth to doe others, that hee might have the higher fall.

PORTUGAL

HOW PEDRO DE COVILHAM WAS SENT TO DISCOVER THE LAND OF PRESTER JOHN AND WHERE THE PEPPER AND CINNAMON GROW [1]

(1487)

FRANCISCO DE ALVAREZ

(*c.* 1465–1541 ?)

WHEREAS I have spoken often in this Booke[2] of Peter de Covillan Portuguez, being an honourable person, and of great credite with Prete Janni and all the Court; It is convenient that I should declare how he came into this Countrey, and the cause thereof as he hath oftentimes told me himselfe. But first I will say, that he is my spirituall sonne, and that I have oftentimes confessed him, because in three and thirtie yeeres while he lived in this Countrey, he told me that he never was confessed, because the custome here is not to keepe that secret which is uttered in confession, and that therefore he went into the Church, when he confessed his sinnes unto God. His beginning was thus: He was borne in the Towne of Covillan in the Kingdome of Portugall, and being a boy, he went into Castile, and gat into the service of Don Alfonso Duke of Sivile; and when the warre began betweene Portugall and Castile, hee returned home with Don John de Gusman, brother to the said Duke, which placed him in the house of Alfonso King of Portugall, who for his valour presently made him a man at Armes, and hee was continually in that warre, and served also abroad in France. After the death of King Alfonso, he was one of the Guard of the King Don John his sonne, until the time of the treasons, when he sent him into Castile, because he spake the Castilian Tongue very well, to spie out who were those Gentlemen of his Subjects, which practised there against him. And returning out of Castile, he was sent into Barbarie, where he stayed a time, and learned the Arabian Tongue, and was afterward sent to conclude a Peace with the King of Tremizen: and being returned, he was sent againe to the King Amoli bela gegi, which restored the bones of the Infant Don Fernando. At his returne, he found that the King Don John, desiring by all means that his ships should find out the Spiceries, had determined to send by land certaine men to discover as much as they might. And Alfonso de Paiva was chosen for this enterprise, a Citizen of Castle Blanco, a very skilfull man, and very expert in the Arabian Tongue.

[1] From *Purchas his Pilgrimes.* [2] *Verdadera Informaçam das Terra do Presto Joam.*

When Peter de Covillan was returned King John called him, and told him secretly, That having alwayes knowne him loyall and his faithfull servant, and readie to doe his Majestie good service, seeing he understood the Arabian tongue, he purposed to send him with another companion, to discover and learne where Prete Janni dwelt, and whether his Territories reached unto the Sea, and where the Pepper and Cinamon grew, and other sorts of Spicerie, which were brought unto the Citie of Venice from the Countries of the Moores; seeing hee had sent for this purpose one of the House of Monterio, and one Frier Anthony of Lisbon, Prior of Porta de Ferro, which could not passe the Citie of Jerusalem, saying, That it was impossible to travell this way without understanding the Arabian tongue, and therefore seeing he understood the same well, hee prayed him to under-take this enterprize, to doe him this so principall service, promising to reward him in such sort, that he should be great in his Kingdome, and all his Posteritie should alwayes live contented. Peter answered him, That he kissed his Majesties hands for the great favour which he had done him, but that he was sorry, that his wisedome and sufficiencie, was not answerable to the great desire he had to serve his Highnesse; and yet neverthelesse, as his faithfull servant he accepted this message with all his heart.

And so in the yeere 1487, the seventh of May, they were both dispatched in Saint Arren, the King Don Emanuel alwayes there present, which at that time was but Duke, and they gave them a Sea-card, taken out of a generall Map of the World, at the making whereof was the Licentiate Calzadilla, Bishop of Viseo; and the Doctor Master Roderigo, inhabitant of Pietre Nere; and the Doctor Master Moyses, which at that time was a Jew; and all this worke was done very secretly in the house of Peter de Alcazova, and all the forenamed persons shewed the uttermost of their knowledge, as though they should have beene Commanders in the Discoverie, of finding out the Countries from whence the Spices come, and as though one of them should have gone into Ethiopia to discover the Countrey of Prete Janni, and as though in those Seas there had beene some knowledge of a passage into our Westerne Seas; because the said Doctors, said, they had found some memoriall of that matter. And for the charges of them both, the King appointed foure hundred Cruzadoes, which were given them out of the Treasurie of the Garden of Almarian: and (as I have said) the King Emanuel was alwayes present, who at that time was Duke. Besides this, the King gave them a Letter of credit in all parts of the Levant, that if they fell into any necessitie or perill, they might be succoured and aided thereby. One halfe of these foure hundred Cruzadoes, they desired to have in readie money, and the other halfe they gave to Bartholmew Marchioni a Florentine, to be payed them in Naples.

And having received the Kings blessing, they departed from Lisbon, and came into Barcelona on Corpus Christi day, and thence unto Naples on Saint Johns day; when their Bills of Exchange were payed them, by the Sonne of Cosmo de Medices. From Naples they went unto the Ile of Rhodes, and here they found two Portugall Knights, the one called Frier Gonsalvo, and the other Frier Fernando, in whose house they lodged; and after certaine dayes, they tooke their voyage for Alexandria, in a ship of Bartholmew de Paredez; having first bought many Jarres of Honey, to shew that they were Merchants. When they were come to Alexandria, they both fell grievously sicke of an ague; and the Cadi tooke all their Honey from them, supposing they would have dyed. But being recovered, they were payed as they would themselves, and having bought sundrie sorts of merchandize, they went to Cairo, where they stayed till they found companie of certaine Moores, called Magabrini, of the Kingdome of Fez and Tremizen, which went to Aden, and in their companie they went by Land to Tor; where taking ship, they sailed to Suachen, upon the Coast of the Abyssins, and from thence unto Aden. And because it was the time of the Monsons or Motions, when those Seas cannot be sailed, they divided themselves the one from the other, and Alfonso passed into Ethiopia, and Peter made his choice to goe into India, as the time served him for to doe. And they agreed together, to meete at a certayne time in the Citie of Cairo, that they might be able to advertize the King of their discoverie.

Peter de Covillan, when time served, tooke shipping, and sailed directly to Cananor, and passed thence to Calecut, and saw the great quantitie of Ginger and Pepper which grow there, and understood that the Cloves and Cinamon were brought thither from farre Countries. Then he went toward Goa, and passed thence to the Ile of Ormuz, and having informed himselfe of certayne other things, he came in a ship toward the Red Sea. Hee landed at Zeila, and with certayne Merchants, which were Moores, he travelled those Seas of Ethiopia, which were shewed him at Lisbon in a Sea Chart, to the intent hee should use all his industrie to discover them. And he went so farre, that he came unto the Towne of Cefala, where he learned of the Mariners and certayne Arabians, that the said Coast might be sailed all along toward the West, and that they knew no end thereof, and that there was a great Ile very rich, which was above nine hundred miles in length, which they call The Ile of the Moone.[1] And having understood these things,

[1] Madagascar.

being very glad thereof, he determined to returne unto Cairo, and so he came back to Zeila, and from thence passed to Aden, and then to Tor, and lastly to Cairo, where he stayed a great time, wayting for Alfonso de Paiva, and at length, had newes that he was dead.

Whereupon he determined to returne into Portugall: but it pleased God, that two Jewes, which went to seeke him, by good lucke found him, and delivered him Letters from the King of Portugall. One of these Jewes was called, Rabbi Abraham, borne in Beggian. The others name was Josepho de Lamego, and was a Shoo-maker. These having beene before in Persia and in Bagadet, told the King many great matters, which they had learned concerning the Spiceries, and the riches which were found in the Ile of Ormuz, whereof the King conceived great pleasure, and commanded them to returne thither againe to see the same themselves; but first, that they should seeke out Peter de Covillan, and Alfonso de Paiva, which hee knew were determined to meet together at a time appointed in Cairo. The contents of the Kings Letters were, that if all the things given them in commission, were searched out by them, then they should returne, because hee would reward them; but if they were not all discovered, that they should send him particular information of those things that they had seene, and then should doe their best endeavour to search out the rest, and above all things, to discover the Countrey of Prete Janni, and to cause Rabbi Abraham to see the Ile of Ormuz. For which cause, Peter de Covillan, purposed to advertise the King of all which hee had seene along the Coast of Calicut, touching the Spiceries, and of Ormuz, and of the Coast of Ethiopia, and of Cefala, and of the great Iland of the Moone, concluding, that his ships which traded into Guinea, sayling along the Coast, and seeking the Coast of that Iland, and of Cefala, might easily enter into these Eastern Seas, and fall upon this Coast of Calicut, for all along there was Sea: he had understood, and that he would returne with Rabbi Abraham to Ormuz, and after his returne he would seeke out Prete Janni, whose Countrey stretched unto the red Sea.

And with these Letters, he dispatched Joseph de Lamego the Jew. And he and the other Jew going againe to Ormuz, and returning to Aden, hee willed him to goe and carrie newes to the King that hee had seene the Ile of Ormuz with his owne eyes. And he himselfe passing into Ethiopia, came into the Court of Prete Janni, which at that time was not farre from Zeila. And having presented his Letters unto him, who at that time was called Alexander, hee was very courteously enteretained, and had great honour done unto him, and was promised that he should speedily be dispatched. But in the meane while, he departed this life, and Nahu his brother succeeded in his stead, which saw him, and made very much of him, but would never give him leave to depart. Afterward Nahu died also, and his sonne David succeeded him, which raigneth at this present, which would not suffer him to depart, saying, that hee came not thither in his time, and that if his Predecessors had given him so great Lands and Revenues, he ought to enjoy them, and to lose none of them: and therefore, seeing they had not given him licence, neither might he give him leave to depart; and so he remained still in the Countrey: and they gave him a wife, with very great riches and possessions, by whom he had children, whom we also saw. And in our time, when he saw that we would depart, he was exceeding desirous to returne into his Countrey, and went to crave leave of the Prete, and we with him, and were very instant on his behalfe, and be sought him very earnestly, yet for all that wee could not obtaine leave. Hee is a man of great spirit and wit, and of his qualitie hee hath not the like in all the Court, and can speake all the Languages, as well of the Christians as of the Moores, Gentiles, and Abassins: and of all things which hee hath knowne and seene, hee can yeeld as particular account, as if they were present. And therefore he is very gracious with the Prete, and all the Court.

HOW BENEDICT GOËS, SEEKING CATHAY, FOUND HEAVEN [1]

(1603)

MATHEW RICCI

(1552–1610)

[*Unaware that Cathay was but another name for China, where the Society was already established, the Jesuit fathers of Agra determined in 1603 to send a missionary in search of the lost empire.*]

So our Benedict[2] began to prepare for his journey, and assumed both the dress and the name of an Armenian Christian merchant, calling himself Abdula, which signifies *Servant of the Lord*, with the addition of *Isáí*, or the Christian. . . . So he was to pass for an Armenian, for in that character he would be allowed to travel feely, whilst if known as a Spaniard he was certain to be stopped. He also carried with him a variety of wares, both that he might maintain himself by selling them, and to keep up his character as a merchant. . . . Father Jerome Xavier, who had for many years been at the head of the Mogul mission, appointed two men acquainted with those

[1] From *Cathay and the Way Thither*, translated and edited by Sir Henry Yule (Hakluyt Society, No. 37 (1866)).

[2] Benedict would then be about forty-two, having been born *c.* 1561.

countries to be the comrades of his journey. One, for Benedict's comfort, was a priest, by name Leo Grimanus, the other a merchant called Demetrius. There were also four servants, Mahomedans by birth and former profession, but converted to Christianity. All of these servants however he discharged as useless when he got to Lahore (the second capital of the Mogul), and took in lieu of them a single Armenian, Isaac by name, who had a wife and family at Lahore. This Isaac proved the most faithful of all his comrades, and stuck to him throughout the whole journey, a regular *fidus Achates*. So our brother took leave of his superior, and set out, as appears from the letter of instructions, on the sixth of January in the third year of this century.

Every year a company of merchants is formed in that capital to proceed to the capital of another territory with a king of its own, called Cascar.[1] These all take the road together, either for the sake of mutual comfort or for protection against robbers. They numbered in the present case about five hundred persons, with a great number of mules, camels and carts. So he set out from Lahore in this way during Lent of the year just mentioned, and after a month's travelling[2] they came to a town called Athec,[3] still within the province of Lahore. After a halt of about a fortnight they crossed a river of a bowshot in width, boats being provided at the passage for the accommodation of the merchants. On the opposite bank of the river they halted for five days, having received warning that a large body of robbers was threatening the road, and then after two months they arrived at another city called Passaur,[4] and there they halted twenty days for needful repose. Further on, whilst on their way to another small town, they fell in with a certain pilgrim and devotee, from whom they learned that at a distance of thirty days' journey there was a city called Capperstam, into which no Mahomedan was allowed to enter, and if one did get in he was punished with death. . . . In the place where they met with that wanderer they halted for twenty days more, and as the road was reported to be infested with brigands they got an escort of four hundred soldiers from the lord of the place. From this they travelled in twenty-five days to a place called Ghideli. In the whole of this journey the baggage and packs were carried along the foot of the hills, whilst the merchants, arms in hand, kept a look out for the robbers from the hill-top. For these latter are in the habit of rolling down stones upon travellers, unless these are beforehand with them on the heights, and meeting violence by violence drive them away. At this place the merchants pay a toll, and here the

[1] Kashgar.

[2] The chronology of the journey is confused; the main facts are that Goës left Agra on January 6, 1603, and reached Su-Chow at the end of 1605.

[3] Attok, on the Indus.

[4] Peshawur.

robbers made an onslaught. Many of the company were wounded, and life and property were saved with difficulty. Our Benedict fled with the rest into the jungle, but coming back at night they succeeded in getting away from the robbers. After twenty days more they reached Cabul, a city greatly frequented for trade, and still within the territories subject to the Mogul. Here our friends halted altogether for eight months. For some of the merchants laid aside the intention of going any further, and the rest were afraid to go on in so small a body. . . .

From this place the Priest Leo Grymanus went back, being unable to stand the fatigues of the journey; and his comrade Demetrius stopped behind in the town on account of some business. So our brother set out, attended by no one but the Armenian, in the caravan with the other merchants. For some others had now joined them, and it was thought that they could proceed with safety.

The first town that they came to was Ciarakár,[1] a place where there is great abundance of iron. And here Benedict was subjected to a great deal of annoyance. For in those outskirts of the Mogul's dominions no attention was paid to the king's *firman*, which had hitherto given him immunity from exactions of every kind. Ten days later they got to a little town called Paruán,[2] and this was the last in the Mogul's territories. After five days' repose they proceeded to cross over very lofty mountains by a journey of twenty days, to the district called Aingharán, and after fifteen days more they reached Calcia. There is a people here with yellow hair and beard like the people of the Low Countries, who occupy sundry hamlets about the country. After ten days more they came to a certain place called Gialalabath.[3] Here are brahmans who exact a toll under a grant made to them by the king of Bruarata. In fifteen days more they came to Talhan, where they halted for a month, deterred by the Civil wars that were going on; for the roads were said to be unsafe on account of the rebellion of the people of Calcia.

From this they went on to Cheman, a place under Abdulahan, King of Samarkan, Burgavia, Bacharata, and other adjoining kingdoms. It is a small town and the governor sent to the merchants to advise them to come within the walls, as outside they would not be very safe from the Calcia insurgents. The merchants, however, replied that they were willing to pay toll and would proceed on their journey by night. The governor of the town then absolutely forbade their proceeding, saying that the rebels of Calcia as yet had no horses, but they would get them if they plundered the caravan, and would thus be able to do much more damage to the country, and be much more troublesome to the town; it would be a much safer arrangement if they would join his men

[1] Charekar. [2] Parwán. [3] Jalalabad.

in beating off the Calcia people. They had barely reached the town walls when a report arose that the Calcia people were coming! On hearing this the bragging governor and his men took to their heels. The merchants on the spur of the moment formed a kind of intrenchment of their packs, and collected a great heap of stones inside in case their arrows should run short. When the Calcia people found this out, they sent a deputation to the merchants to tell them to fear nothing, for they would themselves escort and protect the caravan. The merchants, however, were not disposed to put trust in these insurgents, and after holding counsel together flight was determined on. Somebody or other made this design known to the rebels, upon which immediately they made a rush forward, knocked over the packs, and took whatever they liked. These robbers then called the merchants out of the jungle (into which they had fled) and gave them leave to retire with the rest of their property within the empty city walls. Our Benedict lost nothing but one of his horses, and even that he afterwards got back in exchange for some cotton cloths. They remained in the town in a great state of fear lest the rebels should make a general attack and massacre the whole of them. But just then a certain leading chief, by name Olobet Ebadascan, of the Buchara country, sent his brother to the rebels, and he by threats induced them to let the merchants go free. Throughout the whole journey, however, robbers were constantly making snatches at the tail of the caravan. And once it befel our friend Benedict that he had dropped behind the party and was attacked by four brigands who had been lying *perdus*. The way he got off from them was this: he snatched off his Persian cap and flung it at the thieves, and whilst they were making a football of it our brother had time to spur his horse and get a bowshot clear of them, and so safely joined the rest of the company.

After eight days of the worst possible road, they reached the Tengi Badascian. *Tengi* signifies a difficult road; and it is indeed fearfully narrow, giving passage to only one at a time, and running at a great height above the bed of a river. The townspeople here, aided by a band of soldiers, made an attack upon the merchants, and our brother lost three horses. These, however, also, he was enabled to ransom with some small presents. They halted here ten days, and then in one day's march reached Ciarciunar, where they were detained five days in the open country by rain, and suffered not only from the inclemency of the weather, but also from another onslaught of robbers.

From this in ten days they reached Serpanil; but this was a place utterly desolate and without a symptom of human occupation; and then they came to the ascent of the steep mountain called Sacrithma. None but the stoutest of the horses could face this mountain; the rest had to pass by a roundabout but easier road. Here two of our brother's mules went lame, and the weary servants wanted to let them go, but after all they were got to follow the others. And so, after a journey of twenty days, they reached the province of Sarcil, where they found a number of hamlets near together. They halted there two days to rest the horses, and then in two days more reached the foot of the mountain called Ciecialith. It was covered deep with snow, and during the ascent many were frozen to death, and our brother himself barely escaped, for they were altogether six days in the snow here. At last they reached Tanghetar, a place belonging to the kingdom of Cascar. Here Isaac the Armenian fell off the bank of a great river into the water, and lay as it were dead for some eight hours till Benedict's exertions at last brought him to. In fifteen days more they reached the town of Iakonich, and the roads were so bad that six of our brother's horses died of fatigue. After five days more our Benedict going on by himself in advance of the caravan reached the capital, which is called Hiarchan, and sent back horses to help on his party with necessaries for his comrades. And so they also arrived not long after safe at the capital, with bag and baggage, in November of the same year 1603. . . .

Hiarchan, the capital of the kingdom of Cascar, is a mart of much note, both for the great concourse of merchants, and for the variety of wares. At this capital the caravan of Cabul merchants reaches its terminus; and a new one is formed for the journey to Cathay. . . . A twelvemonth passed away, however, before the new company was formed, for the way is long and perilous, and the caravan is not formed every year, but only when a large number arrange to join it, and when it is known that they will be allowed to enter Cathay. There is no article of traffic more valuable, or more generally adopted as an investment for this journey, than lumps of a certain transparent kind of marble which we, from poverty of language, usually call jasper. They carry these to the Emperor of Cathay, attracted by the high prices which he deems it obligatory on his dignity to give; and such pieces as the Emperor does not fancy they are free to dispose of to private individuals. . . . Out of this marble they fashion a variety of articles, such as vases, and brooches for mantles and girdles, which when artistically sculptured in flowers and foliage certainly have an effect of no small magnificence. . . .

Our brother Benedict went to pay his respect to the king, whose name was Mahomed Khan. The present that he carried with him secured him a good reception, for it consisted of a pocket watch, looking glasses, and other European curiosities. . . . Our friend did not at first disclose his desire to go to Cathay, but spoke only of the kingdom of Cialis, to the eastward of Cascar, and begged a royal passport for the journey thither. . . .

Meantime a certain native named Agiasi was nominated chief of the future caravan of merchants. And having heard that our brother was a man of courage, as well as a merchant of large dealings, he invited him . . . to accompany the caravan all the way to Cathay. He indeed desired nothing better, but experience had taught him how to deal with Saracens, so he was glad that the proposal should come from the other side, and thus that he should seem to be granting rather than accepting a favour. . . .

So he girded up his loins for the journey, and bought ten horses for himself and his comrade and their goods, having already one more at his house, . . . and set out in the middle of November 1604, proceeding first to a place called Iolci, where duties used to be paid and the king's passport to be inspected. After this in twenty-five days, passing successively Hancialix, Alceghet, Hagabateth, Egriár, Mesetelech, Thalec, Horma, Thoantac, Mingieda, Capetal col Zilan, Sarc Guebedal, Canbasci, Aconsersec and Ciacor, they reached Acsu. The difficulties of the road were great, either from the quantities of stones, or from the waterless tracts of sand which they had to pass.

Acsu is a town of the kingdom of Cascar, and the chief there was a nephew of the king's, and only twelve years of age. He sent twice for our brother. The latter carried him presents of sweetmeats and the like, such as would be acceptable to a child, and was most kindly received. A grand dance happening to be performed before them, the young prince asked Benedict how the people of his country used to dance; and so Benedict, not to be churlish with a prince about so small a matter, got up and danced himself to show the way of it. He also visited the prince's mother. . . . To her he presented some little things such as women like, a looking glass, India muslin, and so forth. . . .

In this journey one of the pack-horses belonging to our merchant fell into a very rapid river. In fact, having broken the rope with which its feet (I know not why) were tied, it made off and crossed to the other side of the river. Benedict feeling the loss a serious one invoked the name of Jesus; and the horse of his own accord swam back to join the others, and our friend . . . returned thanks for the benefit vouchsafed. On this part of the journey they crossed the desert which is called Caracathai, or the Black Land of the Cathayans, because 'tis said that the people so called long sojourned there.

At this town (Acsu) they had to wait fifteen days for the arrival of the rest of the merchants. At last they started, and travelled to Oitograch Gazo, Casciani, Dellai, Saregabedal, and Ugan, after which they got to Cucia,[1]

[1] Kucha.

another small town at which they halted a whole month to rest their cattle, for these were nearly done up, what with the difficulties of the road, the weight of the marble which they carried, and the scarcity of barley. . . .

Departing hence, after twenty-five days' journey they came to the city of Cialis, a small place indeed, but strongly fortified. . . . In this city they halted three months, for the chief of the merchants did not wish to set out until a large party should have collected, for the larger it was, the more profitable to him: and for this reason he would not consent on any account that individuals of the company should go on before. Our brother, however, weary of the delay . . . was eager to get away. . . . He was just preparing for his departure . . . when the merchants of the preceding caravan arrived on thier return from Cathay. They had made their way to the capital of Cathay as usual by pretending to be an embassy; and as they had been quartered in Peking at the same hostelry with the members of our Society, they were able to give our brother most authentic information about Father Matthew and his companions, and in this way he learned to his astonishment that China was the Cathay that he was in search of. . . .

These . . . Saracens . . . had dwelt for nearly three months under the same roof with our brethren. They were able to tell therefore how our brethren had made presents to the Emperor of sundry clocks, a clavichord, pictures, and other such matters from Europe. . . . They also described accurately enough the countenances of the members of the Society whom they had seen, but they could not tell their names, it being a Chinese custom to change the names of foreigners. They also produced the strongest corroboration of their story in a piece of paper on which something in the Portuguese language had been written by one of our brethren, and which the travellers had rescued from the sweepings of the rooms and preserved, in order that they might show it as a memorial to their friends at home, and tell them how the people that used this kind of writing had found their way to China. Our travellers were greatly refreshed with all this intelligence, and now they could no longer doubt that Cathay was but another name for the Chinese Empire, and that the capital which the Mahomedans called Cambulu was Peking, which indeed Benedict before leaving India had known, from the letters of our members in China, to be the view taken by them.

As he was departing, the prince granted him letters for his protection, and when a question arose under what name he wished to be described and whether he would have himself designated as a Christian Certainly, said he, "for having travelled thus far bearing the name of Jesus, I would surely bear it unto the end." . . .

He set off at last with his comrade and a few others, and in twenty days came to Pucian, a town of the same kingdom, where they were received by the chief of the place with the greatest kindness, and supplied with the necessary provisions from his house. Hence they went on to a fortified town called Turphan, and there they halted a month. Next they proceeded to Aramuth, and thence to Camul,[1] another fortified town. Here they stopped another month to refresh themselves and their beasts, being glad to do so at a town which was still within the limits of the kingdom of Cialis, where they had been treated with so much civility.

From Camul they came in nine days to the celebrated northern wall of China, reaching it at the place called Chiaicuon,[2] and there they had to wait twenty-five days for an answer from the Viceroy of the province. When they were at last admitted within the wall, they reached, after one more day's travelling, the city of Socieu.[3] Here they heard much about Peking and other names with which they were acquainted, and here Benedict parted with his last lingering doubt as to the identity in all but name of Cathay and China.

The country between Cialis and the Chinese frontier has an evil fame on account of its liability to Tartar raids, and therefore this part of the road is traversed by merchants with great fear. In the day time they reconnoitre from the neighbouring hills, and if they consider the road safe they prosecute their journey by night and in silence. Our travellers found on the way the bodies of sundry Mahomedans who had been miserably murdered. Yet the Tartars rarely slay the natives, for they call them their slaves and shepherds, from whose flocks and herds they help themselves. . . .

In this journey it happened one night that Benedict was thrown from his horse and lay there half dead, whilst his companions who were all in advance went on in ignorance of what had happened. In fact it was not till the party arrived at the halting place that Benedict was missed. His comrade Isaac went back to seek him, but the search in the dark was to no purpose, until at last he heard a voice calling on the name of Jesus. Following the sound, he found Benedict, who had given up all hope of being able to follow his companions, so that his first words were, "What angel has brought thee hither to rescue me from such a plight?" By help of the Armenian he was enabled to reach the halting place and there to recover from his fall. . . .

Our Benedict arrived at Socieu in the end of the year 1605, and it shows how Divine Providence watched over him, that he came to the end of this enormous journey with ample means, and prosperous in every way. He had

[1] Hami, formerly I-gu.

[2] Kia-yu-Koan, or the "Jade Gate" of the Great Wall.

[3] Su-Chow.

with him thirteen animals, five hired servants, two boys, whom he had bought as slaves, and [a] surpassing piece of jade; the total value of his property being reckoned at two thousand five hundred pieces of gold. Moreover both he and his companion Isaac were in perfect health and strength.

At this city of Socieu he fell in with another party of Saracens just returned from the capital, and these confirmed all that he had already been told about our fathers at Peking, adding a good deal more of an incredible and extravagant nature; for example, that they had from the Emperor a daily allowance of silver, not counted to them, but measured out in bulk! So he now wrote to Father Matthew to inform him of his arrival. His latter was entrusted to certain Chinamen, but as he did not know the Chinese names of our fathers, nor the part of the city in which they lived, and as the letter was addressed in European characters, the bearers were unable to discover our people. At Easter however he wrote a second time, and this letter was taken by some Mahomedan who had made his escape from the city, for they also are debarred from going out or coming in, without the permission of the authorities. In this letter he explained the origin and object of his journey, and begged the fathers to devise some way of rescuing him from the prison in which he found himself at Socieu, and of restoring him to the delight of holding intercourse with his brethren, in place of being perpetually in the company of Saracens. He mentioned also his wish to return to India by the sea-route, as usually followed by the Portuguese.

The fathers had long ere this been informed by the Superior's letters from India of Benedict's having started on this expedition, and every year they had been looking out for him, and asking diligently for news of him whenever one of those companies of merchants on their pretended embassy arrived at court. But till now they had never been able to learn any news of him, whether from not knowing the name under which he was travelling, or because the ambassadors of the preceding seasons really had never heard of him.

The arrival of his letter therefore gave great pleasure to the fathers at Peking. It was received late in the year, in the middle of November, and they lost no time in arranging to send a member of the Society to get him away some how or other and being him to the capital. However on re-consideration they gave up that scheme, for the bringing another foreigner into the business seemed likely to do harm rather than good. So they sent one of the pupils who had lately been selected to join the Society but had not yet entered on his noviciate. His name was John Ferdinand; he was a young man of singular prudence and virute, and one whom it seemed safe to entrust with a business of this nature. One of the converts acquainted with that part of the country was sent in company with him. His instructions were to use all possible means to get away Benedict and his party to the capital, but if he should find it absolutely impossible either to get leave from the officials or to evade their vigilance, he was to stop with our brother, and send back word to the members of the Society. In that case it was hoped that by help of friends at Court, means would be found to get him on from the frontier.

A journey of this nature might seem unseasonable enough at a time of the year when winter is at the height of severity in those regions; and the town at which Benedict had been detained was nearly four months' journey from Peking. But Father Matthew thought no further delay should be risked, lest the great interval that had elapsed should lead Benedict to doubt whether we really had members stationed at Peking. And he judged well, for if the journey had been delayed but a few days longer the messengers would not have found Benedict among the living. They carried him a letter from Father Matthew, giving counsel as to the safest manner of making the journey and two other members of the Society also wrote to him, giving full details about our affairs in that capital, a subject on which he was most eager for information.

Our Benedict in the meantime, during his detention at that city, endured more annoyance from the Mahomedans than had befallen him during the whole course of his journey. Also, on account of the high price of food in the place, he was obliged to dispose of his large piece of jade for little more than half its value. He got for it twelve hundred pieces of gold, a large part of which went to repay money which he had borrowed, whilst with the rest he maintained his party for a whole year. Meanwhile the caravan of merchants with their chief arrived. Benedict was obliged to exercise hospitality, and in course of time was reduced to such straits that he had to borrow money to maintain his party; this all the more because owing to his nomination as one of the seventy-two ambassadors he was obliged (again) to purchase some fragments of jade. He hid a hundred pounds of this in the earth to preserve it from any tricks of the Mahomedans, for without a supply of this article he would have been absolutely incapacitated from taking part in the journey to Peking.

John Ferdinand left Peking on the eleventh of December in that year; and his journey also was attended with a new misfortune, for at Singhan, the capital of the province of Sciensi, his servant ran away, robbing him of half his supplies for the journey. Two months more of a fatiguing journey however brought him to Socieu, in the end of March 1607.

He found our Benedict laid low with a disease unto death. The very night before it had been intimated to him, whether by dream or vision, that on the following day one of the Society would arrive from Peking; and upon this he had desired his comrade the Armenian to go to the bazaar and buy certain articles for distribution among the poor, whilst at the same time he earnestly prayed God not to suffer the hopes raised by his dream to be disappointed. Whilst Isaac was still in the bazaar some one told him of the arrival of John Ferdinand from Peking, and pointed him out. The latter followed the Armenian home, and as he entered, saluted our brother Benedict in the Portuguese tongue. From this he at once understood what the arrival was, and taking the letters he raised them aloft with tears of joy in his eyes, and burst into the hymn of *Nunc dimittis*. For now it seemed to him that indeed his commission was accomplished, and his pilgrimage at an end. He then read the letters, and all that night kept them near his heart. The words that were spoken, the questions that were asked, may be more easily conjectured than detailed. John Ferdinand did his best to nurse him, hoping that with recovered strength he might yet be able to undertake the journey to Peking. But strength there was none; as indeed physician there was none, nor proper medicines; nor was there anything to do him good in his illness, unless it were some European dishes which John Ferdinand cooked for him. And thus, eleven days after the latter's arrival, Benedict breathed his last.

THE PERILS OF ÆTHIOPIA[1]

(1622)

JERONIMO LOBO

(1593-1678)

I EMBARKED in March 1622, in the same fleet with the Count Vidigueira, on whom the King had conferred the viceroyship of the Indies, then vacant by the resignation of Alfonso Noronha, whose unsuccessful voyage in the foregoing year had been the occasion of the loss of Ormus, which being by the miscarriage of that fleet deprived of the succours necessary for its defence, was taken by the Persians and English. The beginning of this voyage was very prosperous: we were neither annoyed with the diseases of the climate, nor distressed with bad weather, till we doubled the Cape of Good Hope which was about the end of May. Here began our misfortunes: these coasts are remarkable for the many shipwrecks the

[1] From *Pinkerton's Voyages*, translated by Dr Johnson.

Portuguese have suffered. The sea is for the most part rough, and the winds tempestuous: we had here our rigging somewhat damaged by a strom of lightning, which when we had repaired, we sailed forward to Mosambique, where we were to stay some time. When we came near that coast and began to rejoice at the prospect of ease and refreshment, we were, on the sudden, alarmed with the sight of a squadron of ships, of what nation we could not at first distinguish, but soon discovered that they were three English and three Dutch, and were preparing to attack us. I shall not trouble the reader with the particulars of this fight, in which though the English commander ran himself aground, we lost three of our ships, and with great difficulty escaped with the rest into the port of Mosambique.

This place was able to afford us little consolation in our uneasy circumstances; the arrival of our company almost caused a scarcity of provisions. The heat in the day is introlerable, and the dews in the night so unwholesome that it is almost certain death to go out with one's head uncovered. We staid however in this place from the latter end of July to the beginning of September, when having provided ourselves with other vessels, we set out for Cochim, and landed there after a very hazardous and difficult passage, made so partly by the currents and storms which separated us from each other, and partly by continual apprehensions of the English and Dutch, who were cruising for us in the Indian seas. Here the viceroy and his company were received with so much ceremony as was rather troublesome than pleasing to us who were fatigued with the labours of the passage; and having staid here some time that the gentlemen who attended the viceroy to Goa, might fit out their vessels, we set sail, and after having been detained some time at sea, by calms and contrary winds, and somewhat harassed by the English and Dutch, who were now increased to eleven ships of war, arrived at Goa, on Saturday the 16th of December, and the viceroy made his entry with great magnificence.

I lived here above a year, and completed my studies in divinity; in which time some letters were received from the fathers in Æthiopia, with an account that Sultan Segued, Emperor of Abyssinia, was converted to the church of Rome, that many of his subjects had followed his example, and that there was a great want of missionaries to improve their prosperous beginnings. Every body was very desirous of seconding the zeal of our fathers, and of sending them the assistance they requested; to which we were the more encouraged, because the emperor's letters informed our provincial that we might easily enter his dominions by the way of Dancala, but unhappily the secretary wrote Zeila for Dancala, which cost two of our fathers their lives.

We were, however, notwithstanding the assurances given us by the emperor, sufficiently appraised of the danger which we were exposed to in this expedition, whether we went by sea or land. By sea, we foresaw the hazard we ran of falling into the hands of the Turks, amongst whom we should lose, if not our lives, at least our liberty, and be for every prevented from reaching the court of Æthiopia. Upon this consideration, our superiors divided the eight Jesuits chosen for this mission into two companies. Four they sent by sea, and four by land; I was of the latter number. The four first were the more fortunate, who though they were detained some time by the Turkish bassa, were dismissed at the request of the emperor, who sent him a zeura, or wild ass, a creature of large size and admirable beauty.

As for us, who were to go by Zeila, we had still greater difficulties to struggle with: we were entirely strangers to the ways we were to take, to the manners, and even to the names of the nations through which we were to pass. Our chief desire was to discover some new road by which we might avoid having any thing to do with the Turks. Among great numbers whom we consulted on this occasion, we were informed by some that we might go through Melinda. These men painted that hideous wilderness in charming colours, told us that we should find a country watered with navigable rivers, and inhabited by a people that would either inform us of the way, or accompany us in it. So of we who went by land, two took the way of Zeila, and my companion and I that of Melinda.

Having provided every thing necessary for our journey, such as Arabian habits, and red caps, callicoes, and other trifles to make presents of to the inhabitants, and taking leave of our friends, as men going to a speedy death, for we were not insensible of the dangers we were likely to encounter, amongst horrid deserts, impassable mountains, and barbarous nations, we left Goa on the 26th day of January in the year 1624, in a Portuguese galliot that was ordered to set us ashore at Patè, where we landed without any disaster in eleven days, together with a young Abyssian, whom we made use of as our interpreter. While we stayed here, we were given to understand that those who had been pleased at Goa to give us directions in relation to our journey, had done nothing but tell us lies. That the people were savage, that they had indeed begun to treat with the Portuguese, but it was only from fear, that otherwise they were a barbarous nation, that they ravaged the country, and laid every thing waste, where they came, that they were man-eaters, and were on that account dreadful in all those parts. My companion and I being undeceived by this terrible relation, thought it would be the highest imprudence to expose ourselves both together to a death almost certain and unprofitable, and agreed that I should go with our Abyssin and a Portuguese to observe the country; that if I should prove so happy as to escape being killed by the inhabitants, and to discover a way, I should either return, or send back the Abyssin or Portuguese. Having fixed upon this, I hired a little bark to Juba, a place about forty leagues distant from Patè, on board which I put some provisions, together with my sacerdotal vestments, and all that was necessary for saying mass: in this vessel we reached the coast, which we found inhabited by several nations.

On this coast we landed, with an intention of travelling on foot to Juba, a journey of much greater length and difficulty than we imagined. We durst not go far from our bark, and therefore were obliged to a toilsome march along the widings of the shore, sometimes, clambering up rocks, and sometimes wading through the sands, so that we were every moment in the utmost danger of falling from the one or sinking in the other. Our lodging was either in the rocks or on the sands, and even that incommoded by continual apprehensions of being devoured by lions and tigers. Admidst all these calamities our provisions failed us; we had little hopes of a supply, for we found neither villages, houses, nor any trace of human creature; and had miserably perished by thirst and hunger had we not met with some fishermen's boats, who exchanged their fish for tobacco.

Through all these fatigues we at length came to Juba, a kingdom of considerable extent, situated almost under the line, and tributary to the Portuguese who carry on a trade here for ivory and other commodities. I staid here some time to inform myself whether I might, by pursuing this road, reach Abyssinia; and could get no other intelligence, but that two thousand Galles (the same people who inhabited Melinda) had encamped about three leagues from Juba.

[*At length, "despairing that I should ever come this way to Abyssinia," he returned to Patè and to the Indies, and on April 3, 1625, with the Patriarch of Ethiopia, sailed from Diou for the Red Sea.*]

After some days we discovered about noon the island Socotora, where we proposed to touch. The sky was bright, and the wind fair, nor had we the least apprehension of the danger into which we were falling, but with the utmost carelessness and jollity, held on our course. At night, when our sailors, especially the Moors, were in a profound sleep (for the Mahometans believing every thing forewritten in the decrees of God, and not alterable by any human means, resign themselves entirely to Providence), our vessel ran aground upon a sand-bank at the entrance of the harbour. We got her off, with the utmost difficulty, and nothing but a miracle could have preserved us. We ran along afterwards by the side of the island, but were entertained with no other prospect than of a mountainous country, and of rocks that jutted out over the sea, and seemed ready to fall into it. In the afternoon, putting into the most convenient ports of the island, we came to anchor, very much to the amazement and terror of the inhabitants, who were not used to see any Portuguese ships upon their coasts, and were therefore under a great consternation at finding them even in their ports. Some ran for security to the mountains, others took up arms to oppose our landing, but were soon reconciled to us, and brought us fowls, fish, and sheep, in exchange for India callicoes, on which they set a great value. We left this island early the next morning, and soon came in sight of Cape Gardafui, so celebrated heretofore under the name of the Cape of Spices, either because great quantities were then found there, or from its neigbourhood to Arabia the Happy, even at this day famous for its fragrant products. It is properly at this cape (the most eastern part of Africa) that the Gulf of Arabia begins, which at Babelmandel loses its name and is called the Red Sea.

Having happily passed the straits at the entrance of the Red Sea, we pursued our course, keeping as near the shore as we could. We were however under some concern that we were entirely ignorant in what part of the coast to find Baylur, a port where we proposed landing, and so little known that our pilots, who had made many voyages in this sea, could give us no account of it. We were in hopes of information from the fishermen, but found that as soon as we came near, they fled from us in the greatest consternation. We plied along the coast in this uncertainty two days, till on the first of March having doubled a point of land, which came out a great way into the sea, we found ourselves in the middle of a fair large bay, which many reasons induced us to think was Baylur; that we might be farther assured we sent our Abyssin on shore, who returning next morning confirmed our opinion. It would not be easy to determine whether our arrival gave us greater joy, or the inhabitants greater apprehensions, for we could discern a continual tumult in the land, and took notice that the crews of some barks that lay in the harbour were unlading with all possible diligence, to prevent the cargo from falling into our hands.

We were willing to be assured of a good reception in this port, the patriarch therefore sent me to treat with them. I dressed myself like a merchant, and in that habit received the four captains of gelves which the chec sent to compliment me, and ordered to stay as hostages, whom I sent back, that I might gain upon their affections by the confidence I placed in their sincerity;

this had so good an effect that the chec, who was transported with the account the officers gave of the civilities they had been treated with, came in an hour to visit me, bringing with him a Portuguese, whom I had sent ashore as a security for his return. He informed me that the King, his master, was encamped not far off, and that a chec who was then in the company was just arrived from thence, and had seen the Emperor of Æthiopia's letters in our favour; I was then convinced that we might land without scruple, and to give the patriarch notice of it, ordered a volley of our muskets to be fired, which was answered by the cannon of the two ships, that lay at a distance, for fear of giving the Moors any cause of suspicion by their approach. The chec and his attendants, though I had given them notice that we were going to let off our guns in honour of the King their master, could not forbear trembling at the fire and noise. They left us soon after, and next morning we landed our baggage, consisting chiefly of the patriarch's library, some ornaments for the church, some images, and some pieces of calico, which were of the same use as money.

Our goods were no sooner landed, than we were surrounded with a crowd of officers, all gaping for presents; we were forced to gratify their avarice by opening our bales, and distributing among them some pieces of calico. What we gave to the chec might be worth about a pistole, and the rest in proportion.

The kingdom of Dancali, to which this belongs, is barren, and thinly peopled; the king is tributary to the Emperor of Abyssinia, and very faithful to his sovereign. The Emperor had not only written to him, but had sent a Moor and Portuguese as his ambassadors, to secure us a kind reception.

On Ascension Day we left Baylur, having procured some camels and asses to carry our baggage. The first day's march was not above a league, and the others not much longer. Our guides performed their office very ill, being influenced, as we imagined, by the Chec Furt, an officer whom, though unwilling, we were forced to take with us. This man who might have brought us to the King in three days, led us out of the way through horrid deserts destitute of water, or where what we found was so foul, nauseous and offensive, that it excited a loathing and aversion which nothing but extreme necessity could have overcome.

Having travelled some days, we were met by the King's brother, to whom, by the advice of Chec Furt, whose intent in following us was to squeeze all he could from us; we presented some pieces of Chinese workmanship, such as cases of boxes, a standish, and some earthenware, together with several pieces of painted calico. I was here in danger of losing my life by a compliment which the Portuguese paid the prince of a discharge of twelve muskets; one being unskilfully charged too high, flew out of the soldier's hand, and falling against my leg, wounded it very much; we had no surgeon with us, so that all I could do was to bind it hard with some cloth. I was obliged by this accident to make use of the Chec Furt's horse, which was the greatest service we received from him in all our journey.

When we came within two leagues and an half of the King's court, he sent some messengers with his compliments, and five mules for the chief of our company. Our road lay through a wood, where we found the ground covered over with young locusts, a plague intolerably afflictive in a country so barren of itself. We arrived at length at the bank of a small river, near which the King usually keeps his residence, and found his palace at the foot of a little mountain. It consisted of about six tents and twenty cabins, erected amongst some thorns and wild trees, which afforded a shelter from the heat of the weather. He received us the first time in a cabin about a musketshot distant from the rest, furnished out with a throne in the middle built of clay and stones, and covered with tapestry and two velvet cushions. Over against him stood his horse with his saddle and other furniture hanging by him, for in this country, the master and his horse make use of the same apartment, nor doth the King in this respect, affect more grandeur than his subjects. When we entered, we seated ourselves on the ground with our legs crossed, in imitation of the rest, whom we found in the same posture. After we had waited some time, the King came in, attended by his domestics and his officers. He held a small lance in his hand, and was dressed in a silk robe, with a turban on his head, to which were fastened some rings of very neat workmanship, which fell down upon his forehead. All kept silence for some time, and the King told us by his interpreter, that we were welcome to his dominions, that he had been informed we were to come, by the Emperor his father, and that he condoled the hardships we had undergone at sea. He desired us not to be under any concern at finding ourselves in a country so distant from our own, for those dominions were ours, and he and the Emperor his father would give us all the proofs we could desire of the sincerest affection.

We set out from the kingdom of Dancali, on the fifteenth of June, having taken ourleave of the King, who. . . . dismissed us with a present of a cow, and some provisions, desiring us to tell the Emperor of Æthiopia his father, that we had met with kind treatment in his territories.

Whatever we had suffered hitherto, was nothing to the difficulties we were now entering upon, and which God had decreed us to undergo for the sake of Jesus Christ. Our way now lay through a region scarce passable, and full of serpents, which were continually creeping between our legs; we might have avoided them in the day, but being obliged, that we might avoid the excessive heats, to take long marches in the night, we were every moment treading upon them. Nothing but a signal interposition of providence could have preserved us from being bitten by them, or perishing either by weariness or thirst, for sometimes we were a long time without water, and had nothing to support our strength in this fatigue but a little honey, and small piece of cows' flesh dried in the sun. Thus we travelled on for many days, scarce allowing ourselves any rest, till we came to a channel or hollow worn in the mountains by the winter torrents: here we found some coolness, and good water, a blessing we enjoyed for three days; down this channel all the winter runs a great river, which is dried up in the heats, or to speak more properly hides itself underground. We walked along its side sometimes seven or eight leagues without seeing any water, and then we found it rising out of the ground, at which places we never failed to drink as much as we could, and fill our bottles.

After a march of some days, we came to an opening between the mountains, the only passage out of Dancali into Abyssinia. Heaven seems to have made this place on purpose for the repose of weary travellers, who here exchange the tortures of parching thirst, burning sands, and a sultry climate, for the pleasures of shady trees, the refreshment of a clear stream, and the luxury of a cooling breeze. We arrived at this happy place about noon, and the next day at evening left those fanning winds, and woods flourishing with unfading verdure, for the dismal barrenness of the vast uninhabitable plains, from which Abyssinia is supplied with salt. These plains are surrounded with high mountains, continually covered with thick clouds which the sun draws from the lakes that are here, from which the water runs down into the plain, and is there congealed into salt. Nothing can be more curious than to see the channels and aqueducts that nature has formed in his hard rock, so exact and of such admirable contrivance, that they seem to be the work of men. To this place caravans of Abyssinia are continually resorting, to carry salt into all parts of the empire, which they set a great value upon, and which in their country is of the same use as money. The superstitious Abyssins imagine that the cavities of the mountains are inhabited by evil spirits which appear in different shapes, calling those that pass by their names as in a familiar acquaintance, who, if they go to them, are never seen afterwards.

The heat making it impossible to travel through this plain in the day time, we set out in the evening, and in the night lost our way. It is very dangerous to go through this place, for there are no marks of the right road but some heaps of salt, which we could not see. Our camel drivers getting together to consult on this occasion, we suspected they had some ill design in hand and got ready our weapons; they perceived our apprehensions, and set us at ease by letting us know the reason of their consultation. Travelling hard all night, we found ourselves next morning past the plain; but the road we were in was not more commodious, the points of the rocks pierced our feet; to increase our perplexities we were alarmed with the approach of an armed troop, which our fear immediately suggested to be the Galles, who chiefly beset these passes of the mountains; we put ourselves on the defensive, and expected them, whom upon a more exact examination, we found to be only a caravan of merchants come as usual to fetch salt.

The desire of getting out of the reach of the Galles, made us press forward with great expedition, and indeed, fear having entirely engrossed our minds, we were perhaps less sensible of all our labours and difficulties; so violent an apprehension of one danger made us look on many others with unconcern; our pains at last found some intermission at the foot of the mountains of Duan, the frontier of Abyssinia, which separates it from the country of the Moors, through which we had travelled.

Here we imagined we might repose securely, a felicity we had long been strangers to. Here we began to rejoice at the conclusion of our labours; the place was cool, and pleasant, the water excellent, and the birds melodious; some of our company went into the wood to divert themselves with hearing the birds, and frightening the monkeys, creatures so cunning that they would not stir if a man came unarmed, but would run immediately when they saw a gun. At this place our camel drivers left us, to go to the feast of St Michael, which the Æthiopians celebrate the sixteenth of June. We persuaded them however to leave us their camels and four of their company to take care of them.

We had not waited many days, before some messengers came to us, with an account that father Baradas, with the Emperor's nephew, and many other persons of distinction, waited for us at some distance; we loaded our camels, and following the course of the river, came in seven hours to the place we were directed to halt at. Father Manuel Baradas and all the company, who had waited for us a considerable time, on the top of the mountain, came down when they saw our tents, and congratulated our arrival. It is not easy to express the benevolence and tenderness with which they embraced us, and the concern they showed at seeing us worn away with hunger, labour, and weariness, our cloathes tattered, and our feet bloody.

We left this place of interview the next day, and on the 21st of June, arrived at Fremone the residence of the missionaries, where we were welcomed by great numbers of catholics, both Portuguese and Abyssins, who spared no endeavours to make us forget all we had suffered in so hazardous a journey, undertaken with no other intention, than to conduct them in the way of salvation.[1]

TO THE LAND OF KING CAZEMBE[2]

(1797)

FRANCISCO JOSÉ MARIA DE LACERDA E ALMEIDA

On March 12, 1797, Her Most Faithful Majesty[3]—whom God defend!—having commanded me to ascertain the possibility of overland transit between the eastern and the western coasts of Africa, I sought at Mozambique, Quilimane, Sena, and Tete, for information touching those hitherto untrodden lands. But all was in vain. Those consulted concerning an enterprise not yielding in importance to the discovery of Asia, only represented to me its impossiblity; their reasons were those of men who choose the Royal service rather as a profession that pays than of men who love glory, and who would be useful to the State. . . .

But Providence smiled upon the righteous and benevolent intentions of our august Sovereign. Thirty-three days after my arrival at Tete, I was visited by certain envoys from the Court of the King Cazembe in the distant interior, one Chinimbu, a Muiza, and the other Catára of the same race as the Cazembe, namely the Arunda. I took down their depositions . . . together with those of a native of these parts (the Rios de Sena), and what I could obtain from other strange Caffres who were lodged in the houses at Tete.

Short was the time for organising an expedition, or for finding good porters, trustworthy soldiers, ammunition, and country-money, Caffre cloth, beads, and other necessaries; yet I resolved at once, and at all risks, to carry out the Royal orders. In one point I was fortunate; three or four hundred Caffres were expected at Tete, some composing the escort of Chinimbu and Catára, others bringing their own ivories, and others carrying tusks presented to certain Portuguese inhabitants of the town.

On March 10th and 12th, I wrote officially to the factory and commandants of Sena and Quilimane, directing them to purchase from the resident merchants all that could not be obtained at our ill-provided factories in Tete.

[1] So successful were the missionary efforts of Father Lobo and his companions that they baptized the natives in rows, "crying aloud, 'Those of this rank are named Peter, those of that rank Anthony.' And did the same among the women."

[2] From *The Lands of Cazembe*, translated by Sir Richard Burton.

[3] Queen Maria I.

I offered to repay the loan in kind by drafts upon the Royal treasury at Mozambique. They refused, however, and nothing was to be done without compulsion, a proceeding of which the Crown could not have approved. The Colonel of Maniça (Manisa) Militia, Jeronymo Pereira, who passes for the most respectable man at Sena, proved himself a knave, not only by taking exorbitant prices for his cloth, but also by supplying this primary necessary in Caffre travel of so wretched a quality that it was well-night useless. . . .

As time pressed . . . I resolved to punish the knavery of Jeronymo Pereira by directing the Factor of Sena to take from his warehouses the best cloth, to be repaid in kind from Mozambique. I also warned him that he himself should be at the expense of sending back his vile stuffs to Tete. . . .

I soon found myself in fresh difficulties. An exact muster proved that, of the 300 or 400 Muizas, at most 100 were available as porters, the others having died or disappeared, whilst some refused to carry packs. The Sena Caffres had also fled without a cause, and I expected those of Tete to follow their bad example, because their masters were frightening them. As a last resource, I made the owners responsible for their slaves, yet though many . . . owned more than 200 "captives," and some held valuable Crown lands, they thought much of letting me have ten or fifteen, begging me to be content with fewer as the men leave labour to the more industrious women.

In these straits, I had recource to the heroine of these lands, D. Francisca, Josefa de Moura e Menezes, widow of two officers who had held the captainship. Her boats, and other possessions, are ever at the service of the Crown, and she takes a pride in the Royal service. She replied that, to her legal share of forty, she would add sixty, and retain only those absolutely necessary; also, that the negresses, who were her chief stock, were scattered and working at the mines of Maxinga, where I should pass, and where the rice for our journey was stored.

As the sixty men did not appear, I asked D. Francisca if, in case of need, I could use negresses; she answered, that they would serve me as well as, if not better than men. . . . She at once despatched her freedmen with her negresses, and even her house attendants, to distribute amongst the sixty Caffres and their wives, the rice and the loads lying at Tete.

July 3, 1798. Fearing delay from other troubles, I set out for Nhaufa Fatiola, an estate lying north of the Zambeze River, and distant about three-quarters of a league from Tete; where we had been stationed since the end of June. Our general direction lay north, through Sonte and Cube—Crown properties like Nhaufa. . . . Beyond Sonte there is broken ground, and the path winds up narrow hill-girt valleys. Our day's march lay through troublesome thorns and over lands left incult by want of hands, or by the laziness of their owners. . . .

Some porters deserted, kindly leaving upon the path their packs, which were carried by the bearers of our hammocks. Such flights are fatal to progress, and are the worst of examples. I am in constant dread of fresh cases being reported to me. We could not reach the place where the cooks had been ordered to await us on the second day; consequently our suppers and beds were such as the reader may imagine. . . .

July 4th. We were thrown into confusion by the sudden flight of more than thirty bearers. . . . Upwards of twenty belonged to D. Paulina Anna de Sousa Bragança. This lady, when her quotum had been fixed, showed herself so recalcitrant, that I had sent the Reverned Father Francisco João Pinto . . . to declare, in *verbo sacerdotis*, my unwillingness to punish her, but my determination to carry out the Royal command. D. Paulina yielded, but with delay and bad grace. This desertion . . . compelled me to go a little more than a league further on to "Inhacengeira," where the Expedition was expecting me. Thereon I sent Captain João da Cunha Pereira to Pequizo, where D. Paulina was living, with directions to show that I had ordered the Factor of Tete to sell her lands by public auction, if the twenty fugitives were not forthcoming. . . .

5th. As sailors in a terrible storm throw cargo overboard to lighten the ship, so we reduced our goods to the most needful. I began reforms at the provisions, and divided our salt amongst the soldiers and porters, reserving a little for general use; when it is finished we must do without it, as they say "hungry men want no mustard." . . . Seeing my party down-hearted, I represented to them the honour and glory of our undertaking, and concluded by saying that anyone who liked, might return home. They then recovered some spirit; but only four members of the Expedition betrayed no weakness, namely the chaplain, the chief-serjeant, Pedro Xavier Velasco, the lieutenant-colonel of militia, Pedro Nolasco d'Araujo, and Antonio José da Cruz, fort-lieutenant of Tete. . . .

6th. I spent a sleepless night, thinking of and fearing desertion, and so it again came to pass—thirty-four more porters fled. . . . My firm resolution to push on, despite the lateness of the season, calms my mind and enables me to endure these vexations, as the stormtossed mariner consoles himself with exaggerating the pleasures of port. Disgusted with the place, I marched on till we entered the lands of the Marave, our false friends and fast foes, whose only end is to fleece us of cloth. We passed three little villages, where the males, old and young, stood scattered, and without showing fight; but each armed with his bow and arrows. Caffres, from their childhood, never even visit a neighbour without these weapons. What a well-made, finely-limbed, graceful race it is! I was never tired of looking at them. . . .

7th. The porters set out a at sunrise, I at 7.30 A.M. Half an hour after noon we awaited at a brook those who were behind. Later in the day, the lieutenant came on, and reported that all the porters had halted near a rivulet, distant three-quarters of a league from this place, and that when ordered to advance, they had flown to their inevitable bows and arrows. I neither wondered at, nor cared for, the flight of five Caffres who, shortly after starting, left their loads, including my clothes-box. My mental anxiety is that, to-night, despite all our vigilance, they will disappear in a body. In order to remedy this evil, should it befall us, we must leave early for Maxinga, and thence despatch the necessary aid. . . .

8th. At 2.30 P.M. I reached the Maxinga estate. . . . Here the negresses of D. Francisca, and a few others belonging to two Tete men, were digging for gold. My multitudinous and ever-growing perplexities made me at once send all the Caffres who were found ready, to aid those left behind. Happily they were not required; and on the next day, the whole party arrived safe. I chose out two hundred able-bodied women. . . .

10th. Despite my care to feed the Caffres, who are not supposed to fly from work or blows after meals, last night fifty-two of them deserted. When thrown into bitterest perplexity by the news, I was informed that thirty-seven more had fled. Those who know my activity and zeal for the service of the Crown will appreciate my affliction: yet they will do me the justice to believe that I was resolved to push forward at all risk, and never to return until absolutely necessary. . . .

14th. "*Qui confidit in Deo non confundetur,*" saith the Psalmist. As I was mounting my palanquin at 11 A.M. some twenty-three Caffres arrived with the loads left at "Nhassengeria" (Inhacengeira, July 4th). I was a joyful as if they had been twenty-three thousand. . . .

15th. The Maraves came for their loads, but . . . would not carry them till paid. After long haggling, I gave to each a capotim (two blue cottons) with the chance of losing all by desertion that night. . . . Other Maraves being persuaded to join by these good terms, I divided the remaining loads between them and the Tete Caffres, of whom three had fled during the dark hours. Nothing now remained but a box of crockery destined for the Cazembe, and three arm-chairs, for which he had applied, a case of kitchen-butter for immediate use, and a barrel of gunpowder. . . . Giving orders for these stores to be forwarded, I left Maxinga. . . .

16th. The Maraves ran away, and, unluckily for them, one was captured. This they say will be the source of quarrels and of serious "palavers," as the father and relations of the prisoner must turn against the runaways. Although all the born thieves, robbery amongst themselves is severely punished. . . . Happily appeared other Maraves, who agreed to receive their pay at Java. . . .

17th. All the Caffres assembled and declared their intention of spending the day in the large village. . . . I told them that being ill we would halt at noon, but the brutes were unmoved. Dread of their desertion made me dissimulate, and the better to hide my displeasure I gave them some beads to buy beer. They were delighted, whilst I, having noted the four most maggotty heads of the party, took thought how best to repress and punish such disorders. I gathered the opinions of sundry of my company, especially of José Rodrigues Caleja, who, by the by, had been represented to me as a ready man, well versed in native habits. I blamed their invariable answer to all my perplexities, "We must do what your honour orders us to do." Finally, it was agreed to put up with the porters' insolence till one or two stages after Java, then seize their bows and arrows, and burn these weapons in the presence of their tied-up owners, who would, if properly guarded, march as I might direct.

21st. We arrived at Java. About sunset an envoy of Mussidansáro brought a message from his master that the Maraves, having robbed a packet of porcelain beads, Crown property, which had been entrusted to them for transport, his master would enter the robbers' village, seize three of them, and not release them till the plunder should be restored. He added that he would carry off as much millet as he could, but that the delay would not permit him to visit me at Java. This prince Mussidansáro is a great knave: he came from the Cazembe as a man of business to visit D. Francisca, whom . . . they call Chiponda, that is to say, "the lady that treads all under her feet," to beg that she would send her son to the king. D. Francisca, availing herself of this opportunity, requested her lord the Cazembe to treat me as her son sent under his care, and to defend me from all dangers. . . .

22nd. To-day I have twice crossed the large Aruangôa River. In one place the water reaches the bend of the leg, in another part, somewhat higher up, there is a bridge of canes (bamboos) tied together. I already know in this part of Africa three streams of that name: this is the first; the second is that falling into the Zambeze near Zumbo, dividing the lands of the Maraves and Muizas; and the third is in the lands of the Baróe, between Sena and Maniça.

The mines of Java, here called Bar, were discovered seven or eight years ago by Gonçalo Caetano Pereira; at present they are worked by the negresses of only one inhabitant of Tete, and all these women fled to the bush, justly thinking that I might require their services. These diggings might pay, but they are despised because men ignore working them. . . .

23rd. Until 7 P.M. the expected Marave party did not appear, although I was informed that they were being collected. About 150 are wanted, and if they fail us, it will be troublesome. In such a case only the negresses can extricate me, and even then many loads must be left on the ground. . . .

The two Muizas, Chinimbu and Mussidansáro, took up my time, and stunned me with their disputes, already reckoning upon the honours and gifts of the king (Cazembe). They wish to decide who shall conduct me to him. The former pleaded priority of claim as bearer of the royal message; the latter that he had been sent by the King to request a visit from D. Francisca's "son," in which category I was committed to him. . . . I told them that they must be friendly till we should reach the King, when the weighty matter could be decided. They wished to continue the dispute, but the spirit and eloquence of a flask of strong waters were more convincing than my reasons or the joint tongues of Cicero and Demosthenes would have been. . . .

27th. Tortured with the insatiable thirst and the intense cold of the Sezão (a seasoning fever or fit of ague and fever) which attacked me at 5 A.M., I set out three hours later. Nothing more miserable than to have to do with men wanting common sense like these Caffres, who are absolutely indifferent to good and evil, who feel only when they suffer, and who cannot allow themselves to be persuaded. No reason will convince them that, when possible, we should march together to baffle enemies and robbers, and that we should start early and travel farther, lest the failure of the military chest leave us in woful want. Until they see me *en route* all hide in the bush. . . .

31st. Quinine had prevented the increase of my illness—the only improvement, but no small one. I was carried to my palanquin and took bearings to the best of my power so as not to lose the line of march.

August 7th. Fever prevented my keeping the Diary till to-day. No news except that we have crossed the little streams "Ruy" and the "Bua," which falls into the Chire (Shire). The country traversed is so poor that nothing can be procured but millet, sweet potatoes, yams, ground-nuts, and a few bananas: these, however, are abundant and cheap. My only support is rice-water. Not a chicken during my sickness! not the smallest bird to be seen, and no sign of game: possibly the famished Caffres, after finishing their stores, declare war even upon the butterflies, and have thus exterminated birds and beasts. . . .

9th and 10th. The Caffres, not contented with our halts which, as the Diary shows, were frequent, 'and scandalised by our marching on an average 2½ leagues a day, refused to advance. . . . I had no remedy but to await them in a village called Chitenga. . . .

11th. It was necessary to halt at 10.15 A.M., as the Caffres are accustomed to night in this place—a poor excuse, which would be valid if water lay afar. I am in despair, thinking of the want of supplies, of the necessity for wintering in the interior, and of this delay in carrying out the orders of the Crown. My blood boils to see the likeness between the Caffres and the whites who, introduced to me as knowing the manners and customs of the natives, have adopted only their superstitions and abominations which, added to their own, render them truly detestable. Lieut.-Colonel Pedro Nolasco and the chief sergeant Pedro Xavier Velasco are the only two hitherto found faithful. . . .

13th. At 10.30 A.M. we reached the village of the chief Caperemera, son of the Mocanda. . . . I sent to inform him of my illness, and my wish to see him. The chief presently appeared—a fine-looking man, full of natural grace. Summoning all the servile head-men of porters, I said in their presence that I had much friendship with his father (the Mocanda), in virtue of which he had at my request sent orders to all his vassels and villagers living on or near our road, to seize and bring before him all the Caffres taken without a pass from me, and to sell them for his profit. . . . The truth is, I had failed to obtain this from his father, because the latter had feared to visit me, and moreover because I had neglected, through ignorance of their customs, to delay with him for a day, which they hold a high honour. I added that it was my wish similarly to contract with himself strict friendship, and to open commerce, by which he would be the gainer. By sending to Sena his tusks and gold . . . he would obtain more cloth than from the slave-factors of Mozambique. . . . I expressed, furthermore, a desire that he would respond to my offers of friendship by posting three of his messengers on the different roads, and seize as his own slaves all the fugitive Caffres who could not show my token of dismissal.

The present of a red cloth, a piece of thin Indian cotton, a flagon of rum, and a cloth of cauril, confirmed our friendship. The chief in person leading the Caffres who accompanied him, sent for three of his slaves, and, before all of our head-men of porters, he gave to each a bit of paper, which I had stamped with my arms, and he ordered them at once to carry my plan into execution. . . .

16th. I was getting ready to move forward, but he Muizas had not returned from the villages where they had been to collect millet for the first day's march. Besides which, Caffres never hurry themselves—African Caffres at least. When sold to America they take example from their elders, and become far more diligent. . . . At my request Caperemera sent many couriers to summon the party, who at last arrived; some of them, however, wished to return their pay rather than carry our loads. The Mambo very angrily ordered them, under pain of expulsion and compulsion, to "clear out," and they knew the power of his bow. He was named Caperemera, meaning "the Brave." Sure that our Caffres would not fly, fearing sale at Mozambique, with its consequent exile from Africa . . . and resolved to show them that their reign was over, I summoned them as if to muster them, and when they were gathered together I sent soldiers to their encampment with orders to bring and break before them their bows and arrows. They were seized with consternation, it being a dishonour to travel without weapons, as only criminals and fugitives go unarmed. . . . I left the village at 3.30 P.M. . . .

20th. At the end of the wildest and roughest of our marches lay the village of Mazavamba, a great thief. All the resident Muizas and Botombucas who came to see me were exceedingly drunk, and Mazavamba, who continued his carouse till the 22nd, was too far gone to visit me. . . .

23rd. From Mazavamba's village I made for the Northern Aruangôa River. The ague and fever which attached me so violently on the 21st inst., came on to-day with increased vigour, from 9 A.M. to 9 P.M. Suffering it as best I could, we marched on the River Remimba. . . . I halted at a village near that stream, not so much to nurse my ague as to collect provisions for 3½ to 4 days of march upon the nearest Muiza village. . . .

25th. This day (thirtieth) I resumed my Diary, though still suffering very severely from fever, of which I have had four attacks since the end of March. I did not expect to escape the three first. Perhaps the third would have been less troublesome, had I not been traveling, and in want of everything. Enough to say that his Excellency the Governor of the Rios de Sena, the successor of those heroes who never left the house except in a sedan chair with two large velvet sun-tents (umbrellas) . . . in order that the glances of the Lord of Day, even though setting, might not annoy them; who lived wrapped up in silks, and in the lightest white clothing; who often suffered from indigestion and other inconveniences, the effect of a too splendid and profuse diet, and who finally passed their time in scattering cloth, and in gathering gold and ivory—this successor, I say, spent many an hour shirtless, and wrapped up in a baize, because his clothes were left behind, while during his sickness he had not a chicken for broth. *Deus super omnia!* The route, which I never ceased tracing even at times of my greatest weakness, serves me as a guide to work up this diary. I cannot, however, offer very many details, as my malady often prevented my taking notice of everything. . . .

August 26th, 1798. This day I made a long march to reach a lake or lagoon; all the ground was marked with elephants' trails, the first seen since we left Tete. . . .

29th. A short march to water. Passing the village of Caperempande, I found the people at their orgies with the red wood-dust . . . covering their hair. . . . The place appeared a hell—the Muizas its devils. . . .

Sept. 1st, 1798. As the powerful Muiza kinglet, Mucungure—of whom they say that he is not really a subject, but an ally of the Cazembe—was absent from the village, I marched to meet him in the place where he lives. . . . The country to-day travelled over is high and rocky; the settlements are small, wretched, and starving. . . .

2nd. About midday Mucungure visited me with a long 'tail,' under two very old and broken umbrellas, preceded by many drums, which, with the clamour of his people, made a truly infernal music. He appeared to be in his second childhood; and when I began to talk business about his assisting my people, two of his magnates told me not to trouble myself—that all should be done. He brought a pair of wives: these ladies, like himself and his subjects, wore treebarks with girt waists. The Caffres and their spouses habitually appear in the poorest attires, by this mute language appealing for cloth. Although . . . I have no good opinion of, or trust in, the Muizas, I was satisfied with this chief and his grandees, who gave me 50 men to forward those left behind. . . .

4th. To-day we had three troubles—a long march to water through a depopulated country . . . a thigh-deep marsh near a ridge; and thirdly, the most dangerous, a grass-fire, which surrounded us, and which gave us great trouble to escape. Being sure that the Caffres can no longer fly, I did not administer at the village of Caperemera corporal punishment, that they might be able to march; yet two of those who escorted me, believing that they could escape castigation, did their best to deserve it. After sending an order for them to be flogged, one of them, being a head-man, was put into the bilboes. This example has so altered the Caffres that I no longer recognise them: they are now most obedient; they are ready without murmuring to make any march I please. . . .

6th. To-day the shrubs and bush which cover these lands were so thick that the Caffres who carried our luggage found it had to remove them. The depopulation of the place, the famished state of our party, the marshes, our having to cut lines and paths, and the thirst which often afflicts us, the fevers caused by nightly cold and by fierce suns of day—to say nothing of my sickness—all combine to make the land appear wild and sad. Were there game to supply the want of millet, or small birds to charm us with their song, the transit would have been less tedious. For the last three days we have made much westing. I never supposed that we should have to approach so near the Equinoctial line. . . .

8th. To stifle our hunger and collect six day's rations at the village of Morungabambara, near the Zambeze River, I went to-day a long march through champaign lands clearer than before, and lacking high ridges and difficult swamps. I passed some villages—what villages!—four or five huts, so small and low that one can hardly guess how the Muizas can lodge in them. . . . We raised our hands in thanks to Heaven, when, after abundant difficulty, we bought ten lean cockerels, which seemed to us so many fat turkeys. . . .

10th. After 1 hour 20 minutes' march we reached the Zambeze, measuring some 25 fathoms in breadth, and at this season from 4 to 5 palms. . . . Here end the starvling lands of these high-haired and ringleted people. . . . I sent to inquire about the course of the Zambeze from sundry Mussucumas, a tribe mixed in small numbers with the Muizas on this side of the Zambeze, some of them vassels to the Cazembe. . . . All said that it trends to the river which runs by the city of the Cazembe, whatever be the truth of their information. . . .

14th. A short march placed me at the village of Fumo Chipaco, the largest and the most populous of all. I judge that this must be one of the grandees, as Catára spoke of him with respect. He at once sent him to call upon me, with a civil message that, as a friend of his master, I was in my own country, and that he, as a slave of the Cazembe, was also mine; moreover, that all things in his village, and in those under his command, were at my disposal. . . . As I cannot think of anything but my present undertaking, I begged from him people to assist the 2nd Division, of which he had already heard from Catára. The latter lay sick at a village near the River Zambeze. He answered that he would give me as many as I wanted, and that he would presently order his drums to sound the assembly and to collect all, when I could take what number I pleased. His answer about our provisions is also worthy of being recorded literally. "Tell the Mambo that he is in the village of Chipaco."

16th. With a mind somewhat at ease I continued my march, and, after crossing some rivulets, at the end of the day's work we forded sundry large streamlets, besides others, the Ricena and Mocanda. . . . Some Caffres brought us a few chickens, which, having no large porcelain beads, greatly to our sorrow, we were unable to purchase.

20th. The village of the Fumo Mouro-Atchinto ends the district of Fumo Chipaco, which began at the River Zambeze. Here I halted for three reasons. Firstly, to rest the party and prepare for a forced march of seven or eight days through the waste and desert country before us. Secondly, to collect supplies. . . . Thirdly, to observe the immersions of Jupiter's satellites, if my illness permit, and the bush burnings which begin at 9 to 10 A.M. leave the air clear. Of late the atmosphere has been thick, and only about dawn it thins with the fall of dew, which is cold and heavy. This chill is followed by an intense heat, the effect of sun and grass-smoke, and at 11 A.M. it is at its height. To-day we suffered from the smoke which was all round us, and, fortunately for us, the dried herbage was not very high. . . .

22nd, 23rd, 24th. Many elephant-tracks in these lands; the trees increase in height and thickness. . . .

27th. Feverish and weak, I marched over the desert and crossed some swamps. A Caffre guide assured me that in the highlands to the left hand (westward) is the Great Lake which he and his master Manoel Caetano Pereira—who, however, made it larger—had crossed on their last journey. It must be a continuation of that near which I nighted, perhaps anastomosing with the other water which we have passed, since the owners of certain miserable huts where we are now, there catch, it is said, large fish. . . .

28th. At 1 P.M. I reached a village governed by the Fumo Mouro, of the same grade of vasselhood, but nearer related to the Cazembe. About half a league before our arrival a vast crowd of both sexes and all ages awaited me with festive instruments: so anxious were they to see me that some were perched on tree-tops, and after I had passed they descended and accompanied me, singing, playing instruments, dancing, and at the same time clearing the road. Those who were on the ground ceremoniously rubbed themselves with dust, and showed their wonder of all they saw, not only by the expression of their countenances, but by holding the forefinger in the mouth and by biting the hand. I did not see one Muiza here. In the afternoon Mouro sent me his present of Pombe, four large chickens, and a gazelle almost decomposed, with a message that he did not visit me in person, as he was preparing subsistence for my people. To-day's march was clear of trees; but all suffered from want of water, which was not found till we reached the Daro or halting-place.

29th. As the Fumo did not keep his word touching supplies, I sent my people to buy what was offered, namely manioc flour, as good as any I have seen in Mozambique, millet still in the spike, but very black from the smoke with which they drive away the insects. . . . In the afternoon a visit was paid to me by the Fumo; he exaggerated the honour by assuring me—so infatuated is he with his dignity—that he will explain the extreme measure of leaving his village by considering us to be the Cazembe, the only person who can claim such devoirs.

30th. Leaving a road formerly well-trodden and populous, I followed another shorter and clearer path which was opened, they say, when the Cazembe changed the site of his settlement (Zimboé) for one more easily fortified. This line is at once shorter and clearer. To-day I had news of the chief sergeant Pedro Xaxier Velasco reaching the Zimboé, where the Cazembe had immediately ordered one of his grandees to prepare subsistence and to meet me. They say that the king expects me with transports of delight. May it be true! But I doubt it, having observed that a Caffre's mouth never opens without a lie slipping out. . . .

October 2nd. When beginning the march I met two brothers of the Cazembe and a son of the Fumo Anceva, his relation, escorting a goodly store of manioc, sun-dried 'bush-beef,' and two she-goats for our Caffres: the soldiers had their portion of the same separately.

My intention was to-day to travel as near as possible to the Zimboé, but these messengers told me that being a Mambo, or chief, like the Cazembe, I could not advance until their father, the king, had first rendered to his ancestral Manes due thanks for my arrival in his country. Also that I should advance a little nearer the place, town or house, where the Cazembe's father is buried, and there express proper gratitude for the said benefit. Withal they would not agree for me to enter the place to-day, nor could I do otherwise than conform to their wishes. They begged me to pitch the camp outside, as they had to give me the message of their king. They said that the Cazembe was so much satisfied with my coming that he soon would plaster his body with chalk, in sign of thankfulness to his "spirits," and would send to fetch me.

I was also directed to leave at the burial-place of the royal ancestors a blue cotton (Ardian), 4 fathoms of cotton-cloth, and a small quantity of white and coloured stoneware beads. The king did the same with Manoel Caetano Pereira. As far as I can see, travellers pay up the vows and offerings with which the king supplies the spirits for benefits received. . . .

Whilst they were preparing the hut and bed, between which I am now compelled to live, I called up these officers, but they would not answer a word to my questions. When, wondering at this profound silence, I was told by the interpreter that, though they could listen to all I had to say, they could not speak till after delivering the royal Muromo. Finally, when they brought me the message, I ordered, in token of respect, a mat to be spread for them, but they always seated themselves upon the ground, saying that I was a second Cazembe, and that such was their only place in my presence.

At 6½ A.M. returned the messenger, who was sent forward yesterday by the brothers of the Cazembe. These two officers said that the king asked me not to move to-day as it was unnecessary for me to visit his father's burial-place, that it would be enough for me to forward the cloth yesterday mentioned, and that to-morrow after the ceremonies, I could continue my march. He presented to me two tusks in token of friendship.

It is clear that I must agree to what the Cazembe asks, despite the injury which the delay will cause in my present state of health. But seeing that these exceedingly superstitious Caffres hold their dead to be gods, and reflecting that the faith which the Demon engraves upon the human breast must lie deep, I resolved, by a stately ceremonial, to obtain their good will for myself, and thereby to forward the views of the Crown. Wishing to give an idea of their rites, I sent Lieut.-Colonel Pedro Nolasco and Lieutenant José, Vicente Pereira Salema with soldiers to the grave, and ordered them to fire three salutes with the usual interval, exaggerating as much as possible the obsequies in token of friendship, and carefully noting everything they saw.

This had an excellent effect upon the crowd, and upon the guardian priest, who, externally, was not distinguished from other Caffres. The latter, after consulting his oracle, the ghost of the Cazembe's father, exclaimed that I who had bewailed with them the death of their king was a god who had come to them; that I should go wherever it pleased me, all the country being mine.

[*With only a few more words Lacerda's journal ends. On October 18, worn out with fever, he died.*]

HOLLAND

INTO STRANGE COUNTRIES [1]

(1576)

JAN HUYGEN VAN LINSCHOTEN

(*c.* 1563–1611)

BEEING young, (and living idlelye) in my native Countire, sometimes applying my selfe to the reading of Histories, and straunge adventures, wherein I tooke no small delight, I found my minde so much addicted to see and travaile into strange Countries, thereby to seeke some adventure, that in the end to satisfie my selfe, I determined, and was fully resolved, for a time to leave my Native Countrie, and my friendes (although it greeved me) yet the hope I had to accomplish my desire, together with the resolution taken in the end, overcame my affection and put me in good comfort, to take the matter upon me, trusting in God that he would further my intent. Which done, being resolved, thereupon I tooke leave of my Parents, who as then dwelt at Enckhuysen, and beeing ready to imbarke my selfe, I went to a Fleet of ships that as then lay before the Tassell, staying the winde to sayle for Spaine, and Portingale, where I imbarked my selfe in a ship that was bound for S. Lucas de Barameda, beeing determined to travaile unto Sivill, where as then I had two brethren that had continued there certaine yeares before: so to help my selfe the better, and by their meanes to know the manner and custome of those Countries, as also to learne the Spanish tongue.

And the 6 of December, in the yere of our Lord 1576 we put out of the Tassel, (being in all about 80 ships) and set our course for Spain, and the ninth of the same month, wee passed betweene Dover and Callis, and within three dayes after wee had the sight of the Cape of Finisterra, and the fifteene of the same moneth we saw the land of Sintra, otherwise called the Cape Roexent, from whence the river Tegio, or Tagus, runneth into the maine Sea, uppon the which river lieth the famous citie of Lisbone, where some of our Fleet put in, and left us. The 17 day wee saw Cape S. Vincent, and uppon Christmas day after we entred into the river of S. Lucas de Barameda, where I stayed two or three dayes, and then travailed to Sivill, and the first day of Januarie following, I entred into the citie, where I found one of my brethren, but the other was newly ridden to the Court, lying as then in Madrill. And although I had a speciall desire presently to travaile further, yet for want of the Spanish

[1] From *The Voyage of Jan Huygen van Linschoten to the East Indies.* From the English translation of 1598. Edited by A. C. Burnell (Hukluyt Society, No. 70 (1885)).

tongue without the which men can hardlie passe the countrie, I was constrained to stay there to learne some part of their language. . . .

The fifth day of August in the same yeare, having some understanding in the Spanish tongue, I placed my selfe with a Dutch gentleman, who determined to travaile into Portingale, to see the countrie, and with him stayed to take a more convenient time for my pretended voyage.

Uppon the first of September following we departed from Sivill, and passing through divers Townes and Villages, within eight dayes after we arived at Badaios, where I found my other Brother following the Court. At the same time died Anne de Austria Queene of Spaine, (sister to the Emperour Rodulphus, and Daughter to the Emperour Maximilian) the Kings fourth and last wife, for whom great sorrow was made through all Spaine: her body was convaied from Badaios to the Cloyster of Saint Laurence in Escuriall, where with great solemnitie it was buried. We having stayed certaine dayes in Badaios, departed from thence, and passed through a Towne called Elvas about two or three miles off, being the first towne in the kingdome of Portingale, for that betweene it and Badaios, the borders of Spaine and Portingale are limited: from thence we travailed into divers other places of Portingale, and at the last arived at Lisbone, about the twenty of September following, where at the time wee found the Duke of Alva beeing Governour there for the King of Spaine, the whole Cittie making great preparation for the Coronation of the King, according to the custome of their countrie. Wee beeing in Lisbone, through the change of aire, and corruption of the countrie I fell sicke, and during my sicknes was seaven times let blood, yet by Gods help I escaped: and being recovered, not having much preferment under the gentleman, I left his service, and placed my selfe with a Marchant untill I might attaine to better meanes. About the same time the plague, not long before newly begunne, began againe to cease, for the which cause the King till then had deferred his enterance into Lisbone, which wholly ceased uppon the first day of May, Anno 1581 hee entred with great triumph and magnificence into the cittie of Lisbone, where above all others the Dutchmen had the best and greatest commendation for beautiful shews, which was a Gate and a Bridge that stood uppon the river side where the King must first passe as hee went out of his Gallie to enter into the cittie, being beautified and adorned with many costly and excellent thinges most pleasant to behold, every street and place within the cittie being hanged with rich clothes of Tapistrie and Arras, where they made great triumphes, as the manner is at all Princes Coronations. . . .

Staying at Lisbone, the trade of Marchandize there not beeing great, by reason of the newe and fresh disagreeing of the Spaniards and Portingales, occasion being offered to accomplish my desire, there was at the same time in Lisbone a Monke of S. Dominicks order, named Don frey Vincente de Fonseca, of a noble house: who by reason of his great learning, had of long time beene Chaplen unto Sebastian King of Portingale, who beeing with him in the battaile of Barbarie, where King Sebastian was slain, was taken prisoner, and from thence ransomed, whose learning and good behaviour beeing knowne to the King of Spaine, hee made great account of him, placing him in his own Chappel, and desiring to prefer him, the Archbishopricke of all the Indies beeing voide, with confirmation of the Pope he invested him therewith, although he refused to accept it, fearing the long and tedious travaile hee had to make thether, but in the end through the King's perswasion, hee tooke it upon him, with promise within foure or five yeares at the furthest to recall him home againe, and to give him a better place in Portingale, with the which promise he tooke the voyage upon him.

I thinking upon my affaires, used all meanes I could to get into his service, and with him to travaile the voiage which I so much desired, which fell out as I would wish: for that my Brother that followed the Court, had desired his Master (beeing one of his Majesties secretaries) to make him purser in one of the ships that the same yere should saile unto the East Indies, which pleased me well, in so much that his said Master was a great friend and acquaintance of the Archbishops, by which meanes, with small intreatie I was entertained in the Bishops service, and amongst the rest my name was written downe, wee being in all forty persons, and because my Brother had his choise which ship he would be in, he chose the ship wherein the Archbishop sayled, the better to help each other, and in this manner we prepared our selves to make our voyage, being in all five ships of the burthen of fourteene hundreth Tunnes each ship, their names were the Admirall *S. Phillip*: the Vize Admirall *S. Jacob*. These were two new ships, one bearing the name of the King, the other of his sonne, the other three, *S. Laurence*, *S. Francisco*, and our shippe *S. Salvator*.

Upon the eight of Aprill, beeing good Friday, in the yeare of our Lorde 1583, which commonly is the time when their ships set sayle within foure or five dayes under, or over, wee altogether issued our of the river at Lisbone, and put to sea, setting our course for the Iland of Madera, and so putting our trust in God, . . . we sayled forwards. . . .

The 15 of Aprill we espied the Iland of Madera and Porto Sancto, where the ships use to separate themselves, each ship keeping on his course, that they may get before each other into India for their most commodities, and to dispatch the sooner; whereby in the night, and by tides they leave each others company, each following his owne way.

The 24 of Aprill we fell upon the coaste of Guinea, which beginneth at nine degrees, and stretcheth untill wee come under the Equinoctiall, where wee have much thunder, lightning, and many showers of raine, with stormes of wind, which pass swiftly over, and yet fall with such force, that at every shower we are forced to strike sayle, and let the maine yeard fall to the middle of the mast, and many times cleane down, sometimes ten or twelve times every day: there wee finde a most extreme heate, so that all the water in the ship stinketh, whereby men are forced to stop their noses when they drinke, but when wee are past the Equinoctiall it is good againe, and the nearer wee are unto the land, the more it stormeth, raineth, thundreth and calmeth: so that most commonly the shippes are at the least two monthes before they can passe the line: Then they finde a winde which they name the generall winde, and it is a South east winde, but it is a side wind, and we must alway lie side waies in the wind almost untill wee come to the Cape de Bona Speranza. . . .

The 15 of May being about fiftie miles beyond the Equinoctiall line Northwardes, we espied a French ship, which put us all in great feare, by reason that most of our men were sicke, as it commonly hapneth in those countries through the exceeding heate: and further they are for the most part such as never have beene at Sea before that time, so that they are not able to do much, yet we discharged certaine great shot at him, wherewith he left us (after he had played with us for a small time), and presently lost the sight of him, where-with our men were in better comfort. . . .

The 26 of May wee passed the Equinoctiall line which runneth through the middle of the Iland of Saint Thomas, by the coast of Guinea, and then wee began to see the south star, and to loose the north star, and founde the sunne at twelve of the clocke at noone to be in the north, and after that we had a south east (wind, called a) general wind, which in these partes bloweth all the yeare through.

The 29 of May being Whitsonday, the ships of an ancient custome, doe use to chuse an Emperour among themselves, and to change all the officers in the ship, and to hold a great feast, which continueth three or foure days together, which wee observing chose an Emperour, and being at our banket, by meanes of certaine words that passed out of some of their mouthes, there fell great strife and contention among us, which proceeded so farre, that the tables were throwne downe and lay on the ground, and at the least a hundred rapiers drawne, without respecting the Captaine or any one, for he lay under foote, and they trod upon him, and had killed each other, and thereby had cast the ship away, if the Archbishop had not come out of his chamber among them, willing them to cease, wherwith they stayed their hands, who presently commaunded every man on paine of death, that all their Rapiers, Poynyardes, and other weapons should bee brought into his chamber, which was done, whereby all thinges were pacified, the first and principall beginners being punished and layd in irons, by which meanes they were quiet.

The 12 of June we passed beyond the . . . Flats . . . of Brasillia, whereof all our men were exceeding glad, for thereby we were assured that we should not for that time put backe to Portingale againe, as many doe, and then the generall wind served us untill wee came to the river of Rio de Plata, where wee got before the wind to the cape de Bona Speranza.

The 20 of the same month the *S. Francicus* that so long had kept us company was againe out of sight: and the eleaventh of July after, our Master judged us to bee about 50 miles from the cape de Bona Speranza: wherefore he was desired by the Archbishop to keepe in with the land, that wee might see the Cape. It was then mistie weather, so that as we had made with the land about one houre or more, wee perceived land right before us, and were within two miles thereof, which by reason of the darke and misty weather we could no sooner perceive, which put us in great feare, for our judgement was cleane contrarie, but, the weather beginning to cleare up, we knew the land, for it was a part or bank of the point called Cabo Falso, which is about fifteene miles on this side the cape de Bona Speranza, towards Mossambique: the cape de Bona Speranza, lieth under 34 (35) degrees southward, there wee had a calme and faire weather, which continuing about halfe a day, in the meane time with our lines we got great store of fishes uppon the same land at ten or twelve fadoms water, it is an excellent fish, much like to Haddocks, the Portingales call them Pescados.

The 20 of the same month wee met againe with *Saint Francisco*, and spake with her, and so kept company together till the 24 of June, when wee lost her againe. The same day wee stroke all our sayles, because wee had a contrarie wind, and lay two dayes still driving up and downe, not to loose anie way, meane time wee were against the high land of Tarradonotal,[1] which beginneth in 32 degrees, and endeth in 30 and is distant from Cap de Bona Speranzo 150 miles, in this place they commonly used to take counsell of all the officers of the ship, whether it is best for them to sayle through within the land of S. Laurenso,[2] or without it, for that within (the land) they sayle to Mossambique,

[1] Natal, so called because Vasco da Gama discovered it on Christmas Day, 1497.
[2] The old name of Madagascar.

and from thence to Goa, and sayling without it they cannot come at Goa, by reason they fal down by meanes of the streame, and so must sayle unto Cochin, which lieth 100 miles lower than Goa. . . .

The 1 of August we passed the flats called os Baixos de Judea, that is the Flats of the Jewes(s), which are distant from the cape das Corentes 30 miles, and lie between the Iland of S. Laurence and the firme land . . . there is great care to be taken (lest men fall upon them), for they are very dangerous, and many ships have bin lost there. . . .

The fourth of August we descried the land of Mossambique, which is distant from the Flattes of the Jewes(s) nintie miles under fifteene degrees southwards. The next day we entered into the road of Mossambique, and . . . there we found . . . two more of our ships, *Saint Laurenzo* and *Saint Francisco*. . . .

Being at Mossambique wee were foure of our Fleete in company together, only wanting the *Saint Phillip*, which had holden her course so nere the coast of Guinea, (the better to shun the Flats of Bracillia that are called Abrollios, whereon the yere before she had once fallen), that she was so much becalmed that she could not passe the Equinoctiall line in long time after us, neyther yet the cape de Bona Speranza without great storms and foule weather, as it ordinarilie happeneth to such as come late thether, whereby shee was compelled to compasse about and came unto Cochin about two months after we were al arived at Goa, having passed and endured much misery and foule weather, with sicknes and diseases, as swellings of the legs, and the scorbuicke (and paine in their bellies) . . .

Wee stayed at Mossambique for the space of 15 dayes to provide fresh water and victuails for the supplying of our wants, in the which time divers of our men fel sicke and died, by reason of the unaccustomed ayre of the place, which of it selfe is an unwholesome land, and an evill aire by meanes of the great and unmeasurable heat.

The 20 of August wee set saile with all our companie, that is, our foure shippes of one fleete that came from Portingall, and a shippe of the Captaines of Mossambique. . . .

The 24 of August in the morning wee descryed two Islandes, which are called Insula de Comora and Insula de Don Ian[1] de Castro. The Islande Comora lyeth distant from Mossambique 60 miles, Northwardes under 11 degrees on the South side is a very high land, so high that in a whole dayes saile with a good winde wee could not lose the sight therof. . . .

The third of September we once againe passed the Equinoctiall line,

[1] João.

which runneth betweene Melinde and Brava, townes lying uppon the coast of Abex, and the line is from Mossambique Northwardes 230 miles, and from the line to the Cape de Guardafum are 190 miles. . . . This corner or Cape of Guardafum is the ende of the coast of Abex or Melinde, and by this cape East North east 20 miles within the Sea lyeth the rich Island called Socotora, where they find Aloes . . . and from thence is it carried . . . into al places.

By this corner and Island beginneth the mouth or enterance of the Estreito de Mecka, for that within the same upon the coast of Arabia lyeth the citie of Mecka, where the body of Mahomet hangeth in the ayre in an iron chest, under a sky made of Adamant stone, which is greatly sought unto, and visited by many Turkes and Arabians. This entery is also called the redde sea, not that the water is redde, but onely because there are certaine redde hilles lying about the same, that yeeld redde marble stones: and because the sand in some places is redde, it is the same sea which Moyses with the children of Israel passed through on dry land. . . .

Having againe passed the line, we had the sight of the North Star, whereof upon the coast of Guinea, from the Islande of S. Thomas untill this tyme, wee had lost the sight. The 4 of September wee espyed a shippe of our owne fleete, and spake with him: it was the *S. Francisco*, which sayled with us till the 7 day, and then left us. The 13 of September wee saw an other shippe which was the *S. Jacob*, which sailed out of sight again and spake not to us.

The 20 of September we perceived many Snakes swimming in the sea, being as great as Eeles, and other things like the scales of fish which the Portingals call Vintijns, which are halfe Ryalles of silver, Portingall money, because they are like unto it; these swimme and drive upon the sea in great quantities, which is a certain (sign and) token of the Indian coast.

Not long after with great joy we descried land, and found ground at 47 fadome (deepe) being the land of Bardes, which is the uttermost (ende and) corner of the enterie of the River Goa, of being about three miles from the Citie: it is a high land where the shippes of India do anker and unlade, and from thence by boates their wares are carryed to the towne. That day we ankered without in the sea about three miles from the land, because it was calme, and the fludde was past; yet it is (not) without danger, and hath round about a faire and fast land to anker in, for as then it beganne in those places to be summer.

The 21 being ye next day, there came unto us divers boats called

Almadias, which borded us, bringing with them all manners of fresh victuailes from the land, as fresh bread and fruit, some of them were Indians that are christened: there came likewise a Galley to fetch the Archbishoppe, and brought him to a place called Pangijn, which is in the middle way, betweene Goa and the roade of Bardes, and lyeth upon the same River: Here he was welcommed and visited by the Vice Roy of India, named Don Francisco Mascarenias, and by all the Lordes and Gentlemen of the countrey, as well spirituall as temporall: The Magistrates of the towne desired him to stay there ten or twelve dayes, while preparation might bee made to receive him with triumph into the citie, as their manner is, which hee granted them. The same day in the afternoone we entred the River, into the roade under the lande of Bardes, being the 21 of September Anno 1583 being five monthes and 13 dayes after our putting forth of the River Lisbone, (having stayed 15 daies at Mossambique) which was one of the speediest (and shortest) voyages that in many yeares before and since that time was ever performed. . . .

There dyed in our shippe 30 persons, among the which, some of them were slaves, and one high Dutchman, that had beene one of the King of Spaines garde: every man had beene sicke once or twice and let bloode. This is commonly the number of men that ordinarily dyed in the ships, sometimes more sometimes lesse. . . .

The 30 of September the Archbishoppe, my maister, with great triumph was brought into the towne of Goa, and by the Gentlemen and Rulers of the countrey, led unto the cathedrall Church, singing Te Deum laudamus, and after many ceremonies and auncient customes, they convayed him to his pallace, which is close by the Church.

HOW SIMON VAN DER STEL WENT IN SEARCH OF THE COPPER MOUNTAIN[1]

(1685)

GEORGE McCALL THEAL

(1837-1919)

As soon as the lord of Mydrecht[2] left South Africa, the commander began to make ready for the expedition to Namaqualand which that officer hadsanctioned. He had long been anxious to make an inspection of the countryfrom which the specimens of copper ore had been brought, but it would have been contrary to established rules for him to have gone so far from the castle without special permission. The arrangements were completed by the 25th of August, 1685, and on the morning of that day the baggage waggons were sent forward, the commander himself following on horseback in the afternoon. The secunde Andries de Man, Captain Hieronymus Cruse, and some other members of the council rode with the commander until they overtook the advance party, when his Honour was saluted with three rounds of discharges from the muskets of the whole company.

The train as now completed consisted of fifteen waggons, each drawn by eight oxen, eight carts, and one coach. Of the waggons, eight belonged to burghers, and it was intended to take them no farther than the Elephant river. There were two hundred spare oxen, most of them trained to carry burdens on their backs, thirteen horses, and eight mules. There was a boat for the purpose of crossing the Berg and Elephant rivers, and there were two small cannons to impress the natives with proper respect for the power of the Europeans. The travelling party consisted of Commander van der Stel, with three slaves as personal attendants, fifty-six Europeans of various callings, including soldiers, a Macassar prisoner of state, named Dain Bengale or Manalle, with a slave as his attendant, forty-six drivers and leaders, mostly of mixed blood, and a number of Hottentots to serve as interpreters. Even to-day the train would form an imposing sight, and it must have been considered a very grand spectacle by those who saw it moving slowly northward in that eventful year 1685.

At the Tigerberg the kraals of Schacher and Kuiper were passed, the last of whom presented the commander with an ox for slaughter, according to the

[1] From *History of South Africa under the Administration of the Dutch East India Company.*

[2] Hendrik Adriaan van Rheede, Lord of Mydrecht, whom the Dutch East India Company had sent out to examine into their affairs in Hindostan and Ceylon and at the Cape.

Hottentot custom of treating visitors of rank. The country was covered with grass, which has long since disappeared, and with beautiful flowers of many colours, such as are yet to be seen in the months of August and September. Keeping down the valley of the Berg river, which was found tenantless, Paardenberg, Dassenberg, and Riebeek's Kasteel were passed, while bounding the view on the right was a range of rocky mountains, inhabited solely by Bushmen. These Bushmen lived by the chase and plunder, but savage as they were they have left memorials of their existence in rude paintings upon the rocks, which are still as perfect as if the pigments had been laid on but yesterday.

On the 31st the expedition reached the Sonqua ford of the Berg river, but as the commander preferred to keep along the western bank, he did not cross there. About Twenty-four Rivers and the Honey mountains, many Bushmen huts were seen, but no people. These huts were merely branches of trees fastened together and covered with loose reeds. Farther down two kraals of Cochoquas were passed. On the evening of the 2nd of September an encampment was formed at the Misverstand ford, and next morning at daybreak, after prayers had been said and a psalm sung as usual, the boat was put upon the river and a commencement was made in ferrying the baggage across. Two days were occupied in transferring the camp to the other bank. At this place a trading party which had been sent in advance to purchase slaughter oxen and sheep joined the expedition with an ample supply.

On the second day five natives were seen, who took to flight as soon as they observed the Europeans, but upon a sergeant and two men being sent after them with a present of pipes and tobacco, they were induced to return. They stated that they were Sonquas and lived upon honey and such game as they could shoot, and that they were then following up an eland which they had wounded with a poisoned arrow the day before, and which would die about that time. They were armed with assagais and bows and arrows. Their skins were covered with scurf, as they had undergone great want some time before, and were without grease to rub upon themselves. The commander made them a present of a sheep, which they immediately killed, and they did not cease eating until every particle of the meat and entrails was consumed. They rejected nothing except the gall and four little pieces from the thighs, which they said it was not their custom to eat. They cooked the flesh by laying it in hot ashes. In return for the commander's kindness, they presented him with three wild cats' skins which they had with them.

On the day after leaving the river, when near the Piketberg, an incident occurred which nearly cost the commander his life. Of a sudden an enormous rhinoceros rushed through the middle of the train, and then charged the carriage in which his Honour was seated. The commander sprang out, upon which the rhinoceros made towards him, but was fortunately turned just in time by a ball. The brute then charged in the direction of some horsemen, who in their fright threw themselves from their saddles to the ground and were severely bruised. The cause of the confusion did no further harm, however, but rushed away with incredible swiftness, followed by a volley of musket balls fired at random. Owing to this incident the place received the name Rhenoster Rug.

At the Piketberg the grass was observed to be very rich, and there was timber in abundance in the kloofs, as well as thorn trees for fuel in plenty along the banks of the rivulets. At one encampment an eland weighing a thousand pounds was shot, from which circumstance the place was called Elands Vlakte.

On the 9th of September the Little Elephant river was reached, and the train followed its course through a district which was little better than a solitary wilderness, but where some elephants were seen. On the 14th a hill was passed, which was named Uilenberg, on account of the great number of owls found there. At this place a fountain of sweet water was discovered and named Klipfontein, and a remarkable echo which the hill gave back was noticed. The next encampment was at the foot of Dassenberg, in a spot where there was abundance of wood, water, grass, and game. On the 15th the train passed through Pickenier's Kloof and moved on to the Elephant river, where preparations were made for crossing.

The banks of the river were found to be clothed with willow and thorn trees, and in its waters were fish of large size and good flavour. A kraal of Grigriquas (called in other places Chariguriquas and Gierigriquas) was met with, and it was ascertained that Sonquas were numerous along the whole course of the stream. The burghers now turned back, having first obtained permission from the commander to load their waggons with the flesh of elands, rhinoceroses, and seacows on their homeward journey. It occupied three days to get everything across the river, and in the afternoon of the 18th the train again moved on.

It was by this time evident that the season was an exceptionally favourable one for exploration. In the north, after four years of drought, heavy and continuous rains had fallen, so that there was good hope of meeting with grass and water in the country to be traversed. Where the surgeon Van Meerhof in bygone years, and the ensign Bergh only recently, had found bare and parched ravines, there were now streams of water three feet in depth. Animal life was abundant. The day after crossing the river quails in great numbers were met with, which the Hottentot interpreters knocked over with great dexterity by throwing knobbed sticks at them when on the wing. Hares and antelopes of different kinds were seen sporting about in grass a foot and a half in depth, and were sometimes secured for the table. The whole party was in excellent health and spirits. Every morning and evening they sang a psalm, listened to a chapter of the bible, and repeated a prayer, no one but the cattle herds being permitted to be absent on these occasions. When on the march, a party rode on ahead to select the best paths and the most suitable places for encamping. And when a halt was called, and the cattle were turned loose to graze, the scene resembled a pleasure excursion or a picnic party. If the sun was bright an awning was spread for the commander's use, and if it was dull a tent was pitched; in either case the Batavian tricolour being hoisted in front, and the pennant of the honourable East India Company floating above.

On the 20th the expedition halted in a narrow valley, with the Elephant river on one side of the camp and a rocky mountain on the other. In this neighbourhood most of the Grigriquas were then living, and as a quarrel had broken out among them, in which a section of the clan had rebelled against the chief, the commander was detained four days in making peace. He succeeded in reconciling the belligerents, and in purchasing a number of cattle from them. On the 26th the mountain called Meerhof's Kasteel was passed. The country was now becoming every day more barren in appearance. There was plenty of water, though it was strongly impregnated with salt, and there was a suffciency of grass for the cattle, but there was no wood for fuel. The only inhabitants were Bushmen.

On the 29th the Little Doorn Bosch river was reached, and from an eminence the sea was visible at a distance of about twenty-eight English miles. The following day an encampment was made at the Great Doorn Bosch river, which was found a deep and rapid stream with numerous trees on its banks. Here some Bushmen were seen, and after a little scheming were induced to visit the camp, where they were presented with a sheep and a flask of brandy. They were wretchedly thin, for they were living upon nothing better than tortoises, caterpillars, locusts, and bulbs of wild plants. They made very merry over the feast provided for them, and danced and sang right joyfully. The treatment they received was so much to their liking that for some days they accompanied the expedition, making themselves useful as guides.

On the 4th of October the commander was informed by the Bushmen that there were some Namaqua kraals in the neighbourhood, whereupon a halt was made at a place where there was plenty of grass and water, and four Hottentots were sent with pipes and tobacco as presents to the chiefs. A full week was spent here in making inquiries concerning the country, and in arranging treaties with the chiefs, of whom there were six, over as many kraals. The intercourse was very friendly except with two or three individuals, but the commander asserted and maintained a position of authority, to which they submitted without question. He entertained the chiefs and their wives with European food, but pleased them more by supplying them with a little brandy and tobacco.

On the 11th the march was resumed. The country was now found to be so rugged that progress was very difficult. Fortunately there were water and grass, and Captain Oedeson, who claimed the Copper mountain, and some other Namaquas acted as guides. Along the route various kraals were passed, and at nearly every halting place fresh visitors were found. With all the chiefs treaties of peace and friendship were made, and they further promised not to quarrel with each other or with the Hottentots in the neighbourhood of the Cape, the commander on his part undertaking to prevent these last named from attacking or molesting them, so that they could trade with the Company without let or hindrance.

Sunday, the 14th of October, was the commander's birthday, and in compliment to him the camp, which was in a good position, was not broken up. The cannons were taken from the waggons and loaded, and at noon three volleys of musketry were fired by the whole company, each volley being followed by the discharge of a cannon. There was a large party of Namaquas present, and they arranged a dance, which was their manner of complimenting persons of rank. Twenty men formed a circle, each having a reed in his hand. The reeds were of various sizes and lengths, so that different notes were sounded by blowing into them. A master musician stood in the centre, having in his hand a long rod with which he gave directions, singing a tune, and beating time with his foot as well. The players kept leaping up and down, but produced music which surprised the Europeans by its harmony and power. Outside was a deep circle of men and women, dancing and clapping their hands in time with the music. This entertainment continued until evening, when the commander had an ox slaughtered for his visitors, and distributed a small keg of arrack among them.

The commander here began to obtain information concerning the great river to the north. Many of his visitors had been to it, and they all described it as being about ten days' journey beyond the Copper mountain, as running towards the setting sun, and as being very wide and deep, with banks clothed with large trees. Some of them produced a quantity of glittering sand which they stated they had brought from it. According to the accounts received, the commander conjectured that it must enter the sea about the latitude of the gulf of Voltas of the charts, which is really the correct position of its mouth.

The 15th of October was spent in bartering cattle, and on the 16th the train moved forward. For five days after this the track was through a rugged country, where the waggons and carts were often overturned and where progress was extremely difficult. But on the 21st the commander's perseverance was rewarded, for on the afternoon of that day the camp was pitched at the Copper mountain, the place he had so long desired to see. He calculated that he had travelled three hundred and sixty-five English miles from the castle, and that he had reached the latitude of 29° S. This was not quite correct, owing to the means at the command of the expedition for determining latitudes being faulty. In reality the Copper mountain is more than half a degree farther south. The distance from the castle in a straight line is about three hundred miles, and the direction is a very little to the westward of north.

A fortnight was now occupied in getting out ore and examining the country around. It was found to be a very uninviting district. The Namaquas who were with the party acted as guides and gave all the information they possessed, which was indeed not very much. Aloes were found in abundance, but wood for fuel was very scarce. Barren mountains, naked rocks, and desolate wastes made up the scenery. But copper ore was discovered in great quantities and of surprising richness.

The next object of the commander was to explore the country between the Copper mountain and the sea, and on the 5th of November the camp was broken up for that purpose. A direct route was impracticable, and the expedition was compelled to return some distance to the south before a pathway to the shore could be found. Travelling had now become very difficult. The beds of the rivulets were dried up and baked as hard as brick. Water was rarely met with, and when the guides pointed it out it was so salt that it could hardly be used. The Namaquas—even Captain Oedeson himself, once the most friendly of them all—grew very anxious to hasten southward, and became sulky and stubborn when their wishes were disregarded. But the work of exploration was only half performed, and until the coast was thoroughly examined the commander was unwilling to retreat.

On the twelfth day after leaving the Copper mountain an advance party on foot reached the sea, but it was not until the 22nd of November that the whole expedition encamped at the mouth of a river then nearly dry. Along the shore of the Atlantic much driftwood was seen, in which were many large trees that came, as the Namaquas stated, from the great river of the north. From this circumstance the commander concluded that the river could not be far off, but he was at that time unable to obtain any additional information concerning it, though among the Namaquas with him were some whose usual place of residence was on its banks. One thing, however, was now certain. There was no town of Vigiti Magna. And as this great river of which he had heard so much certainly did not correspond with the Camissa of the old geographers, it would require another name. Thenceforth it was called by the Europeans the river Vigiti Magna, until it obtained from the farmers in the next century the name of the Groote, and from Colonel Gorden that of the Orange. The people who lived upon its banks near the sea, though they were clans of the Nama tribe, were named by Commander van der Stel Camissons, after the Camissa which was now to be removed from the charts.

The place where the expedition was encamped was nearly a degree farther south than the Copper mountain. From the 22nd of November until the 12th of December the time was spent in endeavouring to proceed to the north. A heavy surf was rolling in on the beach, and not a single harbour could be discovered suitable for large vessels to anchor in. One little cove was visited, which was partly protected from the swell of the sea by reefs of rocks that ran out from each side nearly across its entrance, leaving a narrow but deep passage about the centre where boats and small cutters could get in and out. The cove was capable of containing two or three decked boats in a tolerable condition of security, and there was a smooth sandy beach that extended half round it, upon which the sea did not break in calm weather, but no fresh water could be found in the neighbourhood. Parties of men were sent out in all directions to examine the country. One of these proceeded along the coast until the officer in command thought he had reached the position of Angra das Voltas on the charts, but he was in reality still fully seventy miles from it. The Buffalo river was explored a considerable distance upward from its mouth. It was so called on account of some Bushmen stating that they had once seen two buffaloes upon its banks.

Meanwhile the cattle were becoming weak, and were suffering terribly from the scarcity of water. Some of them ran into the sea and drank and immediately afterwards died. The exploring parties were at times reduced to great distress from the same cause. It was evident that everything had been done that was possible, and so on the 12th of December, to the great joy of every one, the commander gave the order to turn homeward. It took the expedition eighteen days to get back to the Elephant river, and they were days of anxiety and suffering. The heat of the sun exhausted both man and beast.

Water was so scarce that at times forced marches had to be made at night to reach a pool which after all would only afford a quart or two for each ox. The little that was obtainable was as bitter with salt as to be nauseous. On the last march some of the cattle lay down exhausted, and were only recovered by sending water back to them in kegs. Four days were spent at the Elephant river refreshing the worn-out animals, during which time the stream was explored some distance upward, and downward to its mouth.

The difficulties of the journey were now over. There was plenty of grass and water in front, and every part of the route was well known. Nothing remained to be done in the way of exploration except to examine a few leagues of the coast. This the commander did, and made a careful inspection of the inlet now known as Lambert's Bay. At the Little Elephant river the Cochoqua kraals were met with, and the men were found with their heads shaven clean as a mark of mourning. They stated that it was on account of the death of the old chief Gonnema, which had recently taken place. At their request, the commander confirmed his son as his successor. Nothing further of any lasting interest occurred on the homeward journey, which ended by the safe arrival of the expedition at the castle on the 26th of January 1686.

The commander had been absent from the seat of government five months and one day.

GERMANY

ALONG THE ORINOCO[1]

(1800)

FRIEDRICH HEINRICH ALEXANDER, BARON VON HUMBOLDT

(1769-1859)

On leaving the Rio Apure we found ourselves in a country presenting a totally different aspect. An immense plain of water stretched before us like a lake, as far as we could see. White-topped waves rose to the height of several feet, from the conflict of the breeze and the current. The air resounded no longer with the piercing cries of herons, flamingos, and spoonbills, crossing in long files from one shore to the other. Our eyes sought in vain those water-fowls, the habits of which vary in each tribe. All nature appeared less animated. Scarcely could we discover in the hollows of the waves a few large crocodiles, cutting obliquely, by the help of their long tails, the surface of the agitated waters. The horizon was bounded by a zone of forests, which nowhere reached so far as the bed of the river. A vast beach, constantly parched by the heat of the sun, desert and bare as the shores of the sea, resembled at a distance, from the effect of the mirage, pools of stagnant water.

In these scattered features of the landscape, in this character of solitude and of greatness, we recognize the course of the Orinoco, one of the most majestic rivers of the New World. The water, like the land, displays everywhere a characteristic and peculiar aspect. The bed of the Orinoco resembles not the bed of the Meta, the Guaviare, the Rio Negro, or the Amazon. These differences do not depend altogether on the breadth or the velocity of the current; they are connected with a multitude of impressions which it is easier to perceive upon the spot than to define with precision. Thus, the mere form of the waves, the tint of the waters, the aspect of the sky and the clouds, would lead an experienced navigator to guess whether he were in the Atlantic, in the Mediterranean, or in the equinoctial part of the Pacific.

The wind blew fresh from east-north-east. Its direction was favourable for sailing up the Orinoco, towards the Mission of Encaramada; but our canoes were so ill calculated to resist the shocks of the waves, that, from the violence of the motion, those who suffered habitually at sea were equally incommoded on the river. The short, broken waves are caused by the conflict of the waters at the junction of the two rivers. We passed the Punta Curiquima, which is

[1] From *Travels in the Equinoctial Regions of America* (1852).

an isolated mass of quartzose granite, a small promontory composed of rounded blocks. There, on the right bank of the Orinoco, Father Rotella founded, in the time of the Jesuits, a Mission of the Palenka and Viriviri or Guire Indians. But during inundations, the rock Curiquima and the village at its foot were entirely surrounded by water; and this serious inconvenience, together with the sufferings of the missionaries and Indians from the innumerable quantity of mosquitoes and *niguas*, led them to forsake this humid spot. It is now entirely deserted, while opposite to it, on the right bank of the river, the little mountains of Coruato are the retreat of wandering Indians, expelled either from the Missions, or from tribes that are not subject to the government of the monks.

We first proceeded south-west, as far as the shore inhabited by the Guaricoto Indians on the left bank of the Orinoco, and then we advanced straight toward the south. The river is so broad that the mountains of Encaramada appear to rise from the water, as if seen above the horizon of the sea. They form a continued chain from east to west. These mountains are composed of enormous blocks of granite, cleft and piled one upon another. . . . What contributes above all to embellish the scene at Encaramada is the luxuriance of vegetation that covers the sides of the rocks, leaving bare only their rounded summits. They look like ancient ruins rising in the midst of a forest.

In the port of Encaramada we met with some Caribs of Panapana. A cacique was going up the Orinoco in his canoe, to join in the famous fishing of turtles' eggs. His canoe was rounded toward the bottom like a *bongo*, and followed by a smaller boat called a *curiara*. He was seated beneath a sort of tent, constructed, like the sail, of palm-leaves. His cold and silent gravity, the respect with which he was treated by his attendants, everything denoted him to be a person of importance. He was equipped, however, in the same manner as his Indians. They were all equally naked, armed with bows and arrows, and painted with *onoto,* which is the colouring fecula of the Bixa orellana. The chief, the domestics, the furniture, the boat, and the sail, were all painted red. These Caribs are men of an almost athletic stature; they appeared to us much taller than any Indians we had hitherto seen. Their smooth and thick hair, cut short on the forehead like that of choristers, their eyebrows painted black, their look at once gloomy and animated, gave a singular expression to their countenances. . . . As none of our Indians of Apure understood the Caribbee language, we could obtain no information from the cacique of Panama respecting the encampments that are made at this season in several islands of the Orinoco for collecting turtles' eggs.

Near Encaramada a very long island divides the river into two branches. We passed the night in a rocky creek, opposite the mouth of the Rio Cabullare, which is formed by the Payara and the Atamaica, and is sometimes considered as one of the branches of the Apure, because it communicates with that river by the Rio Arichuna. The evening was beautiful. The moon illumined the tops of the granite rocks. The heat was so uniformly distributed that, notwithstanding the humidity of the air, no twinkling of the stars was observable, even at four or five degrees above the horizon. The light of the planets was singularly dimmed; and if, on account of the smallness of the apparent diameter of Jupiter, I had not suspected some error in the observation, I should say, that here, for the first time, we thought we distinguished the disk of Jupiter with the naked eye. Towards midnight, the north-east wind became extremely violent. It brought no clouds, but the vault of the sky was covered more and more with vapours. Strong gusts were felt, and made us fear for the safety of our canoe. During this whole day we had seen very few crocodiles, but all of an extraordinary size, from twenty to twenty-four feet. The Indians assured us that the young crocodiles prefer the marshes, and the rivers that are less broad, and less deep. They crowd together particularly in the Caños, and we may say of them, what Abdallatif says of the crocodiles of the Nile, "that they swarm like worms in the shallow waters of the river, and in the shelter of uninhabited islands."

On the 6th of April, whilst continuing to ascend the Orinoco, first southward and then to south-west, we perceived the southern side of the *Serrania*, or chain of the mountains of Encaramada. The part nearest the river is only one hundred and forty or one hundred and sixty toises high; but from its abrupt declivities, its situation in the midst of a savannah, and its rocky summits, cut into shapeless prisms, the Serrania appears singularly elevated. Its greatest breadth is only three leagues. According to information given me by the Indians of the Pareka nation, it is considerably wider toward the east. The summits of Encaramada form the northernmost link of a group of mountains which border the right bank of the Orinoco, between the latitudes of 5° and 7° 30' from the mouth of the Rio Zama to that of the Cabullare. The different links into which this group is divided are separated by little grassy plains. They do not preserve a direction perfectly parallel to each other; for the most northern stretch from west to east, and the most southern from north-west to south-east.

I cannot quit this first link of the mountains of Encaramada without recalling to mind a fact that was not unknown to Father Gili, and which was often mentioned to me during our abode in the Missions of the Orinoco. The natives of those countries have retrained the belief that "at the time of the great waters, when their fathers were forced to have recourse to boats, to escape the general inundation, the waves of the sea beat against the rocks of Encaramada." This belief is not confined to one nation singly, the Tamanacs; it makes part of a system of historical tradition, of which we find scattered notions among the Maypures of the great cataracts; among the Indians of the Rio Erevato, which runs into the Caura; and among almost all the tribes of the Upper Orinoco. When the Tamanacs are asked how the human race survived this great deluge, the 'age of water,' of the Mexicans, they say, "a man and a woman saved themselves on a high mountain, called Tamanacu, situated on the banks of the Asiveru; and casting behind them, over their heads, the fruits of the mauritia palm-tree, they saw the seeds contained in those fruits produce men and women, who repeopled the earth." Thus we find, in all its simplicity, among nations now in a savage state, a tradition which the Greeks embellished with all the charms of imagination! A few leagues from Encaramada, a rock called *Tepumereme*, or ' the painted rock,' rises in the midst of the savannah. Upon it are traced representations of animals, and symbolic figures resembling those we saw in going down the Orinoco, at a small distance below Encaramada, near the town Caycara. Similar rocks in Africa are called by travellers *fetish stones*. I shall not make use of this term, because fetishism does not prevail among the natives of the Orinoco; and the figures of stars, of the sun, of tigers, and of crocodiles, which we found traced upon the rocks in spots now un-inhabited, appeared to me in no way to denote the objects of worship of those nations. Between the banks of the Cassiquiare and the Orinoco, between Encaramada, the Capuchino, and Caycara, these hieroglyphic figures are often seen at great heights, on rocky cliffs which would be accessible only by constructing very lofty scaffolds. When the natives are asked how those figures could have been sculptured, they answer with a smile, as if relating a fact of which only a white man could be ignorant, that "at the period of the great waters, their fathers went to that height in boats."

A fresh north-east breeze carried us full-sail towards the Boca de la Tortuga. We landed, at eleven in the morning, on an island which the Indians of the Missions of Uruana considered as their property, and which lies in the middle of the river. This island is celebrated for the turtle fishery, or, as they say here, the *cosecha*, " the harvest (of eggs)," that takes place annually. We here found an assemblage of Indians, encamped under huts made of palm-leaves. This encampment contained more than three hundred persons. Accustomed, since we had left San Fernando de Apure, to see only desert shores, we were singularly struck by the bustle that prevailed here. We found, besides the Guamos and the Ottomacs of Uruana, who are both considered as savage races, Caribs and other Indians of the Lower Orinoco. Every tribe was separately encamped, and was distinguished by the pigments with which their skins were painted. Some white men were seen amidst this tumultuous assemblage, chiefly *pulperos*, or little traders of Angostura, who had come up the river to purchase turtle oil from the natives. The missionary of Uruana, a native of Alcala, came to meet us, and he was extremely astonished at seeing us. After having admired our instruments, he gave us an exaggerated picture of the sufferings to which we should be necessarily exposed in ascending the Orinoco beyond the cataracts. The object of our journey appeared to him very mysterious. "How is it possible to believe," said he, "that you have left your country, to come and be devoured by mosquitoes on this river, and to measure lands that are not your own?" We were happily furnished with recommendations from the Superior of the Franciscan Missions, and the brother-in-law of the governor of Varinas, who accompanied us, soon dissipated the doubts to which our dress, our accent, and our arrival in this sandy island had given rise among the Whites. The missionary invited us to partake a frugal repast of fish and plantains. He told us that he had come to encamp with the Indians during the time of the 'harvest of eggs,' "to celebrate mass every morning in the open air, to procure the oil necessary for the church-lamps, and especially to govern this mixed republic (*república de Indios y Castellanos*) in which every one wished to profit singly by what God had granted to all."

We made the tour of the island, accompanied by the missionary and by a *pulpero*, who boasted of having, for ten successive years, visited the camp of the Indians, and attended the turtle-fishery. We were on a plain of sand perfectly smooth; and we were told that, as far as we could see along the beach, turtles' eggs were concealed under a layer of earth. The missionary carried a long pole in his hand. He showed us that by means of this pole the extent of the stratum of eggs could be determined as accurately as the miner determines the limits of a bed of marl, of bog iron ore, or of coal. On thrusting the rod perpendicularly into the ground, the sudden want of resistance shows that the cavity, or layer of loose earth containing the eggs, has been reached. We saw that the stratum is generally spread with so much uniformity that the pole finds it everywhere in a radius of ten toises around any given spot. Here they talk continuously of square perches of eggs; it is like a miningcountry, divided into lots, and worked with the greatest regularity. The stratum of eggs, however, is far from covering the whole island: they are not found wherever the ground rises abruptly, because the turtle cannot mount heights.

I related to my guides the emphatic description of Father Gumilla, who asserts that the shores of the Orinoco contain fewer grains of sand than the river contains turtles; and that these animals would prevent vessels from advancing, if men and tigers did not annually destroy so great a number. "*Son cuentos de frails*" "They are monkish legends," said the pulpero of Angostura, in a low voice; for the only travellers in this country being the missionaries, they here call 'monks' stories' what we call 'travellers' tales' in Europe.

Our pilot had anchored at the *Playa de huevos*, to purchase some provisions, our store having begun to run short. We found there fresh meat, Angostura rice, and even biscuit made of wheat-flour. Our Indians filled the boat with little live turtles, and eggs dried in the sun, for their own use. Having taken leave of the missionary of Uruana, who had treated us with great kindness, we set sail about four in the afternoon. The wind was fresh, and blew in squalls. Since we had entered the mountainous part of the country, we had discovered that our canoe carried sail very badly; but the master was desirous of showing the Indians who were assembled on the beach, that by going close to the wind, he could reach, at one single tack, the middle of the river. At the very moment when he was boasting of his dexterity, and the boldness of his manœuvre, the force of the wind upon the sail became so great that we were on the point of going down. One side of the boat was under water, which rushed in with such violence that it was soon up to our knees. It washed over a little table at which I was writing at the stern of the boat. I had some difficulty to save my journal, and in an instant we saw our books, papers, and dried plants, all afloat. M. Bonpland was lying asleep in the middle of the canoe. Awakened by the entrance of the water and the cries of the Indians, he understood the danger of our situation, whilst he maintained that coolness which he always displayed in the most difficult circumstances. The lee-side righting itself from time to time during the squall, he did not consider the boat as lost. He thought that, were we even forced to abandon it, we might save ourselves by swimming, since there was no crocodile in sight. Amidst this uncertainty the cordage of the sail suddenly gave way. The same gust of wind, that had thrown us on our beam, served also to right us. We laboured to bale the water out of the boat with calabashes, the sail was again set, and in less than half an hour we were in a state to proceed. The wind now abated a little. Squalls alternating with dead calms are common in that part of the Orinoco which is bordered by mountains. They are very dangerous for boats deeply laden, and without decks. We had escaped as if by miracle. To the reproaches that were heaped on our pilot for having kept too near the wind, he replied with the phlegmatic coolness peculiar to the Indians, observing "that the whites would find sun enough on those banks to dry their papers." We lost only one book—the first volume of the *Genera Plantarum* of Schreber— which had fallen overboard. At nightfall we landed on a barren island in the middle of the river, near the Mission of Uruana. We supped in a clear moonlight, seating ourselves on some large turtle-shells that were found scattered about the beach. What satisfaction we felt on finding ourselves thus comfortably landed!

The night was intensely hot. We lay upon skins spread on the ground, there being no trees to which we could fasten our hammocks. The torments of the mosquitoes increased every day; and we were surprised to find that on this spot our fires did not prevent the approach of the jaguars. They swam across the arm of the river that separated us from the mainland. Towards morning we heard their cries very near. They had come to the island where we passed the night. The Indians told us that, during the collecting of the turtles' eggs, tigers are always more frequent in those regions, and display at that period the greatest interpidity.

On the following day, the 7th, we passed, on our right, the mouth of the great Rio Auraca, celebrated for the immense number of birds that frequent it; and, on our left, the Mission of Uruana, commonly called *La Conception de Uruana.* This small village, which contains five hundred souls, was founded by the Jesuits, about the year 1748, by the union of the Ottomac and Cavere Indians. It lies at the foot of a mountain composed of detached blocks of granite, which, I believe, bears the name of *Saraguaca.* Masses of rock, separated one from the other by the effect of decomposition, form caverns, in which we find indubitable proofs of the ancient civilisation of the natives. Hieroglyphic figures, and even characters in regular lines, are seen sculputred on their sides; though I doubt whether they bear any analogy to alphabetic writing.

The western bank of the Orinoco remains low farther than the mouth of the Meta; while from the Mission of Uruana the mountains approach the eastern bank more and more. As the strength of the current increases in proportion as the river grows narrower, the progress of our boat became much slower. We continued to ascend the Orinoco under sail, but the high and woody grounds deprived us of the wind. At other times the narrow passes between the mountains by which we sailed, sent us violent gusts, but of short duration. The number of crocodiles increased below the junction of the Rio Arauca, particularly opposite the great lake of Capanaparo, which communicates with the Orinoco, as the Laguna de Cabullarito communicates at the same time with the Orinoco and the Rio Arauca. The Indians told us that the crocodiles came from the inlands, where they had been buried in the dried mud of the savannahs. As soon as the first showers arouse them from their lethargy, they crowd together in troops, and hasten toward the river, there to disperse again. Here, in the equinoctial zone, it is the increase of humidity that recalls them to life; while in Georgia and Florida, in the temperate zone, it is the augmentation of heat that rouses these animals from a state of nervous and muscular debility, during which the active powers of respiration are suspended or singularly diminished. The season of great drought, improperly called the summer of the torried zone, corresponds with the winter of the temperate zone; and it is a curious physiological phenomenon to observe the alligators of North America plunged into a winter-sleep by excess of cold, at the same period when the crocodiles of the Llanos begin their siesta or summer-sleep.

Having passed the mouths of the channels communicating with the lake of Capanaparo, we entered a part of the Orinoco, where the bed of the river is narrowed by the mountains of Baraguan. It is a kind of strait, reaching nearly to the confluence of the Rio Suapure. From these granite mountains the natives heretofore gave the name of Baraguan to that part of the Orinoco comprised between the mouths of the Arauca and the Atabapo. Among savage nations great rivers bear different denominations in the different portions of their course. The Passage of Baraguna presents a picturesque scene. The granite rocks are perpendicular. They form a range of mountains lying north-west and south-east; and the river cutting this dyke nearly at a right angle, the summits of the mountains appear like separate peaks. Their elevation in general does not surpass one hundred and twenty toises, but their situation in the midst of a small plain, their steep declivities, and their flanks destitute of vegetation, give them a majestic character.

We landed in the middle of the strait of Baraguan to measure its breadth. The rocks project so much towards the river that I measured with difficulty a base of eighty toises. I found the river eight hundred and eighty-nine toises broad. In order to conceive how this passage bears the name of a strait, we must recollect that the breadth of the river from Uruana to the junction of the Meta is in general from 1500 to 2500 toises. In this place, which is extremely hot and barren, I measured two granite summits, much rounded; one was only hundred and ten, and the other eighty-five, toises. There are higher summits in the interior of the group, but in general these mountains, of so wild an aspect, have not the elevation that is assigned to them by the missionaries.

We looked in vain for plants in the clefts of the rocks, which are as steep as walls, and furnish some traces of stratification. We found only an old trunk of aubletia, with large apple-shaped fruit, and a new species of the family of the apocyneæ. All the stones were covered with an innumerable quantity of iguanas and geckos with spreading and membraneous fingers. These lizards, motionless, with heads raised, and mouths open, seemed to suck in the heated air. The thermometer placed against the rock rose to 50.2°. The soil appeared to undulate, from the effect of mirage without a breath of wind being felt. The sun was near the zenith, and its dazzling light, reflected from the surface of the river, contrasted with the reddish vapours that enveloped every surrounding object. How vivid is the impression produced by the calm of nature, at noon, in these burning climates! The beasts of the forests retire to the thickets; the birds hide themselves beneath the foliage of the trees, or in the crevices of the rocks. Yet, amidst this apparent silence, when we lend an attentive ear to the most feeble sounds transmitted through the air, we hear a dull vibration, a continual murmur, a hum of insects, filling, if we may use the expression, all the lower strata of the air. Nothing is better fitted to make men feel the extent and power of organic life. Myriads of insects creep upon the soil, and flutter round the plants parched by the heat of the sun. A confused noise issues from every bush, form the decayed trunks of trees, from the clefts of the rocks, and from the ground undermined by lizards, millepedes, and *cecilias*. These are so many voices proclaiming to us that all nature breathes; and that, under a thousand different forms, life is diffused throughout the cracked and dusty soil, as well as in the bosom of the waters, and in the air that circulates around us.

THE ASCENT OF THE BROCKEN [1]

Heinrich Heine

(1797-1856)

With a light heart I began to ascend the mountain. I was soon welcomed by a grove of stately firs, for whom I, in every respect, entertain the most reverential regard. For these trees, of which I speak, have not found growing to be such an easy business, and during the days of their youth it fared hard with them. The mountain is here sprinkled with a great number of blocks of granite, and most of the trees are obliged either to twine their roots over the stones, or split them in two, that they may thus with trouble get at a little earth to nourish them. Here and there stones lie on each other, forming as it were a gate, and over all grow the trees, their naked roots twining down over the wild portals, and first reaching the ground at its base, so that they appear to be growing in the air. And yet they have forced their way up to that startling height, and grown into one with the rocks, they stand more securely than their easy comrades who are rooted in the tame forest soil of the level country. Squirrels climbed amid the fir-twigs, while beneath, yellow-brown deer were quietly grazing. I cannot comprehend when I see such a noble animal, how educated and refined people can take pleasure in its chase or death. Such a creature was once more merciful than man, and suckled the longing Schmerzenreich of the Holy Genofeva.

Most beautiful were the golden sun-rays shooting through the dark green of the firs. The roots of the trees formed a natural stairway, and everywhere my feet encountered swelling beds of moss, for the stones are here covered foot-deep, as if with light-green velvet cushions. Everywhere a pleasant freshness and the dreamy murmur of streams. Here and there we see water rippling silver-clear amid the rocks, washing the bare roots and fibres of trees. Bend down to the current and listen, and you mayhear at the same time the mysterious history of the growth of the plants, and the quiet pulsations of the heart of the mountain. In many places the water jets strongly up, amid rocks and roots, forming little cascades. It is pleasant to sit in such places. All murmurs and rustles so sweetly and strangely, the birds carol broken strains of love-longing, the trees whisper like a thousand girls, odd flowers peep up like a thousand maidens' eyes, stretching out to us their curious, broad, droll-pointed leaves, the sun-rays flash here and there in sport, the soft-souled herds are telling their green legends, all seems enchanted, and becomes more secret and confidential, an old, old dream is realised,

[1] From *Die Harzreise*, translated by C. G. Leland (1866).

the loved one appears—alas, that all so quickly vanishes!

The higher we ascend, so much the shorter and more dwarf-like do the fir-trees become, shrinking up as it were within themselves, until finally only whortle-berries, bilberries and mountain herbs remain. It is also sensibly colder. Here, for the first time, the granite boulders, which are frequently of enormous size, become fully visible. These may well have been the play-balls which evil spirits cast at each other on the Walpurgis night, when the witches came riding hither on brooms and pitch-forks, when the mad unhallowed reverly begins, as our believing nurses have told us, and as we may see it represented in the beautiful Faust-pictures of Master Retsch. Yes, a young poet who in journeying from Berlin to Göttingen, on the first evening in May, passed the Brocken, remarked how certain belle-lettered ladies held their æsthetic tea-circle in a rocky corner, how they comfortably read the Evening Journal, how they praised as an universal genius, their pet billy-goat, who bleating, hopped around their table, and how they passed a final judgment on all the manifestations of German literature. But when they at last fell upon "Ratcliff" and "Almansor," utterly denying to the author aught like piety or Christianity, the hair of the youth rose on end, terror seized him—I spurred my steed and rode onwards!

In fact, when we ascend the upper half of the Brocken, no one can well help thinking of the attractive legends of the Blocksberg, and especially of the great mystical German national tragedy of Doctor Faust. It ever seemed to me that I could hear the cloven foot scrambing along behind, and that some one inhaled an atmosphere of humour. And I verily believe that Mephisto himself must breathe with difficulty when he climbs his favourite mountain, for it is a road which is to the last degree exhausting, and I was glad enough when I at last beheld the long desired Brocken-house.

This house—as every one knows, from numerous pictures—consists of a single story, and was erected in the year 1800 by Count Stollberg Wernigerode, for whose profit it is managed as a tavern. On account of the wind and cold in winter, its walls are incredibly thick. The roof is low. From its midst rises a tower-like observatory, and near the house lie two little out-buildings, one of which, in earlier times, served as shelter to the Brocken visitors.

On entering the Brocken-house, I experienced a somewhat unusual and legend-like sensation. After a long solitary journey, amid rocks and pines, the traveller suddenly finds himself in a house amid the clouds. Far below lie cities, hills and forests, while above he encounters a curiously blended circle of strangers, by whom he is received as is usual in such assemblies, almost like an expected companion—half inquisitively and half indifferently. I found the house full of guests, and, as becomes a wise man, I first reflected on the night, and the discomfort of sleeping on straw. My part was at once determined on. With the voice of one dying I called for tea, and the Brocken landlord was reasonable enough to perceive that the sick gentleman must be provided with a decent bed. This he gave me, in a narrow room, where a young merchant—a long emetic in a brown overcoat—had already established himself.

In the public room I found a full tide of bustle and animation. There were students from different Universities. Some of the newly arrived were taking refreshments. Others, preparing for departure, buckled on their knapsacks, wrote their names in the album, and received bouquests from the housemaid. There was jesting, singing, springing, trilling some questioning, some answering, fine weather, foot path, *prosit*!—luck be with you! Adieu! Some of those leaving were also partly drunk, and these derived a two-fold pleasure from the beautiful scenery, for a tipsy man sees double.

After recruiting myself, I ascended the observatory, and there found a little gentleman, with two ladies, one of whom was young and the other elderly. The young lady was very beautiful A superb figure, flowing locks, surmounted by a helm-like black satin *chapeau,* amid whose white plumes the wind played; fine limbs, so closely enwrapped by a black silk mantle that their exquisite form was made manifest, and great free eyes, calmly looking down into the great free world.

When as yet a boy I thought of naught save tales of magic and wonder, and every fair lady who had ostrich feathers on her head I regarded as an Elfin Queen. If I observed that the train of her dress was wet, I believed at once that she must be a water fairy. Now I know better, having learned from Natural History that those symbolical feathers are found on the most stupid of birds, and that the skirt of a lady's dress may be wetted in a very natural way. But if I had with those boyish eyes seen the aforesaid young lady in the aforesaid position on the Brocken, I would most assuredly have though "That is the fairy of the mountain and she has just uttered the charm which has caused all down there to appear so wonderful."

Yes, at the first glance from the Brocken, everything appears in a high degree marvellous—new impressions throng in on every side, and these, varied and often contradictory, unite in our soul to an overpowring and confusing sensation. If we succeed in grasping the idea of this sensation, we shall comprehend the character of the mountain. This character is entirely German as regards not only its advantages, but also its defects. The Brocken is a German. With German thoroughness he points out to us—sharply and accurately defined as in a panorama—the hundreds of cities, towns, and villages which are principally situated to the north, and all the mountains, forests, rivers and plains which lie infinitely far around. But for this very cause everything appears like an accurately designed and perfectly coloured map, and nowhere is the eye gratified by really beautiful landscapes, just as we German compiliers, owing to the honourable exactness with which we attempt to give all and everything, never appear to think of giving integral parts in a beautiful manner. The mountain in consequence has a certain calm, German, intelligent, tolerant character, simply because he can see things so distant, yet so distinctly. And when such a mountain opens his giant eyes, it may be that he sees something more than we dwarfs, who with our weak eyes climb over him. Many, indeed, assert that the Blocksberg is very Philistine-like, and *Claudius* once sang, "The Blocksberg is the lengthy Sir Philistine." But that was an error. On account of his bald head, which he occasionally covers with a cloud cap, the Blocksberg has indeed something of a Philistine-like aspect, but this with him, as with many other great Germans, is the result of pure irony. For it is notorious that he has his wild-student and fantastic times, as, for instance, in the first night of May. Then he casts his cloud-cap uproariously and merrily on high, and becomes like the rest of us, real German romantic mad.

I soon sought to entrap the beauty into a conversation, for we only begin to fully enjoy the beauties of nature when we talk about them on the spot. She was not *spirituelle*, but attentively intelligent. I developed to my own amazement much geographical knowledge, detailed to the curious beauty the names of all the towns which lay before us, and sought them out for her on the map, which with all the solemnity of a teacher I had spread out on the stone table which stands in the centre of the tower. I could not find many of the towns, possibly because I sought them more with my fingers than with my eyes, which latter were scanning the face of the fair lady, and discovering in it fairer regions than those of Schierke and Elend.

I could not divine the relation in which the little gentleman stood to the ladies whom he accompanied. He was a spare and remarkable figure. A head sprinkled with grey hair, which fell over his low forehead down to his dragonfly eyes, and a round, broad nose which projected boldly forwards, while his mouth and chin seemed retreating in terror back to his ears. The little man never spoke a word, only at times when the elder lady whispered something friendly in his ear, he smiled like a lap dog which had taken cold.

The elder lady was the mother of the younger, and she too was gifted with an air of extreme respectability and refinement. Her eyes betrayed a sickly, dreamy depth of thought, and about her mouth there was an expression of confirmed piety, yet withal, it seemed to me that she had once been very beautiful, and often smiled, and taken and given many a kiss. Her countenance resembled a *codex palimpsestus*, in which, from beneath the recent black monkish writing of some text of a Church Father, there peeped out the half obliterated verse of an old Greek love-poet. Both ladies had been that year with their companion in Italy, and told me many things of the beauties of Rome, Florence and Venice.

While we conversed, the sun sank lower and lower, the air grew colder, twilight stole over us, and the tower platform was filled with students, travelling mechanics, and a few honest citizens with their spouses and daughters, all of whom were desirous of witnessing the sunset. That is a truly sublime spectacle which elevates the soul to prayer. For a full quarter of an hour all stood in solemn silence, gazing on the beautiful fire-ball as it sank in the west; faces were rosy in the evening red; hands were involuntarily folded; it seemed as if we, a silent congregation, stood in the nave of a giant church, that the priest raised the body of the Lord, and that Palestrina's everlasting choral song poured forth from the organ.

As I stood thus lost in piety, I heard some one near me exclaim, "Ah! how beautiful Nature is, as a general thing!" These words came from the full heart of my room-mate, the young shopman. This brought me back to my weekday state of mind, and I found myself in tune to say a few neat things to the ladies, about the sunset, and to accompany them, as calmly as if nothing had happened, to their room. They permitted me to converse an hour longer with them. Our conversation, like the earth's course, was about the sun. The mother declared that the sun as it sunk in the snowy clouds seemed like a red glowing rose, which the gallant heaven had thrown upon the white and spreading bridal-veil of his loved earth. The daughter smiled, and thought that a frequent observation of such phenomena weakened their impression. The mother corrected the error by a quotation from Goethe's *Letters of Travel*, and asked me if I had read *Werther*. I believe that we also spoke of Angora cats, Etruscan vases, Turkish shawls, maccaroni and Lord Byron, from whose poems the elder lady, while daintily lisping and sighing, recited several sunset quotations. To the younger lady, who did not understand English, and who wished to become familiar with those poems, I recommended the translation of my fair and gifted country-woman, the Baroness Elise von Hohenhausen. On this occasion, as is my custom, when talking with young ladies, I did not neglect to speak of Byron's impiety, heartlessness, cheerlessness, and heaven knows what beside.

After this business I took a walk on the Brocken, for there it is never quite dark. The mist was not heavy, and I could see the outlines of the two hills known as the Witch's Altar and the Devil's Pulpit. I fired my pistol, but there was no echo. But suddenly I heard familiar voices, and found myself embraced and kissed. The new comers were fellow-students, from my own part of Germany, and had left Göttingen four days later than I. Great was their astonishment at finding me alone on the Blocksberg.

TIMBUKTU THE MYSTERIOUS[1]

(1853)

HEINRICH BARTH

(1821-65)

[*With James Richardson (who had been sent out by the British Government to open up commercial relations with the states of the Central and Western Sudan) and Adolf Overweg, Barth had left Tripoli early in 1850. In March 1851 Richardson died, and in the following September Overweg, Barth being thus left to carry on the mission alone.*]

MONDAY, SEPT. *5 (1853)*. Thus the day broke which, after so many months' exertion, was to carry me to the harbour of Timbúktu. We started at a tolerably early hour, crossing the broad sheet of the river, first in a north-easterly, then in an almost northerly direction, till finding ourselves opposite the small hamlet Tásakal, mentioned by Caillié, we began to keep along the windings of the northern bank which, from its low character, presented a very varying appearance, while a creek, separating from the trunk, entered the low ground. The river a month or two later in the season inundates the whole country to a great distance, but the magnificent stream, with the exception of a few fishing-boats, now seemed almost tenantless, the only objects which in the present reduced state of the country animated the scenery being a number of large boats lying at anchor in front of us near the shore of the village Koróme. But the whole character of the river was of the highest interest to me as it disclosed some new features for which I had not been prepared; for, while the water on which Koróme was situated formed only by far the smaller branch, the chief river, about three-quarters of a mile in breadth, took its direction to the south-east, separated from the former by a group of islands called Day, at the headland of which lies the islet of Tárashám.

[1] From *Travels and Discoveries in North and Central Africa.*

It was with an anxious feeling that I bade farewell to that noble river as it turned away from us, not being sure whether it would fall to my lot to explore its further course, although it was my firm intention at the time to accomplish this task if possible. Thus we entered the branch of Koróme, keeping along the grass which here grows in the river to a great extent, till we reached the village, consisting of nothing but temporary huts of reed, which, in the course of a few weeks, with the rising of the waters, were to be removed further inland. Notwithstanding its frail character, this poor little village was interesting on account of its wharfs, where a number of boats were repairing. The master of our own craft residing here (for all the boatmen on this river are serfs, or nearly in that condition), we were obliged to halt almost an hour and a half; but in order not to excite the curiosity of the people, I thought it prudent to remain in my boat. But even there I was incommoded with a great number of visitors, who were very anxious to know exactly what sort of person I was. It was here that we heard the unsatisfactory news that El Bakáy, whose name as a just and intelligent chief alone had given me confidence to undertake this journey, was absent at the time in Gúndam, whither he had gone in order to settle a dispute which had arisen between the Tuarek and the Berabísh; and as from the very beginning, when I was planning my journey to Timbúktu, I had based the whole confidence of my success upon the noble and trustworthy character which was attributed to the Sheikh El Bakáy by my informants, this piece of information produced a serious effect upon me.

At length we set out again on our interesting voyage, following first a south-easterly, then a north-easterly direction along this branch, which, for the first three miles, and a half, retained some importance, being here about two hundred yards wide, when the channel divided a second time, the more considerable branch turning off towards Yélluwa and Zegália, and other smaller hamlets situated on the islands of Day, while the water-course which we followed dwindled away to a mere narrow meadow-water, bearing the appearance of an artificial ditch or canal, which, as I now heard, is entirely dry during the dry season, so that it becomes impossible to embark directly at Kábara for places situated higher up or lower down the river. The navigation of this water became so difficult, that all my people were obliged to leave the boat, which with great difficulty was dragged on by the boatmen, who themselves entered the water and lifted and pushed it along with their hands. But before we reached Kábara, which is situated on the slope of a sandy eminence, the narrow and shallow channel widened to a tolerably large basin of circular shape; and here, in front of the town, seven good-sized boats were lying giving to the whole place some little life.

At length we lay to, and sending two of my people on shore, in order to obtain quarters, I followed them as soon as possible, when I was informed that they had procured a comfortable dwelling for me. The house where I was lodged was a large and grand building (if we take into account the general relations of this country) standing on the very top of the mound on the slope of which the town is situated. It was of an oblong shape, consisting of very massive clay walls, which were even adorned, in a slight degree, with a rude kind of relief; and it included, besides two ante-rooms, an inner courtyard, with a good many smaller chambers, and an upper story. The interior, with its small stores of every kind, and its assortment of sheep, ducks, fowls, and pigeons, in different departments, resembled Noah's Ark, and afforded a cheerful sight of homely comfort.

Having taken possession of two ante-rooms for my people and luggage, I endeavoured to make myself as comfortable as possible, while the busy landlady, a tall and stout personage, in the absence of her husband, a wealthy Songhay merchant, endeavoured to make herself agreeable, and offered me the various delicacies of her store for sale; but these were extremely scanty, the chief attraction to us, besides a small bowl of milk seasoned with honey, being some onions, of which I myself was not less in want than my people for seasoning our simple food. Besides this article so necessary for seasoning the food, I bought a little buláanga, or vegetable butter, in order to light up the dark room where I had taken up my quarters; but the night which I passed here was a very uncomfortable one, on account of the number of mosquitoes which infest the whole place.

Thus broke September 6th, a very important day for me, as it was to determine the kind of reception I was to meet with in this quarter. But notwithstanding the uncertainty of my prospects, I felt cheerful and full of confidence; and, as I was now again firmly established on dry soil, I went early in the morning to see my horse, which had successfully crossed all the different branches lying between Kábara and Sarayámo; but I was sorry to find him in a very weak and emaciated condition.

While traversing the village, I was surprised at the many clay buildings which are to be seen here, amounting to between one hundred and fifty and two hundred; however, these are not so much the dwellings, of the inhabitants of Kábara themselves, but serve rather as magazines for storing up the merchandise belonging to the people of, and the foreign merchants residing in, Timbúktu and Sansándi. There are two small market-places, one containing about twelve stalls or sheds, where all sorts of articles are sold, the other being used exclusively for meat. Although it was still early in the day, women were already busy boiling rice, which is sold in small portions, or made up into thin cakes boiled with bulánga, and sold for five shells each.

Having returned to my quarters from my walk through the town, I had to distribute several present's to some people whom El Waláti chose to represent as his brothers and friends. Having then given to himself a new, glittering, black tobe of Núpe manufacture, a new 'half,' and the white bernús which I wore myself, I at length prevailed upon him to set out for the town, in order to obtain protection for me; for as yet I was an outlaw in the country, and any ruffian who suspected my character might have slain me, without scarcely anybody caring anything about it; and circumstances seemed to assume a very unfavourable aspect: for there was a great movement among the Tuarek in the neighbourhood, when it almost seemed as if some news of my real character had transpired. Not long after my two messengers were gone, a Tárki chief, of the name of Knéha, with tall and stately figure, and of noble expressive features, as far as his shawl around the face allowed them to be seen, but, like the whole tribe of Kél-hekíkan to which he belongs, bearing a very bad character as a freebooter, made his appearance, armed with spear and sword, and obtruded himself upon me while I was partaking of my simple dish of rice; notwithstanding which, he took his seat at a short distance opposite to me. Not wishing to invite him to a share in my poor frugal repast by the usual 'bismillah,' I told him, first in Arabic and then in Fulfúlde, that I was dining, and had no leisure to speak with him at present. Whereupon he took his leave, but returned after a short while, and in a rather peremptory manner, solicited a present from me, being, as he said, a great chief of the country; but as I was not aware of the extent of his power, and being also afraid that others might imitate his example, I told him that I could not give him anything before I had made due enquiries respecting his real importance from my companion who had just gone to the town. But he was not at all satisfied with my argument; representing himself as a great 'dhálem' or evil-doer, and that as such he might do me much harm; till at length, after a very spirited altercation, I got rid of him.

He was scarcely gone, when the whole house was filled with armed men, horse and foot, from Timbúktu, most of them clad in light blue tobes, tightly girt round the waist with a shawl, and dressed in short breeches reaching only to the knee, as if they were going to fight, their head being covered with a straw hat of the peculiar shape of a little hut with regular thatchwork, such as is fashionable among the inhabitants of Másina and of the provinces further west. They were armed with spears, besides which some of them wore also a sword: only a few of them had muskets. Entering the house rather abruptly, and squatting down in the ante-chambers and courtyard, just where they could find a place, they stared at me not a little, and began asking of each other who this strange-looking fellow might be, while I was reclining on my two smaller boxes, having my larger ones and my other luggage behind me. I was rather at a loss to account for their intrusion, until I learned, upon inquiry of my landlady, that they were come in order to protect their cattle from the Tuarek, who at the time were passing through the place, and who had driven away some of their property. The very person whom they dreaded was the chief Knéha, who had just left me, though they could not make out his whereabouts. Having refreshed themselves during the hot hours of the day, these people started off; but the alarm about the cattle continued the whole of the afternoon, and not less than two hundred armed men came into my apartments in the course of an hour.

My messengers not returning at the appointed time from their errand in the town, I had at length retired to rest in the evening, when shortly before midnight they arrived, together with Sídi Álawáte, the Sheikh El Bakáy's brother, and several of his followers, who took up their quarters on the terrace of my house in order to be out of the reach of the mosquitoes; and after they had been regaled with a good supper, which had been provided beforehand by some of the townspeople, I went to pay my respects to them.

It was an important interview; for, although this was not the person for whom my visit was specially intended, and whose favourable or unfavourable disposition would influence the whole success of my arduous undertaking, yet for the present I was entirely in his hands, and all depended upon the manner in which he received me. Now my two messengers had only disclosed to himself personally, that I was a Christian, while at the same time they had laid great stress upon the circumstance that, although a Christian, I was under the special protection of the sultan of Stambúl; and Sídi Álawáte inquired therefore of me, with great earnestness and anxiety, as to the peculiar manner in which I enjoyed the protection of that great Mohammedan sovereign.

Now it was most unfortunate for me that I had no direct letter from that quarter. Even the firmán with which we had been provided by the Bashá of Tripoli had been delivered to the governor for whom it was destined, so that at the time I had nothing with me to show but a firmán which I had used on my journey in Egypt, and which of course had no especial relation to the case in question. The want of such a general letter of protection from the sultan of Constantinople, which I had solicited with so much anxiety to be sent after me, was in the sequel the chief cause of my difficult and dangerous position in Timbúktu; for, furnished with such a letter, it would have been easy to have imposed silence upon my adversaries and enemies there, and especially upon the merchants from Morocco, who were instigated by the most selfish jealousy to raise all sorts of intrigues against me.

Having heard my address with attention, although I was not able to establish every point so clearly as I could have wished, the sheikh's brother promised me protection, and desired me to be without any apprehension with regard to my safety; and thus terminated my first interview with this man, who, on the whole, inspired me with a certain degree of confidence, although I was glad to think that he was not the man upon whom I had to rely for my safety. Having then had a further chat with his telamíd or pupils, with whom I passed for a Mohammedan, I took leave of the party and retired to rest in the close apartments of the lower story of the house.

Wednesday, Sept. 7. After a rather restless night, the day broke when I was at length to enter Timbúktu; but we had a great deal of trouble in performing this last short stage of our journey, deprived as we were of beasts of burden; for the two camels which the people had brought from the town in order to carry my boxes, proved much too weak, and it was only after a long delay that we were able to procure eleven donkeys for the transport of all my luggage. Meanwhile the rumour of a traveller of importance having arrived had spread far and wide, and several inhabitants of the place sent a breakfast both for myself and my protector. Just at the moment when we were at length mounting our horses, it seemed as if the Tárki chief Knéha was to cause me some more trouble, for in the morning he had sent me a vessel of butter in order thus to acquire a fair claim upon my generosity; and coming now for his reward, he was greatly disappointed when he heard that the present had fallen into the hands of other people.

It was ten o'clock when our cavalcade at length put itself in motion, ascending the sandhills which rise close behind the village of Kábara, and which, to my great regret, had prevented my obtaining a view of the town from the top of our terrace. The contrast of this desolate scenery with the character of the fertile banks of the river which I had just left behind was remarkable. The whole tract bore decidedly the character of a desert, although the path was thickly lined on both sides with thorny bushes and stunted trees, which were being cleared away in some places in order to render the path less obstructed and more safe, as the Tuarek never failed to infest it, and at present were particularly dreaded on account of their having killed a few days previously three petty Tawáti traders on their way to Árawán. It is from the unsafe character of this short road between the harbour and the town, that the spot, about halfway between Kábara and Timbúktu, bears the remarkable name of "Ur-immándes" ("He does not hear"), meaning the place where the cry of the unfortunate victim is not heard from either side.

Having traversed two sunken spots designated by especial names, where, in certain years when the river rises to an unusual height, as happened in the course of the same winter, the water of the inundation enters and occasionally forms even a navigable channel; and leaving on one side the talha tree of the Welí Sálah, covered with innumerable rags of the superstitious natives, who expect to be generously rewarded by their saint with a new shirt, we approached the town; but its dark masses of clay not being illuminated by bright sunshine, for the sky was thickly overcast and the atmosphere filled with sand, were scarcely to be distinguished from the sand and rubbish heaped all round; and there was no opportunity for looking attentively about, as a body of people were coming towards us in order to pay their compliments to the stranger and bid him welcome. This was a very important moment, as, if they had felt the slightest suspicion with regard to my character, they might easily have prevented my entering the town at all, and thus even endangered my life.

I therefore took the hint of Álawáte, who recommended me to make a start in advance in order to anticipate the salute of these people who had come to meet us; and putting my horse to a gallop, and gun in hand, I galloped up to meet them, when I was received with many saláms. But a circumstance occurred which might have proved fatal, not only to my enterprise, but even to my own personal safety, as there was a man among the group who addressed me in Turkish, which I had almost entirely forgotten; so that I could with difficulty make a suitable answer to his compliment; but avoiding further indiscreet questions, I pushed on in order to get under safe cover.

Having then traversed the rubbish which has accumulated round the ruined clay wall of the town, and left on one side a row of dirty reed huts which encompass the whole of the place, we entered the narrow streets and lanes, or, as the people of Timbúktu say, the tijeráten, which scarcely allowed two horses to proceed abreast. But I was not a little surprised at the populous and wealthy character which this quarter of the town, the Sáne-Gúngu, exhibited, many of the houses rising to the height of two stories, and in their façade evincing even an attempt at architectural adornment. Thus, taking a more westerly turn, and followed by a numerous troop of people, we passed the house of the Sheikh El Bakáy, where I was desired to fire a pistol; but as I had all my arms loaded with ball I prudently declined to do so, and left it to one of my people to do honour to the house of our host. We thus reached the house on the other side of the street, which was destined for my residence, and I was glad when I found myself safely in my new quarters.

It had been arranged that, during the absence of the Sheikh El Bakáy, whose special guest I professed to be, my house should be locked up and no one allowed to pay me a visit. However, while my luggage was being got in, numbers of people gained access to the house, and came to pay me their compliments, and while they scrutinised my luggage, part of which had rather a foreign appearance, some of them entertained a doubt as to my nationality. But of course it could never have been my intention to have impressed these people with the belief of my being a Mohammedan; for having been known as a Christian all along my road as far as Libtáko, with which province the Arabs of Ázawád keep up a continual intercourse, although there the people would scarcely believe that I was a European, the news of my real character could not fail soon to transpire; and it was rather a fortunate circumstance that, notwithstanding our extremely slow progress and our roundabout direction, the news had not anticipated us. I had been obliged to adopt the character of a Mohammedan, in order to traverse with some degree of safety the country of the Tuarek, and to enter the town of Timbúktu, which was in the hands of the fanatical Fúlbe of Hamda-Alláhi, while I had not yet obtained the protection of the chief whose name and character alone had inspired me with sufficient confidence to enter upon this enterprise.

Thus I had now reached the object of my arduous undertaking; but it was apparent from the very first, that I should not enjoy the triumph of having overcome the difficulties of the journey in quiet and repose. The continuous excitement of the protracted struggle, and the uncertainty whether I should succeed in my undertaking, had sustained my weakened frame till I actually reached this city; but as soon as I was there, and almost at the very moment when I entered my house, I was seized with a severe attack of fever. Yet never were presence of mind and bodily energy more required; for the first night which I passed in Timbúktu was disturbed by feelings of alarm and serious anxiety.

On the morning of September 8th, the first news I heard was, that Hammádi the rival and enemy of El Bakáy had informed the Fúlbe, or Fullán, that a Christian had entered the town, and that, in consequence, they had come to the determination of killing him. However, these rumours did not cause me any great alarm, as I entertained the false hope that I might rely on the person who, for the time, had undertaken to protect me: but my feeling of security was soon destroyed, this very man turning out my greatest tormentor. I had destined for him a very handsome gift, consisting of a fine cloth bernús, a cloth kaftán, and two tobes, one of silk and the other of indigo-dyed cotton, besides some small er articles; but he was by no means satisfied with these, and peremptorily raised the present to the following formidable proportions:

	SHELLS
Two blue bernúses of the best quality, worth . . .	100,000
One kaftán	40,000
Two waistcoats; one red and one blue.	15,000
Two silk tobes	35,500
Two Núpe tobes	30,000
A pair of small pistols, with 7 lb. of fine powder .	
Ten Spanish dollars	
Two English razors, and many other articles . .	

While levying this heavy contribution upon me, in order to take from the affair its vexatious character, my host stated, that as their house and their whole establishment were at my disposal, so my property ought to be at theirs. But even this amount of property did not satisfy him, nor were his pretensions limited to this; for, the following day, he exacted an almost equal amount of considerable presents from me, such as two cloth kaftáns, two silk hamáil, or sword-belts, three other silk tobes, one of the species called jellábi, one of that called harír, and the third of the kind called filfil, one Núpe tobe, three túrkedís, a small six-barrelled pistol, and many other things. He promised me, however, on his part, that he would not only make presents of several of these articles to the Tuarek chiefs, but that he would also send a handsome gift to the governor of Hamda-Alláhi; but this latter condition at least, although the most important, considering that the town was formally subjected to the supremacy of the ruler of Másina, was never fulfilled; and although I was prepared to sacrifice all I had for the purposes of my journey, yet it was by no means agreeable to give up such a large proportion of my very limited property to a younger brother of the chief under whose protection I was to place myself. Thus my first day at Timbúktu passed away, preparing me for a great deal of trouble and anxiety which I should have to go through; even those who professed to be my friends treating me with so little consideration.

However, the second day of my residence here was more promising. I received visits from several respectable people, and I began to enter with spirit upon my new situation, and to endeavour by forbearance to accommodate myself to the circumstances under which I was placed. The state of my health also seemed to improve, and I felt a great deal better than on the preceding day. I was not allowed to stir about, but was confined within the walls of my house. In order to obviate the effect of this want of exercise as much as possible, to enjoy fresh air and at the same time to become familiar with the principal features of the town, through which I was not allowed to move about at pleasure, I ascended as often as possible the terrace of my house. This afforded an excellent view over the northern quarters of the town. On the north was the massive mosque of Sánkoré, which had just been restored to all its former grandeur through the influence of the Sheikh El Bakáy, and gave the whole place an imposing, character. Neither the mosque Sídi Yáhia, nor the "great mosque" or Jíngeré-bér, was seen from this point; but towards the east the view extended over a wide expanse of the desert, and towards the south the elevated mansions of the Ghadámsíye merchants were visible. The style of the buildings was various. I could see clay houses of different characters, some low and unseemly, others rising with a second story in front to greater elevation, and making even an attempt at architectural ornament, the whole being interrupted by a few round huts of matting. The sight of this spectacle afforded me sufficient matter of interest, although the streets being very narrow, only little was to be seen of the intercourse carried on in them, with the exception of the small market in the northern quarter, which was exposed to view on account of its situation on the slope of the sand-hills which, in course of time, have accumulated round the mosque.

But while the terrace of my house served to make me well acquainted with the character of the town, it had also the disadvantage of exposing me fully to the gaze of the passers-by, so that I could only slowly and with many interruptions succeed in making a sketch of the scene thus offered to my view.

Meanwhile I began to provide what was most necessary for my comfort, and bought for myself and my people a piece of good bleached calico, "shígge" or "sehen híndi," as it is called here, for 13,500 shells, and three pieces of unbleached calico for 8000 each. At the same time I sent several articles into the market, in order to obtain a supply of the currency of the place 3000 shells being reckoned equal to one Spanish dollar.

Thus I had begun to make myself a little more comfortable, when suddenly on the morning of the 10th, while I was suffering from another attack of fever, I was excited by the report being circulated, that the party opposed to my residence in the town was arming in order to attack me in my house. Now, I must confess that, notwithstanding the profession of sincere friendship made to me by Sídi Álawáte, I am inclined to believe that he himself was not free from treachery, and, perhaps, was in some respect implicated in this manœuvre, as he evidently supposed that, on the first rumour of such an attack being intended, I should abandon my house, or at least my property, when he might hope to get possession underhand of at least a good portion of the latter before the arrival of his brother, whom he knew to be a straightforward man, and who would not connive at such intrigues. With this view, I have no doubt, he sent a famale servant to my house, advising me to deposit all my goods in safety with the Táleb el Wáfi, as the danger which threatened me was very great; but this errand had no other effect than to rouse my spirits. I armed immediately, and ordered my servants to do the same, and my supposed protector was not a little astonished, when he himself came shortly afterwards with the Waláti (who, no doubt, was at the bottom of the whole affair), and found me ready to defend myself and my property, and to repulse any attack that might be made upon my residence, from whatever quarter it might proceed. He asked me whether I meant to fight the whole population of the town, uttering the words "gúwet e' Rúm," "strength of the Christians"; and protested that I was quite safe under his protection and hand nothing to fear, and certainly, for the moment, my energetic conduct had dispersed the clouds that might have been impending over my head.

But not withstanding his repeated protestations of sincere friendship, and although he confirmed with his own mouth what I had already heard from other people, that he himself was to accompany me on my return journey as far as Bórnu, he did not discontinue for a moment his importunity in begging for more presents day by day.

One day he called on me in company with his principal pupils, and earnestly recommended me to change my religion, and from an unbeliever to become a true believer. Feeling myself strong enough in arguments to defend my own religious principles, I challenged him to demonstrate to me the superiority of his creed, telling him that in that case I should not fail to adopt it, but not till then. Upon this, he and his pupils began with alacrity a spirited discussion, in the firm hope that they would soon be able to overcome my arguments; but after a little while they found them rather too strong, and were obliged to give in, without making any further progress at the time in their endeavours to persuade me to turn Mohammedan. This incident improved my situation in an extraordinary degree, by basing my safety on the sincere esteem which several of the most intelligent of the inhabitants contracted for me.

While thus gaining a more favourable position, even in the eyes of this unprincipled man, I had the pleasure of receiving a letter from his elder, more intelligent, and straightforward brother, the Sheikh el Bakáy himself, late in the evening of the 13th, full of the most assuring promises that I should be quite safe under his protection, and that he would soon arrive to relieve me from my unsatisfactory position. And although I felt very unwell all this time, and especially the very day that I received this message, I did not lose a moment in sending the Sheikh a suitable answer, wherein I clearly set forth all the motives which had induced me to visit this city, in conformity with the direct wish of the British Government, whose earnest desire it was to open friendly intercourse with all the chiefs and princes of the earth; mentioning among other Mohammedan chiefs with whom such a relation existed, the Sultan 'Abd el Mejíd, Múlá 'Abd e' Rahmán, and the Inám of Maskat; and whose attention the region of the Great River (Niger) together with Timbúktu, had long attracted. At the same time I assured him that his own fame as a just and highly intelligent man, which I had received from my friends far to the east in the heart of Negroland, had inspired me with full confidence that I should be safe under his protection. In consequence of the view which I set forth in this letter, I was so fortunate as to gain the lasting esteem of this excellent man, who was so much pleased with the contents of it, that on its arrival in Gúndam, where he was at the time, he read it to all the principal men, Tuarek, Songhay, and even Fullán, in whose company he was staying.

After my fever had abated for a day or two it returned with greater violence on the 17th, and I felt at times extremely unwell and very weak, and in my feverish state was less inclined to bear with tranquillity and equanimity all the exactions and contributions levied upon me by Sídi Álawáte. We had a thunderstorm almost every day, followed now and then by a tolerable quantity of rain; the greatest fall of rain, according to the information which I was able to gather, annually occurring during the month of September, a phenomenon in entire harmony with the northerly latitude of the place. This humidity, together with the character of the open hall in which I used to pass the night as well as the day, increased my indisposition not a little; but the regard for my security did not allow me to seek shelter in the store-room wherein I had placed my luggage, and which, being at the back of the hall, was well protected against cold, and, as it seemed at least, even against wet. For, not to speak of the oppressive atmosphere and almost total darkness which prevailed in that close place, in taking up my residence there I should have exposed myself to the danger of a sudden attack, while from the hall where I was staying I was enabled to observe everything which was going on in my house; and through the screen which protected the opening, close by the side of my couch, I could observe everybody that entered my yard long before they saw me. For this reason I preferred this place even to the room on the terrace, although the latter had the advantage of better air. I may observe that these upper rooms in general form the private residence of most of the people in the town who have the luxury of such an upper story.

Monday, Sept. 26th. About three o'clock in the morning, while I was lying restlessly on my couch, endeavouring in vain to snatch a moment's sleep, the Sheikh Sídi Áhmed el Bakáy arrived. The music, which was immediately struck up in front of his house by the women, was ill-adapted to procure me rest; while the arrival of my protector, on whose disposition and power the success of my whole undertaking and my own personal safety fully depended, excited my imagination in the highest degree, and thus contributed greatly to increase my feverish state.

The following day I was so ill as to be quite unable to pay my respects to my protector, who sent me a message begging me to quiet myself, as I might rest assured that nothing but my succumbing to illness could prevent me from safely returning to my native home. Meanwhile, as a proof of his hospitable disposition he sent me a handsome present, consisting of two oxen, two sheep, two large vessels of butter, one camel load, or "suníye" of rice, and another of negrocorn, cautioning me, at the same time, against eating any food which did not come from his own house. In order to cheer my spirits, he at once begged me to choose between the three roads by which I wanted to return home—either through the country of the Fúlbe, or in a boat on the river, or, by land, through the district of the Tuarek.

As from the first I had been fully aware that neither the disposition of the natives, and especially that of the present rulers of the country, the Fúlbe, nor the state of my means, would allow me to proceed westward, and as I felt persuaded that laying down the course of the Niger from Timbúktu to Sáy would far outweigh in importance a journey through the upper country towards the Senegal, I was firm in desiring from the beginning to be allowed to visit Gógó. For not deeming it prudent, in order to avoid creating unnecessary suspicion, to lay too great stress upon navigating the river, I preferred putting forward the name of the capital of the Songhay empire; as in visiting that place I was sure that I should see at least the greater part of the river, while at the same time I should come into contact with the Tuarek, who are the ruling tribe throughout its whole course.

But the generous offer of my friend was rather premature; and if at that time I had known that I was still to linger in this quarter for eight months longer, in my feeble condition, I should scarcely have been able to support such an idea; but fortunately Providence does not reveal to man what awaits him, and he toils on without rest in the dark.

RUSSIA

ACROSS THE GOBI DESERT[1]

NIKOLAI PREJEVALSKY

(1839-88)

THE second week in June we left the high lands of Kan-su and crossed the threshold of the desert of Ala-shan. The sanddrifts now lay before us like a boundless sea, and it was not without sundry misgivings that we entered this forbidding realm.

Without sufficient means top enable us to hire a guide, we went alone, risking all dangers and difficulties, the more imminent because the year before, while travelling with the Tangutan caravan, I could only note down by stealth, and often at haphazard, the landmarks and direction of the route. This itinerary was of course inaccurate, but now it served as our only guide.

We were fifteen days marching from Tajing to Din-yuan-ing, and safely accomplished this difficult journey, only once nearly losing ourselves in the desert. This happened on the 21st June between Lake Serik-dolon and the well of Shangin-dalai. Having left Serikdolon early in the morning, we marched through miles of loose sands, and at last came to an expanse of clay where the track divided. We had not noticed this spot on the outward journey, and had therefore to guess which of the two roads would lead to our destination. What made it worse was that the angle of bifurcation being acute, we could not decide, even with the aid of a compass, which we ought to take. The track to the right being more beaten, we determined to follow it, but after all we were mistaken, for having gone a few miles a number of other tracks crossed ours. This fairly puzzled us; however, we still pressed forward, till at length a well-beaten road joined the one we had first chosen. This we durst not follow, for it went we knew not whither, nor could we return to the place where the roads first branched off. Choosing the lesser of two evils, we resolved to persevere in our first route, hoping soon to see the group of hills at whose foot lies the well of Shangin-dalai. But it was midday, and the intense heat obliged us to halt for two or three hours. On resuming out march, with the aid of the compass we steered in the same direction as before, till at length we discerned a small group of hills to our right. These we supposed to be the landmark of the Shangin-dalai, but they were still a long way off, and the dust which pervaded the atmosphere the whole day prevented our seeing their outline distinctly even with a glass.

[1] From *Mongolia, the Tangut Country, and the Solitudes of Northern Tibet*, translated by E. Delmer Morgan.

Evening fell and we halted for the night, fully confident that these hills were indeed those we were in search of. But on projecting our line of march on the map, I became aware how far we had diverged to the right of our proper course, and doubts arose as to whether we were really in the right road or not. In the meanwhile only five gallons of water were left for the night; our horses had had none, and were suffering such agonies of thirst that they could hardly move their legs. The question of finding the well on the morrow became one of life and death. How can I decribe our feelings as we lay down to rest! Fortunately the wind fell and the dust in the air cleared off. In the morning, with the first glimmer of light, I climbed on to the top of the pile of boxes containing our collections, and carefully scanned the horizon with a glass. I could see distinctly the group of hills we had remarked the previous day, but in a direction due north of our halting-place: I could also distinguish the summit of another, which might perhaps be that of Shangin-dalai. Towards which should we direct our steps? Having taken careful bearings of the latter, and having compared its position on the map with that noted down last year, we decided to march in that direction.

In doubt and anxiety we loaded our camels and started, the hill now and then visible above the low ridges, and now and again hidden from sight. In vain we strained our eyes through the glass to see the cairn of stones ("obo") piled upon its summit; the distance was still too great to distinguish anything so small. At length, after having gone nearly seven miles from the halting-place, we descried what we sought; with strength renewed by hope we pressed onwards; and in a few more hours we stood by the side of the well, to which our animals, tortured with thirst, rushed eagerly forward.

On one of the marches through Southern Ala-shan we met a caravan of Mongol pilgrims on their way from Urga to Lhassa. . . . The pilgrims were marching in echelons, some distance apart, having agreed to rendezvous at Koko-nor. As the foremost files met us, they exclaimed, "See where our brave fellows have got to!" and could hardly believe at first that we four had actually penetrated into Tibet. But what must have been the appearance of the Russian *molodtsi*? Exhausted with fatigue, half starved, unkempt, with ragged clothes and boots worn into holes, we were regular tatterdemalions! Socompletely had we lost the European aspect that when we arrived at Din-yuan-ing the natives remarked that we were the very image of their own people! i.e., of the Mongols. . . .

In accordance with the plan we had previously sketched, we purposed marching straight to Urga from Din-yuan-ing, by way of the Central Gobi, a route which had never before been travelled by any European, and was therefore of the greatest scientific interest. Before starting, however, we determined to rest, and to take this opportunity of exploring more thoroughly than last time the mountains of Ala-shan. . . . Here we stayed three weeks, and finally came to the conclusion that the mountains of Ala-shan are rich neither in flora nor in fauna. . . .

In such arid mountains as these one would have supposed that we should not have incurred the slightest risk from water; but fate willed that we should experience every misfortune which can possibly overtake the traveller in these countries, for, without giving us the slightest warning, a deluge, such as we never remember to have seen, swept suddenly down upon us.

It was on the morning of the 13th July; the summits of the mountains were enveloped in mist, a sure indication of rain. Towards midday, however, it became perfectly clear and gave every promise of a fine day, when, three hours later, all of a sudden, clouds began to settle on the mountains, and the rain poured down in buckets. Our tent was soon soaked through, and we dug small trenches to drain off the water which made its way into the interior. This continued for an hour without showing any sign of abatement, although the sky did not look threatening. The rainfall was so great that it was more than could be absorbed by the soil or retained on the steep slopes of the mountains; the consequence was that streams formed in every cleft and gorge, even falling from the precipitous cliffs, and uniting in the principal ravine, where our tent happened to be pitched, descended in an impetuous torrent with terrific roar and speed. Dull echoes high up in the mountains warned us of its approach, and in a few minutes the deep bed of our ravine was inundated with a turbid, coffee-coloured stream, carrying with it rocks and heaps of smaller fragments, while it dashed with such violence against the sides that the very ground trembled as though with the shock of an earthquake. Above the roar of the waters we could hear the clash of great boulders as they met in their headlong course. From the loose banks and from the upper parts of the defile whole masses of smaller stones were detached by the force of the current and thrown up on either side of the channel, whilst trees were torn up by their roots and rent into splinters. . . . Barely twenty feet from our tent rushed the torrent, destroying everything in its course. Another minute, another foot of water, and our collections, the fruit of our expedition, were irrevocably gone! . . .

Fortune, however, again befriended us. Before our tent was a small projecting ledge of rock upon which the waves threw up stones which soon formed a breakwater, and this saved us. Towards evening the rain slackened, the torrent quickly subsided, and the following morning beheld only a small stream flowing where the day before the waters of a mighty river had swept along. . . .

On returning to Din-yuan-ing we equipped our caravan, bartered away our bad camels, bought new ones, and on the morning of the 26th July started on our journey. Thanks to our Peking passport and still more to the presents we bestowed on the *tosalakchi* who acted as regent during the Prince's[1] absence, we were able to hire two guides to escort us to the border of Ala-shan, where we were to obtain others, and for this purpose the yamen (or magistracy) of Ala-shan issued an official document: in this way we continued to obtain guides from one banner to another; a matter of great importance, for our road lay through the wildest part of the Gobi, in a meridional direction from Ala-shan to Urga, and we could not possibly have found our way without them.

Another long series of hardships now awaited us. We suffered most from the July heat, which at midday rose to 113° Fahr. in the shade, and at night was never less than 73°. No sooner did the sun appear above the horizon than it scorched us mercilessly. In the daytime the heat enveloped us on all sides, above from the sun, below from the burning ground; the wind, instead of cooling the atmosphere, stirred the lower strata and made it even more intolerable. On these days the cloudless sky was of a dirty hue, the soil heated to 145° Fahr., and even higher where the sands were entirely bare, whilst at a depth of two feet from the surface is was 79°.

Our tent was no protection, for it was hotter within than without, although the sides were raised. We tried pouring water on it, and on the ground inside, but this was useless, in half an hour everything was as dry as before, and we knew not whither to turn for relief.

The air, too, was terribly dry; no dew fell, and rain-clouds dispersed without sending more than a few drops to earth. . . . Thunderstorms rarely occurred, but the wind was incessant night and day, and sometimes blew with great violence, chiefly from the south-east and south-west. On calm days tornadoes were frequent about the middle of the day or a little later. To avoid the heat as much as possible we rose before daybreak; tea-drinking and loading the camels, however, took up so much time that we never got away before four or even five o'clock in the morning. We might have lightened the fatigue considerably by night-marching, but in that case we should have had to forego the survey which formed so important a part of our labours. . . .

The commencement of our journey was unpropitious, for on the sixth day

[1] The Prince of Ala-shan.

after we left Din-yuan-ing, we lost our faithful friend Faust,[1] and we ourselves nearly perished in the sands.

It was on the 31st July; we had left Djaratai-dabas and had taken the direction of the Khan-ula mountains; our guide having informed us that a march of eighteen miles lay before us that day, but that we should pass two wells about five miles apart.

Having accomplished that distance, we arrived at the first, and after watering our animals, proceeded, in the full expectation of finding the second, where we intended to halt; for though it was only seven in the morning, the heat was overpowering. So confident were we that the Cossacks proposed to throw away the supply of water that we had taken in the casks, in order not to burden our camels needlessly, but fortunately I forbade their doing this. After nearly seven miles more, no well was to be seen, and the guide announced that we had gone out of our road. So he proceeded to the top of a hillock in the immediate neighbourhood to obtain a view over the surrounding country, and soon afterwards beckoned to us to follow. On rejoining him, he assured us that although we had missed the second well, a third, where he purposed passing the night, was scarcely four miles farther. We took the direction indicated. In the meanwhile it was near midday and the heat intolerable. A strong wind stirred the hot lower atmosphere, enveloping us in sand and saline dust. Our animals suffered frightfully; especially the dogs, obliged to walk over the burning sand. We stopped several times to give them drink, and to moisten their heads as well as our own. But the supply of water now failed! Less than a gallon remained, and this we reserved for the last extremity. "How much farther is it?" was the question we constantly put to our guide, who invariably answered that it was near, that we should see it from the next sand hill or the one after; and so we passed on upwards of seven miles without having seen a sign of the promised well. In the meanwhile the unfortunate Faust lay down and moaned, giving us to understand that he was quite unable to walk. I then told my companion and guide to ride on, charging the latter to take Faust on his camel as he was completely exhausted. After they had ridden a mile in advance of the caravan the guide pointed out the spot where he said the well should be, apparently about three miles off. Poor Faust's doom was sealed; he was seized with fits, and Mr Pyltseff, finding it was impossible to hurry on, and too far to ride back to the caravan for a glass of water, waited till we came up, laying Faust under a clump of *saxaul* and covering him with saddle-felt. The poor dog became less conscious every minute, gasped two or three times, and expired. Placing his body on one of

[1] Colonel Prejevalsky's setter.

the packs, we moved on again, sorely doubting whether there were really any well in the place pointed out to us by the guide; for he had already deceived us more than once. Our situation at this moment was desperate. Only a few glasses of water were left, of which we took into our mouths just enough to moisten our parched tongues; our bodies seemed on fire, our heads swam, and we were close upon fainting. In this last extremity I desired a Cossack to take a small vessel and to ride as hard as he could to the well, accompanied by the guide, ordering him to fire at the latter if he attempted to run away. They were soon hidden in a cloud of dust which filled the air, and we toiled onwards in their tracks in the most anxious suspense. At length, after half an hour, the Cossack appeared. What news does he bring? and spurring our jaded horses, which could hardly move their legs to meet him, we learned with the joy of a man who has been snatched from the jaws of death that the well had been found! After a draught of fresh water from the vesselful that he brought, and, having wet our heads, we rode in the direction pointed out, and soon reached the well of Boro-Sondji. It was now two o'clock in the afternoon; we had, therefore, been exposed for nine consecutive hours to frightful heat, and had ridden upwards of twenty miles.

After unloading the camels, I sent a Cossack back with the Mongol for the pack which had been left on the road, by the side of which our other (Mongol) dog, who had been with us nearly two years, was laid. The poor brute had lain down underneath the pack but was still alive, and after getting a draught of water he was able to follow the men back to camp. Notwithstanding the complete prostration of our physical and moral energies, we felt the loss of Faust so keenly that we could eat nothing, and slept but little all night. The following morning we dug a small grave and buried in it the remains of our faithful friend. As we discharged this last duty to him my companion and I wept like children. Faust had been our friend in every sense of the word! How often in moments of trouble had we caressed and played with him, half forgetting our griefs! For nearly three years had he served us faithfully through the frost and storms of Tibet, the rain and snow of Kan-su, and the wearisome marches of many thousand miles, and at last had falled a victim to the burning heat of the desert; this too within two months of the termination of the expedition!

The route taken by most of the caravans of pilgrims from Urga to Ala-shan on their way to Tibet turns a little to the west at the Khan-ula mountains, afterwards taking the direction of the Khalka country. We did not follow this road because the wells along it were not sufficiently numerous. . . . Our course lay due north, and after crossing some spurs of the Kara-narin-ula entered the country of the Urutes, which lies wedge-shaped between Ala-shan and the Khalka country.

This country is considerably higher than Ala-shan, but soon begins to sink towards the Galpin Gobi plain, where the elevation is only 3200 feet; north of this again it rises towards the Hurku mountains which form a distinct definition between the barren desert on the south and the more steppe-like region on the north. There is also a slope from the ranges bordering the valley of the Hoang-ho westward to the Galpin Gobi, which forms a depressed basin, no higher than Djaratai-dabas, extending as we were informed by the Mongols, for twenty-five days' march from east to west.

The soil of the Galpin Gobi, in that eastern portion of it which we crossed, consists of small pebbles or of saline clay almost devoid of vegetation; the whole expanse of country to the Hurku range being a desert as wild and barren as that of Ala-shan, but of a somewhat different character. The sand-drifts, so vast in the latter country, are here of comparatively small extent, and in their stead we find bare clay, shingle, and naked crumbling rocks (chiefly gneiss) scattered in low groups. Vegetation consists of stunted half-withered clumps of *saxual, karmyk, budarhana,* and a few herbaceous plants, the chief amongst which is the *sulhir*; the elms are the most striking features in the Urute country, forming in places small clumps; bushes of wild peach are also occasionally met with, such as are never seen in the desert of Ala-shan. Animal life in these regions is very scant; birds and mammals are the same as in Ala-shan. You may often ride for hours together without seeing a bird, not even a stone-chat or a *kolodjoro*; nevertheless, wherever there are wells or springs, Mongols are to be found, with a few camels, and large numbers of sheep and goats.

During our progress through this country, in the latter half of August, the heat was excessive, although never so high as in Ala-shan. Winds blew ceaselessly night and day, often increasing to the violence of a gale, and filling the air with clouds of saline dust and sand, the latter choking up many of the wells; but these were more frequently destroyed by the rains, which, although rare, came down with terrific force, and for an hour or two afterwards large rivers continued to flow, silting up the wells (always dug on the lower ground) with mud and sand. It would be impossible to travel here without a guide throughly acquainted with the country; for destruction lies in wait for you at every step. In fact this desert, like that of Ala-shan, is so terrible that, is comparison with it, the deserts of Northern Tibet may be called fruitful. There, at all events, you may often find water and good pasture-land in the valleys; here, there is neither the one nor the other, not even a single oasis; everywhere the silence of the valley of death.

The well-known Sahara can hardly be more terrible than these deserts, which extend for many hundreds of miles in length and breadth. The Hurku hills, where we crossed, are the northern definition of the wildest and most sterile part of the Gobi, and form a distinct chain with a direction from S.E. to W.N.W.; how far either way we could not say positively; but, according to the information we received from the natives, they are prolonged for a great distance towards the south-east, reaching the mountains bordering the valley of the Hoang-ho, while on the west they extend, with a few interruptions, to other far distant mountains of no great elevation. If the latter statement may be relied upon, we may conclude that they unite with the Thian Shan, and supply, as it were, a connecting link between that range and the In-shan system; an extremely interesting fact and one worthy the attention of future explorers.

Their width where we crossed them is a little over seven miles, and their apparent height hardly above a thousand feet. . . .

South of the Hurku lies the great trade route from Peking, *via* Kuku-khoto and Bautu, to Hami, Urumchi and Kulja, branching off near the spring of Bortson, where we encamped for the night. . . .

On crossing the frontier of the Khalka country we entered the principality of Tushetu-khan, and hastened by forced marches to Urga, which was now the goal we were so desirous of reaching. Nearly three years of wanderings, attended by every kind of privation and hardship, had so worn us out physically and morally that we felt most anxious for a speedy termination of our journey; besides which, we were now travelling through the wildest part of the Gobi, where want of water, heat, storms of wind, in short every adverse condition combined against us, and day by day undermined what little of our strength remained. . . .

The mirage, that evil genius of the desert, mocked us almost daily, and conjured up such tantalising visions of tremulous water that even the rocks of the neighbouring hills appeared as though reflected in it. Severe heat and frequent storms of wind prevented our sleeping quietly at night, much as we needed rest after the arduous day's march.

But not to us alone was the desert of Mongolia an enemy. Birds which began to make their appearance in the latter half of August suffered equally from thirst and hunger. We saw flocks of geese and ducks resting at the smallest pools, and small birds flew to our tent so exhausted with starvation as to allow us to catch them in the hand. We found several of these feathered wanderers quite dead, and in all probability numbers of them perish in their flight across the desert.

The chief migration of birds was in September, and by the 13th of that month we had counted twenty-four varieties. From our observations the geese directed their flight not due south but south-east towards the northern bend of the Hoang-ho.

Eighty-seven miles north of the Hurku hills we crossed another trade route from Kuku-khoto to Uliassutai; practicable for carts although the traffic is mostly on camels. . . .

Northwards the character of the Gobi again changes, and this time for the better. The sterile desert becomes a steppe, more and more fruitful as we advance to the north. The shingle and gravel are in turn succeeded by sand mixed in small quantities with clay. The country becomes extremely undulating. The gradual slopes of low hills intersect one another in every possible direction, and earn for this region the Mongol name, *Kangai—i.e.*, hilly. This continues for upwards of a hundred miles to the north of the Uliassutai post road, when the waterless steppe touches the margin of the basin of Lake Baikal; here finally, at Hangin-daban, you find yourself among groups and ridges of rocky hills, beyond which lie the well-watered districts of Northern Mongolia. . . .

Our impatience to reach Urga kept ever increasing as we approached it, and we counted the time no longer by months or weeks but by days. At length after crossing the Hangin-daban range we arrived on the banks of the Tola, the first river we had made acquaintance with in Mongolia. For 870 miles, *i.e.*, between Kan-su and this river, we had not seen a single stream or lake, only stagnant pools of brackish rain-water. Forests now appeared, darkening the steep slopes of the Mount Khan-ola. Under these grateful circumstances we at last accomplished our final march, and on the 17th September entered Urga, where we received a warm welcome from our Consul. I will not undertake to describe the moment when we heard again our mother-tongue, when we met again our countrymen, and experienced once more European comforts. We enquired eagerly what was going on in the civilised world; we devoured the contents of the letters awaiting us; we gave vent to our joy like children; it was only after a few days that we came to ourselves and began to realise the luxury to which our wanderings had rendered us for so long a time strangers. . . . After resting a week at Urga, we proceeded to Kiakhta, which we reached on the 1st October, 1873.

Our journey was ended. Its success had surpassed all the hopes we entertained when we crossed for the first time the borders of Mongolia. Then an uncertain future lay before us; now, as we called to mind all the difficulties and dangers we had gone through, we could not help wondering at the good fortune which had invariably attended us everywhere. Yes! in the most adverse circumstances, Fortune had been ever constant, and ensured the success of our undertaking: many a time when it hung on a thread a happy destiny rescued us, and gave us the means of accomplishing, as far as our strength would permit, the exploration of the least known and most inaccessible countries of Inner Asia.

ICELAND

THE MAP-MAKER[1]

THORVALDUR THORODDSEN

(1855-)

IN the year 1881, I conceived the idea of trying to fill up piece by piece some of the biggest gaps in our knowledge of the geography and geology of Iceland. Considering the extremely modest resources I had at my command, I could scarcely hope to examine the entire island. The task I set myself was to go systematically to work and, instead of making a hasty survey of a large area, to confine myself to relatively narrow districts, examining one or more every year as thoroughly as I was able. By adopting this plan, I hoped, with patience, to gain a tolerably accurate knowledge of some of the less-known quarters of the island; and, time and opportunity favouring me, I might possibly go on, and in this way gradually lay the foundations for a general survey of the whole country.

The first nine years I was sadly hampered through lack of means; but as time went on, this hindrance was gradually removed. First, the Icelandic Althing made me a grant. After that the Danish Rigsdag and two private gentlemen—Mr Oscar Dickson, of Gothenburg, and Mr A. Gamél, of Copenhagen—generously provided me with the means to procure a better equipment; so that I was enabled to continue my work under much more favourable conditions than before. Thanks to this valuable support, I succeeded, during the years 1881-98, in travelling over and exploring the entire island.

My first object was to acquire a pretty accurate knowledge of the interior of the island. The coast was surveyed during the first nineteen years of the nineteenth century by various Danish and Norwegian naval officers. In the years 1831-43 Björn Gunnlögsson surveyed the inhabited districts, and also took a few trips into the interior. The map of Iceland which he drew up, in four sheets, was an excellent piece of work; but the interior of the island, which was very little known, was laid down from mere observation and the reports of shepherds and others. Indeed, of the area represented on Gunnlögsson's map, some 17,500 square miles, representing the interior, had never been subjected to scientific examination, and certain other regions (including 3500 square miles of the ice-mountains) had never been trodden by human foot.

[1] Translated by J. T. Bealby.

Amongst the latter I may especially mention a portion of Odádahraun, the desert regions north-east of Fiskivötn, besides a few other places scattered up and down the island. The sources of several of the larger streams had never been seen, and the situation of some of the large groups of lakes was uncertain. My first immediate object then was to obtain a general and reliable view of the topography. At the same time there were also a number of geographical and geological questions urgently demanding solution. I intended, amongst other things, to collect materials for a geological map, on which I hoped to indicate with tolerable accuracy the extent of the several formations and species of rocks; in the next place, to attempt to trace out the broad lines of the structural history of the island; to examine and map the volcanoes and lava-streams, to study the history of the volcanic eruptions, as well as the origin, distribution, and geological relations of the warm springs, solfataras, and earth-tremors. In addition to these objects, it would also be desirable to make observations upon the modern glaciers, the altitude of their snowline, their glacial changes and formations, the glacial scratchings, the marine deposits, marine terraces, and so forth. When I embarked upon this enterprise, I fully realized the magnitude of the task I was setting myself. I knew full well how audacious it was for a single private individual, with such limited resources as I possessed, to attempt the exploration of a country stretching over an area of 40,450 square miles, possessing an arctic climate, and being in many parts extremely difficult of access. But I took courage from the Horatian maxim:

Est quadam prodire tenus, si non datur ultra,

and counted upon the friendly consideration of my scientific colleagues over sea to extend to me that indulgence which is one of the brightest features of the modern scientific world. In a word, I hoped that generous allowance would be made for the difficult circumstances under which I worked. Iceland is destitute of scientific institutions and laboratories. For many years I never had opportunity to exchange a word with anyone who had an interest in geology. I am, therefore, all the more deeply grateful to those men of science in both America and Europe who have encouraged me by letters and helped me with presents of books. . . .

As I have already remarked more than once, my first object was to explore the interior. Now, as the interior consists for the greater part of deserts, lava-fields, and glaciers, and as it is almost entirely destitute of vegetation, exploring trips in that direction obviously demand both time and patience, as well as a good equipment of tents, provisions, horses, instruments, and so forth. Most of the earlier attempts to explore the most difficult parts of the interior failed from want of grass for the horses. To carry sufficient fodder to last over a prolonged stay in the highly-lying desert regions is an absolute impossibility. The large expedition which was sent out in 1840, under the leadership of T. C. Schythe, in order to explore the southern part of Odádahraun, was unsuccessful from that very cause—want of grass, coupled with snowstorms. Nearly all the horses died, whilst the members of the expedition barely struggled back to the inhabited districts alive. Others which followed had no better fortune. With the view of avoiding a failure from the same cause, I went to work on a plan which had not previously been attempted. I never carried hay with me from the settled districts. Scattered round the outer border of the interior plateau there are a few small oases yielding scanty supplies of grass. These are known to certain shepherds and others, who in autumn have had occasion to follow straying sheep into the desert wilds, and I got them to tell me where these spots were situated. The knowledge thus obtained proved extremely useful to me in my expeditions. Although frequently not greater than a few score chains square, these patches of grass served for camping-grounds, and temporary centres from which to make flying excursions to this or the other point of interest in the immediate vicinity. I used to take a scythe and rake with me, mow the grass, pack it into sacks, and in that way carry it as food for the horses whilst journeying from one oasis to another. As a rule, the desert wastes between the oases could be traversed in from two to three days. My equipment was in nearly all respects typically Icelandic, although during the first nine years, owing to lack of pecuniary means, extremely primitive and inadequate. I and my attendants lived upon the plain ordinary food of the Icelandic peasant. During our tent life in the interior we drank large quantities of coffee, but no alcoholic liquors. Surveying in the interior of Iceland is wont to be frequently interrupted by bad weather—rain, fogs, storms of sand and snow. Owing to fog, I often had to ascend the same mountain several times before I was able to get a proper observation for measurement. In fact, the principal *desiderata* for successful exploration work in the interior of Iceland are a thoroughly good equipment and an unlimited stock of patience.

In the year 1876 I took part in Prof. Johnstrup's expedition to the northern parts of the island, to study the volcanoes at Mývatn and the volcano of Askja. My own independent investigations I began five years later, in 1881, when I made a hurried journey obliquely across the island, working in with it trips to the south-west corner, where I studied the volcanoes and warm springs near Œlfus and Thingvallavatn. I made my first long exploring journey in the summer of 1882, and with it began the execution of my plan, my former expeditions having partaken more of the nature of trial trips. That year I went from Akureyri to Mývatn, and thence to the fjord districts of Eastern Iceland; besides which I made two or three excursions into the interior—for example, to the east side of Hofsjökull, which no traveller had previously visited. Amongst other work which I accomplished on that journey, I investigated the well-known "double spar" quarry at Reydarfjord, in the vicinity of Helgustadir, mapping it and taking drawings of it in profile. But the year 1882 was for several reasons unfavourable for travel. The whole of the north coast was blocked by the Greenland drift-ice until the very end of August. The summer was so cold that very little grass grew, and some of my horses broke down. In addition to these drawbacks, the entire island was ravaged by an epidemic of measles, which carried off nearly two thousand people. Wherever I went there were sick folk, so that but little assistance was to be procured. Before the end of the journey my own men fell ill, and I was obliged to bring my summer's work to an abrupt termination.

In the summer of 1883 I explored the peninsula of Reykjanes. Although lying so near to Reykjavik, the greater portion of this remarkable volcanic peninsula had never been visited by a geologist. Except for a few fishing-stations along the coast, it is almost entirely buried under lava, and uninhabited and barren waste. Although it was no easy matter to use horses in that region, owing to the uneven surface of the lava and the numerous rents in the ground, I nevertheless managed to cross it backwards and forwards sufficiently to examine its remarkable geological conditions. I counted some thirty volcanoes, with over seven hundred craters of different sized, as well as a great number of volcanic fissures, out of which the lava had flowed. I estimated that the lavas thus ejected covered an area of 730 square miles.

The following summer I spent the time at my disposal in investigating the vast lava desert of Odádahraun and the adjacent parts of the interior plateau, ranging at altitudes of 1500 to 3000 feet above the level of the sea. The country was difficult to travel through; besides which we had to contend against a deficiency of grass, glacier streams so swollen as to be actually dangerous, and unfavourable weather. In spite of these obstacles, I was successful in ascending the greater part of the mountains, in crossing the desert backwards and forwards, both on horseback and on foot, and in covering it with a network of trigonometrical triangles drawn from mountain to mountain. That same year I made a trip to the little island of Grimsey, lying off the north coast, immediately above the arctic circle.

In the year 1885 I undertook no long journey, but contented myself with short geological excursions in both the north and the south of the island. But in the two following years, 1886-87, I visited the north-west peninsula of the island, and explored its many fjords. During the summer of 1886 I traversed the coast districts lying on the north side of Breidifjördr, where I found a good deal that was of geological interest—well-marked profiles of basalt formations, deposits of lignite, petrified vegetation, as well as glacial formations and marine terraces. In August of that same year I travelled along the north-east coast of the peninsula, through the so-called Hornstrandir, as far as Cape North (the Horn). The southern portion of that coast had not been visited since the year 1754, when it was traversed by E. Olafsson; the northern portion had never been visited by any traveller. My journey along that coast was the most toilsome of any I have ever undertaken in Iceland. We had wretched weather all the time. The drift-ice had penetrated close in to the shore. The fjords and glens were shrouded in the cold fogs which generally accompany the drift-ice. All August it snowed and rained without intermission; so that we were obliged to quit the tent, and take refuge in the miserable huts of the peasantry. We used up all the provisions we had brought with us, and for several weeks had to live upon half-decayed seafowl, shark's flesh, and such like delicacies of the native inhabitants of the region. When we stumbled upon an occasional bowl of porridge, it came as a veritable feast. We got wet through every day, and had no opportunity to dry our clothes. No wonder, then, that we looked thin and wretched when we returned home.

The inhabitants of these parts of the coast dwell at vast distances apart. The mountain spurs which divide fjord from fjord are lofty, narrow, and very steep, and to climb up and down them entailed severe labour upon both horses and men. In many places the only means of getting up is along mere ribbons of footpath, that wind up the faces of the precipices, and demand the utmost caution in moving along them, whilst the surf rolls in with a thundering roar several hundred feet below. At other times the horses had to scramble over slippery blocks of stone down on the very edge of the sea, both horses and men constantly drenched by the bursting waves. At the most dangerous places we were obliged to unload the horses and carry their loads on our own backs, whilst the horses were led across one by one after us. In the valleys it rained without ceasing . On the tops of the mountains it snowed so heavily that the snow often lay knee-deep, and the horses kept sticking fast in the snow-drifts.

The people who inhabit those tracts have a terribly hard struggle to exist. During one-half of the year the drift-ice lies wedged up against the coast, or drifts close to it. So much of the summer's warmth is consumed in melting the ice that it is always cold and raw during that season, and nearly always excessively damp. For this reason the people experience very great difficulty in drying the small quantity of hay they require for their few domestic animals. Their principal means of subsistence is wild-fowling, a dangerous occupation, frequently costing human lives. It would scarcely be possible to conceive anything more lonely and desolate than a cottage on the Hornstrandir. The wretched hut clings like an eyrie to the face of the steep sea-cliffs, several hundred fathoms above the water. No stranger ever shows his face within sight of it. Often the nearest neighbour lives an entire day's journey distant. The inhabitants are almost entirely ignorant of what goes on in the world, for it is extremely seldom that an odd number of an Icelandic newspaper finds its way into those remote regions.

I devoted the summer of 1887 to the exploration of the north-west fjords of the same peninsula. Travel on that side of the peninsula is beset with well-nigh the same difficulties as on the east side, especially towards the northern extremity, round about Adalvik, west from Cape North. In that part we were unable to take our horses, but were obliged to make our way entirely on foot. That summer those remote northern districts were suffering from famine, and a malignant form of typhus and scurvy. In the widely separated and poverty-stricken huts, where we spent the nights, there was scarcely any food to be had; and unfortunately we were not able to carry much else with us beyond the instruments we needed most. By good fortune we escaped the infection.

To the geologist that coast presents many features of interest. I discovered several deposits of *surtarbrand*, or lignite, and explored the glaciers which stretch down to the sea from Drangajökull.

In the year 1888 I directed my investigations to the southern parts of the interior plateau, more particularly the tracts around Langjökull and Hofsjökull. On that journey I was for the most part favoured with fine weather, and in the districts which I visited there were adequate supplies of grass. My first excursion was to the so-called Thjórsárdalur, where the ruins of twenty thousand homesteads remain as melancholy witnesses of a destructive volcanic outburst in the fourteenth century. Here too there was much to interest a geologist. Thence we travelled beside the Hvítá (White river), up into the interior, where I spent several weeks, for I soon perceived that the existing maps of the districts I was visiting needed considerable revision. Whilst examining the liparite mountains of Kerlingarfjöll, I had the good fortune to discover some exceptionally fine solfataras—in fact, the finest in all Iceland. I also explored the glaciers around Lake Hvítárvatn, the lava-fields of Kjalhraun, and the warm springs at Hveravellir. I made my way home by the north and west roads, and was so fortunate as to discover some hitherto unknown places with fossil plants.

The next year, 1889, I explored the portion of the interior which was least known, namely, the tracts west of Vatnajökull, including the lakes which bear the name Fiskivötn. In that journey I travelled over long distances which had never before been trodden by human foot. Before visiting them, I believed that the lakes of Fiskivötn, like other similar groups in the interior of Iceland, were of glacial origin—depressions lying between ancient moraine ridges. I was, therefore, not a little surprised to discover that the greater part of them were crater lakes, and that they lay ensconced among a large cluster of volcanoes with extensive lava-fields, forming a link of connection between the volcanic regions of the south and the north of the island. To the north and east of these lakes there was nothing but deserts of sand and lava, utterly destitute of vegetation. We had to carry with us every blade of fodder we needed for the horses. I made several long excursions through those deserts, visiting, amongst other places, Lake Thorisvatn, which I found to be a little over 25 square miles in extent. In the course of another excursion I touched Vatnajökull, discovered the sources of the (river) Tungná, and also a long narrow lake, to which I gave the name of Langisjór (Long lake). On my return journey I came across some extremely interesting currents of obsidian lava.

The exploration of the peninsula of Snæfellsnes and the districts at the head of Faxafjord claimed my attention in 1890. There was plenty of scope for geological work. I opened up several fresh fields, discovering, amongst other things, some new beds of liparite, extensive deposits of *nagelflüh,* numerous groups of craters which had never previously been examined by any geologist, warm springs, carbonic acid springs, and similar features. The summer of the following year was occupied with short excursions to the west side of the island, more especially to the neighbourhood of Borgarfjord, where I completed certain investigations which I began in 1890; for instance, observations of warm springs and different glacial deposits and rockstriations.

In 1892 I did no exploring work in Iceland. An illness compelled me to go abroad for the summer. The rest and change, however, restored me to good health.

Next year I worked the county of Vester Skaptafell and the littleknown parts of the interior plateau which fringe the south-west slopes of Vatnajökull. Travelling was anything but easy in that quarter, because of the great irregularities of surface of the lava-streams, the broken and rifted character of the mountain ridges, the want of grass, and the drift-sand. In spite of these drawbacks I was successful in penetrating to the sources of the two streams—the Skaptá and the Hvfrtisfljót—which had never previously been visited. I also was the first explorer to examine the mountainous country north of Fljótshverfi. All these districts, and especially the stretch of country between the Tungná and the Skaptá, are amongst the most interesting in Iceland. I investigated the border glaciers of Mýrdalsjökull and the western side of Vatnajökull, and discovered thirteen hitherto unknown glaciers, as well as took the altitudes of the snow-line and of the edges of the glaciers in many places. But the features of greatest interest were the volcanoes. Amongst other notable discoveries I made in that quarter was a gigantic volcanic fissure (Eldgjá) which ran to a length of nearly twenty miles, with a depth of 400 to 650 feet. This fissure has in three different places ejected streams of lava, which now cover a combined area of 268 square miles. Later on in the summer I explored the chain of craters at Laki, amounting to about one hundred in number. They were the scene of a violent eruption in 1783, which left behind it a lava-stream 220 square miles in extent and having a volume equal to a cube measuring 3 miles along each of its sides. These gigantic outflows of lava have occasioned great changes in the appearance of the country, altering the coast-line and the channels of the rivers. I made a close study of the geological development of this part of Iceland, and embodied the results in a series of maps.

The summer of 1894 was devoted to an examination of the southern flank of Vatnajökull, and that part of the plateau which borders upon the north-east side of the same glacial tract, as well as a portion of the northerly fjords on the east side of the island. For the most part the mountains in the latter region consist of basalt, but there are also a good many dykes of liparite and granophyr. I discovered close upon fifty new deposits of these eruptive rocks. At Lón I studied the gabbro mountains and their relations to other species of rocks. The only places in Iceland where gabbro occurs are the districts adjacent to the south-east corner of Vatnajökull. A great number of large glaciers radiate from the southern flank of Vatnajökull, and the narrow sandy belt of coast between the mountain and the sea is traversed by numerous rivers, conveying considerable volumes of water. I studied the physical conditions of the glaciers, and found that some of them have sensibly increased in dimensions within his toric times, as well as moved nearer down to the sea. On the plateau to the north-east of Vatnajökull I investigated other glaciers, as well as discovered some new lakes and surveyed certain of the less-known districts.

In the following summer I bent my steps towards the extreme north-east of the island, the peninsulas of Melrakkaslétta and Langanes, and the portions of the plateau which lie immediately behind them. These districts had never previously been surveyed; and they revealed several features of geological importance. For instance, I ascertained that the more recent volcanic formations of Iceland, extend very much further to the east than had hitherto been supposed. Here again I discovered and measured some new volcanoes of lavastreams. In the interior I found several chains of tuff hills, as well as rivers and lakes, which had never been shown on any map. Towards the end of that summer's journey I fell ill of typhus, and had to stay some time in a peasant's house. By the time I had recovered and got back my normal strength, autumn was come, and the snow and frost made it impossible to continue my work. However, I had pretty nearly done all I had planned to do that year.

I next directed my attention, in the summer of 1896, to the northern parts of the island, namely the mountainous peninsulas between Skjálfandi and Húnaflói, and undertook a longer excursion to Arnarfellsjökull (or Hofsjökull), in the interior, for the purpose of exploring districts there which were but little known including the glaciers. In that quarter the plateau consists for the most part of stony deserts without a vestige of grass, so that we were obliged to carry all the hay for the horses with us.

In the summer of 1897 I laboured in the southern lowlands of the island, in special in those districts which were the scene of the violent seismic disturbances of the preceding autumn. My principal object was to gather details that would serve as a basis for a general view of the geology of that region, in the hope that I might thus trace out the cause of the earthquake tremors, and ascertain their connection with the fundamental structure of the island, as also to collect materials for a descriptive account of the disturbance itself. Towards the close of the summer I made an excursion to the north of the island, and travelled through the *syssel* (county) of Húnavatn, studying its geology, especially its glacial deposits. In the last summer, 1898, I explored the interior plateau north-west of Langjökull and the mountains behind the Borgarfjord.

From all this it will be seen that I have pretty well travelled over the whole of Iceland—the interior plateau, the inhabited and cultivated parts, the promontories, peninsulas, and fjords, and I have carried through my original plan of making a geographical and geological reconnaissance of the entire country.

NORWAY

THE SAGA OF SIGURD THE CRUSADER [1]

(1107-11)

ANONYMOUS

AFTER King Magnus Barefoot's fall, his sons, Eystein, Sigurd and Olaf took the kingdom of Norway. Eystein got the northern and Sigurd the southern parts of the country. King Olaf was then four or five years old and the third part of the country which he had was under the management of his two brothers. King Sigurd was chosen king when he was thirteen or fourteen years old, and Eystein was a year older. When King Magnus's sons were chosen kings, the men who had followed Skopte Ogmundsson returned home. Some had been to Jerusalem, some to Constantinople; and there they had made themselves renowned, and they had many kinds of novelties to talk about. By these extraordinary tidings many men in Norway were incited to the same expedition. . . . Then these Northmen desired much that one of the two kings, either Eystein or Sigurd, should go as commander of the troop which was preparing for this expedition. The kings agreed to this, and carried on the equipment at their common expense. Many great men, both of the lendermen and bonders, took part in this enterprise; and when all was ready for the journey, it was determined that Sigurd should go, and Eystein, in the mean time, should rule the kingdom upon their joint account.

Four years after the fall of King Magnus, King Sigurd sailed with his fleet of sixty ships from Norway. So says Thorarin Stutfeld:

A young king just and kind,
People of loyal mind:
Such brave men soon agree—
To distant lands they sail with glee.
To the distant Holy Land,
A brave and pious band,
Magnificent and gay,
In sixty long ships glide away.

King Sigurd sailed in autumn to England, where Henry, son of William the Bastard, was then king, and Sigurd remained with him all winter. So says Einar Skuleson:

The king is on the waves!
The storm he boldly braves.

[1] From *The Heimskringla,* translated by Samuel Laing.

His ocean steed,
With winged speed,
O'er the white-flashing surges,
To England's coast he urges;
And there he stays the winter o'er:
More gallant king ne'er trod that shore.

In spring King Sigurd and his fleet sailed westward to Valland,[1] and in autumn came to Galicia,[2] where he staid the second winter. So says Einar Skuleson:

Our king, whose land so wide
No kingdom stands beside,
In Jacob's land next winter spent,
On holy things intent;
And I have heard the royal youth
Cut off an earl who swerved from truth.
Our brave king will endure no ill—
The hawks with him will get their fill.

It went thus: The earl who ruled over the land made an agreement with King Sigurd, that he should provide King Sigurd and his men a market at which they could purchase victuals all the winter; but this he did not fulfil longer than to about Yule. It began then to be difficult to get food and necessaries, for it is a poor barren land. Then King Sigurd with a great body of men went against a castle which belonged to the earl; and the earl fled from it, having but few people. King Sigurd took there a great deal of victuals and of other booty, which he put on board his ships, and then made ready and proceeded westward to Spain. It so fell out, as the King was sailing past Spain, that some pirates who were cruising for plunder met him with a fleet of galleys, and King Sigurd attacked them. This was his first battle with heathen men; and he won it, and took eight galleys from them. So says Halldor Skualldre:

Bold vikings, not slow
To the death-fray go,
Meet our Norse king by chance,
And their galleys advance.
The bold vikings lost
Many a man of their host,
And eight galleys too,
With cargo and crew.

[1] The west of France. [2] North-west Spain.

Thereafter King Sigurd sailed against a castle called Sintre,[1] and fought another battle. This castle is in Spain, and was occupied by many heathens, who from thence plundered Christian people. King Sigurd took the castle, and killed every man in it, because they refused to be baptized; and he got there an immense booty. So sings Halldor Skualldre:

From Spain I have much news to tell
Of what our generous king befell.
And first he routs the viking crew,
At Cintra next the heathens slew;
The men he treated as God's foes,
Who dared the true faith to oppose.
No man he spared who would not take
The Christian faith for Jesus' sake.

After this King Sigurd sailed with his fleet to Lisbon, which is a great city in Spain, half Christian and half heathen; for there lies the division between Christian Spain and heathen Spain, and all the districts which lie west of the city are occupied by heathens. There King Sigurd had his third battle with the heathens, and gained the victory, and with it a great booty. So says Halldor Skualldre:

The son of kings on Lisbon's plains
A third and bloody battle gains.
He and his Norsemen boldly land,
Running their stout ships on the strand.

Then King Sigurd sailed westwards along heathen Spain, and brought up at a town called Alkassi; and here he had his fourth battle with the heathens, and took the town, and killed so many people that the town was left empty. They got there also immense booty. So says Halldor Skualldre:

A fourth great battle, I am told,
Our Norse king and his people hold
At Alkassi; and here again
The victory fell to our Norsemen.

And also this verse:

I heard that through the town he went,
And heathen widows' wild lament
Resounded in the empty halls;
For every townsman flies or falls.

[1] Cintra.

King Sigurd then proceeded on his voyage, and came to Niorfa Sound; and in the Sound he was met by a large viking force, and the king gave them battle: and this was his fifth engagement with heathens since the time he left Norway. So says Halldor Skualldre:

> Ye moistened your dry swords with blood,
> As through Niorfa Sound ye stood:
> The screaming raven got a feast,
> As ye sailed onward to the East.

King Sigurd then sailed eastward along the coast of Serkland,[1] and came to an island there called Formentara. There a great many heathen Moors had taken up their dwelling in a cave, and had built a strong stone wall before its mouth. It was high up to climb to the wall, so that whoever attempted to ascend was driven back with stones or missile weapons. They harried the country all round, and carried all their booty to their cave. King Sigurd landed on this island, and went to the cave; but it lay in a precipice, and there was a high winding path to the stone wall, and the precipice above projected over it. The heathens defended the stone wall, and were not afraid of the Northmen's arms; for they could throw stones, or shoot down upon the Northmen under their feet: neither did the Northmen, under such circumstances, dare to mount up. The heathens took their clothes and other valuable things, carried them out upon the wall, spread them out before the Northmen, shouted, and defied them, and upbraided them as cowards. Then Sigurd fell upon this plan: he had two ship's boats, such as we call barks, drawn up the precipice right above the mouth of the cave; and had thick ropes fastened round the stem, stern, and hull of each. In these boats as many men went as could find room, and then the boats were lowered by the ropes down in front of the mouth of the cave; and the men in the boats shot with stones and missiles into the cave, and the heathens were thus driven from the stone wall. Then Sigurd with his troops climbed up the precipice to the foot of the stone wall, which they succeeded in breaking down, so that they came into the cave. Now the heathens fled within the stone wall that was built across the cave; on which the King ordered large trees to be brought to the cave, made a great pile in the mouth of it, and set fire to the wood. When the fire and smoke got the upper hand, some of the heathens lost their lives in it; some fled; some fell by the hands of the Northmen; and part were killed, part burned; and the Northmen made the greatest booty they had got on all their expeditions. So says Halldor Skualldre:

[1] North Africa.

Formentara lay
In the victor's way;
His ships' stems fly
To victory.
The bluemen there
Must fire bear,
And Norsemen's steel
At their hearts feel.

And also thus:

'Twas a feat of renown—
The boat lowered down,
With a boat's crew brave,
In front of the cave;
While up the rock scaling,
And comrades up trailing,
The Norsemen gain,
And the bluemen are slain.

And also Thorarin Stuttfeld says:

The king's men up the mountain's side
Drag two boats from the ocean's tide:
The two boats lay,
Like hill-wolves gray.
Now o'er the rock in ropes they're swinging,
Well manned, and death to bluemen bringing:
They hang before
The robbers' door.

Thereafter King Sigurd proceeded on his expedition, and came to an island called Ivitsa [Ivica], and had there his seventh battle, and gained a victory. So says Halldor Skualldre:

His ships at Ivica now ride,
The king's whose fame spreads far and wide;
And here the bearers of the shield
Their arms again in battle wield.

Thereafter King Sigurd came to an island called Minorca, and held there his eighth battle with heathen men, and gained the victory. So says Halldor Skualldre:

On green Minorca's plains
The eighth battle now he gains:
Again the heathen foe
Falls at the Norse king's blow.

In spring King Sigurd came to Sicily, and remained a long time there. There was then a Duke Roger in Sicily, who received the King kindly, and invited him to a feast. King Sigurd came to it with a great retinue, and was splendidly entertained. Every day Duke Roger stood at the company's table, doing service to the King; but the seventh day of the feast, when the people had come to table, and had wiped their hands, King Sigurd took the Duke by the hand, led him up to the high seat, and saluted him with the title of king; and gave the right that there should be always a king over the dominion of Sicily, although before there had only been earls or dukes over that country.

In summer King Sigurd sailed across the Greek sea to Palestine, and came to Acre, where he landed, and went by land to Jerusalem. Now when Baldwin, King of Palestine, heard that King Sigurd would visit the city, he let valuable clothes be brought and spread upon the road, and the nearer to the city the more valuable; and said, "Now ye must know that a celebrated king from the northern part of the earth is come to visit us; and many are the gallant deeds and celebrated actions told of him, therefore we shall receive him well; and in doing so we shall also know his magnificence and power. If he ride straight on to the city, taking little notice of these splendid preparations, I will conclude that he has enough of such things in his own kingdom; but, on the other hand, if he rides off the road, I shall not think so highly of his royal dignity at home." Now King Sigurd rides to the city with great state; and when he saw this magnificence, he rode straight forward over the clothes, and told all his men to do the same. King Baldwin received him particularly well, and rode with him all the way to the river Jordan, and then back to the city of Jerusalem. Einar Skuleson speaks thus of it:

Good reason has the scald to sing
The generous temper of the king,
Whose sea-cold keel from Northern waves
Ploughs the blue sea that green isles laves.
At Acre scarce were we made fast,
In holy ground our anchors cast,
When the King made a joyful morn
To all who toil with him had borne.

And again he sang:

To Jerusalem he came,
He who loves war's noble game,
(The scald no greater monarch finds
Beneath the heaven's wide all of winds)
All sin and evil from him flings
In Jordan's wave: for all his sins
(Which all must praise) he pardon wins.

King Sigurd staid a long time in the land of Jerusalem in autumn, and in the beginning of winter.

King Baldwin made of magnificent feast for King Sigurd and many of his people, and gave him many holy relics. By the orders of King Baldwin and the patriarch, there was taken a splinter off the holy cross; and on this holy relic both made, oath, that this wood was of the holy cross upon which God himself had been tortured. Then this holy relic was given to King Sigurd; with the condition that he, and twelve other men with him, should swear to promote Christinity with all his power, and erect an archbishop's seat in Norway if he could; and also that the cross should be kept where the holy King Olaf reposed, and that he should introduce tithes, and also pay them himself. After this King Sigurd returned to his ships at Acre; and then King Baldwin prepared to go to Syria, to a town called Saet, which some think had been Sidon. This castle, which belonged to the heathens, he wished to conquer, and lay under the Christians. On this expedition King Sigurd accompanied him with all his men, and sixty ships; and after the Kings and besieged the town some time it surrendered, and they took possession of it, and of a great treasure of money; and their men found other booty. King Sigurd made a present of his share to King Baldwin. So says Halldor Skualldre:

He who for wolves provides the feast
Seized on the city in the east,
The heathen nest; and honour drew,
And gold to give, from those he slew.

Einar Skuleson also tells of it:

The Norsemen's king, the scalds, relate,
Has ta'en the heathen town of Saet:
The slinging engine, with dread noise,
Gables and roofs with stones destroys.
The town wall totters too—it falls;
The Norsemen mount the blackened walls.

He who stains red the raven's bill.
Has won—the town lies at his will.

Thereafter King Sigurd went to his ships, and made ready to leave Palestine. They sailed north to the island of Cyprus; and King Sigurd staid there awhile, and then went to the Greek country, and came to the land with all his fleet at Engilsness. Here he lay still for a fortnight, although every day it blew a breeze for going before the wind to the north; but Sigurd would wait a side wind, so that the sails might stretch fore and aft in the ship; for in all his sails there was silk joined in, before and behind in the sail, and neither those before nor those behind the ships could see the slightest appearance of this, if the vessel was before the wind; so they would rather wait a side wind.

When King Sigurd sailed into Constantinople, he steered near the land. Over all the land there are burghs, castles, country towns, the one upon the other without interval. There from the land one could see into the bights of the sails; and the sails stood so close beside each other, that they seemed to form one inclosure. All the people turned out to see King Sigurd sailing past. The Emperor Alexius had also heard of King Sigurd's expedition, and ordered the city port of Constantinople to be opened, which is called the Gold Tower, through which the Emperor rides when he has been long absent from Constantinople, or has made a campaign in which he has been victorious. The Emperor had precious cloths spread out from the Gold Tower to Loktiar, which is the name of the Emperor's most splendid hall. King Sigurd ordered his men to ride in great state into the city, and not to regard all the new things they might see; and this they did. The Emperor sent signers and stringed instruments to meet them; and with this great splendour King Sigurd and his followers were received into Constantinople. It is told that King Sigurd had his horse shod with golden shoes before he rode into the city, and managed so that one of the shoes came off in the street, but that none of his men should regard it. When King Sigurd came to the magnificent hall, everything was in the grandest style; and when King Sigurd's men had come to their seats, and were ready to drink, the Emperor's messengers came into the hall, bearing between them purses of gold and silver, which they said the Emperor had sent to King Sigurd; but the King did not look upon it, but told his men to divide it among themselves. When the messengers returned to the Emperor, and told him this, he said, "This king must be very powerful and rich not to care for such things , or even give a word of thanks for them"; and ordered them to return with great chests filled with gold. They come again to King Sigurd, and say, "These gifts and presents are sent thee from the Emperor." King Sigurd said, "This is a great and handsome treasure, my men; divide it among you." The messengers return and tell this to the Emperor. He replies, "This king must either exceed other kings in power and wealth, or he has not so much understanding as a king ought to have. Go now thou the third time, and carry him the costliest purple, and these chests with ornaments of gold": to which he added two gold rings. Now the messengers went again to King Sigurd, and told him the Emperor had sent him this great treasure. Then he stood up, and took the rings, and put them on his hand; and the King made a beautiful oration in Greek, in which he thanked the Emperor in many fine expressions for all this honour and magnificence, but divided the treasure again very equitably among his men. King Sigurd remained here some time. The Emperor Alexius sent his men to him to ask if he would rather accept from the Emperor six skifpound [one ton] of gold, or would have the Emperior give the games in his honour which the Emperor was used to have played at the Padreimr. [1] King Sigurd preferred the games, and the messenger said the spectacle would not cost the emperor less than the money offered. Then the Emperor prepared for the games, when were held in the usual way: but this day every thing went on better for the King than for the Queen; for the Queen has always the half part in the games, and their men, therefore, always strive against each other in all games. The Greeks accordingly think that when the King's men win more games at the Padreimr than the Queen's, the King will gain the victory when he goest into battle. People who have been in Constantinople tell that the Padreimr is thus constructed: A high wall surrounds a flat plain, which may be compared to a round bare Thing-place,[2] with earthen banks all around at the stone wall, on which banks the spectators sit; but the games themselves are in the flat plain. There are many sorts of old events represented concerning the Asers, Volsungers, and Giukungers, in these games; and all the figures are cast in copper, or metal, with so great art that they appear to be living things; and to the people it appears as if they were really present in the games. The games themselves are so artfully and carefully managed, that people appear to be riding in the air, and at them also are used shot-fire, and all kinds of harpplaying, singing, and music instruments.

It is related that King Sigurd one day was to give the Emperor a feast, and he ordered his men to provide sumptuously all that was necessary for the entertainment; and when all things were provided which are suitable for an entertainment given by a great personage to persons of high dignity, King Sigurd ordered his men to go to the street in the city where fire-wood was

[1] Hippodrome. [2] Place of public assembly.

sold, as they would require a great quantity to prepare the feast. They said the King need not be afraid of wanting fire-wood, for every day many loads were brought into the town. When it was necessary, however, to have fire-wood, it was found that it was all sold, which they told the King. He replied, "Go and try if you can get walnuts. They will answer as well as wood for fuel." They went and got as many as they needed. Now came the Emperor, and his grandees and court, and sat down to table. All was very splended; and King Sigurd received the Emperor with great state, and entertained him magnificently. When the Queen and the Emperor found that nothing was wanting, she sent some persons to inquire what they had used for fire-wood; and they came to a house filled with walnuts, and they came back and told the Queen. "Truly," said she, "this is a magnificent King, who spares no expense where his honour is concerned." She had contrived this to try what they would do when they could get no firewood to dress their feast with.

King Sigurd soon after prepared for his return home. He gave the Emperor all his ships; and the valuable figure-heads which were on the King's ships were set up in Peter's church, where they have since been to be seen. The Emperor gave the King many horses and guides to conduct him through all his dominions, and appointed markets for him in his territories at which he could buy food and drink. Then King Sigurd left Constantinople; but many Northmen remained, and went into the Emperor's pay. Then King Sigurd travelled from Bulgaria, and through Hungary, Pannonia, Suabia, and Bavaria. In Suabia he met the Roman Emperor Lotharius, who received him in the most friendly way, gave him guides through his dominions, and had markets established for him at which he could purchase all he required. When King Sigurd came to Sleswick in Denmark, Earl Eilif made a sumptuous feast for him; and it was then midsummer. In Heidaby he met the Danish King Nicolaus, who received him in the most friendly way, made a great enteratinment for him, accompanied him north to Jutland, and gave him a ship provided with every thing needful. From thence the King returned to Norway, and was joyfully welcomed on his return to his kingdom. It was the common talk among the people, that none had ever made so honourable a journey from Norway as this of King Sigurd. He was twenty years of age, and had been three years on these travels.

THE FIRST CROSSING OF GREENLAND [1]

(1888)

FRIDTJOF NANSEN

(1861-1930)

[*It was in the summer of 1882 that Nansen, on board a Norwegian sealer which was caught in the ice off the east coast of Greenland, first conceived the idea of crossing Greenalnd on ski from east coast to west coast. Six years later he put the idea into action. With Otto Sverdrup, Oluf Dietrichson, Kristian Kristiansen Trana, and two Lapps, Balto and Ravna, Nansen, in May 1888, left Leith for Iceland, there to join the Norwegian sealer "Jason." Landing on the east coast of Greenland, they began the ascent of the inland ice on August 15, and on September 28 successfully reached the west coast at Ameralikfjord.*]

On the morning of August 15 the boats were hauled up to their last resting-place, a little cleft in the rocks, which promised them a tolerable degree of shelter and protection. We placed them carefully with their keels uppermost, blocked them with stones to keep them steady in a wind, and it is to be hoped they are still there just as we left them. But it is quite possible, of course, that the Eskimo have already found them, and appropriated the iron parts and fittings of the boats and many other wonderful things. If this be so, it is not easy to imagine what kind of supernatural beings they have taken us for, who have thus abandoned our valuable possessions and so mysteriously disappeared. . . .

As it was now too warm in the daytime, and the snow consequently soft, we determined to do our hauling work at night. So at nine in the evening the sledges were finally loaded and we started on our way for Christianshaab.

At first our progress was slow. The snow came nearly down to the sea, so we could begin hauling at once; but the gradient was steep, and we had to put three men to each sledge. Our loads were heavy, too, each sledge weighing somewhat more than two hundred-weight. When we had got so high that we could think of dragging them singly, we redistributed the weight, so that four of them were about two hundred pounds; and the fifth, which had two to pull it, weighed about double as much. This first night we had fine weather, and just enough frost to make the snow hard. The ground was favourable except for the steepness of the incline, and of crevasses we as yet found none. Towards morning, however, we reached some unpleasant ice, which was full of depressions and irregularities, but had at the same time a hardish surface

[1] From *The First Crossing of Greenland*, translated from the Norwegian by H. M. Gepp.

on which the sledges travelled well. After a first stage of some two or three miles we pitched our tent at a height of about five hundred feet. It was a pleasure almost divine to get half a dozen cups of good hot tea with condensed milk and then to creep into our sleeping-bags after this our first spell of sledge-hauling. . . . Just as we were proposing to go off to sleep it was dicovered that we had left our only piece of Gruyère cheese at the place where we had halted for our midnight dinner. To leave this cheese behind was scarcely to be thought of, and yet to fetch it, tired as we were, was also too much to be expected. But then Dietrichson came forward and offered to go and get it, declaring that there was nothing he should like so much, as it would give him a little morning walk before he went to bed, and a look round besides, which would be to the advantage of his map. I remember that it was with a feeling of simple admiration that I saw him start gaily off on his errand, and that I could not myself conceive that anyone could find pleasure in such an expedition after the work we had had already.

On the evening of the day we broke up again and went on over ice of the same rough kind. Towards midnight it grew so dark that we could no longer see, so at eleven o'clock we encamped, made some chocolate, and waited for daylight. Before we started off again we took a photograph of the tent and the ice to the south stretching downwards towards the sea.

We now got on to some smoother ice, but the snow grew looser and crevasses began to appear, though the first were negotiable without any great difficulty. Towards morning it began to rain; as the hours passed things grew worse and worse, and existence to us less joyous. We all got into our waterproofs, of course, but waterproof these garments were certainly not, and the rain poured down upon us till every rag we had on was wet through. There was no chance of our getting chilled or frozen, though there was a moderately sharp wind blowing, as our work kept us warm, and we had to put forth all our strength. But to feel one's clothes cling to one's limbs and hinder every movement is not a state of things to make hard work pleasanter. We kept on till past noon; the ascent was not too steep to allow of the sledges being brought up with tolerable ease, but we had to put two men to each of them. Crevasses were plentiful, so we had to go warily. We could not rope ourselves together, as that made the hauling work too difficult, so we had to be content with attaching ourselves to the sledges by our strong tow-ropes, which were again made fast to the stout hauling-strap and belt we each wore. If we went through the snow-bridges which crossed the fissures, we were left hanging securely, as long as the sledge did not follow us, which, owing to its length, was not very likely out happen. As a mater of fact, we fell through rarely, and then only to the armpits, so that by the help of our staffs we were able to get out again without other assistance. . . .

This day we did not stop till early noon, when we encamped on flat ledge between two huge crevasses, the weather being now altogether impracticable. . . .

For three whole days, from noon on August 17 to the morning of August 20, we were now confined to the tent by a violent storm and uninter rupted rain. . . . The greater part of the time we spent in sleep, beginning with an unbroken spell of twenty-four hours. Rations were reduced to a minimum, the idea being that as there was no work to do, there was no need for much food, though we had to take just enough to keep ourselves alive, the whole consumption amounting to about one full meal a day. . . . Our waking moments were . . . perhaps chiefly spent in gazing at the tent roof and listening to the rain splashing overhead and the wind tearing and shrieking round the walls and among the guy-ropes. It is pleasant, no doubt, to lie snugly housed while tempests rave outside, but there is also no gainsaying that we longed to hear the rain beat a little less pitilessly and the wind howl a little more gently round our tent.

At last, on the morning of August 20, the weather so far improved that we could resume our journey, and in preparation we fortified ourselves with a supply of hot lentil soup, to make up for the famine rations of the three preceding days.

The ice was still much fissured, and as we were about to attempt the ascent of a ridge which lay in front of us, we found the crevasses so numerous and formidable that there was no possibility of passing them. Here they ran not only parallel, but also across each other, a combination before which one is completely powerless. We had to turn back and try more to the north, and sitting on the sledges we slid down the slope again between the crevasses. Below we found the ice less broken and the gradient less steep. Progress was here comparatively easy, and at places we could even haul our sledges singly, Sverdrup and I going on in front with the heaviest to choose the route. . . .

Towards eight o'clock that evening the sky looked as if it would clear, and as well felt sure that this would bring us frost, we stopped and camped at once to wait till the snow got harder. Next morning August 21, we turned out at four. The sky was clear, and though the thermometer showed that there was still a certain amount of warmth in the air, the crust on the snow was nevertheless sufficiently hard to bear us. The gradient was still steep, and the crevasses large and numerous, but we pushed on fast and without mishap in the most glorious weather, keeping at work till well into the morning, when the blazing sun began to make the snow softer and softer. This work under such conditions is terribly exhausting, and we suffered from an unquenchable thirst. We had already passed the limit of drinking-water, and were destined to find no more till we reached the west side. All we get is what we can melt by the warmth of our own bodies in the tin flasks which we carry at the breast inside our clothes and sometimes next the very skin. Few of us are long-suffering enough to wait till the snow is turned to water, but as it grows a little moist we suck out the few drops which it produces.

About eleven we had reached the top of a ridge which we had set as our goal for the day's march, a distance of some three or four miles. Beyond, the ice sloped gently inwards, and was particularly free from crevasses. So we thought we must have already overcome the first difficulty of our ascent, and felt justified in marking the occasion by a festal meal, distinguished by extra rations of cheese, jam, and oatmeal biscuits. We were now all but 3000 feet above the sea, and could see 'nunataks'[1] here and there in front of us, while we already had a whole row of them alongside us to the north.

At two o'clock on the morning of August 22 we went on again. There had been nine degrees of frost in the night and the snow was as hard as iron, but the surface was exceedingly rough, so rough indeed that a sledge occasionally upset. By nine o'clock the sun had such power that we were obliged to halt after having again accomplished a stage of three or four miles. . . .

We started off again the same evening about nine o'clock. The ice was still very rough; we had now to haul our sledges up on to the crests of the steep waves, now to let them rush down into the hollows. The strain on the upper part of the body was very trying, and Balto was quite right in saying that our shoulders felt as if they were burnt by the rope.

But if we often suffered a good deal in the way of work, we had full compensation during these nights in the wonderful features of the sky, for even this tract of the earth has its own beauty. When the ever-changing northern lights filled the heavens to the south with their fairylike display—a display, perhaps, more brilliant in these regions than elsewhere—our toils and pains were, I think, for the most part forgotten. Or when the moon rose and set off upon her silent journey through the fields of stars, her rays glittering on the crest of every ridge of ice, and bathing the whole of the dead frozen desert in a flood of silver light, the spirit of peace reigned supreme and life itself became beauty. I am convinced that these night marches of ours over the "Inland ice" left a deep and ineffaceable impression upon the minds of all who took part in them. . . .

[1] Crags peeping through the ice.

For days [1]—I might almost say weeks—we toiled across an interminable flat desert of snow; one day began and ended like another, and all were characterised by nothing but a wearisome, wearing uniformity which no one who has not experienced the like will easily realise. Flatness and whiteness were the two features of this ocean of snow; in the day we could see three things only—the sun, the snowfield, and ourselves. We looked like a diminutive black line feebly traced upon an infinite expanse of white. There was no break or change in our horizon, no object to rest the eye upon, and no point by which to direct the course. We had to steer by a diligent use of the compass, and keep our line as well as possible by careful watching of the sun and repeated glances back at the four men following and the long track which the caravan left in the snow. We passed from one horizon to another, but our advance brought us no change. We knew to a certain extent where we were, and that we must endure the monotony for a long time to come. . . .

As the middle of September approached, we hoped every day to arrive at the beginning of the western slope. To judge from our reckoning it could not be far off, though I had a suspicion that this reckoning was some way ahead of our observations. These, however, I purposely omitted to work out, as the announcement that we had not advanced as far as we supposed would have been a bitter disappointment to most of the party. Their expectations of soon getting the first sight of land on the western side were at their height, and they pushed on confidently, while I kept my doubts to myself and left the reckoning as it was.

On September 11 the fall of the ground was just appreciable, the theodolite showing it to be about a third of a degree. On September 12 I entered in my diary that "we are all in capital spirits, and hope for a speedy change for the better, Balto and Dietrichson being even confident that we shall see land to-day. They will need some patience, however, as we are still 9000 feet above the sea" (we were really about 8250 feet that day), "but they will not have to wait very long. This morning our reckoning made us out to be about seventy-five miles from bare land, and the ground is falling well and continuously." The next day or two the slope grew more and more distinct, but the incline was not regular, as the ground fell in great undulations, like those we had had to climb in the course of our ascent.

On September 14 the reckoning showed that it was only about thirty-five miles to land. But even now we could see nothing, which the Lapps thought was very suspicious. Ravna's face began to get longer and longer, and one evening about this time he said, "I am an old Lapp, and a silly old fool, too;

[1] It was September now.

I don't believe we shall ever get to the coast." I only answered, "That's quite right, Ravna; you are a silly old fool." Whereupon he burst out laughing: "So it's quite true, is it—Ravna is a silly old fool?" and he evidently felt quite consoled by this doubtful compliment. These expressions of anxiety on Ravna's part were very common.

Another day Balto suddenly broke out: "But how on earth can any one tell how far it is from one side to the other, when no one has been across?" It was of course, difficult to make him understand the mode of calculation; but, with his usual intelligence, he seemed to form some idea of the truth one day when I showed him the process on the map. The best consolation we could give Balto and Ravna was to laugh at them well for their cowardice.

The very pronounced fall of the ground on September 17 certainly was a comfort to us all, and when the thermometer that evening just failed to reach zero we found the temperature quite mild, and felt that we had entered the abodes of summer again. It was now only nine miles or so to land by our reckoning.

It was this very day two months that we had left the *Jason*. This happened to be one of our butter-mornings, the very gladdest mornings of our existence at the time, and breakfast in bed with a good cup of tea brought the whole party into an excellent humour. It was the first time, too, for a long while that the walls of our tent had not been decorated with fringes of hoar-frost. As we were at breakfast we were no little astonished to hear, as we thought, the twittering of a bird outside; but the sound soon stopped, and we were not at all certain of its reality. But as we were starting again after our one o'clock dinner that day we suddenly became aware of twitterings in the air, and, as we stopped, sure enough we saw a snow-bunting come flying after us. It wandered round us two or three times, and plainly showed signs of a wish to sit upon one of our sledges. But the necessary audacity was not forthcoming, and it finally settled on the snow in front for a few moments, before it flew away for good with another encouraging little twitter.

Welcome, indeed, this little bird was. It gave us a friendly greeting from the land we were sure must now be near. . . . We blessed it for its cheering song, and with warmer hearts and renewed strength we confidently went on our way, in spite of the uncomfortable knowledge that the ground was not falling by any means so rapidly as it should have done. In this way, however, things were much better next day, September 18; the cold consistently decreased, and life grew brighter and brighter. In the evening, too, the wind sprang up from the south-east, and I hoped we should really get a fair sailing breeze at last. We had waited for it long enough, and sighed for it too, in spite of Balto's assurances that this sailing on the snow would never come to anything.

In the course of the night the wind freshened, and in the morning there was a full breeze blowing. Though, as usual, there was no great keenness to undertake the rigging and lashing together of the sledges in the cold wind, we determined, of course, to set about the business at once. Kristiansen joined Sverdrup and me with his sledge, and we rigged the two with the tent-floor, while the other three put their two sledges together.

All this work, especially the lashing, was anything but delightful, but the cruellest part of it all was that while we were in the middle of it the wind showed signs of dropping. It did not carry out its threat, however, and at last both vessels were ready to start. I was immensely excited to see how our boat would turn out, and whether the one sail was enough to move both the sledges. It was duly hoisted and made fast, and there followed a violent wrenching of the whole machine, but during the operations it had got somewhat buried in the snow and proved immovable. There was enough wrenching and straining of the mast and tackle to pull the whole to pieces, so we harnessed ourselves in front with all speed. We tugged with a will and got our boat off, but no sooner had she begun to move than the wind brought her right on to us, and over we all went into the snow. We were soon up again for another try, but with the same result; no sooner are we on our legs than we are carried off them again by the shock from behind.

This process having been gone through a certain number of times, we saw plainly that all was not right. So we arranged that one of us should stand in front on his *ski* and steer by means of a staff fixed between the two sledges, like the pole of a carriage, leaving himself to be pushed along by his vessel, and only keeping it at a respectful distance from his heels. The other two members of the crew were to come behind on their *ski,* either holding on to the sledges or following as best they could.

We now finally got under way, and Sverdrup, who was to take the first turn at steering, had no sooner got the pole under his arm than our vessel rushed furiously off before the wind. I attached myself behind at the side, riding on my *ski* and holding on by the back of one of the sledges as well as I could. Kristiansen thought this looked much too risky work, and came dragging along behind on his *ski* alone.

Our ship flew over the waves and drifts of snow with a speed that almost took one's breath away. The sledges struggled and groaned, and were strained in every joint as they were whirled over the rough surface, and often indeed they simply jumped from the crest on one wave on to another. I had quite enough to do to hang on behind and keep myself upright on the *ski*. Then the ground began to fall at a sharper angle than any we had had yet. The pace grew hotter and hotter, and the sledges scarcely seemed to touch the snow. Right in front of me was sticking out the end of a *ski* which was lashed fast across the two sledges for the purpose of keeping them together. I could not do anything to get this *ski*-end out of the way, and it caused me a great deal of trouble, as it stuck out across the points of my own *ski*, and was always coming into collision with them. It was worst of all when we ran along the edge of a drift, for my *ski* would then get completely jammed, and I lost all control over them. For a long time I went on thus in a continual struggle with this hopeless *ski*-end, while Sverdrup stood in front gaily steering and thinking we were both sitting comfortably on behind. Our ship rushed on faster and faster; the snow flew round us and behind us in a cloud, which gradually hid the others from our view.

Then an ice-axe which lay on the top of our cargo began to get loose and promised to fall off. So I worked myself carefully forward, and was just engaged in making the axe fast when we rode on to a nasty drift. This brought the projecting *ski*-end just across my legs, and there I lay at once gazing after the ship and its sail, which were flying on down the slope, and already showing dimly through the drifting snow. It made one quite uncomfortable to see how quickly they diminished in size. I felt very foolish to be left lying there, but at last I recovered myself and set off bravely in the wake of the vessel, which was by this time all but out of sight. To my great delight I found that, thanks to the wind, I could get on at a very decent pace alone.

I had not gone far before I found the ice-axe, in trying to secure which I had come to grief. A little further on I caught sight of another dark object, this time something square, lying in the snow. This was a box which contained some of our precious meat-chocolate, and which of course was not to be abandoned in this way. After this I strode gaily on for a long time in the sledge-track, with the chocolate box under one arm and the ice-axe and my staff under the other. Then I came upon several more dark objects lying straight in my path. These proved to be a fur jacket belonging to me, and no less than three pemmican boxes. I had now much more than I could carry, so the only thing to be done was to sit down and wait for succour from the others who were following behind. All that could be seen of our proud ship and its said was a little square patch far away across the snowfield. She was going ahead in the same direction as before, but as I watched I suddenly saw her brought up to the wind, the tin boxes of her cargo glitter in the sun, and her sail fall. Just then, Kristiansen came up with me, followed not long after by the other vessel. To them we handed over some of our loose boxes, but just as we were stowing them away Balto discovered that they had lost no less than three pemmican tins. These were much too valuable to be left behind, so the crew had to go back and look for them.

Meanwhile Kristiansen and I started off again, each with a tin box under his arm, and soon overtook Sverdrup. We now sat down to wait for the others, which was not an agreeable job in this bitter wind.

Sverdrup told us that he had sailed merrily off from the very start, had found the whole thing go admirably, and thought all the time that we two were sitting comfortably on behind. He could not see behind him for the sail, but after a long while he began to wonder why there was not more noise among the passengers in the stern. So he made an approach to a conversation, but got no answer. A little further on he tried again and louder, but with the same result. Then he called louder still,and lastly began to shout at the top of his voice, but still there was no response. This state of things needed further investigation; so he brought his boat up to the wind, went round behind the sail to see what was the matter, and was not a little concerned to find that both his passengers had disappeared. He tried to look back along his course through the drifting snow, and he thought he could see a black spot far away behind. This must have been my insignificant figure sitting upon the lost tin boxes. Then he lowered his sail, which was not an easy matter in the wind that was blowing, and contented himself to wait for us.

We had to sit a long time before the others caught us up again. We could just see the vessel through the snow, but her sail was evidently not up, and of her crew there was not a sign. At last we caught sight of three small specks far away up the slope and the glitter of the sun on the tins they were carrying. Presently the sail was hoisted, and it was not long before they joined us.

We now lashed the sledges better together and made the cargo thoroughly fast, in order to escape a repetition of this performance. Then we rigged up some ropes behind, to which the crew could hold or tie themselves, and thus be towed comfortably along. In this way we got on splendidly, and never in my life have I had a more glorious run on *ski*.

A while later Sverdrup declared that he had had enough of steering, and I therefore took his place. We had now one good slope after another and a strong wind behind us. We travelled as we should on the best of *ski*-hills at home, and this for hour after hour. The steering is exciting work. One has to keep one's tongue straight in one's mouth, as we say at home, and whatever one does, take care not to fall. If one did, the whole conveyance would be upon one, and once under the runners and driven along by the impetus, one would fare badly indeed, and be lucky to get off without a complete smash up. This was not to be thought of, so it was necessary to keep one's wits about one, to hold the *ski* well together, grip the pole tight, watch the ground incessantly, so as to steer clear of the worst drifts, and for the rest take things as they came, while one's *ski* flew on from the crest of one snow-wave to another.

Our meals were not pleasant intervals that day, and we therefore got through them as quickly as we could. We stopped and crept under shelter of the sails, which were only half lowered on purpose. The snow drifted over us as we sat there, but the wind at least was not so piercing as in the open. We scarcely halted for the usual chocolate distributions, and took our refreshment as we went along.

In the middle of the afternoon—this notable day by the way was September 19—just as we were sailing our best and fastest, we heard a cry of joy from the party behind, Balto's voice being prominent as he shouted "Land ahead."

And so there was; through the mist of snow, which was just now a little less dense, we could see away to the west a long, dark mountain ridge, and to the south of it a smaller peak. Rejoicings were loud and general, for the goal towards which we had so long struggled was at last in sight.

SWEDEN

HOW PRINCESS CECILIA OF SWEDEN JOURNEYED TO THE COURT OF QUEEN ELIZABETH[1]

JAMES BELL

WHAT time the Duke of Finland, Duke John, brother unto the Princess Cecilia, about five years past arrived here in England . . . being sent . . . in embassadge from the puissant Gustavus, King of Sweden, Goths and Vandals . . . as he was of your Majesty in most princely wise received and entertained, so he spared not at his return to make such honourable report unto the king his father, with the princes his brothers and sisters, as well became his personage and as your bounty well deserved: the sweet sound and very rehearsal of which princely courtesy kindled in them all (as it were) a secret love and singular admiration of your highness. Amongst whom the gentle and vertuous Princess Madame Cecilia, being no less moved with the report of your noble vertues than the Queen of Sheba was with the fame of Solomon's wisdom, gave ear to the relation of her brother much more attentively than any of the rest. . . . And as of few and slender sparks are often increased great and fervent fires, so she of bare report conceived such great and fervent thirst to enjoy the presence of your Majesty . . . that ever since that time thus hath been her care, her travail, her chief petition of God and men that once she might enjoy your happy sight, her heart's desire. And since this hath been her practice by all manner and ways convenient to bring to pass her just affection, so much that it seemed she took no delight to greatly in any time as in that she employed in the talk of England. . . . There came not at any time any Englishman into that country of any honest name or serviceable behaviour, but that she would receive him herself, yea, and would think it an injury done unto her if she might not have retained him: yea, so much she fed and nourished the incredible affection planted in her breast, that before she could get opportunity to come into England, she endeavoured herself altogether to be an Englishwoman. And . . . she laboured so fervently, as well by great study as by continual conference, that within four years' space she hath attained the English tongue, and, as your Grace doth well perceive, speaketh the same very well: a language not very easy to be learned . . . yet . . . she hath not only learned perfectly to pronounce, but also can perfectly read and somewhat write our natural English tongue, yea, (I weene) more natural than many our natural Englishmen. . . . To show the

[1] From *Transactions of the Royal Historical Society,* new series, vol. xii.

fruits of her study gotten, as I have said before, she sought all occasions how she might with all expedition in England speak English with Englishmen, for she omitted no time, no place, no occasion that might conveniently be ministered, but it was wholly applied to the entreaty of her brother Eric, the king that now is, his goodwill for her journey into England . . . and would not spare openly to affirm that whosoever should take her to wife, should solemnly vow to bring her into England within one year next after her espousals; yea, some hold opinion that it was a covenant in contract betwixt her Grace and the Marquis now her husband.

Now . . . when she had obtained to be a good English scholar, she . . . imagined every day to be a year until she could win her brother to her desire so that whereas he was in Denmark in the wars, forth from his own court, by the space of three hundred English miles, for the more expedition she thought it not good to expect his return, but would in her own person travel where he then was, touching her departure into England. And the eighteenth day of September in the year of our Lord God, 1564, at Stockholm (a city in Sweden where her brother's court is kept), entering a small vessel, began her journey by water towards a town called Tellinge; who, being accompanied with my Lord Marquis and a few others, was in this beginning of her enterprise like to have been intercepted, for, though it was but a fresh water whereupon they sailed, yet the surges thereof were so cruel that my Lord himself was compelled, with the rest of the company, to help to lade out the water that overflowed the vessel exceedingly : and if the greater grace of God had not in time plucked down the rage of the boisterous whirlwinds, they must by likelihood all have perished. What might her Grace think of the rest of her purposed journey, that before her lies in this small beginning, [when she] beheld such imminent danger in so small a river, far unequal either for the high surges or boiling waves to the swelling rage of the foaming seas? Might this not rather have daunted the mind of a Princess not inured with such fearful frights, and forced her to retire and forsake her enterprise? She did not know your Grace. She was by no proof of her part assured how acceptable her coming should be unto your highness. . . . She was also by others always persuaded to the contrary. She found her brother always unwilling to grant her request. She did not continually hear the lamentable entreaties and natural requests of her brothers and sisters, to whom nature bindeth to be most dearest. She tasted her entry wonderful perilous. She might well suspect of this small journey what was most like to ensue of that which remained. Yet such was her incredible desire and constancy that all those could not move her. . . . But forward she would, and came to Tellinge, from thence to

Horneshollome, where my Lord, not being able to provide for her Grace and her train as became her estate, . . . requested her to abide his return, . . . and taking post horses rode towards the king: who, being gone before no more but one day's journey, contrary to all expectation, she, furnished only with pad and pannell such as the boors and husbandmen do occupy (a furniture no less uncomely than uneasy) took horses likewise and followed after in post. So that in the space of one day and one night she attained to Sowercopinge, where she did meet with the king her brother, and making there but one day's abode, rode back to Stockholm from whence they first set forth. And here remaining longer than her goodwill was, being assailed of all parts with sweet and loving persuasions either wholly to cut off her purposed journey or at least to defer the same until a better time of the year more apt and easy for travel, would not by any means be dissuaded, but remained invincible. . . . But she, altogether persuaded and armed at all points with the inward love of your highness, neither with the terror of the raging seas, neither with the pernicious air of the bitter winter, neither with . . . sweet alluring of the king her brother, could anything be altered from her fixed purpose. But still continuing her suit, at the last overcame her brother, and was addressed to her voyage, ready to take shipping at Stockholm aforesaid the twelfth day of November than next ensuing. Where (although quite against their hearts) the king with the rest of her brothers and sisters did honourably conduct her to the water-side. What did I say? Honourably? Nay, rather mournfully as to her grave. . . . There were sweet kissings intermixed with salt tears. There were countenances without words. There were clippings betwixt the sisters not able scarce to be unclosed. . . . The most virtuous Princess Sophia, sister to her grace, was so deeply wounded with sorrow for this her departure, that whiles they were embracing each other, she fell in a swoon before her sister's feet, and could scarcely be revived, being carried out of the press as one whose soul had departed from the body . . . .

The thirteenth of November she sailed to Waxehollome, the fourteenth, fifteenth and sixteenth being continually at sea. They haled over to Hellengenhaven in Eolande. This day, the ship sailing round about the huge and monstrous rocks of Finland . . . there began to arise so loud and fierce a tempest that the steersman himself . . . gave over, and pointing to a rock with his finger: "Yonder, on yonder rock," quoth he; "by sooth we shall all be cast away," and with the same words forsook the helm, ready to leap overboard, had he not been stayed by one of the company. Yet such was the goodness of God, and rather favour of the winds than well guiding of the pilot, that even now upon the wreck, the ship shoven aside from the rock,overpassed so great and present peril. Overpassed I say, for escaped how should I say, since immediately, by necessity forced, they must venture upon no less dangerous a coast . . . for directing forward their course, they approached near a point named the Quinelaxe, a marvellous dangerous passage, where being under sail the seventeenth of November, not able to stay their course, saw before their eyes one ship rashte in pieces, and the mariners crying for help to them that even now were like to be helpless themselves, for the same course that the other ran before, they must needs and did run presently after. But by the grace of God escaped.

After this, sailing still betwixt the rocks on the one side and in the face of their enemies the Danes on the other side, [they] arrived at last at User in the same country of Finland the fifth day of December, and there remaining till the ninth of the same (the country not being able to provide them victual) standing betwixt two extremities, chose rather to hazard themselves in the terrible seas than by longer abode to fall into extreme penury of necessaries. So that they took shipping in a most terrible tempest what time the storm coming upon them wonderful fast, and the wind being outrageous, and the ship boy, (for want of heed) having cut the sail before the anchor was weighed. The ship, betwixt the full sail and the fast anchor-hold was like to put her nose quite under water, or with the recoiling of the surges and waves in danger to be crashed in pieces. And yet this storm with like hap overpassed, they sailed forward betwixt the rocks.

And towards night, as the wind waxed more calm, the seas also abating somewhat in courage, and her Grace, almost wearied in these perplexities, was desirous to repose herself ashore. So that somewhat before night she was set ashore in her ship's boat in a land to her unknown, in wild and desert woods, forsaken (as it were) for the unfriendliness thereof as well of brute and savage beasts as every other inhabitant. And her grace, accompanied but with a very few, and contrary to her expectation without house or harbour, having no victual in a desert nor entertainment in a barren country, must needs with gladsome will, yield over all that winter night in all the extremity of cold to the cold ground . . . and must be contented to shroud herself in her servants' clocks, whiles they were enforced to skip about therewhiles in their jerkins to get heat to their limbs. . . . Besides this they had no meat to refresh their hungry bodies, but such fowl as some of the servants might haply kill with their guns. A very fresh entertainment to refresh a wearied princess. But such was the extremity of the time, and the wildness of the savage wilderness, wherewith she seemed almost nothing to be dismayed, but cheerfully calling her servants together:

"Come hither," quoth she. "What is this for a cold lodging? Let us now talk of the Queen of England, who knoweth not in what case I am now, the remembrance of whom hath always hitherto put away all troubles, fears, and dangers out of my head."

And so passed over all that cold night.

The next day [they] took shipping and arrived at Renell, a city within the province of Lyfeland. At which place (as the solemnities of the time required) staying for a season, prepared with all possible reverence and religion to celebrate the feast of the Nativity of Christ. During which time, for that her Grace's necessary journey did lie directly through part of the dominion of the King of Poland (being not in league with the King of Sweden) she was constrained by way of request to obtain his favourable passport to pass over his country, with her train, without interruption : which being obtained with much difficulty the second day of March, [she] renewed her desired journey . . . that is to say, was carried in a sled by many days' journey, drawn with horses altogether upon ice. Which kind of travel how unpleasant it was, the late terrible winter did plainly declare and shew us here in England, both for the cruelty of the cold, and likewise for the peril and danger of ice, which, if at any time should have resolved, must needs have cut off their purposed journey. But she, refusing no danger to attain her desire, departed in this sort from Renell by Regel to Pades and so to Pernone, the uttermost frontier of all Sweden, where began a new broil: for here, notwithstanding the King of Poland's passport, they were in danger of the Moskovyter, who bordereth upon Pades and is enemy to the King of Sweden, into whose hands, if they had fallen, they must needs have perished . . . for the avoiding whereof, having before determined to have reposed herself here (being wearied as well with long turmoil by sea as want of refreshing by land) she was constrained to hazard herself in the dark night in an unknown and perilous country. And so the whole train, travelling without victual for themselves or forrage for their horses all that night and until the afternoon of the next day, with swift and never-ceasing travel came to Sales, the seventh day of March, where the Heremaster of Lyfelande received her, and the next day convoyed her to Lemsey, where she reposed herself until the eleventh day of the same month. And from thence [she] set forward to Rie, a city subject to the King of Poland, yet a free city, such a one as hath free access of all strangers for the use of traffic or otherwise. And here she determined somewhat to refresh her wearied body : but, contrary to her expectation, the Burgomaster of Rie would not permit her so much as once to enter into their city. By which their uncourtesy compelled, she turned from thence to Newemyll, betwixt Hensken, where being received after the Polish manner (which is no less strange than stately) she was so much grieved with the ungrateful refusal of the men of Rie that through the same and her former restless toil, she fell into such an extreme sickness as all the company seemed well near to despair of her health and recovery. Yet after two days' only tarriance, she proceeded from thence to Mysse, being scarce any iota recovered of her painful and sharp sickness: by reason whereof and the too speedy renewing of her troublesome toil, she became more grievously sick than before, for at this place the rage of her cruel disease bereft her so of memory that it seemed her wits were scarce her own. But lo, though weakness and very extremity of sickness caused her senses to fail, so that she knew them not whom daily she saw, and which had been continual partakers of her sorrows, yet could not the same sickness bereave the joyful remembrance of your Majesty from her faithful breast; for what time to her, almost fainting, drink being brought by Master North, and she not knowing him, demanded who he was, after that she had heard his name—

"Nay, nay," quoth she, "if my servant North were here, I am assured we should have some mention of the Queen of England."

Seeming even with the name somewhat to have conceived of better courage.

New whiles she had continued here a few days by occasion of her sick and weak body, she departed from Mysse the eighteenth day of March, and the nineteenth came to Sallade in Lyttome, the most barbarous country in the world : a people as rude of manners as froward of stomach. . . . Here her Grace . . . being very much dismayed therewith, with as much speed as she possibly might, passed that unfriendly country and came the thirtieth day of March to Cowyne, a town in Samozitche within the Dukedom of Lyttome, where she made an end of her perilous journey by ice. Certainly a voyage (as seemeth to our ears that have not proved the like) no less dangerous with coursers in chariot to cut the swelling seas than it was sometime marvellous the aged Dedalus (if old report be true) with waxed wings to cut the Candiane skies.

At Cowyne she remained until the eighteeth of April, during which time began new tidings to spring . . . full of discomfort . . . for here, upon the view of the King of Poland's passport, the inhabitants of Cowyne practiced to defeat the same and . . . alleged that, contrary to the grant of her passport, she had passed those countries which she ought not to have passed, whereby they would have entrapped her and betrayed her into the hands of the Duke of Olyka, an old and ancient enemy to the King of Sweden . . . out of whose hands, when she, by long entreaty, by sweet and loving words, had won herself, with glad and speedy course, she at the last recovered Ragnette, a castle of the Duke of Prussia, where resting not above two days, she travelled forth to Tylzey, a town which lieth within the dukedom of Prussia. At which place (Easter drawing near) she, only for the honour of the feast, continued four days' space. . . . After which . . . renewing eftsoons her long and painful voyage, so far she travelled those countries till after eight days' journey she attained to Queensburgh . . . and there . . . the Duke of Prussia . . . welcomed her. . . in as princely a manner as might be devised : so now began the first sign and (as I might say) the kalends of better hope to enter in, the grisly face of passed dangers to seem more mild : for the Duke himself for his own part entreated her not as a stranger, but as if she had been the sovereign lady and princess of his country . . . stirred with respect of her estate, and desire (as he himself confessed) to have his country honoured with the birth of her offspring, which otherwise, by shortness of time . . . or by the turmoil of so long and tedious travel, might haply have been born in an obscure and unknown country . . . . But she, still fixed in her former purpose, amidst all her joys, chief joy, she deemed this to think upon your Majesty : as well appeared what time she, with the Duke honouring with their persons the marriage day an English merchant, called to her, then sitting at meat, the bridegroom, and taking in her hands a piece filled with wine, with glad semblant and smiling countenance. . . .

"I drink," quoth she, "a carouse unto the Queen of England, whom, I pray God, I may once see before I die : then should I think my travel both well bestowed and fully recompensed. . . ."

Hastening her journey forward, she attained at the last to Dantzig, a city subject to the King of Poland, where, through the immoderate haste that she made to shorten her travel, she distempered her body and renewed her sickness, so that she was constrained to abide in this city by the space of six weeks, although altogether against her will. But there was no remedy, expect she would wilfully put her life and her charge withal in adventure. Wherefore, after she was somewhat (as it were) gravely recovered of her sickness perceiving her time to approach daily near and near, she addressed herself to a fresh toil, and making scarce two days' abode in any place, with all expedition passed the countries of Pomerlande, Mechelbourghe, Saxone, Lunenburghe, Bremme, Oldenburghe, and after thirty days' continual travel, came at last to Steckuzen, a castle in East Friselande, where the lady of Embden, being her own natural sister, received her as princely and lovingly as reason and nature might devise . . . and perceiving by conference and computation of time that she had then but eight weeks to accomplish, fearing the most likely event of her perilous attempt, comparing the shortness of time to the length of the remaining voyage, and the disturbance she must needs endure in the common waggons, began to dissuade her with all the arguments she could devise. She laid before her eyes the long unquiet and loathsome travel, the extremity of the hot summer, the necessary doubt . . . whether in the case that she was in, she might ever have achieved her desire. She charged her with the common usage of the inferior estates, who, being with child, commonly take up their chambers six or seven weeks before their time, lest haply the careful mother by some little motion or stirring of the body, be an occasion of prejudice to her charge. But she, whom neither her brother's slights, nor swelling seas, nor threatening rocks, nor grisly winter winds, nor (worse than this) the rude and faithless Lyttowane could move . . . would not yield unto the soft persuasions of her sister. She had (she said) no seas of ice to slide again, no wild untamed Dane, no Moskovite, no other Olykane, whom either as her cruel murderer or proud disdainful master she needed now to fear. Her short time she had to go with child, she would with speedy course prevent. The hard toil she would make easy with remembrance of the end. . . .

Therefore, through not so soon as she desired, yet lo, after ten days' abode at Steckhusen and Embden, leaving her sister and (as to her sister seemed) her safety and health withal behind her, she set forward with all celerity from Embden, and in six days' travel passed through the regions of East and West Fryselande and Brabant, and by continual restless race of almost four hundered English miles in length, entered Antwerp . . . where, reposing herself by the space of five days only, with like celerity hastened through Flanders, and at the last recovered to Calais.

Here, lo, a day or two awaiting for the weather, she all the day continued wishing and praying for the happy winds and, as the air was clear, feeding her eyes from afar with the glad sight of the white rocks of the English shore. Till at the last the winds agreeing some what to her will, the seas notwithstanding going very high, she with her train took shipping, and sailing in her forward course with so jocund a courage that (when all the passengers were terribly sick with the cruel surges of the water, and the rolling of the unsavoury ship) she was not only not sick, but also standing above the hatches, feeding her eyes upon the English coast, was unto the sick passengers a princely nurse and an especial comfort. . . .

But as the son of Ixion, having water at the brink of his thirsty lips, by want of what he saw increased more his thirst, so she, even in the view of the desired haven, the end of all her travels, must be contented to suffer the repulse and recoil of the same: for upon the sudden a contrary gale of wind rising compelled the shipmaster to seek his shifts, to turn and return, to fetch the wind (as they term it) to apply and reply every way whereby he might achieve the haven of Dover. But when she perceived no hope left of attaining the port and that of force she must needs retire:

"Alas," quoth she, "now must I needs be sick both in body and mind! I can endure no longer."

And therewith immediately taking to her cabin, betwixt plaints and sorrows, she waxed wonderful sick: and so continued until the ship was brought into Calais haven again, where scare willing to come on shore, overcome at last with the entreaty of the company, she would, notwithstanding, not receive any comfort, but accusing her cruel hap all the night, not ceasing before she was informed of a fair and large wind to serve for her new passage, she expressed nothing but countenances of heaviness.

But after she was once called upon to make ready to shipboard, she prepared herself with no less joyful cheer than Theseus (I think), when from the mazy labyrinth in Crete he set forth with Ariadne to his desired country of Athens. Her colour, that was a little before altogether appalled, wan and dead, appeared again and showed as fresh a hue as at any time before, that a man might well have marvelled to see in her countenance in so small a time so great an alteration.

The second time joyously entering the ship, she provoketh the mariners with gentle request to weigh the anchors and hoist the sails, that no time may be lost, and notwithstanding the tempestuous sea furiously raged with her wonted surges and compelled the passengers as before to be extremely sick, yet she, sitting always upon the hatches, passed the time in singing the English psalms of David after the English note and ditty, and would many times in mirth and disport call the passengers weaklings, not worthy to bear the names of men, that were not able to endure, with her, being but a weak woman.

But what prevailed it to hope well? What helpeth glad courage, what undaunted cheer? The weather, always contrary to her good endeavour, seemed again to express the conspiracy between Juno and the god Œolus, ruler of the winds, in chasing away of Æneas' navy from the coast of Italy. So were the skies suddenly overcast with clouds. So strove the froward winds with backward course to bear the unwilling sails again towards the place from whence they last set forth. So grisly from the bottom the surging waves bare up the boiling sands: which she beholding, through fear and pensiveness changeth her lay, with salt tears trickling down her paled cheeks, with a doleful sigh accuseth her mishap, and kneeling on her knees, with rung hands beholding the heavens, breaketh out in this complaint.

"O Lord, since by Thy working will it may seem we are come in place more like to spill than save, for me Thy will be done in the seas as in the heavens. But yet the little one with whom now great I go, would God in England might I wish, even in the hands of that most noble Queen, that at the least it might be nourished to some better chance than this."

Which said, dropping (as it were) almost in a swoon, she entereth her cabin where, through bitterness of her sighing and sobbing, she altered her stomach and was very sore sick, insomuch that the company feared much lest she would even there amongst them have fallen into travail. But she, being in this perplexity of mind, altogether unwilling to look back, desired the shipmaster not to apply into Calais haven, but to cast anchor rather, and abide the adventure, if perhaps God would cause the wind to turn and blow fortunately again; whose request . . . the master . . . trusting thereby somewhat to assuage the same, cast anchor, and lay at anchor by the sands by the space of two or three hours.

But it booteth not to strive against the secret determination of God. The seas went so high, and the winds wax so rough, that of necessity they must cut cable and betake themselves to the winds and weather in hope to get Calais again, for all hope to proceed was clearly and utterly cut off. Therefore, as the time served, with much danger she at last arrived within Calais again, no less grieved with her backward course than Andromache is said to have bewailed her exile from Troy, when she was led as captive by Achilles' son to Scyros Isle: and in such sort and plight she endured at Calais till the weather began somewhat to clear, what time she was not so much moved with the envious storm of her peril, as grieved with the prolonging of her weary travel almost finished.

Before that the seas were quieted (such was her thoughtful care and inward thirst to win the land) she embarked herself again with all her train, sustaining so, with better hope, her long and tedious delay. And now at the last, once to wind up the long clew of her toilsome travel, after many a sour blast, many a boisterous billow, many nights passed without rest, many days without comfort, many embracings of friends, many dangers of her enemies, she hardly hath attained the happy land, the end of all her travels, and certain hope of present joys. Even here she seemed to challenge again her long forsaken lightsomeness of heart. Even as (when grisly winter's flaws are faded . . . and lusty April begins to cloth herself in gladsome green) the nightingale, forgetting then her former griefs of woeful winter storms, beginneth to record her sweet abashed song with doubtful voice; so she, the noble princess, half overcome with present hap and joy of passed sorrows, with tears . . . breaks out in praising God for this her good success and happy end of travel.

Thus fully fraught with comfort, she marched forward, and with easy journey (as being conveyed in your Grace's horse-litter) . . . came with good speed to Canterbury, where the honourable Lord Cobham, Lord Warden of the Cinque Ports, and his virtuous Lady, accompanied with the honourable and worshipful of the Shire, received her and conveyed her to Rochester, where God increased her joy, for being likely there in her inn to travail, it pleased Him to reserve the same until a better time, which she perceiving, passed forth the next day from thence to Gravesend, where the honourable the Lord of Hunsden meeting her (as the time and water tide would serve) did most honourably conduct her to Bedford House in London.

[*Princess Cecilia reached London at two o'clock in the afternoon of September 11, 1565, and her baby—a son—was born four days latter.*]

A TOUR IN LAPLAND[1]

(1732)

CARL VON LINNÉ (LINNÆUS)

(1707-78)

HAVING been appointed by the Royal Academy of Sciences to travel through Lapland, for the purpose of investigating the three kingdoms of Nature in that country, I prepared my wearing apparel and other necessaries for the journey as follows.

My clothes consisted of a light coat of Westgothland linsey-woolsey cloth without folds, lined with red shalloon, having small cuffs and collar of shag; leather breeches; a round wig; a green leather cap, and a pair of half boots. I carried a small leather bag, half an ell in length, but somewhat less in breadth, furnished on one side with hooks and eyes, so that it could be opened and shut at pleasure. This bag contained one shirt; two pair of false sleeves; two half shirts; an inkstand, pencase, microscope, and spying-glass; a gauze cap to protect me occasionally from the gnats; a comb; my journal, and a parcel of paper stitched together for drying plants, both in folio; my manuscript Ornithology, *Flora Uplandica*, and *Characteres generici*. I wore a hanger at my side, and carried a small fowling-piece, as well as an octangular stick,

[1] From *Lachesis Lapponica; or, a Tour in Lapland* (1811).

graduated for the purpose of measuring. My pocket book contained a passport from the Governor of Upsal, and a recommendation from the Academy.

MAY 12, 1732, OLD STYLE

I set out alone from the city of Upsal on Friday May 12, 1732, at eleven o'clock, being at that time within half a day of twenty-five years of age. As the summer seemed to be fast advancing, I thought it not advisable to lose time by the way, nor to stray far from the road, in the early part of the tour, but only to observe attentively what readily presented itself, that I might reach Lapland with all possible dispatch.

MAY 13

By eleven o'clock I arrived at Gefle, where I was obliged to stay all the day, for it was evening before I received from the governor of the province (of Gestrickland) the requisite passport, which was accompanied by orders to all the public officers in his district to give me all requisite assistance to penetrate, if possible, into Asila Lapmark.

MAY 14

Owing to the above delay, and my attending morning service the next day at Gefle church, I could not quit that place till one o'clock. Proceeding without stopping to Hudwickswald, I there merely spoke a few words to Mr Broman the clergyman, and pursued my way to Knorby Knylen, the highest mountain in Medelpad, from whence I went to Sundswall, and further. In my way I examined a cave formed by nature in a very hard rocky mountain, formerly a retreat for thieves and highwaymen.

I was so unfortunate, in my journey through Medelpad, as not to meet with a single horse that did not tumble with me several times, in consequence of which I was at one time so serverly hurt as to be scarcely able to remount. Having already collected together a number of stones and minerals, which were no less burthensome than unnecessary to carry along with me further, I rode to Hernosand, where I left these incumbrances. I did not, however, stay there above two hours.

MAY 20

At length I reached the famous mountain of Skula in Angermanland, at the very top of which is a large grotto, so neatly formed by nature that art could scarcely have excelled it. This grotto was represented to me as quite inaccessible, and it was said that not more than two or three persons had ever been there; nor was it without great difficulty that I prevailed on two men to accompany me, every body deeming the project impracticable. As we climbed up towards it, we sometimes crept forwards, sometimes slid back again. Now we mounted a considerable way by catching hold of branches and roots of trees, and then, meeting with steep inaccessible rocks, were obliged to turn back. After following one of my guides for about two hours, I thought the other seemed to make more progress; which induced me to go after the latter. I was scarcely got two ells out of my former path, than the man whose track I had left loosened a large stone with his foot, which fell on the very spot I had quitted, with such violence, that I was surrounded by fire and smoke, and should certainly, but for the protecting hand of Providence, have been crushed to pieces. We reached the grotto at length, after much labour and trouble, and descended the mountain with much greater facility. Laying hold of the tops of spruce firs which grew close to the rocks, we slid down upon them, dragging them after us down the precipices.

MAY 23

I, at length, after twelve days journey, reached Umœa.

It had originally been my design to go to Asila Lapmark, in order to observe what plants are able to endure the very hard winters of that region, but I was obliged to change my plan. The summer would not have been long enough, nor my stock of money sufficient to enable me to reach that most northern part of the country, where the severity of the climate is augmented by the cold north wind and the vast snowy mountains. I applied, therefore, to baron Grundell, governor of Umœa, for a passport to the nearer parts of Lapland, which was immediately granted. This gentleman showed the greatest readiness to befriend me, and appeared to take much interest in the success of my undertaking. He gave such orders as might cause the public officers in Lapland to lay no obstacles in my way, but rather to assist me by every means in their power. He himself gave me much curious information, and showed me his own garden, that I might observe what plants would stand the winter here: concluding by expressing, in the most flattering terms, his approbation of my appointment.

MAY 25

The following morning I set out on my way towards Lapmark. Leaving the highway, I came to one of the most unpleasant roads I ever travelled. It was covered with stones, betwixt which were thick entangled roots of trees, and among them were deep holes full of water. The whole ground was a marsh, which the frost was at this time just about quitting. Large pine-trees, that had been blown down in the course of the stormy winter, frequently crossed my path; and the more flexible birches, weighed down by the snow, interrupted my course on all sides. I frequently came to such steep heathy places that my horse could scarcely climb or descend them, and in the bottoms between them were marshy tracts, with rivulets destitute of bridges, so that my beast slipped down several times; and as I passed the streams, the water reached up to my saddle. I then regretted, what I had in the former part of my journey so much detested, travelling on the highway on these stumbling horses, and would rather have descended the steepest hill in Angermannia than have chosen the present road, or at every step the horse took, I thought he would have fallen.

In the evening of

MAY 28

however, I arrived at Genom, the last village in Westbothland, seven miles from the great road which leads westward from Umœa. Not having reposed since I left the place last mentioned, I slept here all night.

MAY 29

The next morning I proceeded in a boat up the river of Umœa as far as Lycksele church, which is the first in Umœan Lapmark, and situated five miles distant from Grano. This was Whitsun-eve.

MAY 30

Being Whitsunday, I determined to stay here. Indeed, Mr Gran the minister of the place, wished me to wait till the next Sabbath day, as he did not think it advisable for me to proceed, so as to come suddenly among the Laplanders, before he had made my design known from the pulpit. He was apprehensive that I might meet with the same accident as his own wife had done, who, coming unexpectedly upon these people, had a fire-lock presented to her breast. Notwithstanding this, the rise of the water in the river, in consequence of the advancing summer among the Alps, was so rapid, that I was on that account induced to hasten my departure, after having engaged one of the colonists to accompany me by water to the nearest habitation of some one of the native Laplanders.

MAY 31

The divine service of this day being over, I left Lycksele, taking with me only three loaves of bread, and some reindeer tongues, by way of provision. I presumed that I should procure among the Laplanders flesh of the reindeer, cheese, milk, fish, fowl, etc. Nor, indeed, could I well take anything more at present; for, whenever we came at any shoals or falls in the river, it was necessary for my companion to take our boat on his head, over mountains and valleys, so that I had not only my own luggage to carry at such time, but his likewise.

JUNE 1

Having by morning come within the territories of the nearest Laplander, we left our boat on the shore of the river, and went in search of this man through the wild forests, where we saw no more traces of roads or enclosures than if the country were entirely uninhabited. We met, however, with several deserted huts, where he had at one time or other resided.

Being exceedingly tired with this walk, I was glad to repose myself here in the desert, while my Finland conductor went in search of my future guide. Nor was I without considerable fears that this man, when he had met with the Laplander, might not be able to find me again. However, about noon he returned, accompanied by a Laplander, who took charge of me, inviting me home to his hut, where he treated me with fish, and fresh water.

I was afterwards conducted from one Laplander to another, till I came to a part of the river, about twenty-five miles above Lycksele. I shall not dwell on the inconveniences I was obliged to undergo every time we had to seek for any of the Laplanders, while I was quite destitute of provisions. These poor people themselves had, at this season, nothing but fish to eat, as they had not yet begun to slaughter their reindeer, nor to go a fowling; neither had they, as yet milked any of their reindeer.

JUNE 2

On coming to the place just mentioned, we found it impracticable to proceed by water, the river being so rapid, and so much impeded by falls, that we were obliged to undertake a walk of a few miles further, which I was told would bring us to a more navigable stream. After walking for some time, a fen or marsh lay before us, seemingly half a mile broad, which we had to cross. At every step the water was above our knees, and the ice was at the bottom. Where the frost was quite gone, we often sunk still deeper. When we had traversed this marsh, we sought in vain for any human creature, and were therefore under the necessity, a little further on, of crossing another bog, still worse than the former, and a mile in extent. I know not what I would not rather have undertaken than to pass this place, especially as the elements were all adverse, for it blowed and rained violently.

JUNE 3

By four o'clock this morning, having conquered all our difficulties, we still could not meet with any Laplander. I was so fatigued that I could proceed no further without some repose. We therefore made a fire; and having dried my clothes, I lay down by the side of it, in hopes of taking a little rest. But in this I had no success. The fire scorched me on one side, while the cold north wind pinched me on the other; and the gnats so stung my hands, face, and legs, that it was impossible to sleep. Thus I remained in expectation of my Lapland conductor, who had set out in search of another, till two o'clock in the afternoon. I could not help thinking how miserably I might have to end my days here, in case he should think proper to desert me entirely. At length, however, he returned, bringing with him a little, black-looking woman, whose hair hung loose about her shoulders, with a red cap upon her head. I scarcely think that any poet could have described a fury so hideous as this woman. She addressed me in Swedish to the follwoing effect.

"Oh, thou poor man! what misfortune can have brought thee into my country? Seest thou what miserable living we have? I have never yet seen any stranger here in summer. Whence dost thou come, and whither dost thou intend to do?"

Having tasted nothing for four days past but a little fresh fish, without any bread, I asked her, seeing a small kettle in her hand, what she could give me to eat. She immediately set about boiling a pike which she had brought with her; but when I was going to taste it, Observed heaps of vermin between the gills, which made me loathe it altogether, and rather continue to fast, though my strength suffered much. This woman informed me there was no boat to be had on the next river, and that I had only to return the way I came; which words were like a stroke of thunder to me. I know not anything I would less willingly have undertaken than to traverse again these Stygian marshes, which were now not to be avoided. However, this good woman conducted us to a side path, whereby we avoided about half a mile of the way we had come. In traversing the forest, we arrived at a shed, supported by four posts, and covered with a roof. Here hung some clothes, and a small reindeer cheese, which last I immediately wished to obtain. But the woman refused, saying she should want it hereself for the next holiday. My hunger was such, that I could not lose sight of this cheese, and I was induced to offer her any thing she was pleased to ask for it telling her I verily believed I should hardly survive another day if I had it not. At length she complied, and the cheese proved afterwards of the most signal service to me. We then took leave of our female companion, and began to measure back our steps. I was thus obliged to return by the course of the river, having, with the thoughtlessness of youth, undertaken more than it was possible to perform.

We continued our voyage down the river, being carried with great velocity by the current, the whole of the next day. At length coming to an island, the Laplander failed in his attempt to weather it, and the boat, striking against to rock, was dashed to pieces. We both found ourselves in the water; but the depth being inconsiderable, we soon landed on the island. My conductor lost not only his boat, but a hatchet and pike. I lost two stuffed birds, one of them a large Heron (*Ardea cinerea*?) which was black with a white breast; the other a Red-bird, or *Gvousach* as the Laplanders call it (*Corvus,* or *Lanius infaustus*). It was with great difficulty we got from this island to the shore. The sun shone warm; and after having wrung the water out of our clothes, we walked on for about a mile, along the bank of the river, amongst thickets and bogs, till we came in sight of a colonist, who was fishing for pike. He gave me some provision, and conducted me to Grano, where I only stopped to rest one night, and on the evening of the 8th of June arrived at Umœa.

June 12

Early this morning I set out by land towards Pithoea, where I arrived after two days' journey, for the night was as pleasant for travelling as the day. Here I met with kind entertainment from Mr Solander, the principal clergyman of the place.

June 19

I went out to sea in a boat for some miles, to explore the neighbouring coast and islands, and returned at length to the new town. Here however I made no long stay, but proceeded in one day from thence to Lulea. I was anxious to lose as little time as possible, being very desirous of reaching the alps of Lulean Lapland time enough to see the sun above the horizon at midnight, which is seen to greater advantage there than at Tornea.

JUNE 25

Taking leave of the town, I embarked on the river of Lulea, which I continued to navigate upwards for several successive days and nights, having good accommodation both as to food and boat. The boats here are excellent, far unlike those in the district of Umœan Lapland, which are, in a manner, only sewed together, so that a foot set on one of their sides is sufficient to stave them; and if the passengers are not careful how they sit down, the boat is overset. After three days and three nights, we reached Quickjock situated close to the alps. Here I received from the famous wife of the curate Mr Grot provisions sufficient to last me for eight days.

JULY 6

After several days' travelling, on the evening of July 6th I ascended *Wallavari*, the first mountain of the alps on this side, which is indeed of a very considerable height. My companion was a Laplander, who served me both as servant and interpreter. In the latter capacity his assistance was highly requisite, few persons being to be met with on these alps who are acquainted with the Swedish language; nor was I willing to trust myself alone among these wild people, who were ignorant for what purpose I came. I had hardly suffered much in the Lapland part of Umœa for want of knowing the language. Nor was my companion wanted less to assist me in carrying what was necessary, for I had sufficient incumbrances of my own, without being the bearer of our provisions into the bargain.

On my first ascending these wild alps, I felt as if in a new world. Here were no forests to be seen, nothing but mountains upon mountains, larger and larger as I advanced, all covered with snow. No road, no tracks, nor any signs of inhabitants were visible. The verdure of summer seemed to shun this frozen region, retiring into the deep valleys between the mountains. I saw very few birds, except some Ptarmigans, which the Laplanders call *Cheruna* (*Tetrao Lagopus*), running with their young along the vales. The delightful season of spring, whose cheering influence on man and all living nature I had so lately experienced in the beginning of my journey, seemed an alien here. The declining sun never disappeared sufficiently to allow any cooling shade, and by climbing to the more elevated parts of these lofty mountains, I could see it at midnight above the horizon. When I cast my eyes over the grass and herbage, there were few objects I had seen before, so that all nature was alike strange to me. I sat down to collect and describe these vegetable rarities, while the time passed unperceived away, and my interpreter was obliged to remind me that we had still five or six miles to go to the nearest Laplander, and that if we had a mind for any reindeer meat, we ought to bestir ourselves quickly. We proceeded therefore up and down the snowy hills, sometimes passing along their precipitous sides, which was the most difficult travelling of all, and for many a long way we walked over heaps of stones. About the evening of the following day we reached the nearest spot where any Laplander was at that time settled. The man we met with gave me a very good reception, and furnished me with a couple of reindeer skins to sleep between. Immediately after my arrival, the herd, consisting of seven or eight hundred head of reindeer, came home. These were milked, and some of the milk was boiled for my entertainment, but it proved rather too rich for my stomach. My host furnished me with his own spoon, which he carried in his tobacco-bag. On my expressing a wish, through my interpreter, to have the spoon washed, my Lapland friend immediately complied, taking a mouthful of water and spitting it over the spoon.

After having satisfied my hunger, and refreshed myself with sleep, I steered my course directly South-west, towards the alps of Pithoea, proceeding from thence to the lofty icy mountains, or main ridge of the country. A walk of scarcely above four or five miles further brought me to the western edge of this ridge, for I was desirous of examining that side of the mountains, to see how it agreed with the eastern part. I had no sooner arrived at the icy mountains than a storm overtook me, accompanied by a shower of thin pieces of ice, which soon formed an icy crust over my own clothes and those of my conductor. The severity of the cold obliged me to borrow the gloves and lappmudd (coat of reindeer skin) from the man who accompanied me. But the weather proved more favourable as soon as we had crossed the summit of the ridge. From hence the verdant appearance of Norway, lying far beneath us, was very delightful. The whole country was perfectly green, and, notwithstanding its vast extent, looked like a garden in miniature, for the tallest trees appeared not above a span high. As we began to descend the alps it seemed as if we should soon arrive at the lower country, but our calculations were very inadequate to what we found its actual distance. At length, however, we reached the plains of which we had enjoyed so stupendous a prospect. Nothing could be more delightful to my feelings than this transition, from all the severity of winter, to the warmth and beauty of summer. The verdant herbage, the sweet-scented clover, the tall grass reaching up to my arms, the grateful flavour of the wild fruits, and the fine weather which welcomed me to the foot of the alps, seemed to refresh me both in mind and body.

Here I found myself close to the sea-coast. I took up my abode at the house of a ship-master, with whom I made an agreement to be taken in a boat, the following day, along the coast. I much wished to approach the celebrated whirlpool, called the *Maelstrom*, but I could find nobody willing to venture near it.

We set sail the next morning according to appointment, but the wind proved contrary, and the boat-men were, after a while, exhausted with rowing. Meantime I amused myself in examining various petrifactions, zoophytes, and submarine plants of the *Fucus* tribe, which occupied every part of the coast. In the evening I arrived at the house of Mr Rask, the pastor of Torfjorden, who gave me a kind reception.

Next day we proceeded further on our voyage; but the contrary wind exhausted our patience, and we veered about, soon reaching the place from whence we had first set out, the wind being directly in our favour for that purpose.

On the following morning I climbed one of the neighbouring mountains, with the intention of measuring its height. While I was reposing in perfect tranquillity on the side of the hill, busied only in loosening a stone which I wanted to examine, I heard the report of a gun at a small distance below. I was however too far off to receive any hurt, so, thanks to Providence, I escaped, but my alarm may be easily imagined. Perceiving the man who had fired the gun, I pursued him to a considerable distance, in order to prevent his charging his piece a second time, and I determined never to go there again without some protection. I inquired who it could be that had made this unprovoked attack, but I found it impossible to gain any information on the subject.

On the 15th of July we set out on our return, and that whole day was employed in climbing the mountains again, to our no small fatigue and exhaustion, the ground we had to pass over being so extremely steep as well as lofty. When we reached the cold snowy mountains, indeed, we had sufficient opportunity to cool ourselves.

From hence we turned our course towards the alps of Tornea, which were described to me as about forty miles distant. What I endured in the course of this journey is hardly to be described. How many weary steps was I obliged to set to climb the precipices that came in my way, and how excessive were my perspiration and fatigue! Nor were these the worst evils we had to encounter before we reached Caituma. Sometimes we were enveloped with clouds, so that we could not see before us; sometimes rivers impeded our progress, and obliged us either to choose a very circuitous path, or to wade naked through the cold snow water. This fresh snow water however proved a most welcome and salutary refreshment, for without it we should never have been able to encounter the excessive heat of the weather. Water was our only drink during this journey, but it never proved so refreshing as when we sucked it out of the melting snow. Having nearly reached the Lapland village of Caituma, the inhabitants of which seemed perfectly wild, running away from their huts as soon as they perceived us approaching, from a considerable distance, I began to be tired of advancing further up into this inhospitable country. We had not at this time tasted bread for several days, the stock we had brought with us being entirely exhausted. The rich milk of the reindeer was too luscious to be eaten without bread, and the ordinary or second-rate cheese occasioned such a degree of costiveness as I could not longer endure. I determined therefore to return towards Quickjock, which was forty miles from this spot. In the course of my journey thither, walking rather carelessly over the snow, without noticing a hole which the water had made, I fell through the icy crust into the deep snow. The interpreter and guide were totally unable to assist me, the cavity in which I lay being very steep, and so hollowed out by the water that it surrounded me like a wall. It was not in their power to reach me without a rope, which they luckily were able to procure to drag me out of the hole. I had received a blow on my thigh in the fall, the effects of which I felt for a month afterwards. One of my guides had met with a similar accident but a week before.

At length we arrived at Quickjock, after having been four weeks without tasting bread. Those who have not experienced the want of this essential support of life, can scarcely imagine how hard it is to be deprived of it so long, even with a superfluity of all other kinds of food. I remained four days at Quickjock to recruit my strength, and afterwards descended the river again to Lulea. There being no boat to be had north of Purkijaur, we were obliged to construct a raft for ourselves. Our voyage was very perilous, for the wind and current both combined to overset us, so that it was not without the greatest exertion we saved ourselves, and it being night, nobody heard our cries for assistance.

The next day I was conducted to the river of Calatz, to see the manner of fishing for pearls, and on the 30th of July arrived at Lulea.

Here I rested for a day or two, then proceeded to Tornea, and from thence to Kimi, and some way up the river of that name. Afterwards I entered East Bothland; but not understanding the Finnish language, I found it inconvenient to proceed, and preferred returning four miles back again. I made several excursions to an adjacent island. At the town of Calix I became acquainted with the judge of a neighbouring district, and we accompanied each other to Tornea, from whence I proceeded in a boat to Kengis, Jonesvando, and within four miles of Juckesceni; but as the frost was beginning to set in very hard, it being late in autumn, had there being nothing, as far as I could discover, very remarkable to see, I descended the river again in the same boat, and had a quick passage back. Having noted down the Finnish names for such articles as I should be most likely to want at the inns, I ventured once more to enter East Bothland, in order to pursue my journey that way homeward. I considered that in a new country there is always something new to be seen, and that to travel the same road I had come, would probably afford but little entertainment or instruction. I had still less inclination, at this advanced season of the year, to encounter the hazard of a sea voyage. Several merchants who wanted to sail from Tornea to Stockholm, had long been waiting for a fair wind.

I therefore pursued my way along the coast through East Bothland and Finland, visiting Ulea, Brakestad, Old and New Carleby, Wasa, Christina, Biorreborg and Abo, remaining four days at the place last mentioned. I then went by the post yacht to Aland, crossed the sea of Aland, and on the 10th of October reached Upsal.

The whole extent of my journey amounts to 633 Swedish miles (about 3798 English miles).

DENMARK

THE NORTH-WEST PASSAGE TO THE INDIES[1]

JENS MUNCK

(1579-1628)

IN the Name of the Holy Trinity, Amen.

Anno Domini, 1619; His Royal Majesty[2] our most gracious Master's ship *Enhiörningen*[3] and the sloop *Lamprenen*[4] having, according to His said Majesty's gracious orders, been properly made ready, provided, and prepared with crew, equipment, provisions, ammunition and other necessaries for the voyage and expedition to search for the North-west Passage: I, Jens Munck, in the name of God, sailed with the said two ships from Copenhagen into the Sound on the 9th of May; and there were then on the ship *Enhiörningen* forty-eight, and on the sloop *Lamprenen*, sixteen persons. . .

[*Sighting Cape Farewell on June 30, Munck crossed Davis Strait in search of the inlet which was supposed to lead to the North-west Passage. Entering Hudson Strait on July 13, he began his long battle with the ice. On August 10 he at last found himself in that mysterious inland sea—Hudson Bay—which Hudson had discovered nine years before, and which was supposed to lead to the still more mysterious North-west Passage to the Indies. Sailing south-west, Munck crossed the 'sea' only to find himself embayed at the mouth of the river now known as the Churchill.*]

September 7th. When I now had come into the harbour . . . though with great difficulty, on account of wind and storm, snow, hail, and fog, I at once ordered my shallop, which was divided into six parts, to be put together; and, during the night following, we kept a watch on the land, and maintained a fire, in order that *Lamprenen*, which, during the great gale and storm, had strayed from us, might find us again. She joined us on the 9th of September, having been under the northern land, where an open passage was supposed to exist, but there was none. The crew having suffered much from the before-mentioned gale, and in other hardship and trouble, and a part in consequence being down with illness, I caused, during these days, the sick people to be brought from the ship on shore; and we gathered . . . some cloud-berries, gooseberries, and other berries, which in Norway are called Tydebær and Kraghær. I also had a good fire made on shore every day for the sick, whereby

[1] From "The Expedition of Captain Jens Munck," in *Danish Arctic Expeditions, 1605-20,* edited by C. C.A. Gosch (Hakluyt Society, No. 97 (1897)).

[2] Christian IV.

[3] The *Unicorn,*

[4] The *Lamprey.*

they were comforted, and in time nicely regained their health.

On the 10th and 11th of September there was such a terrible snowstorm and gale that nothing could be done.

September 12th. In the morning early, a large white bear came down to the water near the ship, which stood and ate some Beluga flesh, off a fish so named which I had caught the day before. I shot the bear, and the men all desired the flesh for food, which I also allowed. I ordered the cook just to boil it slightly, and then to keep it in vinegar for a night, and I myself had two or three pieces of this bear-flesh roasted for the cabin. It was of good taste and did not disagree with us.

On the 13th of September, I sent out both my shallop and the ship's boat, under the command of my second mates, Hans Brock and Jan Pettersen, with orders to proceed 8 or 9 miles along the shore, one on the western, the other on the eastern side, and to examine what accommodation the land afforded, and whether there were any better harbours there than the one we were in.

On the 16th of September, Jan Pettersen returned, who had been investigating the localities on the western side; and he reported that... no harbours could be found. . . .

September 18th. As we experienced nothing but frost and snow, we deliberated together as to what measures to take. Then all the officers thought it best, and it was finally resolved, that, inasmuch as the winter was coming on us very hard and severe, increasing and getting worse day by day, we should have the ship brought in some where . . . behind some promontory, where she might be safe from drift-ice. . . .

On the 19th of September we sailed up the river, with the ship and the sloop, as far as we could, and stayed one night at anchor. On that night, the new drift-ice cut into both sides of the ship and of the sloop, to the depth of about two fingers'-breadths, so that I was obliged to have the ship brought nearer to the western shore by 8 cables' lengths, across a flat. It was a distance of nearly 900 fathoms across the flat, where the ship was in great danger, because the ground was covered with stones, and the ship could not well rest on it, on account of her being sharp-built. As the drift-ice got the upper hand, the ship stuck on a stone and became quite leaky, so that all the carpenters had enough to do during the ebb in order to make her tight again before the return of the flood.

September 25th. As we had now secured the ship close under the land and brought the sloop on shore by means of a high tide, I caused the ship's keel to be dug down into the ground, and branches of trees to be spread under the bilge, packed together with clay and sand, in order that the ship might rest evenly on the bilge on both sides, and thus suffer less damage.

On the same day, Hans Brock, the mate, returned, having been to the eastward to ascertain whether better harbours could be found. He also reported that there were no harbours suitable for winter quarters in the places where he had been, but only flat, bare, and swampy land. . . .

September 27th. Whilst we now thought that the ship was well protected against drift-ice and bad weather, such a tremendous drift of ice came upon us with a low ebb, that if the ship had not been resting so firmly on the ground, we should have been carried away by the ice. We were obliged to let go all four hawsers by which the ship was moored, and part of them went to pieces. By this breaking up of the ice, the ship also became so leaky that, at flood time, we pumped out quite 2,000 strokes of water; the ship was, on the same occasion, moved out of the dock which we originally had made for her. . . .

On the 28th of September, at high tide, we had the ship replaced in position and moored by six hawsers; and , during the lowest ebb, the leaks were looked for and made good again. Thereupon I had a fresh dock made as before, in which the ship again was placed; and, at the same time, I ordered the carpenters and others who could ply an axe, to make five bridge-piles . . . which I caused to be placed before the bow of the ship, in order to turn off the ice so that it should not hurt us.

October 1st. Everything being now well finished, and the ship and the sloop well protected against ice and tempest, I ordered the hold to be cleared out, the cannon to be placed in the hold, and a part of our goods to be brought on shore, in order that the deck might be clear and the men have more space to move about, and also that the ship should not suffer too much from the great weight resting on her deck. . . .

On the 4th of October, I distributed to the crew, clothes, shirts, shoes, and boots, and whatever else could be of use as a protection against the cold.

On the 5th of October, I caused two large fireplaces, round each of which 20 men might easily sit, to be arranged on the deck, one before the mast, the other behind the mast, as well as a fireplace on the steerage, round which likewise 20 persons could be accomodated, in addition to that in the cook's galley, where he did his cooking; that he required to have for himself.

On the 7th of October . . . I myself journeyed up the river to see how far I could get with a boat; but, about a mile and a half up, there were so many stones in it, that I could not advance any further, and had to return. I had brought with me all sorts of small goods, intending, if I had met any natives, to present them with some in order to become acquainted with them, but I could neither find nor perceive any. . . .

In many places where we came we could quite well see where people had been and had their summer abodes. Even in the place where the ship is lying there are certain signs . . . of people having been there. In the forest there are, likewise, in many places, great heaps of chips, where they have cut wood or timber; and the chips look as if they had been cut off with curved iron tools. . . . As regards their food and mode of living, it would seem that they use much in a half-cooked state, because, wherever we found that they had had their meals the bones did not seem to have been very well roasted. . . . I went on shore on the 7th of November with 19 men, and penetrated nearly three miles into the country, in order to ascertain whether any inhabitants were to be found. As, however, there was a sudden great fall of snow, which was too heavy for us to make our way through, we were obliged to return without effecting anything by the journey. But, if we had had snowshoes, such as are used in Norway, and men that knew how to run on them, it is not improbable that we might have got far enough to find people. Otherwise it is impossible to get along in these countries in the winter.

On the 10th of November, which was St Martin's Eve, the men shot some ptarmigan, with which we had to content ourselves, instead of St Martin's goose; and I ordered a pint of Spanish wine for each bowl to be given to the men, besides their daily allowance; wherewith the whole crew were well satisfied, even merry and joyful. . . .

November 14th. In the night a large black dog came to the ship on the ice, when the man on the watch observed him, and, not knowing but that it was a black fox, at once shot him, and, with much exultation, dragged him into the cabin, thinking that he had got a great prize. But when, in the morning, we examined it, we found it to be a large dog, which no doubt had been trained to catch game, because he had been tied round the nose with small cords, so that the hair was rubbed off there. . . . I should myself have been glad to have caught him alive, in which case I should have made a pedlar of him, and have let him go home to where he had come from with small goods.

November 21st. During these days the weather was very beautiful—as fine as could be expected in Denmark at that time of the year; the sea outside us was also quite clear, and the water open as far as we could see over the sea. It is, however, to be noticed that the ice on the sea drifts mostly according to the strength of the wind. . . .

On the 3rd of December, the weather being very mild, I went out into the middle of the estuary, with some of the men, in order to ascertain how thick the ice was in the middle of the channel; and we found that the ice was seven

[1] About 3 ft. 7 in.

Seeland quarters thick;[1] and this thickness it retained until long after Christmas. . . .

On the 12th of December, one of my two surgeons, the one on *Lamprenen*, David Velske by name, died, and his corpse had to remain on the ship unburied for two days, because the frost was so very severe that nobody could get on shore to bury him before the 14th of December; and the cold was then so intense that many of the men got frostbites on the nose and the cheeks when they met the wind with uncovered face. . . .

On the 24th of December, which was Christmas Eve, I gave the men wine and strong beer, which they had to boil afresh, for it was frozen to the bottom; so they had quite as much as they could stand, and were very jolly, but no one offended another with as much as a word.

The Holy Christmas Day we all celebrated and observed solemnly, as a Christian's duty is. We had a sermon and Mass; and, after the sermon, we gave the priest an offertory, according to ancient custom, each in proportion to his means. There was not much money among the men, but they gave what they had; some of them gave white fox-skins, so that the priest got enough wherewith to line a coat. However, sufficiently long life to wear it was not granted to him. . . . The crew, most of whom were, at that time, in good health . . . had all sorts of larks and pastimes; and thus we spent the Holy Days with . . . merriment. . . .

ANNO DOMINI 1620

January 1st. On New Year's Day there was a tremendously sharp frost . . . the sharpest frost that we had yet experienced during the whole winter, and at the time we suffered more severely from that terrible frost than from anything else. . . . On the 8th of January . . . one of my sailors died. . . .

On the 10th of January the priest, Mr Rasmus Jensen, and the surgeon, M. Casper Caspersen, took to their beds, having for some time felt very unwell; and after that time violent sickness commenced amongst the men which day by day prevailed more and more. . . .

On the 21st of January it was fine clear weather and sunshine; and, on that date, thirteen of us were down with sickness. Then, as I had often done before, I asked the surgeon, M. Casper Caspersen aforesaid, who was also lying mortally ill, whether he knew of any good remedy that might be found in his chest and which might serve for the recovery or comfort of the crew, as well as of himself, requesting him to inform me of it. To this he answered that he had already used as many remedies as he had with him to the best of his ability and as seemed to him advisable, and that, if God would not help, he could not employ any further remedy at all. . . .

On the 23rd of January died one of my two mates, Hans Brock by name, who had been ill, in and out of bed, for nearly five months. On the same day, it was fine weather and beautiful sunshine; and the priest sat up in his berth and gave the people a sermon, which sermon was the last he delivered in this world. . . .

On the 25th of January, when I had the body of my mate, the before-mentioned Hans Brock, buried, I ordered two falconets to be discharged, which was the last honour that I could show him. . . . But the trunnion burst off both falconets, and the man who fired them very nearly lost both his legs, so very brittle had the iron become on account of the sharp and severe frost.

On the 27th January, died Jens Helsing, seaman. On the same day my lieutenant, the well-born Mauritz Stygge, took to his bed for good, after having been ailing some time. . . .

On the 6th of February, I went with three men to the opening by which we had entered, to see how matters stood with the ice in the sea; but at that time we could not see any open water, and in the evening we returned to the ship. . . .

February 16th. During all these days, there was nothing but sickness and weakness; and every day the number of the sick was continually increased, so that, on this day, there were only seven persons in health that could fetch wood and water, and do whatever work there was to be done on board. . . .

On the 17th of February, one of my men, Rasmus Kiöbenhauffn, died; and, of the crew, there had then already died twenty persons. . . .

On the 20th of February, in the evening, died the priest, Mr Rasmus Jensen aforesaid, who had been ill and had kept his bed a long time. . . .

On the 29th of February the frost was so severe that nobody could get on shore to fetch water or wood; and that day the cook was obliged to take for fuel whatever he could find. Towards evening, however, I got a man on shore to fetch wood. On that same day I was obliged to mind the cabin myself: otherwise we should have got nothing to eat all day, because my servant had then also fallen ill and taken to his bed altogether.

On the 1st of March, died Jens Borringholm and Hans Skudenes; and, the sickness having now prevailed so far that nearly all of the crew lay sick, we had great difficulty in getting the dead buried. . . .

March 21st. During all these days, the weather was changeable. Some times it was fine and clear; at other times, sharp and severe, so that nothing particular can be recorded on that score. But as regards the crew, the most part of them were, alas, down with illness, and it was very miserable and melancholy either to hear or see them. On that same day, died the surgeon, M. Casper before-mentioned, and Povel Pedersen, who had both been ill almost since Christmas. . . .

On the 27th of March I looked over the surgeon's chest and examined its contents in detail, because, having no longer any surgeon, I had now to do the best I could myself. But it was a great neglect and mistake that there was not some little list, supplied by the physicians, indicating what those various medicaments were good for, and how they were to be used. I am also certain, and would venture to stake my life on it, that there were many kinds of medicaments in that surgeon's chest which the surgeon I had did not know; much less did he know for what purpose, and in what way, they were to be employed; because all the names were written in Latin, of which he had not forgotten much in his lifetime; but whenever he was going to examine any bottle or box, the priest had to read the description out for him. . . .

On the 30th of March . . . died Suend Arffuedsen, carpenter; and at this time commenced my greatest sorrow and misery, and I was then like a wild and lonely bird. I was now obliged myself to run about in the ship, to give drink to the sick, to boil drink for them, and get for them what I thought might be good for them, to which I was not accustomed, and of which I had but little knowledge.

On the 31st of March died my second mate, Johan Pettersen. . . . On the 1st of April, died my late nephew, Erich Munck, and his and Johan Pettersen's dead bodies were placed together in one grave.

On the 3rd of April it was a fearfully sharp frost, so that none of us could uncover himself for cold. Nor had I now anybody to command, for they were all lying under the hand of God, so that there was great misery and sorrow. . . .

On the 8th of April died Villom Gorden,[1] my chief mate, who had long been ill, in and out of bed. On the same day, towards evening, died Anders Sodens, and his dead body and that of the above-mentioned Villom Gorden were buried together in one grave, which we who then were alive could only manage with great difficulty, on account of the miserable weakness that was upon us. . . .

On April the 10th died the honourable and well-born gentleman Mauritz Stygge, my lieutenant . . . and I took some of my own linen wherein to wrap his body as well as I could. It was with great difficulty that I got a coffin made for him. . . .

[1] William Gordon, the English pilot.

On the 13th of April I took a bath in a wine-cask, which I had caused to be prepared for the purpose; and I utilized for this purpose all the kinds of herbs which we found in the surgeon's chest and thought serviceable. After that, my men likewise had a bath, as many of them as could move about and were not too weak; which bath (thanks be to God) did us much good, myself in particular.

On the 14th of April . . . only four beside myself had strength enough to sit up in the berth and listen to the homily for Good Friday. . . .

On the 21st of April the sunshine was beautiful; wherefore some of the sick crawled forth from their berths in order to warm themselves by the sun. But as they were so very weak some of them swooned, so that it did not do them any good; and I had enough to do before I got them back again, each to his berth. . . .

On the 25th of April the wild geese began to arrive; at which we were delighted, hoping that the summer would now soon come; but in this expectation we were disappointed, for the cold lasted on much longer. . . .

May 3rd and 4th. During all these days not a man left his berth save myself and the under-cook, who still could do a little. . . .

May 10th. On this day the weather was fine and mild, and great numbers of geese arrived; we got one of them, which sufficed us for two meals. We were, at that time, eleven persons alive, counting the sick. . . .

On the 12th of May died Jens Jörgensen, carpenter, and Suend Marstrand; and God knows what misery we suffered before we got their bodies buried. These were the last that were buried in the ground. . . .

May 28th. During these days there was nothing particular to write about, except that we seven[1] miserable persons, who were still lying there alive, looked mournfully at each other, hoping every day that the snow would thaw and the ice drift away. . . .

During these days, when we were lying in bed so altogether bad, there died Peder Nyborg, carpenter, Knud Lauritzsen Skudenes, and Jörgen, the cook's boy, all of whom remained on the steerage; for there was then nobody that could bury their bodies or throw them overboard.

On the 4th of June, which was Whit-Sunday, there remained alive only three beside myself, all lying down, unable to help one another. . . . The cook's boy lay dead by my berth, and three men on the steerage; two men were on shore, and would gladly have been back on the ship, but it was impossible for them to get there, as they had not sufficient strength in their limbs . . . so that both they and I were lying quite exhausted, as we had now for four entire days

[1] Two more had died since the 12th. The disease was doubtless scurvy.

had nothing for the sustenance of the body. Accordingly I did not now hope for anything but that God would put an end to this my misery and take me to Himself and His Kingdom; and thinking that it would have been the last I wrote in this world, I penned a writing as follows:

> Inasmuch as I have now no more hope of life in this world, I request, for the sake of God, if any Christian men should happen to come here, that they will bury in the earth my poor body, together with the others which are found here, expecting their reward from God in Heaven; and, furthermore, that this my journal may be forwarded to my most gracious Lord and King (for every word that is found herein is altogether truthful) in order that my poor wife and children may obtain some benefit from my great distress and miserable death. Herewith, good-night to all the world; and my soul into the hand of God, etc.
>
> JENS MUNCK

June the 8th. As I could not now any more stand the bad smell and stench from the dead bodies, which had remained in the ship for some time, I managed, as best I could, to get out of the berth (which no doubt was due to God's fatherly Providence, He being willing still to spare my life), considering that it would not matter where, or among what surroundings, I died—whether outside amongst the others that were lying dead, or remaining in the berth. When, by the assistance of God, I had come out of the cabin, I spent that night on the deck, using the clothes of the dead. But next day, when the two men who were on shore saw me and perceived that I was still alive—I, on my part, had thought that they were dead long ago—they came out on the ice to the ship, and assisted me in getting down from the ship to the land, together with the clothes which I threw to them; for the ship was not farther from the shore than about twelve or fourteen fathoms. For some time we had our dwelling on shore under a bush . . . and there we made a fire in the daytime. Later on, we crawled about everywhere near, wherever we saw the least green growing out of the ground, which we dug up and sucked the main root thereof. This benefited us, and, as the warmth now commenced to increase nicely, we began to recover.

While we thus continued on shore, the sailmaker, who before had been extremely weak, died in the ship.

June 18th. When the ice drifted away from the ship, we got a net for catching flounders out of the sloop; and, when the ebb had run out one quarter, we went out dryshod and set it. When the flood returned, God gave us six large trout, which I cooked myself, while the two others went on board *Lamprenen* to fetch wine, which we had not tasted for a long time, none of us having had an appetite for it.

As we now thus every day got fresh, fish which was well cooked, it comforted us much, although we could not eat any of the fish, but only the broth, with which we drank wine, so that by degrees we recovered somewhat. At last, we got a gun on shore and shot birds, from which we obtained much refreshment; so that, day by day, we got stronger and fairly well in health.

June 26th. In the name of Jesus, and after prayer and supplication to God for good fortune and counsel, we now set to work to bring *Lamprenen* alongside *Enhiörningen*, and worked as diligently as we could in getting sails ready for us. But herein we encountered a great difficulty and much anxiety, because *Lamprenen* stood high on the shore, having been carried up by the winter's flood. We were consequently obliged first to unload all that was in her, and then to look out for a high spring tide in order to haul her out. In this we succeeded, and brought her alongside *Enhiörningen*. When we got on board *Enhiörningen,* we were obliged first of all to throw overboard the dead bodies, which were then quite decomposed, as we could not move about or do anything there for bad smell and stench, and yet were under the necessity of taking out of *Enhiörningen* and placing on board *Lamprenen* victuals and other necessaries for our use in crossing the sea, as far as we three persons could manage.

On the 16th of July, which was Sunday, in the afternoon, we set sail from there in the name of God. At that time it was as warm in that country as it might have been in Denmark, and the cloud-berries were in bud. There was such a quantity of gnats that in calm weather they were unbearable. A quantity of rain also fell every day at this time of the year. Before setting out from there, I drilled two or three holes in *Enhiörningen,* in order that the water which might be in the ship might remain when the ebb was half out, so that the ship should always remain firm on the ground whatever ice might come. . . . And I have called the same harbour after myself, JENS MUNCKES BAY. . . .

[*It took them seven weeks to work their way through the ice to Mansfield Island. Five days later—August 18—they were out once more upon the Atlantic, and on September 1 "Before a wind that could move men."*]

September 2nd and 3rd. Again storm and tempest from the South-east. Towards evening we were obliged to take in the sails altogether and to lie-to, working the pump.

On the 4th of September we had tremendous rain and wind, amounting to a gale, and we could not at all leave the pump. Towards the evening the wind commenced to be more favourable; and, as we were quite exhausted with pumping, we drifted the whole night without sails, in order to get some rest, as far as the pump would allow of it. . . .

On the 9th, 10th, and 11th of September we had all kinds of wind and foggy weather; but in the evening, towards night, a gale sprang up, and our foresail was torn from the bolt-rope, so that we three men had plenty to do to get it in, and then the ship was half full of water.

September 12th. In the course of the night the wind shifted to the west and blew hard; our topsail-sheet was blown to pieces, the topmost-stay broken asunder, and the great parrel too; so that it was very anxious work for us three. . . .

On the 14th of September we made the Orkney Islands. . . .

On the 16th of September we sailed 20 miles, steering East by North, towards Norway, as near to the wind as possible. . . .

On the 21st of September we came to harbour South of Allen[1] in a flying gale, not knowing the locality. When I had come inside the rocky islands into a large fjord, I could find no anchorage, and was obliged all day to beat to and fro inside the rocks, because I had only half an anchor. Towards evening, when I saw that nobody came out, I steered into a bay, where I dropped that half of an anchor, and this remained, without being moored, as I had no boat wherewith to carry a hawser on shore. Late in the evening, a peasant came there by accident; and I was obliged to threaten him with a gun to make him come and assist me in getting a hawser on shore. In the morning, I at once proceeded in the same boat to His Majesty's bailiff in Sundfiord,[2] and requested him to procure fresh victuals and men that could run the ship into Bergen.

As I now had seen the ship safe, and had returned into a Christian country, we poor men could not hold our tears for great joy, and thanked God that He had graciously granted us this happiness.

On the 25th of September I came myself to Bergen, and went at once to physicians to obtain advice and remedies. I also ordered at once drink and medicines to be prepared and forwarded to my two men by the hands of a skipper whom I sent to the ship to take care of it in my place.

On the 27th of September I wrote home to Denmark, to the High Authorities, to report that I had arrived there.

[1] Alden. [2] Söndfjord.

SLEDGE-TRACKS NORTHWARD[1]

(1902-4)

KNUD RASMUSSEN

(1879-1933)

I

WE had reached our goal!

But one of our number was dangerously ill, and we were powerless to relieve him; the people we had hoped to meet with at Cape York settlement had left their houses, and our famished dogs were circling madly round us; we had hardly enough food left for one good meal, even for ourselves. To lighten our sledges we had stored our chests of supplies at Cape Murdoch, and a considerable proportion of the provisions that we had calculated would suffice for the journey thence to Cape York had been devoured by the dogs.

The forced pace of the last two days and nights had greatly exhausted us; for the moment, however, we were so much struck by all the new sights around us, by the strange, primitive human dwellings, that we forgot our fatigue in exploring the settlement. But it was not long before we flung ourselves down by our sledges and dropped asleep.

It is but a short rest, though, that a traveller can permit himself under critical circumstances. One of us soon woke again and roused the others. A more careful examination of the snow huts then revealed that it could not have been long since their owners had left them. In one of them there was a large seal, not cut up, which provided our dogs with a very welcome feast.

There were numerous sledge-tracks running northward, with only a light powdering of snow upon them; consequently men could not be far away.

I remembered a story told us by an old Greenlander whom we had visited in Danish West Greenland, on our way north.

He knew that they had kinsmen a long way north; but no one was certain exactly whereabouts. It was so far away. The following tradition he had heard as a child:

"Once upon a time there was a man who lived farther north than any of the settlements. He hunted bears every spring on a dogsledge.

"Once, during the chase, he came upon strange sledge-tracks, and made up his mind to seek out the people who had made them. So he set out on his bear-hunts the next year earlier than he was wont to do. The third day he came to houses different in appearance from those to which he was accustomed. But he met with no people; fresh tracks, though, showed that the

[1] From *The People of the Polar North.*

settlement had been only recently left.

"When the bear-hunter drove off the following year he took wood with him, as a gift to the strangers; for he thought they must suffer greatly from the want of wood, as they used narwhal's tusks for the roof-beams of their houses.

"But he did not meet with the strangers on his second visit either. True, the tracks were newer than they had been the last time, but he did not dare to follow them up, and thus put a still greater distance between himself and his own village. He contented himself with burying the wood he had brought with him in the snow near the houses, and then, having presented his gifts, he went home.

"The third year he raised the best team of dogs that he had ever had, and earlier than was his custom he drove north after bears and the strange people. When at last he reached the village it was just as it had been the other years; the inhabitants had gone; but in the snow, where he had left his wood, they had hidden a large bundle of walrus tusks, and inside, in the entrance passage, lay a magnificent bitch and puppies. These were the return gifts of the strangers.

"He put them on his sledge and drove back home; but the people who lived north of all other men he never found."

And now, just as had been the case then, many sledge-tracks ran north, and again, as in the legend, it could not have been many days since they had been made.

It was an odd experience, creeping through the long, low tunnel entrances into the houses; with our furs on we could hardly pass. At the end, we came to a hole up through which we had to squeeze ourselves, and then we were in the house. There was a strong smell of raw meat and fox inside.

The first time one sees a house of this description one is struck by the little with which human beings can be content. It is all so primitive, and has such an odour of paganism and magic incantation. A cave like this, skilfully built in arch of gigantic blocks of stone, one involuntarily peoples mentally with half supernatural beings. You see them, in your fancy, pulling and tearing at raw flesh, you see the blood dripping from their fingers, and you are seized yourself with a strange excitement at the thought of the extraordinary life that awaits you in their company.

We walked round, examining all these things, which, in their silent way, spoke to us of the men and women who lived their lonely life up here. A little way from the houses, in a circle, were some large round stones, shining with stale grease. "Here they must have had their meals," suggested one of our

Greenlanders. Already our imagination was at work.

Farther up, just under the overhanging cliff, lay a kayak with all its appurtenances, covered over with stones. Behind it was a sledge, with dead dogs harnessed to it, almost wholly hidden by the drifting snow. There, then, men lay buried with all their possessions, as Eskimo custom prescribes.

All that we saw was new to us and absorbingly interesting. At last we were on Polar Eskimo ground, and our delight at having reached our goal was unmeasured. If only we had been spared the calamity of our comrade's serious illness! He lay dazed and feverish, unable to stir, and had to be fed when he required to eat. At a council among ourselves, it was agreed that Mylius-Erichsen should remain with him, keeping the two seal-hunters, while Jörgen Brönlund and I drove on north as fast as our almost exhausted dogs could take us, to look for people. We calculated that at a distance of about sixty-four English miles from Cape York we ought to come across Eskimos at Saunders Island, and if not there, then at Natsilivik, some forty English miles farther north. All the provisions we could take were a few biscuits and a box of butter. Still we had our rifles to fall back upon.

The sealers had gone out to try their luck, and we waited for them to return— which they did empty-handed. Then we drank a little cocoa, and drove off along the glorious rocky coast, into the clear, light night.

In the neighbourhood of Cape Atholl we discovered fresh sledgetracks, which we followed up. They led to a stone cairn, under a steep wall of rock, which cairn contained a large deposit of freshly-caught bearded seal. Ah! then we could not be far from human beings. The intense suspense of it! For it almost meant our comrade's life.

We had driven all night—some twelve hours, and a little way beyond Cape Atholl were obliged to pull up, to give the dogs a rest and breathing time. We had covered about fifty-six English miles at full gallop, and, should we be forced to drive all the way to Natsilivik, should have to make reasonable allowance for the empty stomachs of our poor animals. We flung ourselves down on the ice, discussed our prospects, ate a little butter—we simply dared not eat our biscuits—lay down on our sledges and went to sleep.

After three hours' rest we went on again.

We had only driven a little way when a black dot became visible in front. It developed and grew into a sledge.

"Jörgen!—Knud!—Jörgen!—Knud!"

We were half mad with relief and delight, and could only call out each other's names.

Speed signal! The dogs drop their tails and prick up their ears. We murmur the signal again between our teeth, and the snow swirls up beneath their hind legs. A biting wind cuts us in the face. At last! at last! people, other people, the new people—the Polar Eskimos!

A long narrow sledge is coming towards us at full speed, a whip whistles through the air, and unfamiliar dog-signals are borne on the wind to our ears. A little fur-clad man in a pair of glistening white bearskin trousers springs from the sledge and runs up to his team, urging the dogs on still faster with shouts and gesticulations. Behind him, sitting astride the sledge, sits another person, dressed in blue fox, with a large pointed hat on her head: that is his wife.

Our dogs begin to bark, and the sledges meet to the accompaniment of loud yelps. We spring off and run up to each other, stop and stare at one another, incapable of speech, both parties equally astonished.

I explain to him who we are, and where we come from.

"White men! White men!" he calls out to his wife. "White men have come on a visit!"

We have no difficulty in understanding or making ourselves understood.

I hasten to the woman, who has remained seated on the sledge. All sorts of strange emotions crowd in upon me, and I do not know what to say. Then, without thinking what I am doing, I hold out my hand. She looks at me, uncomprehending, and laughs. And then we all laugh together.

The man's name is Maisanguaq (the little white whale skin), his wife Meqo (the feather); they live at Igfigsoq, from twelve to sixteen English miles south of our meeting-place, and we learn that three or four other families live at the same place.

In our eagerness to arrive at Agpat (Saunders Island) we had cut across outside the bay on which Igfigsoq lies.

The snow on the ice at the entrance to the bay being hard, we had not been able to detect sledge-tracks which might have led us to enter it. But when we heard that there were far more people at Agpat, and that the hunting and sealing there were particularly good, I decided to drive straight on, and, by sledge post, advise my comrades to do the same.

Maisanguaq promptly seated himself across my sledge, his wife driving theirs, and we all set off together towards Agpat, carrying on the liveliest conversation meanwhile. The two ought really to have been at home by this time, but had turned back to show us the way.

Meqo was a capital dog-driver, and wielded her long whip as well as any man. In West Greenland you never see a woman drive, so I expressed my surprise; Maisanguaq laughed out with pride, and called out to her gaily to lash hard with her whip, it amused the white men, and Meqo swung her whip, and off we dashed, she leading.

"*Tugto! tugto*!" she cried, and the dogs bounded forward, and soon we began to near the high-lying little island on which Agpat lay.

Maisanguaq then told me that "many" people lived at Agpat: there were three stone houses and five snow huts; and the burst into peals of laughter each time he thought of the surprise he was going to witness. "White men! White men!" he called out, whenever an instant's pause in the conversation occurred, and rubbed his hands with glee.

Suddenly he stopped short and listened, then jumped up in my sledge and looked behind. Another sledge had come in sight a long way to our rear.

"*Aulavte! aulavte!*" he called out. (That is the signal for a halt.) But my dogs did not understand him, and I had to come to the rescue by whistling to them.

Then he jumped out on the one side, and began to hop up in the air and slap himself on the legs. He continued to indulge in these extraordinary antics till he was quite red in the face from his exertions. This was an indication that something unusual was going on. The strange sledge came on at a gallop; as it approached, two young fellows sprang out and ran alongside, shouting. Maisanguaq began to yell too, and continued to flounder about like a madman.

At last the sledge came up to ours and stopped. The two young men were named Qulutana and Inukitsoq. First, of course, they wanted to know who we were, and Maisanguaq delivered himself of his lesson. Then the whole caravan drove on, laughing and shouting, towards Agpat.

Never in my life have I felt myself to be in such wild, unaccustomed surroundings, never so far, so very far away from home, as when I stood in the midst of the tribe of noisy Polar Eskimos on the beach at Agpat. We were not observed till we were close to the land, so the surprise and confusion created by our arrival were all the greater.

Maisanguaq recommenced his jumping antics by the side of the sledge as soon as we arrived within calling distance of the place, and then screamed out a deafening "White men! White men!"

The people, who had been moving briskly about among the houses, stood still, and the children left off their play.

"White men! White men!" repeated the young fellows who had joined us. Our dogs drooped their tails and pricked up their ears as a many-tongued roar from the land reached us. And then, like a mountain-slide, the whole swarm rushed down to the shore, where we had pulled up—a few old grey-haired men and stiff-jointed old crones, young men and women, children who could hardly toddle, all dressed alike in these fox and bear-skin furs, which create such an extraordinarily barbaric first impression. Some came with long knives in their hands, with bloodstained arms and upturned sleeves, having been in the midst of flaying operations when we arrived, and all this produced a very savage effect; at the moment it was difficult to believe that these "savages," "the neighbours of the North Pole," as Astrup called them, were ever likely to become one's good, warm friends.

Our dogs were unharnessed, and quantities of meat flung to them at once. Meat there was in abundance, and everywhere, in between the houses, you saw cooking-hearths. It was immediately apparent that these people were not suffering from privation.

On one's arrival at a settlement in Danish West Greenland, it is usual for the young women to help the newcomers off with their outdoor clothes. Now, for a moment, I forgot where I was, and as the Greenlandic custom is, stretched out my foot towards a young girl who was standing by my side, meaning her to pull off my outer boots. The girl grew embarrassed, and the men laughed. There was that winning bashfulness about her that throws attraction over all Nature's children; a pale blush shot across her cheek, like a ripple over a smooth mountain lake; she half turned away from me, and her black eyes looked uneasily out over the frozen sea.

"What is thy name?"

"Others will tell thee what my name is," she stammered.

"Aininâq is her name," put in the bystanders, laughing.

A jovial old paterfamilias them came up to her and said with gravity:

"Do what the strange man asks thee!" And she stooped down at once and drew off my boots.

"Move away; let me come!" called out an old woman from the crowd, and she elbowed the people aside and forced her way through to my sledge.

"It was my daughter thou wast talking to!" she burst out eagerly. "Dost thou not think her beautiful?" and she rolled her little selfconscious eyes around.

But Aininâq had slipped quietly away from the crowd to curious beholders and hidden herself. It was only later that I learnt my request to her had been construed into a proposal of marriage.

Jörgen and I were now conducted up to the houses. Sheltering walls of snow had been built up here and there to form cooking-places, and round these the natives clustered. A young fellow came up carrying a frozen walrus liver, raw, which was our first meal; all the men of the village ate of it with us, to show their hospitable intent. Curious youngsters gaped at us greedily from every side, and ran away when we looked at them.

When the pot had boiled, we were called in to the senior of the tribe, the magician Sagdloq ("The Lie"); the boiled meat was placed on the floor, and a knife put in our hands.

A lively conversation got under way. The people were not difficult to understand, as their dialect differed but little from the ordinary Greenlandic; they were surprised themselves at the ease with which they understood us, who yet came from such a distance.

After the meal, they immediately set about building us a snow hut.

"There is a sick man with you, so you must be helped quickly," they said.

They hewed large blocks out of the hard snow: those were to be the walls of our new house. Then they set it up in a hollow in the snow, and in the course of half an hour it stood complete.

A sledge was sent for our comrades, and by early morning we were all together.

The reception these pagan savages gave us was affectingly cordial; it seemed that they could not do enough for us. And just as they were on our arrivel—helpful as they could possibly be, and most generious with their gifts—so they remained the whole time that we spent among them. . . .

II

Our sick comrade, Count Harald Moltke, was by this time so far on the road to recovery that he could take a walk every day on the big flat outside our tent on Saunders Island. But in spite of the steady progress he was making, we dared not expose him to another winter in this harsh climate and under these primitive conditions, if we could possibly avoid it.

Two Scottish captains, whom we had met on June 27, would not undertake the responsibility of transporting him by vessel, but they had told us that not far behind them was another whaler, the *Vega*, which would be able to lend us a boat; they themselves could not spare one. If Moltke's health continued to improve, towards the autumn, when the channels were clear of ice, we might make an attempt to penetrate, along the Melville Glaciers, to Upernivik. We waited for the *Vega*, and went up the hills, on the look-out, whenever it was clear. But the waiting-time grew long. The *Vega* did not come. As is well known, she was packed in the ice in Melville Bay and lost.

By the middle of July we came to the conclusion that we must seek some other way out of our difficulties, if we wanted to reach Upernivik before the winter. And as an Eskimo, named Sâmik, in the Northern District, possessed a whaling sloop that he had received from Robert Peary, the American, we decided to place ourselves in communication with him and try to induce him to lend us his boat, which could be returned to him later by a whaler from Upernivik.

The time of year was not a favourable one for the journey. Ice still lay over the fjord, and made kayak travelling impossible. The attempt would have to be made with dog-sledges. It was decided, therefore, that Mylius-Erichsen and the Greenlander Gabriel should remain behind with Harald Moltke, while I, with the Greenlandic Catechist Jörgen Brönlund, was to drive north and open negotiations with Sâmik. In addition to Jörgen, I chose, as escorts, two young Eskimos of about twenty years of age, Sitdluk and Qisunguaq.

So two sledges left our encampment in Saunders Island on July 17 at midnight and proceeded north. All the ice on the south side of the island had disappeared, but on the north coast there was still a narrow bridge of ice connecting it with the mainland: we should be able to cross by that. But first we had to get out sledges over the high land, 2000 feet in height and bare of snow, and that was no easy matter, as our way up and down led through ravines where the streams had long since burst their ice covering and rushed down with great force. Foreseeing what the dificulties of our journey would be, we had limited our baggage to our sleeping-bags and a little clothing, all the provisions we had being a handful of biscuits and a little tea and sugar; we should fall in with food enough on the way.

"Men don't drag meat with them in the height of summer!" as the Eskimos said. Nor did we take a tent with us. We owned two, but one had to be left for Moltke; the other had been torn by the dogs, and was consequently unusable in wet weather. We should have to manage Eskimo fashion; if it rained we must seek shelter among the rocks.

Along wretched, half-melted ice, intersected by streams, and after a twelve hours' journey, we reached the mainland, where we had to camp, as the heat was too much for the dogs. Towards midnight we went on, at first on ice. We passed a few small islands, where we collected eider-ducks', terns' and long-tailed ducks' eggs. The first ice came to an end at the islands, and we went on for a little way on floating ice-floes, but at last we were compelled to fall back on the land, though bare of snow. The inland streams gave us a great deal of trouble. We were obliged to pull the sledges ourselves, barelegged, when we wanted to cross them, and, being glacier streams, they were icily cold; our flaming scarlet legs tingled with the freezing water.

We then came to the great bay, Iterdlagssuaq, across the mouth of which it was easy going; but farther inland the ice was cut up by the current and covered with water, which often reached above the cross-bars of our sledges. Towards midnight we succeeded in making the opposite coast of the bay, without a dry thread upon us. There we encamped, by a little stream-bed.

July 18. Towards evening we were awakened by pouring rain and obliged to seek shelter in a cave near by. Here we were protected from the south-west gale and the driving sleet. We remained thritysix hours in the cave.

July 20. Towards morning it cleared up; we sprang half-naked about the rocks, and dried our clothes and sleeping-bags. We made a little tea, and boiled some seal's skin—starvation fare. During the strom the dogs broke in and ate our meat. We set out again towards evening. Towards camping time, shot three seals; men and dogs ate what they could. Sweet sleep followed.

July 21. Rain and storm again; we are sadly wet.

July 22. Good drying weather. We went on. The ice unfortunately broken up; we had to drive on floes, the ice-foot and on land. At the head of the fjord we made a halt to reconnoitre; from there we had to travel along the glacier. Jörgen, who had gone on in front, saw a reindeer, which he shot. While we were engaged in skinning and cutting up, the rain came on again. At the same time, a storm rose amongst the rocks and glaciers, so violent that it swept sand and stones down with it. We hastily erected a little shelter, constructed of our sledges, covered with blubber, and the freshly flayed seal-skins, and crawled inside.

For the third time we are weather-bound, even before we have our clothes dried from the last wetting.

July 23. Rain and wind. We sit under an uninviting dripping of blubber. When we are tired of telling tales—and by degrees we have worked through the whole of our childhood and our taste of manhood—we lie down to sleep, or Jörgen begins to read aloud to us from his Bible. I read the Revelation of St John, which impresses me greatly in its imposing Greenlandic translation. Jörgen clings to St Paul, and reads me the Eqistle to the Romans. Now and again an illusion of comfort visits us, and as we grow absorbed in each other's narrations we manage to forget that we are wet and hungry. It is only when silence has fallen upon us all again that we notice how we are slowly being pickled in the wet. The sleeping-bags are drenched, the reindeer hair on them is beginning to fall off in patches, and our clothes are smelling musty. Our feet are white and swollen from the damp, and we are cold.

Our spirits are on the verge of a breakdown, and we are beginning to talk of our comrades at Agpat, who, on the thorns of expectation, probably think that we have already reached our goal.

When shall we be able to go on? Will it be possible to get through at all? Or is this expedition, which was started upon in such high hopes, to end merely in disappointment—disappointment for us, and for those behind who are waiting?

"Talk, Knud, talk! There will be no standing it, if we are both silent. Tell us something, no matter what!" And Jörgen rolls me over in my sleeping-bag. Sitdluk thrusts his head out and shouts hopelessly into the roaring gale, "*Qanigtailivdlugo! qanigtailivdlugo*!" which in translation means, " Stop the rain! stop the rain!" For he believes that up among the rocks there live powerful spirits who can cammand the wind and stop the downpours of rain.

And Qisunguaq begins to reproach me with avarice. "You are so strange, you white men! You collect things you will never require, and you cannot leave even the graves alone. All this calamity is the revenge of the dead. Perhaps we shall die of hunger. Just because you took those stupid things!"

A few days before I had taken a scratching-pin, a needle-case, and a curved knife from an old grave. I console him by saying that the corpse would certainly have been satisfied with my exchange gifts to the soul. It had had tea, matches, blubber and meat, just as they had stipulated. But Qisunguaq would not be appeased.

"The thoughts of the dead are not as our thoughts; the dead are incomprehensible in their doings!" he sighed.

"Stop, stop the rain!" calls Sitdluk despairingly up to the rocks.

"Tell us about Marianne, or Ellen, or Sara. Tell tales, and do not stop till we have forgotten where we are and think we are with them," demands Jörgen.

And memory hypnotises us back to experiences that lie behind; and fancy draws us ever in the same direction—back to vanished well-being, when we knew no privations; back to the delicacies of the Danish-Greenlandic kitchen, to the magnificent splendour of the shops. And thus, when one of us gets well under way with his narrative, we succeed in forgetting for a moment where we are, and friends, who perhaps think of us no more, Danes and Greenlanders, file past us, while the roaring stream outside thunders and swells with the rain.

The dogs, lying drenched in the wet, whine plintively now and again; but the hills merely play withtheir yelping, and the echo of it rings across and across the fjord head.

July 24. Rained all night. Towards morning the storm gave over. The clouds parted and the sun streamed down upon us. We attempted at three different places to cross the stream separating us from the drive up the glacier leading to Itivdleq on the other side of the mainland, but in vain.

By the time the water was up to our knees, the current was so strong that we almost lost our footing and were in danger of being carried off with it. Originally there were two streams only at the head of the bay, but in the last few days they have multiplied sadly. The terrific downpour has transformed the little valley into a whole network of streamlets. Altogether I counted eighteen, large and small.

An attempt at low water along the beach, leaping from one floe to another, was likewise unsuccessful. And the middle of the bay is now open water; the ice we were driving upon has been broken up by the storm. We are under siege. Seven glaciers shoot down to the head of the bay where we are; on the other side is the valley with the eighteen streams, and below it, the open bay itself.

July 25. Qisunguaq discovered a way up over a cliff about 2000 feet high, bare of snow. It was no easy matter to get the sledges up. Driving across the glacier was not without danger, either; there were many rushing streams, the passage of which gave plenty of trouble; I fell off twice and got wet through, but as there was a strong wind I soon got dry again. Some of the streams, with soft, deep snow on the sides, we had to cross by hurling ourselves over, to fall flat, rather than on our feet or legs, as otherwise we were in danger of disappearing altogether.

Late in the evening we have reached the place where begins the descent to Itivdleq, whence we were to cross to Qanâ. We are 2400 feet above the level of the sea and there is a superb view; but all our efforts have been wasted; Qanâ, where the boat is, is inaccessible. The ice is all broken up into floes.

It is night, and our journey has been a hard one; our provisions are at an end; we can only fling ourselves down on our sledges and sleep our fatigue away. On the top of the hill, a terrific storm is howling.

July 26. We cannot get back to Agpat; and we must get into communication with men somewhere as soon as possible. Food we must have, and new footgear. We have tried to bind the soles of our kamiks (soft leather boots) together with thread; but they are so worn from the crumbling sandstone rocks and the sharp glacier ice that they are in holes that leave our feet bare. It is painful walking on the rocks, and it is abominably cold travelling on the ice.

We must attempt to reach Natsilivik; perhaps ther are men there.

We break up towards midday and drive to the top of the glacier ridge, about 3400 feet up. We drive all day in a glorious sunshine through deep snow. Marvellously lovely glacier landscapes spread themselves out before us; there is a view over the whole of Whale Sound, with its islands, and the island of Agpat, and Wolstenholme with Jának. The sea is like a mirror, but up here, where we are driving, a fresh north wind is blowing, and it is cold—in spite of the sun.

The glacier drops gently down to Natsilivik, and we have an enjoyable drive downhill of two to three hours, with, when the snow is not too deep, good going.

We are above the clouds, for there hangs a thick fog down over Natsilivik while we are driving along in sunshine.

Down at the edge of the glacier, where we have to guide our team with great caution, as there is no snow, there are great glacier fountains, and several magnificent red water-springs, which give birth to red streamets.

"It is the glacier bleeding!" says Qisunguaq of these great red springs, which gush up through narrow openings and rise in a thick stream, till they are scattered by the wind and fall away to the sides, like a waving crown of flowers.

At the edge of the glacier we leave our sledges and baggage behind and walk down to Natsilivik, where we arrive towards midnight.

No one there!

July 27. A dense fog further increases the difficulty of all search. Jörgen and Sitdluk have gone down to the houses at Natsilivik to see if there are meat deposits to be found.

Qisunguaq and I cross a ridge and make our way down to a creek, Narssaq, where there used to be tents.

We advance through the fog, seeing nothing and hoping for no more, our feet sore and our stomachs empty. After a few hours' toilsome march, we reach a rapid stream which we cannot cross; and we lie down under a great boulder, discuss the position, and decide which of the dogs we shall be obliged to shoot, it we do not meet with people. We have eaten nothing for forty hours, and the last few days' traveling have been exhausting. Just as we are dropping asleep the fog lifts suddenly and we are inspired with fresh hope. We fling large stones into the stream, but the current carries them with it. At last one stone remains in place and we dare the crossing.

We are over; we run up the opposite bank, which is steep and high, and both utter wild cries of delight: at a distance of about 200 yards there are five tents . . . people!—and food . . . food!

CHINA

HOW FA-HIAN WENT IN SEARCH OF THE SACRED BOOKS[1]

Fa-Hian

(*fl.* A.D. 399-414)

He sets out for India

Fah hian, when formely resident at Tchang'an,[2] was grieved at noticing the fragmentary character of the Rules of the Buddhist Discipline (as they were then known in China). Whereupon, in the second year of Hung Chi, the cyclical characters being Ki Hae, he agreed with Hwui King, Tao Ching, Hwui Ying and Hwui Wu, to go together to India to seek for complete copies of these Rules.

Setting out, therefore, from Tchang'an they first of all crossed the Lung (Mountains), and arrived at the country of Kon Kwei, where they sojourned during the season of the Rains. After this they pushed forward, and arrived at the country of Niu Tan; then crossing the Yang Lau Hills they reached the great frontier station of Chang Yeh. This place was in such an unsettled condition that the roads were unsafe forb passsengers. The Prince of the country prevailed on them to remain there for some time, and himself afforded them hospitality. It was here they fell in with Chi Yen, Hwui Kan, Sang Chau, Po Wan and Sang King, and pleased to find they all had one common aim in view, they remained together during the season of the rains.[3] After this they again set out and arrived at Tun Wang. . . . They all stopped here a month and some odd days, after which Fah Hian and his four companions made arrangements to set out in advance of the others, and so they were again separated.

He crosses the River of Sand—

The military governor of Tun Wang, Li Ho by name, provided them with all necessaries for crossing the Desert.[4] In this desert there are great many evil demons, there are also sirocco winds, which kill all who encounter them. There are no birds or beasts to be seen; but so far as the eye can reach, the route is marked out by the bleached bones of men who have perished in the attempt to cross the desert. After travelling thus for seventeen days, a distance of about fifteen hundred li, they at the kingdom of Shen-Shen.

[1] From *Travels of Fah Hian and Sung-Yun,* translated by Samuel Beal (1869).

[2] Si-Gan Fu.

[3] This shows that nine months had gone since they left Kon Kwei.

[4] The Gobi Desert.

And the Little Snowy Mountains

In the second month of winter, Fah Hian and his two companions going to the South, crossed the Little Snowy Mountains. The snow continually accumulates on these mountains, both in winter and summer. The exceeding cold which came on suddenly in crossing the Northern slope of the mountain, which lies in the shade, caused the men generally to remain perfectly silent [to shut their mouths] through fear. The pilgrim Hwui Ying was unable, after repeated efforts, to proceed any further. His mouth was covered with a white foam; at last he addressed Fah Hian and said, "It is impossible for me to recover; whilst there is time, do you press forward, lest we all perish," and upon this the presently died. Fah Hian cherished him [to supply warmth] and piteously invoked him by his familiar name, but it was all ineffectual to restore life. Submitting therefore to his destiny, he once more gathered up his strength and pressed forward.

He reaches the Vulture Peak

Entering the valley, and skirting the mountains along their south-eastern slope for a distance of fifteen li, we arrive at the hill called Gridhrakôuta[1] (Ki-che-kiu). Three li from the top is a stone cavern facing the south. Buddha used in this place to sit in profound meditation (*dhyâna*). Thirty paces to the north-west is another stone cell, in which Ânanda practiced meditation (*dhyâna*). The Dêva Mâra Pâpîyan having assumed the form of a vulture, took his station before the cavern, and terrified Ânanda. Buddha, by his spiritual power (of Irrdhi) penetrated the rock, and with his outspread hand touched the head of Ânanda. On this he bore up against his fear, and found peace. The traces of the bird and of the hand-hole still plainly exist, and from this circumstance the hill is called "the hill of the vulture cave." Fah Hian, having bought flowers, incense, and oil and lamps, in the New Town, procured the assistance of two aged Bikshus to accompany him to the top of the peak. Having arrived there, he offered his flowers and incense, and lit his lamps, so that their combined lustre illuminated the gloom of the cave. Fah Hian was deeply moved, even till the tears coursed down his cheeks, and he said, "Here it was in bygone days Buddha dwelt, and delivered the Surañgama Sutra. Fah Hian, not privileged to be born at a time when Buddha lived, can but gaze on the traces of his presence, and the place which he occupied." Then taking his position in front of the cave, he recited the Surañgama (Sutra), and remained there the entire night.

[1] Near Patna.

He transcribes the Sacred Books

From Benares going eastward in a retrograde order, we arrive at the town of Pâtaliputra again. The purpose of Fah Hian was to seek for copies of the Vinaya Pitaka. But throughout the whole of Northern India the various masters trusted to tradition only for their knowledge of the Precepts, and had no written copies of them at all. Wherefore Fah Hian had come even so far as Mid-India [without effecting his purpose]. But here in the Sañghârâma of the Great Vehicle (at Patna) he obtained one copy of the Precepts, viz., the collection used by the school of the Mahâsañghikas, which was that used by the first great assembly of priests convened during Buddha's lifetime. Moreover, he obtained one copy of Precepts in manuscript, comprising about 7000 gâthas. Moreover he obtained a collection of Sutras in their abbreviated form, consisting altogether of 2500 verses. Moreover he obtained an expanded volume of the Parinirvâna Sûtra, containing about 5000 verses. Moreover he procured a copy of the Abhidharma according to the school of the Mahâsañghikas. On this account Fah Hian abode in this place for the space of three years engaged in learning to read the Sanskrit books, and to converse in that language, and in copying the precepts. When To-ching arrived in Mid-India and saw the customary behaviour of the Shamans, and the strict decorum observed by the assembly of priests, and their religious deportment, even in the midst of worldly influences—then, sorrowfully reflecting on the meagre character of the Precepts known to the different assemblies of priests in the border land of China, he bound himself by a vow and said, "From the present time for ever till I obtain the condition of Buddha, may I never again be born in a frontier country." And in accordance with this expression of his wish, he took up his permanent abode in this place, and did not return. And so Fah Hian, desiring with his whole heart to spread the knowledge of the Precepts throughout the land of Han (China), returned alone.

He reaches the Country of the Lions—

Following down the river Ganges in an easterly direction for eighteen yôjanas distance, we find the great kingdom of Tchen-po (Champa) on its southern shore. From this, continuing to go eastward nearly fifty yôjanas, we arrive at the kingdom of Tamralipti (Tamluk). Here it is the river empties itself into the sea. Fah Hian remained here for two years, writing out copies of the Sacred books, and taking impressions of the figures [used in worship]. He then shipped himself on board a great merchant vessel. Putting to sea, they proceeded in a south-westerly direction, and, catching the first fair wind of the winter season (*i.e.*, of the north-east monsoon), they sailed for fourteen days and nights and arrived at the country of the Lions (Siñhala, Ceylon). Men of that country (Tamralipti) say that the distance between the two is about 700 yôjanas. This kingdom [of Lions] is situated on a great island [and] had originally no human inhabitants, but only demons and dragons dwelt in it. Merchants of different countries [however] resorted here to trade. At the time of the traffic, the demons did not appear in person, but only exposed their valuable commodities with the value affixed to them. Then the merchant men, according to the prices marked, purchased the goods and took them away. Buddha came to this country (in the first instance) from a desire to convert a malevolent dragon. Fah Hian had now been absent from China (the land of Han) many years. Moreover his fellow travellers were now separated from him—some had remained behind and some were dead—to think upon the past was all that was left him! And so his heart was continually saddened.

Is nearly shipwrecked—and reaches Home

Fah Hian resided in this country for two years. Continuing his search (for the sacred books), he obtained a copy of the Vinaya Pitaka, according to the school of the Mahisasikas. He also obtained a copy of the Great Âgama (Dirgâgama), and of the Miscellaneous Âgama (Sanyuktâgama) and also a volume of miscellaneous collections from the Pitakas (Samyukta Pitaka). All these were hitherto entirely unknown in the land of Han.

Having obtained these works in the original language, he forthwith shipped himself on board a great merchant vessel, which carried about two hundred men. Astern of the great ship was a smaller one, as a provision in case of the large vessel being injured or wrecked during the voyage. Having got a fair wind they sailed eastward for two days, when suddenly a tempest (tyfoon) sprung up, and the ship sprang a leak. The merchants then desired to haul up the smaller vessel, but the crew of that ship, fearing that a crowd of men would rush into her and sink her, cut the towing cable and fell off. The merchant men were greatly terrified, expecting their death momentarily. Then dreading lest the leak should gain upon them, they forthwith took their goods and merchandize and cast them overboard. Fah Hian also flung overboard his water-pitcher and his washing basin, and also other portions of his property. He was only afraid lest the merchants should fling into the sea his sacred books and images. And so with earnestness of heart he invoked Avâlokitèswara, and paid reverence to the Buddhist saints (the priesthood) of the land of Han—speaking thus:

"I, indeed, have wandered far and wide in search of the Law. Oh! would that by your spiritual power, you would turn back the flowing of the water, and cause us to reach some resting-place."

Nevertheless, the hurricane blew for thirteen days and nights, when they arrived at the shore of a small island, and on the tide going out, they found the place of the leak; having forthwith stopped it up, they again put to sea on their onward voyage. In this ocean there are many pirates, who, coming on you suddenly, destroy everything. The sea itself is boundless in extent—it is impossible to know east or west, except by observing the sun, moon, or stars in their motions. If it is dark, rainy weather, the only plan is to steer by the wind without guide. During the darkness of night, one only sees the great waves beating one against the other and shining like fire, whilst shoals of sea monsters of every description [surround the ship].

The merchant men were now much perplexed, not knowing towards what land they were steering. The sea was bottomless and no soundings could be found, so that there was not even a rock for anchorage. At length, the weather clearing up, they got their right bearings, and once more shaped a correct course and proceeded onwards.

Thus they voyaged for ninety days and more, when they arrived at a country called Yo-po-ti (Java). Stopping here the best portion of five months, Fah Hian again embarked on board another merchant vessel, having also a crew of 200 men or so. They took with them fifty days provisions, and set sail on the 15th day of the fourth month. Fah Hian was very comfortable on board this ship. They shaped a course north-east for Kwang Chow (Canton province in China). After a month and some days, at the stroke of two in the middle watch of the night, a black squall suddenly came on, accompanied with pelting rain. The merchant men and passengers were all terrified. Fah Hian at this time also, with great earnestness of mind, again entreated Avâlokitèswara and all the priesthood of China to exert their Divine power in his favour, and bring them daylight.

When the day broke, all the Brahmans, consulting together, said: "It is because we have got this Shaman on board with us that we have no luck, and have incurred this great mischief—come let us land this Bikshu on the first island we meet with, and let us not, for the sake of one man, all of us perish."

The religious patron (Danapati) of Fah Hian then said:

"If you land this Bikshu, you shall also land me with him; and if not, you had better kill me: for if you really put this Shaman on shore (as you threaten), then, when I arrive in China, I will go straight to the King and tell him what you have done. And the King of that country is a firm believer in the Law of Buddha, and greatly honours the Bikshus and priests."

The merchant men on this hesitated, and [in the end] did not dare to land him. The weather continuing very dark, the pilots began to look at one another in mutual distrust. Nearly seventy days had now elapsed. The rice for food, and the water for congee was nearly all done. They had to use salt water for cooking, whilst they gave out to every man about two pints of fresh water. And now, when this was just exhausted, the merchants held a conversation and said:

"The proper time for the voyage to Kwang Chow is about fifty days, but now we have exceeded that time these many days—shall we then undertake the navigation ourselves?"

On this, they put the ship on a north-west course to look for land. After twelve days' continuous sailing, they arrived at the southern coast of Lau Shan which borders on the prefecture of Chang Kwang. They then obtained good fresh water and vegetables; and so, after passing through so many dangers, and such a succession of anxious days, they suddenly arrived at this shore. On seeing the Le-ho vegetable (a sort of reed), they were confident that this was, indeed, the land of Han. But not seeing any men or traces of life, they scarcely knew what to take for granted. Some said they had not yet arrived at Kwang Chow, others maintained they had passed it. In their uncertainty, therefore, they put off in a little boat, and entered a creek to look for some one to ask what place it was they had arrived at. Just at this moment, two men who had been hunting were returning home; on this, the merchants requested Fah Hian to act as interpreter and make inquiries for them. Fah Hian having first tried to inspire them with confidence, then asked them:

"What men are you?"

They replied, "We are disciples of Buddha."

Then he asked, "What do you find in these mountains here, that you should have gone hunting in them?"

They prevaricated and said, "To-morrow is the 15th day of the 7th month, and we were anxious to catch something to sacrifice to Buddha."

Again he asked, "What country is this?"

They replied, "This is Tsing Chow, on the borders of the prefecture of Chang Kwang, dependent on the Leou family."

Having heard this, the merchants were very glad, and, immediately begging that their goods might be landed, they deputed men to go to Chang Kwang. The Prince Lai Ying, who was a faithful follower of the law of Buddha, hearing that there was a Shaman on board with sacred books and images, took ship and embarked and came on board [to see Fah Hian]. Then, immediately engaging men from the nearest shore, he dispatched the books and sacred figures to be landed and taken forthwith to the seat of his government. After this the merchants returned towards Yang Chow.

Meanwhile Leou of Tsing Chow entertained Fah Hian for the whole winter and summer. The summer period of rest being over, Fah Hian dismissed all the doctors of religion [who had been with him]. He had been anxious for a long time.to get back to Tchang'an. But as the engagements he had entered into were pressing ones, he directed his course first towards the southern capital, where the different doctors edited the sacred books he had brought back.

After Fah Hian left Tchang'an, he was five years in arriving at Mid-India. He resided there during six years, and was three years more before he arrived at Tsing Chow. He had successively passed through thirty different countries. In all the countries of India, after passing the Sandy Desert (of Gobi), the dignified carriage of the priesthood and the surprising influence of religion [amongst the people] cannot be adequately described. But, because our learned doctors had not heard of these things, he was induced, regardless of all personal considerations, to cross the seas, and to encounter every conceivable danger in returning home. Having been preserved, therefore, by Divine power (by the influences of the Three Honourable Ones), and brought through all dangers safely he was further induced to commit to writing these records of his travels, desiring that the virtuous of all ages may be informed of them together, as well as himself.

In this year Kea-yin, being the twelfth of the reign of I Hi of the Tsin dynasty, when the star Sheou was just emerging from the summer mansion, Fah Hian, the pilgrim, arrived home.

HOW HIUEN-TSIANG CAME TO I-GU[1]

THE SHAMAN HWUI-LI

(A.D. 630)

AT the birth of the Master of the Law[2] his mother had dreamt that she saw him going to the West clothed in a white robe—on which she said: "You are my son, where then are you going?" In reply he said, "I am going to seek for the Law." This was the first indication, then, of his foreign travels.

In the third year and the eighth month of the period Chêng Kwan (A.D. 630), he was prepared to make a start. Desiring some happy omen, he dreamt at night that he saw in the middle of the great sea the Mount Sumeru, perfected with the four precious substances—its appearance supremely bright and majestic. He thought he purposed to scale the Mount, but the boisterous waves arose aloft and swelled mightily. Moreover, there was neither ship nor raft; nevertheless, he had no shadow of fear, but with fixed purpose he entered [*the waves*]. Suddenly he saw a lotus of stone burst as it were exultingly from the deep; trying to put his foot on it, it retired; whilst he paused to behold it, it followed his feet and then disappeared;—in a moment he found himself at the foot of the Mount, but he could not climb its craggy and scarped sides: as he tried to leap upwards with all his strength, there arose in a moment a mighty whirlwind which raised him aloft to the summit of the Mount. Looking around him on the four sides from the top he beheld nought but an uninterrupted horizon; ravished with joy he awoke.

On this he forthwith started on his journey. He was then twentysix years of age. At this time there was a Tsin-Chow priest called Hiau-Ta who lived in the capital and studied the Nirvâna Sûtra. His study being finished he was returning to his home—they both went together therefore so far as Tsin-Chow. Having stopped there one night, he met with an associate from Lan-Chow; going on with him he came to Lan-Chow; and stopped there one night. Here he met with some mounted men who were returning to Liang-Chow, after escorting an officer. Going with them, he came to that place, and stopped there a month and some days. The priests and laymen invited him to explain the Nirvâna Sûtra and the Shi-lun, and the Pan-jo-king. The Master of the Law accordingly opened out the meaning of these works. Now Liang-Chow is the place of rendezvous for people dwelling to the west of the River: moreover merchants belonging to the borders of Si-Fan (*Tibet*) and countries

[1] From *The Life of Hiuen-Tsiang*, translated by Samuel Beal.

[2] *I.e.*, Hiuen-Tsiang.

to the left of the T'sung-Ling Mountains, all come and go to this place without hindrance.

On the day of opening the Religious Conference, these men all came together to the place and offered jewels and precious things, as they bowed down and uttered the praises of the Master. And on their return to their several countries they loudly applauded the Master of the Law to their Rulers, saying that he was about to go westwards to seek the Law in the country of the Brahmans.

In consequence of this throughout the kingdoms of the West all persons were prepared with joyful heart to entertain him on his arrival, with magnificence.

The day of the Conference being ended, they offered him in charity abundant gifts, gold and silver money, and white horses without number. The Master of the Law, accepting one half, caused the lamps of the different convents to be lit, and as for the rest of the money he distributed it among the various religious establishments. At this time the administration of the country was newly arranged, and the frontiers did not extend far. There were severe restrictions placed on the people, who were forbidden to go abroad into foreign parts. Just then the governor of Liang-Chow was called Li-ta-liang. Obedient to the Royal mandate he strictly adhered to the rules of prohibition. And now there came a man who addressed Liang thus:—"There is a priest here from Chang'an who is intending to go to the western regions—I do not know his plans." Liang, full of anxiety, called the Master of the Law to his presence and asked him the object of his arrival. The Master replied, "I wish to go to the West to seek for the Law." Liang hearing this, urged him to return to the capital.

There was then at Liang-Chow a Master of the Law called Hwuiwei, the most renowned of all priests of the region West of the River, for his spiritual perception and vast abilities. He greatly admired the profound reasoning of the Master of the Law, and hearing of his intention to go in search of the Law, he was very greatly rejoiced. Secretly sending two of his disciples, one called Hwui-lin, the other Taou-ching, he bade them conduct the Master in secret towards the West.

From this time he dare not be seen in public—during the daytime he hid himself, at night he went on.

In process of time he came to Kwa-chow; the governor To-Kiu having heard of his coming was greatly pleased, and provided him with all necessary provisions in plenty.

The Master of the Law inquiring as to the Western roads, he was told in reply that north from this point fifty *li* or more there was the river Hu-lu, the lower part of which is wide, the upper course narrow. Its stream is very impetuous and suddenly becomes deep, so that no boat can pass over it. It On the upper part is fixed the Yuh-men barrier, so that one must pass by this; thus it is the key to the Western frontiers. North-west beyond the barrier there are five signal towers in which officers, charged to watch, dwell—they are one hundred *li* apart. In the space between them there is neither water nor herb. Beyond the five towers stretches the desert called Mo-Kia-Yen, on the frontiers of the kingdom of I-gu.

On hearing these particulars he was filled with anxiety and distress. His horse was dead, and he did not know what steps to take; he remained there a month or so, sad and silent. Before his departure there came certain spies from Liang-Chow, who said: "There is a priest called Hiuen-Tsiang who is purposing to enter on the Si-Fan territory. All the governors of provinces and districts are ordered to detain him." The Governor of the Province, Li-Chang, was a man of a religious turn (a man of religion and faith), and he suspected in his heart that the Master of the Law was [*the person named*]; accordingly he secretly brought the mandate and showing it to Hiuen-Tsiang he said: "Is not the Master the person here named?" The Master of the Law hesitated and made no reply; on which Chang said: "The Master ought to speak the truth, and your disciple will make some plan for you to escape." The Master of the Law then replied truthfully. Chang, hearing it, was filled with admiration and surprise: and then he said, "Since the Master is indeed capable of such a project, I will for his sake destroy the document"; and forthwith he tore it up before him. "And now, Sir," he said, "you must depart in all haste."

From this time his anxieties and fears greatly increased. Of the two novices who accompanied him, one, called Taou-ching, returned at once to Tun-hwang; the other, called Hwui-Lin, alone remained, but because the Master knew that he had not strength for so distant a journey he let him also return. He now procured a horse by exchange; his only sorrow was that he had no guide to accompany him. On this he proceeded to the temple where he was staying, and bowing before the image of Maitrêya, he fervently prayed that he would find him a guide who would lead him past the barrier.

That night there was a foreign priest in the temple who had a dream. His name was Dharma, and in his dream he saw the Master sitting on a lotus flower and going towards the West. Dharma was lost in surprise, and on the morrow he told his dream to the Master of the Law, whose heart was rejoiced thereat, taking it as a sign of his being able to go. He answered Dharma, however, thus: "Dreams are vain and deceptive: what need is there to examine into this matter?" Again he entered the Sacred precinct and worshipped in prayer.

And now suddenly a foreign person came into the temple to worship Buddha, after doing which he saluted the Master of the Law by turning round him three times. The Master then asked him his family and personal name, on which he said, "My family name is Shi, my personal name is Pan-to [Bandha?]." The foreigner then asked to be allowed to take on him the five Rules,[1] and having done so he was greatly rejoiced, and asked permission to come back; after a little while he returned with cakes and fruit. The Master of the Law observing his intelligence and strong build, and also his respectful manner, accordingly spoke to him about his purpose to go westwards. The foreigner readily acquiesced, and said he would conduct the Master beyond the five signal towers. The Master of the Law was filled with joy, and gave him some clothes and other property to exchange for a horse, and appointed a time of meeting.

On the morrow at sundown he proceeded towards the bush, were shortly afterwards the foreigner with an old greybeard, likewise a foreign person, riding on a lean horse of a red colour, came to meet him. The Master of the Law was not easy in his mind; on which the young foreigner said: "This venerable greybeard is intimately acquainted with the Western roads, and has gone to and come back from I-gu more than thirty times: I have therefore brought him to go with you, hoping it may give you assurance." Then the senior man said: "The Western roads are difficult and bad; sand-streams stretch far and wide; evil sprites and hot winds, when they come, cannot be avoided: numbers of men travelling together, although so many, are misled and lost; how much rather you, sir, going alone! how can you accomplish such a journey? I pray you, weigh the thing with yourself well, and do not trifle with your life."

The Master replied: "This poor priest [*i.e., Hiuen-Tsiang*] aims to reach the Western world to search after the great Law—if he does not in the end reach the land of the Brahmans—there is no return to the Eastward, it matters not if he dies in the mid-route."

The foreign greybeard then said. "If, sir, you will go you must ride this horse of mine: he has gone to and fro to I-gu some fifteen times. He is strong and knows the road; your horse, sir, is a small one and not suitable for the journey."

The Master of the Law then recalled to himself the following circum-

[1] Of a lay disciple.

stance: when he was at Chang'an forming his purpose of visiting the Western World, one day there was a diviner named Ho-wang-ta, who by reciting spells and prognosticating, could tell a great deal about the matters in which one was engaged. The Master of the Law requested him to prognosticate about his journey. *Ta* said, "Sir! you may go; the appearance of your person as you go is that of one riding an old red horse, thin and skinny; the saddle is varnished, and in front it is bound with iron."

Now having observed that the horse which the old foreigner was riding was lean and of a red colour, and that the varnished saddle was bound with iron, agreeing with the words of the diviner, he made up his mind that this was the fulfilment of the augury, and accordingly he exchanged his horse. The old greybeard was much rejoiced thereat, and making his respectful obeisance, they separated.

And now having packed his baggage, he went on through the night with the young foreigner. In the third watch they came to the river, and saw the guard-house called the Yuh-Mên a good way off. At ten *li* from the barrier the upper stream is not more than ten feet wide; on each side there is a scrub composed of the Wutung tree; the foreigner, cutting down some wood, made a bridge and spread over it branches, filling it up with sand. Thus they led over the horses and went on.

The Master of the Law having crossed the river was filled with joy. Being fatigued, he dismounted and sought some repose. The foreign guide also, separated about fifty paces or so from the Master, spread his mat on the ground, and so they both slept. After a while the guide took his knife in his hand, and rising up, approached towards the Master of the Law; when about ten paces off, he turned round. Not knowing what his intention was, and being in doubt about the matter, the Master rose from his mat and repeated some Scripture, and called on *Kwan-yin* Bôdhisattva. The foreigner having seen this went back, and slept.

At the first dawn of day the Master called to him and bade him fetch water. Having washed and taken some little food, he purposed to go onwards. The guide said: "Your disciple is leading you forward on a way full of danger and very remote; there is no water or grass; only beyond the fifth tower there is water. It will be necessary to go there at night-time and get the water and pass on. But if at any one place we are perceived we are dead men! Is it not better to return and be at rest?" The Master of the Law having positively refused to return, they both went forward. [Now the guide], with his knife drawn and his bow strung, begged the Master to go on in front; but the Master of the Law would not consent to the proposal. The foreigner going by himself, after a few *li* stopped and said: "Your disciple can go no further—he has great family concerns to attend to, and he is not willing to transgress the laws of his country." The Master of the Law, knowing his purpose, let him go back.

The young foreigner replied: "It is impossible for the Master to carry out his plan: how can you avoid being seized and brought back?"

The Master of the Law answered: "Though they cause my body to be cut up as small as the very dust, I will never return; and I here take an oath to this."

So the matter rested; he gave the young man his horse[1] as a mark of his obligation to him, and so they parted.

And now, alone and deserted, he traversed the sandy waste; his only means of observing the way being the heaps of bones and the horse-dung, and so on; thus slowly and cautiously advancing, he suddenly saw a body of troops, amounting to several hundreds, covering the sandy plain; sometimes they advanced and sometimes they halted. The soldiers were clad in fur and felt. And now the appearance of camels and horses, and the glittering of standards and lances met his view; then suddenly fresh forms and figures changing into a thousand shapes appeared, sometimes at an immense distance and then close at hand, and then they dissolved into nothing.

The Master of the Law when he first beheld the sight thought they were robbers, but when he saw them come near and vanish, he knew that they were the hallucinations of demons. Again, he heard in the void sounds of voices crying out: "Do not fear! do not fear!" On this he composed himself, and having pushed on eighty *li* or so, he saw the first watch-tower. Fearing lest the look-outs should see him, he concealed himself in a hollow of sand until night; then going on west of the tower, he saw the water; and going down, he drank and washed his hands. Then as he was filling his water-vessel with water an arrow whistled past him and just grazed his knee, and in a moment another arrow. Knowing then that he was discovered, he cried with a loud voice: "I am a priest come from the capital: do not shoot me!" Then he led his horse towards the tower, whilst the men on guard opening the gate, came out; after looking at him they saw that he was indeed a priest, and so they entered in together to see the commander of the guard-house, whose name was Wang-siang. Wang, having ordered the fire to be well lit up for the purpose of inspecting the Master, said: "This is no priest of our country of Ho-si,[2] he is indeed one from the capital": then he asked him about his object in travelling.

The Master of the Law replied: "Captain! have you not heard men of

[1] *I.e.*, the one the young man rode, Hiuen-Tsiang's being the "old red horse."

[2] Tangut.

Liang-chow talk about a priest named Hiuen-Tsiang, who was about to proceed to the country of the Brahmans to seek for the Law?" He answered: "I have heard that Hiuen-Tsiang has returned already to the East. Why have you come here?" The Master of the Law then took him to his horse, and showed him various places on which were written his name and familiar title. On this the other was convinced. He then said: "Sir, the western road is dangerous and long, you cannot succeed in your plan. But I have no fault to find with you. I myself am a man of Tun-hwang and I will conduct you there. There is a Master of the Law there called Chang-kiau, he reveres men of virtue (sages) and honours the priesthood: he will be rejoiced to see you: I ask your consent to this."

The Master of the Law replied: "My birthplace is Lo-yang; from a child I have been zealous for religion; in both capitals all those engaged in the study of the Law, in Wu and Shuh the most eminent priests without exception, have come to me for instruction; for their sakes I have explained and discussed and preached on religion; and I may boldly say that I am the leading authority of the time. If I wished for further renown and encouragement, should I seek a patron at Tun-hwang? But being afflicted because I found the sacred books of the religion of Buddha were not always in agreement, and were imperfect, forgetful of my own comfort and disregarding all dangers, I have sworn to go to the West to seek for the Law bequeathed to the world. But you, my patron, instead of rousing me to effort in my undertaking, would exhort me rather to turn back and give it up. How then can you profess to have in common with myself distaste for the follies of life, and wish with me to plant the seed, leading to Nirvâna? But if you must needs detain me here—let me be punished with death! Hiuen-Tsiang will never return one step to the East, nor give up his first intention!"

Siang, hearing these words, filled with emotion, said: "I am indeed fortunate in having met with you! How can I but rejoice? But now, sir, you are fatigued and worn; take some sleep before the day dawns. I will then myself conduct you, and show you the proper route." He then spread out a mat for him to rest upon.

When the morning came, the Master of the Law having taken some food, Siang sent a man to fill his water-vessel, and providing him with some cakes made of flour, he himself conducted him for ten *li* or so, and then he said: "From this point, sir, the road goes straight on to the fourth watch-tower; the man there is a good-hearted person; moreover, he is a near relation of mine. His family name is Wang, his private name is Pi-lung. When you come to see him you can say that I have sent you to him." Then, with tearful salutations, they parted.

Having gone on till night he came to the fourth watch-tower, and fearing lest he should be detained, he purposed to get some water quietly, and to go on. Coming to the water, and scarcely there, there came an arrow flying towards him; turning round he called out as before, and went forward to the tower. Then the men coming down, he entered the building. The officer of the tower having spoken to him, he answered: "I purpose going to India, and my way is in this direction. Wang-siang, the officer of the first tower, has commissioned me to meet you." Hearing this he was much pleased, and detained him for the night; moreover he gave him a great leather bottle for water, and fodder for his horse. Then conducting him by his side he said: "You had better not, sir, go towards the fifth tower, for the men there are rude and violent, and some mishap may befall you. About 100 *li* from this is the Ye-ma spring, where you can replenish your supply of water."

Having gone on from this he forthwith entered on the *Mo-kia-Yen* desert, which is about 800 *li* in extent. The old name for it is Sha-ho. There are no birds overhead, and no beasts below; there is neither water nor herb to be found. On occasions, according to the sun's shadow, he would, with the utmost devotion, invoke the name of Kwan-shai-yin Bôdhisattva, and also [recite] the Pan-jo-sin Sûtra (*Prajña-pâramîta-hridaya Sûtra*).

At first when the Master of the Law was dwelling in Shuh he saw a diseased man whose body was covered with ulcers, his garments tattered and filthy. Pitying the man he took him to his convent, and gave him clothing and food; the sick man, moved by a feeling of deep gratitude, gave to the Master of the Law this little Sûtra-book, and on this account he was in the habit of reciting it continually. Arriving at the *Sha-ho* as he passed through it, he encountered all sorts of demon shapes and strange goblins, which seemed to surround him behind and before. Although he invoked the name of Kwan-Yin, he could not drive them all away; but when he recited the Sûtra, at the sound of the words they all disappeared in a moment. Whenever he was in danger, it was to this alone that he trusted for his safety and deliverance.

After going a hundred *li* or so, he lost his way, and searching for the fountain called *Ye-ma* he could not find it, to get water from. Then when he was going to drink from the pipe of his water-vessel, because of its weight it slipped from his hands, and the water was wasted; thus, a supply enough for 1000 *li* was lost in a moment. Then again, because of the winding character of the road, he did not know which way to follow it. At length, purposing to return eastward to the fourth watch-tower, after going ten *li*, he thought thus within himself, "I made a vow at the first that if I did not succeed in reaching India I would never return a step to the East; what then am I now doing here? It is better to die in the attempt to go to the West, than to live by returning to the East." Then turning the bridle he invoked *Kwan-Yin*, and proceeded in a northwest direction.

At this time [*as he looked*] in the four directions, the view was boundless; there were no traces either of man or horse, and in the night the demons and goblins raised fire-lights as many as the stars; in the daytime the driving wind blew the sand before it as in the season of rain. But notwithstanding all this his heart was unaffected by fear; but he suffered from want of water, and was so parched with thirst that he could no longer go forward. Thus for four nights and five days not a drop of water had he to wet his throat or mouth; his stomach was racked with a burning heat, and he was well-nigh thoroughly exhausted. And now not being able to advance he lay down to rest on the sands, invoking *Kwan-Yin* without intermission, although worn out with sufferings. And as he addressed the Bôdhisattva, he said: "Hiuen-Tsiang in adventuring this journey does not seek for riches or worldly profit, he desires not to acquire fame, but only for the sake of the highest religious truth does his heart long to find the true Law. I know that the Bôdhisattva lovingly regards all living creatures to deliver them from misery! Will not mine, bitter as they are, come to his knowledge!"

Thus he spake, [*praying*] with earnest heart and without cessation the while, till the middle of the fifth night, when suddenly a cool wind fanned his body, cold and refreshing as a bath of icy water. His eyes forthwith recovered their power of sight and his horse had strength to get up. His body being thus refreshed, he lay still and fell asleep for a little while. Whilst he slept thus he had a dream, and in his sleep he thought he saw a mighty spiritual being, several *chang*[1] in height, holding in his hand a halberd used for signalling, who spake thus: "Why are you still sleeping and not pressing on with all your might?"

The Master of the Law, rousing himself from slumber, pushed on for ten *li*, when his horse suddenly started off another way and could not be brought back or turned. Having gone some *li* in the new direction, he saw all at once several acres of green grass; getting off his horse, he let him graze; when leaving the grass, purposing to resume his journey, about ten paces off he came to a pool of water, sweet, and bright as a mirror; dismounting again, he drank without stint, and so his body and vital powers were restored once more, and both man and horse obtained refreshment and ease. Now we may

[1] A *change* = 141 inches.

conclude that this water and grass were not natural supplies, but undoubtedly were produced through the loving pity of Bôdhisattva, and it is a proof of his guileless character and spiritual power.

Having bivouacked near the grass and fountain of water for a day, on the day following he filled his water-vessel and cut some grass, and proceeded onward. After two days more they got out of the desert and arrived at I-gu.